HAMMOND

THE TIMES

CONCISE

ATLAS OF WORLD HISTORY

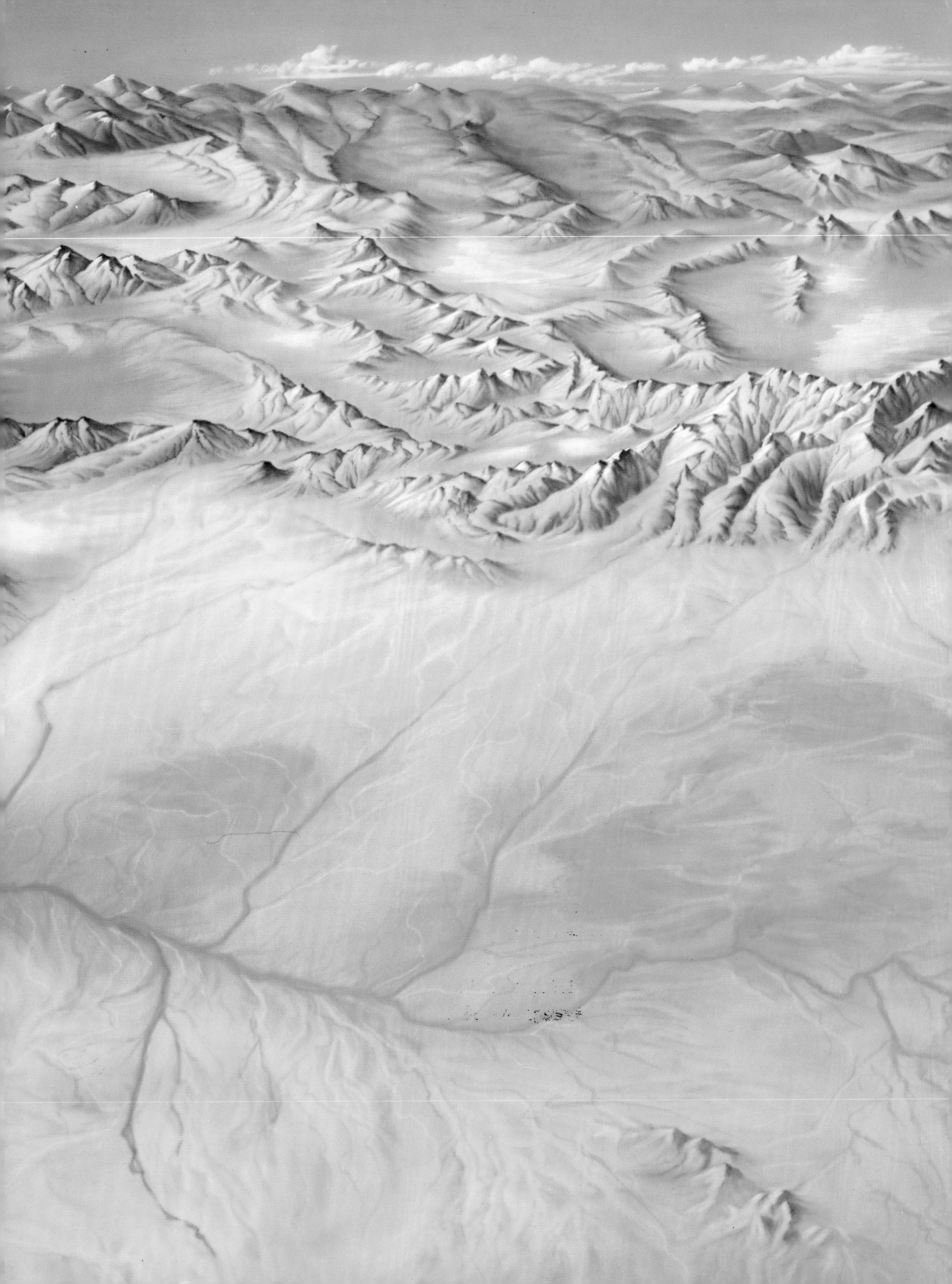

HAMMOND

THE TIMES CONCISE ATLAS OF WORLD HISTORY

Edited by
GEOFFREY BARRACLOUGH

MAPLEWOOD, NEW JERSEY 07040-1396

Times Books, a division of
HarperCollins*Publishers*
77–85 Fulham Palace Road
Hammersmith
London W6 8JB

First published in 1982
Revised editions 1986, 1988, 1992, 1994

Library of Congress Cataloging in Publication Data
Main entry under title:

The Times concise atlas of world history

ISBN 0-7230-0674-1 Order No. 1147-7

HAMMOND
INCORPORATED
MAPLEWOOD, NEW JERSEY 07040-1396

EDITORIAL DIRECTION Barry Winkleman
Ailsa Heritage

DESIGN & ART DIRECTION Ivan and Robin Dodd

MAP DESIGN AND ARTWORK Swanston Graphics Ltd., Derby
P.S.G. Ltd., Derby
Peter Sullivan
Ivan and Robin Dodd

PLACE NAMES AND INDEX P.J.M. Geelan

COLOUR SEPARATION City Ensign Ltd., Hull
D.S. Colour International Ltd., London

PRINTED AND BOUND Hong Kong

EDITORIAL CONSULTANTS *(Fourth edition)*
Dr Chris Scarre, *McDonald Institute, University of Cambridge*
Geoffrey Parker, *Robert A. Lovett Professor of Military and Naval History, Yale University*
Dr Richard Overy, *Reader in History, King's College London*

ACKNOWLEDGEMENTS
This atlas contains the work of many of the contributors to THE TIMES ATLAS OF WORLD HISTORY (Fourth edition, 1993) who are listed in that volume. We also wish to thank:
Frederick W. Boal, *Professor of Human Geography, Queens University, Belfast*
Professor Michael Crowder, late of the *University of Botswana*
Dr Elizabeth Dunstan, *International African Institute*
David Hickman
Raymond Hutchings, *Senior Editor, Abstract, Soviet and Eastern European Series*
Morton Keller, *Spector Professor of History, Brandeis University, Massachusetts*
John Lynch, *Professor of Latin American History and Director, Institute of Latin American Studies, University of London*
W.H. McNeill, *Robert A. Millitin Distinguished Services Professor of History, University of Chicago*
W.H. Parker, *formerly Lecturer of the Geography of the USSR, University of Oxford*
R.L. Sims, *Lecturer in the History of the Far East, School of Oriental and African Studies, University of London*
Peter Sluglett, *Lecturer in Modern Middle Eastern History, Durham University*

CONTENTS

1 INTRODUCTION

Part One

Early man and the civilisations of the ancient world

2 HUMAN ORIGINS
1 The origin and development of life
2 The spread of Homo sapiens
3 Traces of human origins

4 THE ICE AGES
1 The world 20,000 years ago
2 The colonisation of the Americas
3 Palaeolithic art in Europe

6 FROM HUNTING TO FARMING
1 World economies
2 Adoption of the plough
3 The decline of hunter-gathering
4 The agricultural revolution in the Near East
5 Centres of plant and animal domestication

8 EARLY CULTURES OF ASIA
1 India: Stone Age and Iron Age
2 Early Chinese agriculture
3 Prehistoric sites in South-East Asia
4 Shang China
5 The Indus civilisations of Harappa and Mohenjo-Daro
6 China under the Western Chou c.1027–771 BC

10 PREHISTORIC AFRICA AND AUSTRALASIA
1 Africa: the Stone Age to the Iron Age
2 Early settlement in the South Seas
3 The settlement of New Zealand

12 PEOPLES AND CULTURES OF THE AMERICAS
1 American peoples and cultures c.AD 500
2 The Classic Period in Mesoamerica AD 300–800
3 Eastern North America, 300 BC–AD 500
4 Early cultural centres of the Andes
5 The empires of Tiahuanaco and Huari, AD 600–800

14 THE DEVELOPMENT OF EUROPE 6000–300 BC
1 The spread of agricultural settlement
2 The introduction of metallurgy to Europe
3 Megalithic monuments
4 Amber trade
5 The expansion of the Celts

16 EGYPT AND MESOPOTAMIA 3500–1600 BC
1 The spread of civilisation
2 Sumerian Mesopotamia c.2500–2000 BC
3 Old Kingdom Egypt c.3000–2000 BC
4 Early empires of Mesopotamia

18 THE FIRST CIVILISATIONS OF EUROPE 3000–600 BC
1 The Aegean, 2500–1200 BC
2 Mycenaean trade, 1500–1150 BC
3 Post-Mycenaean Greece, c.1150–950 BC
4 Greek colonisation, 750–550 BC

20 NEAR EASTERN EMPIRES, 1600–330 BC
1 Kingdoms and empires of the Near East, c.1500–1200 BC
2 Palestine at the time of David
3 The growth of the Assyrian Empire
4 The Babylonian Kingdom, 604–539 BC
5 The Persian Empire, 550–331 BC

22 THE GREEK WORLD
1 The Persian wars, 490–479 BC
2 The Peloponnesian War, 431–404 BC
3 The empire of Alexander the Great
4 The Hellenistic world in 185 BC

24 TRADING LINKS OF THE ANCIENT WORLD
1 Eurasian trade routes, c.AD 200
2 The economy of the Roman Empire c.AD 200
3 The spread of epidemics

26 THE WORLD RELIGIONS c.500 BC–AD 500
1 The diffusion of religions
2 The spread of Christianity
3 Judaea, 63 BC–AD 73

28 INDIA AND CHINA: THE FIRST EMPIRES
1 The unification of China, 328–221 BC
2 The expansion of the Han Empire
3 Han China in AD 2
4 India's first empires, 297 BC–AD 150
5 Gupta India

30 THE ROMAN EMPIRE, 264 BC–AD 565
1 Roman expansion in Italy
2 The Punic Wars, 264–146 BC
3 The Roman Empire, AD 14–280
4 The later Empire, AD 284–565

Part Two

Decline and recovery: the emergence of a new world

32 THE BARBARIAN INVASIONS
1 Barbarian invasions of the ancient world
2 Germanic invasions of Europe
3 Anglo-Saxon invasions of Britain c.440–650
4 The Lombards in Italy
5 The expansion of the Slavs, c.700

34 GERMANIC KINGDOMS OF WESTERN EUROPE
1 Germanic kingdoms in AD 493
2 Early Frankish expansion
3 Anglo-Saxon England, c.AD 800
4 The Frankish Empire, 714–814
5 Treaty of Verdun, 843
6 Partition of Meersen, 870

36 INVASION AND RECOVERY: EUROPE 814–1149
1 Viking, Magyar and Saracen invasions
2 The Western reconquest of the Mediterranean
3 Norman England, 1066–1087
4 The Christian reconquest of Spain 1080–1492

38 CHRISTIANITY AND JUDAISM c.600–1500
1 Christianity in Asia
2 Christianity in Europe
3 Irish and Anglo-Saxon missions
4 The Jews in medieval Europe

40 THE ISLAMIC WORLD, 632–1517
1 The expansion of Islam, 632–936
2 The Middle East and North Africa 786–1260
3 The Muslim reconquest of Palestine
4 Islam in India
5 Islam in S.E. Asia

42 THE BYZANTINE WORLD, 610–1453
1 The Byzantine Empire, 628–1143
2 The 'themes' and the Arab invasions
3 The Crusades and the decline of Byzantium
4 The Muslim conquest of Anatolia

44 EARLY RUSSIA, 862–1245
1 Varangian Russia, 862–1054
2 Kievan Russia, 1054–1242
3 Mongol invasions, 1223–40

46 THE MONGOL EMPIRE, 1206–1696
1 The Mongol Empire before 1259
2 The Mongol invasion of Europe 1237–42
3 The break-up of the Mongol Empire after 1259
4 The conquests of Timur, 1370–1405

48 THE MUSLIM RESURGENCE 1301–1639
1 The Ottoman advance 1300–1520
2 The resurgence of Muslim power

50 CHINA AND ITS NEIGHBOURS 618–1644
1 The T'ang Empire of China
2 South-East Asia, 500–1500
3 Civil war in Japan, 1467–1590
4 China under the Ming, 1368–1644

52 NORTHERN AND WESTERN EUROPE 960–1314
1 The rise of Poland
2 The expansion of the French monarchy, 987–1328
3 The rise of Denmark
4 The empire of Canute the Great 1014–1035
5 The Northern Kingdoms, c.1035
6 The British Isles, 1215–1307
7 The conquest of Wales, 1283–84

54 THE MEDIEVAL GERMAN EMPIRE 962–1356
1 The East Frankish Kingdom of Otto I
2 German eastward expansion
3 The Hohenstaufen Empire 1152–1250
4 The conquest of Prussia
5 The rise of the Swiss Confederation

56 FOURTEENTH CENTURY EUROPE
1 Europe at the time of the Black Death
2 Eastern Europe, 1278–1389
3 Italy, c.1310
4 The Anglo-Scottish Wars 1296–1402
5 The Hundred Years' War
6 The Western Schism, 1378–1417

58 MEDIEVAL TRADE ROUTES c.1000–1500
1 Trade routes in Western Europe c.1000–1150
2 Hanseatic trade
3 Eurasian trade routes c.1000–1500

60 AFRICAN STATES AND EMPIRES c.900–1800
1 Africa, 900–1500
2 Africa, 1500–1800
3 African languages

62 AMERICA ON THE EVE OF EUROPEAN CONQUEST
1 The American peoples, c.1500
2 The Aztec Empire in Mexico
3 The Inca Empire in Peru
4 Archaeological sites in North America from AD 1000

Part Three

The rise of the West

64 EUROPEAN VOYAGES OF DISCOVERY 1487–1780
1 The Portuguese in Africa 1418–1488
2 Voyages of discovery, 1480–1630
3 Voyages in the Caribbean 1493–1519
4 Voyages in the Pacific, 1720–1780

66 EUROPEAN EXPANSION OVERSEAS
1 Spanish and Portuguese trade and settlement by c.1600
2 Commercial expansion to the East 1600–1700
3 European settlement in North America
4 The West Indies

68 COLONIAL AMERICA, 1519–1783
1 The Spanish invasion of Mexico 1519–20
2 The Spanish invasion of Peru 1531–33
3 The development of colonial America
4 Population and settlement
5 Trading posts and forts

70 SOUTH-EAST ASIA, 1511–1826
1 South-East Asia in 1500
2 Trade and politics
3 European rivalries, 1511–1682
4 Dutch expansion in Java
5 The Malay states in 1826

72 NEW MONARCHY IN EUROPE 1453–1547
1 The new monarchies
2 The reunification of France 1440–1589
3 The Low Countries, 1467–1548
4 Extension of Tudor power in Britain
5 Renaissance Italy, 1454

74 THE REFORMATION IN EUROPE 1517–1648
1 The religious situation in 1560
2 The European sectaries 1525–1620
3 The French wars of religion
4 The Thirty Years' War in Germany 1618–48

76 WESTERN EUROPE, 1558–1648
1 The Dutch revolt, 1572–1648
2 Revolts in France
3 The rise of the Swedish Empire
4 The English Civil War, 1642–45
5 Depopulation during the Thirty Years' War

78 GERMANY AND ITS NEIGHBOURS 1648–1806
1 Germany in 1648
2 The rise of Prussia
3 The growth of the Habsburg Empire
4 The partitions of Poland

80 FRANCE AND EUROPE, 1648–1715
1 France under Louis XIV
2 The north-east frontier 1648–1714
3 The Anglo-Dutch wars 1652–1673
4 The wars of Louis XIV, 1667–1697
5 The war of the Spanish Succession 1702–1713

82 THE EUROPEAN ECONOMY c.1500–1815
1 The emancipation of the peasantry
2 The introduction of the potato
3 Land reclamation in the Netherlands
4 Trade and industry in the 18th century
5 The main trading flows, c.1775

84 THE EXPANSION OF RUSSIA 1462–1905
1 Muscovy and the Russian Empire 1462–1815
2 Russian expansion in Siberia 1581–1800
3 Russia in Asia, 1815–1900
4 The industrialisation of the Ukraine 1861–1913

86 THE STRUGGLE FOR EMPIRE 1713–1805
1 The North Atlantic and North America, 1754–63
2 The Franco-British conflict in India
3 The growth of British power in India to 1805

88 THE AGE OF REVOLUTION 1773–1810
1 Revolts and revolutions in Europe and America
2 The French Revolution, 1789–94
3 The expansion of revolutionary France, 1793–99

90 NAPOLEONIC EUROPE
1 The empire of Napoleon
2 The Egyptian campaign
3 The Anglo-French naval conflict
4 Napoleonic Germany, 1806

92 THE UNITED STATES, 1783–1865
1 The American War of Independence, 1775–1783
2 Territorial expansion, 1803–1853
3 Slaves in 1850
4 Union and Confederate states
5 The Civil War, 1861–1865

94 THE EXPANSION OF THE UNITED STATES, 1803–1898
1 The opening of the continent
2 The Indian wars
3 Railroads and agriculture
4 Immigration in the 19th century

96 INDEPENDENT LATIN AMERICA 1808–1910
1 Political development
2 Population and immigration
3 Exports and foreign investment
4 The War of the Pacific, 1879–93

98 THE INDUSTRIAL REVOLUTION IN EUROPE, 1760–1914
1 The beginning of the Industrial Revolution: Great Britain c.1750–1820
2 The Industrial Revolution in Europe, 1860–1914
3 The economic unification of Germany, 1828–88

100 EUROPEAN IMPERIALISM 1815–1914
1 Colonial expansion, 1815–70
2 The colonial empires in 1914
3 British control of the Indian Ocean

102 NINETEENTH CENTURY AFRICA
1 European exploration in Africa 1769–1887
2 South Africa, 1818–81
3 European penetration after 1880
4 The Boer War and the Union of South Africa, 1899–1910
5 Africa after partition, 1914

104 INDIA UNDER BRITISH RULE 1805–1947
1 India, 1805–57
2 The annexation of Burma 1826–86
3 The Indian Empire in 1931
4 The Indian Nationalist Movement 1915–47
5 The partition of India, 1947

106 CHINA UNDER THE CH'ING DYNASTY 1644–1911
1 Imperial expansion, 1644–1760
2 17th century trade
3 Rebellions and foreign attacks 1840–1901
4 The dismemberment of the Chinese Empire, 1842–1911

108 THE WORLD ECONOMY, 1850–1929
1 Industrialisation outside Europe
2 Population movements 1820–1910
3 Trade and investment
4 Shorter journeys via the Suez and Panama Canals
5 Balance of world trade 1860 and 1913

110 THE UNITED STATES AND CANADA 1865–1920
1 The development of Canada 1867–1920
2 Urban and industrial growth 1860–1920
3 United States economic growth
4 American expansion in the Pacific and Caribbean, 1867–1917
5 Population density in 1900

112 AUSTRALIA AND NEW ZEALAND 1788
1 The settlement and development of Australia
2 The settlement and development of New Zealand
3 Anglo-Maori conflict
4 Early trade
5 The exploration of Australia

114 EUROPEAN NATIONALISM 1815–1914
1 Peoples, languages and political divisions in the 19th century
2 The unification of Germany 1815–71
3 The unification of Italy, 1859–70
4 The Scandinavian kingdoms
5 Belgian independence, 1830–39

116 THE EUROPEAN POWERS, 1878–1914
1 The Balkans, 1878–1913
2 European alliances
3 The arms race

118 THE FIRST WORLD WAR, 1914–1918
1 The line-up of the Powers
2 The German attack in the West, August 1914
3 The war in Europe, 1914–18
4 Allied shipping losses, 1914–18

Part Four

The modern world

120 THE RUSSIAN REVOLUTION 1905–1925
1 The first Russian revolution, 1905
2 Russia in war and revolution
3 Red star over Europe
4 Red star over Asia

122 THE CHINESE REVOLUTION 1911–1949
1 The revolution of 1911
2 The Northern Expedition 1926–27
3 China under the Kuomintang 1928–37
4 The Chinese Communist movement to 1945
5 The establishment of Communist rule, 1945–49

124 THE OTTOMAN EMPIRE, 1800–1923
1 The disintegration of the Ottoman Empire, 1805–1923
2 The Middle East in the First World War, 1914–18
3 Agreements between the powers
4 The Greco-Turkish War, 1920–22

126 MODERN JAPAN, 1868–1941
1 Japan in 1868
2 Industrialisation and economic growth, c.1880–1922
3 The growth of the Japanese empire 1872–1918
4 The Russo-Japanese War, 1904–05
5 Japanese expansion, 1931–41

128 EUROPEAN POLITICAL PROBLEMS 1919–1939
1 The European security system 1921–36
2 National conflicts and frontier disputes, 1919–34
3 The refugee problem
4 The Spanish Civil War, 1936–39
5 German and Italian expansion 1935–39

130 THE GREAT DEPRESSION 1929–1939
1 The world economy, 1929–39
2 The Depression in the United States
3 Social unrest and political movements in Europe

132 THE WAR IN THE WEST, 1939–1945
1 The German advance, 1939–43
2 The defeat of Germany, 1943–45
3 The battle of the Atlantic, 1941–45

134 THE WAR IN ASIA AND THE PACIFIC 1941–1945
1 The Japanese advance, 1941–42
2 The Allied counter-offensive
3 The bombardment of Japan, 1945

136 EUROPE AFTER 1945
1 Territorial change and population movements, 1945–49
2 Military and economic blocs, 1949–86
3 Post-war Germany to 1990
4 The fall of communism in Eastern Europe, 1989–93

138 RETREAT FROM EMPIRE AFTER 1947
1 Decolonisation, 1947–90
2 Indonesia and Malaysia, 1945–65
3 The Algerian Civil War, 1954–62
4 The Congo crisis, 1960–65

140 ASIA AND AFRICA AFTER INDEPENDENCE
1 Post-independence wars and revolutions
2 Nigeria and the Biafran War 1967–70
3 Israel and Palestine, 1947–85
4 Japanese industrial production 1945–80

142 LATIN AMERICA SINCE 1930
1 Social and political movements 1930–92
2 Economic development
3 Population growth and change

144 THE UNITED STATES FROM 1945
1 Movement of population, 1930–79
2 Growth of metropolitan areas 1940–75
3 Civil rights and urban unrest 1960–68
4 Economic growth, 1939–77
5 Agricultural development

146 THE SOVIET UNION, 1926–90
1 Industrial expansion, 1926–80
2 The constituent republics
3 The different nationalities in the USSR

148 THE COLD WAR FROM 1947
1 The Soviet and American blocs 1949–59
2 The Korean War, 1950–53
3 The war in Vietnam, 1957–73
4 The Middle East during the Cold War 1955–68
5 The Cuban crisis, 1962

150 THE WORLD IN THE 1990s
1 Gross national product and foreign investment
2 Population growth, 1985–90
3 Infant mortality and life expectancy, 1950–92
4 The successor states of the Soviet Union

152 ACKNOWLEDGEMENTS

153 INDEX

INTRODUCTION

The welcome given to THE TIMES ATLAS OF WORLD HISTORY, first published in English in September 1978, and now available in nine languages, shows how widespread an interest there is today in the human story. It also led us to think that there might be a place for a shorter, less elaborate atlas on a reduced scale.

The present volume is the result. Nevertheless THE TIMES CONCISE ATLAS OF WORLD HISTORY is not merely a condensed and abbreviated version of the earlier work. No fewer than 70 of the 320 maps here presented are entirely new or radically changed, and many others have been revised and redesigned. THE TIMES CONCISE ATLAS is intended to stand on its own feet as a compact, easily available reference book covering the whole story of mankind from the earliest beginnings, when man's ancestors first emerged from the tropical forests of Africa, to the complex, highly articulated world in which we live.

Although the present volume incorporates new material and differs in a number of other ways from the larger work on which it is based, the principles which have guided us are the same. As in THE TIMES ATLAS OF WORLD HISTORY, we have endeavoured to make the coverage as universal as is possible in the present state of knowledge, and in particular to provide full and clear accounts of the civilisations of Asia, Africa and the Americas, both before and after the coming of the Europeans. We have paid close attention to the relations and interactions between these different regions in all their manifestations – cultural and economic, peaceful and warlike, including invasions and migrations, the spread of agriculture and the diffusion of technologies – because we believe these to be some of the main threads of world history. Although we have given more space in this volume to the intricate web of politics (wars, treaties, frontier changes) and to the internal development of particular countries (e.g. England, Russia, Japan, and the U.S.A.), it is our view that world history is more than a combination of national histories, and we have planned this work accordingly.

A long view and a wide historical perspective are vitally important in the world as it is constituted today. If THE TIMES CONCISE ATLAS OF WORLD HISTORY has succeeded in providing such a view, it will have fulfilled one of its objectives. Nevertheless it is important to emphasise that this is not an atlas of current affairs. We have sought, in the concluding plates, to pick out and illustrate some of the more significant trends and movements in the contemporary world, but no attempt has been made to cover the years between 1945 and 1980 in detail. That was not our purpose; but we believe that informed knowledge of the past is a key to the understanding of the present and – as the great Victorian historian, Lord Acton, said it should be – 'a power that goes to the making of the future.'

GEOFFREY BARRACLOUGH
Oxford, March 1982

This fourth edition brings many changes and updates to Professor Barraclough's first edition and to the edition overseen by Professor Norman Stone. The world order is changing so fast that Professor Barraclough's warning that this is not an atlas of current affairs must be repeated. Nonetheless the final plates have been updated extensively.

TIMES BOOKS
January 1994

Human origins

In the vast time perspective of earth history the human species is a relative newcomer. The first life on earth of which we have any trace, simple single-celled organisms, date back some 4600 million years (diagram 1). In contrast, fully modern *Homo sapiens sapiens* originated a mere 120,000 years ago. Yet within that short period of time we have become one of the most successful species ever, colonising virtually every corner of the globe, increasing enormously in numbers and manipulating the earth's resources and environment in a way never attempted by any other organism on our planet.

Study of chromosomes shows that our nearest relatives in the animal kingdom are the African apes (gorillas and chimpanzees). With them we share a common descent from various ape-like species such as the *Dryopithecines* which lived in Africa, Europe and south Asia some 20–15 million years ago. The parting of the ways, when the human line diverged from that of the chimpanzees and gorillas (diagram), may have come as recently as 8 million years ago, a tiny interval in the 4600 million years of life on earth.

The origins of the earliest hominids lie in equatorial Africa, and it is here that the oldest remains have been found (map 3). These are of a small creature known as *Australopithecus* or 'southern ape', from the first discovery at Taung in South Africa in 1924. No fewer than four separate species of *Australopithecus* have now been distinguished in the fossil record, all restricted to Africa and living in the period from 5 million to 1 million years ago. We know that they walked upright on two legs from footsteps left in the mud at Laetoli in east Africa.

These *Australopithecines* were small agile creatures, only around four feet tall, and they lived almost exclusively on nuts, fruits and berries. But they already displayed some of the trends which were to lead to modern humans. The bipedal posture freed the hands for other tasks, in turn stimulating the development of a larger brain. At the same time, the jaw and snout became less prominent as hands could be used to break off foods

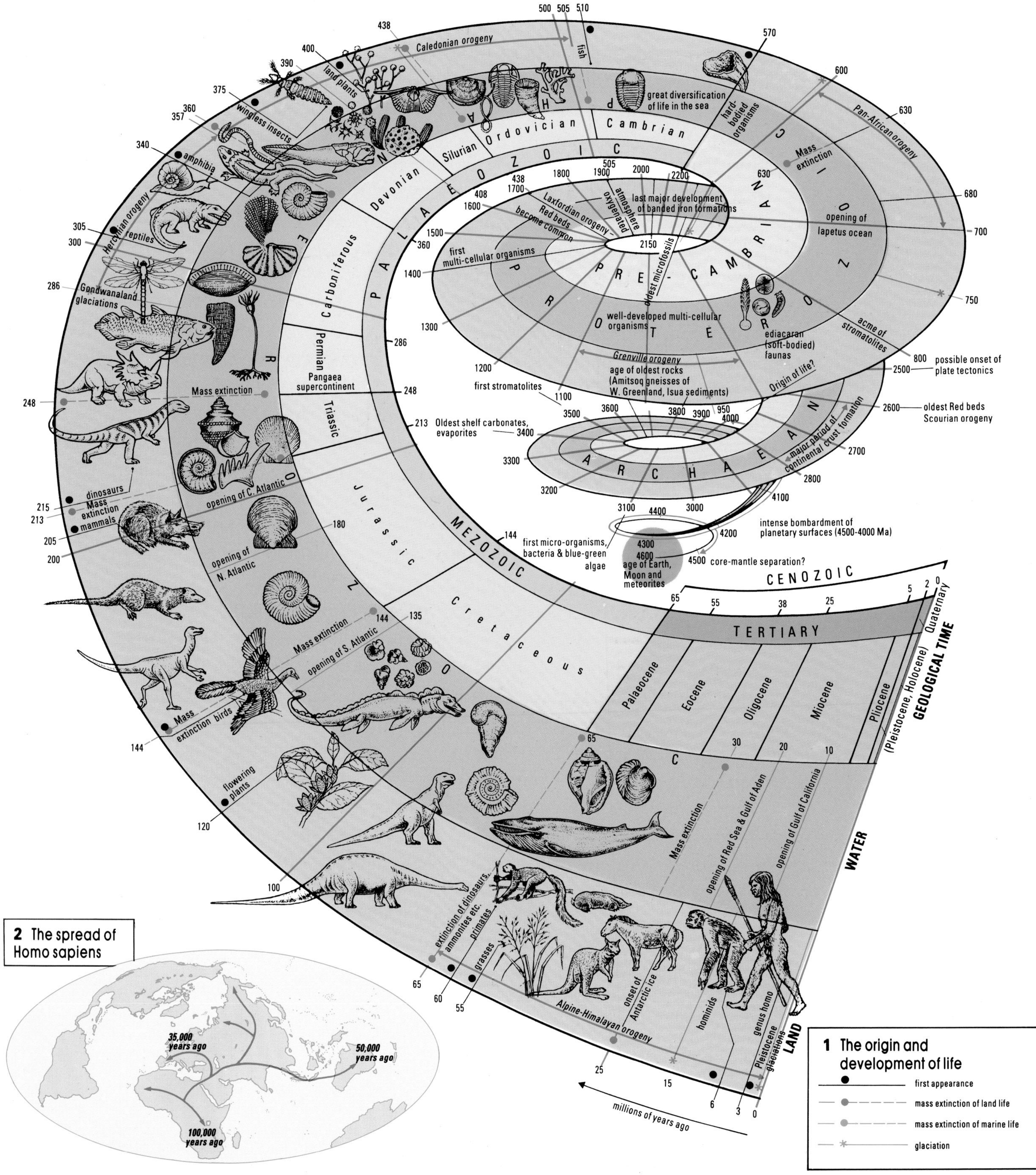

and bring them to the mouth.

A crucial stage in the development of modern man was the appearance of a new species, *Homo habilis* or 'handy man', in East Africa around 2 million years ago. These may have been the first hominids to make and use stone tools, and probably the first to scavenge for meat as a regular part of their diet. They were followed around 1.5 million years ago by *Homo erectus*, a larger and more intelligent creature, and the first human ancestor to spread beyond the confines of Africa to Europe, China and South-East Asia.

The colonisation of the Old World by *Homo erectus* was a considerable achievement given the environmental conditions of the period. *Homo erectus* and his descendants were able to make use of clothes and artificial shelters. They may also have started to hunt. Most important, however, was their mastery of fire. With more sophisticated tools, a larger brain, and command of fire, *Homo erectus* was able to survive north of the frost line at sites such as Chou-k'ou-tien (Zhoukoudian) near Peking around half a million years ago.

Homo erectus survived for a million years or more, but some time after 500,000 years ago new types of hominid began to develop in Europe and Africa. In Europe, these changes led c.100,000 BC to the appearance of Neanderthal man, named after a skull found in the Neander valley in Germany in 1856. The line of development leading to modern humans, however, was based in Africa. Here, a little over 100,000 years ago, developed the first members of our own species, *Homo sapiens sapiens*: larger-brained creatures, able hunters and gatherers, equipped with sophisticated language and technology. From Africa the new species spread throughout the whole of the territory which had been occupied by *Homo erectus* and its descendants (map 2), and beyond into the hitherto unsettled regions of Australia and the Americas. For a while, Neanderthals hung on in parts of Europe, as the last Ice Age gathered pace; but their days were numbered. By 30,000 years ago, of the many species of hominid which had walked the earth during the past 5 million years of human development, only one, *Homo sapiens sapiens*, was left.

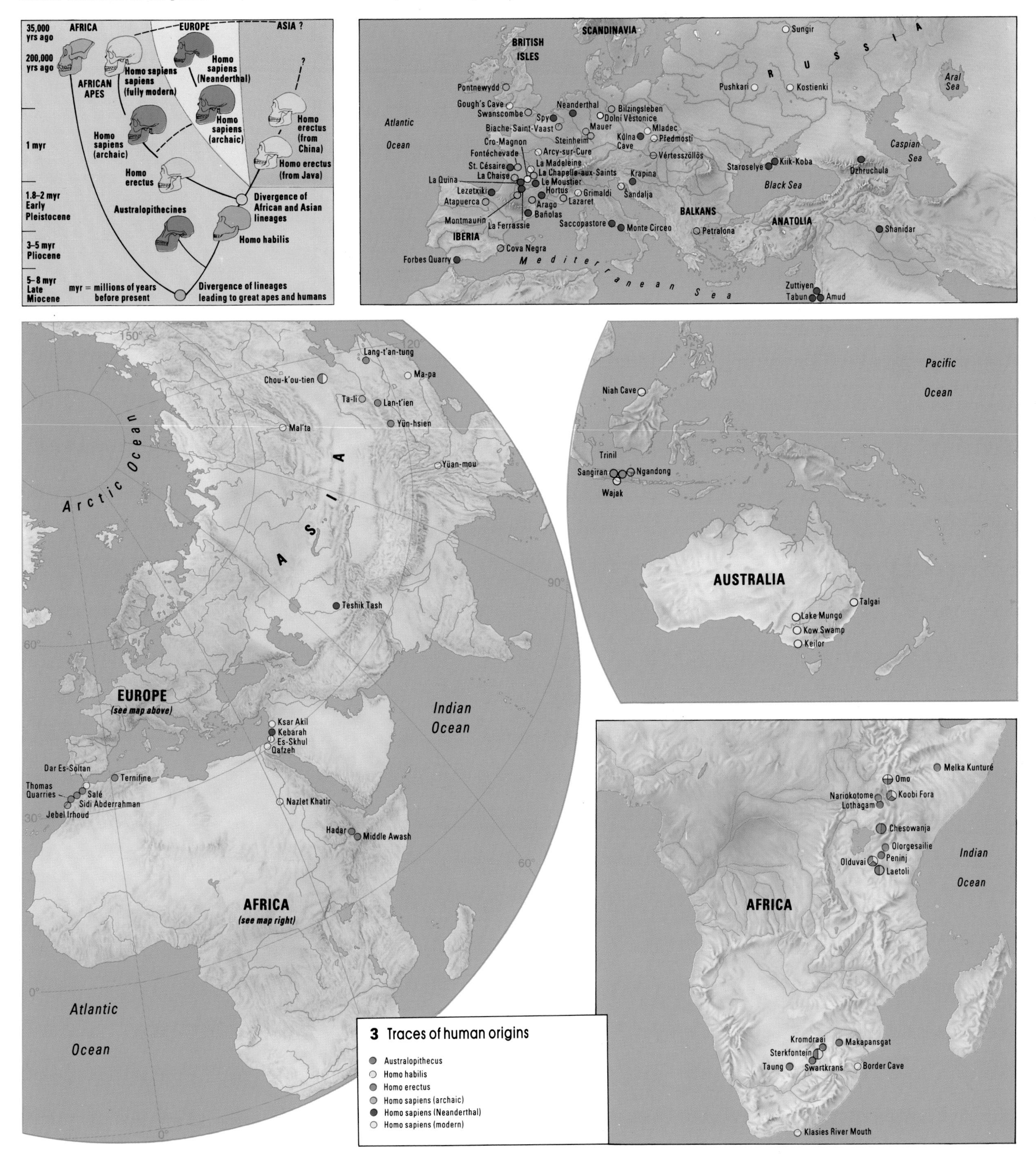

The Ice Ages

We are well aware today that the earth's climate is not a stable, static phenomenon. Indeed, for at least 14 million years world climate has gradually been cooling. Around 2 million years ago this process intensified, and by 800,000 years ago the earth was in the grip of the first of the great ice ages which were to come and go roughly every 100,000 years, and to dominate human history until the last of them receded only 10,000 years ago.

The ice ages were periods of intense cold in northern and southern latitudes away from the equator. Temperatures fell by up to 15°C, and ice sheets advanced across the frozen wastes of northern Eurasia and North America. As more and more of the earth's water became locked into the growing ice sheets, sea levels fell, and even equatorial regions did not escape the effects of climatic adversity as rainfall diminished, turning half of all the land area between the tropics into desert.

The glaciers advanced and retreated several times, reaching a climax every 100,000 years but also giving way for short periods of 10,000 years or so to more temperate regimes. With each ice advance the plants and animals of the northern hemisphere withdrew before them to warmer latitudes waiting, perhaps several thousand years, for the ice to retreat and allow them to move northwards again. Hominids too such as *Homo erectus* must have migrated with the changing climate. Yet despite the harshness of the coldest periods, the human species continued to develop during these millennia. It was indeed at this time that the human species spread from its original African homeland to east and south-east Asia and Europe. The mastery of fire and the invention of clothing and shelter were crucial to this achievement, but so were new social and communication skills. The human species as we know it today is the product of the long process of adaptation to the harsh conditions of the ice age.

The final phase of the ice ages began 75,000 years ago with the advance of the Würm glaciers in central Europe and the associated Weichsel and Wisconsin glacier fields in northern Europe and North America. By tying up water on a grand scale these reduced sea levels, and land bridges appeared, linking most of the major land areas and many present-day islands (including the British Isles) into one single continental mass. It was at this time, too, that a new species of human, fully modern *Homo sapiens sapiens*, began to spread from Africa, replacing or interbreeding with existing hominid populations in Europe and Asia. It was thus modern humans that were able to take advantage of the short sea crossing caused by sea-level fall and colonise Australasia in about 50,000 BC. A little later, perhaps as early as 40,000 BC, humans also colonised America (map 2), either by crossing the land bridge which joined the two sides of the Bering Straits at certain periods or by use of boats. With the onset of warmer conditions some 10,000 years ago rising sea levels cut off these human communities in Australia and the Americas from further contact with Eurasia. Henceforward, these regions pursued their own independent lines of development.

Modern humans were relatively late arrivals in western Europe, replacing earlier Neanderthal populations only around 35,000 years ago. Yet here, as in Australia and South America, the new communities soon developed new levels of cultural expression which still impress us today (map 3). In the Dordogne area of south-west France, in the Pyrenees and in the Cantabrian region of northern Spain, hundreds of caves were decorated with paintings of symbols and animals, sometimes in rich polychrome style.

As hunting techniques and tool technology became more sophisticated, human communities became more and more able to cope with their environment. It was, however, change in the environment itself which was most important in opening up new opportunities. Around 20,000 years ago, the last ice age was at its peak (map 1); ten thousand years later, it was in its closing stages. As temperatures rose, vegetation spread and animals began to recolonise the cold northern wastes. With them went the human hunters and gatherers. By 8000 BC, in certain crucial corners of the world such as Central America and the Near East, people had begun to move beyond their existing resources to investigate new ways of producing food, manipulating plants and animals in the first experiments in farming.

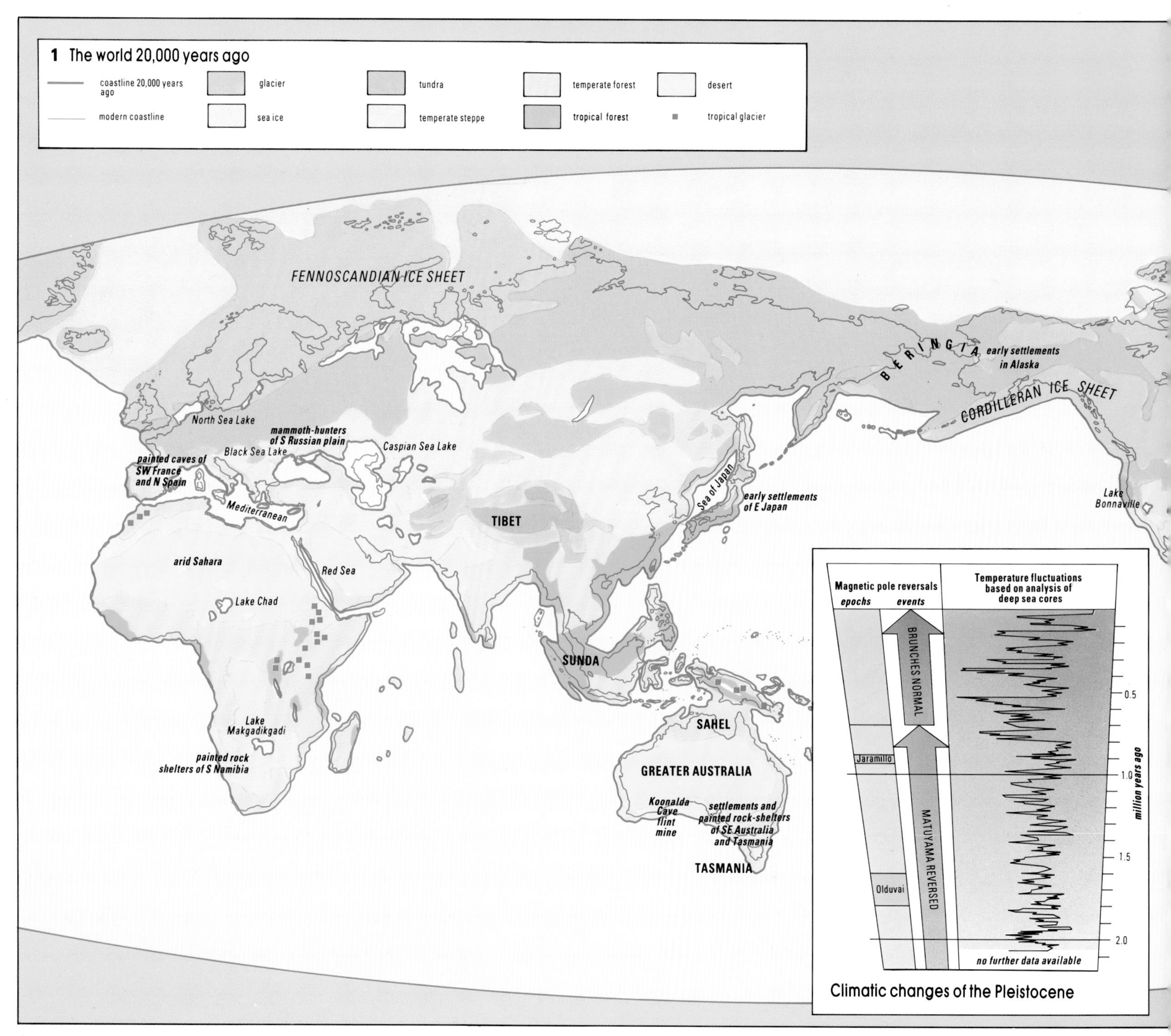

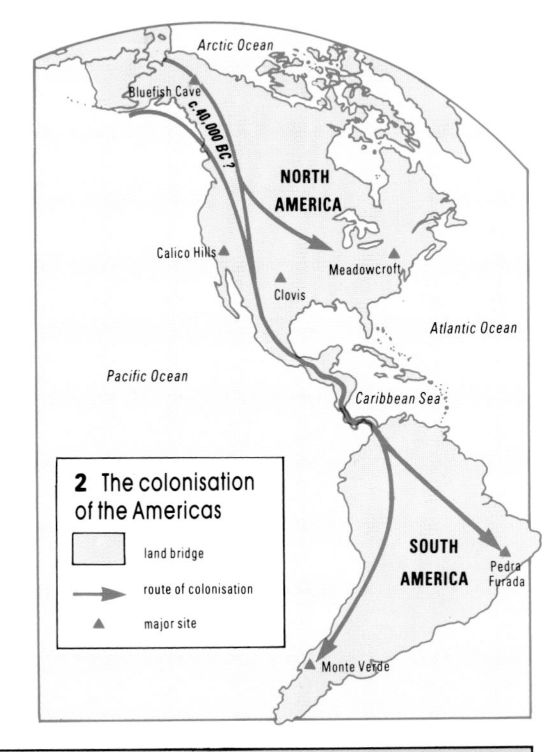

2 The colonisation of the Americas

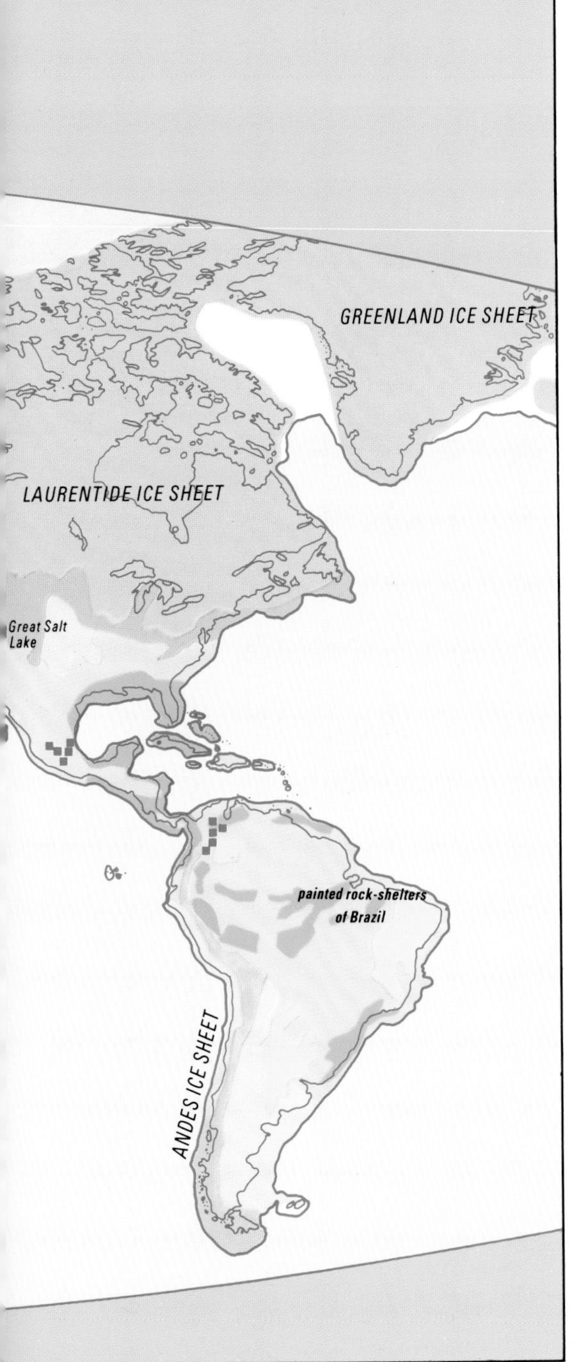

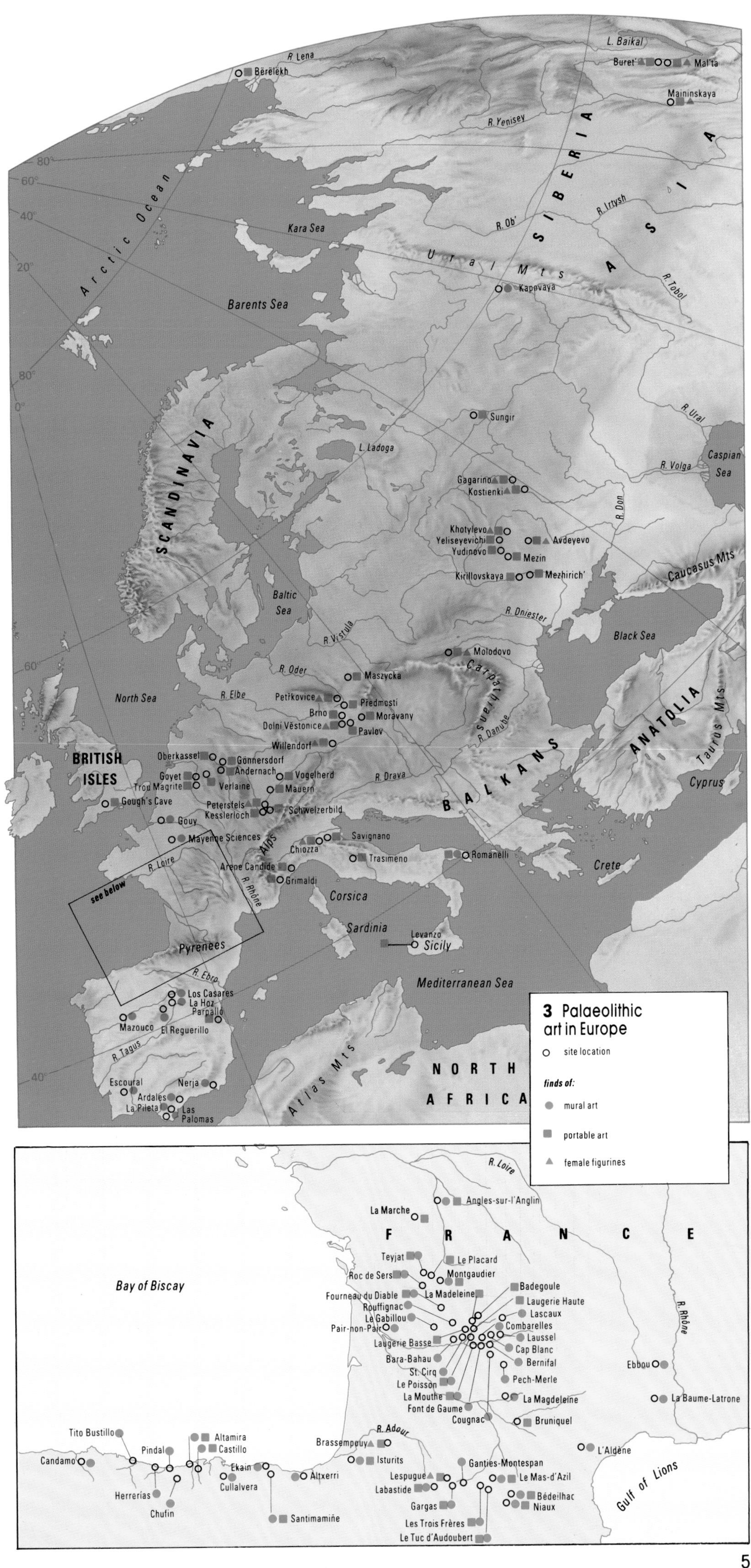

3 Palaeolithic art in Europe

From hunting to farming

Somewhere around 8000 BC human communities began to select, breed, domesticate and cultivate various species of plant and animal. This was the beginning of agriculture and is sometimes called the Neolithic or agricultural revolution. In fact, it was a slow and partial process which occurred at different times and speeds in different parts of the world and was never complete, if only because climatic and soil variations precluded agriculture in many areas. The arid zones were the home of mobile pastoralists, who domesticated sheep and horses and colonised the grazing grounds of the steppes, while the densely afforested areas, in northern Europe and elsewhere, were inhabited, as earlier, by hunters. The result, following the spread of agriculture, was a differentiated world economy, with well defined zones, cereal and root-crop cultivation being characteristic of the temperate and tropical regions respectively (map 1).

The transformation from a hunter and fisher to an agriculturalist, and from a migratory to a sedentary life, was a decisive event in world history. The increase in food resources which followed made possible a spectacular growth of human population calculated to have multiplied sixteen times between 8000 and 4000 BC. It also required co-operative effort, particularly after the introduction of irrigation c.5000 BC, leading to the establishment of settled, organised societies, at first villages, then towns and cities. Urban civilisation dates from c.3500 BC, but already before 6000 BC there were 'proto-cities' covering extensive sites (up to 30 acres) at Jericho in the Jordan valley and Çatal Hüyük in Anatolia. Here also there is evidence of long-distance trade.

There is no doubt that agriculture developed independently in different parts of the world, presumably in response to similar stimuli, but the beginnings of cereal cultivation are clearly associated with the Near East. Here, on the remote mountain uplands, were found the wild ancestors of wheat and barley, and the villages where they were first cultivated (c.8000 BC) grew up on the edge of this zone, within the critical rainfall limit of 300 mm (12 ins) a year (map 4). Only with the introduction of irrigation was it possible to extend cultivation into the adjacent dry plains. This occurred during the fifth and fourth millennia BC. At about the same time the ox-drawn plough began to be adopted throughout much of Eurasia, enlisting animal traction to increase the efficiency of farming (map 2). In much of the world, however, hoe agriculture persisted and human muscle power remained the basis of farming until relatively recent times.

Many other parts of the globe contributed their quota at different times to the supply of domesticated plants and animals (map 4). Their diffusion from their original habitat not only supplemented native food resources, but also affected human diet. Rice, which originated in South-East Asia and southern China, passed into the Near East and Mediterranean Europe, where it became a staple foodstuff. The yam and banana, later to be major African food crops, were introduced from Asia during the first millennium BC.

As farming spread, hunting and gathering was increasingly relegated to the more marginal world environments where agriculture was unable to secure a foothold (map 3). The gradual decline of hunters and gatherers can be traced across the centuries, until in recent times their sole surviving representatives have been found only in hot deserts such as the Kalahari and Australia, in the dense rain forests of the Amazon basin, central Africa and South-East Asia, and in the frozen wastes of the Arctic.

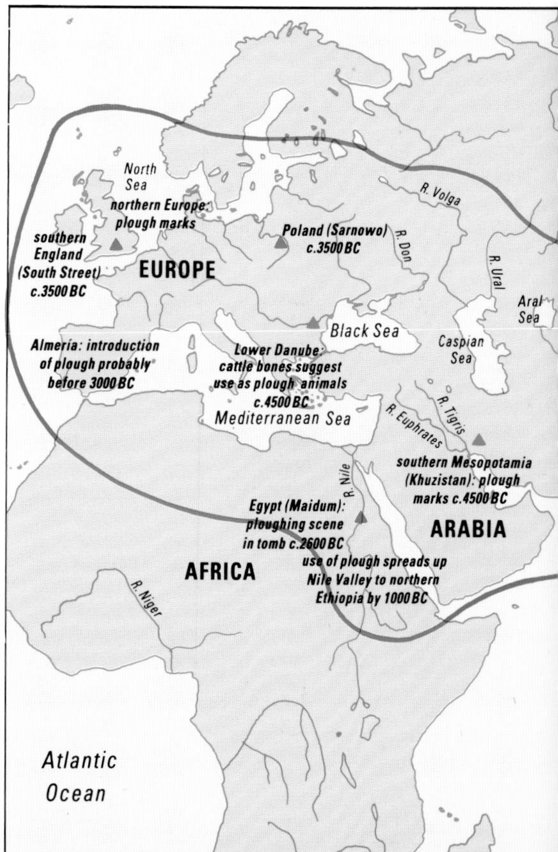

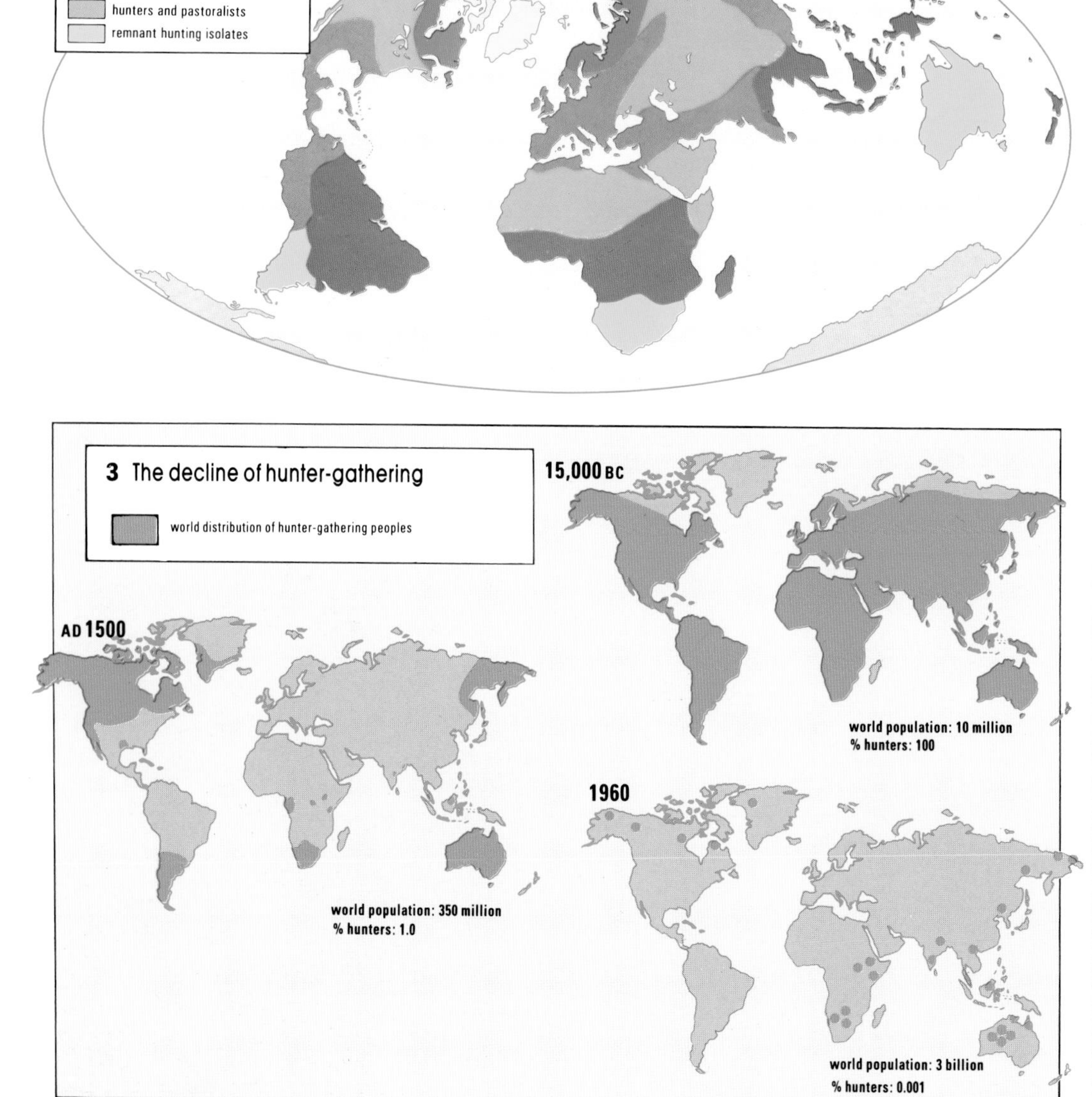

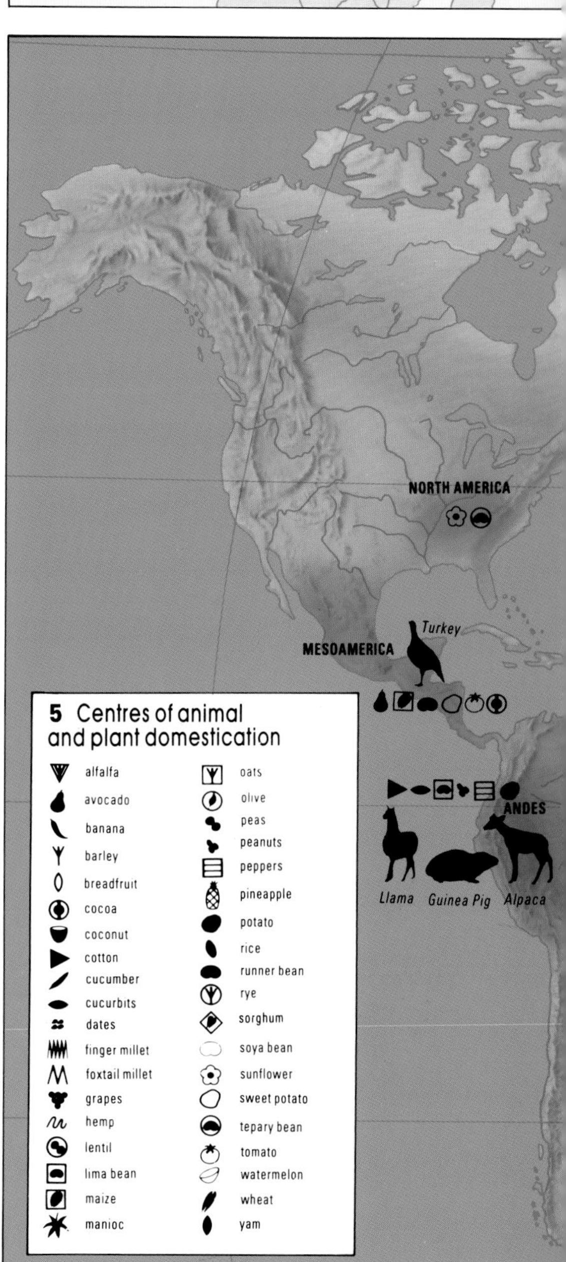

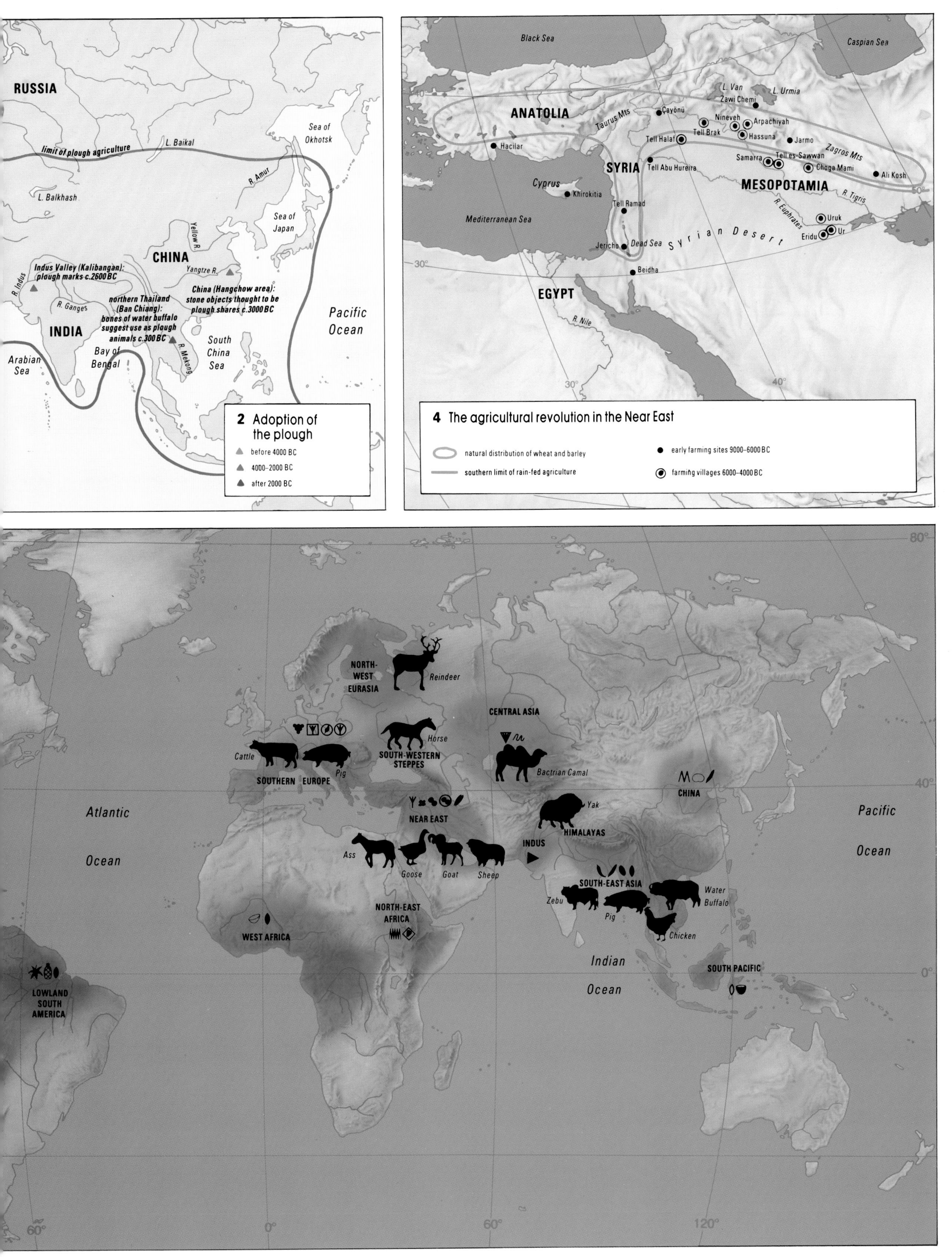

RUSSIA
limit of plough agriculture
L. Baikal
Sea of Okhotsk
R. Amur
L. Balkhash
Sea of Japan
Yellow R.
CHINA
Yangtze R.
Indus Valley (Kalibangan): plough marks c.2600 BC
R. Indus
R. Ganges
northern Thailand (Ban Chiang): bones of water buffalo suggest use as plough animals c.300 BC
China (Hangchow area): stone objects thought to be plough shares c.3000 BC
INDIA
Bay of Bengal
Arabian Sea
R. Mekong
South China Sea
Pacific Ocean
2 Adoption of the plough
before 4000 BC
4000–2000 BC
after 2000 BC
Black Sea
Caspian Sea
L. Van
L. Urmia
Zawi Chemi
ANATOLIA
Taurus Mts
Çayönü
Nineveh
Arpachiyah
Tell Brak
Hassuna
Tell Halaf
Jarmo
Hacilar
Zagros Mts
SYRIA
Tell Abu Hureira
Samarra
Tell es-Sawwan
Choga Mami
Ali Kosh
Cyprus
Khirokitia
MESOPOTAMIA
R. Tigris
Tell Ramad
R. Euphrates
Mediterranean Sea
Uruk
Eridu
Ur
Jericho
Dead Sea
Syrian Desert
Beidha
EGYPT
R. Nile
4 The agricultural revolution in the Near East
natural distribution of wheat and barley
southern limit of rain-fed agriculture
early farming sites 9000–6000 BC
farming villages 6000–4000 BC
NORTH-WEST EURASIA
Reindeer
CENTRAL ASIA
Horse
SOUTH-WESTERN STEPPES
Cattle
Pig
SOUTHERN EUROPE
Bactrian Camal
CHINA
Atlantic Ocean
NEAR EAST
Yak
HIMALAYAS
Pacific Ocean
Ass
Goose
Goat
Sheep
INDUS
SOUTH-EAST ASIA
Zebu
Pig
Water Buffalo
Chicken
NORTH-EAST AFRICA
WEST AFRICA
Indian Ocean
SOUTH PACIFIC
LOWLAND SOUTH AMERICA

Early cultures of Asia

From an origin in Africa, *Homo erectus* or its close relatives had spread widely through Asia by the Middle Pleistocene period (400–200,000 years ago). It is not possible to establish the precise history of this colonisation process, but it is reasonable to assume that these hominids first reached India, where hand-axes, chopping tools and flakes of the early Stone Age are found not only in the foothills of the Punjab but as far east as southern Bihar and northern Orissa and as far south as Madras (map 1). It was not long before *Homo erectus* also became established in both East and South-East Asia, as shown by skeletal remains from Java and China. Here they remained until replaced some 60,000 years ago by our own fully modern species, *Homo sapiens sapiens*.

Little is known of the development of human societies in this part of the world until the advent of agriculture. At about the same time as farming communities were getting under way in western Asia, the first experiments in agriculture were also being made in East and South Asia. In China, the most important centre of early farming was the Yellow River valley in the north, where crops of millet were raised on the well-drained loess terraces of the river valleys from around 6000 BC (map 2). A little later, rice cultivation spread northwards from its original heartland in South-East Asia, giving a second productive staple crop. The early villages grew and prospered, and new technologies made their appearance: jade-carving, silk-weaving and very high quality pottery production using the fast wheel.

In about 1800 BC the thriving villages and small towns which had developed in northern China gave rise to the first Chinese civilisation. Early dynasties soon gave way to the Shang, who ruled much of the North China plain and parts of the Yangtze valley from the 16th to the 11th century BC (map 4). Great cities developed, notably at Cheng-chou and An-yang, and rulers were given lavish burial in royal tombs.

The first civilisation of South Asia developed in the valley of the Indus river. Again, this was founded on a secure agricultural base which had been developing since c.6000 BC or earlier. Large-scale settlement of the fertile river plain seems to have occurred in the 4th millennium BC, and soon afterwards the first cities appear, notably those of Harappa and Mohenjo-daro (map 5). These were highly-developed cities covering nearly 1,295,000 sq.kms, and surviving for over 1000 years. A standardised system of weights and measures was devised, and trade with the Persian Gulf brought Indus products to the great cities of southern Mesopotamia. Influences from South Asia also reached South-East Asia, where the distinctive Dong Son drums were produced by communities of village farmers from 1500–500 BC (map 3).

The Indus cities were abandoned soon after 2000 BC, overtaken perhaps by environmental change or natural disaster, and it was over 1000 years before cities reappeared in the sub-continent. The focus had by this time shifted to the Ganges, where the historic cities and states of northern India began to form in about 500 BC. By that time China too was divided between a number of major kingdoms, as the unified rule of the Shang and their successors the Chou broke down and fragmented (map 6). Yet despite the divisions, the basic foundations of Chinese and Indian civilisation had been laid.

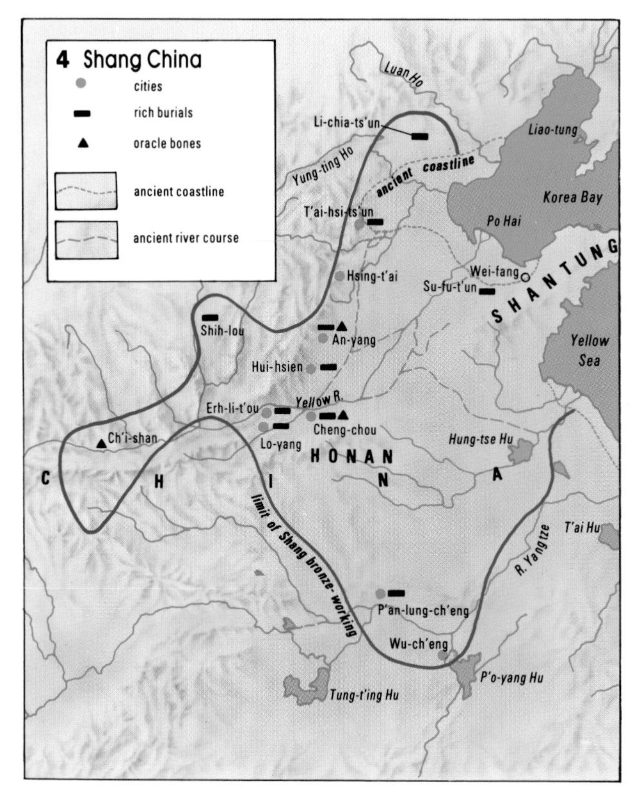

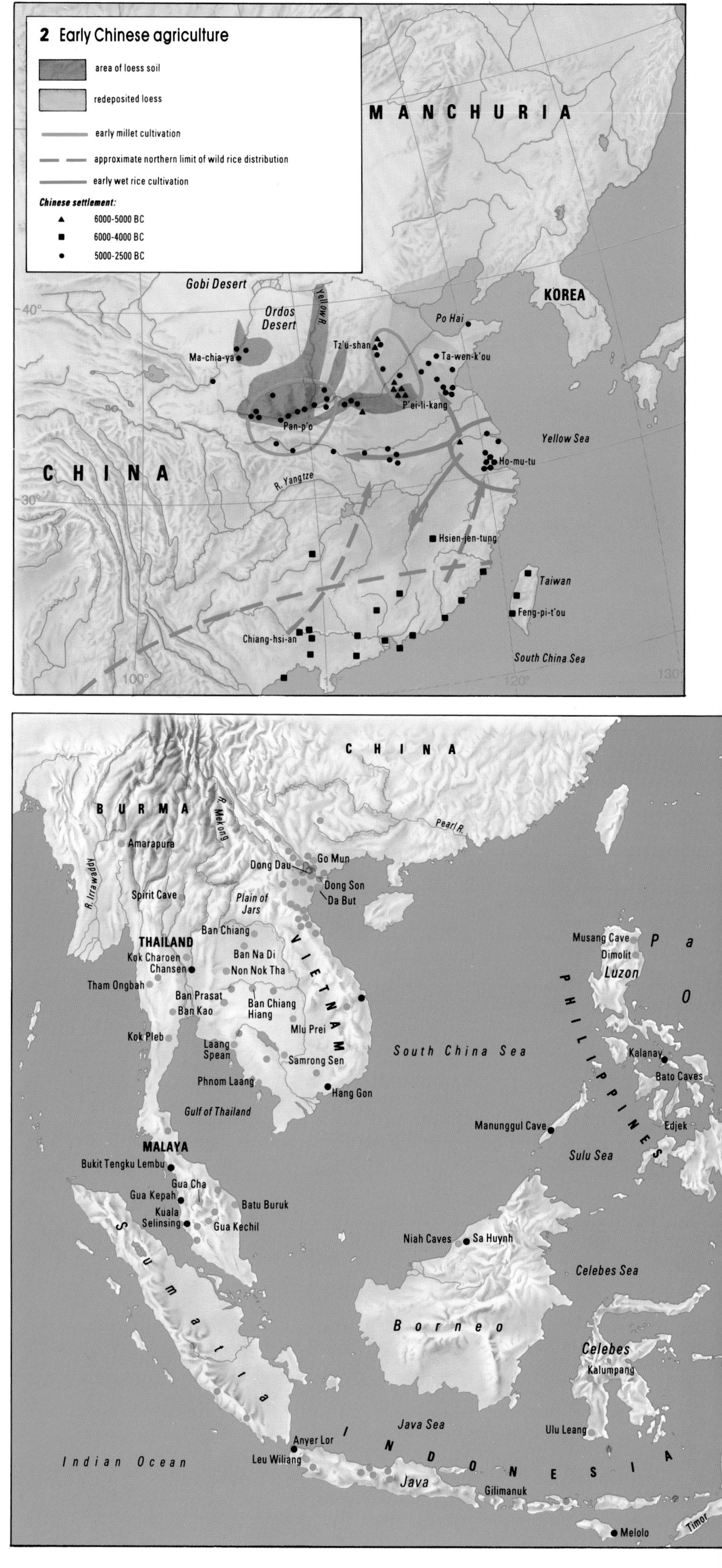

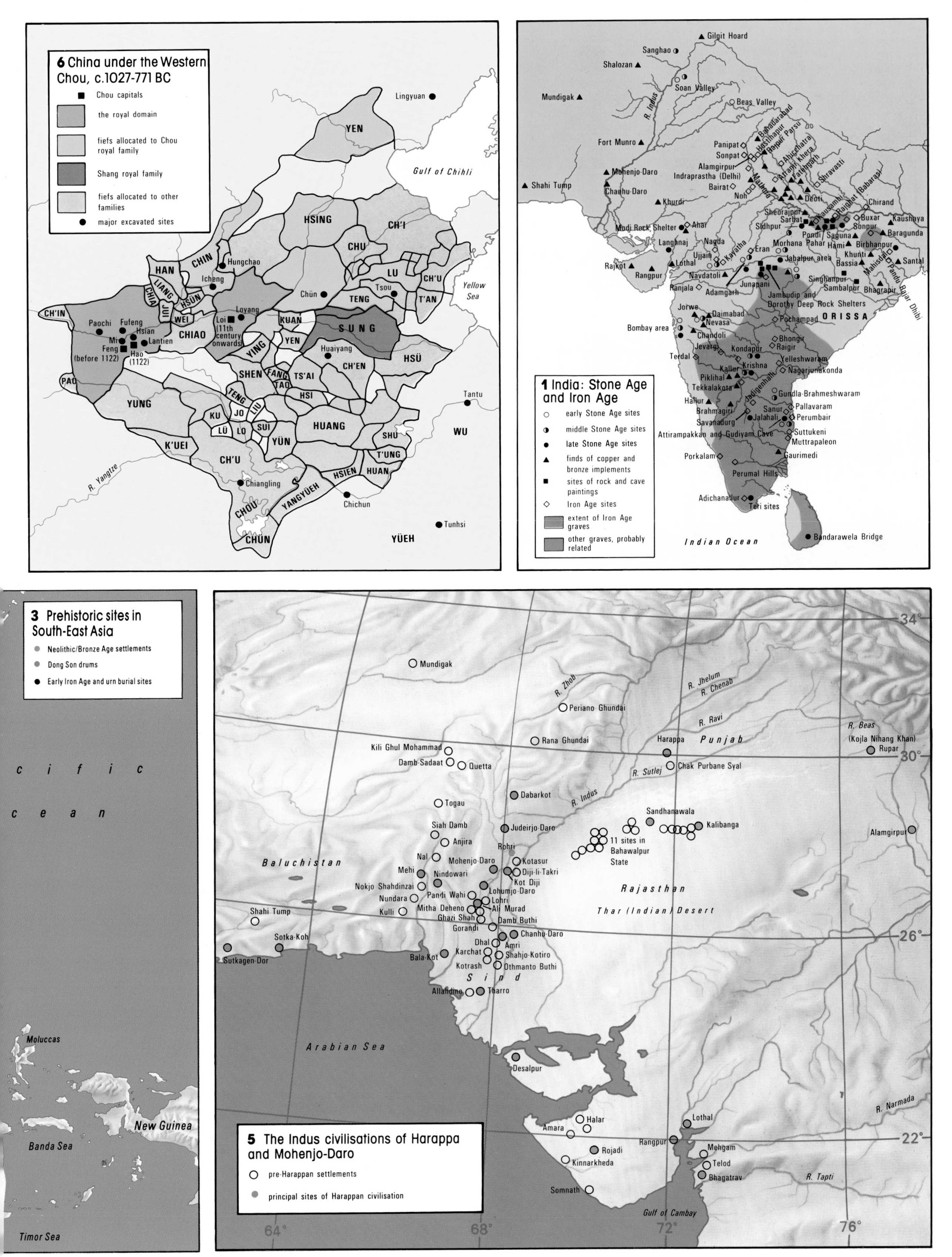

6 China under the Western Chou, c.1027-771 BC

1 India: Stone Age and Iron Age

3 Prehistoric sites in South-East Asia

5 The Indus civilisations of Harappa and Mohenjo-Daro

Prehistoric Africa and Australasia

Climatic change, between 5–6000 years ago, profoundly influenced the early history of Africa and Australasia. North Africa developed in close association with western Asia, and by 3000 BC an advanced civilisation was established in Egypt. But Africa south of the equator, almost certainly the original home of humans, was cut off from the mainstream for centuries by the desiccation of the Sahara. Similar changes occurred in Australia which had been populated during the late Pleistocene ice age via the land bridge from New Guinea (page 4). Here the rise of the sea level drowned large areas of coastal lowland and severed the land link with New Guinea. The Australasian continent developed thenceforth in geographical isolation. The colonisation of the islands of Melanesia occurred considerably later, when settlers from New Guinea, associated with the distinctive Lapita pottery, reached Fiji (c.1300 BC) and then made their way into Polynesia via Tonga and Samoa, reaching the Marquesas Islands c.AD 300 (map 2). From here they spread north to Hawaii (c.AD 800) and south-west via the Cook Islands to New Zealand between 850 and 1100 (map 3).

Geographical isolation was an important factor in shaping the cultures of southern Africa and of Oceania. In much of Australia the aborigines remained hunters and gatherers and there was no use of iron, but they were prolific in their decoration of rock shelters with deeply symbolic designs. Elsewhere in Oceania, notably in New Zealand, a mixed hunting-farming society developed and settlement spread inland. But population remained small, about 300,000 in Australia and 100,000 in New Zealand when the Europeans arrived. The isolation of southern Africa was never so complete. In East Africa settlers spread down the Rift Valley from Ethiopia during the first millennium BC, and trans-Saharan trade increased in importance after the introduction of the camel from Asia c.100 BC (map 1). This facilitated the spread of iron tools and weapons, introduced in the north by Greeks and Carthaginians in the eighth and seventh centuries. Aided by the new iron technology, Bantu-speaking farmers and cattle-herdsmen began to colonise southern Africa in the early centuries AD. By the thirteenth century powerful Bantu chiefdoms had emerged, such as that centred on the Great Zimbabwe enclosure, cattle-raising communities already engaged in trade when the Portuguese arrived at the close of the fifteenth century.

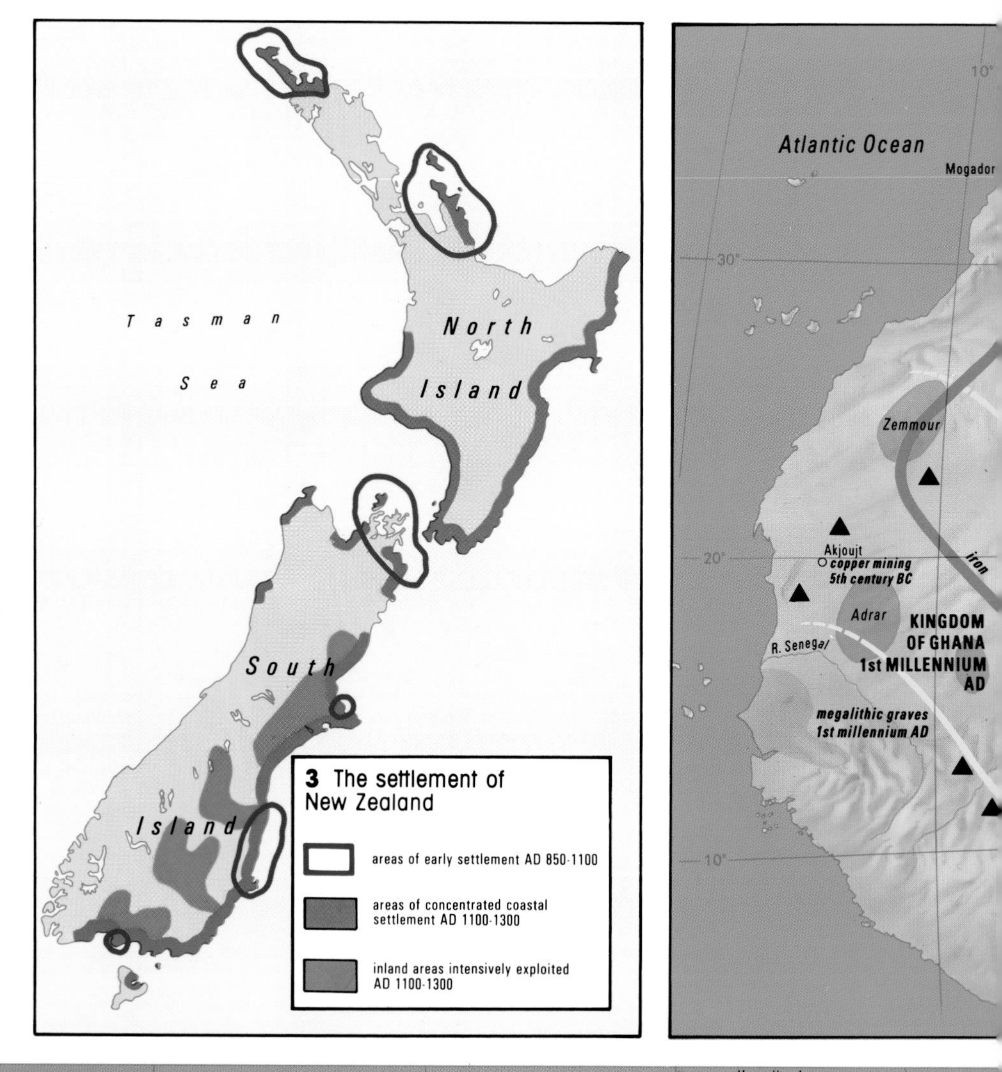

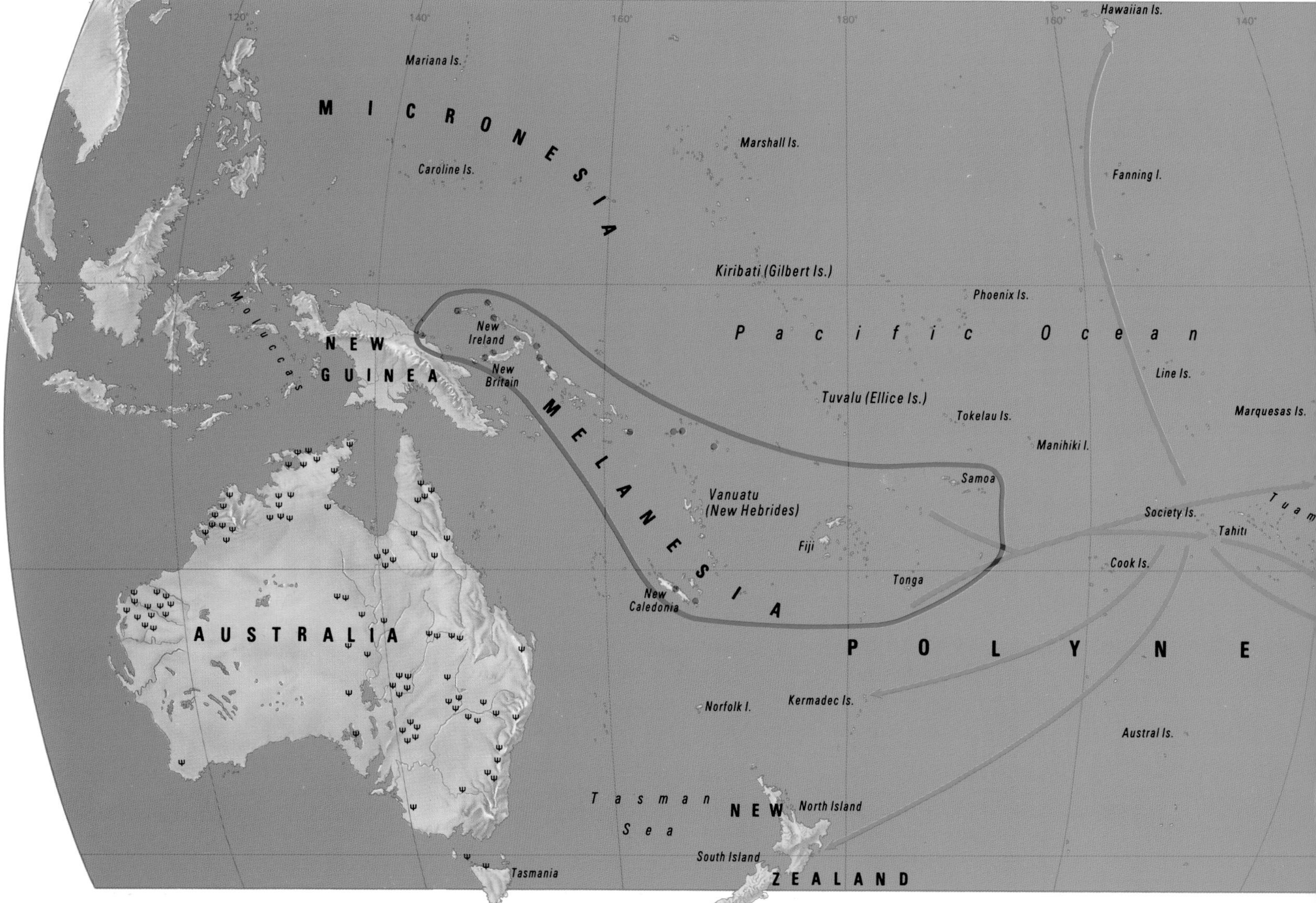

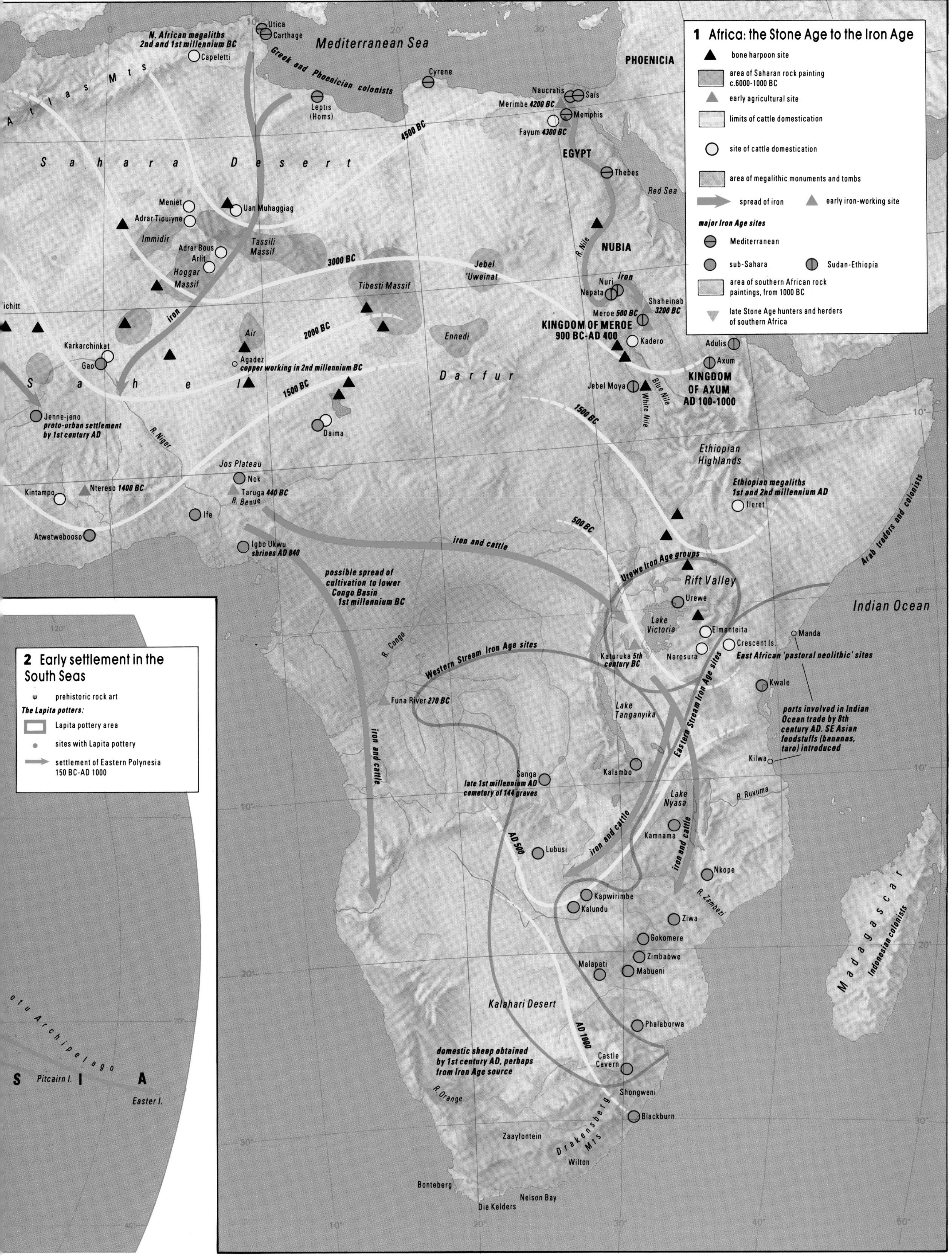
1 Africa: the Stone Age to the Iron Age
bone harpoon site
area of Saharan rock painting c.6000-1000 BC
early agricultural site
limits of cattle domestication
site of cattle domestication
area of megalithic monuments and tombs
spread of iron
early iron-working site
major Iron Age sites
Mediterranean
sub-Sahara
Sudan-Ethiopia
area of southern African rock paintings, from 1000 BC
late Stone Age hunters and herders of southern Africa
Mediterranean Sea
N. African megaliths 2nd and 1st millennium BC
Utica
Carthage
Capeletti
Greek and Phoenician colonists
Cyrene
Leptis (Homs)
PHOENICIA
Naucratis
Sais
Merimbe 4200 BC
Memphis
Fayum 4300 BC
EGYPT
Thebes
Red Sea
Atlas Mts
Sahara Desert
4500 BC
Meniet
Uan Muhaggiag
Adrar Tiouiyne
Immidir
Adrar Bous
Arlit
Tassili Massif
Hoggar Massif
3000 BC
Tibesti Massif
Jebel 'Uweinat
R. Nile
NUBIA
Nuri
Napata
iron
Shaheinab 3200 BC
Meroe 500 BC
KINGDOM OF MEROE 900 BC-AD 400
Kadero
Adulis
Axum
KINGDOM OF AXUM AD 100-1000
Jebel Moya
Blue Nile
White Nile
Tichitt
Karkarchinkat
Gao
Air
2000 BC
Ennedi
Agadez
copper working in 2nd millennium BC
Sahel
1500 BC
Darfur
Jenne-jeno
proto-urban settlement by 1st century AD
R. Niger
Daima
1500 BC
Ethiopian Highlands
Jos Plateau
Nok
Kintampo
Ntereso 1400 BC
Taruga 440 BC
R. Benue
Ife
Atwetwebooso
Ethiopian megaliths 1st and 2nd millennium AD
Ileret
500 BC
iron and cattle
Igbo Ukwu shrines AD 840
possible spread of cultivation to lower Congo Basin 1st millennium BC
Urewe Iron Age groups
Rift Valley
Urewe
Arab traders and colonists
Indian Ocean
Lake Victoria
Elmenteita
Manda
Crescent Is.
Narosura
Katuruka 5th century BC
East African 'pastoral neolithic' sites
R. Congo
Western Stream Iron Age sites
Kwale
Funa River 270 BC
iron and cattle
Lake Tanganyika
Eastern Stream Iron Age sites
ports involved in Indian Ocean trade by 8th century AD. SE Asian foodstuffs (bananas, taro) introduced
Kilwa
Kalambo
Sanga
late 1st millennium AD cemetery of 144 graves
Lake Nyasa
R. Ruvuma
Kamnama
iron and cattle
AD 500
Lubusi
Nkope
Kapwirimbe
Kalundu
R. Zambezi
Ziwa
Madagascar
Indonesian colonists
Gokomere
Zimbabwe
Malapati
Mabueni
Kalahari Desert
AD 1000
Phalaborwa
domestic sheep obtained by 1st century AD, perhaps from Iron Age source
Castle Cavern
R. Orange
Shongweni
Blackburn
Drakensberg Mts
Zaayfontein
Wilton
Bonteberg
Nelson Bay
Die Kelders
2 Early settlement in the South Seas
prehistoric rock art
The Lapita potters:
Lapita pottery area
sites with Lapita pottery
settlement of Eastern Polynesia 150 BC-AD 1000
Tuamotu Archipelago
Pitcairn I.
Easter I.

Peoples and cultures of the Americas

America, like Australia (page 10), was colonised from Asia during the last Ice Age more than 10,000 years ago, and like Australia was later cut off from the Old World by the melting of the ice and the rise of the sea level which submerged the land bridge across the Bering Strait (page 4). Unlike the Australian aborigines, however, who never progressed beyond a Stone Age hunting and gathering culture, geographic isolation did not prevent the American Indians from developing independently a high level of civilisation, based on agriculture (particularly the cultivation of maize), mining (particularly obsidian for tools and weapons), pottery manufacture and gold, silver and copper working. It was a civilisation distinguished not only by magnificent art and remarkable mathematical and astronomical skills, but also by monumental building on a grand scale. In its prime, around AD 600, the city of Teotihuacán in the basin of Mexico covered 20 sq. km (8 sq. miles) and had a population of 125,000.

The first civilisations arose in the climatically favourable regions of Mesoamerica and the central Andes, where maize farming, permitting a rapid increase in population, became widespread from c.1500 BC. Between 800 and 500 BC the Olmecs on the Gulf of Mexico, the Zapotecs at Monte Albán, and the inhabitants of Chavín in Peru had developed complex societies with populations numbering tens of thousands, possibly a professional priesthood, and several social ranks including craftsmen and traders. Mesoamerica and the central Andes remained the main centres of civilisation, but the diffusion of agriculture and growing commercial exchanges soon affected other regions. In North America the introduction of maize, beans and squashes from Mexico initiated a period of rapid development between 300 BC and AD 550. Its centre was the Hopewell territory in Illinois and Ohio, but trading contacts (mainly for precious metals) extended its influence as far as Florida and the Rockies (map 3). In South America a number of separate centres, each with its own distinctive artistic style, developed in the Andes (map 4), and were fused after AD 600 into the empires of Tiahuanaco and Huari (map 5). But this precarious unity broke down after AD 800 and it was not until the fifteenth century under the Incas that Peru was once again united (page 62).

In Mesoamerica, the early Olmec and Zapotec civilisations were complemented by new influences, including the Maya in Yucatán from the fourth century BC, then the Toltecs in the ninth century and finally the Aztecs in the thirteenth century. The classic period of Maya civilisation falls between AD 300 and AD 900; but influences radiating from Teotihuacán were strong (map 2), and Maya civilisation, like all the other civilisations of the classical period, was essentially a variant of a common Mesoamerican culture pattern. Internecine warfare appears to have weakened these civilisations and left them prey to invaders or local instability. Teotihuacán was destroyed c.750, Monte Albán allowed to go to ruin during the tenth century, and Maya civilisation collapsed between AD 800 and 900.

For all their brilliant architectural and artistic achievements, the civilisations of Mesoamerica and the Andes account for only a small area of the Americas taken as a whole (map 1). Climatic variation alone dictated disparate ways of life. Particularly in the far north and far south, where conditions were too harsh for farming, the small nomadic populations depended on hunting and fishing. Climate was also a determining factor for the desert gatherers in the interior. The continent the Europeans encountered when they arrived in the sixteenth century was at widely different levels of development; but even the simpler societies had adapted themselves to the environment and its requirements.

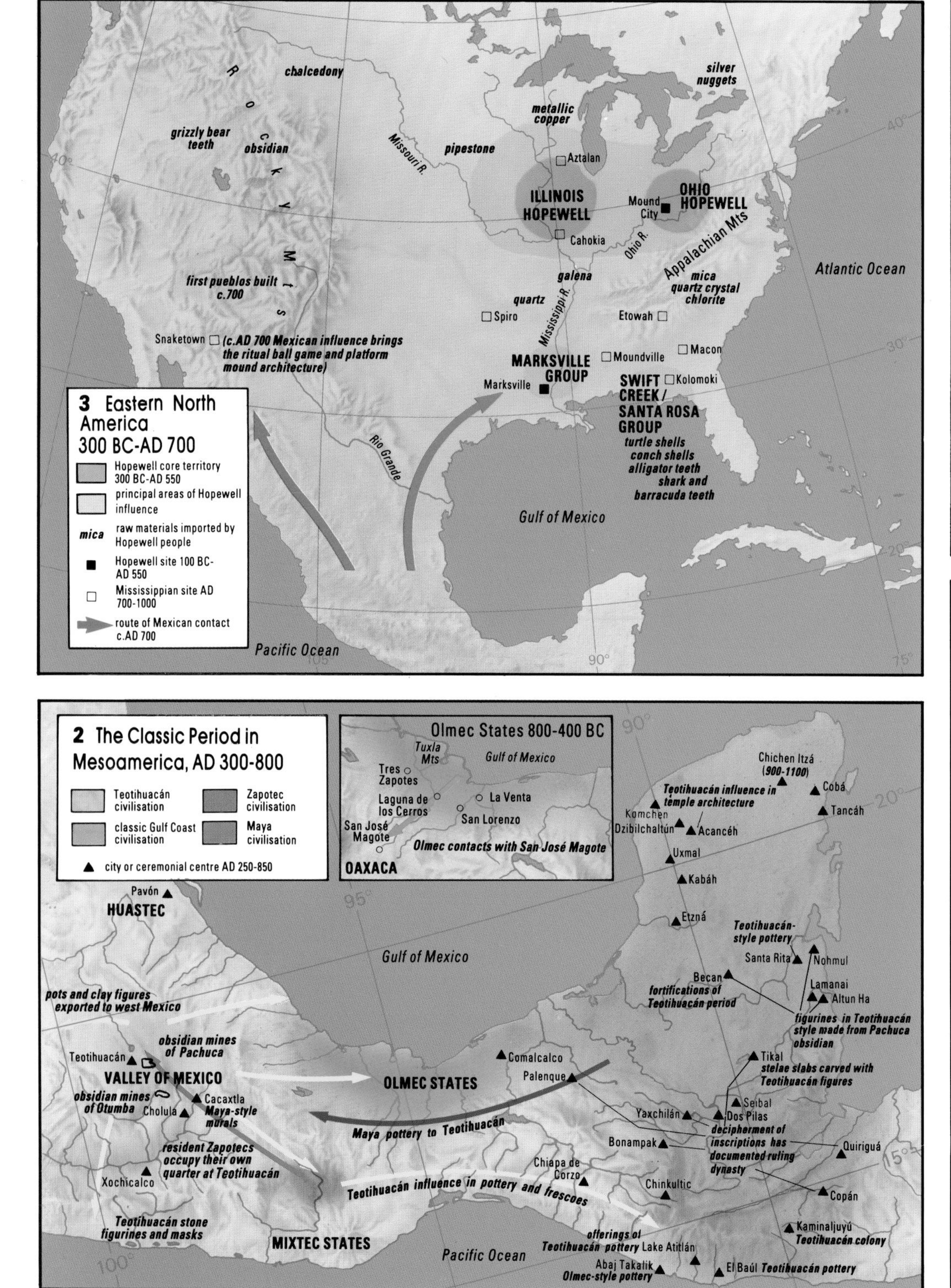

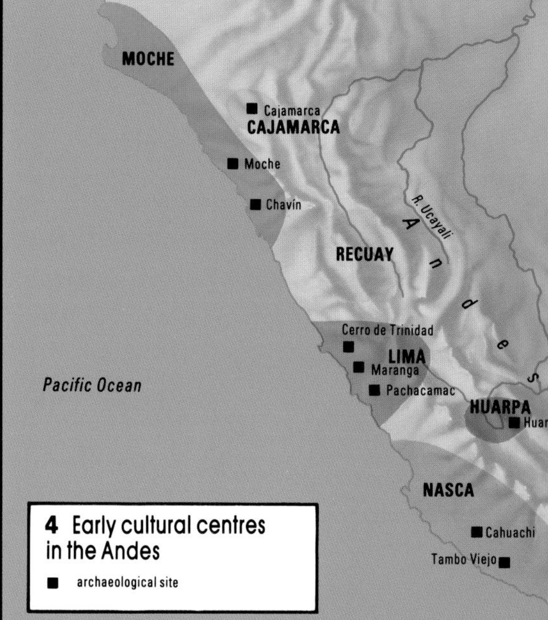

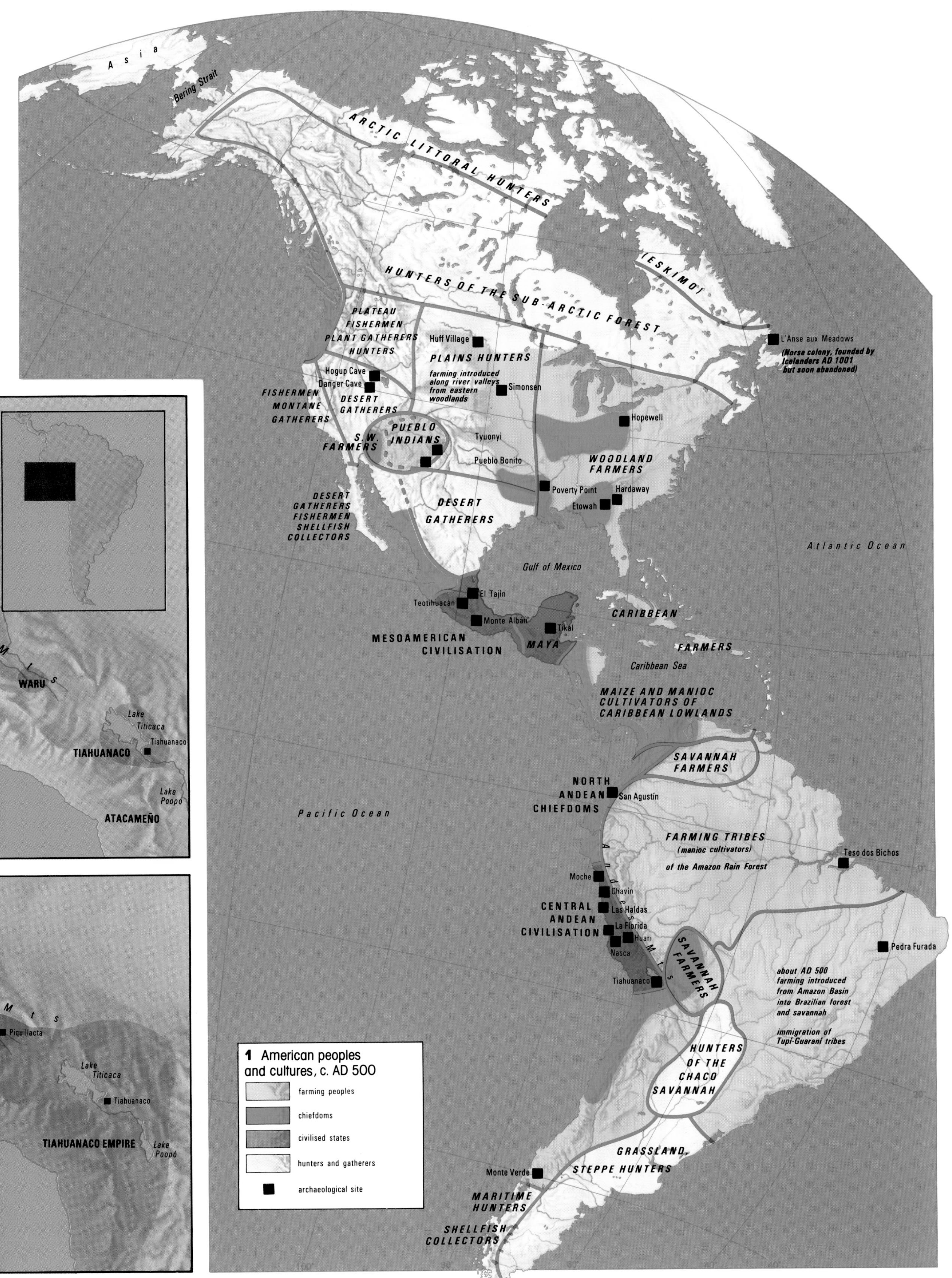
Asia
Bering Strait
ARCTIC LITTORAL HUNTERS
(ESKIMO)
HUNTERS OF THE SUB-ARCTIC FOREST
PLATEAU FISHERMEN PLANT GATHERERS HUNTERS
Huff Village
PLAINS HUNTERS
farming introduced along river valleys from eastern woodlands
Simonsen
L'Anse aux Meadows
(Norse colony, founded by Icelanders AD 1001 but soon abandoned)
Hogup Cave
Danger Cave
FISHERMEN MONTANE GATHERERS
DESERT GATHERERS
PUEBLO INDIANS
S.W. FARMERS
Tyuonyi
Pueblo Bonito
Hopewell
WOODLAND FARMERS
Poverty Point
Hardaway
Etowah
DESERT GATHERERS FISHERMEN SHELLFISH COLLECTORS
DESERT GATHERERS
Atlantic Ocean
Gulf of Mexico
El Tajín
Teotihuacán
Monte Albán
Tikal
MAYA
MESOAMERICAN CIVILISATION
CARIBBEAN FARMERS
Caribbean Sea
MAIZE AND MANIOC CULTIVATORS OF CARIBBEAN LOWLANDS
SAVANNAH FARMERS
NORTH ANDEAN CHIEFDOMS
San Agustín
Pacific Ocean
FARMING TRIBES
(manioc cultivators)
of the Amazon Rain Forest
Teso dos Bichos
Andes Mts
Moche
Chavín
Las Haldas
CENTRAL ANDEAN CIVILISATION
La Florida
Huari
Nasca
Tiahuanaco
SAVANNAH FARMERS
Pedra Furada
about AD 500 farming introduced from Amazon Basin into Brazilian forest and savannah
immigration of Tupí-Guaraní tribes
HUNTERS OF THE CHACO SAVANNAH
GRASSLAND, STEPPE HUNTERS
Monte Verde
MARITIME HUNTERS
SHELLFISH COLLECTORS
Mts
WARU
Lake Titicaca
Tiahuanaco
TIAHUANACO
Lake Poopó
ATACAMEÑO
Piquillacta
TIAHUANACO EMPIRE
1 American peoples and cultures, c. AD 500
farming peoples
chiefdoms
civilised states
hunters and gatherers
archaeological site

The development of Europe, 6000-300BC

It was only after farming had been established in the Near East for several hundred years that it first spread westwards to Europe. The earliest European agriculturalists settled in farming villages on the plains of Thessaly and Crete c.6000 BC (map 1). The crops of wheat and barley which these communities grew were of Near Eastern type, and they relied heavily on the Near Eastern animal domesticates sheep and goat. As farming spread north and west into temperate Europe, however, major adjustments were necessary. New types of wheat and barley replaced those of Greece and the Near East, and cattle and pig became the dominant species of livestock in forested parts of central, western and northern Europe in place of sheep and goat.

The new farming technology, including not only domesticated species of plants and animals but also pottery and polished stone tools, spread rapidly across Europe in the 6th and 5th millennia BC, reaching Britain and Denmark by 4000 BC. In the centuries of consolidation which followed, the early farmers of western and northern Europe built great burial mounds with megalithic chambers in which dozens if not hundreds of dead bodies were deposited. They also raised circles of standing stones (map 3).

By this time a new technology was spreading across Europe, supplementing the stone tools of the previous centuries: metallurgy (map 2). South-east Europe became an important centre of gold and copper-working as early as 4500 BC. By 2500 BC it had become common to alloy the copper with tin to produce bronze, an alloy of greater hardness, thus initiating the period known as the Bronze Age. The need to obtain access to the raw materials copper and tin led to the development of extensive trade networks along which other materials also travelled, such as the Baltic amber which is found as far afield as Mycenae (map 4).

Around 1200 BC a more closely articulated political organisation began to emerge, centred upon hillforts built to house and defend a warrior-aristocracy. The upper Rhine/upper Danube became an important core area where a distinctive Celtic culture emerged in the 1st millennium BC (map 5). Ironworking was introduced c.1000–700 BC, which together with population growth fuelled a period of Celtic expansion in the La Tène period (from 480 BC). Contact with the Mediterranean world stimulated Celtic civilisation, but it also prepared the way for Caesar's campaigns. Thus it was that by 50 BC most of the western Celtic world was under Roman control.

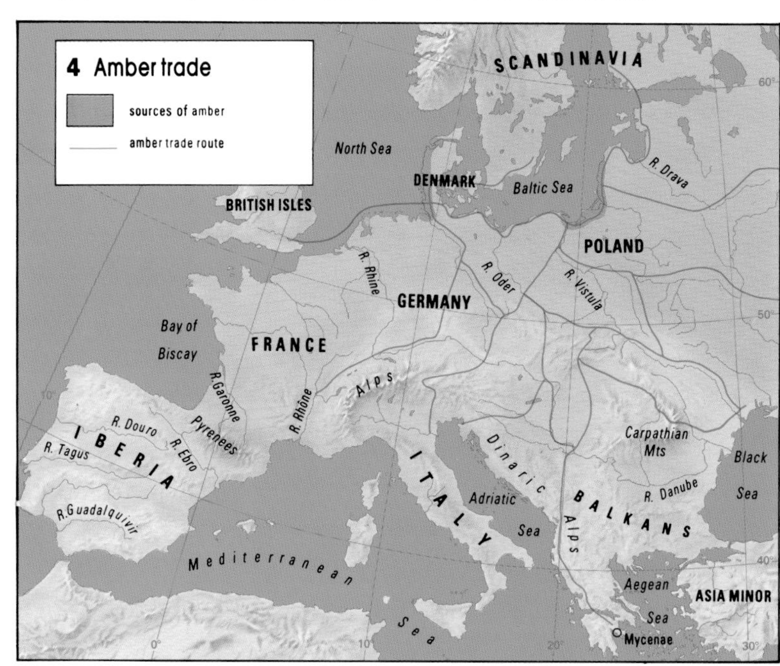

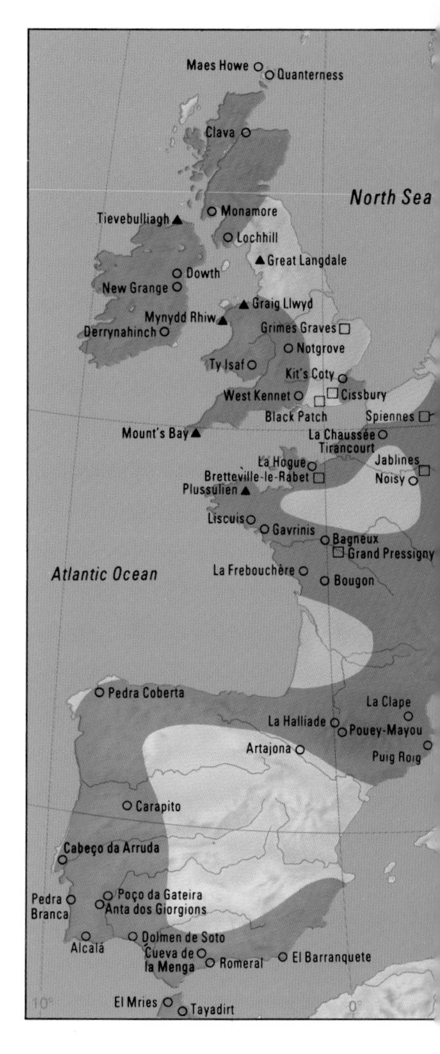

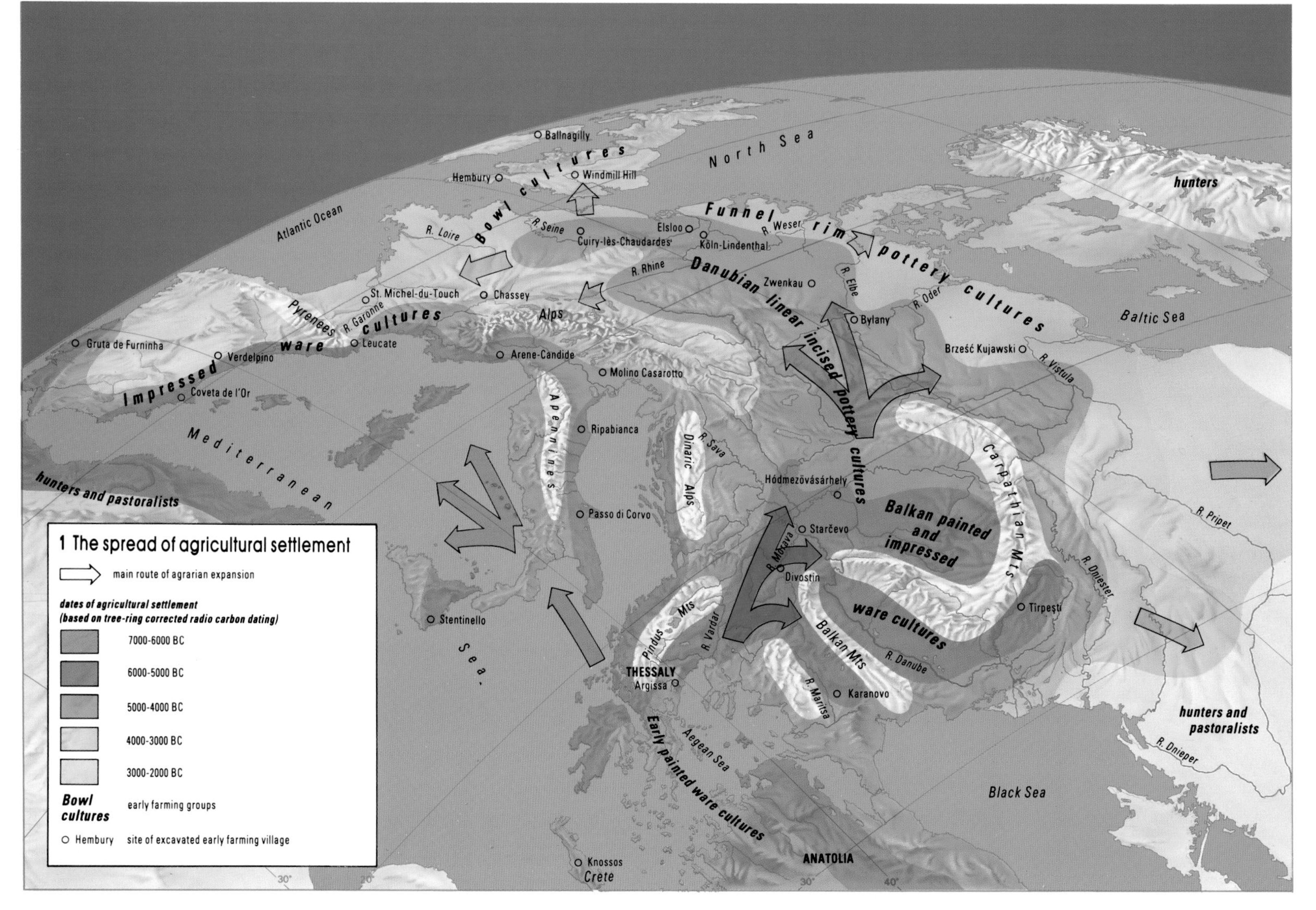

1 The spread of agricultural settlement

main route of agrarian expansion

dates of agricultural settlement (based on tree-ring corrected radio carbon dating)

7000-6000 BC
6000-5000 BC
5000-4000 BC
4000-3000 BC
3000-2000 BC

Bowl cultures — early farming groups

○ Hembury — site of excavated early farming village

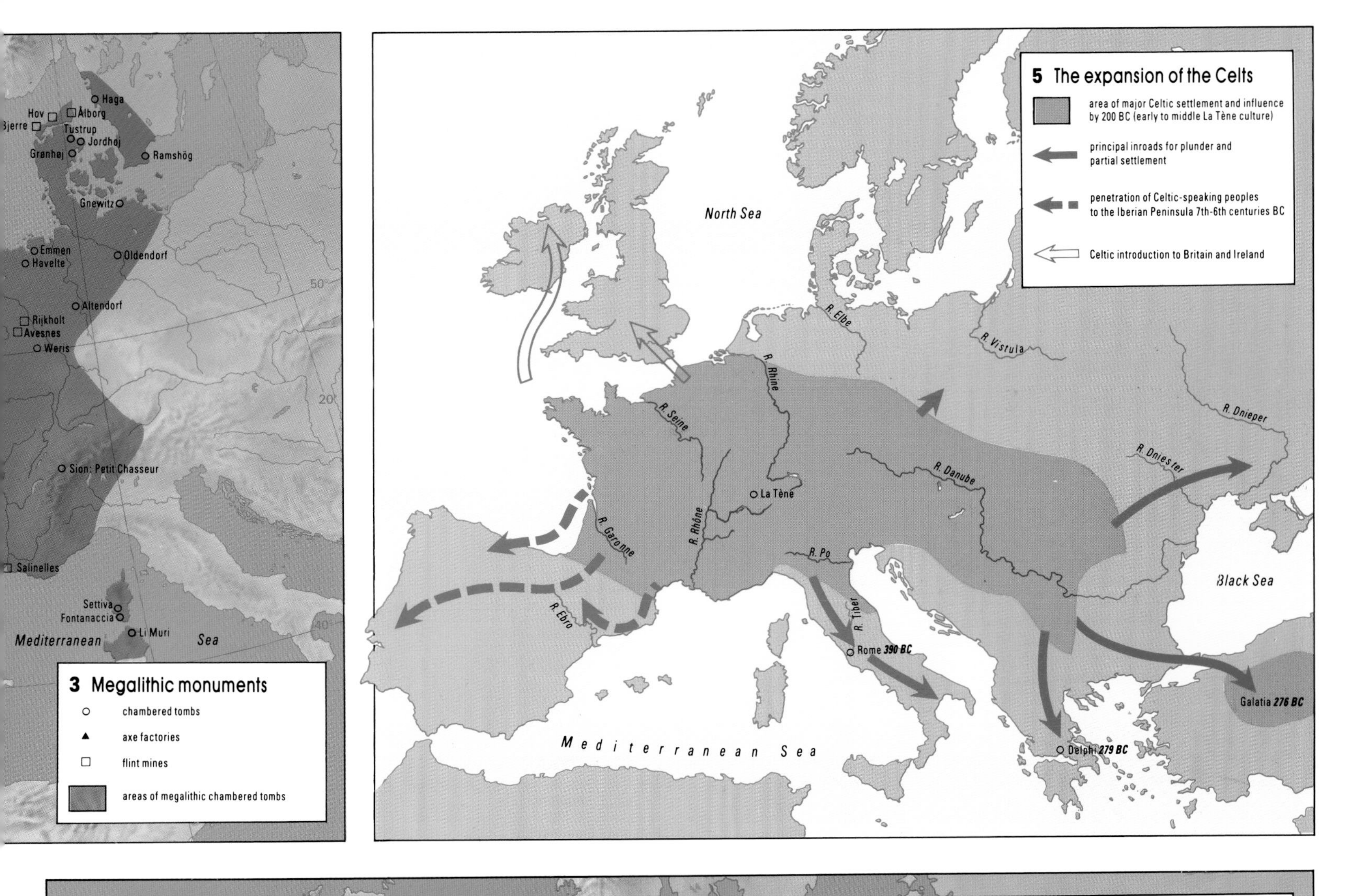
3 Megalithic monuments
chambered tombs
axe factories
flint mines
areas of megalithic chambered tombs
Haga
Hov
Ålborg
Tustrup
Jordhøj
Grønhøj
Ramshög
Gnewitz
Emmen
Havelte
Oldendorf
Altendorf
Rijkholt
Avesnes
Weris
Sion: Petit Chasseur
Salinelles
Settiva
Fontanaccia
Li Muri
Mediterranean
Sea
5 The expansion of the Celts
area of major Celtic settlement and influence by 200 BC (early to middle La Tène culture)
principal inroads for plunder and partial settlement
penetration of Celtic-speaking peoples to the Iberian Peninsula 7th-6th centuries BC
Celtic introduction to Britain and Ireland
North Sea
R. Elbe
R. Vistula
R. Rhine
R. Seine
R. Dnieper
R. Dniester
R. Danube
La Tène
R. Rhône
R. Garonne
R. Po
R. Ebro
R. Tiber
Rome 390 BC
Black Sea
Galatia 276 BC
Delphi 279 BC
Mediterranean Sea

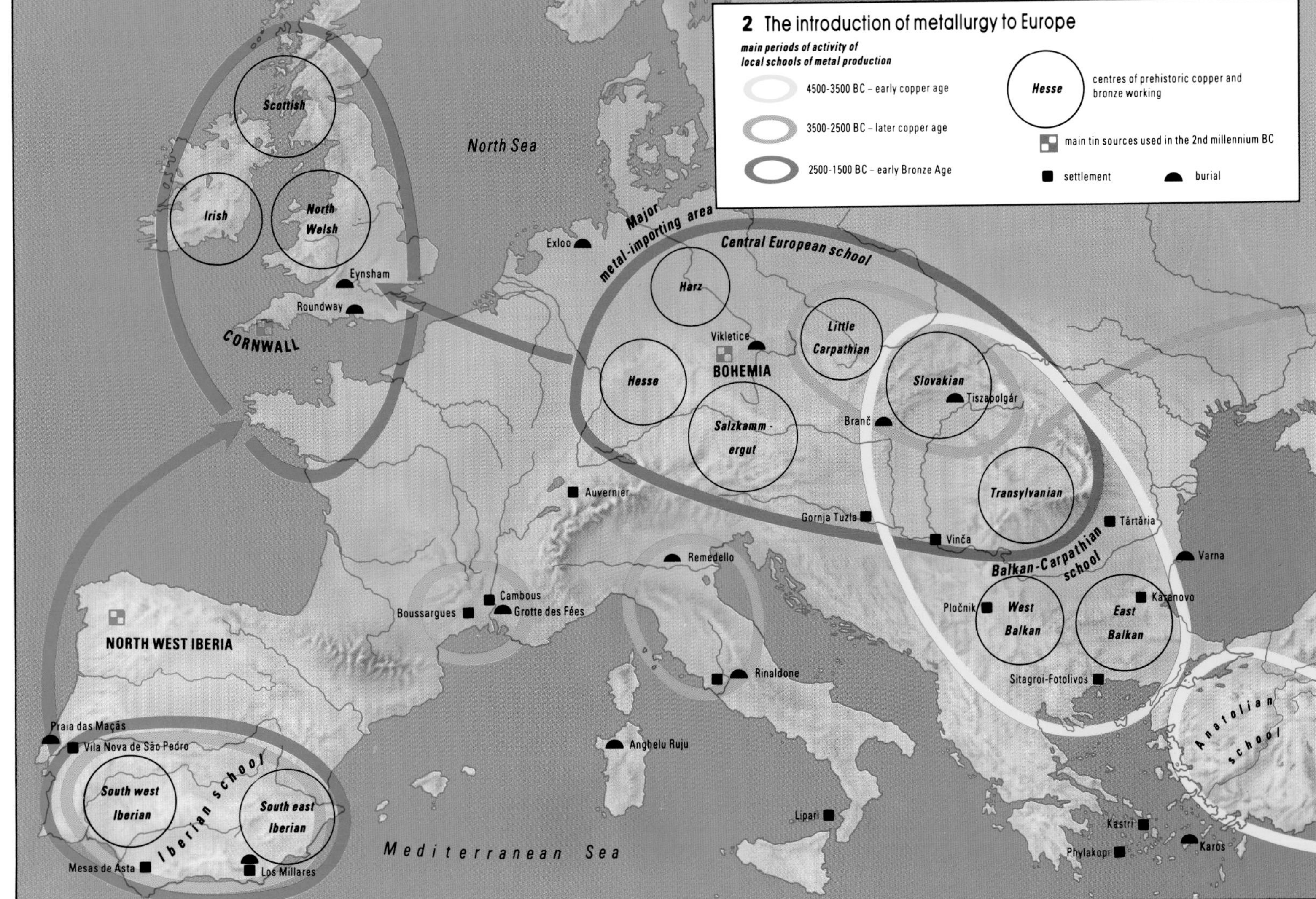
2 The introduction of metallurgy to Europe
main periods of activity of local schools of metal production
4500-3500 BC – early copper age
3500-2500 BC – later copper age
2500-1500 BC – early Bronze Age
centres of prehistoric copper and bronze working
main tin sources used in the 2nd millennium BC
settlement
burial
Scottish
Irish
North Welsh
North Sea
Major metal-importing area
Central European school
Exloo
Eynsham
Roundway
CORNWALL
Harz
Vikletice
BOHEMIA
Little Carpathian
Hesse
Slovakian
Tiszapolgár
Salzkamm-ergut
Branč
Transylvanian
Auvernier
Gornja Tuzla
Vinča
Tărtăria
Varna
Balkan-Carpathian school
Remedello
Cambous
Boussargues
Grotte des Fées
Pločnik
West Balkan
East Balkan
Karanovo
NORTH WEST IBERIA
Rinaldone
Sitagroi-Fotolivos
Anatolian school
Praia das Maçãs
Vila Nova de São Pedro
Anghelu Ruju
South west Iberian
South east Iberian
Iberian school
Lipari
Kastri
Phylakopi
Karos
Mesas de Asta
Los Millares
Mediterranean Sea

Egypt and Mesopotamia
3500-1600BC

The rise of the great riverine civilisations in the fertile valleys of the Nile in Egypt, the Euphrates and Tigris in Mesopotamia, and the Indus valley in north-west India (map 1), was a decisive stage in the development of human society. The springboard for this development was provided by the prosperous farming communities which had grown up in the hill country around the foothills of the Fertile Crescent from 8000 BC. Some of these settlements, such as Jericho and Catal Hüyük, had been of considerable size and were already small towns rather than mere villages. But the alluvial valleys of Egypt and Mesopotamia offered far greater potential, and it was here, around 3500 BC, that cities and city-states distinguished by size, planning, architecture and fortifications first appeared. It was here also, because of the need for accounting procedures in the collection and distribution of agricultural produce, that writing was first invented.

The early cities of Egypt and Mesopotamia were entirely dependent on the agricultural productivity of the alluvial plains. Water was the key to life in these semi-arid environments. In Egypt, the River Nile did most of the work, its annual flood bringing not only water but a deposit of rich alluvial silt to the farmlands of the valley and delta. In Mesopotamia, the rivers Tigris and Euphrates provided the water but to bring it to the fields an extensive network of irrigation canals was created.

Because of geographical factors political unification came early to Egypt. It was King Menes of Upper (southern) Egypt who in c.3100 BC conquered the delta kingdoms and founded a new capital at Memphis, which remained the administrative centre of Egypt for almost 2000 years. During the Old Kingdom period (map 3) (2685–2180 BC) Egyptian rulers built a series of massive pyramid-tombs along the desert edge opposite Memphis which emphasised their power and prestige and are among the greatest constructions of their age. Despite a period of setback in the political anarchy of the First Intermediate Period, the Egyptian state was sufficiently firmly established to recover and entered a second period of impressive cultural achievement under the able rulers of the Middle Kingdom (2040–1783 BC).

In Mesopotamia the basic political pattern until the second half of the third millennium BC remained one of city states, with a shifting hegemony between them but no centralised control. The Sumerians who built these cities (map 2) were also responsible for the invention of writing, at first pictographic but soon developing into the cuneiform script used on clay tablets and in inscriptions on stone. An important factor in Mesopotamian economic organisation was the need to acquire scarce resources. Southern Mesopotamia lacked stone, metals and timber, which led the Sumerians to exploit the Zagros mountains and to develop trading relations with Iran and Asia Minor. Egypt was more self-sufficient, but here also the need for timber stimulated trade with Syria, and Syria served as a link between Egypt and Mesopotamia.

The first significant attempt at empire in Mesopotamia came when Sargon (2371–16 BC), of Akkadian immigrant descent, founded the city of Agade (site uncertain) and made it his task to bring the old Sumerian city states under centralised control (map 4). From this base he and his successors, notably his grandson, Naram-Sin (2291–55 BC), undertook conquests from Elam in south-west Iran to Syria, including the recently excavated city of Ebla, and possibly also into south-eastern Asia Minor. Motivated by trade, this expansion extended sea-links which reached as far east as the Indus valley.

Sargon's empire collapsed as a result of internal stresses and the invasion of hillmen from the central Zagros, and was followed by a revival of the Sumerian city-state system, in which Ur emerged as the dominant element. This was a highly bureaucratic empire, more stable than that of Agade; but it collapsed in turn (c.2000 BC) under the pressure of a new wave of Semitic invaders, the Amorites from the Syrian desert, who established control over the whole region from Syria to southern Mesopotamia, where they set up a number of small kingdoms, among which Assyria and Babylon eventually won pre-eminence. The former emerged under the Amorite Shamshi-Adad I (1813–1781 BC), who annexed the kingdom of Mari on the middle Euphrates and formed a powerful state extending from the Zagros mountains to the border of the Anatolian plateau. But the pre-eminence of Assyria was short-lived, and after Shamshi-Adad's death its place was taken by Babylon under Hammurabi (1792–50 BC). By the seventeenth century BC a new power centre was developing further north, in Anatolia, where the Hittites set up a kingdom with its capital at Hattushash. After 1650 BC they began to spread southwards and in 1595 they sacked Babylon. In the dislocation which ensued the first Babylonian dynasty collapsed; but the ideal of a single south Mesopotamian kingdom with Babylon as its capital, survived as Hammurabi's enduring legacy.

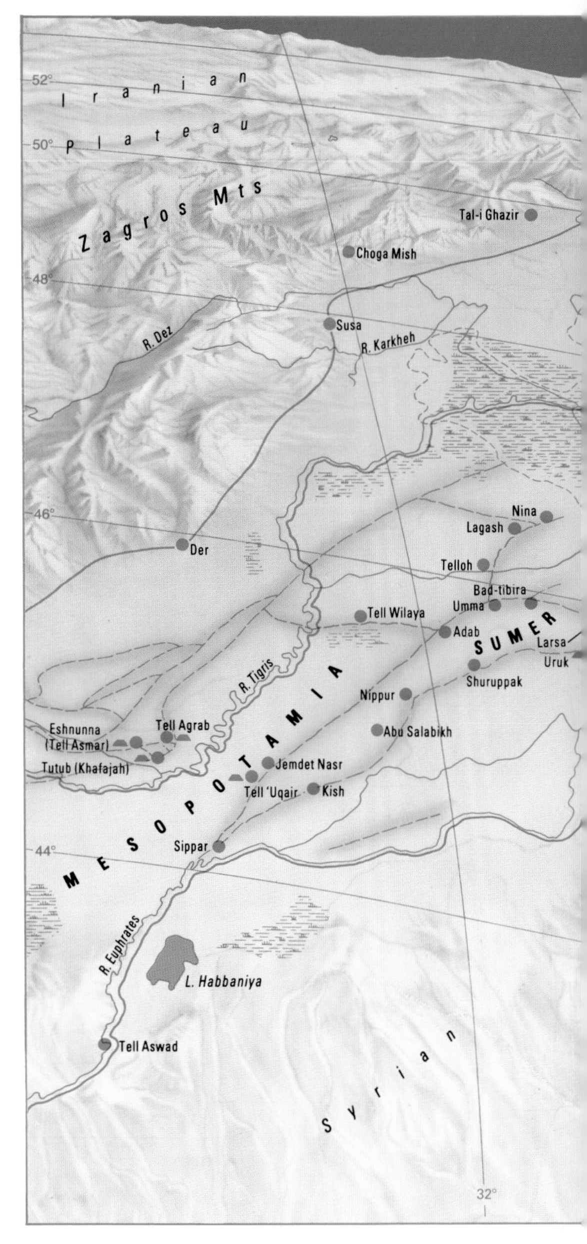

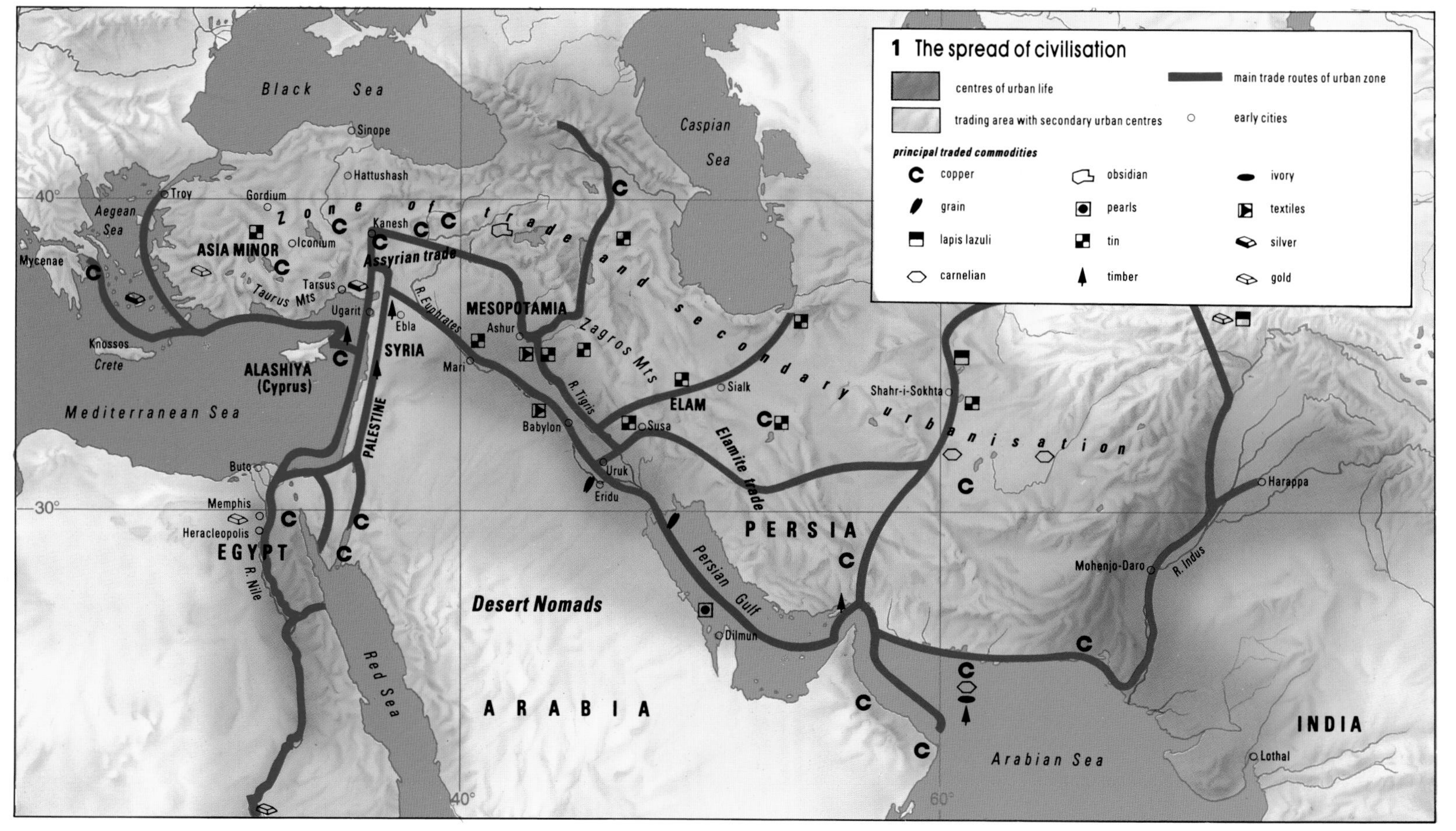

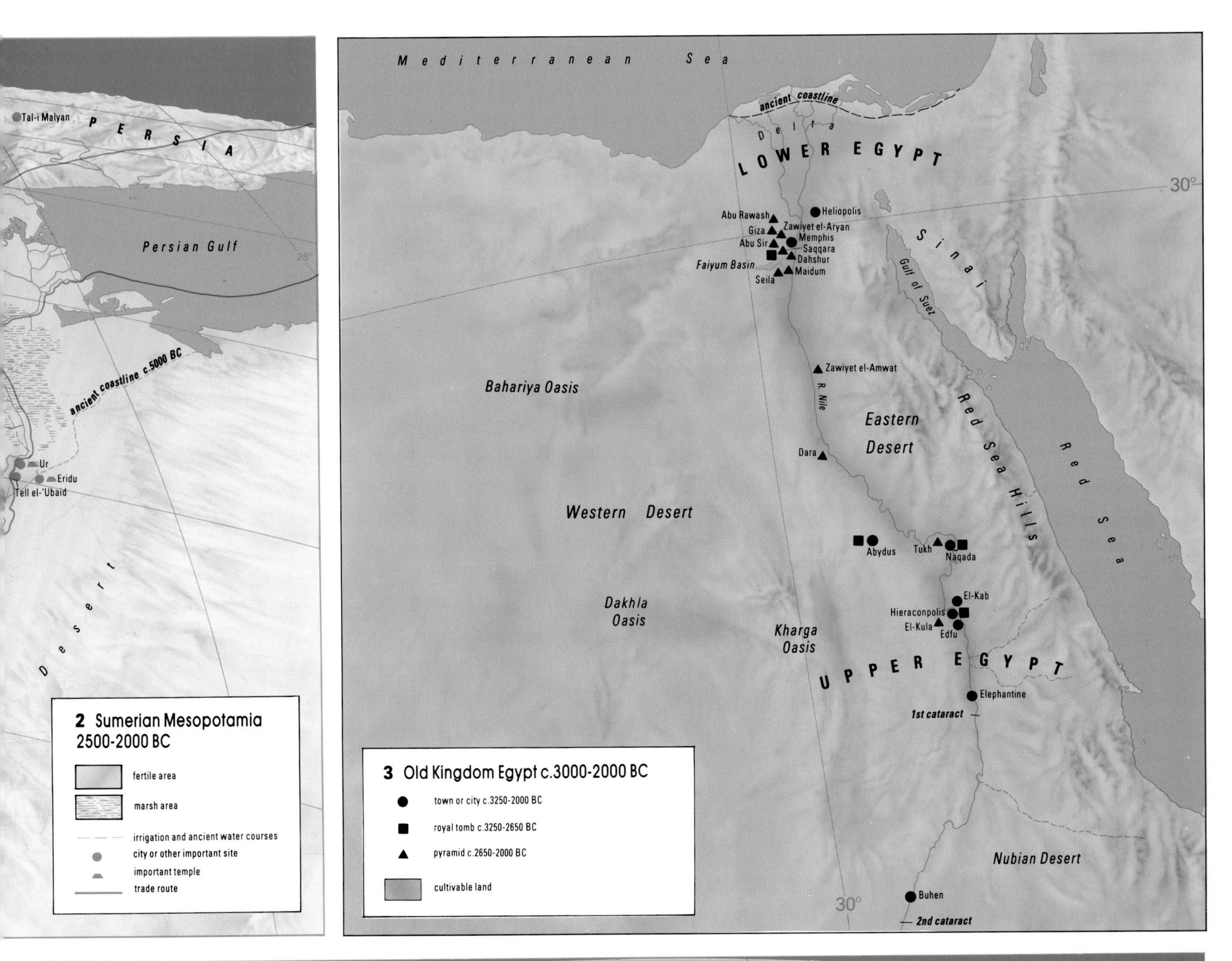

Tal-i Malyan
P E R S I A
Persian Gulf
28°
ancient coastline c.5000 BC
Ur
Eridu
Tell el-'Ubaid
D e s e r t
2 Sumerian Mesopotamia 2500-2000 BC
fertile area
marsh area
irrigation and ancient water courses
city or other important site
important temple
trade route
M e d i t e r r a n e a n S e a
ancient coastline
D e l t a
LOWER EGYPT
30°
Abu Rawash
Heliopolis
Giza
Zawiyet el-Aryan
Abu Sir
Memphis
Saqqara
Dahshur
Faiyum Basin
Seila
Maidum
S i n a i
Gulf of Suez
Zawiyet el-Amwat
Bahariya Oasis
R. Nile
Eastern Desert
Red Sea Hills
R e d S e a
Dara
Western Desert
Abydus
Tukh
Naqada
Dakhla Oasis
El-Kab
Hieraconpolis
El-Kula
Edfu
Kharga Oasis
U P P E R E G Y P T
Elephantine
1st cataract
3 Old Kingdom Egypt c.3000-2000 BC
town or city c.3250-2000 BC
royal tomb c.3250-2650 BC
pyramid c.2650-2000 BC
cultivable land
Nubian Desert
30°
Buhen
2nd cataract

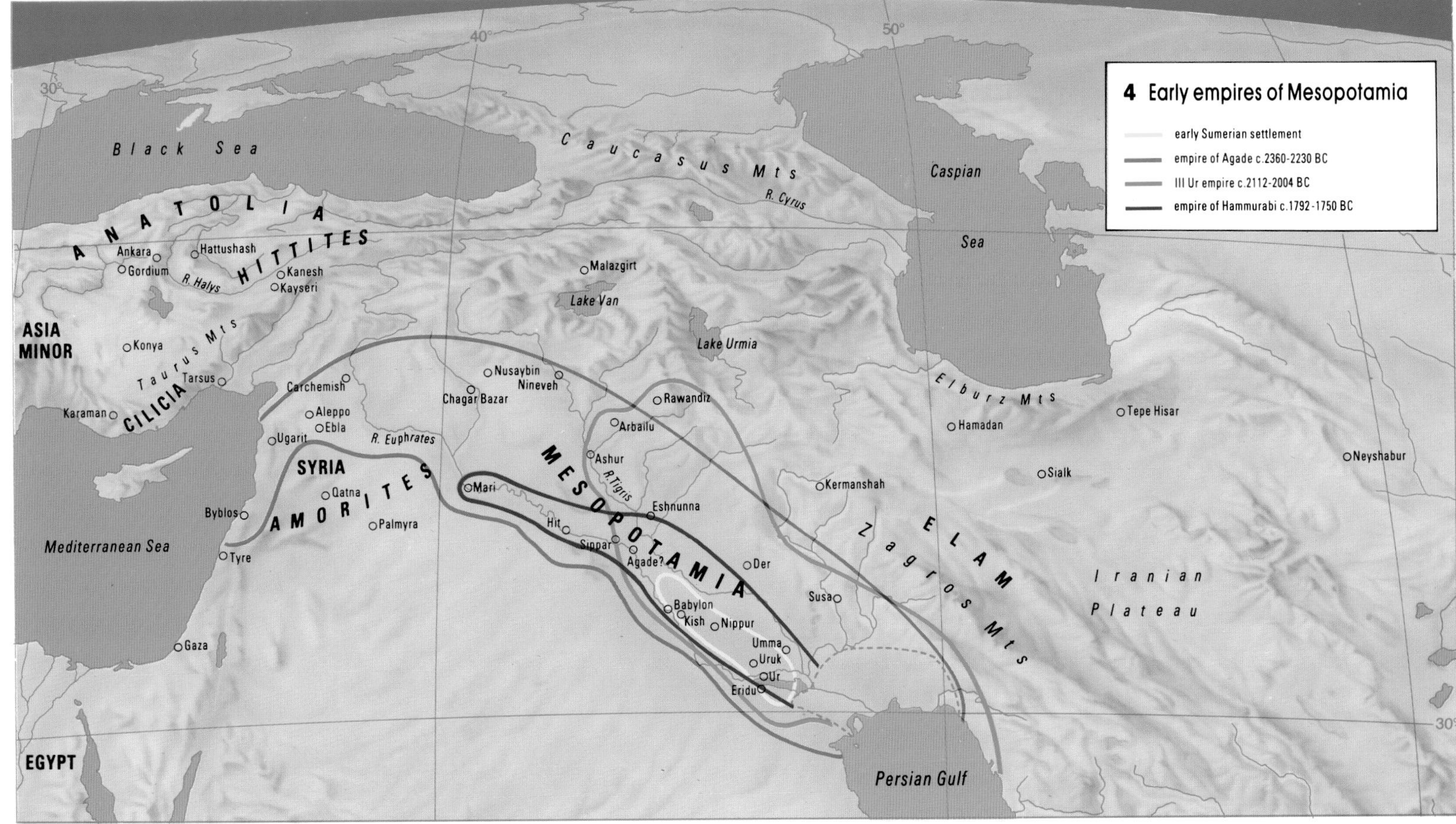

40°
50°
30°
4 Early empires of Mesopotamia
early Sumerian settlement
empire of Agade c.2360-2230 BC
III Ur empire c.2112-2004 BC
empire of Hammurabi c.1792-1750 BC
B l a c k S e a
C a u c a s u s M t s
R. Cyrus
Caspian Sea
A N A T O L I A
Ankara
Gordium
Hattushash
R. Halys
H I T T I T E S
Kanesh
Kayseri
Malazgirt
Lake Van
ASIA MINOR
Konya
T a u r u s M t s
Tarsus
Lake Urmia
Nusaybin
Nineveh
Chagar Bazar
Carchemish
Karaman
CILICIA
Aleppo
Ebla
Rawandiz
Arbailu
E l b u r z M t s
Tepe Hisar
Hamadan
Ugarit
R. Euphrates
SYRIA
Ashur
R. Tigris
M E S O P O T A M I A
Sialk
Neyshabur
Mari
Qatna
A M O R I T E S
Kermanshah
Byblos
Palmyra
Eshnunna
E L A M
Hit
Sippar
Agade?
Z a g r o s M t s
Mediterranean Sea
Tyre
Der
I r a n i a n P l a t e a u
Susa
Babylon
Kish
Nippur
Umma
Uruk
Ur
Eridu
Gaza
EGYPT
Persian Gulf
30°

The first civilisations of Europe
3000-600BC

The earliest civilisations in the western world arose in western Asia and the Nile valley in the fourth millennium BC, but within two thousand years new civilisations, distinctively different in character, had appeared around the shores of the Aegean in Crete, Greece, and western Asia Minor.

The first European civilisation was that of Minoan Crete, based on elaborate palaces which were both the seats of rulers and the centres of a bureaucratic administration. The most famous of the Minoan palaces is that of Knossos in northern Crete, in later Greek legend the home of King Minos. Cretan civilisation reached a level of considerable sophistication in the middle of the second millennium BC. The palaces were decorated with colourful frescoes and equipped with elaborate sanitary and drainage systems. Cretan traders visited Egypt, and spread Minoan influence among the Aegean islands. Bureaucracy flourished with the adoption of writing in around 1600 BC, using the locally-invented Linear A script. With a powerful fleet giving security at sea, the development of Minoan civilisation appears to have been interrupted only by the recurrent earthquakes of the region.

The development of civilisation on the Greek mainland owed something to contact with Crete but was nonetheless a largely independent process. Soon after 1600 BC rich graves make their appearance at important centres such as Mycenae, with sumptuous offerings of gold and jewellery, testifying to the rise of a wealthy and powerful artistocracy. These warlike rulers built themselves fortified palaces and drove to battle in horse-drawn chariots. The Mycenaeans were not only warriors, however, but also cultivated the arts and became successful traders whose products are found throughout the east and central Mediterranean (map 2).

In the fifteenth century BC the Mycenaeans conquered Minoan Crete and became the principal political and military power in the Aegean (map 1). They adapted the Minoan Linear A script and carried their modified version, Linear B, back to the mainland where it was used in the administration of their own kingdoms. Within two hundred years their ambitions had stretched still further to the coast of Asia Minor. The legend of the Trojan war is generally thought to be a memory of a successful Mycenaean campaign of c.1250 BC against a rival power, the city of Troy, strategically situated at the mouth of the Dardenelles, controlling access to the Black Sea.

The Trojan war, if indeed it really happened, must have been the final fling of the Mycenaean warlords. By 1200 BC, most of their palaces were in ruins, overthrown perhaps by civil strife, perhaps by piracy and a rebellious peasantry. With the demise of the Mycenaean kingdoms Greece entered a Dark Age which lasted some 400 years. It was only in the eighth century BC that trade and city life began to recover. The recovery was rapid, however, and two centuries later Greek colonies had been established all along the northern Mediterranean and Black Sea coasts (map 4). Writing was reintroduced, using an alphabetic script adapted from the Phoenician, and new styles of sculpture, architecture and vase-painting developed. Yet while sharing a common language and culture the Greek world of the eighth century was divided between hundreds of independent city-states, and was to remain so throughout the Classical age of the fifth and fourth centuries BC until conquered and united by Philip of Macedon in 338 BC.

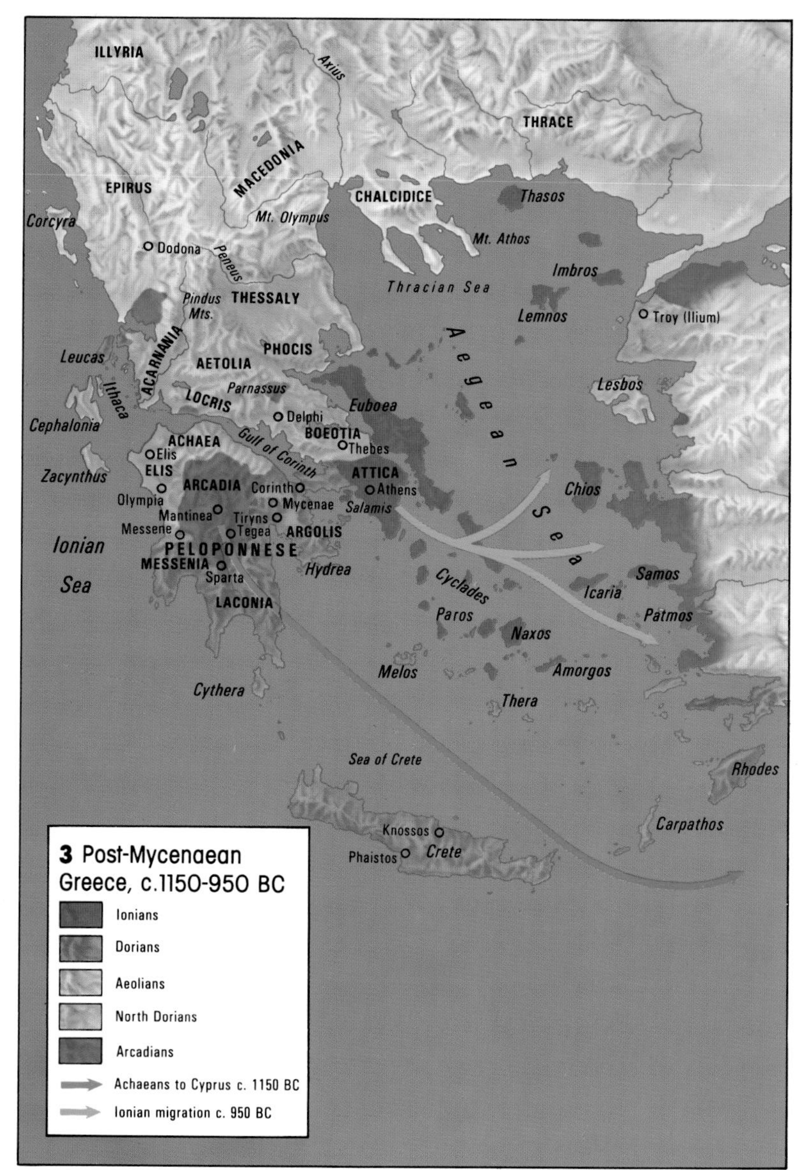

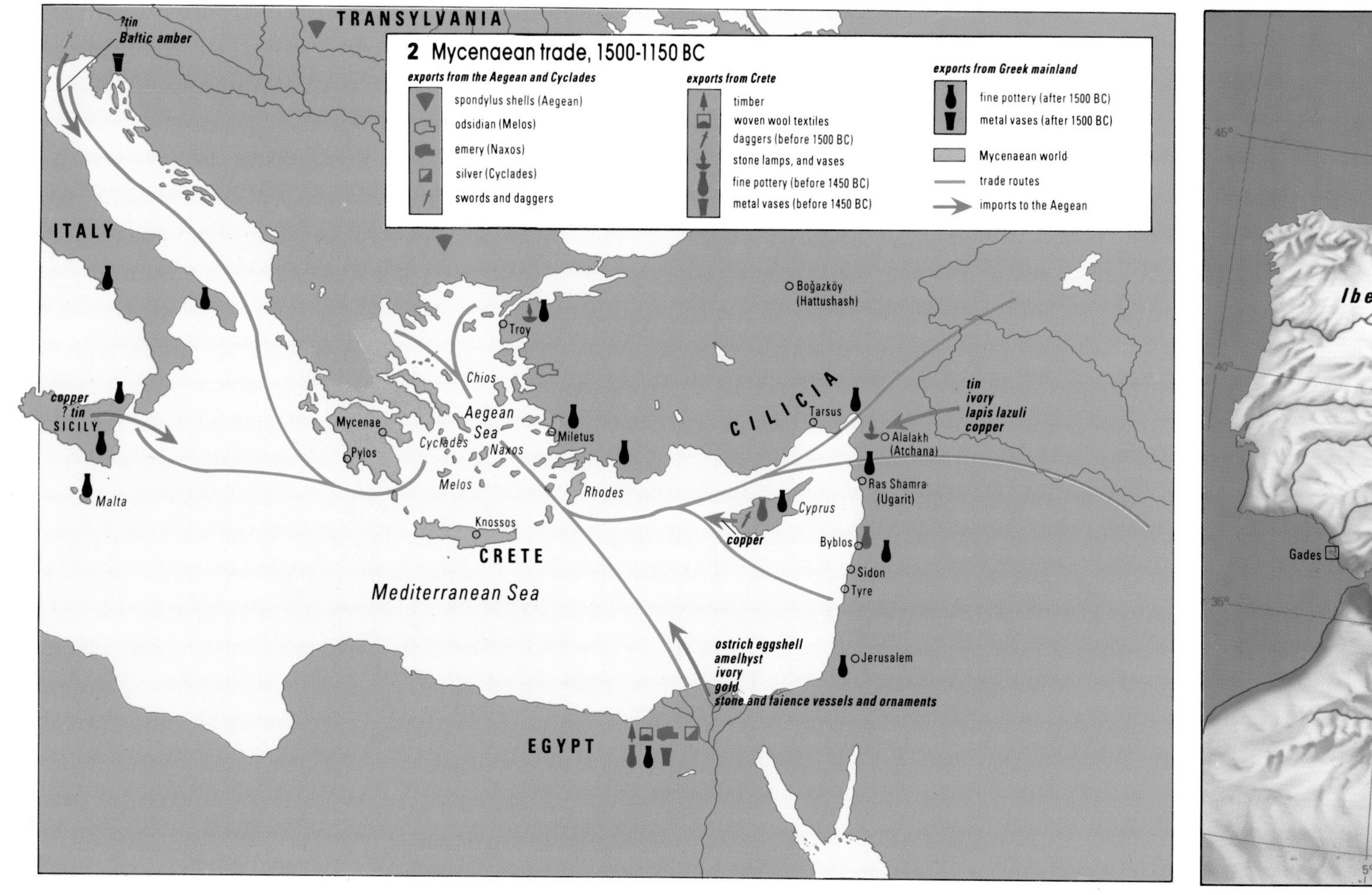

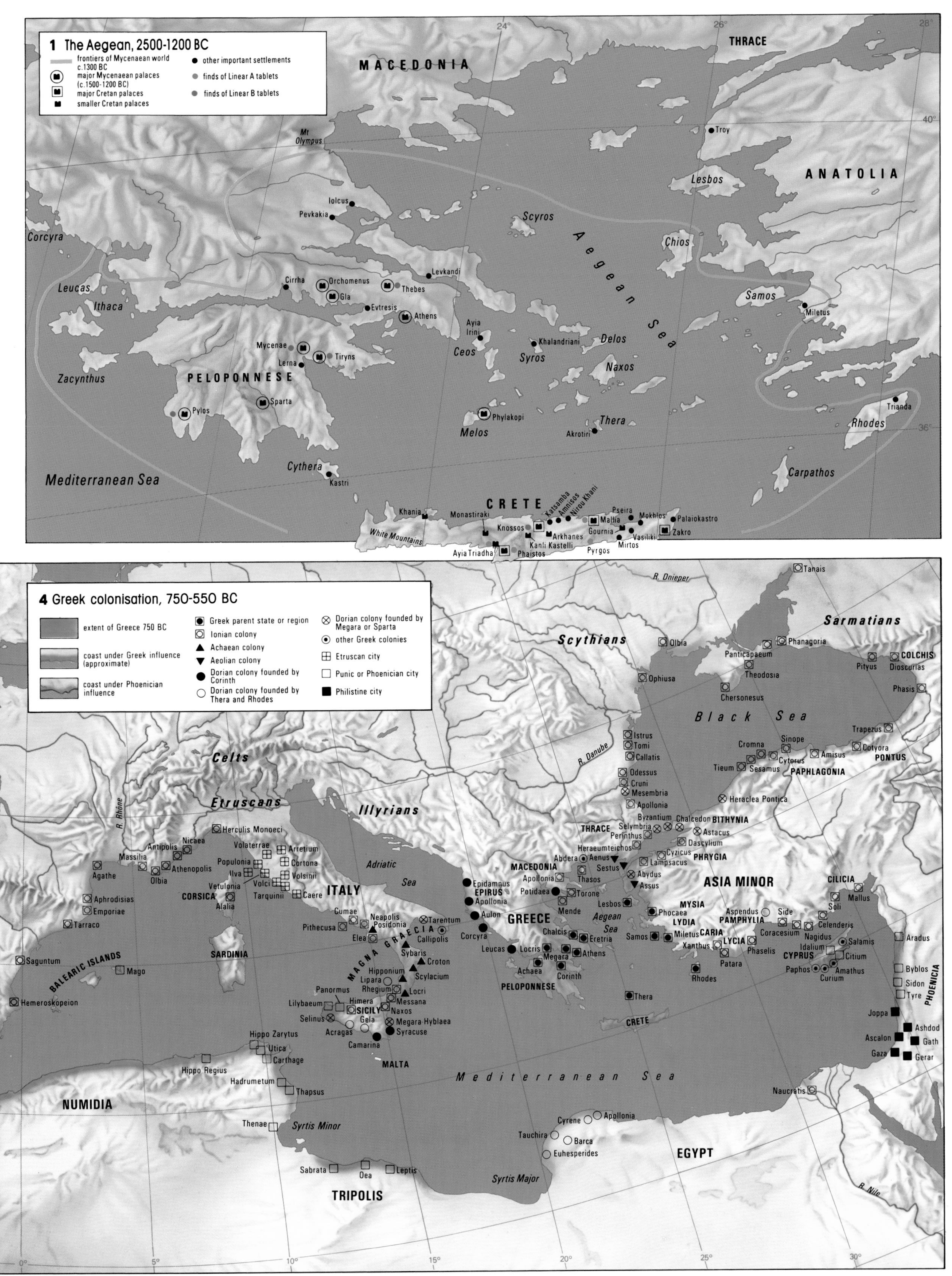

1 The Aegean, 2500-1200 BC
frontiers of Mycenaean world c.1300 BC
major Mycenaean palaces (c.1500-1200 BC)
major Cretan palaces
smaller Cretan palaces
other important settlements
finds of Linear A tablets
finds of Linear B tablets
MACEDONIA
THRACE
ANATOLIA
Mt Olympus
Troy
Lesbos
Iolcus
Pevkakia
Scyros
Aegean Sea
Chios
Corcyra
Leucas
Ithaca
Cirrha
Orchomenus
Gla
Thebes
Levkandi
Evtresis
Athens
Samos
Miletus
Ayia Irini
Ceos
Khalandriani
Syros
Delos
Naxos
Mycenae
Tiryns
Lerna
Zacynthus
PELOPONNESE
Sparta
Pylos
Phylakopi
Melos
Thera
Akrotiri
Trianda
Rhodes
Cythera
Kastri
Mediterranean Sea
Carpathos
CRETE
Khania
Monastiraki
Katsamba
Amnisos
Nirou Khani
Knossos
Arkhanes
Mallia
Pseira
Mokhlos
Palaiokastro
Gournia
Vasiliki
Zakro
White Mountains
Kanli Kastelli
Mirtos
Pyrgos
Ayia Triadha
Phaistos
4 Greek colonisation, 750-550 BC
extent of Greece 750 BC
coast under Greek influence (approximate)
coast under Phoenician influence
Greek parent state or region
Ionian colony
Achaean colony
Aeolian colony
Dorian colony founded by Corinth
Dorian colony founded by Thera and Rhodes
Dorian colony founded by Megara or Sparta
other Greek colonies
Etruscan city
Punic or Phoenician city
Philistine city
R. Dnieper
Tanais
Sarmatians
Scythians
Olbia
Phanagoria
Panticapaeum
Theodosia
Pityus
COLCHIS
Dioscurias
Phasis
Ophiusa
Chersonesus
Black Sea
Istrus
Tomi
Callatis
R. Danube
Trapezus
Sinope
Cromna
Cytorus
Amisus
Cotyora
PONTUS
Tieum
Sesamus
PAPHLAGONIA
Odessus
Cruni
Mesembria
Heraclea Pontica
Apollonia
Celts
Etruscans
R. Rhône
Illyrians
Byzantium
Chalcedon
BITHYNIA
THRACE
Selymbria
Perinthus
Astacus
Dascylium
Heraeumteichos
Cyzicus
Abdera
Aenus
Lampsacus
PHRYGIA
Herculis Monoeci
Nicaea
Antipolis
Volaterrae
Arretium
Massilia
Populonia
Cortona
Agathe
Athenopolis
Ilva
Volsinii
Olbia
Vetulonia
Volci
Tarquinii
Caere
CORSICA
Alalia
ITALY
Adriatic Sea
Aphrodisias
Emporiae
Tarraco
MACEDONIA
Apollonia
Thasos
Sestus
Abydus
Assus
ASIA MINOR
CILICIA
Mallus
Soli
Epidamnus
EPIRUS
Apollonia
Aulon
Corcyra
Potidaea
Torone
Mende
Lesbos
MYSIA
Phocaea
LYDIA
Aspendus
Side
PAMPHYLIA
Celenderis
Coracesium
Nagidus
Aradus
Cumae
Neapolis
Posidonia
Pithecusa
Tarentum
Callipolis
Elea
MAGNA GRAECIA
GREECE
Aegean Sea
Chalcis
Eretria
Samos
Miletus
CARIA
Xanthus
LYCIA
Phaselis
Idalium
Salamis
Citium
Saguntum
BALEARIC ISLANDS
Mago
SARDINIA
Sybaris
Croton
Scylacium
Hipponium
Lipara
Rhegium
Locri
Messana
Naxos
Leucas
Locris
Megara
Athens
Achaea
Corinth
PELOPONNESE
Patara
CYPRUS
Paphos
Curium
Amathus
Rhodes
Byblos
Sidon
Tyre
PHOENICIA
Hemeroskopeion
Panormus
Himera
Lilybaeum
SICILY
Selinus
Gela
Megara Hyblaea
Acragas
Syracuse
Camarina
MALTA
Thera
CRETE
Joppa
Ashdod
Ascalon
Gath
Gaza
Gerar
Hippo Zarytus
Utica
Carthage
Hippo Regius
Hadrumetum
Thapsus
Mediterranean Sea
Naucratis
NUMIDIA
Thenae
Syrtis Minor
Cyrene
Apollonia
Tauchira
Barca
Euhesperides
EGYPT
Sabrata
Oea
Leptis
Syrtis Major
TRIPOLIS
R. Nile

Near Eastern empires, 1600-330BC

Since the third millennium BC the rich lands of the Fertile Crescent had been subject to periodic invasion by warlike but less prosperous peoples from adjoining steppes and mountains, jealous of their civilisation and greedy for their riches. Egypt alone was sheltered by the desert; but even Egypt fell prey about 1730 BC to an Asiatic people known as the Hyksos, who conquered the Delta and the Nile valley as far as Cusae, and ruled there until 1567 BC. But the Hyksos occupation stimulated a great revival and, under the XVIIIth dynasty (1570–1320 BC), a policy of expansion was initiated to preclude any further occupation. Egypt advanced through Palestine into Syria and created an empire which extended almost to the Euphrates for the next four hundred years.

Egyptian control over Syria and Palestine may in part have been an attempt to shield the Nile valley from further invasions, but it in fact brought it directly into conflict with the Hittites of Asia Minor and the Mitannians of north-central Syria (map 1). In the fourteenth century BC the Hittites defeated Mitanni, which ceased to be a major actor in the struggle for the Levant. Egyptian power remained strong, however, and after the drawn battle of Kadesh in 1279 BC Hittites and Egyptians agreed to respect each other's sphere of influence.

The Egyptian pharaohs channelled the profits of empire into vast building programmes, such as the so-called 'Colossi of Memnon' built by Amenhotep III at Thebes (1391–1353 BC) or the massive rock-cut temple at Abu Simbel created by Ramesses II (1290–1224 BC). Memphis remained the administrative capital, but the power of Thebes as the religious centre of Egypt steadily grew.

The balance of power between Egyptians and Hittites in the Levant did not last long after Kadesh, since the Hittite empire collapsed around 1200 BC under internal pressure and attacks by their northern neighbours and by seaborne invaders – the so-called 'peoples of the sea'. Egypt successfully fought off similar attacks, but only with the loss of its Levantine possessions. Into the gap created by the decline of the Hittites and Egyptian empires new peoples entered; Phrygians in Asia Minor, Hebrews and Philistines in Palestine. The power vacuum enabled the Israelites under King David (c.1006–966 BC) to create a kingdom briefly controlling Palestine and Syria (map 2); but after Solomon (966–926 BC) the kingdom, inherently unstable because of its disparate tribal origins, quickly disintegrated. But change and fluidity had the effect of breaking down old geographical and cultural barriers and fusing the whole regior 'nto a single cosmopolitan society, over which, after 539 BC, Persia established hegemony.

The immediate beneficiary was Assyria, the political successor of Mitanni (map 3). Already in the thirteenth century this city-state had joined the ranks of the great powers of the ancient Near East. Early in the ninth century, the Assyrian kings again began to flex their military muscle, embarking on a policy of conquest which soon brought them to the shores of the Mediterranean (map 3). The profits were ploughed back into the construction of the successive capitals of the Assyrian empire: Nimrud, Khorsabad and Nineveh. At its greatest extent, in the seventh century BC, the empire stretched from the Nile valley to the Persian Gulf and northwards into Armenia and eastern Turkey. But during the long reign of Ashurbanipal (668–627 BC) Assyria began to lose its military dominance and soon afterwards the assault of Medes and Scythians, combined with the secession of Babylonia, brought Assyrian power to ruin. The capital Nineveh was destroyed in 612 BC, and Assyria disappeared for ever in 605 BC. After an interlude in which Medes, Chaldeans and Egyptians divided the legacy, another semi-barbarian conqueror, Cyrus the Persian, rebelled against his Median overlord, captured the Median capital Ecbatana in 550 BC, and quickly overran most of the Middle East. When his son Cambyses (529–522 BC) conquered Egypt (525 BC), the Persian empire extended from the Nile to the Oxus (map 5). The ancient world was for the first time united under one administration. Persian attempts to extend their power to the west, however, met with resistance from the Greeks and defeat at Marathon (490 BC), Salamis (480 BC) and Plataea (479 BC), and the Persian empire entered a period of slow decline. The way was opened for the ultimate triumph of Hellenism and the conquest of Persia by Alexander the Great a century and a half later.

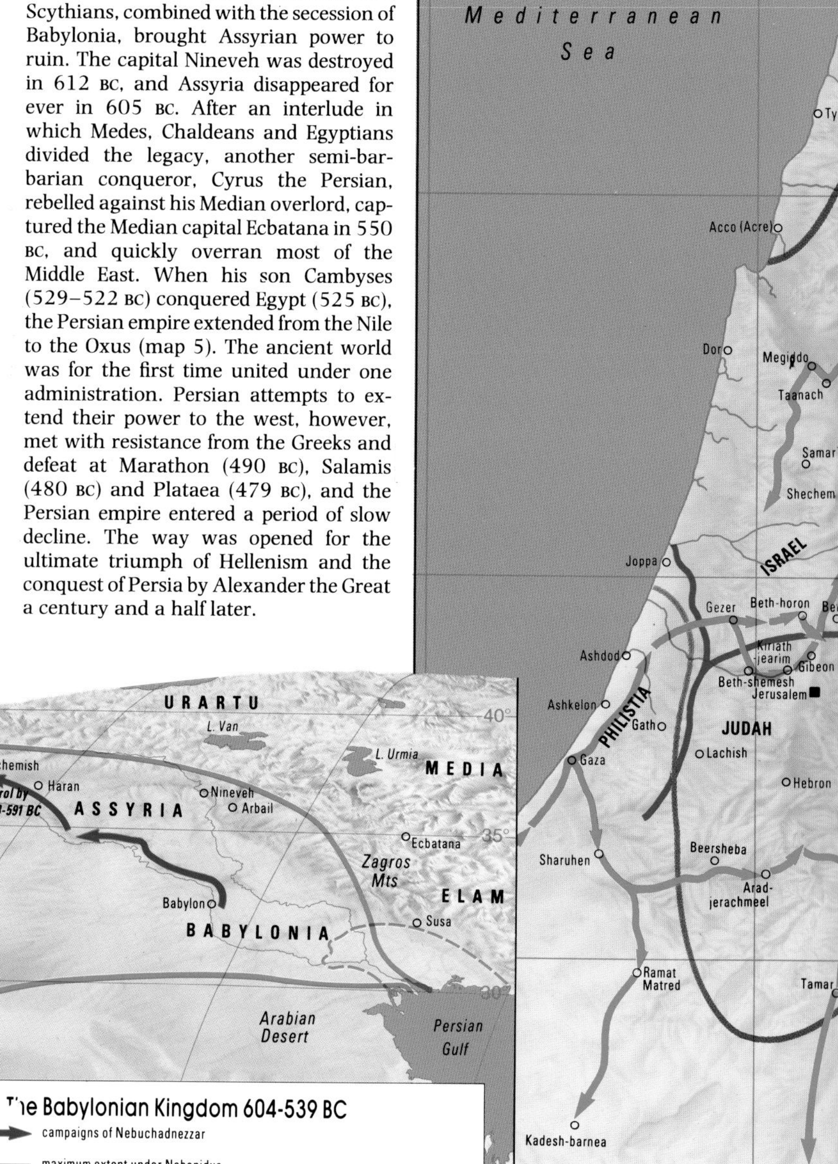

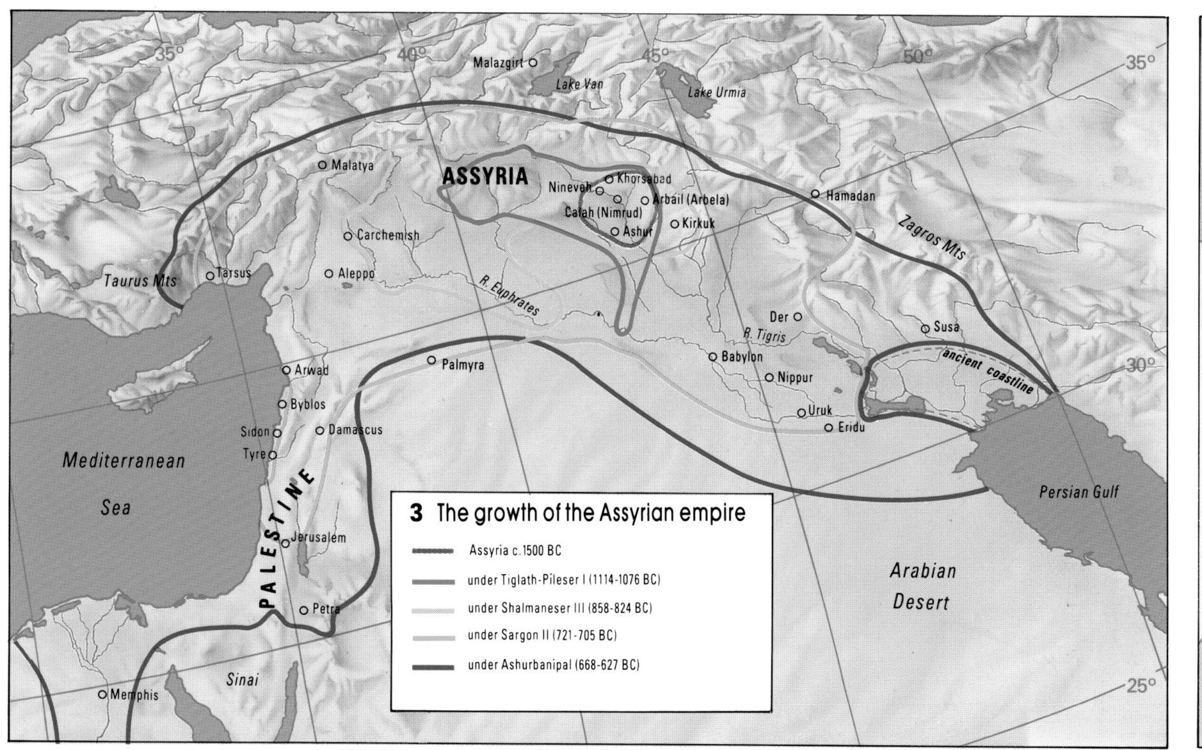

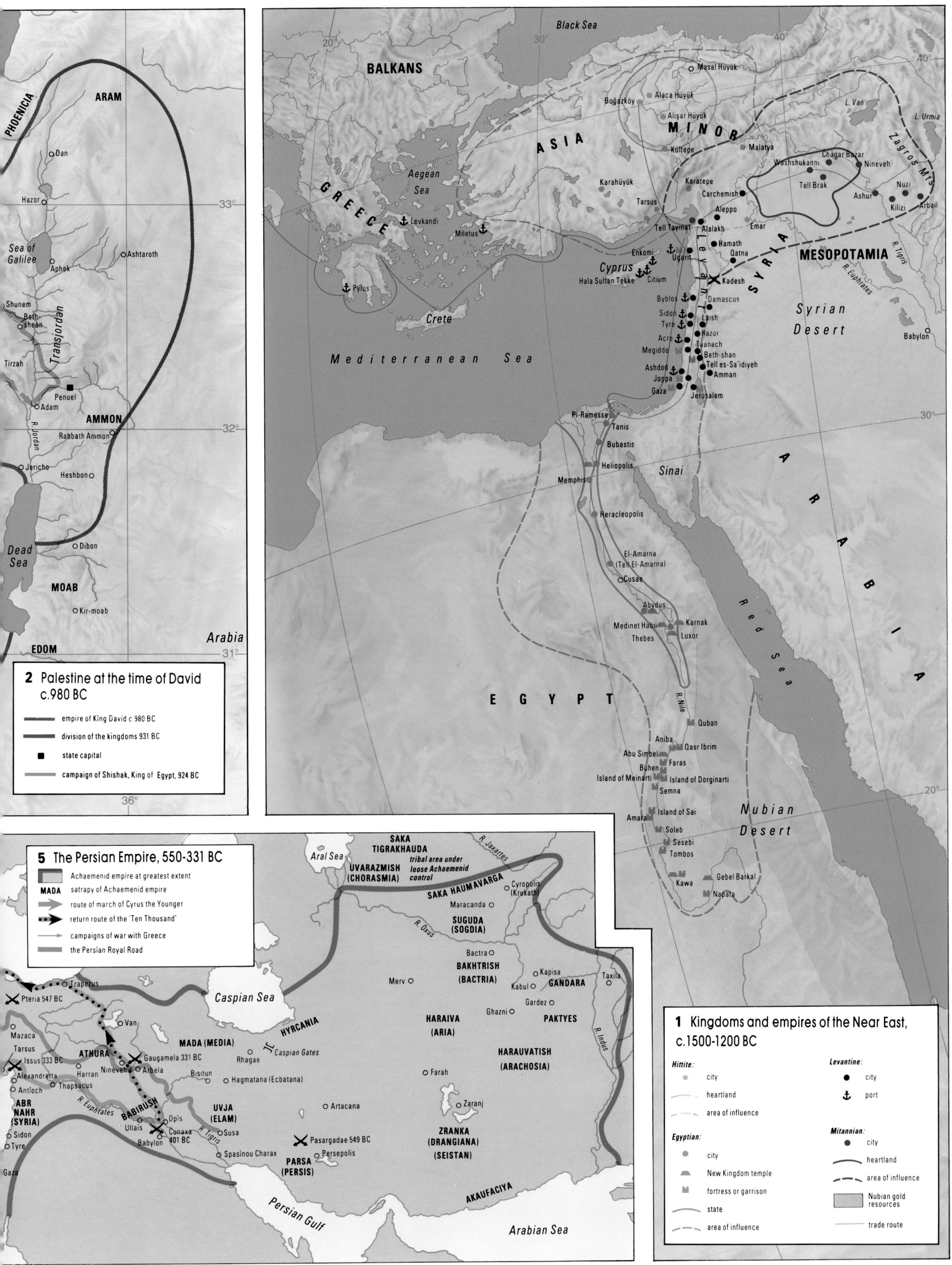

2 Palestine at the time of David c.980 BC
empire of King David c.980 BC
division of the kingdoms 931 BC
state capital
campaign of Shishak, King of Egypt, 924 BC
PHOENICIA
ARAM
Dan
Hazor
Sea of Galilee
Aphek
Ashtaroth
Shunem
Beth-shean
Transjordan
Tirzah
Penuel
Adam
AMMON
Rabbath Ammon
R. Jordan
Jericho
Heshbon
Dead Sea
Dibon
MOAB
Kir-moab
Arabia
EDOM
33°
32°
31°
36°
1 Kingdoms and empires of the Near East, c.1500-1200 BC
Hittite:
city
heartland
area of influence
Egyptian:
city
New Kingdom temple
fortress or garrison
state
area of influence
Levantine:
city
port
Mitannian:
city
heartland
area of influence
Nubian gold resources
trade route
Black Sea
BALKANS
Maşat Hüyük
Boğazköy
Alaca Hüyük
Alişar Hüyük
ASIA
MINOR
Kültepe
Malatya
L. Van
L. Urmia
Zagros Mts
Chagar Bazar
Washshukanni
Nineveh
Tell Brak
Nuzi
Ashur
Kilizi
Arbail
Aegean Sea
GREECE
Levkandi
Miletus
Pylos
Crete
Karahüyük
Tarsus
Karatepe
Carchemish
Aleppo
Emar
Tell Tayinat
Alalakh
Hamath
Qatna
Enkomi
Ugarit
Cyprus
Hala Sultan Tekke
Citium
Kadesh
SYRIA
Levant
MESOPOTAMIA
R. Tigris
R. Euphrates
Byblos
Damascus
Sidon
Tyre
Laish
Hazor
Acre
Taanach
Megiddo
Beth-shan
Tell es-Sa'idiyeh
Ashdod
Joppa
Amman
Gaza
Jerusalem
Syrian Desert
Babylon
Mediterranean Sea
Pi-Ramesse
Tanis
Bubastis
Heliopolis
Memphis
Sinai
Heracleopolis
El-Amarna (Tell El-Amarna)
Cusae
Abydus
Medinet Habu
Thebes
Karnak
Luxor
ARABIA
Red Sea
EGYPT
R. Nile
Quban
Aniba
Abu Simbel
Qasr Ibrim
Faras
Buhen
Island of Meinarti
Island of Dorginarti
Semna
Amara
Island of Sai
Soleb
Sesebi
Tombos
Nubian Desert
Kawa
Gebel Barkal
Napata
20°
30°
40°
5 The Persian Empire, 550-331 BC
Achaemenid empire at greatest extent
MADA satrapy of Achaemenid empire
route of march of Cyrus the Younger
return route of the 'Ten Thousand'
campaigns of war with Greece
the Persian Royal Road
Aral Sea
SAKA TIGRAKHAUDA
tribal area under loose Achaemenid control
UVARAZMISH (CHORASMIA)
R. Jaxartes
SAKA HAUMAVARGA
Cyropolis (Krukath)
Maracanda
SUGUDA (SOGDIA)
R. Oxus
Bactra
BAKHTRISH (BACTRIA)
Merv
Kapisa
Kabul
GANDARA
Taxila
Trapezus
Pteria 547 BC
Caspian Sea
Gardez
Ghazni
PAKTYES
HYRCANIA
Van
HARAIVA (ARIA)
R. Indus
Mazaca
Tarsus
MADA (MEDIA)
Caspian Gates
Issus 333 BC
ATHURA
Gaugamela 331 BC
Rhagae
HARAUVATISH (ARACHOSIA)
Alexandretta
Harran
Nineveh
Arbela
Bisitun
Antioch
Thapsacus
Hagmatana (Ecbatana)
Farah
ABR NAHR (SYRIA)
R. Euphrates
BABIRUSH
Opis
Zaranj
Ullais
Artacana
Sidon
Tyre
Cunaxa 401 BC
Babylon
R. Tigris
Susa
UVJA (ELAM)
Pasargadae 549 BC
Persepolis
ZRANKA (DRANGIANA) (SEISTAN)
Gaza
Spasinou Charax
PARSA (PERSIS)
AKAUFACIYA
Persian Gulf
Arabian Sea

The Greek world
497-185 BC

The fifth century BC was the great age of Greece – the age of Pericles and Socrates, of Sophocles and Euripides, of the Parthenon and the sculptures of Phidias. It was also the century when internal strains (the growing conflict between oligarchy and democracy) and internecine war undermined the stability of the Greek city states and their ability to withstand external pressures. Colonisation had already carried Greek civilisation and Greek city life to Asia Minor (page 18). But here it came up against the Persian empire under Darius and Xerxes (page 20). Persian attempts to subdue Athens, which had been supporting the rebellious Ionians, were almost miraculously defeated at Marathon (490) and Salamis (480), (map 1). But thereafter the cities which had united against Persia fell apart, and the Peloponnesian war between Athens and Sparta and their allies (map 2) permanently weakened Greek resistance, and ensured the victory of Philip of Macedon (338). Under Philip's son, Alexander the Great, Macedonia became a world power, its dominion stretching from the Adriatic to India (map 3). Alexander's death in 323 BC at the age of 32 prevented the consolidation of his empire. In the succeeding struggles between his generals three major powers arose: Macedonia, shorn of its Asiatic conquests but still dominant in northern Greece; Egypt under the Ptolemies, with its capital at Alexander's newly founded city of Alexandria; and the Seleucid kingdom comprising the bulk of the Persian empire (map 4). To these were added in the east the Bactrian kingdom, extending over Afghanistan into northern India, and the Parthian empire, founded in 247 BC when a dissident provincial governor broke away from the Bactrian Greeks. This Parthian state eventually stretched from the Euphrates to the Indus and successfully withstood Roman expansion until it was displaced in AD 224 by a resurgent Persia under the Sasanian dynasty.

Although politically the empire of Alexander the Great proved ephemeral, in other respects its consequences were epoch-making. Alexander himself founded some 70 cities, not merely as military strongholds but as cultural centres – a policy continued by his Seleucid successors – and thus carried Greek civilisation far to the east. Greek culture was now no longer the preserve of separate city-states but infused and Hellenised the whole civilised world (*oikoumene*) as far as India and China. Greek itself became the *lingua franca* of the whole region, though more subtly the Greek world itself was permeated by oriental influences as its contacts with the ancient civilisations of the Near East intensified. When Rome asserted control over the Hellenistic world after its defeat of Macedon at Cynoscephalae in 197 and of the Seleucids at Magnesia in 190 BC, this was its inheritance; and the longer the Roman empire existed, the greater was the part played by the Hellenic and oriental elements in its civilisation.

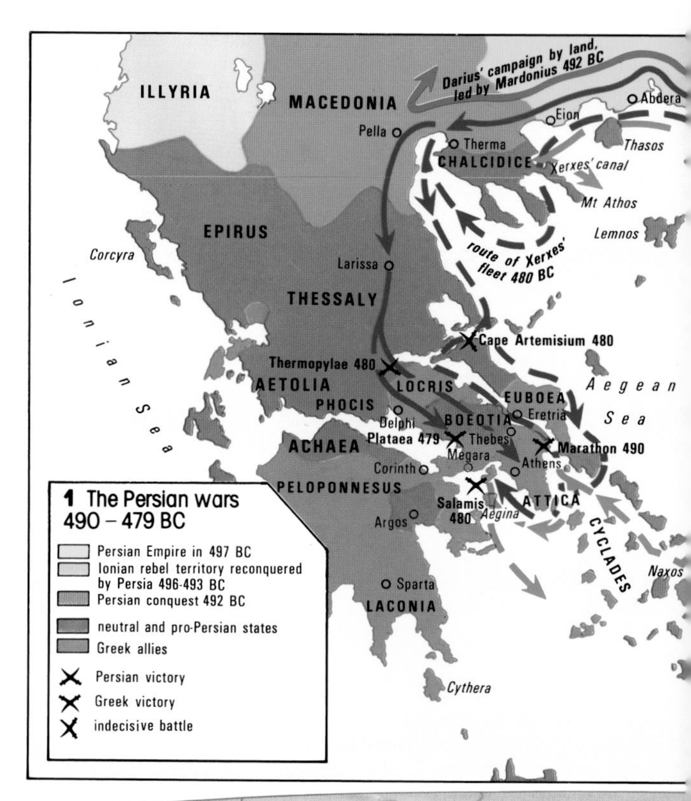

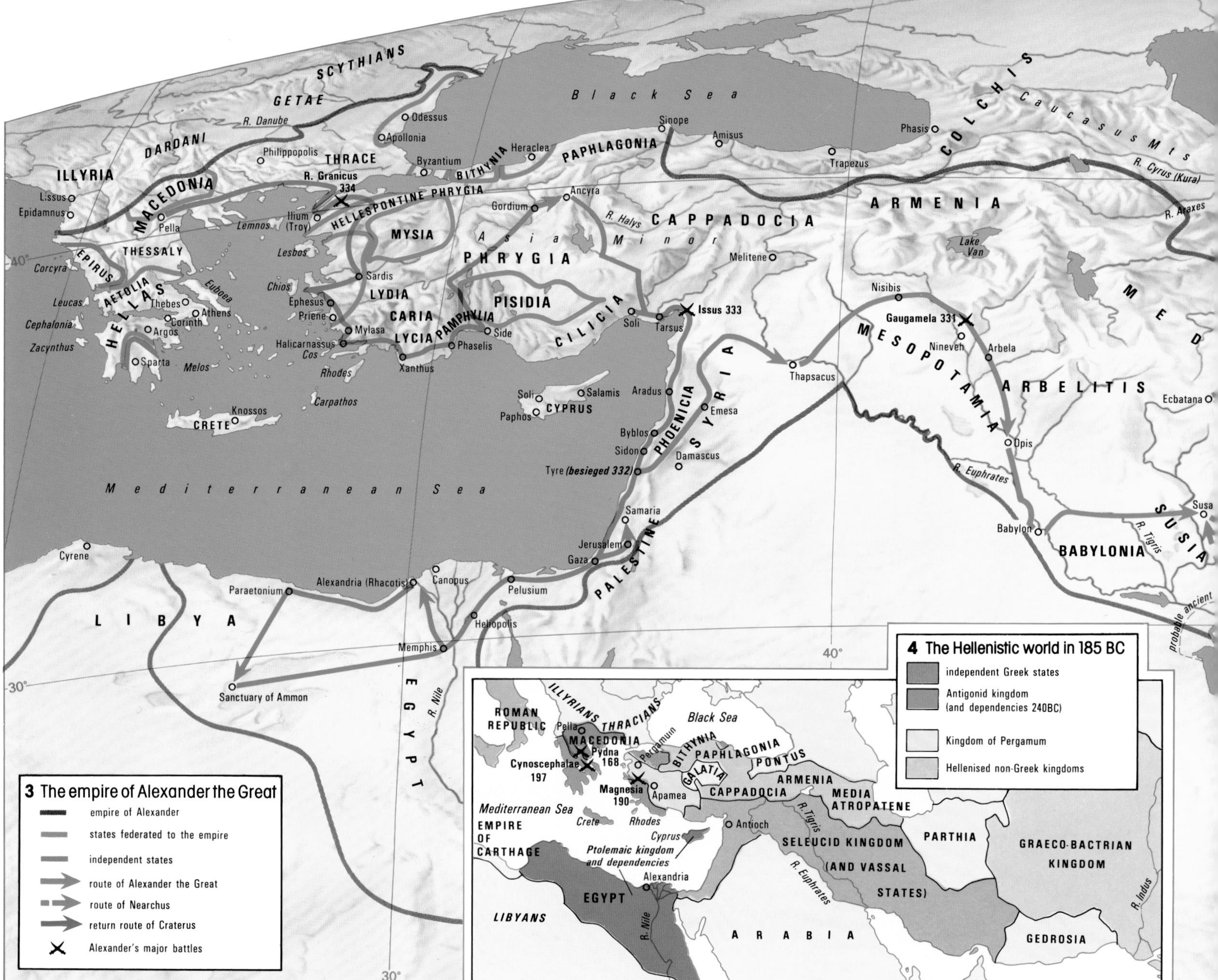

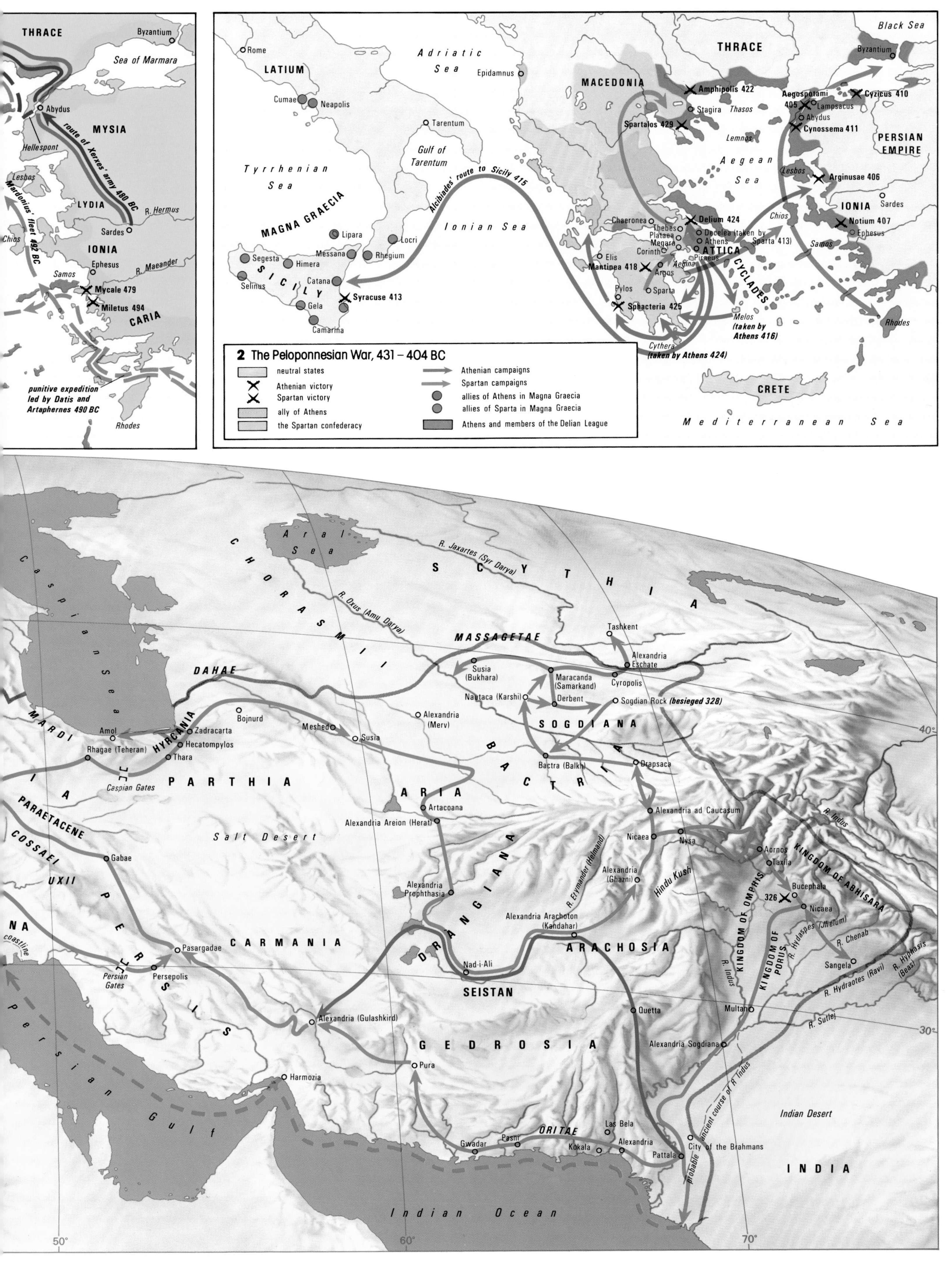
THRACE
Byzantium
Sea of Marmara
Abydus
MYSIA
Hellespont
route of Xerxes' army 480 BC
Lesbos
Mardonius' fleet 492 BC
LYDIA
R. Hermus
Chios
Sardes
IONIA
Ephesus
R. Maeander
Samos
Mycale 479
Miletus 494
CARIA
punitive expedition led by Datis and Artaphernes 490 BC
Rhodes
2 The Peloponnesian War, 431 – 404 BC
neutral states
Athenian victory
Spartan victory
ally of Athens
the Spartan confederacy
Athenian campaigns
Spartan campaigns
allies of Athens in Magna Graecia
allies of Sparta in Magna Graecia
Athens and members of the Delian League
Rome
LATIUM
Adriatic Sea
Epidamnus
Cumae
Neapolis
Tarentum
Gulf of Tarentum
Tyrrhenian Sea
MAGNA GRAECIA
Alcibiades' route to Sicily 415
Ionian Sea
Lipara
Locri
Messana
Rhegium
Segesta
Himera
SICILY
Catana
Selinus
Syracuse 413
Gela
Camarina
MACEDONIA
THRACE
Black Sea
Byzantium
Amphipolis 422
Stagira
Thasos
Aegospotami 405
Lampsacus
Abydus
Cyzicus 410
Cynossema 411
Spartalos 429
Lemnos
PERSIAN EMPIRE
Aegean Sea
Lesbos
Arginusae 406
IONIA
Sardes
Chaeronea
Thebes
Plataea
Megara
Corinth
Delium 424
Decelea (taken by Sparta 413)
Athens
ATTICA
Piraeus
Chios
Notium 407
Ephesus
Samos
Elis
Mantinea 418
Argos
Aegina
CYCLADES
Pylos
Sparta
Sphacteria 425
Melos (taken by Athens 416)
Rhodes
Cythera (taken by Athens 424)
CRETE
Mediterranean Sea
Aral Sea
CHORASMII
R. Jaxartes (Syr Darya)
SCYTHIA
R. Oxus (Amu Darya)
Caspian Sea
MASSAGETAE
Tashkent
Alexandria Eschate
DAHAE
Susia (Bukhara)
Maracanda (Samarkand)
Cyropolis
Nautaca (Karshi)
Derbent
Sogdian Rock (besieged 328)
SOGDIANA
MARDI
Bojnurd
Alexandria (Merv)
Amol
Zadracarta
HYRCANIA
Meshed
Susia
Hecatompylos
Rhagae (Teheran)
Thara
BACTRIA
Bactra (Balkh)
Drapsaca
Caspian Gates
PARTHIA
ARIA
Artacoana
Alexandria Areion (Herat)
Alexandria ad Caucasum
PARAETACENE
Salt Desert
Nicaea
Nysa
Aornos
COSSAEI
Taxila
KINGDOM OF ABHISARA
R. Indus
Gabae
UXII
R. Etymander (Helmand)
Alexandria (Ghazni)
Hindu Kush
KINGDOM OF OMPHIS
Alexandria Prophthasia
DRANGIANA
326
Bucephala
Nicaea
Alexandria Arachoton (Kandahar)
R. Hydaspes (Jhelum)
R. Chenab
PERSIS
CARMANIA
Pasargadae
ARACHOSIA
KINGDOM OF PORUS
R. Indus
Sangela
R. Hyphasis (Beas)
Persian Gates
Persepolis
Nad-i-Ali
SEISTAN
R. Hydraotes (Ravi)
R. Sutlej
Quetta
Multan
Alexandria (Gulashkird)
GEDROSIA
Alexandria Sogdiana
Persian Gulf
Pura
Harmozia
probable ancient course of R. Indus
Indian Desert
ORITAE
Las Bela
Gwadar
Pasni
Kokala
Alexandria
Pattala
City of the Brahmans
INDIA
Indian Ocean
40°
30°
50°
60°
70°
NA
coastline

Trading links of the ancient world

Trade is as old as the beginning of settled urban life. Though ordinary needs were met by local agriculture and local manufacture, even the earliest cities had requirements that could not be satisfied locally. Jericho imported stone for tools from Anatolia (page 6); the Sumerians, who lacked timber, stone and minerals, developed trading links with Asia Minor and by sea with Dilmun on the Persian Gulf. But the formation of an intensive trading network spanning the whole Eurasian world only became possible after the rise of empires which could provide peace and security, build roads and maintain harbours. The Achaemenids made a beginning in sixth-century Persia, where Darius's Royal Road ran 1420 well-garrisoned miles (2300 km) from Sardis to Susa (page 20). But the decisive step forward was the rise, after 202 BC, of the Roman empire in the west and the Han empire in China. By the close of the first century BC Rome's conquests from the Atlantic to Syria formed a single vast trading area, gathered round a Mediterranean axis (map 2), and the expansion of Han China under Wu-ti (140–87 BC) created an economic bloc of similar dimensions in the east (page 28). Both possessed an elaborate network of roads and a highly organised system of transport and marketing, which encouraged regional specialisation and an unprecedented interchange of goods and manufactures. In the west the requirements of the legions in the frontier provinces of Gaul and the Balkans were a further stimulus. Spain became a large-scale producer and exporter of wine and olive oil; but the most important export of all was grain from Egypt, North Africa and the Pontine provinces, upon which Rome itself and many cities of Greece and Asia Minor were dependent.

Nor did trade halt at the frontier. China sent a mission to Ferghana, Bukhara and Bactria in 128 BC, and shortly afterwards the famous Silk Route came into operation (map 1). It started at Tunhwang on China's far western boundary, and skirted north or south of the Takla Makan Desert to Kashgar, before crossing the Pamirs and debouching into Bactria, Persia and the Mediterranean coastal belt. But the Silk Route, spectacular though it was, was less important in economic terms than the sea route to India and the Far East, traffic along which increased greatly after the discovery of the monsoon around 100 BC. Previously there had been coastal traffic, mainly in Arab or Indian hands. Now up to 120 Greek vessels a year, some with a carrying capacity of up to 500 tons, plied direct to the Indian ports of Barbaricum, Barygaza and Muziris, where they picked up eastern cargoes shipped by Indian merchants from Go Oc Eo in southern Cambodia, and carried them to Berenice and other Red Sea ports for transport on to Alexandria and thence to all parts of the Roman empire.

These far-flung trading links are impressive, but their economic importance should not be exaggerated. Both the Roman and the Han empires were self-sufficient in all essential commodities, and foreign trade was essentially a luxury trade, marginal to everyday needs. On the other hand, there is no doubt that foreign trade contributed directly to cultural interchange and to the spread of the great world religions (page 26). However, it also had other less happy consequences, particularly the spread of disease and pestilence (map 3). Earlier epidemics, like that which smote Athens in 430–29 BC, may have been transmitted by armies; but their incidence after about 100 BC leaves little doubt that, both in east and west, they were carried by caravans or merchant shipping from India or tropical Africa. Their precise character is not easily determined, though they seem to fall into two main groups, smallpox or measles, and bubonic plague; but there is no doubt about their devastating effects on vulnerable populations. 'One or two out of a hundred survived,' wrote the Chinese historian Ssu-ma Kuang of the epidemic of AD 317, and some later historians have attributed the failure both of China and of Rome to withstand the barbarian onslaughts of the fourth and fifth centuries to the sharp fall in manpower caused by imported pestilences.

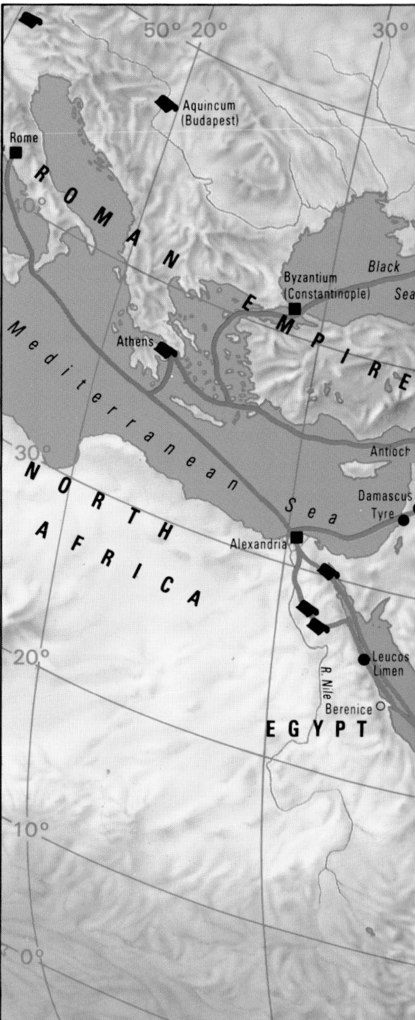

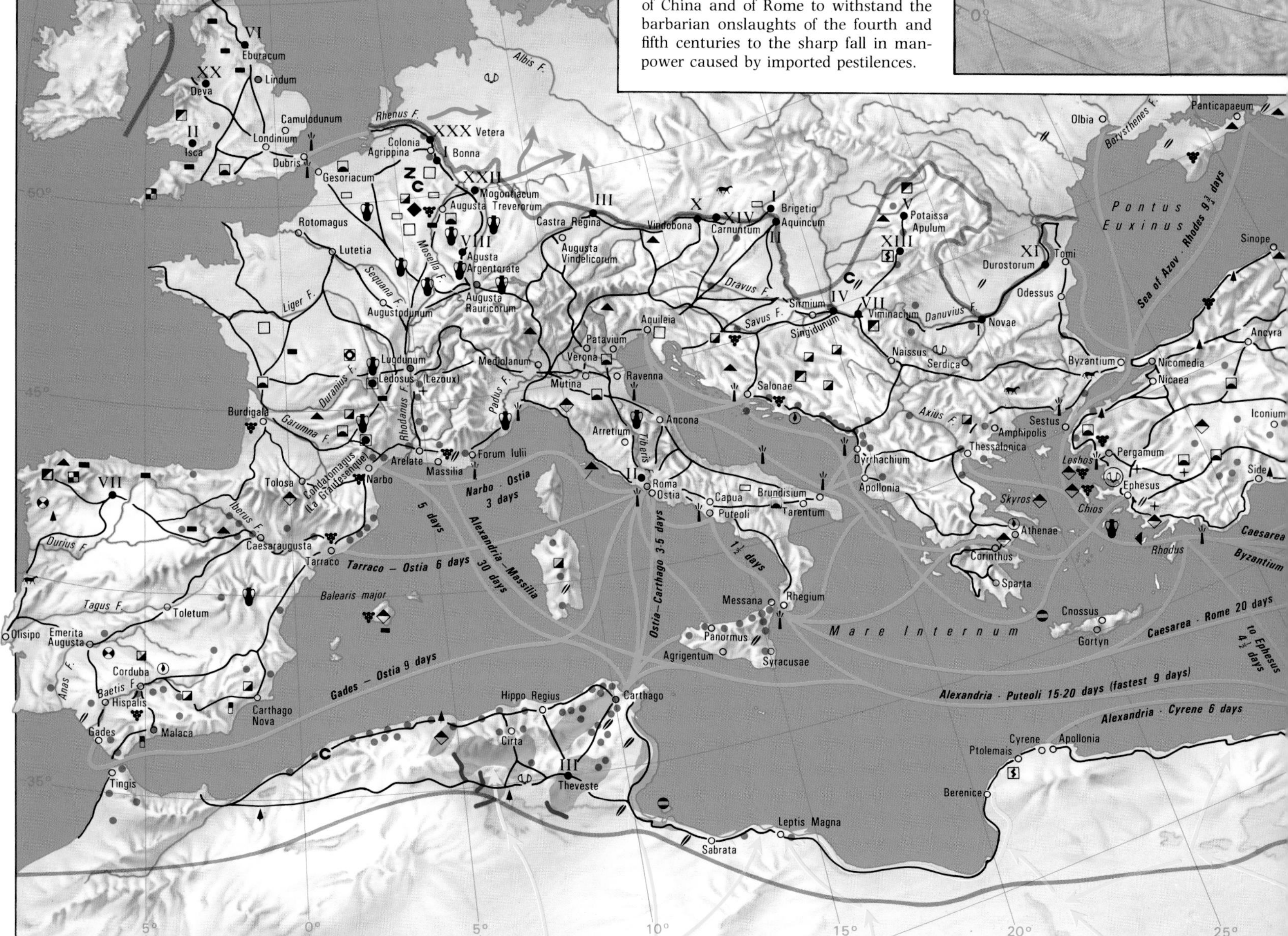

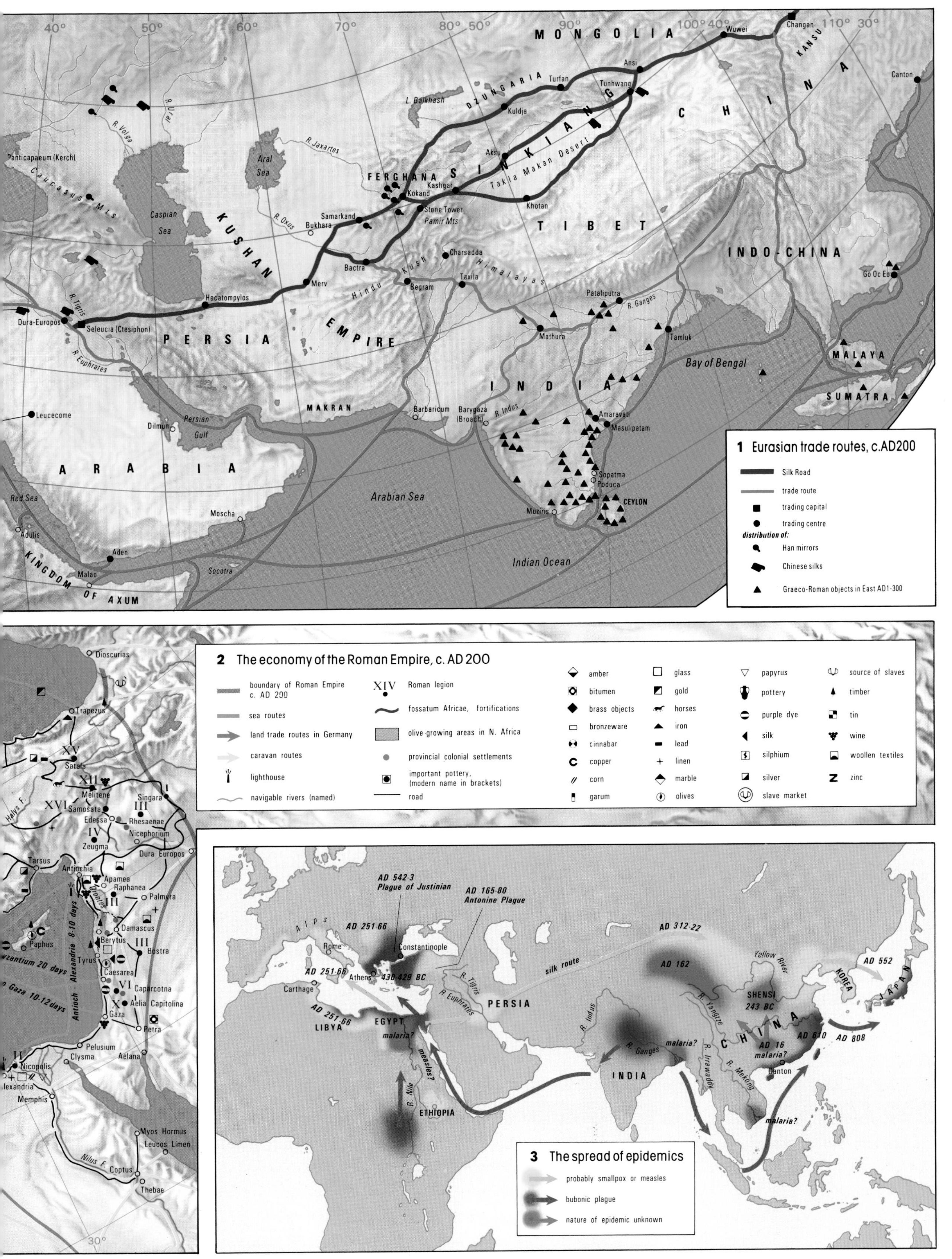
1 Eurasian trade routes, c.AD200
Silk Road
trade route
trading capital
trading centre
distribution of:
Han mirrors
Chinese silks
Graeco-Roman objects in East AD1-300
M O N G O L I A
C H I N A
T I B E T
INDO-CHINA
K U S H A N
E M P I R E
P E R S I A
I N D I A
A R A B I A
KINGDOM OF AXUM
MALAYA
SUMATRA
CEYLON
MAKRAN
FERGHANA
S I N K I A N G
DZUNGARIA
KANSU
Takla Makan Desert
Pamir Mts
Hindu Kush
Himalayas
Caucasus Mts
Caspian Sea
Aral Sea
L. Balkhash
Persian Gulf
Red Sea
Arabian Sea
Bay of Bengal
Indian Ocean
R. Volga
R. Ural
R. Jaxartes
R. Oxus
R. Tigris
R. Euphrates
R. Indus
R. Ganges
Changan
Wuwei
Ansi
Tunhwang
Turfan
Kuldja
Aksu
Kashgar
Kokand
Stone Tower
Khotan
Samarkand
Bukhara
Bactra
Merv
Hecatompylos
Charsadda
Begram
Taxila
Pataliputra
Mathura
Tamluk
Canton
Go Oc Eo
Panticapaeum (Kerch)
Dura-Europos
Seleucia (Ctesiphon)
Leucecome
Dilmun
Barbaricum
Barygaza (Broach)
Amaravati
Masulipatam
Sopatma
Poduca
Muziris
Moscha
Adulis
Aden
Malao
Socotra
2 The economy of the Roman Empire, c. AD 200
boundary of Roman Empire c. AD 200
sea routes
land trade routes in Germany
caravan routes
lighthouse
navigable rivers (named)
XIV Roman legion
fossatum Africae, fortifications
olive-growing areas in N. Africa
provincial colonial settlements
important pottery, (modern name in brackets)
road
amber
bitumen
brass objects
bronzeware
cinnabar
copper
corn
garum
glass
gold
horses
iron
lead
linen
marble
olives
papyrus
pottery
purple dye
silk
silphium
silver
slave market
source of slaves
timber
tin
wine
woollen textiles
zinc
Dioscurias
Trapezus
XV
Satala
XII
Melitene
XVI
Samosata
Singara
III
Edessa
Rhesaenae
IV
Nicephorium
Zeugma
Dura Europos
Halys F.
Tarsus
Antiochia
Apamea
Raphanea
Palmyra
Orontes
Damascus
Paphus
Berytus
Tyrus
Bostra
Caesarea
VI
Caparcotna
X
Aelia Capitolina
Gaza
Petra
Pelusium
Clysma
Aelana
II
Nicopolis
Alexandria
Memphis
Myos Hormus
Leucos Limen
Nilus F.
Coptus
Thebae
Byzantium 20 days
Gaza 10-12 days
Antioch - Alexandria 8-10 days
3 The spread of epidemics
probably smallpox or measles
bubonic plague
nature of epidemic unknown
AD 542-3 Plague of Justinian
AD 165-80 Antonine Plague
AD 251-66
AD 312-22
AD 162
AD 552
AD 808
AD 610
AD 16 malaria?
SHENSI 243 BC
430-429 BC
Alps
Rome
Constantinople
Athens
Carthage
LIBYA
EGYPT
malaria?
measles?
ETHIOPIA
R. Nile
PERSIA
R. Tigris
R. Euphrates
silk route
R. Indus
R. Ganges
INDIA
R. Irrawaddy
R. Mekong
R. Yangtze
Yellow River
CHINA
KOREA
JAPAN
Canton

The world religions c.500BC-AD500

The period 550–500 BC saw the birth of great world religions in all the main centres of civilisation. Their appearance perhaps reflected a need in the rising empires of the old world for more universal creeds than the local tribal deities could provide, and their diffusion – particularly the spread of the great missionary religions, Buddhism and Christianity – was an important factor in linking together the different areas of civilisation (map 1). Their other major contribution – seen, for example, in the work of Anglo-Saxon missionaries in Germany or of Russian missionaries among the heathen tribes of the Urals (page 38) – was to carry civilisation to peoples outside the frontiers of the civilised world.

All the great religions shared, to one degree or another, a belief in a single spiritual reality. Not all were inspired by a missionary spirit. Hinduism, the oldest, was essentially the religion of the people of India, and Judaism, the religion of 'the chosen people of the Lord', was also exclusive. But Buddhism, originally a reformist movement within Hinduism, became perhaps the greatest of all missionary religions when it assumed its universalist, or Mahayana, form some 500 years after the death of its founder, Gautama (c.563–483 BC). Judaism also spread as a result of the persecution of the Jews by more formidable neighbours, beginning with the Babylonian exile (586 BC). After the Roman destruction of the temple in Jerusalem in AD 70 (map 3) the Jewish diaspora carried Judaism far and wide from its home in Palestine, until in time it became a worldwide religion. It also gave birth, directly or indirectly, to two of the world's great missionary religions, Christianity and Islam.

In the Far East the same period saw the rise of the ethical system of Kung Futzu or Confucius (551–479 BC) and the mystical religion of the Tao, or 'the Way', associated with the shadowy figure of Lao-tzu. Later Buddhism spread eastward along the Silk Route through central Asia and with Taoism and Confucianism became one of the 'three religions' of traditional China. Buddhism also reached Japan in the sixth century AD, where it effectively displaced spirit-worship and traditional Shinto until the revival of the latter in the nineteenth century.

The other great religion of the period was Zoroastrianism, which originated in Persia and is associated with another shadowy figure, Zarathustra. Zoroastrianism, which sees life as a battleground between the forces of good and the forces of evil, spread rapidly through the Roman world in the form of Mithraism, with shrines as far afield as northern Britain. It was one of the many oriental cults which permeated the Roman empire when, after the beginning of the Christian era, belief in the Greek pantheon and the household deities broke down. Until the end of the third century AD it was undecided which of the oriental mystery cults would prevail; but with the conversion of the emperor Constantine to Christianity and its recognition by the Edict of Milan (AD 313), still more after it became the official religion of the Roman empire under Theodosius (374–95), the die was cast. Heathen temples were uprooted; rival cults were condemned.

Christianity had begun as a Jewish splinter-movement; its founder, Jesus of Nazareth, saw himself as the Messiah, or Saviour, sent to liberate the Jews from the Roman yoke. But when, after Jesus's condemnation and crucifixion (AD 29), Jewish orthodoxy rejected his message, his disciples, notably Paul of Tarsus, turned instead to the conversion of the 'gentiles', or people outside the law. Paul's journeys (map 2) were a turning point. Thereafter Christianity spread rapidly, both in the Roman empire and also further east. Here the great Christian centres were Antioch and Edessa, the home of the Nestorian church which carried Christ's teaching to Persia and from there to China and India (page 38). This was the situation until the rise of Islam (page 40) changed the scene.

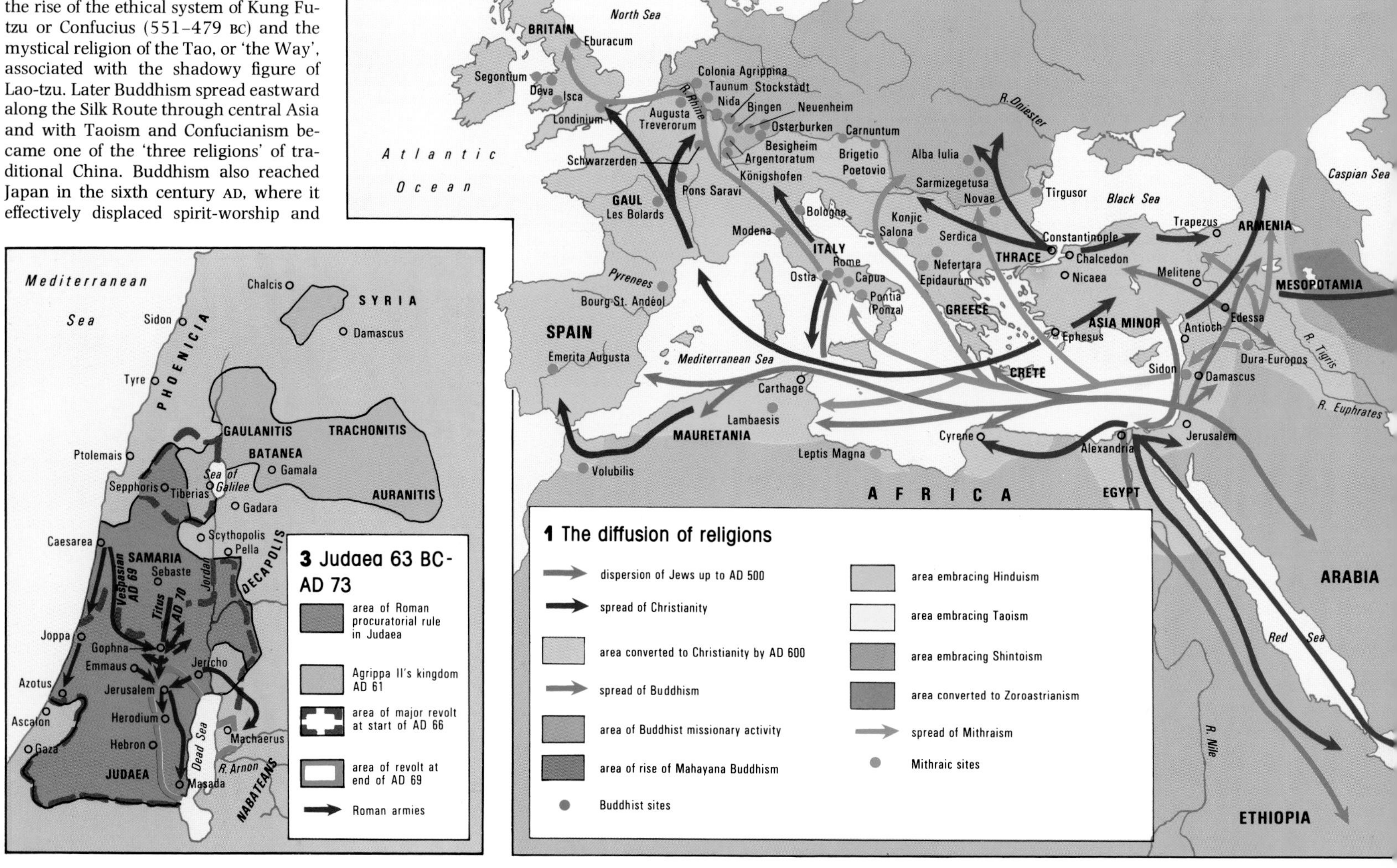

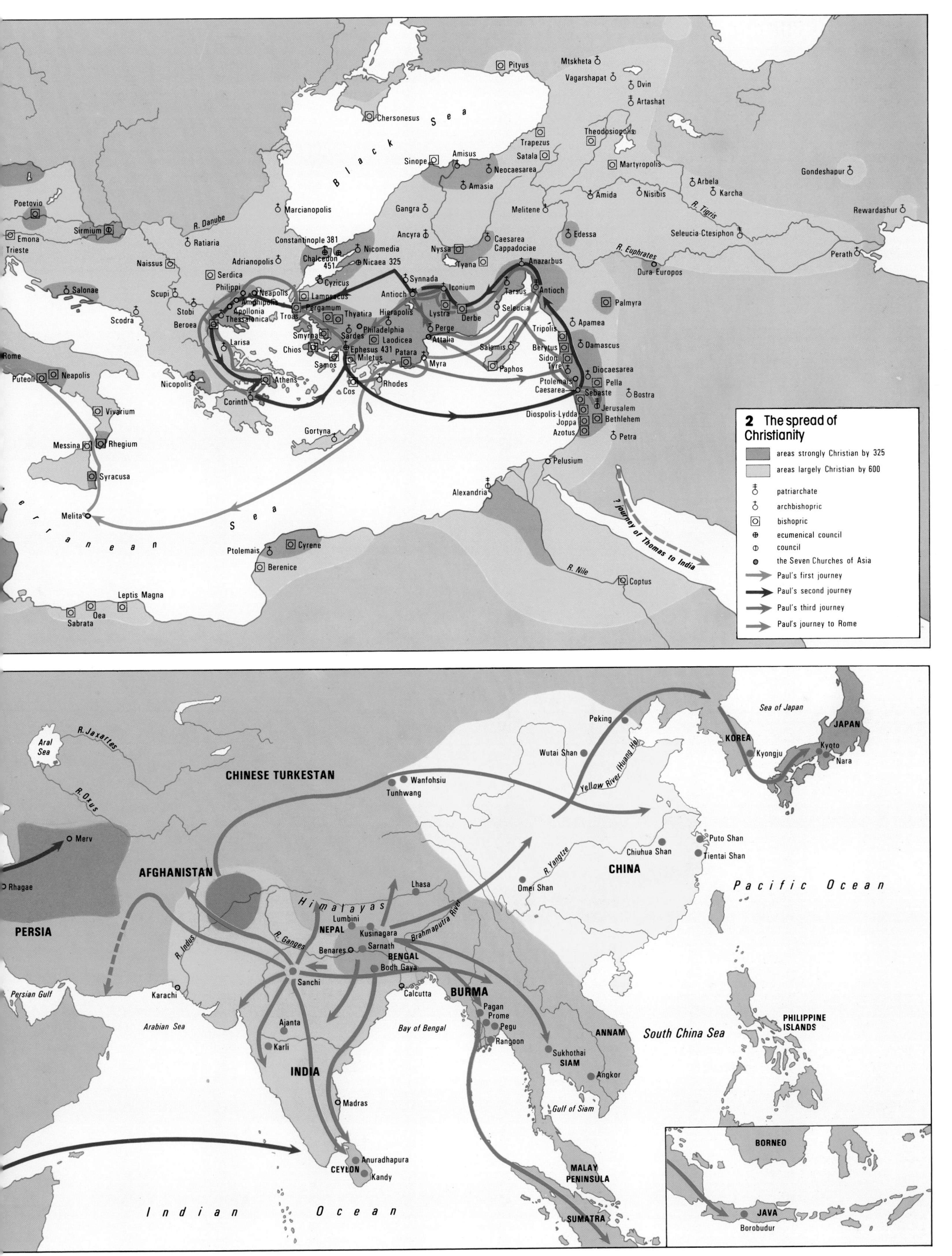
2 The spread of Christianity
areas strongly Christian by 325
areas largely Christian by 600
patriarchate
archbishopric
bishopric
ecumenical council
council
the Seven Churches of Asia
Paul's first journey
Paul's second journey
Paul's third journey
Paul's journey to Rome
Black Sea
Mediterranean Sea
? Journey of Thomas to India
R. Danube
R. Tigris
R. Euphrates
R. Nile
Rome
Constantinople 381
Chalcedon 451
Nicaea 325
Ephesus 431
Jerusalem
Antioch
Alexandria
CHINESE TURKESTAN
AFGHANISTAN
PERSIA
INDIA
NEPAL
BENGAL
BURMA
CHINA
KOREA
JAPAN
ANNAM
SIAM
CEYLON
MALAY PENINSULA
SUMATRA
BORNEO
JAVA
PHILIPPINE ISLANDS
Himalayas
Pacific Ocean
Indian Ocean
South China Sea
Bay of Bengal
Arabian Sea
Sea of Japan
Persian Gulf
Gulf of Siam
Aral Sea
R. Jaxartes
R. Oxus
R. Indus
R. Ganges
Brahmaputra River
R. Yangtze
Yellow River (Huang Ho)
Merv
Rhagae
Wanfohsiu
Tunhwang
Peking
Wutai Shan
Kyongju
Kyoto
Nara
Puto Shan
Tientai Shan
Chiuhua Shan
Omei Shan
Lhasa
Lumbini
Kusinagara
Sarnath
Benares
Bodh Gaya
Sanchi
Karachi
Calcutta
Ajanta
Karli
Madras
Anuradhapura
Kandy
Pagan
Prome
Pegu
Rangoon
Sukhothai
Angkor
Borobudur

India and China: the first empires

The fifth and sixth centuries BC were a period of consolidation in India and China. In India by the end of the fifth century the 16 political units in existence in 600 BC had been reduced to four. In China, by 400 BC, instead of the multiple feudal principalities of the Chou period (page 8) seven major states were contending for supremacy. In both countries iron tools increased both agricultural productivity and the resources of the rising states. In China the area of civilisation had expanded from the Yellow river to the Yangtze valley and beyond. In India the deforestation of the north shifted the centre of power from the Indus, the seat of the earliest civilisations (page 8), to the fertile plain of the Ganges. Here the kingdom of Magadha emerged as the nucleus of the first Indian empire.

Politically, nevertheless, it was a period of continuous strife, and the resulting social tensions were a major factor in the emergence of the great religious and ethical systems, Buddhism, Taoism, Confucianism and Jainism (page 26), which, in various ways, expressed a yearning for a more stable world order. In India the turning point came in 320 BC when Chandragupta Maurya seized the Magadhan throne, annexed the lands east of the Indus, occupied large parts of central India north of the Narmada river, and in 303 BC annexed the Seleucid province of Trans-Indus. Chandragupta's grandson, Asoka (273–236), conquered Kalinga on the Bay of Bengal, and the greater part of the subcontinent was brought under one rule. His edicts, inscribed on pillars and rocks, evidence Asoka's conversion to Buddhism (map 4).

In China the turning point came with the rise of the state of Ch'in (328–308), which finally dominated China in 221 BC (map 1). But the ruthless centralising policy of the first Ch'in emperor, Shih Huang-ti (221–206), provoked a reaction, and after his death his empire collapsed. It was revived, after a period of civil war, by the Han dynasty, which compromised between centralising policies and the feudal principalities. In India, also, the death of Asoka introduced a long period of decentralisation, punctuated by invasion from the north, which was not overcome until AD 320 when the Guptas, based again on Magadha, imposed a new imperial rule (map 5). This classical age of Indian civilisation survived beyond the collapse of the Gupta empire caused by the barbarian invasions of the fifth century (page 32).

The barbarian invasions were also a turning point in China. The Ch'in and the Han built and extended the Great Wall against the nomad Hsiungnu in the north. Under the emperor Wu-ti (140–87) the Han extended their power to central Asia (map 2). With its efficient administration, a large export trade, and an extensive network of roads and canals, Han China, with its capital at Changan was extremely prosperous (map 3). But control over south China was tenuous, while in the north feudal magnates still exercised great power, which grew with the threat of war. Crisis came in AD 9, and although Han rule was restored, disintegration set in after c.AD 160. When in 304 the Hsiungnu broke through the Great Wall, China remained divided until 589.

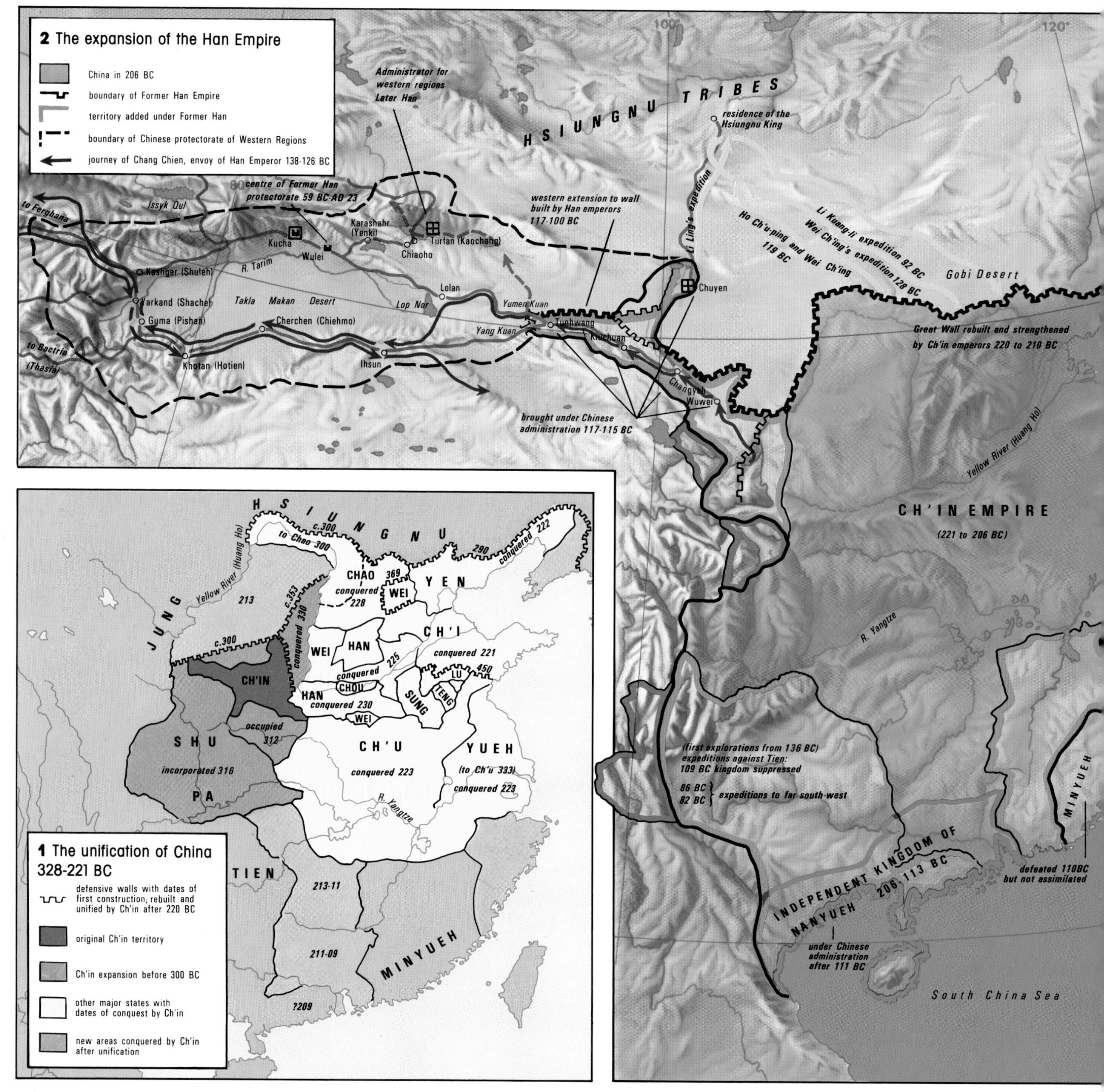

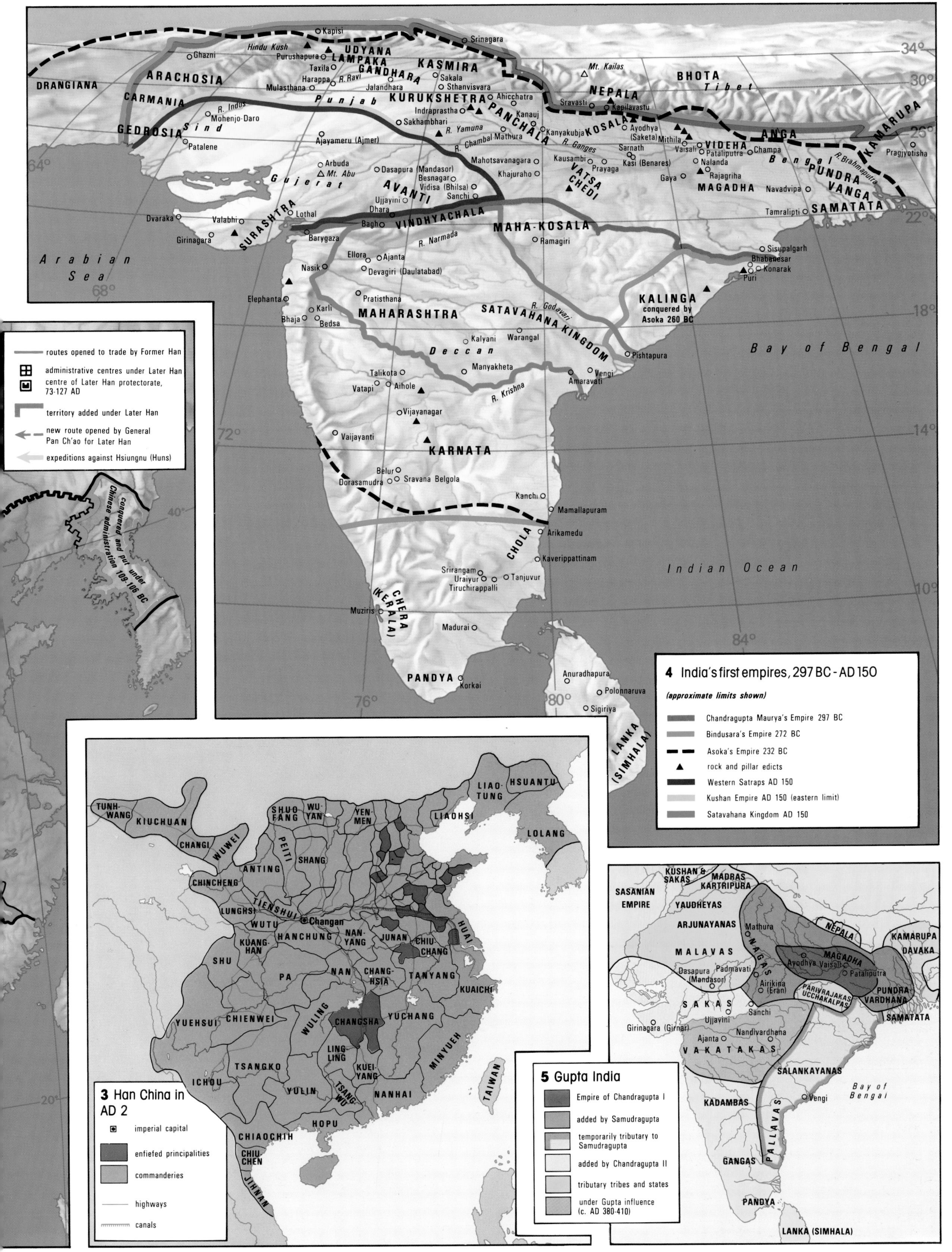

4 India's first empires, 297 BC - AD 150
(approximate limits shown)
Chandragupta Maurya's Empire 297 BC
Bindusara's Empire 272 BC
Asoka's Empire 232 BC
rock and pillar edicts
Western Satraps AD 150
Kushan Empire AD 150 (eastern limit)
Satavahana Kingdom AD 150
routes opened to trade by Former Han
administrative centres under Later Han
centre of Later Han protectorate, 73-127 AD
territory added under Later Han
new route opened by General Pan Ch'ao for Later Han
expeditions against Hsiungnu (Huns)
conquered and put under Chinese administration 109-106 BC
DRANGIANA
ARACHOSIA
CARMANIA
GEDROSIA
UDYANA
LAMPAKA
GANDHARA
KASMIRA
KURUKSHETRA
PANCHALA
NEPALA
BHOTA
Tibet
KOSALA
VIDEHA
ANGA
KAMARUPA
PUNDRA
VANGA
SAMATATA
MAGADHA
VATSA
CHEDI
AVANTI
SURASHTRA
VINDHYACHALA
MAHA-KOSALA
Punjab
Sind
Gujerat
Bengal
KALINGA
conquered by Asoka 260 BC
MAHARASHTRA
SATAVAHANA KINGDOM
Deccan
KARNATA
CHOLA
CHERA (KERALA)
PANDYA
LANKA (SIMHALA)
Arabian Sea
Bay of Bengal
Indian Ocean
Kapisi
Srinagara
Ghazni
Hindu Kush
Purushapura
Taxila
Harappa
R. Ravi
Mulasthana
Jalandhara
Sakala
Sthanvisvara
Ahicchatra
Mt. Kailas
Sravasti
Kapilavastu
Indraprastha
Kanauj
Kanyakubja
Ayodhya (Saketa)
Mithila
Vaisali
Pataliputra
Champa
Nalanda
Rajagriha
Gaya
R. Indus
Mohenjo-Daro
Sakhambhari
R. Yamuna
Mathura
R. Chambal
R. Ganges
Sarnath
Kasi (Benares)
Kausambi
Prayaga
Mahotsavanagara
Khajuraho
Ajayameru (Ajmer)
Patalene
Arbuda
Mt. Abu
Dasapura (Mandasor)
Besnagar
Vidisa (Bhilsa)
Sanchi
Ujjayini
Dhara
Bagh
Lothal
Dvaraka
Valabhi
Girinagara
Barygaza
R. Narmada
Ramagiri
Navadvipa
Tamralipti
R. Brahmaputra
Pragjyotisha
Sisupalgarh
Bhabanesar
Konarak
Puri
Ellora
Ajanta
Devagiri (Daulatabad)
Nasik
Elephanta
Pratisthana
Karli
Bhaja
Bedsa
R. Godavari
Kalyani
Warangal
Pishtapura
Manyakheta
Talikota
Vatapi
Aihole
Vengi
Amaravati
R. Krishna
Vijayanagar
Vaijayanti
Belur
Dorasamudra
Sravana Belgola
Kanchi
Mamallapuram
Arikamedu
Kaverippattinam
Srirangam
Uraiyur
Tiruchirappalli
Tanjuvur
Muziris
Madurai
Korkai
Anuradhapura
Polonnaruva
Sigiriya
3 Han China in AD 2
imperial capital
enfiefed principalities
commanderies
highways
canals
TUNHWANG
KIUCHUAN
CHANGI
WUWEI
SHUO FANG
WU-YAN
YEN-MEN
LIAO-TUNG
HSUANTU
LIAOHSI
LOLANG
PEITI
SHANG
ANTING
CHINCHENG
TIENSHUI
LUNGHSI
WUTU
Changan
HANCHUNG
NAN-YANG
JUNAN
CHIU-CHANG
HUAI
KUANG-HAN
SHU
PA
NAN
CHANG-HSIA
TANYANG
KUAICHI
YUEHSUI
CHIENWEI
WULING
CHANGSHA
YUCHANG
LING-LING
KUEI-YANG
MINYUEH
TSANGKO
ICHOU
YULIN
TSANG-WU
NANHAI
HOPU
TAIWAN
CHIAOCHIH
CHIU-CHEN
JIHNAN
5 Gupta India
Empire of Chandragupta I
added by Samudragupta
temporarily tributary to Samudragupta
added by Chandragupta II
tributary tribes and states
under Gupta influence (c. AD 380-410)
KUSHAN & SAKAS
MADRAS
KARTRIPURA
SASANIAN EMPIRE
YAUDHEYAS
ARJUNAYANAS
Mathura
NEPALA
KAMARUPA
DAVAKA
MALAVAS
NAGAS
MAGADHA
Ayodhya
Vaisali
Pataliputra
Dasapura (Mandasor)
Padmavati
Airikina (Eran)
PARIVRAJAKAS
UCCHAKALPAS
PUNDRA-VARDHANA
SAMATATA
SAKAS
Sanchi
Ujjayini
Girinagara (Girnar)
Nandivardhana
Ajanta
VAKATAKAS
SALANKAYANAS
KADAMBAS
Vengi
Bay of Bengal
PALLAVAS
GANGAS
PANDYA
LANKA (SIMHALA)

The Roman Empire
264 BC–AD 565

The rise of Rome from a collection of shepherds' huts on the hills overlooking the Tiber to a great world empire is a story of seven centuries of constant warfare. According to tradition, the city of Rome was founded in 754 BC by descendants of Aeneas, the legendary hero who had fled to Italy after the sack of Troy. Archaeology shows that it was only in the sixth century that it began to take on the trappings of a city.

In 510 BC the citizens of Rome expelled the last of the Etruscan kings and formed a republic. Over the next 300 years victories over Etruscans, Greeks and Celts gradually extended Roman control over the whole of Italy (map 1), but this expansion brought her into direct conflict with the imperialist ambitions of Carthage on the North African coast. Three fierce Punic Wars were fought for supremacy between the two powers (map 2). In the second (218–201 BC), the Carthaginians under the brilliant generalship of Hannibal inflicted a series of crushing defeats on the Romans. But Roman resolve held, Hannibal was ultimately defeated, and some fifty years later Carthage itself was destroyed in the Third Punic War (146 BC).

The Punic Wars gave Rome control over Sicily (241 BC), Spain (206 BC), and North Africa (146 BC). At the same time, conflict with the Hellenistic kingdoms of the East Mediterranean resulted in the conquest of Macedon, Greece and western Asia Minor. In this way, almost by accident, Rome became an imperial power with far-flung possessions. In the first century BC the growing power of successful war-leaders led to fierce rivalries and civil wars, culminating in the struggle between Caesar and Pompey (49–45 BC), from which Caesar emerged victorious. His assassination in 44 BC, however, initiated a further thirteen years of conflict, only ending with Augustus' victory over Antony and Cleopatra at Actium in 31 BC.

Augustus' rule initiated a period of two centuries of unprecedented peace and prosperity in the extensive lands of the Roman empire (map 3). Population increased, trade flourished, and cities grew. Civic authorities and wealthy individuals embellished their cities with theatres, baths and temples, while roads, aqueducts and harbours brought in essential supplies from outside. This vast common market was further united by Roman law and by the use of Latin.

This peace was broken in the middle of the third century AD by Germanic invasions in the west and Persian victories in the east which brought the empire temporarily to its knees (map 4). Reform and reorganisation under Diocletian (AD 284–305) and Constantine (306–337) ensured the continued survival of the eastern half of the empire, with its new capital at Constantinople (Byzantium), but Rome itself fell to the Goths in AD 410 and Justinian's abortive efforts to recover the western provinces in the mid-sixth century showed clearly that the unified empire was a thing of the past. The ghost of the Roman empire lived on in the west, however, in the continued importance of Roman law and the continued use of Latin by the Christian church.

2 The Punic Wars, 264-146 BC

1 Roman expansion in Italy

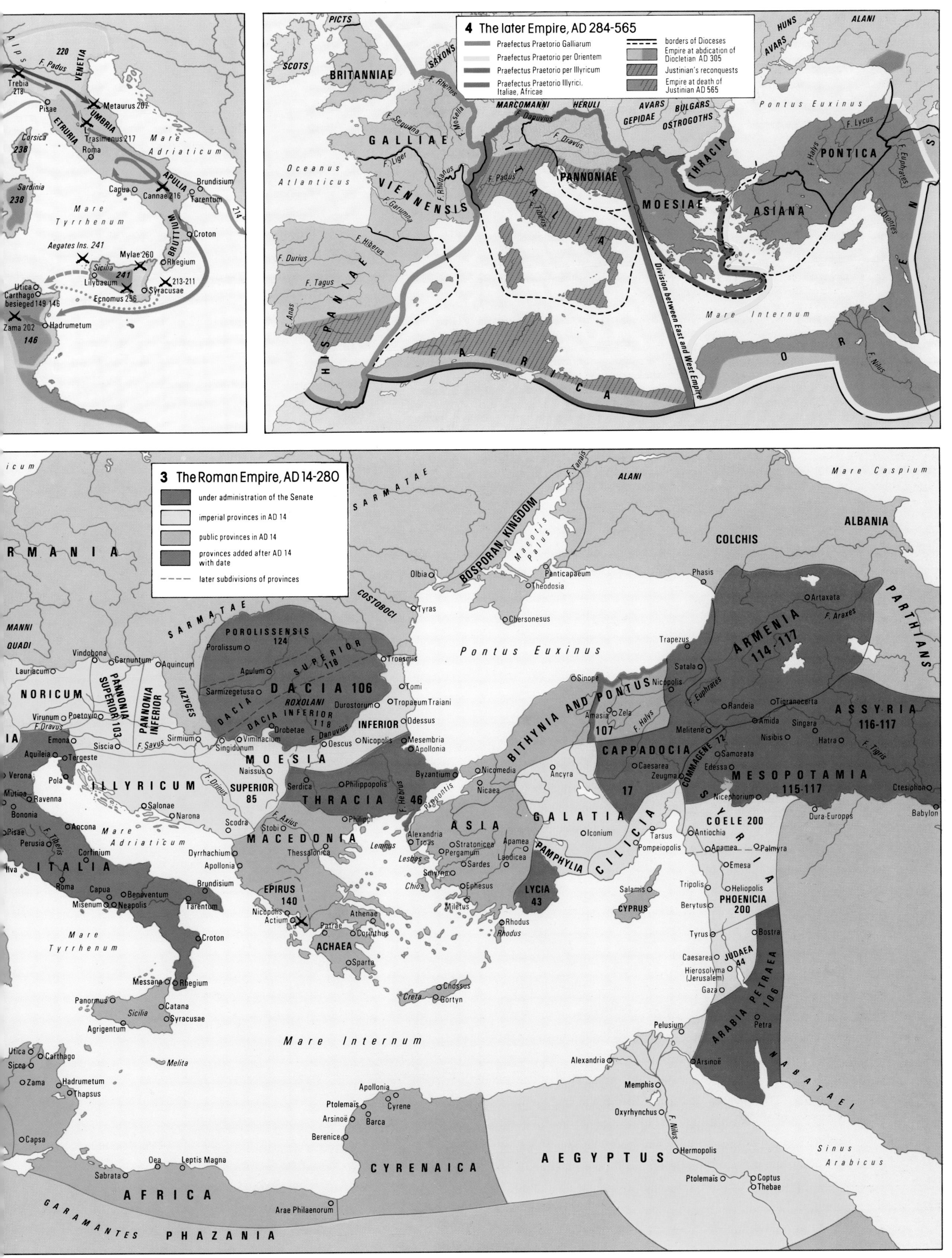
4 The later Empire, AD 284-565
Praefectus Praetorio Galliarum
Praefectus Praetorio per Orientem
Praefectus Praetorio per Illyricum
Praefectus Praetorio Illyrici, Italiae, Africae
borders of Dioceses
Empire at abdication of Diocletian AD 305
Justinian's reconquests
Empire at death of Justinian AD 565
BRITANNIAE
GALLIAE
VIENNENSIS
HISPANIAE
ITALIA
AFRICA
PANNONIAE
MOESIAE
THRACIA
ASIANA
PONTICA
ORIENS
Division between East and West Empire
Pontus Euxinus
Mare Internum
Oceanus Atlanticus
3 The Roman Empire, AD 14-280
under administration of the Senate
imperial provinces in AD 14
public provinces in AD 14
provinces added after AD 14 with date
later subdivisions of provinces
NORICUM
PANNONIA SUPERIOR 103
PANNONIA INFERIOR
DACIA 106
MOESIA
THRACIA 46
MACEDONIA
EPIRUS 140
ACHAEA
ASIA
BITHYNIA AND PONTUS
GALATIA
CAPPADOCIA 17
LYCIA 43
CILICIA
ARMENIA 114-117
ASSYRIA 116-117
MESOPOTAMIA 115-117
SYRIA
PHOENICIA 200
JUDAEA 44
ARABIA PETRAEA 106
AEGYPTUS
CYRENAICA
AFRICA
ITALIA
ILLYRICUM
Pontus Euxinus
Mare Internum
Mare Caspium
Sinus Arabicus

The barbarian invasions

In the fourth and fifth centuries AD the irruption of nomadic peoples from central Asia threw the civilised world into disarray. The invading nomads were under no form of central control though their movements radiated from a common centre. They were mostly Mongoloid and their languages mostly of the Turkish family; they were largely pastoralists with mobile encampments of tents and their success in war owed much to their mounted archers. All the established centres of civilisation were affected by them: China, the Gupta empire in India, Sasanian Persia and the Roman empire in the west (map 1). In 304 the Great Wall of China was breached by the Hsiung-nu, forbears of the Huns; in 367, Picts and Scots broke through Hadrian's Wall into Britain. The setbacks were lasting. China remained disunited until 589, and western Europe (if we except the short-lived Carolingian revival) only began to recover from invasion around the middle of the eleventh century (page 36).

The appearance of the Huns in Europe c.370 immediately caused a great involuntary movement among the Germanic peoples who had long been settled in northern and central Europe beyond the confines of the Roman empire. The details, beginning with the Visigoths, who defeated the Roman emperor at Adrianople in 378, sacked Rome in 410 and were settled in Aquitaine in 418, can be followed on map 2. Behind the Visigoths followed other east and west Germanic peoples: Alans, Vandals, Sueves, Alemans, Franks, and finally the Ostrogoths who, having earlier been forced into subjection, liberated themselves after the defeat of the Huns in 451, and descended into Italy, where they were in control by 493. Only the Anglo-Saxon invasion of Britain, beginning c.440, followed a different course. Here scattered bands of warriors and settlers, moving by ship up the estuaries of the Humber, Thames and the Wash, met with stubborn resistance. It was to be almost two centuries before the invaders, following their victories at Deorham (577) and Chester (616), established control of Britain (map 3). Here continuity with the Roman past was at a modest level at best.

In continental Europe continuity was more evident. Political control passed from Roman officials to German kings; but, except for the Anglo-Saxons and Franks, who could draw manpower from their homeland, the invaders were too few in number to change decisively the character of Roman society. Hence the success of the counter-offensive which Justinian launched in 533 (page 30). But Justinian's wars, and the havoc they wrought, left the way open for another wave of invasion from Asia, this time the Avars, and it was their onslaught, beginning c.560, that drove the Lombards into Italy (568). But they were too few in number to occupy the whole peninsula, and Italy remained divided between the Lombards, the Byzantine emperor and the Papacy (map 4). When the Lombard ruler Aistulf advanced south, seeking to establish his authority over the Lombard dukes of Spoleto and Benevento, occupied Ravenna in 751 and drove out the Byzantine exarch, the Pope, fearing for his independence, called on the Franks for aid. Thus was sealed the momentous alliance of the Carolingians and the Papacy, which resulted in Charles the Great's invasion, conquest and annexation of the Lombard kingdom in 774.

The appearance of the Avars also unsettled the Slav peoples who had greatly extended their settlement in eastern Europe following the Germanic migration westwards. Beginning c.600 Slav warbands descended into Greece and the Balkans, while the Bulgars took control of the western shore of the Black Sea (map 5). The arrival of the Slavs, cutting the landbridge between Byzantium and the west, was a cardinal fact in European history. The rise of the Bulgarian Empire and the gradual consolidation of Serbia and Croatia left a permanent imprint on the demography and historical geography of Europe.

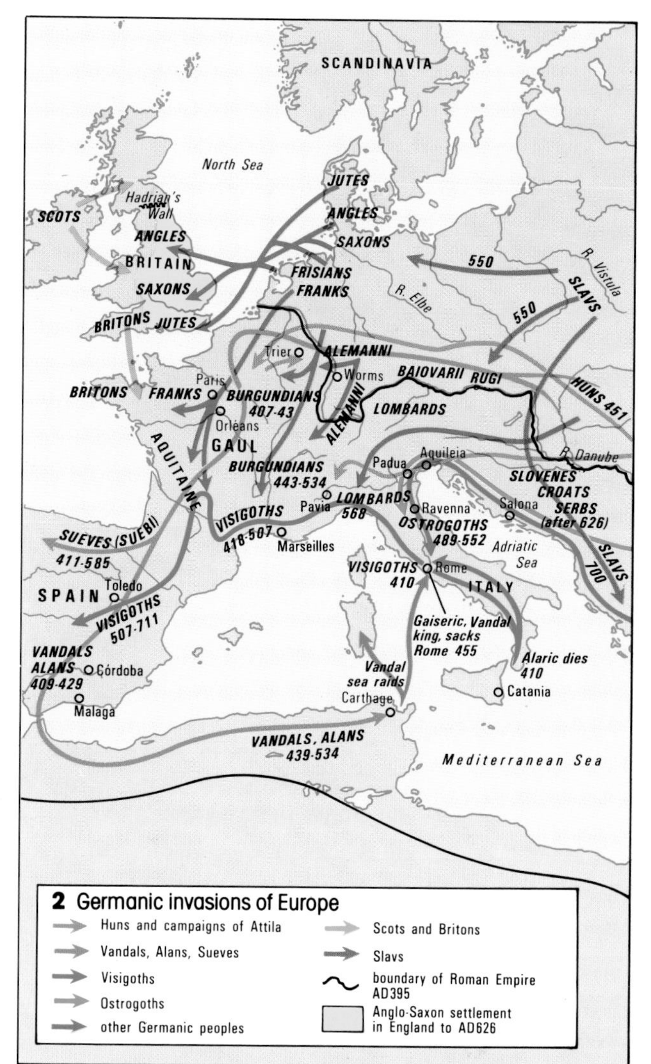

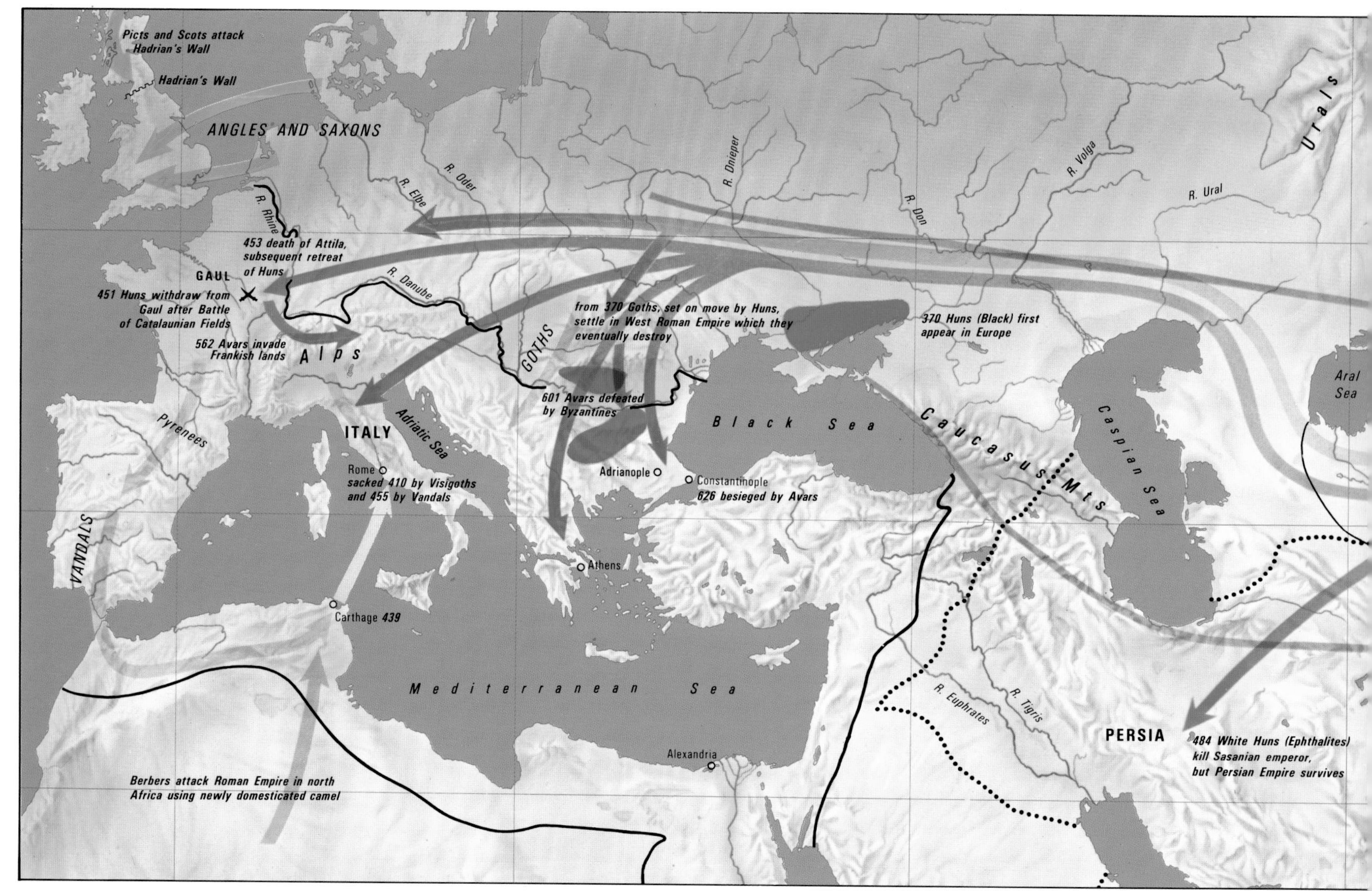

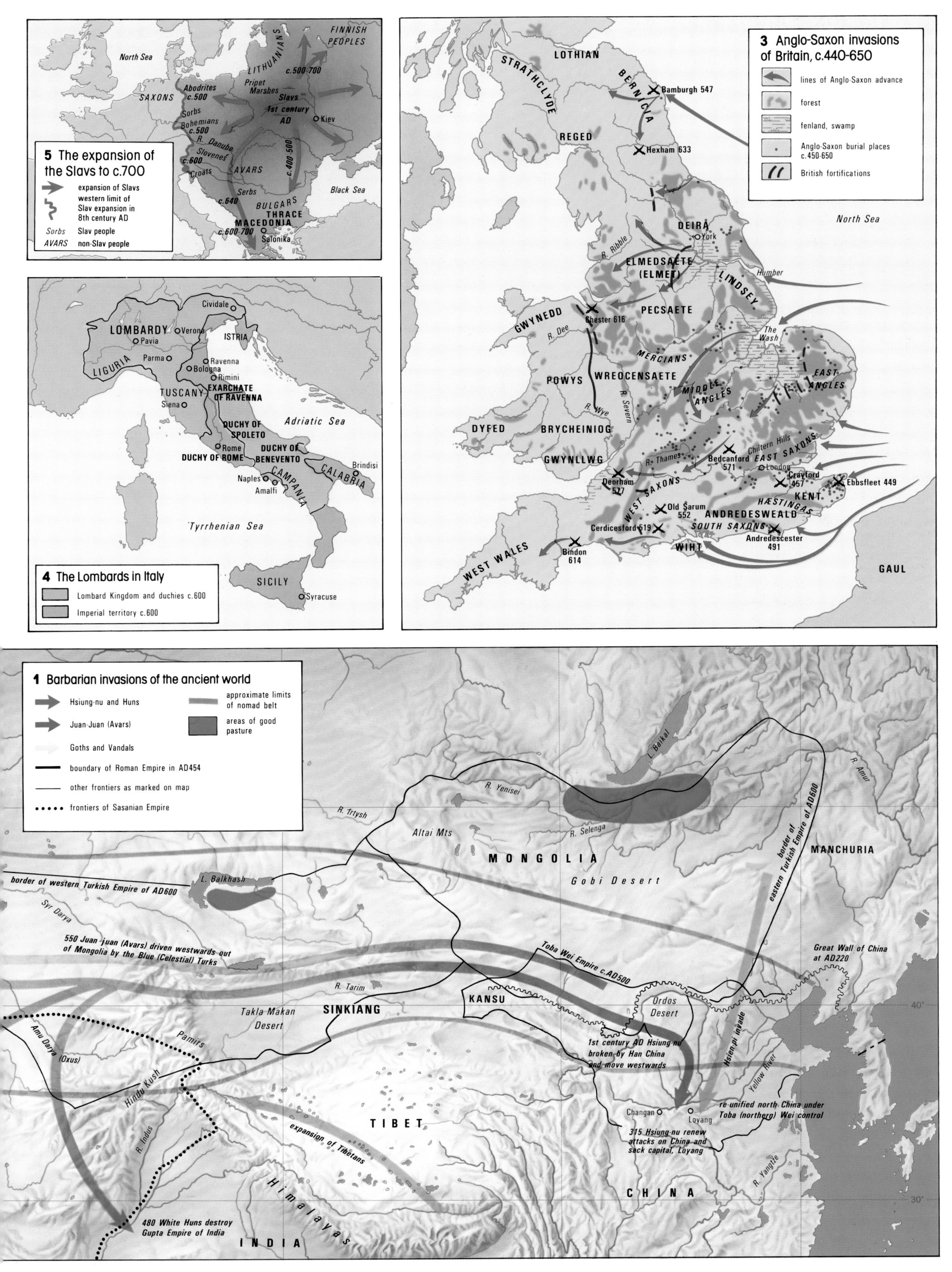

5 The expansion of the Slavs to c.700
expansion of Slavs
western limit of Slav expansion in 8th century AD
Sorbs Slav people
AVARS non-Slav people
North Sea
FINNISH PEOPLES
LITHUANIANS
c.500-700
Pripet Marshes
Slavs 1st century AD
Kiev
SAXONS
Abodrites c.500
Sorbs
Bohemians c.500
R. Danube
Slovenes
c.600
Croats
AVARS
c.400-500
Serbs
c.640
BULGARS
THRACE
MACEDONIA
c.600-700
Salonika
Black Sea
4 The Lombards in Italy
Lombard Kingdom and duchies c.600
Imperial territory c.600
Cividale
LOMBARDY
Verona
Pavia
ISTRIA
LIGURIA
Parma
Ravenna
Bologna
Rimini
TUSCANY
EXARCHATE OF RAVENNA
Siena
DUCHY OF SPOLETO
Adriatic Sea
Rome
DUCHY OF ROME
DUCHY OF BENEVENTO
CAMPANIA
CALABRIA
Brindisi
Naples
Amalfi
Tyrrhenian Sea
SICILY
Syracuse
3 Anglo-Saxon invasions of Britain, c.440-650
lines of Anglo-Saxon advance
forest
fenland, swamp
Anglo-Saxon burial places c.450-650
British fortifications
LOTHIAN
STRATHCLYDE
BERNICIA
Bamburgh 547
REGED
Hexham 633
DEIRA
York
North Sea
R. Ribble
ELMEDSAETE (ELMET)
LINDSEY
Humber
GWYNEDD
Chester 616
R. Dee
PECSAETE
The Wash
MERCIANS
POWYS
WREOCENSAETE
R. Severn
MIDDLE ANGLES
EAST ANGLES
R. Wye
DYFED
BRYCHEINIOG
Chiltern Hills
EAST SAXONS
GWYNLLWG
R. Thames
Bedcanford 571
London
Deorham 577
Crayford 457
Ebbsfleet 449
WEST SAXONS
KENT
Old Sarum 552
HÆSTINGAS
ANDREDESWEALD
Cerdicesford 519
SOUTH SAXONS
Andredescester 491
WIHT
Bindon 614
WEST WALES
GAUL
1 Barbarian invasions of the ancient world
Hsiung-nu and Huns
Juan-Juan (Avars)
Goths and Vandals
approximate limits of nomad belt
areas of good pasture
boundary of Roman Empire in AD454
other frontiers as marked on map
frontiers of Sasanian Empire
L. Baikal
R. Amur
R. Yenisei
R. Irtysh
Altai Mts
R. Selenga
MONGOLIA
MANCHURIA
border of eastern Turkish Empire of AD600
L. Balkhash
border of western Turkish Empire of AD600
Gobi Desert
Syr Darya
550 Juan-juan (Avars) driven westwards out of Mongolia by the Blue (Celestial) Turks
Toba Wei Empire c.AD500
Great Wall of China at AD220
R. Tarim
KANSU
Ordos Desert
Takla Makan Desert
SINKIANG
Amu Darya (Oxus)
Pamirs
1st century AD Hsiung-nu broken by Han China and move westwards
Hsien-pi invade
Yellow River
Hindu Kush
Changan
Loyang
re-unified north China under Toba (northern) Wei control
R. Indus
TIBET
expansion of Tibetans
315 Hsiung-nu renew attacks on China and sack capital, Loyang
Himalayas
R. Yangtze
CHINA
480 White Huns destroy Gupta Empire of India
INDIA
40°
30°

Germanic kingdoms of Western Europe

Within a century of the Germanic invasions there were settled kingdoms in western Europe, except in Britain where invaders still met resistance. Among these (map 1) the Ostrogothic kingdom of Theodoric the Great (493–526) was outstanding. In Spain, the kingdom of the Visigoths was to endure from the late fifth century until the Arab conquest in 711. But monarchical institutions were still weak and religious differences divided the Arian rulers from their Catholic subjects. Justinian's attack on the Ostrogothic kingdom (page 30) destroyed equilibrium in the west and opened the way for the advance of the Franks (map 2).

The Franks also had appeared on the scene as scattered warbands, but Clovis (486–511) ruthlessly eliminated his rivals, made himself sole king,, and reconciled the Gallo-Roman population by embracing the Catholic faith (497). He then turned against the neighbouring peoples, the Alemanni and Burgundians, defeated the Visigoths at Vouillé (507), near Poitiers, and forced them to withdraw to Spain and Septimania. But Theodoric's support for the other Germanic kingdoms checked further advance, and only after his death was a new phase of Frankish expansion possible. Deprived of Ostrogothic support, the Thuringians (531), Burgundians (532–4), and Alemanni (535) succumbed, and in 537 the Franks seized Provence.

Once the initial wave of conquest was spent, however, decline set in. Division of the royal patrimony, dynastic quarrels and alienation of the royal estates to buy aristocratic and ecclesiastical support, seemed after the death of Dagobert I (629–39) to presage the break-up of the kingdom. In Britain, on the other hand, the seventh century saw the emergence and consolidation of the kingdoms known as the Heptarchy. It seems that the kingdoms of the south-east (Sussex, Kent, Essex, East Anglia) were prevented from expanding by geographical obstacles, and leadership passed first to Northumbria and then to Mercia. The progress of Northumbria was helped by its early conversion to Christianity, but it was resisted by pagan Mercia under Penda (632–54), sometimes in alliance with the Britons, and by the time of Offa (757–96) the pre-eminence of Mercia, now Christian, was unquestionable. It controlled the four eastern kingdoms (map 3), and even Wessex recognised Mercian overlordship.

In the Frankish lands the turning point came with the battle of Tertry (687), when the leaders of the Austrasian aristocracy established their preponderance. This was the beginning of the rise of the Carolingian dynasty. Ruling at first indirectly, but after 751 with the royal title, the Carolingians restored Frankish fortunes and inaugurated a great surge of territorial expansion (map 4). Charles Martel (714–41) won a famous victory over the Arabs at Poitiers (732). His son Pepin (751–68) expelled them from Aquitania (752). Charles the Great, or Charlemagne (768–814), conquered Lombardy (774) and established Frankish rule in Italy. But his greatest victories were in the east, against the Bavarians (788), the Avars (796), and the Saxons (finally subdued in 804). His coronation as emperor by Pope Leo III in 800 marked the apogee of Frankish success.

However, Charlemagne's last ten years were beset by problems, the frontier marches never safe from attack; and after his death the inherent institutional weaknesses quickly became apparent. Civil war led to a first partition in 843. But the famous treaty of Verdun (map 5) was only a first step, and at Meersen (870) the 'Middle Kingdom' was eliminated (map 6) and the familiar outlines of Europe began to take shape. In 888 the Carolingian empire collapsed but its legacy to European civilisation remained.

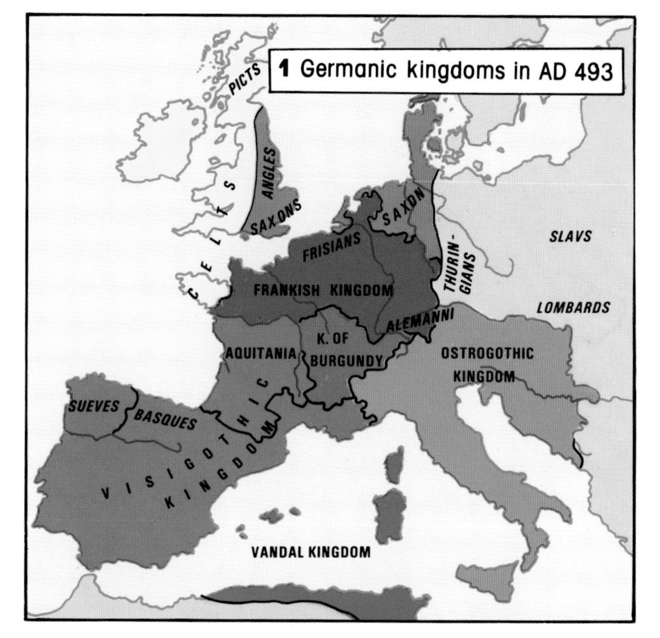

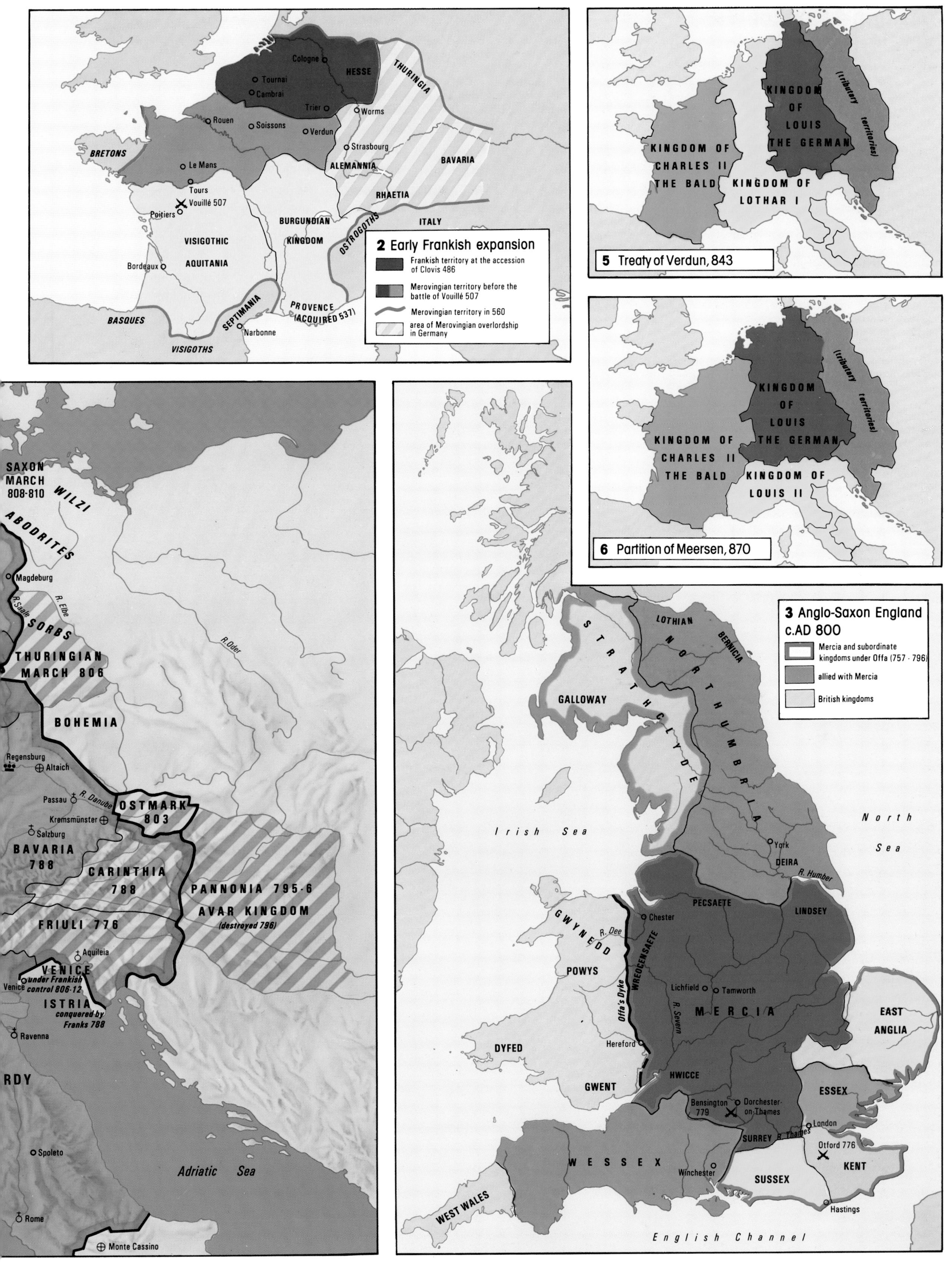

2 Early Frankish expansion
Frankish territory at the accession of Clovis 486
Merovingian territory before the battle of Vouillé 507
Merovingian territory in 560
area of Merovingian overlordship in Germany
Cologne
Tournai
Cambrai
HESSE
THURINGIA
Trier
Worms
Rouen
Soissons
Verdun
Strasbourg
BRETONS
Le Mans
ALEMANNIA
BAVARIA
Tours
Vouillé 507
Poitiers
RHAETIA
BURGUNDIAN KINGDOM
OSTROGOTHS
ITALY
VISIGOTHIC AQUITANIA
Bordeaux
BASQUES
SEPTIMANIA
PROVENCE (ACQUIRED 537)
Narbonne
VISIGOTHS
5 Treaty of Verdun, 843
KINGDOM OF LOUIS THE GERMAN
(tributary territories)
KINGDOM OF CHARLES II THE BALD
KINGDOM OF LOTHAR I
6 Partition of Meersen, 870
KINGDOM OF LOUIS THE GERMAN
(tributary territories)
KINGDOM OF CHARLES II THE BALD
KINGDOM OF LOUIS II
SAXON MARCH 808-810
WILZI
ABODRITES
Magdeburg
R. Saale
R. Elbe
SORBS
R. Oder
THURINGIAN MARCH 806
BOHEMIA
Regensburg
Altaich
Passau
R. Danube
OSTMARK 803
Kremsmünster
Salzburg
BAVARIA 788
CARINTHIA 788
PANNONIA 795-6
AVAR KINGDOM
(destroyed 796)
FRIULI 776
Aquileia
VENICE
under Frankish control 806-12
Venice
ISTRIA
conquered by Franks 788
Ravenna
RDY
Spoleto
Adriatic Sea
Rome
Monte Cassino
3 Anglo-Saxon England c.AD 800
Mercia and subordinate kingdoms under Offa (757 - 796)
allied with Mercia
British kingdoms
LOTHIAN
BERNICIA
STRATHCLYDE
NORTHUMBRIA
GALLOWAY
Irish Sea
North Sea
York
DEIRA
R. Humber
PECSAETE
LINDSEY
Chester
GWYNEDD
R. Dee
WREOCENSAETE
POWYS
Offa's Dyke
Lichfield
Tamworth
R. Severn
MERCIA
EAST ANGLIA
DYFED
Hereford
HWICCE
GWENT
ESSEX
Bensington 779
Dorchester-on-Thames
London
SURREY
R. Thames
Otford 776
WESSEX
Winchester
KENT
SUSSEX
WEST WALES
Hastings
English Channel

Invasion and recovery: Europe, 814-1149

The relative stability of western Europe under Charles the Great (Charlemagne) and of England under Offa of Mercia (page 34) was shattered in the ninth century by attacks by Saracens in the south, Magyars in the east, and Norwegians and Danes in the north and west (map 1). The Saracens pillaged Rome in 846, and after establishing a base at Fraxinetum in 890 raided deep into southern Gaul. Northern Italy and Germany were a prey to the Magyars who had moved into the Hungarian plain after Charlemagne's destruction of Avar power. The Vikings of Norway and Denmark also began as raiders; but in their case an initial phase of plunder was followed by settlement and colonisation, first in Orkney and Shetland, then in Ireland where Dublin was founded c.841, later (c.870) in Iceland and in England, where the Danish armies occupied the countryside round the Five Boroughs of the Midlands after 876. In France the West Frankish king conferred the lands at the mouth of the Seine – the later duchy of Normandy – on the Danish leader Rollo in 911.

The invasions were accompanied by widespread devastation and depopulation. Inevitably recovery was slow. In Germany (page 54) Otto I's defeat of the Magyars at the river Lech (955) was a turning point. In England only determined resistance by Alfred the Great of Wessex (871–99) held the Danes at bay. After 909 his successors went over to the offensive and by 939 Scandinavian England had been subjugated. But after the death of Edgar (959–75) a second wave of Danish invasion began.

In southern Europe, where most of Spain had been in Arab hands for over two centuries, the Mediterranean was by 950 virtually a 'Muslim lake'. But the collapse of Arab unity after 936 (page 40) facilitated a Christian revival. After the fall of Fraxinetum in 972 the fleets of Pisa and Genoa went over to the offensive, attacking the Muslim bases in North Africa, while Venice cleared the Adriatic (map 2). After the First Crusade (1096–99) and the great Venetian naval victory off Ascalon in 1123, the Italian cities dominated Mediterranean trade. The period of the First Crusade also saw the beginning of the Christian reconquest of Spain under Alfonso VI (1065–1109), king of León and Castile, who actually advanced as far as Toledo in 1084 (map 4). But the first wave of reconquest was halted by the great Islamic revival under the Almoravid and Almohad dynasties. The Christian advance only resumed in the thirteenth century after the decisive victory at Las Navas de Tolosa (1212) which led to the conquest of Córdoba (1236), Valencia (1238), Murcia (1243), Seville (1248) and Cádiz (1262).

The ninth and tenth century invasions also disrupted royal authority and created political fragmentation. In Gaul the Frankish rulers virtually capitulated to the Vikings, leaving defence to the local magnates. The result was a great upsurge of feudalism. Peasant freemen virtually disappeared and society was polarised between nobles and serfs. In Germany power devolved into the hands of dukes and margraves who defended the frontiers, and in Italy only the walled cities could withstand the Magyar onslaught. The kingdom of Wessex was the exception, unique in tenth century Europe beyond the borders of Muslim Spain and Byzantium. Here the monarchy took control, creating during the reconquest of the Danelaw a system of shires and hundreds administered by sheriffs who were officials, not feudatories. But this royal government could not withstand the renewal of Danish attacks during the reign of Aethelred II (978–1016). By the beginning of the eleventh century England seemed destined to pass into a Scandinavian orbit (page 52). The Norman Conquest (map 3) decisively halted this development. William the Conqueror quickly established control in the south; but in the north, where Danish and Scottish intervention underpinned resistance, he only made his authority secure by systematic devastation (1069). Danish reconquest was still a threat until 1085; but after 1066 England was permanently aligned with the Christian and feudal civilisation of western Europe. The period of invasions had irrevocably changed the structure of Western society.

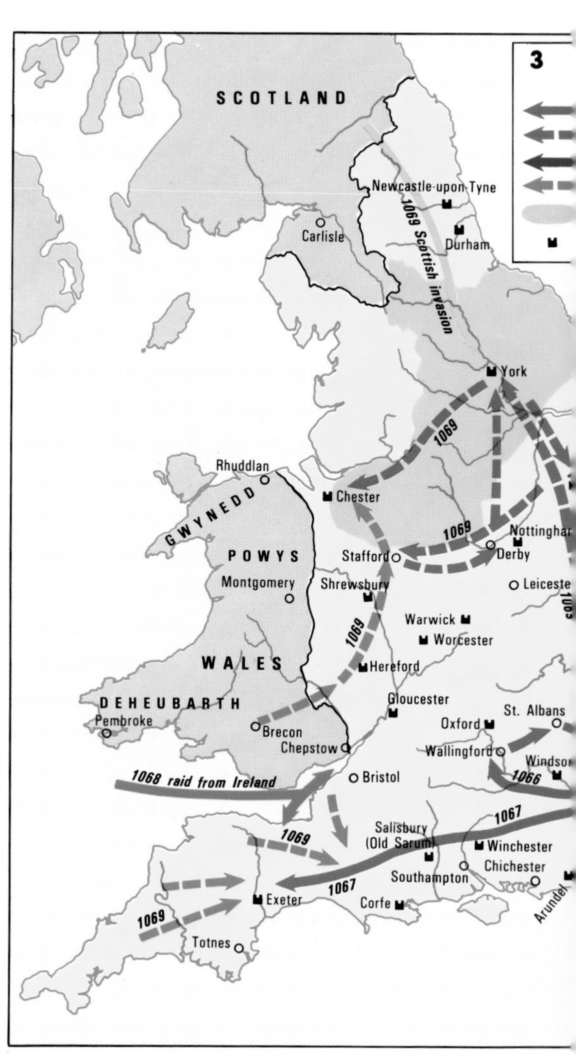

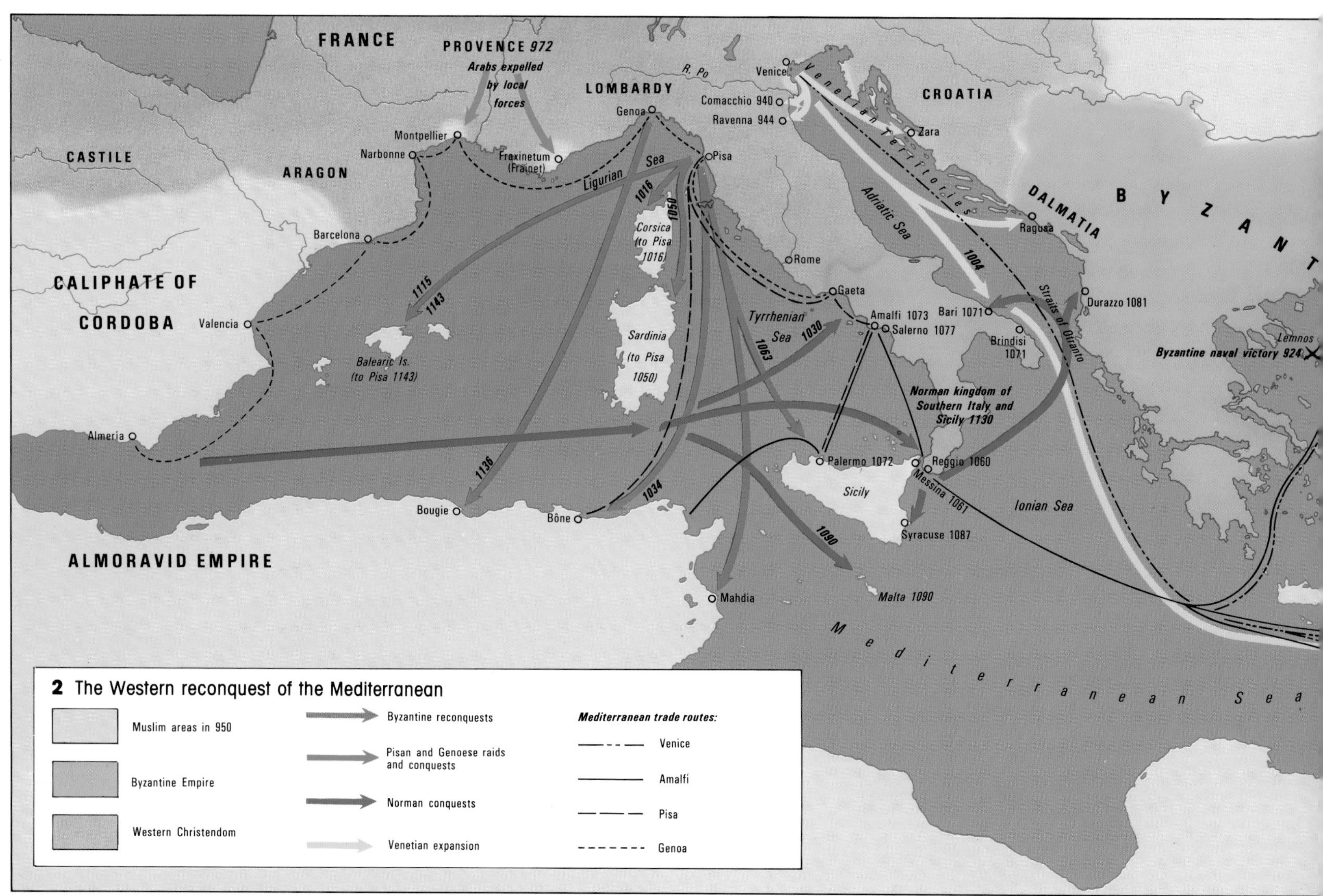

2 The Western reconquest of the Mediterranean

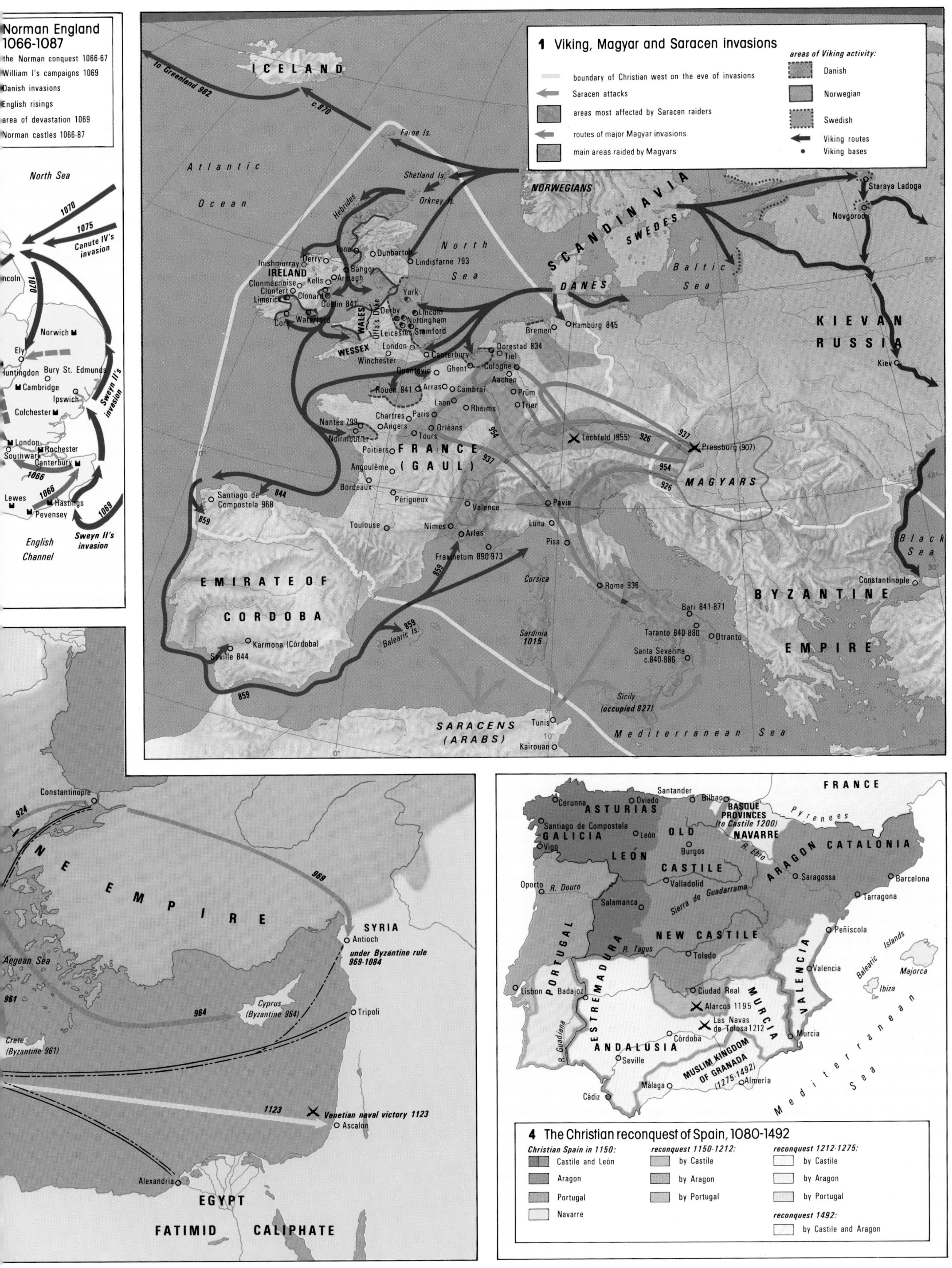

Norman England 1066-1087
the Norman conquest 1066-67
William I's campaigns 1069
Danish invasions
English risings
area of devastation 1069
Norman castles 1066-87
North Sea
Canute IV's invasion
Sweyn II's invasion
English Channel
1 Viking, Magyar and Saracen invasions
boundary of Christian west on the eve of invasions
Saracen attacks
areas most affected by Saracen raiders
routes of major Magyar invasions
main areas raided by Magyars
areas of Viking activity:
Danish
Norwegian
Swedish
Viking routes
Viking bases
ICELAND
Atlantic Ocean
NORWEGIANS
SCANDINAVIA
SWEDES
DANES
Baltic Sea
North Sea
IRELAND
WALES
WESSEX
KIEVAN RUSSIA
FRANCE (GAUL)
MAGYARS
EMIRATE OF CORDOBA
BYZANTINE EMPIRE
SARACENS (ARABS)
Mediterranean Sea
Black Sea
4 The Christian reconquest of Spain, 1080-1492
Christian Spain in 1150:
Castile and León
Aragon
Portugal
Navarre
reconquest 1150-1212:
by Castile
by Aragon
by Portugal
reconquest 1212-1275:
by Castile
by Aragon
by Portugal
reconquest 1492:
by Castile and Aragon
ASTURIAS
GALICIA
LEÓN
OLD CASTILE
NEW CASTILE
BASQUE PROVINCES (to Castile 1200)
NAVARRE
ARAGON
CATALONIA
PORTUGAL
ESTREMADURA
ANDALUSIA
MURCIA
VALENCIA
MUSLIM KINGDOM OF GRANADA (1275-1492)
FRANCE
SYRIA
EGYPT
FATIMID CALIPHATE

Christianity and Judaism, c.600-1500

By the time of Pope Leo I (440–461) an organised Christian church existed with a hierarchy of bishops and a full-scale framework of patriarchates, provinces and dioceses. But the attempt to enforce orthodoxy, particularly at the Council of Chalcedon (451), caused serious internal conflict. The Monophysite or Coptic Christians of Egypt were alienated, the Nestorians driven into exile in Persia. Here they carried on great missionary work (map 1), only halted centuries later by the advance of Islam (page 40). In the west, however, where Christianity was the official religion of the Roman empire, the church suffered from the setbacks inflicted by the Germanic invasions of the western provinces (page 32), and subsequent rivalry between Rome and Constantinople resulted after 1054 in schism between Catholicism and Orthodoxy. A period of stagnation had set in, only ended by the Irish and later Anglo-Saxon missionaries (map 3), who converted the heathen tribes of Germany, reformed the Frankish church, and inaugurated a great missionary drive to Scandinavia and eastern Europe. In addition a counter-offensive against Islam was launched in a series of Crusades beginning in 1096. The general outline of the Christian thrust, north and east from the Rhine and Danube, can be followed on map 2.

The resurgence of Christianity, particularly marked after the pontificate of Leo IX (1048–54) was a disaster for the Jewish communities which had spread throughout Europe before and after the suppression of the Jewish revolts in Palestine by the Romans in AD 66 and 132. The Jews suffered no restrictions in the Roman empire and, with their widespread international connections, were welcomed as traders by the Carolingians and other early medieval kings. But the Crusades inaugurated a wave of intolerance, and the third and fourth Lateran Councils (1179, 1215) passed discriminatory legislation. The rise of a native merchant class also made Jews less indispensable to Christian rulers, and later they became the scapegoats for the economic setbacks of the fourteenth century (page 56). The result was the series of expulsions, beginning in England in 1290. In 1492 the Sephardic Jews were expelled from Spain, in 1497 from Portugal. The Ashkenazi in the German lands took refuge in Poland and Lithuania, where they formed tight communities in what later was called 'the Pale'. Only the eighteenth-century Enlightenment brought a beginning of reconciliation, but the Nazi experience was to show that it was far from complete.

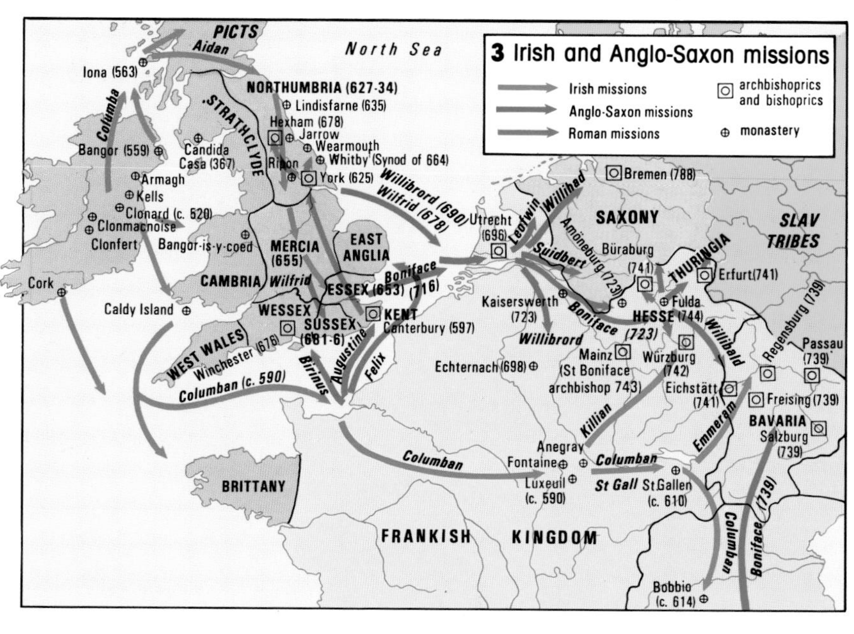

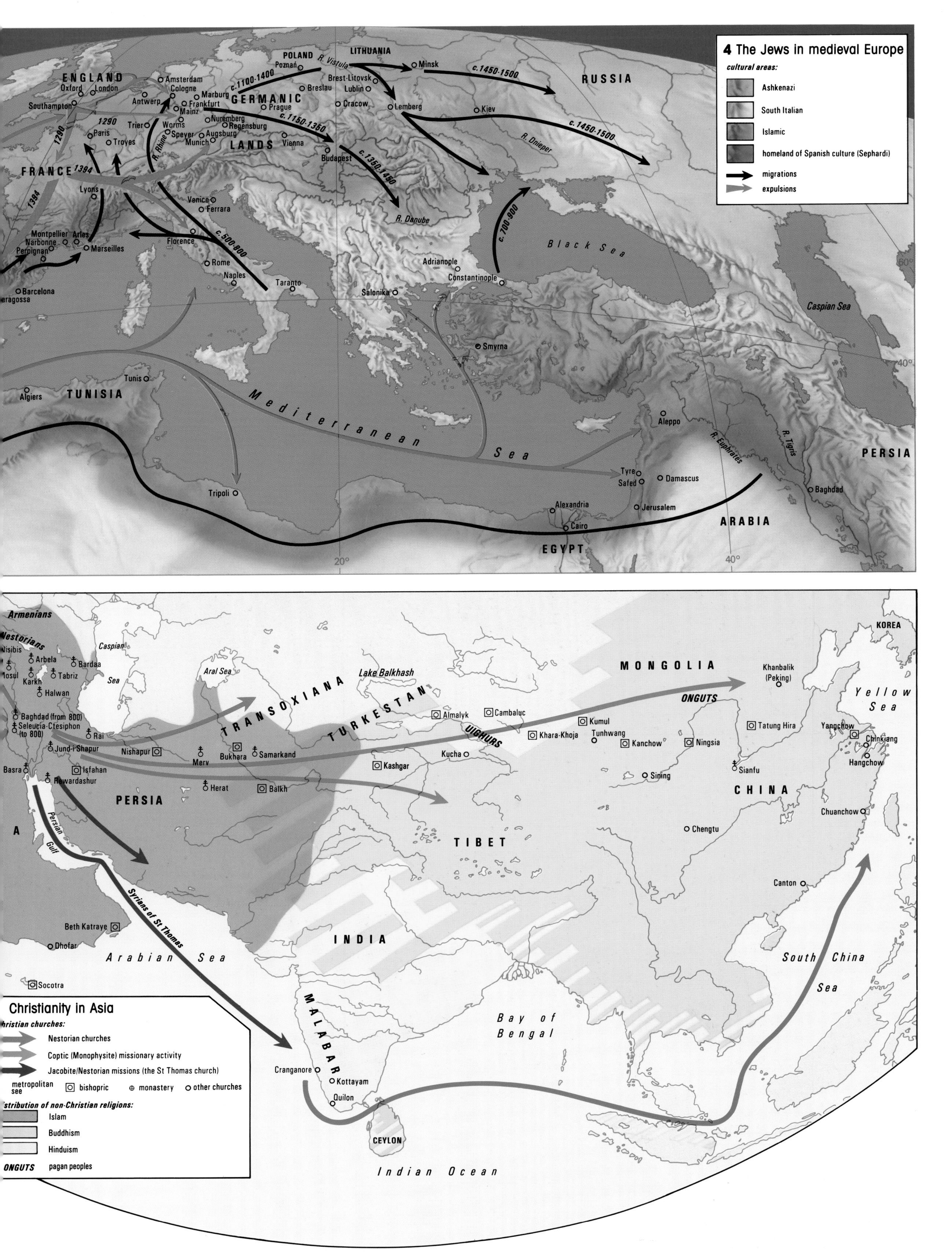

4 The Jews in medieval Europe
cultural areas:
Ashkenazi
South Italian
Islamic
homeland of Spanish culture (Sephardi)
migrations
expulsions
ENGLAND
FRANCE
GERMANIC LANDS
POLAND
LITHUANIA
RUSSIA
TUNISIA
EGYPT
ARABIA
PERSIA
Mediterranean Sea
Black Sea
Caspian Sea
Christianity in Asia
Christian churches:
Nestorian churches
Coptic (Monophysite) missionary activity
Jacobite/Nestorian missions (the St Thomas church)
metropolitan see
bishopric
monastery
other churches
Distribution of non-Christian religions:
Islam
Buddhism
Hinduism
ONGUTS pagan peoples
MONGOLIA
TRANSOXIANA
TURKESTAN
TIBET
CHINA
INDIA
MALABAR
CEYLON
KOREA
Arabian Sea
Bay of Bengal
Indian Ocean
South China Sea
Yellow Sea
Syrians of St Thomas

The Islamic world
632-1517

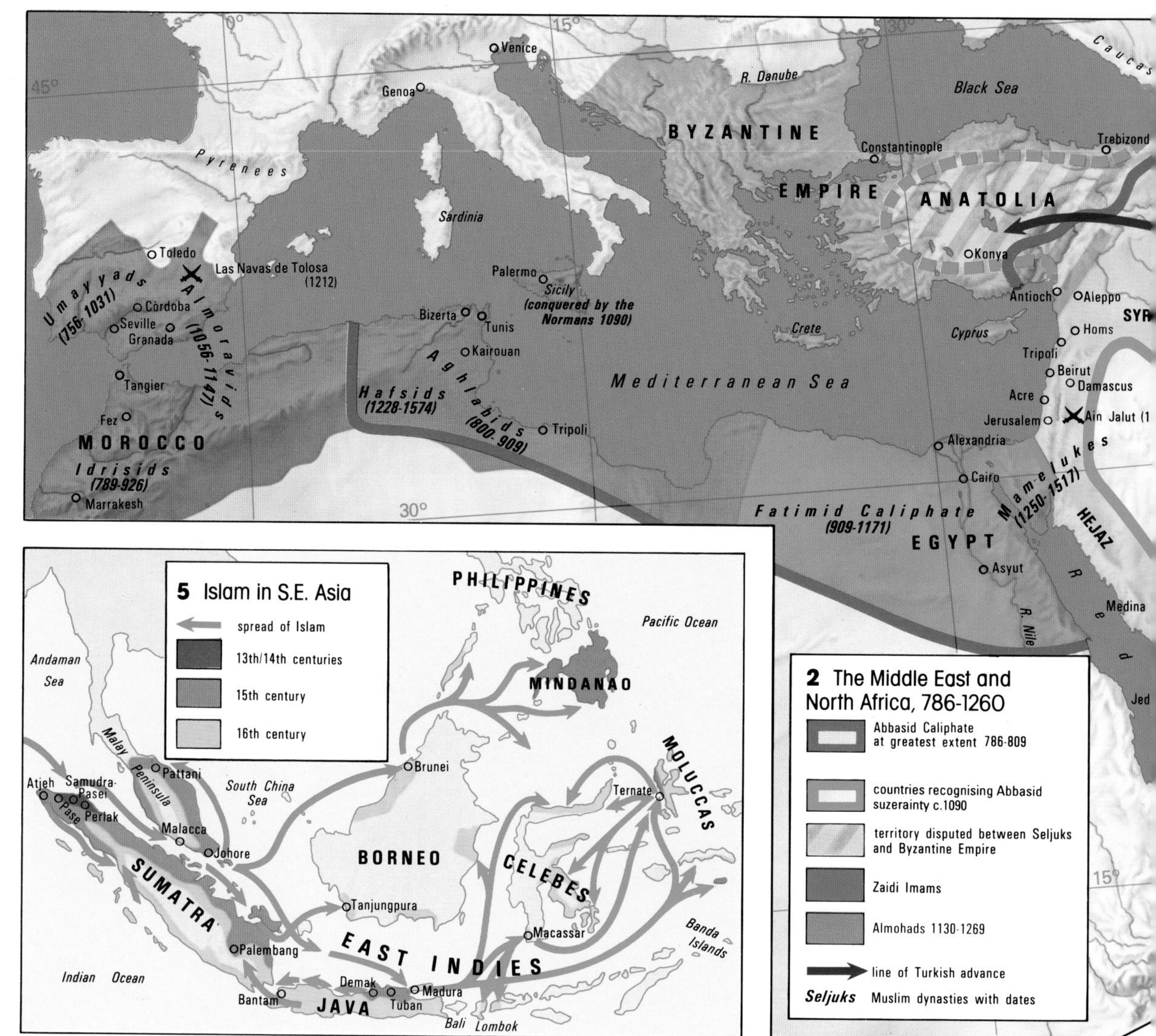

The rise and expansion of Islam was one of the most significant and far-reaching events in modern history. 'Islam' means 'submission to the will of God'; God's message has been conveyed to mankind through a series of prophets, culminating in Mohammed. The Koran is the Word of God; Mohammed is the Seal of the Prophets, and no others will come after him. Mohammed was born in Mecca about AD 570, and received his first revelations in 610. As his followers grew in number they aroused the hostility of the merchant aristocracy of Mecca, and the group was eventually obliged to withdraw to Medina, some 280 miles north-east of Mecca. This migration, *hijra* in Arabic, marks the beginning of the Islamic era and of the Muslim calendar. Mohammed eventually returned to Mecca in triumph in 630. He died in 632, but Islam expanded rapidly; over the next century Arab armies brought the new religion as far west as Spain and the Mediterranean islands and as far east as northern India (map 1).

In 661 the political control of the Arab-Islamic empire passed to the Umayyads, a dynasty originating from the pre-Islamic Meccan aristocracy, whose power was now centred on Damascus. In 750 the Umayyads were replaced by the Abbasids, a family claiming direct descent from Mohammed. The capital now shifted from Syria to Baghdad, and power began to pass from the Arab minority to the non-Arab Muslims, who had always formed the numerical majority in the Muslim Empire. The Abbasid period was a time of great prosperity and cultural and intellectual achievement, although the Muslim world gradually lost its political unity and split into a number of local dynastic entities (map 2). Among these were the Umayyads and Almoravids of Spain and North Africa, the Fatimids of Egypt and the Ghaznavids of north India.

In 945, the centre of the empire itself was captured by the Buyids, who ruled in the Abbasids' name for over a century. These were displaced in their turn by the Seljuks, Turks from central Asia, who gradually expanded into Anatolia. Their defeat of the Byzantine army at Manzikert in 1071 caused the Byzantines to seek the aid of Western Christendom which was to materialise in the form of the Crusades, principally in the late eleventh and twelfth centuries (map 3). The Crusades had little impact upon Arab society, but the Norman conquest of southern Italy and the southward expansion of the Christian states of northern Spain combined to push the Muslims out of Europe by the end of the fifteenth century, and to move the centre of gravity of the Muslim world permanently further east.

In the twelfth and thirteenth centuries the Islamic world was disrupted by a new wave of invaders, the Mongols, who founded states in Iran, central Asia and south Russia (page 46). The Mongols defeated the Seljuk Turks in 1243 and sacked Baghdad in 1258, bringing about the end of the Abbasid Empire, but their defeat by the Mamelukes of Egypt at Ain Jalut in Palestine in 1260 marked their furthest westward advance. The Mongols' retreat created a vacuum which was filled by the rise of a number of Turcoman dynasties, one of which, the Ottomans, had risen to pre-eminence by the beginning of the fourteenth century. Islam continued to expand in India (map 4), Indonesia (map 5) and in sub-Saharan Africa (page 60); today there are about 400 million Muslims, forming about one seventh of the population of the world.

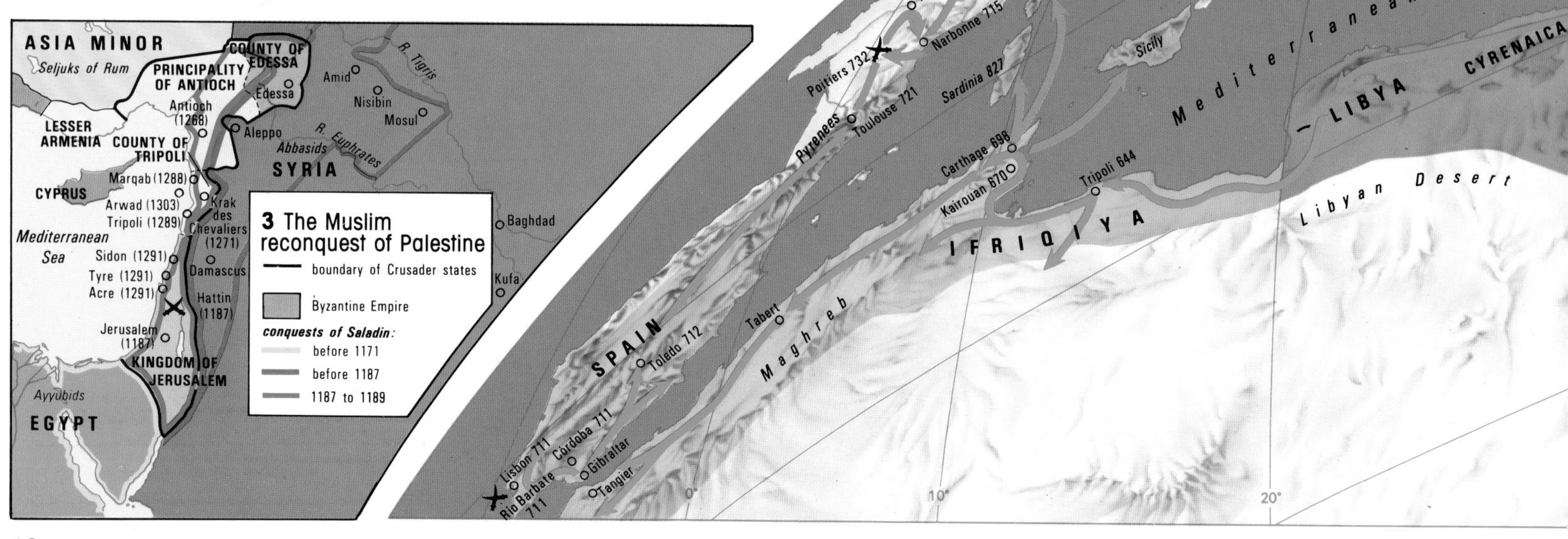

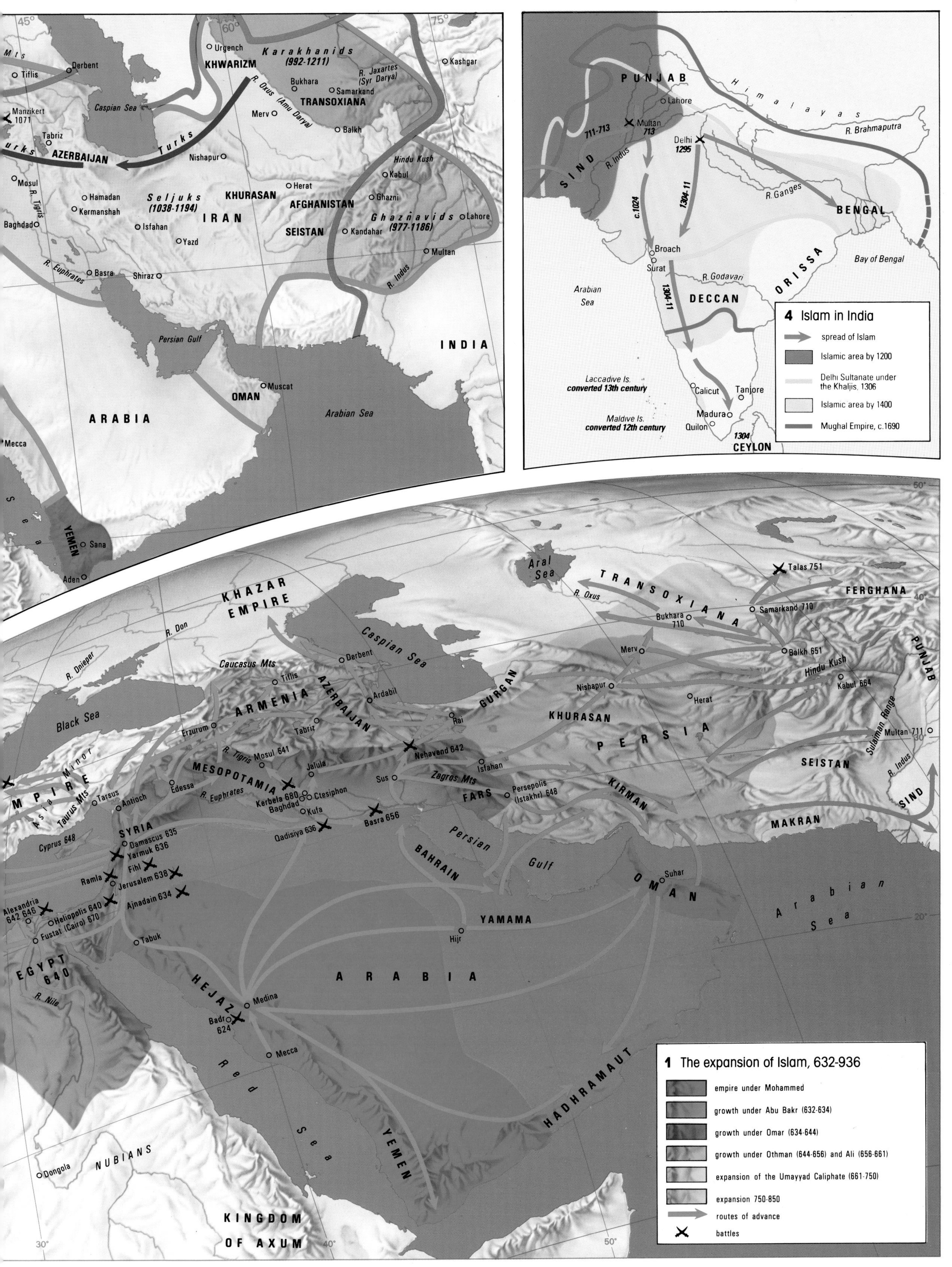
4 Islam in India
spread of Islam
Islamic area by 1200
Delhi Sultanate under the Khaljis, 1306
Islamic area by 1400
Mughal Empire, c.1690
PUNJAB
Himalayas
Lahore
Multan 713
711-713
SIND
R. Indus
Delhi 1295
R. Brahmaputra
c.1024
1304-11
R. Ganges
BENGAL
Broach
Surat
R. Godavari
ORISSA
Bay of Bengal
Arabian Sea
DECCAN
Laccadive Is. converted 13th century
Maldive Is. converted 12th century
Calicut
Tanjore
Madura
Quilon
1304
CEYLON
1 The expansion of Islam, 632-936
empire under Mohammed
growth under Abu Bakr (632-634)
growth under Omar (634-644)
growth under Othman (644-656) and Ali (656-661)
expansion of the Umayyad Caliphate (661-750)
expansion 750-850
routes of advance
battles
Urgench
KHWARIZM
Karakhanids (992-1211)
Kashgar
Derbent
Tiflis
Caspian Sea
Manzikert 1071
Tabriz
AZERBAIJAN
Turks
R. Oxus (Amu Darya)
Bukhara
Samarkand
R. Jaxartes (Syr Darya)
TRANSOXIANA
Merv
Balkh
Nishapur
Hindu Kush
Kabul
Mosul
R. Tigris
Hamadan
Kermanshah
Seljuks (1038-1194)
KHURASAN
Herat
AFGHANISTAN
Ghazni
IRAN
Baghdad
Isfahan
Ghaznavids (977-1186)
Lahore
Yazd
SEISTAN
Kandahar
Multan
R. Euphrates
Basra
Shiraz
R. Indus
Persian Gulf
INDIA
Muscat
OMAN
ARABIA
Arabian Sea
Mecca
YEMEN
Sana
Aden
KHAZAR EMPIRE
R. Don
R. Dnieper
Caucasus Mts
Black Sea
Aral Sea
TRANSOXIANA
R. Oxus
Talas 751
FERGHANA
Samarkand 710
Bukhara 710
Merv
Balkh 651
Hindu Kush
Kabul 664
PUNJAB
Nishapur
Herat
GURGAN
Rai
Ardabil
ARMENIA
AZERBAIJAN
Tabriz
Erzurum
KHURASAN
PERSIA
Sulaiman Range
Multan 711
Nehavend 642
Isfahan
SEISTAN
R. Indus
Mosul 641
MESOPOTAMIA
Jalula
Sus
Zagros Mts
Edessa
R. Euphrates
Kerbela 680
Ctesiphon
Baghdad
Kufa
FARS
Persepolis (Istakhr) 648
KIRMAN
SIND
Asia Minor
Taurus Mts
Tarsus
Antioch
SYRIA
Damascus 635
Yarmuk 636
Qadisiya 636
Basra 656
Persian Gulf
MAKRAN
Cyprus 648
Fihl
Ramla
Jerusalem 638
Ajnadain 634
BAHRAIN
OMAN
Suhar
Alexandria 642 646
Heliopolis 640
Fustat (Cairo) 670
Arabian Sea
YAMAMA
Hijr
Tabuk
EGYPT 640
ARABIA
R. Nile
HEJAZ
Medina
Badr 624
Mecca
Red Sea
HADHRAMAUT
YEMEN
NUBIANS
Dongola
KINGDOM OF AXUM

The Byzantine world, 610-1453

The history of the Roman empire was marked almost from the outset by a shift of focus to the east. The original cause was the lure of the wealth of the older oriental civilisations and the economic strength of the great commercial centres of Egypt and western Asia (page 24). Later, the loss of the western provinces to Germanic invaders (page 34) hastened the trend. Simultaneously the great Persian revival under the Sasanians forced Rome to concentrate its efforts on defence of its eastern frontier. After Justinian (page 30) the west was neglected, the Roman empire became an eastern, Greek-speaking dominion. The change is conventionally placed in the reign of Heraclius (610–641). From this time it is customary to speak of a Byzantine rather than a Roman empire.

Heraclius brought the long contest with Persia to a victorious close at Nineveh (628), but almost immediately was confronted by an even more redoubtable foe: Islam. The struggle with Islam (page 40) and with the Slavs, pressing against the European frontier in the Balkans (page 32), now became the dominant fact in Byzantine history. What is remarkable is Byzantine resilience. To meet the Arab threat, Asia Minor was reorganised into military districts, or 'themes', manned by a peasant militia (map 2). After two long Arab sieges of Constantinople had been repelled (674–8, 717–8), the new Macedonian dynasty (867–1056) launched a vigorous counter-offensive. By the death of Basil II (976–1025) the frontiers had been pushed back almost to their earlier limits. The Arabs were driven back to Jerusalem (976), and Bulgaria was finally reduced to a group of Christian provinces. Even later Manuel I (1143–80) still planned to recover the former Byzantine territories in Italy. But constant war imposed heavy financial strains, as well as profound and debilitating social change, and in spite of phases of aggressive counter-offensive and expansion, the frontiers steadily shrank (map 1).

After Basil I, the decisive fact was the appearance of a new foe, the Seljuk Turks (page 40). The crushing Seljuk victory at Manzikert (1071) induced Alexios I (1081–1118) to call on the west for help, thus initiating the sequence of events that led to the First Crusade. In retrospect, it was a disastrous move. The Franks were less concerned to aid Byzantium than to set up their own principalities in Palestine and Asia Minor. The Normans, by now in control of Sicily and Byzantine Italy, were greedy for Byzantine territory in the Morea (Peloponnese) and further east. The Italian cities, Venice to the fore, were striving to engross the oriental trade (page 36). The outcome, after a century of vicissitudes, was the Fourth Crusade (1202–4), the conquest and pillage of Constantinople, the partition of the Byzantine empire, and the establishment in its place of a Latin empire (map 3). But the Latin empire proved short-lived. The Greek-speaking population resented it, and a new dynasty, the Palaeologi, restored the Greek empire in 1261.

It was, nevertheless, only a shadow of the former Byzantine empire; and when a new Turkish people, the Ottomans, established itself in Anatolia, and then, outflanking Constantinople, advanced into Byzantium's European territories (page 48), its fate was sealed (map 4). The rest of the story is an epilogue, ending with the fall of Constantinople in 1453. Nevertheless the story of Byzantium is not without greatness and lasting achievements. For centuries it was ahead of the west in government and in the arts of civilisation. It also passed on its culture and its religion to the Balkan peoples and to Russia. 'Two Romes have fallen,' a Russian monk wrote shortly after 1453, 'but the third is standing, and there shall be no fourth.' He was speaking of Moscow. Russia, gradually consolidated under its Varangian rulers and their Muscovite successors (page 44), now emerged as heir to the Byzantine inheritance. This was to be a fact of lasting importance in world history.

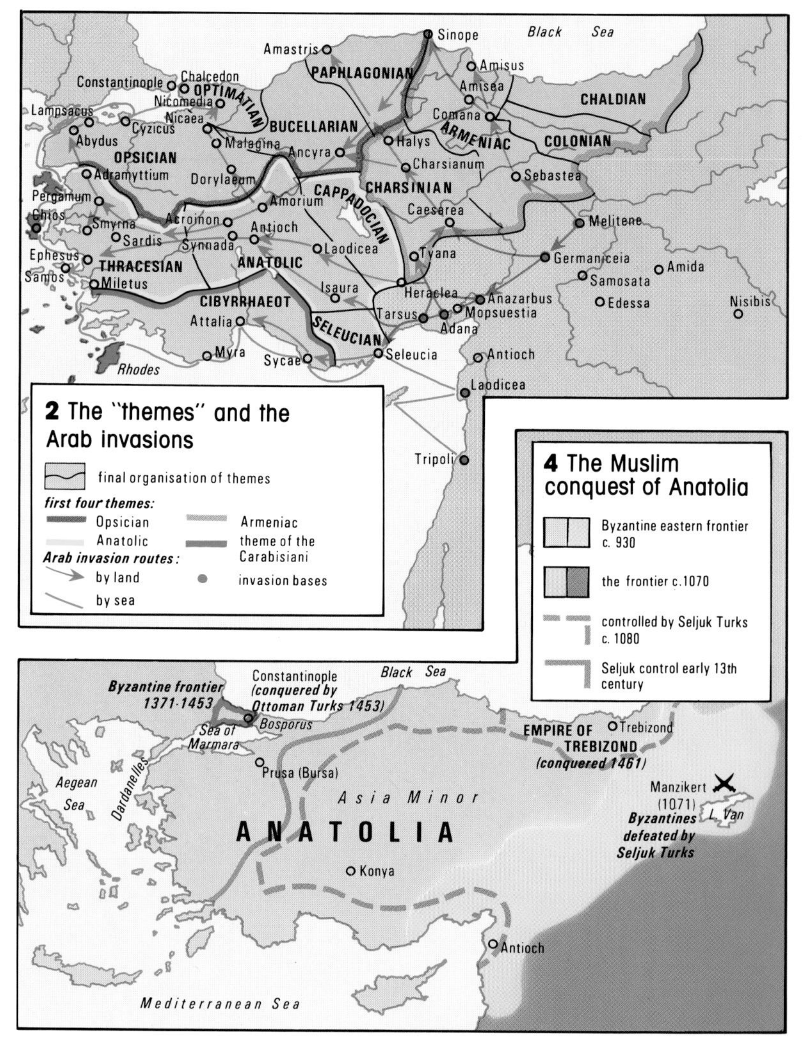

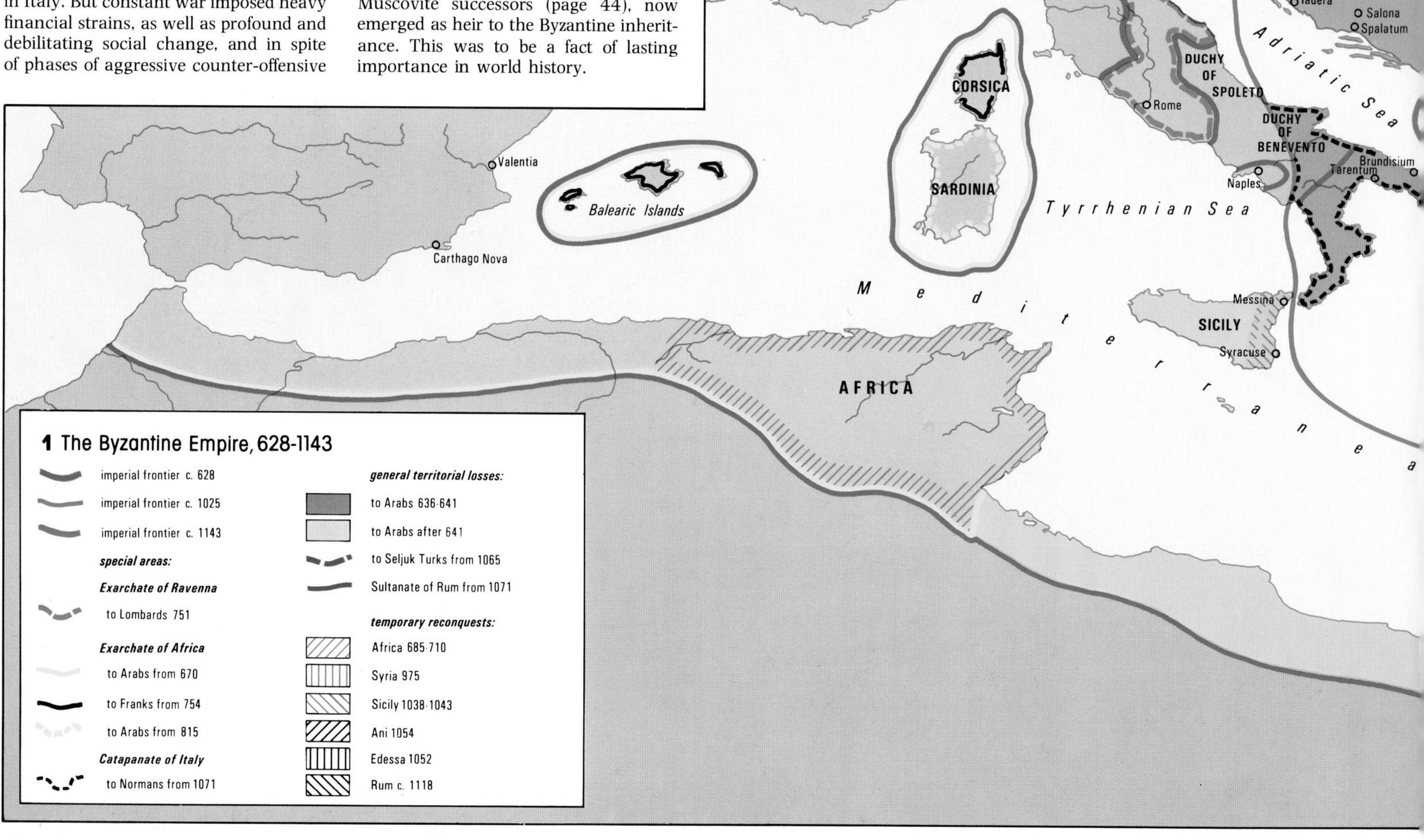

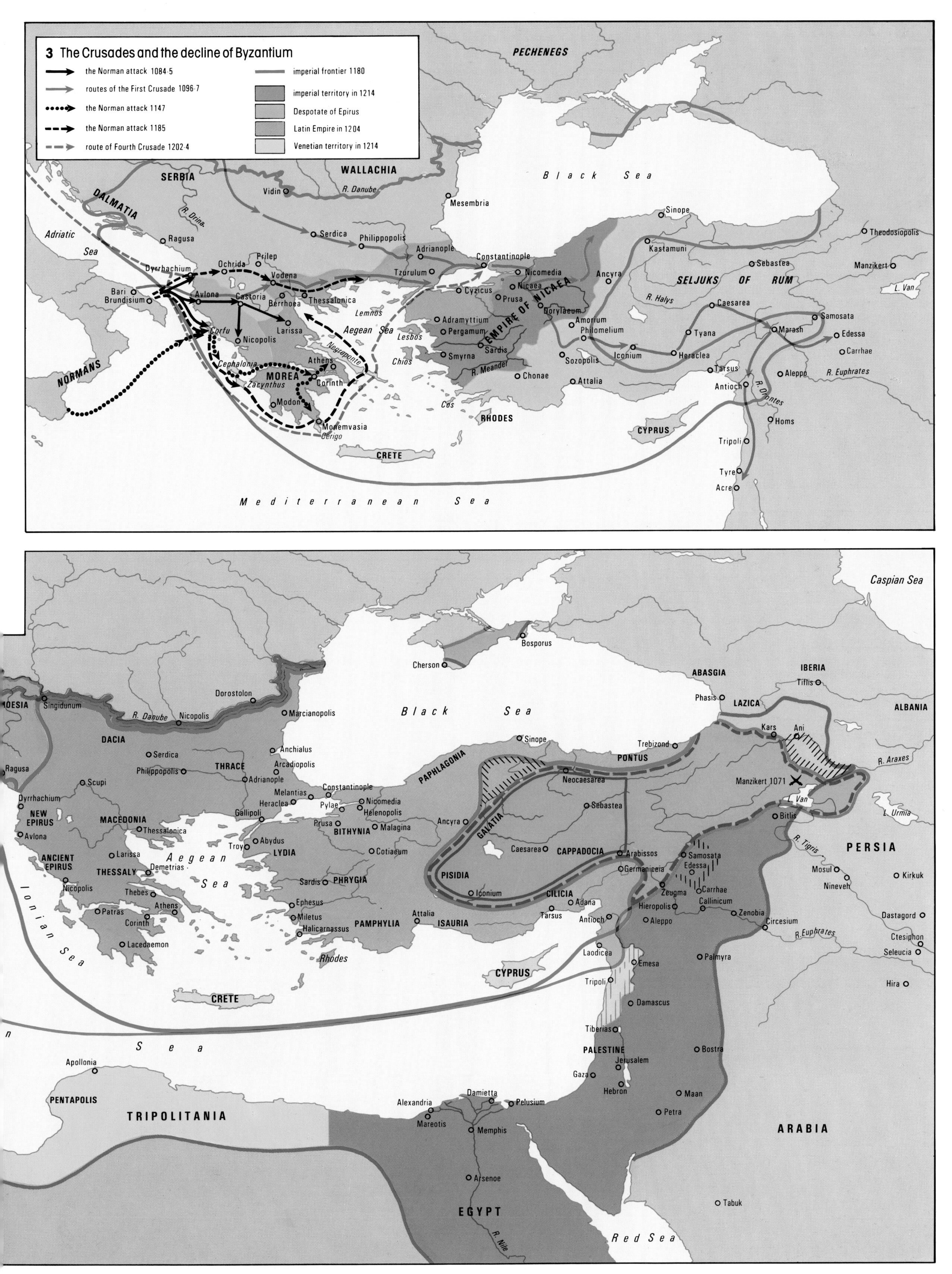

3 The Crusades and the decline of Byzantium
the Norman attack 1084-5
routes of the First Crusade 1096-7
the Norman attack 1147
the Norman attack 1185
route of Fourth Crusade 1202-4
imperial frontier 1180
imperial territory in 1214
Despotate of Epirus
Latin Empire in 1204
Venetian territory in 1214
PECHENEGS
WALLACHIA
SERBIA
DALMATIA
Black Sea
Mediterranean Sea
Aegean Sea
SELJUKS OF RUM
EMPIRE OF NICAEA
MOREA
NORMANS
CRETE
CYPRUS
RHODES
Constantinople
Caspian Sea
PERSIA
ARABIA
EGYPT
TRIPOLITANIA
PENTAPOLIS
Red Sea
Ionian Sea

Early Russia
862-1245

Three factors shaped the early history of Russia: the movement eastward of Slav tribal settlers; the impact of the Vikings or Varangians, seafaring raiders and traders from Sweden who entered northern Russia c.850 (page 36) and imposed tribute on the neighbouring Slavs and Finns; the basic geography of the region, particularly the division between the forests of central and northern Russia and the treeless steppes of the south through which successive waves of invaders from Asia poured into Europe. Fierce Pechenegs controlled the fertile steppelands. To avoid them Slav colonists moved into central Russia, where they settled in the river basins, clearing the forests and living by agriculture, hunting, trapping and by the fur trade.

At first the Slavs resisted the Varangians. But in 862 they called in 'Rurik the Viking' to restore order and protect them from Pecheneg raiders. Rurik occupied Novgorod, but the Varangians immediately pushed south to Smolensk and then along the Dnieper to Kiev (882). They thus controlled the trade route from the Baltic to the Black Sea. At the same time they imposed their rule over the Slav tribes on both sides of the river (map 1). It was nevertheless only a loose tributary overlordship, and it was not until the time of Vladimir I of Kiev (980–1015) that the tribal regions were welded together into a single state.

The reign of Vladimir's son, Yaroslav I (1019–54) was the high point of Kievan Russia. Converted to Christianity under Vladimir and in close contact with Constantinople, Kiev ranked high among European cities. But the new state had grown too quickly and after 1054 its decline was rapid. Dynastic conflict was incessant, and the administration ineffective. At the same time the destruction of the Khazar empire by Svyatoslav (965) opened the way for a new wave of Asiatic nomads, the Polovtsy, who broke through the defences erected by Vladimir I and sacked Kiev in 1093. The result was a great exodus of peasants northwards to the region between the Oka and the Volga, where many new towns were founded including Vladimir, Suzdal, Rostov, Moscow and Tver. Novgorod-Seversk, and in the west, Galich and Vladimir-Volynsk broke away from Kiev. After 1125 the axis of Russian life shifted north and the state broke up into warring principalities (map 2), among which Vladimir-Suzdal was outstanding.

The final blow to the old order was the Mongol invasions, which fell upon the Volga region before turning south against Kiev which was sacked in 1240 (map 3), while Novgorod was exposed simultaneously to German and Swedish attack. Mongol control was only indirect, but its results were far-reaching. Kievan Russia, already debilitated, disappeared for ever, and the way was open for the rise of Moscow.

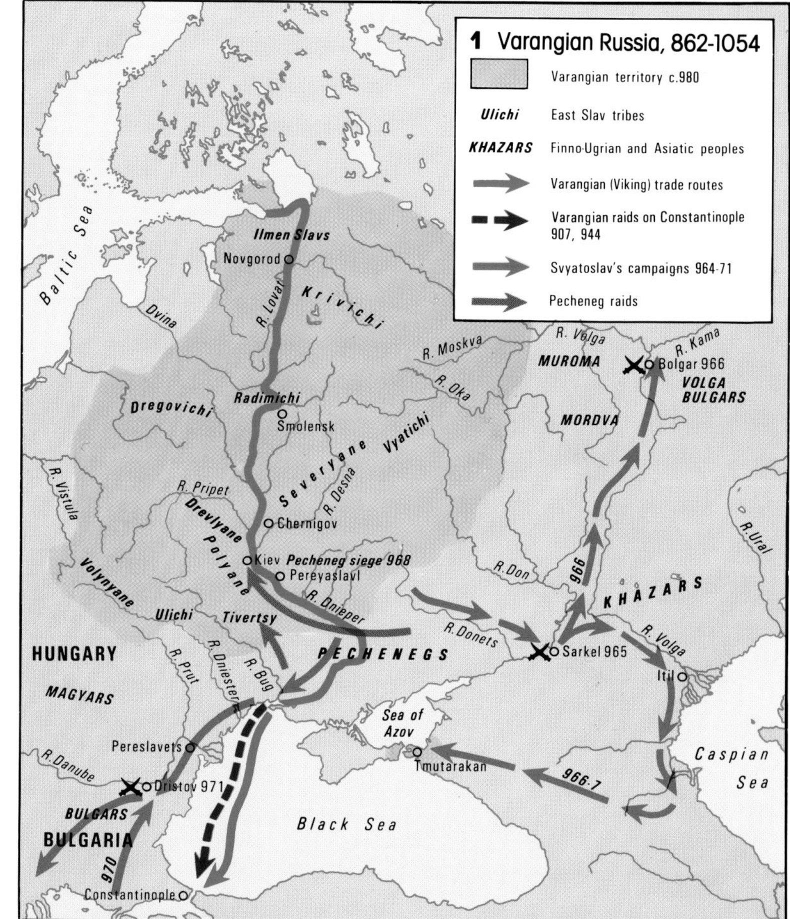

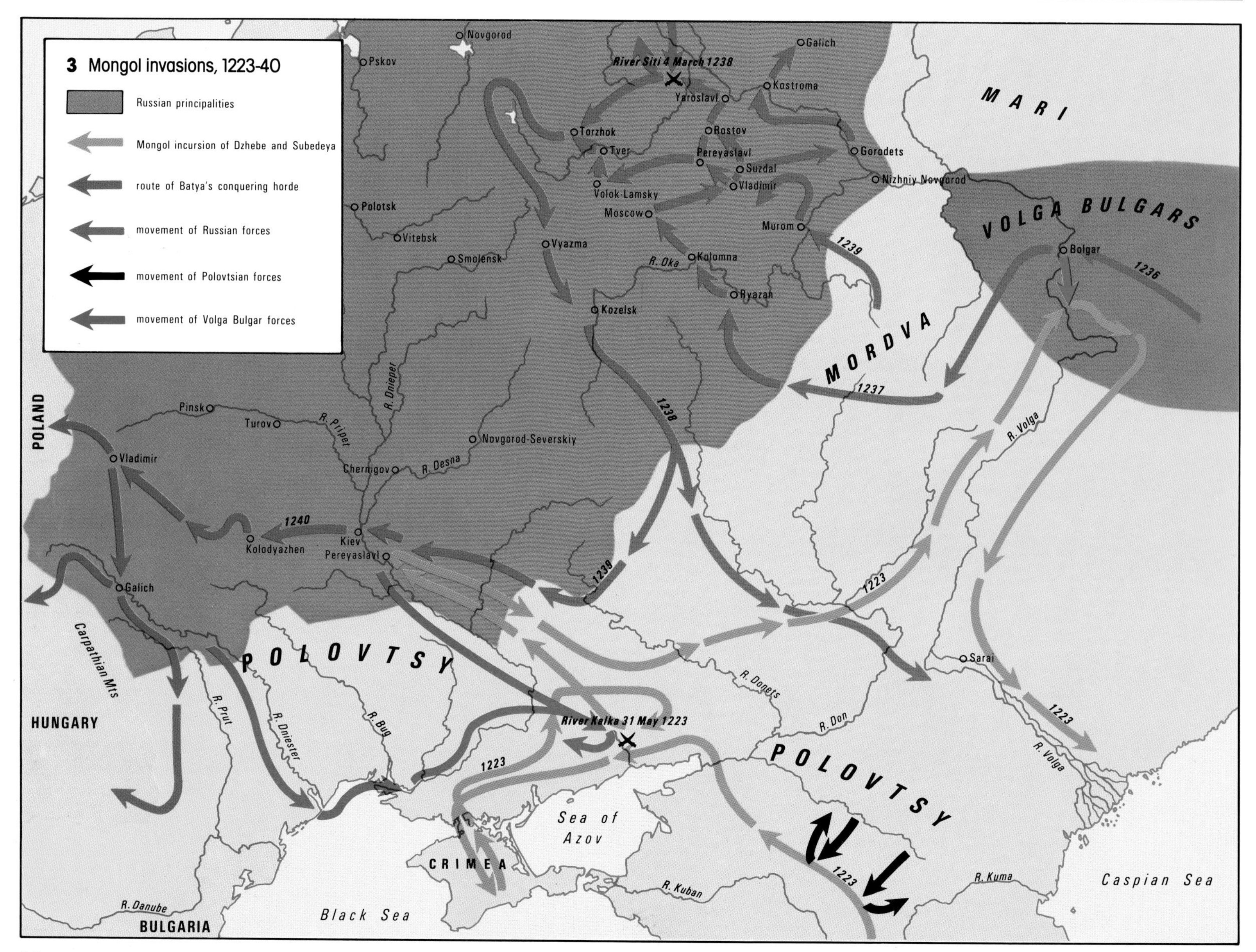

2 Kievan Russia, 1054-1242
towns and places of significance 1054
towns and places of significance 1054-1200
MARI
tribes
movement of steppe nomads in 11th century
defensive works built against nomads
boundaries of Russian principalities c. 1200
Prince Igor Svyatoslavich's campaign against Polovtsy 1185
waterway trade routes
tundra
coniferous and deciduous forest
steppe and desert
mountain vegetation
White Sea
Arctic Circle
SAMOYED
YUGRA
PERM
KARELIA
NOVGOROD EMPIRE
CHUD
Pinega
R. Mezen
R. Pechora
Ural Mts
Northern Dvina
R. Onega
R. Vychegda
L. Onega
L. Ladoga
Gulf of Finland
Baltic Sea
ESTS
Ladoga
R. Neva 1240
L. Peipus 1242
Yuriev
Novgorod
R. Volkhov
L. Ilmen
Beloozero
R. Sukhona
VYATKA TERRITORY
Gulf of Riga
ORDER
Pskov
Izborsk
KURS
Riga
LIVONIAN
Kukeynoys
Gertsike
Western Dvina
ZHMUD
TEUTONIC ORDER
LITVA
Polotsk
POLOTSK
Vitebsk
Orsha
Smolensk
SMOLENSK
Kopys
Toropets
R. Lovat
Torzhok
Tver
Volok-Lamsky
Galich
MARI
Yaroslavl
Rostov
Kostroma
VLADIMIR-SUZDAL
Pereyaslavl
Suzdal
Dmitrov
Vladimir
R. Klyazma
Nizhniy Novgorod
R. Kama
Moscow
R. Moskva
Murom
Kolomna
Ryazan
R. Oka
MUROM-RYAZAN
MORDVA
Bolgar
Bilyar
VOLGA BULGARS
Suvar
Gorodno
Minsk
Nesvizh
Klechesk
Berestye
Drogochin
TUROV-PINSK
Pinsk
Turov
VLADIMIR-VOLYNSK
Kholm
Vladimir
Cherven
Belz
Koselsk
CHERNIGOV
Bryansk
Karachev
Novosil
R. Desna
NOVGOROD-SEVERSK
Rechitsa
Listem
Novgorod-Severskiy
Vruchy
Korosten
Lyubech
Chernigov
Rylsk
Kursk
R. Ural
Gorodets
KIEV
Kiev 1093
PEREYASLAVL
Pereyaslavl
Rodnya
Donets
R. Don
Peremyshl
Terebovl
Galich
GALICH
Kamenets
Kolomyya
Poltava
POLOVTSY
(in 1054)
TORKI
PECHENEGS
POLOVTSY
in 1200
R. Volga
R. Donets
SAKSINY
R. Prut
Peresechen
HUNGARIAN KINGDOM
R. Dniester
Southern Bug
R. Dnieper
Sarkel
Belgorod
Oleshe
Carpathian Mts
Pereslavets
Sea of Azov
Itil
R. Danube
Dristov
Tmutarakan
Khersones
Sugdeya
R. Kuban
R. Kuma
Caspian Sea
BULGARIA
Black Sea
KASOGI
YASI
R. Terek
70°
60°
50°
30°
40°

The Mongol Empire, 1206-1696

The Mongols, a primitive nomadic people from the depths of Asia, had tremendous influence on the course of world history. Few in number, but augmented by Turcoman auxiliaries, they threw themselves against the old centres of civilisation in east and west (map 1). After overrunning the Ch'in empire in north China between 1211 and 1234, they defeated the Sung army and ruled over the whole of China from 1280 to 1367 (page 50). They even launched seaborne expeditions against Java and Japan, though neither was successful. In the west their first victim was the Muslim empire of Khwarizm (1220), after which they turned against the Abbasid caliphate, sacking Baghdad in 1258. But the decisive Mameluke victory at Ain Jalut (1260) halted their advance in this direction. Meanwhile, they had thrown themselves against Christian Europe, overrunning the northern Russian principalities in 1237–8 and sacking Kiev in 1240 (page 44), before advancing into Hungary and Poland and destroying a German-Polish army at Legnica in 1241 (map 2).

The architect of these amazing victories was a certain Temujin, known to history as Genghis Khan, son of a Mongol chief, who united the different Mongol tribes under his leadership (1206) and subdued other neighbouring, mainly Turcoman, tribes, before turning against China in 1211. Genghis died in 1227, but his wars of conquest were continued by his sons and grandsons, among whom Ogedei, elected Great Khan in 1229, and Möngke, who succeeded in 1251, were outstanding. But the vast empire lacked coherence and stability, and the Mongols failed to develop appropriate institutions. Genghis himself divided his empire among his four sons, like earlier Frankish rulers in the west (page 34), and with similar results. Already on the death of Ogedei (1241), Genghis' grandson Batu, commander-in-chief in the west, withdrew his army from Poland to the base on the lower Volga, in order to take part in the choice of a successor. It never returned and western Europe was spared, though Russia remained a Mongol tributary for over two centuries. Finally, on the death of Möngke (1259), the brittle unity dissolved. Kublai (d. 1294) was elected Great Khan, but instead of a general overlordship, his authority was confined to the east, and the western khanates (Chagatai, Il-Khan and the Golden Horde) went their own way (map 3). By the sixteenth century only the eastern khanate survived: in Persia the Ilkhanids were displaced by a local Turcoman dynasty in 1353, and later the successors of the Golden Horde, which had broken up into a number of smaller khanates at the time of Tamerlane the Great, were mopped up by a resurgent Russia.

It was, paradoxically, Timur, or Tamerlane (1336–1405), traditionally the last great Mongol conqueror (though he was in fact a Turcoman from Transoxiana), whose victorious career initiated the decline. Timur's vast empire (map 4) fell apart rapidly after his death while leading an expedition against China; but in the course of his conquests he destroyed the Chagatai khanate, which ceased to exist in 1405, and dislocated the Golden Horde. Henceforward the Mongols were under attack from all sides, increasingly at a disadvantage as the introduction of firearms weighed the balance on their adversaries' side. In the west Russia absorbed the former territories of the Golden Horde (page 84). In the east, the Mongols threw back a major Chinese assault in 1449 (page 50) and resumed their offensive under Altan Khan (1507–82); but in the end Mongolia itself was brought under Chinese dominion in 1696 by the new Ch'ing dynasty (page 106). Nevertheless the Mongol impact had lasting results. All the older civilisations were affected; faced by the Mongol challenge, their history took a new course.

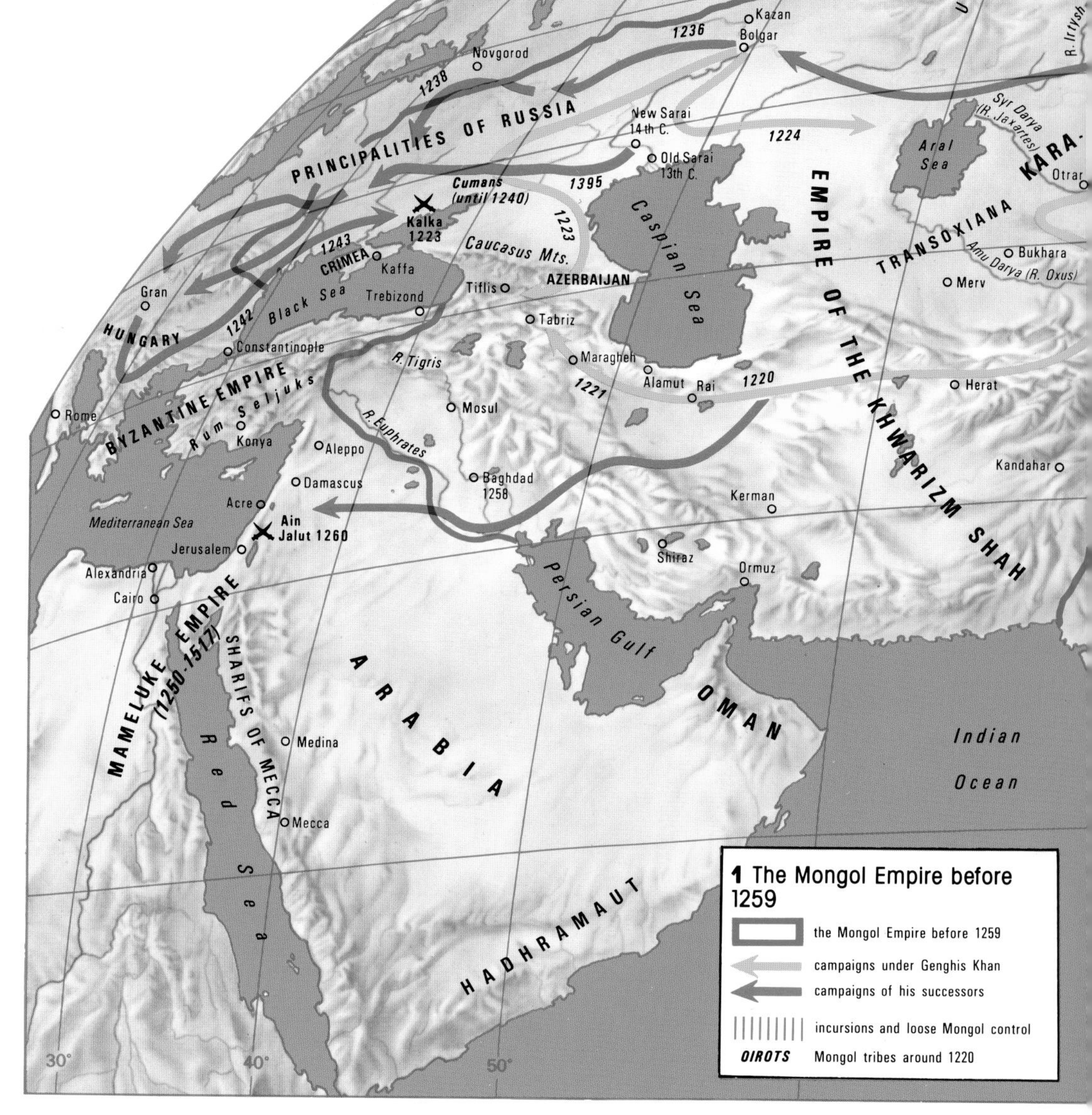

1 The Mongol Empire before 1259

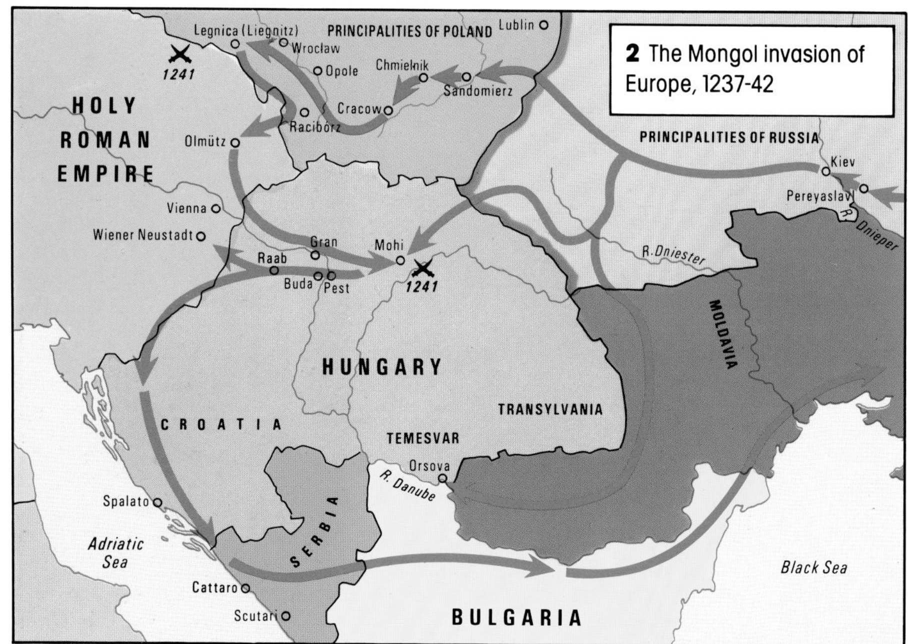

2 The Mongol invasion of Europe, 1237-42

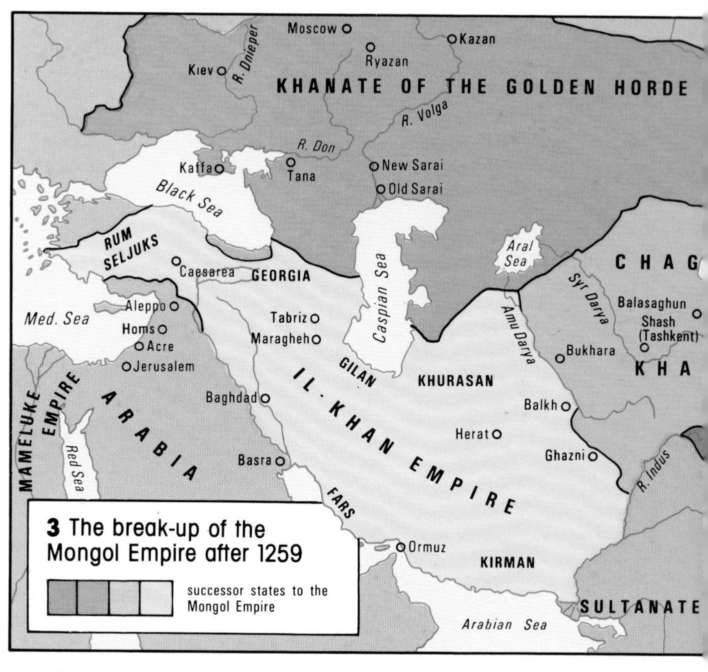

3 The break-up of the Mongol Empire after 1259

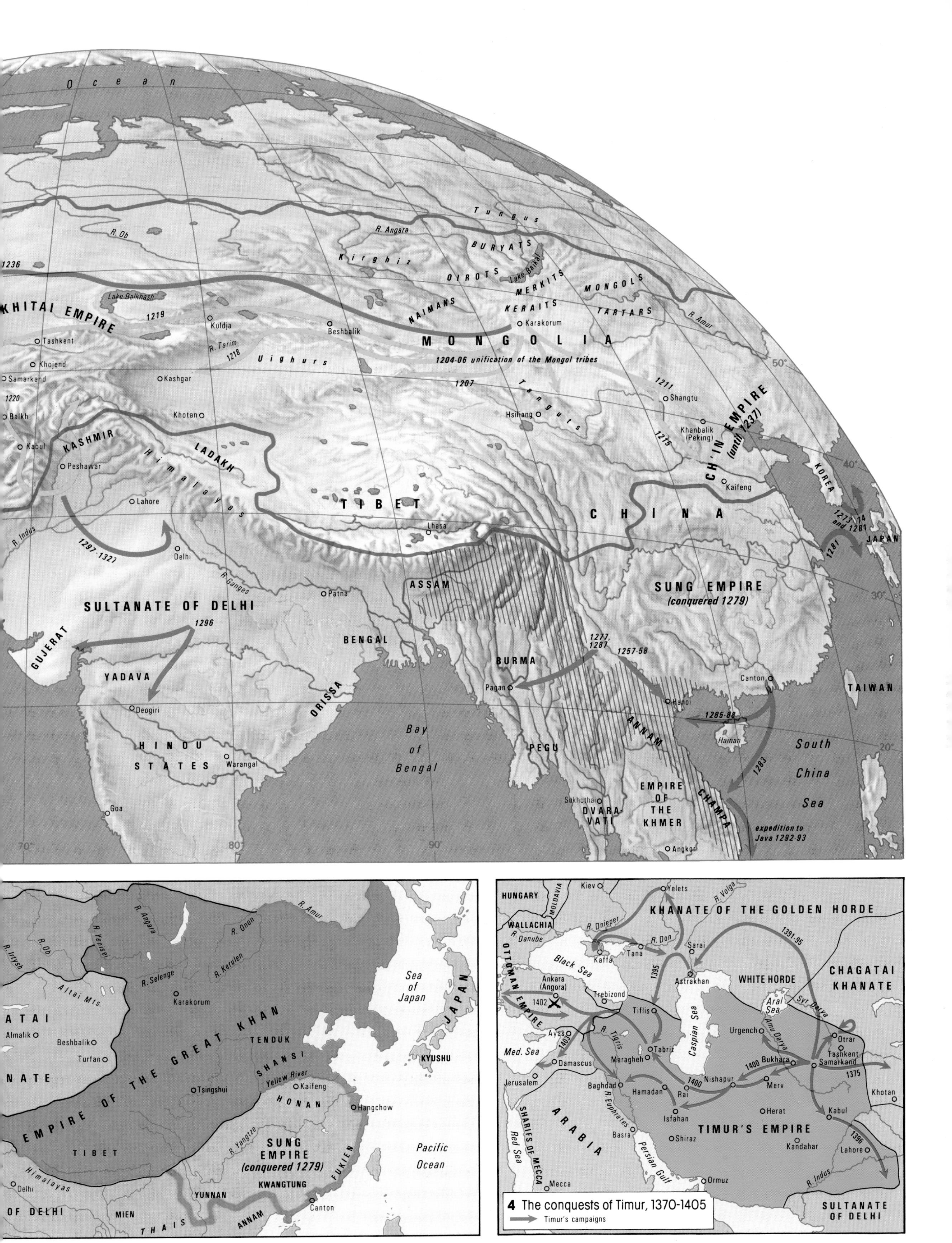

4 The conquests of Timur, 1370-1405

Timur's campaigns

The Muslim resurgence
1301-1639

The revival of Islam after 1300 and the great wave of Muslim expansion that followed, dominated the next four centuries, far more so than European expansion, which had only marginal effects before 1700. After 1354 the Christian west stood on the defensive, while the Turks conquered the whole of Europe east of the Adriatic and south of the Danube. The progress of Islam in the east was equally remarkable. By 1500 northern India was under Muslim rule, and most of the south after 1565 when the last surviving Hindu state, Vijayanagar, succumbed. It prevailed also in the oases of central Asia, in the outlying provinces of Ming China, and was making rapid headway in Java.

This amazing revival was the more remarkable because in 1258, when the Mongols sacked Baghdad and overthrew the caliphate (page 46), the Muslim world was in disarray. The Seljuk sultanate (page 40) had broken up after half a century, and only the Mamelukes of Egypt and Syria maintained any sort of political stability. Two factors transformed the situation. One was the revitalisation of Islam itself under the impact of Sufi mysticism. The other was the infiltration, with or in the wake of the Mongols, of Turkic peoples from central Asia, who, after conversion and assimilation, became the spearhead of Muslim advance. It was they who, in 1206, set up the Delhi Sultanate, the leading Indian state until the appearance in 1526 of Babur, another warrior from inner Asia. In the west Turkish warriors settled around 1265 in north-west Anatolia, and here in 1301 their leader, Osman, founded a state which became the core of the future Ottoman empire (map 1). By 1354 the Turks had crossed the Dardanelles to Gallipoli, and their victory at Kosovo (1389) and repulse of a Christian counter-offensive at Nicopolis (1396) left them masters of the Balkans. Only the invasion of Timur (page 46) and his destruction of the Turkish army at Ankara (1402) gave hard-pressed Byzantium respite. But the renewal of expansion under Murad II (1421–51) and Mehemmed II (1451–81) sealed its fate. In 1453 Constantinople fell, and Mehemmed went on to extend control over Moldavia, the Crimea and Trebizond, turning the Black Sea into an Ottoman lake.

By the time that Suleiman the Magnificent (1520–66) succeeded to the throne, the Ottoman empire was one of the world's leading powers, comparable with Ming China or Charles V's empire in the west. But now two other empires arose to share pre-eminence in the Muslim world. The one was the Mughal empire, founded by Babur in 1526, but only consolidated by his grandson, Akbar (1556–1605). The other was Persia, which had been in a state of chaos ever since it was overrun by Timur. Here, in 1500, the leader of a fanatical Shi'i sect, Ismail Safavi, seized Tabriz, crowned himself shah as Ismail I (1500–24), and quickly reunited the country. Safavid Persia reached its peak under Abbas I (1587–1629), by which time the three Muslim empires controlled a wide belt of territory from the frontiers of Austria and Morocco to the borders of China, the foothills of the Himalayas and the Bay of Bengal (map 2). But their divisions and rivalries, particularly the clash between Sunni Turkey and Shi'i Persia, drove a wedge into the Muslim world, comparable to the conflict between Catholics and Protestants in western Europe. Shi'ism had originated centuries earlier over the question of the true succession to the Prophet Mohammed; but wider issues, religious and political, were involved. In Persia a resurgent nationalism certainly played a part. The Safavids were the first native Persian dynasty since Sasanian times, and Ismail I's decision to make Shi'ism the Persian state religion was a challenge to the Sunni Turkish sultan. The Ottoman reaction was swift. In 1514 Ismail's armies were defeated at Çaldiran, and in 1516–17 the Ottomans captured Syria and Egypt from the Mamelukes. These successes enabled Suleiman to resume the Ottoman advance in Europe. After the battle of Mohács (1526) Hungary was overrun and Vienna was besieged (1529). But Persia remained a thorn in the Ottoman side. The long wars against the Safavids (1534–35, 1554–55, 1577–90, 1603–19) were not the only reason for the Muslim decline which became apparent after 1560, but they certainly hastened it. This was a great age of Islamic art and architecture, particularly in Persia and India. But in a changing world Islam remained static. All three Muslim empires were essentially land-based; but now hegemony was passing to the sea, and to the peoples on the fringe – the Dutch, the French, the English – who knew how to master and exploit it.

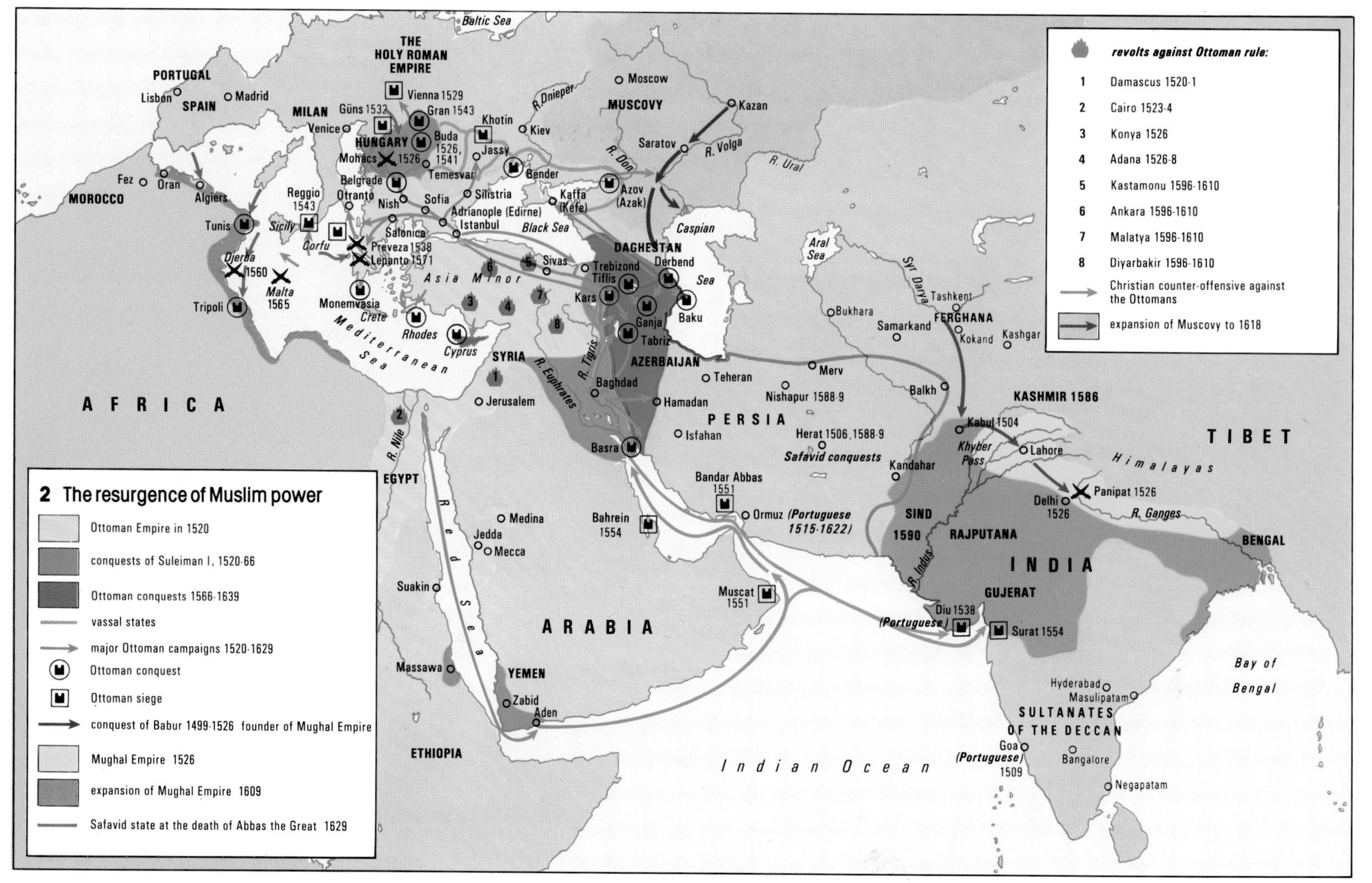

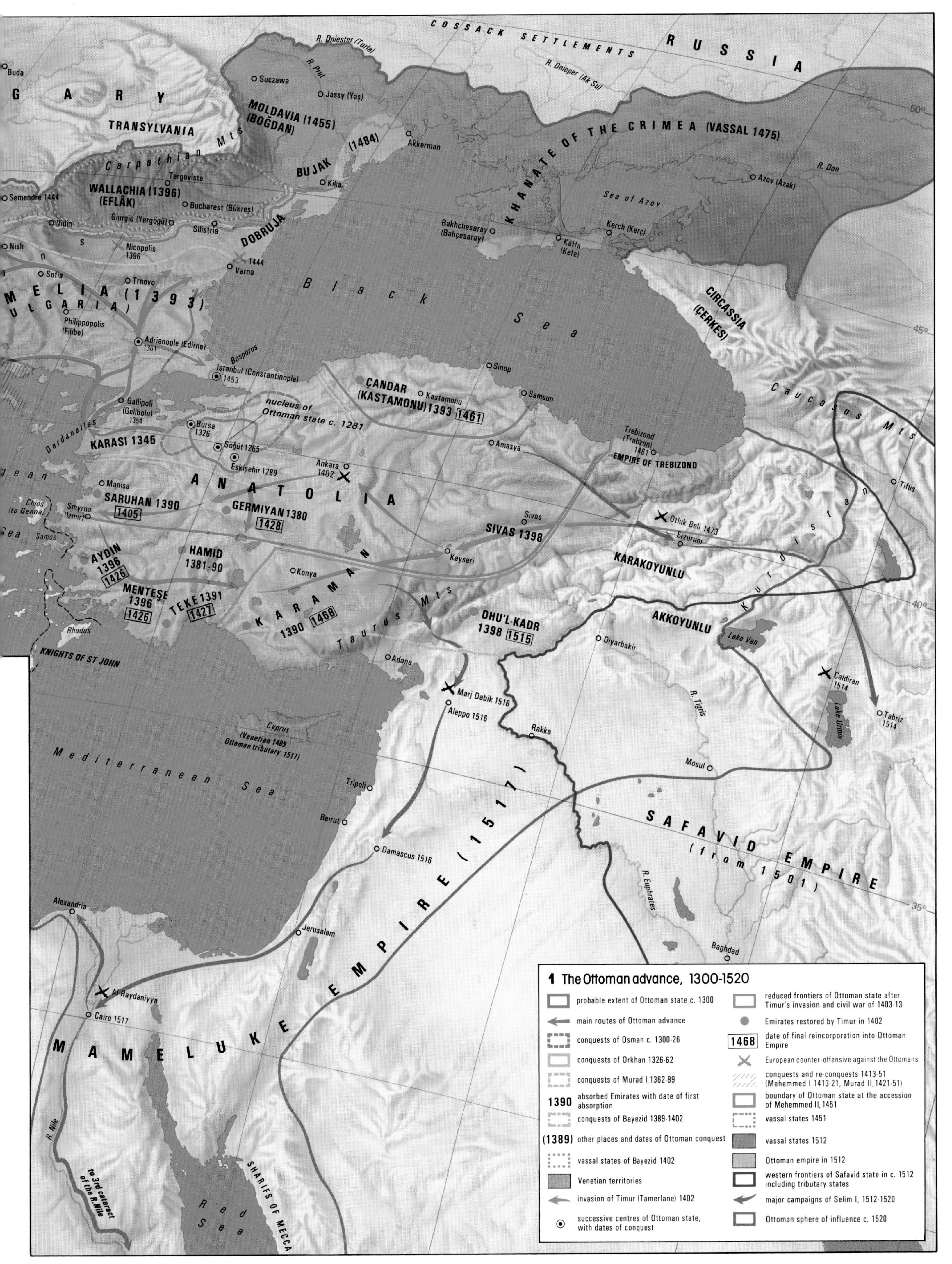

COSSACK SETTLEMENTS
RUSSIA
R. Dniester (Turla)
R. Prut
R. Dnieper (Ak Su)
Buda
Suczawa
Jassy (Yaş)
MOLDAVIA (1455) (BOĞDAN)
TRANSYLVANIA
Carpathian Mts
(1484)
Akkerman
KHANATE OF THE CRIMEA (VASSAL 1475)
R. Don
Azov (Azak)
Sea of Azov
Tergoviste
WALLACHIA (1396) (EFLÂK)
BUJAK
Kilia
Semendre 1444
Bucharest (Bükreş)
Vidin
Giurgiu (Yergögü)
Silistria
DOBRUJA
Bakhchesaray (Bahçesaray)
Kerch (Kerç)
Kaffa (Kefe)
Nish
Nicopolis 1396
1444
Varna
Sofia
Trnovo
Black Sea
ÇIRÇASSIA (ÇERKES)
Philippopolis (Filibe)
Adrianople (Edirne) 1361
Bosporus
Istanbul (Constantinople) 1453
Sinop
Samsun
ÇANDAR (KASTAMONU) 1393 1461
Kastamonu
Caucasus Mts
Gallipoli (Gelibolu) 1354
nucleus of Ottoman state c. 1281
Dardanelles
Bursa 1326
Söğüt 1265
KARASI 1345
Eskişehir 1289
Trebizond (Trabzon) 1461
EMPIRE OF TREBIZOND
Amasya
Ankara 1402
Tiflis
Manisa
ANATOLIA
SARUHAN 1390 1405
Chios (to Genoa)
Smyrna (Izmir)
GERMIYAN 1380 1428
Samos
Sivas
SIVAS 1398
Otluk-Beli 1473
Erzurum
Kurdistan
AYDIN 1396 1426
HAMID 1381-90
Kayseri
KARAKOYUNLU
Konya
MENTEŞE 1396 1426
TEKE 1391 1427
KARAMAN 1390 1468
Taurus Mts
DHU'L-KADR 1398 1515
AKKOYUNLU
Lake Van
Rhodes
KNIGHTS OF ST JOHN
Diyarbakir
Adana
Çaldiran 1514
Marj Dabik 1516
Aleppo 1516
R. Tigris
Tabriz 1514
Lake Urmia
Cyprus (Venetian 1489, Ottoman tributary 1517)
Rakka
Mediterranean Sea
Mosul
Tripoli
Beirut
SAFAVID EMPIRE (from 1501)
Damascus 1516
R. Euphrates
Alexandria
Jerusalem
Baghdad
MAMELUKE EMPIRE (1517)
Al Raydaniyya
Cairo 1517
R. Nile
to 3rd cataract of the R. Nile
Red Sea
SHARIFS OF MECCA
1 The Ottoman advance, 1300-1520
probable extent of Ottoman state c. 1300
main routes of Ottoman advance
conquests of Osman c. 1300-26
conquests of Orkhan 1326-62
conquests of Murad I, 1362-89
1390 absorbed Emirates with date of first absorption
conquests of Bayezid 1389-1402
(1389) other places and dates of Ottoman conquest
vassal states of Bayezid 1402
Venetian territories
invasion of Timur (Tamerlane) 1402
successive centres of Ottoman state, with dates of conquest
reduced frontiers of Ottoman state after Timur's invasion and civil war of 1403-13
Emirates restored by Timur in 1402
1468 date of final reincorporation into Ottoman Empire
European counter-offensive against the Ottomans
conquests and re-conquests 1413-51 (Mehemmed I, 1413-21, Murad II, 1421-51)
boundary of Ottoman state at the accession of Mehemmed II, 1451
vassal states 1451
vassal states 1512
Ottoman empire in 1512
western frontiers of Safavid state in c. 1512 including tributary states
major campaigns of Selim I, 1512-1520
Ottoman sphere of influence c. 1520

China and its neighbours
618-1644

The recovery of China from the barbarian invasions of the fourth and fifth centuries (page 32) was the work of the Sui dynasty (581–617). But it was the T'ang (618–907) who ushered in one of the great ages of Chinese history. Under the T'ang and their successors, the Sung (960–1279), China attained a level of prosperity, social stability and civilisation far ahead of contemporary Europe; and it was only another wave of invasion from inner Asia, this time the Mongols (page 46), that brought this era of wellbeing to a temporary halt. During the period of Mongol domination (1280–1368) much of the land was devastated, particularly in the north, and the population, which in 1280 probably topped 100 million, was reduced by 1393 to 60 million. The Ming dynasty (1368–1644) reversed these setbacks and put China back on the course charted by its T'ang predecessors.

T'ang China (map 1) was a centralised empire with a uniform administrative organisation of prefectures, in which the old ruling aristocracy was replaced by officials recruited by an examination system which lasted into the twentieth century. A massive movement of population into the fertile Yangtze valley and southern China produced large agricultural surpluses which stimulated trade and urban development. The T'ang also embarked on an ambitious programme of external expansion which carried them in the north-west to the Tarim Basin before they were halted by the Arabs at the Talas river in 751. By 649, the end of the reign of T'ai-tsung, 88 Asiatic peoples recognised Chinese overlordship. But the widespread military expeditions over-extended the empire's resources, many of the gains proved only temporary, and after 1127 even north China was lost and only recovered after the fall of the Mongol dynasty in 1386. Their successors, the Ming, also engaged in an active foreign policy, particularly against the Mongols in the north (map 4), but these ventures proved too costly and sparked off a series of rebellions which, coupled with external pressures from the Manchus in Liaotung and Japanese raiders, toppled the dynasty.

Military and political reverses did not impede the expansion of Chinese culture and political institutions to all her neighbouring states. Those most directly affected were Korea, under Chinese rule from 668 to 676 and a vassal state after 1392, Japan and South-East Asia, though in the latter region, where they came into contact with Indian and (from about AD 1300) Islamic influences, they were largely confined to north Vietnam. In South-East Asia the small temple states of the ninth to twelfth centuries (Prambanan, Angkor, Pagan), established under Hindu and Buddhist influence, gave way after the thirteenth century to new political centres (Ava, Pegu, Phnom Penh), while in Vietnam, where Chinese attempts at reconquest failed, a new kingdom of Dai Viet arose. But behind the fluctuating political fortunes the outstanding fact was the formative influence of Hinduism, Buddhism and Confucianism; their assimilation defined the distinctive character of South-East Asian civilisation (map 2).

In Japan Chinese influence was more direct. As early as AD 645 the whole administration had been remodelled on the pattern of T'ang China. The two capitals, Nara (710) and Kyoto (794), were copied from the T'ang capital of Changan, and Buddhism was introduced from China. But after 1192 the bureaucratic state was displaced by a feudalised society, until finally, between 1467 and 1590, the country broke up into a series of warring Daimyo clans (map 3). It was the work of Oda Nobunaga (1534–82) and Hideyoshi Toyotomi (1535–98) to bring the anarchy under control, and prepare the way for the Tokugawa shogunate which gave Japan 250 years of internal peace and prosperity until, in the middle of the nineteenth century the western powers forced Japan into the modern world (page 126).

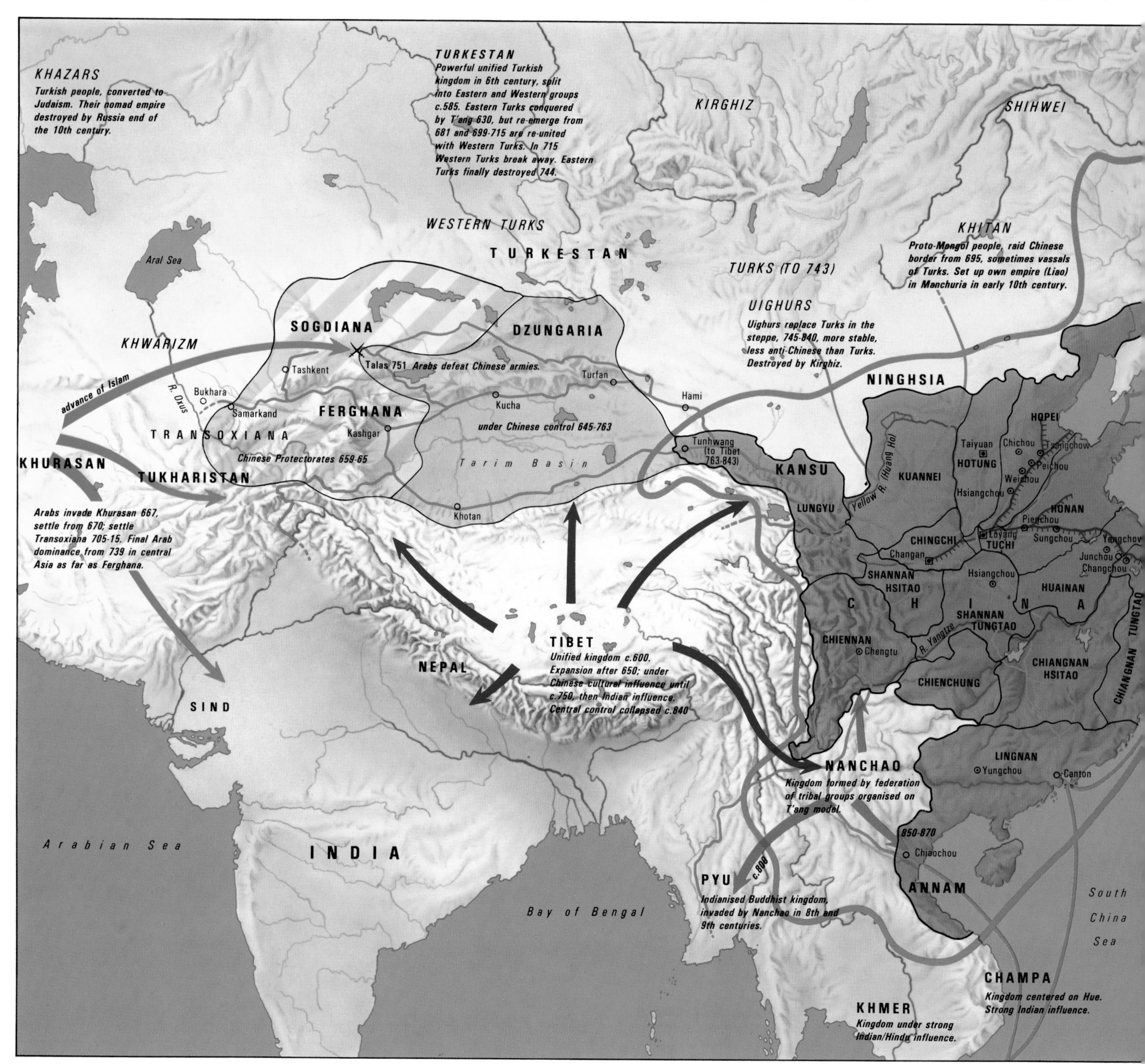

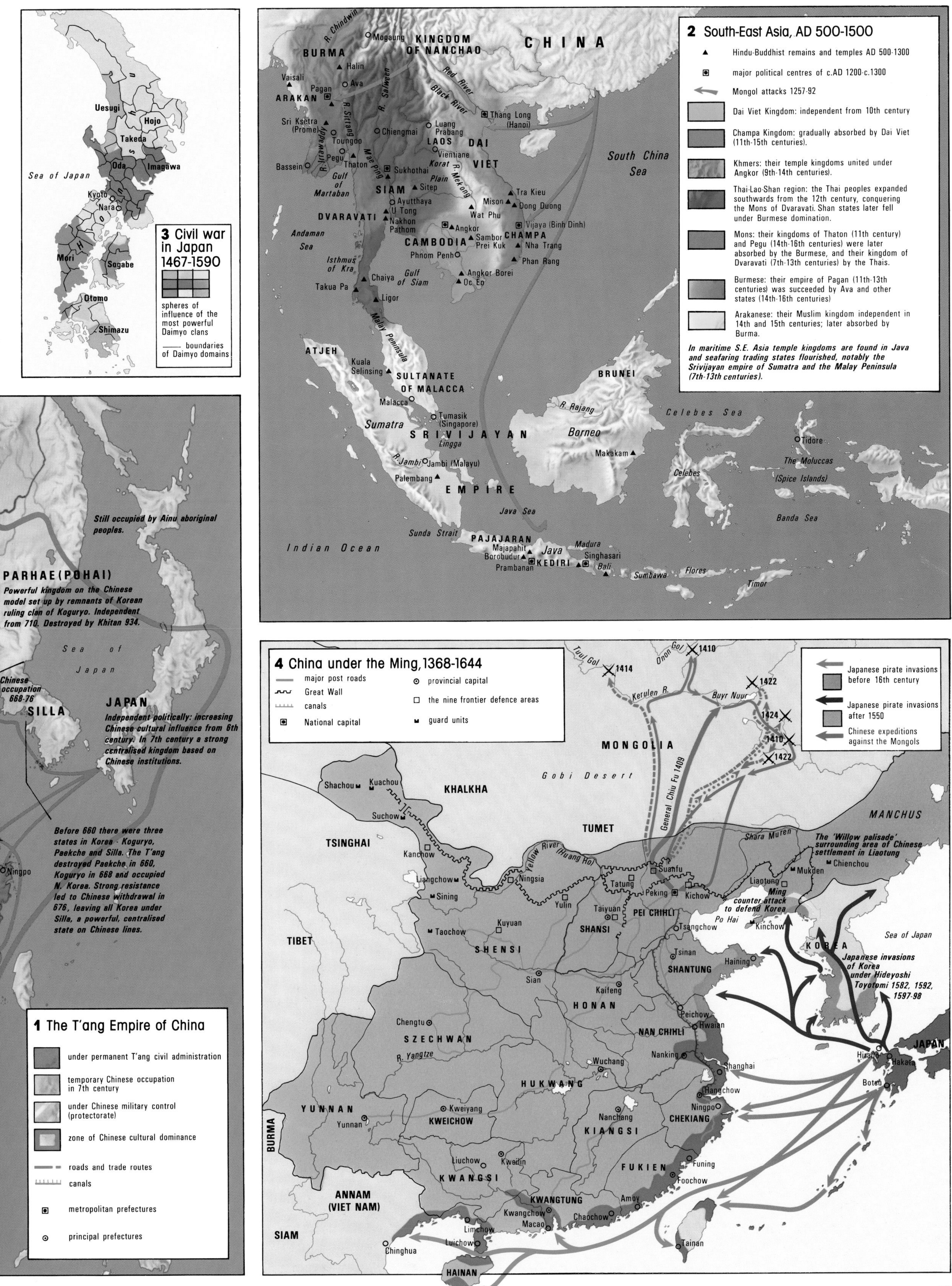
2 South-East Asia, AD 500-1500
Hindu-Buddhist remains and temples AD 500-1300
major political centres of c.AD 1200-c.1300
Mongol attacks 1257-92
Dai Viet Kingdom: independent from 10th century
Champa Kingdom: gradually absorbed by Dai Viet (11th-15th centuries).
Khmers: their temple kingdoms united under Angkor (9th-14th centuries).
Thai-Lao-Shan region: the Thai peoples expanded southwards from the 12th century, conquering the Mons of Dvaravati. Shan states later fell under Burmese domination.
Mons: their kingdoms of Thaton (11th century) and Pegu (14th-16th centuries) were later absorbed by the Burmese, and their kingdom of Dvaravati (7th-13th centuries) by the Thais.
Burmese: their empire of Pagan (11th-13th centuries) was succeeded by Ava and other states (14th-16th centuries)
Arakanese: their Muslim kingdom independent in 14th and 15th centuries; later absorbed by Burma.
In maritime S.E. Asia temple kingdoms are found in Java and seafaring trading states flourished, notably the Srivijayan empire of Sumatra and the Malay Peninsula (7th-13th centuries).
CHINA
KINGDOM OF NANCHAO
BURMA
ARAKAN
DAI VIET
LAOS
SIAM
DVARAVATI
CAMBODIA
CHAMPA
South China Sea
Andaman Sea
Gulf of Martaban
Gulf of Siam
Isthmus of Kra
Malay Peninsula
ATJEH
SULTANATE OF MALACCA
SRIVIJAYAN EMPIRE
Sumatra
BRUNEI
Borneo
Celebes Sea
Celebes
The Moluccas (Spice Islands)
Banda Sea
Java Sea
Sunda Strait
Indian Ocean
PAJAJARAN
KEDIRI
Java
3 Civil war in Japan 1467-1590
spheres of influence of the most powerful Daimyo clans
boundaries of Daimyo domains
Sea of Japan
Uesugi
Hojo
Takeda
Oda
Imagawa
Kyoto
Nara
Mori
Sogabe
Otomo
Shimazu
Still occupied by Ainu aboriginal peoples.
PARHAE (POHAI)
Powerful kingdom on the Chinese model set up by remnants of Korean ruling clan of Koguryo. Independent from 710. Destroyed by Khitan 934.
Sea of Japan
Chinese occupation 668-76
SILLA
JAPAN
Independent politically: increasing Chinese cultural influence from 6th century. In 7th century a strong centralised kingdom based on Chinese institutions.
Before 660 there were three states in Korea - Koguryo, Paekche and Silla. The T'ang destroyed Paekche in 660, Koguryo in 668 and occupied N. Korea. Strong resistance led to Chinese withdrawal in 676, leaving all Korea under Silla, a powerful, centralised state on Chinese lines.
Ningpo
1 The T'ang Empire of China
under permanent T'ang civil administration
temporary Chinese occupation in 7th century
under Chinese military control (protectorate)
zone of Chinese cultural dominance
roads and trade routes
canals
metropolitan prefectures
principal prefectures
4 China under the Ming, 1368-1644
major post roads
Great Wall
canals
National capital
provincial capital
the nine frontier defence areas
guard units
Japanese pirate invasions before 16th century
Japanese pirate invasions after 1550
Chinese expeditions against the Mongols
MONGOLIA
Gobi Desert
General Chiu Fu 1409
KHALKHA
TUMET
MANCHUS
TSINGHAI
TIBET
The 'Willow palisade' surrounding area of Chinese settlement in Liaotung
Ming counter-attack to defend Korea
Po Hai
KOREA
Sea of Japan
Japanese invasions of Korea under Hideyoshi Toyotomi 1582, 1592, 1597-98
JAPAN
SHENSI
SHANSI
PEI CHIHLI
SHANTUNG
HONAN
SZECHWAN
NAN CHIHLI
HUKWANG
YUNNAN
KWEICHOW
KIANGSI
CHEKIANG
FUKIEN
KWANGSI
KWANGTUNG
BURMA
ANNAM (VIET NAM)
SIAM
HAINAN

Northern and Western Europe, 930-1314

Two features marked the period following the Viking and Magyar invasions in northern and western Europe: the emergence of settled states and the spread of Christianity. The two went hand in hand. Both in Scandinavia and in the Slavonic east the Christian church, introduced in Denmark by Harold Bluetooth in 965, in Norway by Olaf Tryggveson (995–1000), in Bohemia by Boleslav II (967–99), and in Poland by Miesko I (960–92), contributed substantially to political cohesion. The rise of powerful kingdoms in Poland and Denmark was also in part a response to German pressure. In Poland (map 1) the Piast dynasty united the tribes of Great (or northern) Poland. Boleslav Chrobry (992–1025) not only added Little Poland, Silesia and Lausitz but also temporarily Bohemia and Moravia. In Denmark Harold Bluetooth (940–86) defended Slesvig from German attack, strengthening and extending the fortified Danevirke (map 3). In Norway and Sweden development was hampered by formidable geographical obstacles (map 5). Under Sweyn I, who also became king of England in 1013, both countries were under Danish control; and Sweyn's son Canute the Great (1014–35) ruled a great but short-lived Anglo-Scandinavian empire (map 4). Following an interlude under Edward the Confessor (1042–66) England passed under Norman rule (page 36). Norway achieved independence and was united under Magnus the Good (1033–47). Sweden (except for the southern provinces which remained under Danish rule) was welded together by the kings of Uppland, and Denmark itself settled down within its frontiers after the death of Sweyn II (1047–74).

Nevertheless all countries were plagued by dynastic conflict and aristocratic resistance. In Poland Boleslav Chrobry's ambitious foreign policy provoked a sharp reaction after his death. In England William the Conqueror was faced by baronial unrest as early as 1074. But it was France that suffered most from feudal disruption. The Capetian kings, who displaced the Carolingians in 987, were confined to the Ile de France, and even here royal authority was insecure until the reign of Louis VI (1108–37). Even then the Capetians lagged behind the feudal princes. The continental possessions of Henry II of England (the so-called Angevin Empire) far outmatched the French royal domain (map 2). When Philip Augustus (1180–1223) conquered Normandy (1204) and the Angevin Empire collapsed, English rule was confined to Gascony, and the Capetians embarked on a policy of expansion which carried them to the Mediterranean by 1229.

In England expansion had begun on the morrow of the Conquest when Norman barons invaded Wales and set up extensive marcher lordships. A century later they moved on to Ireland. By 1250 two-thirds of the country had been occupied, but Ireland remained divided and rebellious. So also did Wales which had seen a remarkable national resurgence under Llewellyn the Great (1197–1240). But Edward I (1272–1307) would not brook Welsh independence. After a first campaign (1276), followed by systematic castle building to enforce English control, a second campaign in 1283 (map 7) placed the principality directly under royal administration in 1284. Edward's attempt in 1296 to repeat the process in Scotland was a costly failure, culminating in the English defeat at Bannockburn in 1314. Like his French contemporary, Philip the Fair (1285–1314), defeated by the Flemings in 1302, Edward had overreached himself. The great baronial families, still firmly ensconced (map 6), forced him in 1297 to confirm the charters wrested from King John in 1215. It was a prelude to the aristocratic reaction and the setbacks of the fourteenth century.

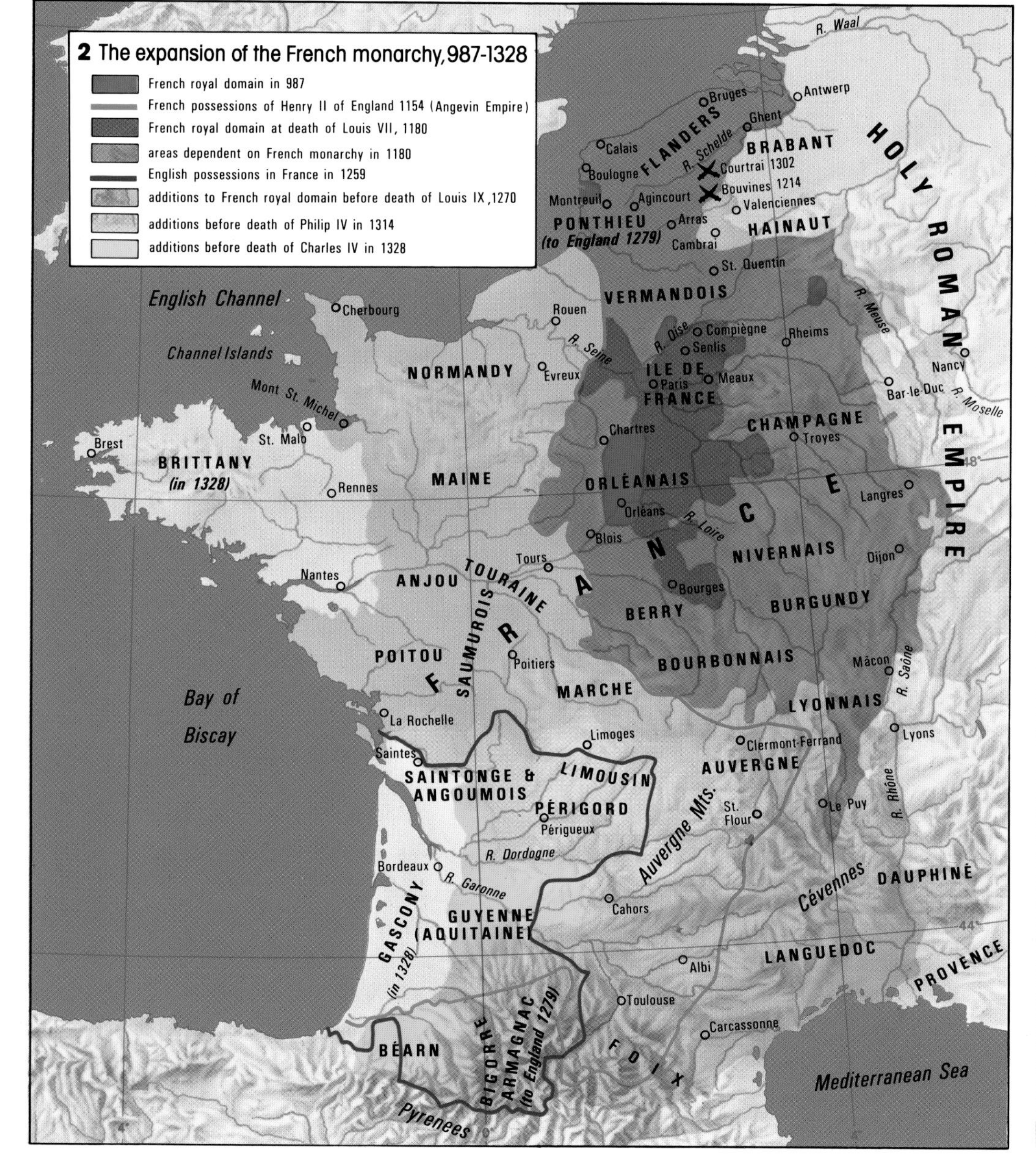

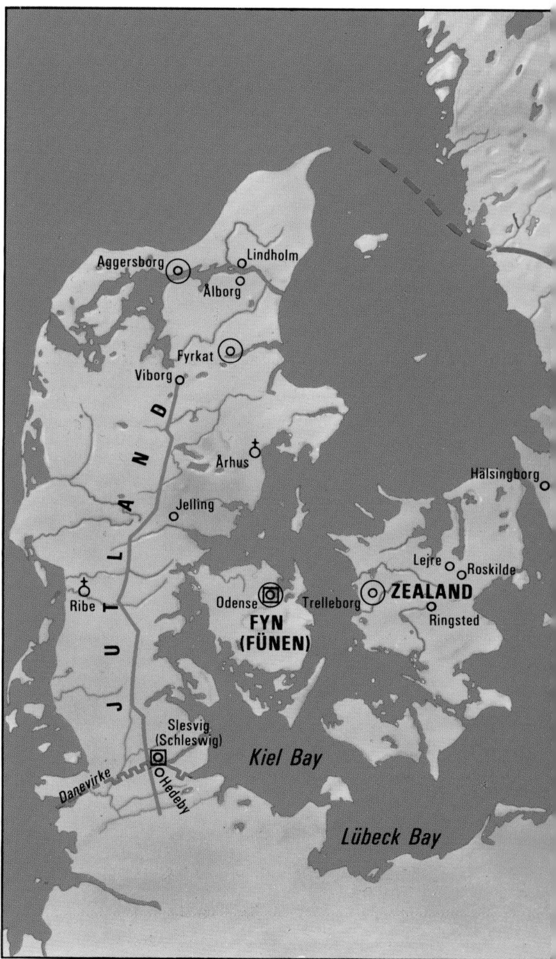

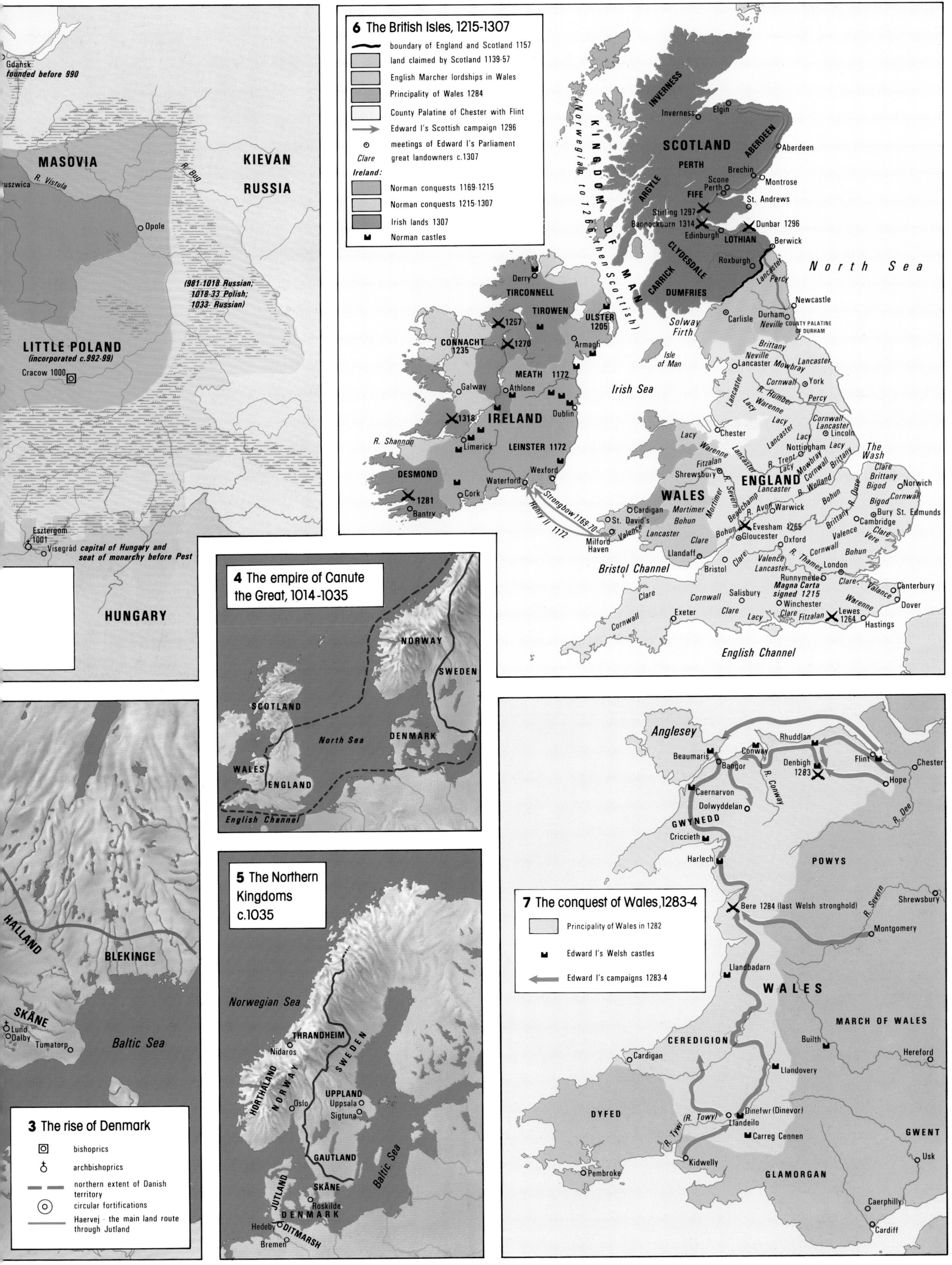

6 The British Isles, 1215-1307
boundary of England and Scotland 1157
land claimed by Scotland 1139-57
English Marcher lordships in Wales
Principality of Wales 1284
County Palatine of Chester with Flint
Edward I's Scottish campaign 1296
meetings of Edward I's Parliament
Clare great landowners c.1307
Ireland:
Norman conquests 1169-1215
Norman conquests 1215-1307
Irish lands 1307
Norman castles
SCOTLAND
ENGLAND
WALES
IRELAND
North Sea
Irish Sea
English Channel
Bristol Channel
Magna Carta signed 1215
Strongbow 1169-70
Henry II 1172
Kingdom of Man (Norwegian to 1266, then Scottish)
4 The empire of Canute the Great, 1014-1035
NORWAY
SWEDEN
SCOTLAND
North Sea
DENMARK
WALES
ENGLAND
English Channel
5 The Northern Kingdoms c.1035
Norwegian Sea
Baltic Sea
THRANDHEIM
NORWAY
SWEDEN
UPPLAND
GAUTLAND
SKÅNE
DENMARK
JUTLAND
DITMARSH
3 The rise of Denmark
bishoprics
archbishoprics
northern extent of Danish territory
circular fortifications
Haervej - the main land route through Jutland
MASOVIA
KIEVAN RUSSIA
LITTLE POLAND (incorporated c.992-99)
Cracow 1000
(981-1018 Russian; 1018-33 Polish; 1033- Russian)
Gdansk founded before 990
Esztergom 1001
Visegrád capital of Hungary and seat of monarchy before Pest
HUNGARY
HALLAND
BLEKINGE
SKÅNE
Baltic Sea
7 The conquest of Wales, 1283-4
Principality of Wales in 1282
Edward I's Welsh castles
Edward I's campaigns 1283-4
Anglesey
GWYNEDD
POWYS
WALES
MARCH OF WALES
CEREDIGION
DYFED
GLAMORGAN
GWENT
Bere 1284 (last Welsh stronghold)

The medieval German Empire
962-1356

Germany, or the eastern half of the Frankish empire, was the first country in Europe to recover from the setbacks of the ninth century invasions (page 36). This fact assured its predominance for upward of three centuries. German rulers never sought to assert control over the West Frankish lands, but, as heirs to the Carolingians, they claimed the imperial title and the right to rule over Italy and the lands of the former 'Middle Kingdom.' Germany's control of the Alpine passes between Lombardy and the Rhinelands assured not only its political preponderance but also gave it a leading place in the cultural exchange between Mediterranean and northern Europe.

There was, at first, no sense of a common German, or East Frankish, identity, and the effective control of the first German ruler, Henry I of Saxony (919–936), scarcely extended beyond Saxony and Franconia (map 1). But his son, Otto I (936–973), brought the other German duchies under royal control. Also, by defeating the Magyars at the battle of Lechfeld (955), he freed Germany from external threats and was able, in 951 and 961, to intervene effectively in Italy. His coronation as emperor (962) sealed the historic connexion between Germany and Italy. As heir to the Carolingian tradition, he also inaugurated a Christian drive against the pagan Slavs on the eastern frontier. But the great Slav revolt of 983 halted this advance until the twelfth century, and German efforts were concentrated instead on the south and south-west. The result, in 1034, was the addition of Burgundy to the imperial domains.

In spite of these successes, aristocratic resistance to royal centralisation was never overcome, and an opportunity to renew it came in 1075, when the outbreak of conflict between the emperor Henry IV (1056–1106) and the papacy, which saw imperial power in Italy as a threat to its independence, played into the German princes' hands. The ensuing civil war (1076–1122) was a turning point in German history. Although the monarchy emerged successful, its position was permanently weakened. German power was apparently restored during the reign of Frederick I (1152–1190), but it depended increasingly on the riches of Italy, and this embroiled Frederick not only with the papacy but also with the Italian cities. The marriage of his son, Henry VI, with Constance, the heiress of Sicily (1186), held out new possibilities. But the prospect of the union of Sicily and the empire alarmed the papacy, which saw itself being encircled, and led to the final struggle between Frederick II (1212–1250), and Pope Innocent IV (1243–1254).

Meanwhile Germany was being overtaken by the western monarchies (page 52). The empire under Frederick II was still the most imposing political body in Europe (map 3), but by 1200 Paris was the intellectual and cultural centre of Europe, and by comparison with England and Sicily Germany's financial organisation was antiquated. Eastward expansion had begun again after 1138 (map 2). It added two-thirds to the German territories and shifted the seat of power from Rhine to Elbe. But the beneficiaries were the princes on the eastern frontier, not the monarchy. Later, the Teutonic Knights conquered heathen Prussia (map 4), but within the empire the tendency was to fragmentation rather than expansion, and gains in the east were offset by loss of control over Italy which now went its own way (page 56). In default of royal authority local leagues were formed to resist princely encroachments and to preserve the peace. The most famous and enduring was the Swiss Confederation, formed in 1291 (map 5). The Golden Bull of 1356, formally recognising the autonomy of the princes, marked the beginning of a new era in German history; but the age of German preponderance in Europe had already ended a century earlier.

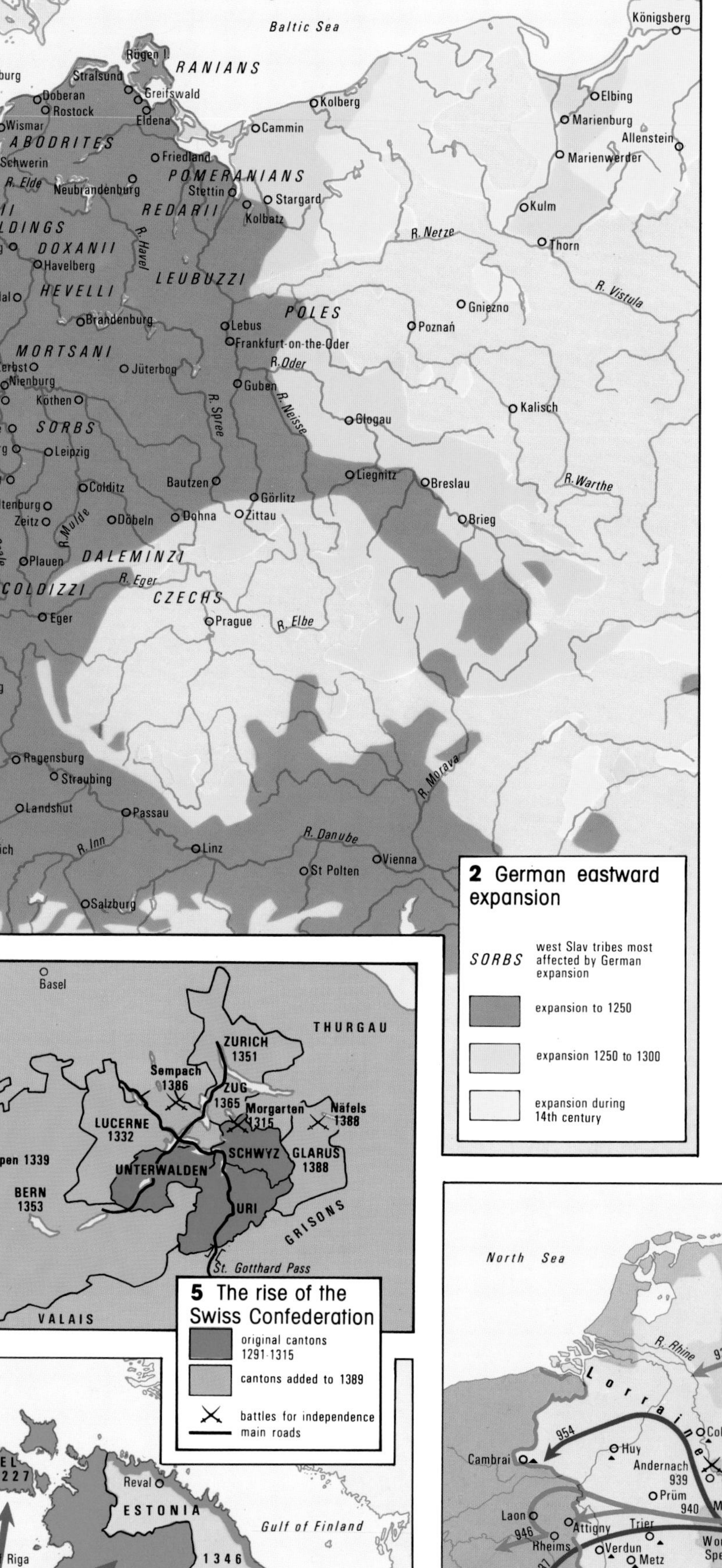

2 German eastward expansion

1 The East Frankish Kingdom of Otto I

5 The rise of the Swiss Confederation

4 The conquest of Prussia

3 The Hohenstaufen Empire 1152-1250
eastward spread of German peasant settlement 12th century
German settlement by 1200-1250
city with over 10,000 inhabitants
member of Lombard Leagues of 1167 and 1226
member of 1167 League only
member of 1226 League only
German invasions 1190-94
Henry VI's Genoese and Pisan fleet 1194
main Hohenstaufen palaces and castles
mountain pass
North Sea
Baltic Sea
Holstein
Saxony
Altmark
DUCHY OF BRUNSWICK (after 1235)
DUCHY OF WESTPHALIA (after 1180)
ANHALT (After 1180)
Thuringia
Lusatia
Meissen
Pomerania
Silesia
Lower Lorraine
Brabant
Hainaut
KINGDOM OF GERMANY
KINGDOM OF BOHEMIA
Moravia
Franconia
Swabia
Bavaria
Austria
Styria
Carinthia
Tyrol
Friuli
Carniola
Upper Lorraine
Alsace
Burgundy
KINGDOM OF ARLES
Savoy
Provence
KINGDOM OF ITALY
Lombardy
Verona
Tuscany
PAPAL PATRIMONY
VENETIAN TERRITORIES
expansion of Papal States under Innocent III
Adriatic Sea
KINGDOM OF SICILY
SICILY
Bornhöved 1227
Bouvines 1214
Tagliacozzo 1268
Brenner
Septimer
St. Gotthard
St. Bernard
Mont Cenis
Pontebba
Semmering
Alps
Baltic Sea
Pomerania
WAGRIANS
ABODRITES
WARNABI
March of the Billungs c.937-92
REDARII
POLABII
VELETIANS
Nordmark
HEVELLI
Saxony
Lusatia
LUSIZZI
SORBS
Meissen
MILIZI
DALEMINZI
Mark Zeitz
POLAND
Franconia
Bohemia (tributary from 950)
Swabia
Bavaria
Ostmark
Pitten
HUNGARY
Styria
Carinthia (Duchy 976)
Lechfeld 955
new bishopric with date of foundation
bishopric destroyed in Slav rising of 983
visited more than once by Henry I
MILIZI Slav tribes
frontier c.950

Fourteenth century Europe

After the rise and consolidation of national monarchies in Spain, France and England in the thirteenth century (page 52), the fourteenth century was a period of setbacks on all fronts in western Europe. In part, this may be attributed to a sudden climatic deterioration (the onset of the 'little ice age') which brought to an end the agricultural boom that had been virtually continuous since 1150. Already in 1315–17 Europe experienced a 'great famine', and the weakening of human powers of resistance induced by inadequate nourishment may have been one factor accounting for the rapid spread of the Black Death, or bubonic plague, which first appeared in the Crimea in 1346 and spread from there first by ship to Italy and then to the west (map 1). But there were also other factors. All the western monarchies had over-extended themselves financially, and the economic setback accentuated their difficulties. Philip IV's unsuccessful attempts to subdue Flanders played after his death (1314) into the hands of the aristocracy; so also did the involvement of Catalonia in Italy after the death of James II (1285–1327); and in England the attempt to subdue Scotland (map 4) proved to be a running sore. Ireland also virtually went its own way until Tudor times (page 72), and Wales, conquered but not subdued by Edward I (page 52), had a great national revival under Owain Glyndwr (1400–1409). Germany broke apart into rival principalities after the extermination of the Hohenstaufen dynasty (page 54), and Italy went the same way once Hohenstaufen rule was removed, breaking up into a number of local lordships or *signorie* (map 3). In the end, even the Catholic church was affected by the economic and fiscal stringency. From 1378 to 1417 it was divided by schism (map 6), which undermined its authority, while its financial extortions gave impetus to the anti-papal, reformatory movements of Hus in Bohemia and Wyclif in England.

Eastern Europe, on the other hand, was in process of recovery from the Mongol incursions of the thirteenth century (page 46). Bohemia under Charles IV (1333–78), Poland under Casimir III (1339–70), and Hungary under Louis the Great (1342–82), all made rapid strides, helped perhaps by the fact that the impact of the Black Death was less severe in the east than in the west, and also by exploitation of their natural resources, such as the silver mines of Kutna Hora (map 2). In the west, on the other hand, the setback was lasting. Two English kings, Edward II (1327) and Richard II (1399) were murdered. The Hundred Years' War between England and France (map 5) resulted in widespread devastation. Overall, the Black Death reduced the population of Europe by roughly one-third. Further, the misery caused by economic recession and military ravages sparked off a series of popular risings, the Jacquerie in France and the Peasants' Revolt in England being best known (map 1), although urban discontent – the weavers' rising in Flanders under Artevelde, or the Ciompi in Florence – was no less significant in the long run. It was not until after c.1450 that recovery began (page 82); but even then under-currents of popular resentment persisted, which found their outlet in the Peasants' War of 1524–5 and the messianic movements of the Reformation.

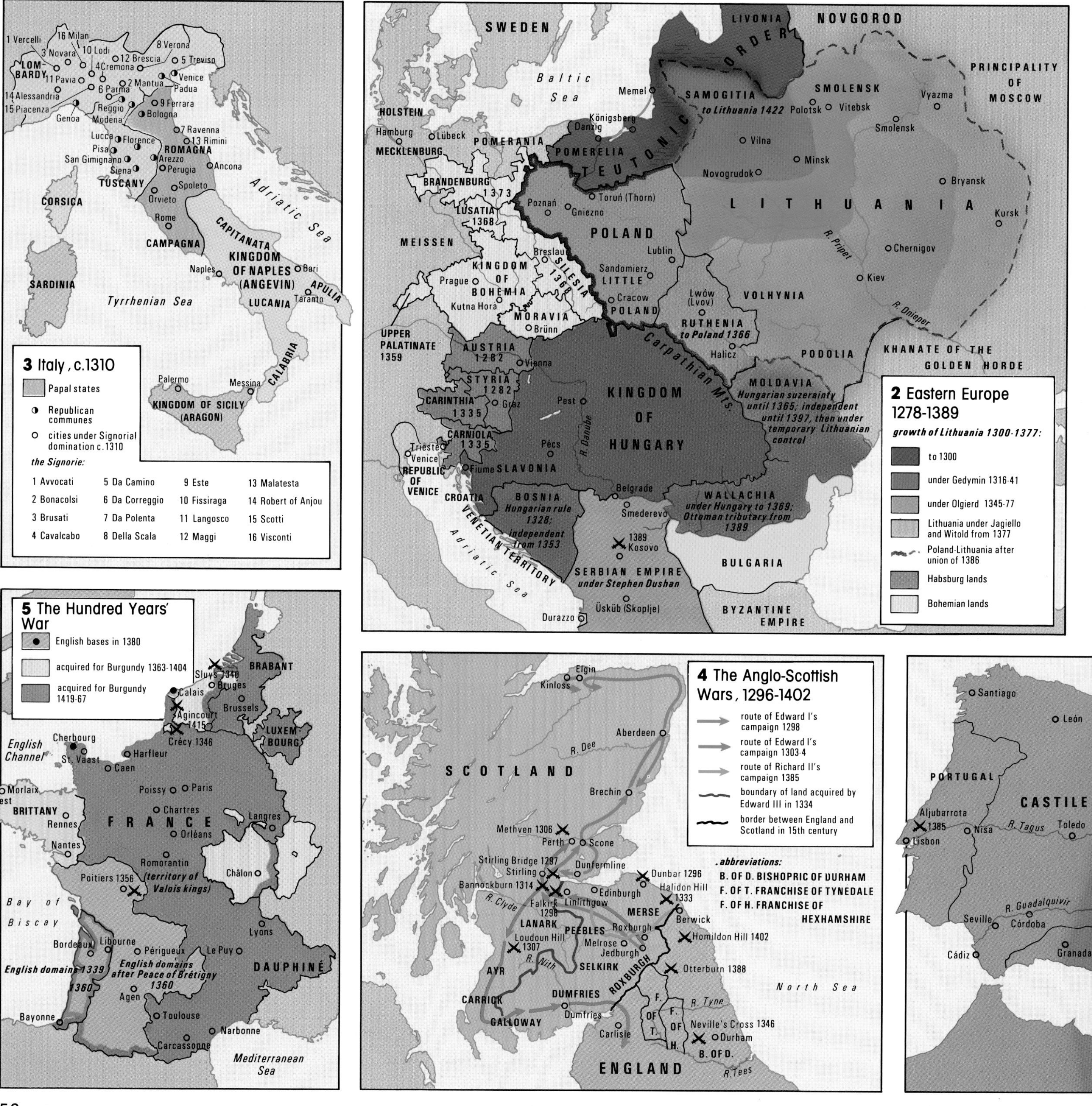

1 Europe at the time of the Black Death
extent of spread of Black Death:
1346
1347
mid 1348
end 1348
mid 1349
end 1349
1350
c. 1351
c. 1353
little or no plague mortality
political change:
union of Kalmar 1397
Milanese territory under Giangaleazzo Visconti 1378-1402
territory under Florentine control, end 14th century
Luxembourg lands
Wittelsbach lands
Habsburg lands
social unrest:
areas of disturbance during Great Peasant Revolt in England 1381
centre of urban revolt
rural uprisings
defeats in battle of lower class
battle
religious unrest:
spread of Lollardry in England to death of Richard II, 1399
area of Hussite influence
Hussite centre
the Western Schism (inset map right):
areas giving allegiance to Pope in Rome
areas giving allegiance to Pope in Avignon
allegiance officially to Rome but shifting local allegiances
6 The Western Schism, 1378-1417
Avignon
Rome
NORWAY
SWEDEN
DENMARK
RUSSIAN STATES
PRINCIPALITY OF MOSCOW
ORDER
TEUTONIC
LITHUANIA
POLAND
UKRAINE
MOLDAVIA
HUNGARY
WALLACHIA
BULGARIA
SERBIAN PRINCES
BOSNIA
PRINCIPALITY OF ALBANIA
OTTOMAN TURKS
DUCHY OF ATHENS
ACHAEA
HOLY ROMAN EMPIRE
SCOTLAND
ENGLAND
WALES
FRANCE
BRITTANY
BURGUNDY
AQUITAINE
ENGLISH GASCONY
NAVARRE
ARAGON
CATALONIA
PROVENCE
DAUPHINÉ
SAVOY
SWISS CONFED.
SWABIA
BAVARIA
AUSTRIA
CARINTHIA
BOHEMIA
MORAVIA
SILESIA
FRANCONIA
LORRAINE
FLANDERS
HOLLAND
FRIESLAND
SAXONY
BRANDENBURG
POMERANIA
REPUBLIC OF VENICE
PAPAL STATES
KINGDOM OF NAPLES
KINGDOM OF SICILY
Hebrides
Orkneys
North Sea
Baltic Sea
Black Sea
Adriatic Sea
Mediterranean Sea
Corsica
Sardinia
Balearic Islands
Crete
Rhodes
R. Loire
R. Dordogne
R. Rhône
R. Rhine
R. Elbe
R. Oder
R. Danube
R. Dniester
R. Dnieper
Oslo
Uppsala
Stockholm
Visby
Novgorod
Riga
Smolensk
Königsberg
Danzig
Copenhagen
Edinburgh
Armagh
Carlisle
Newcastle
York
Chester
Lincoln
Norwich
Bury St Edmunds
London
Bristol
Winchester
Roosebeke 1382
Bruges
Antwerp
Ghent
Ypres
Aachen
Cologne
Agincourt
Crécy
Liège
Amiens
Rouen
Mello 1358
Meaux 1358
Rheims
Paris
Chartres
Troyes
Orléans
Poitiers
Bordeaux
Cahors
Toulouse
Montpellier
Narbonne
Avignon
Marseilles
Lyons
Geneva
Lausanne
Basle
Constance
Strasbourg
Trier
Mainz
Frankfurt
Amsterdam
Bremen
Hamburg
Lübeck
Brunswick
Magdeburg
Prague
Tabor
Regensburg
Passau
Augsburg
Munich
Salzburg
Vienna
Warsaw
Cracow
Kiev
Buda
Pest
Belgrade
Bucharest
Ragusa
Adrianople
Constantinople
Salonica
Athens
Milan
Venice
Trieste
Turin
Genoa
Ravenna
Pisa
Florence
Ancona
Siena
Rome
Naples
Amalfi
Palermo
Messina
Saragossa
Barcelona
Valencia

Medieval trade routes
c.1000-1500

Trading connexions had been remarkably widespread during late antiquity, and they had brought with them important cultural interchanges (page 24). The barbarian invasions, beginning c.300 AD and lasting some 200 years, had disastrous results. The Silk Route from Rome to China was cut, and even within the Roman empire communications broke down. There was a short-lived recrudescence in Carolingian times, involving trade in the North Sea, centred on Dorestad and Quentovic; but it was only after c.1000, with the restoration of relatively stable conditions, that trade picked up. In particular, the Italian cities, already in contact with the Near East (page 36), established connexions with north-west Europe, where the fairs of Champagne were becoming clearing-houses for trade between Italy and the rising industrial centres of Flanders (map 1).

The consolidation of the German empire under the Saxon and Salian dynasties gave impetus to trade from west to east, along a line running from the Low Countries via Cologne to Magdeburg, and along the Main valley to Bamberg and Prague. German control of the Alpine passes, particularly after the opening of the Septimer and St. Gotthard passes during the Hohenstaufen period, stimulated trade with Italy, which contributed to the growing wealth of the south German cities, among them Augsburg, which later became a major commercial and financial centre after the rise of the Fugger merchant family in the fifteenth century. In the north the most important city was Lübeck (founded 1158), the key point controlling trade between the North Sea and the Baltic and the seat of the Hanseatic League, an association of German merchants which took shape in 1259 and was formally constituted in 1358. With its far-flung network of associated cities, and with branches in London, Bruges and Bergen, the Hansa dominated the trade of northern Europe in the fourteenth and fifteenth centuries. It also had connexions with Venice and Genoa, the cities which dominated Mediterranean and Levantine commerce (map 2).

Levantine trade fell into two broad categories: the spice trade, in which Venice predominated, and the silk trade, largely in the hands of Genoa and its merchant colonies in Constantinople and at Kaffa, Tana and Trebizond. The latter profited greatly from the restoration of order and settled government in central Asia by the Mongols (page 46), which allowed a resumption of overland trade, and for a time there was extensive east-west traffic, exemplified by the famous journeys of Marco Polo between 1271 and 1295 (map 3). But the roads opened by the rise of the Mongol empire in the thirteenth century were closed by its decline in the mid-fourteenth century. The important spice trade from Ormuz to the Black Sea was also badly affected; but the trade via the Red Sea and Alexandria to Venice continued without interruption until the Ottoman conquest of Egypt in 1517 (page 48).

Spices were indispensable, easy to handle and highly profitable, and they were the staple of intercontinental trade in this period. Both Europe and China were dependent for supplies on the spice-producing regions of Asia, particularly the Moluccas and the Malay archipelago, and the resultant transactions, largely in the hands of Arab and Indian middlemen, created a complicated network of sea routes, hinging on Malacca, which stretched from the Red Sea and the Persian Gulf to the South China Sea (map 3). In the early fifteenth century, between 1405 and 1433, the Chinese sent seven expeditions through the Strait of Malacca to the Indian Ocean and beyond; but this enterprise ceased abruptly after 1440. Meanwhile, Portugal was probing down the west coast of Africa (page 64) in search of gold; but later, when Genoa, which had lost its eastern markets after the fall of Constantinople in 1453, provided financial backing for the Portuguese ventures, the main objective became the search for an alternative route to the east, to cut out Genoa's rival, Venice. When the Portuguese reached India in 1498, and Columbus, despatched by Portugal's rival, Spain, reached America, a new era had begun. The thousand-year-old pattern, centred on the Mediterranean, gave way to an Atlantic economy (page 82), and the whole economic and political balance in Europe shifted dramatically.

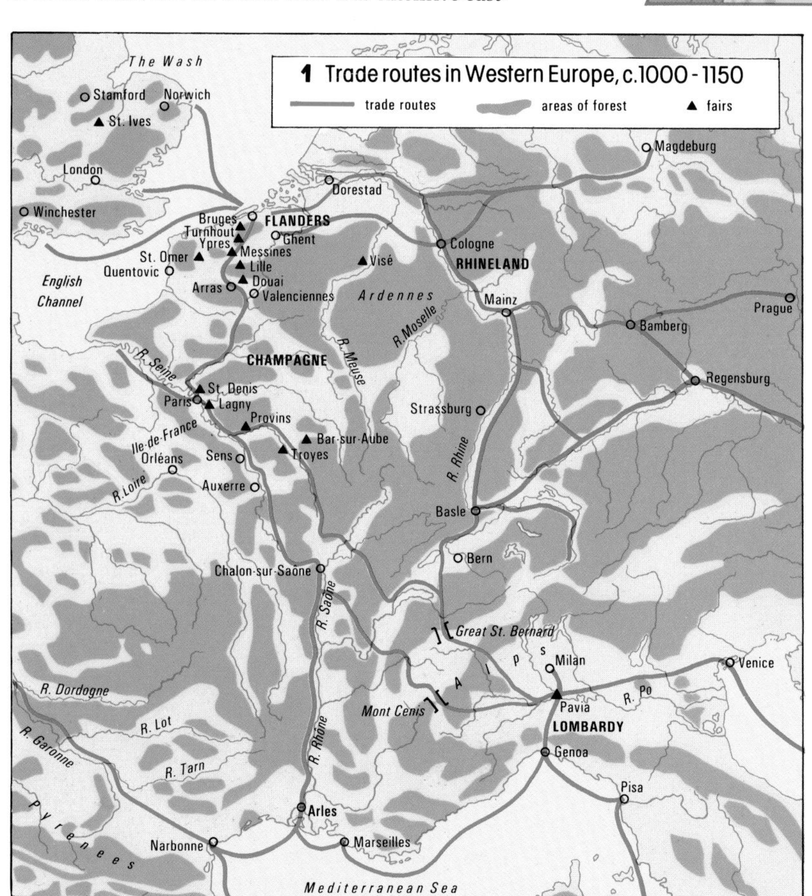

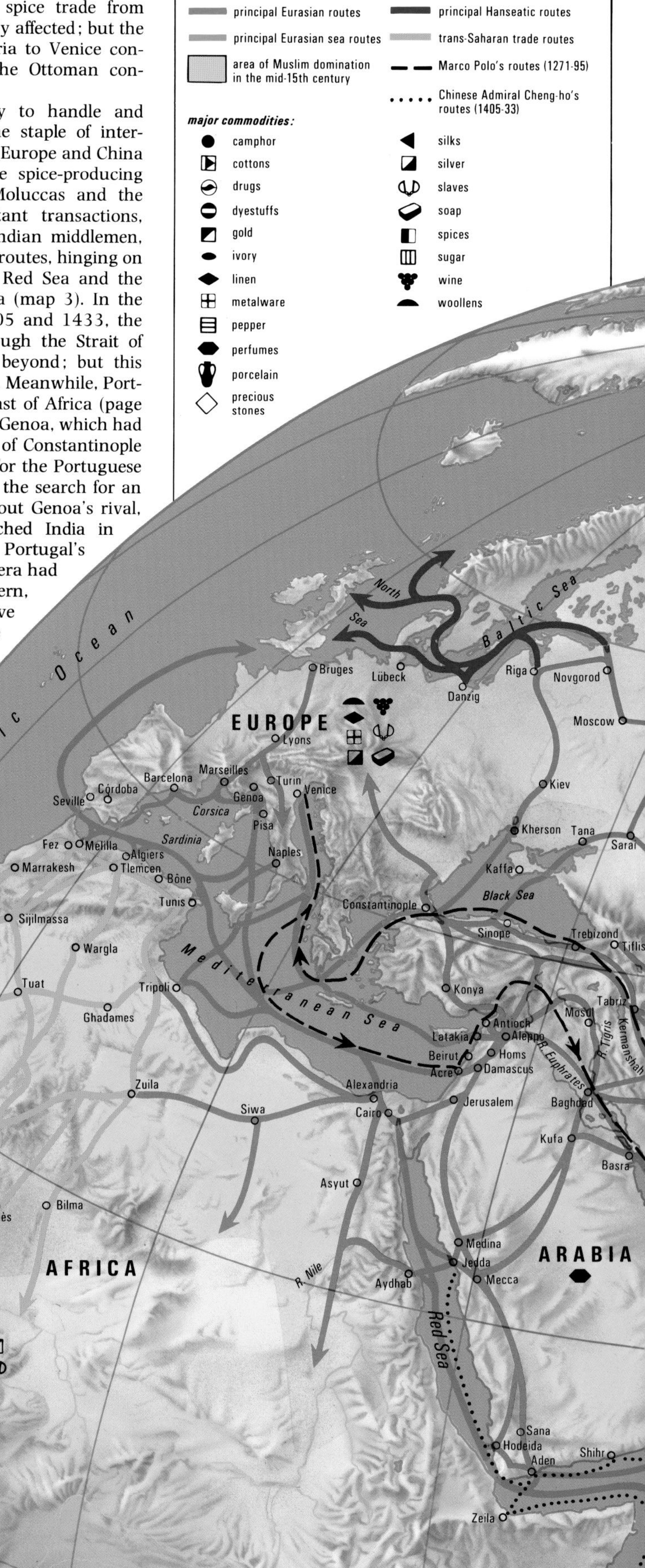

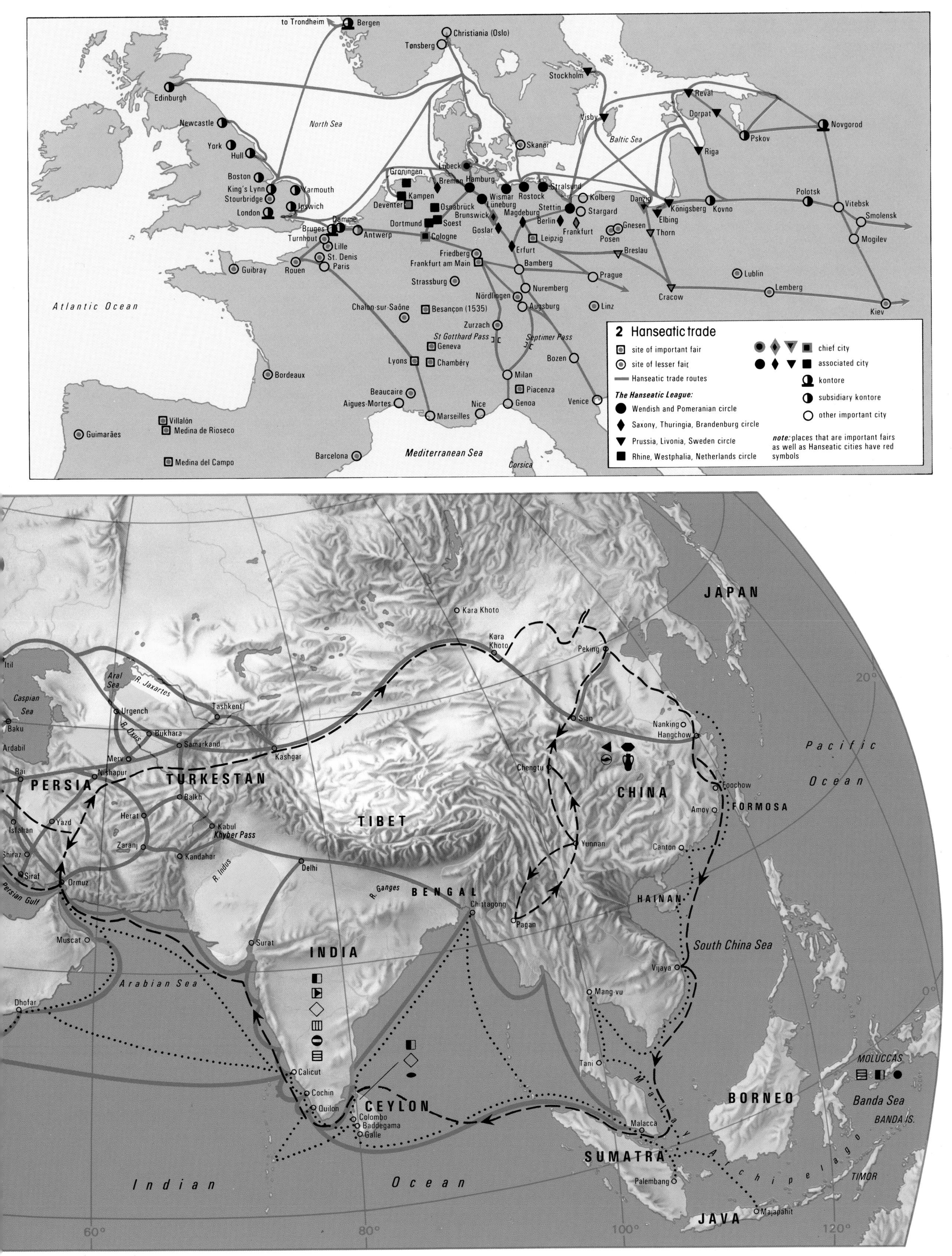

2 Hanseatic trade
site of important fair
site of lesser fair
Hanseatic trade routes
The Hanseatic League:
Wendish and Pomeranian circle
Saxony, Thuringia, Brandenburg circle
Prussia, Livonia, Sweden circle
Rhine, Westphalia, Netherlands circle
chief city
associated city
kontore
subsidiary kontore
other important city
note: places that are important fairs as well as Hanseatic cities have red symbols
to Trondheim
Bergen
Christiania (Oslo)
Tønsberg
Stockholm
Edinburgh
Newcastle
York
Hull
Boston
King's Lynn
Stourbridge
Yarmouth
Ipswich
London
North Sea
Baltic Sea
Visby
Reval
Dorpat
Novgorod
Pskov
Riga
Skanör
Groningen
Lübeck
Hamburg
Bremen
Kampen
Deventer
Osnabrück
Lüneburg
Wismar
Rostock
Stralsund
Kolberg
Stettin
Stargard
Danzig
Königsberg
Elbing
Kovno
Polotsk
Vitebsk
Smolensk
Mogilev
Brunswick
Magdeburg
Berlin
Frankfurt
Soest
Dortmund
Goslar
Gnesen
Posen
Thorn
Bruges
Damme
Turnhout
Antwerp
Cologne
Leipzig
Breslau
Lille
St. Denis
Paris
Rouen
Guibray
Erfurt
Friedberg
Frankfurt am Main
Bamberg
Prague
Lublin
Strassburg
Nördlingen
Nuremberg
Cracow
Lemberg
Augsburg
Linz
Kiev
Atlantic Ocean
Chalon-sur-Saône
Besançon (1535)
Zurzach
St Gotthard Pass
Septimer Pass
Geneva
Lyons
Chambéry
Bozen
Milan
Bordeaux
Piacenza
Beaucaire
Aigues-Mortes
Nice
Genoa
Venice
Marseilles
Villalón
Medina de Rioseco
Guimarães
Medina del Campo
Barcelona
Mediterranean Sea
Corsica
JAPAN
Kara Khoto
Peking
Itil
Aral Sea
R. Jaxartes
Caspian Sea
Urgench
Tashkent
Baku
R. Oxus
Bukhara
Samarkand
Ardabil
Merv
Kashgar
Sian
Nanking
Hangchow
Pacific Ocean
Rai
Nishapur
PERSIA
TURKESTAN
Chengtu
Foochow
Balkh
CHINA
Herat
Kabul
Khyber Pass
TIBET
Amoy
FORMOSA
Yazd
Isfahan
Zaranj
Yunnan
Canton
Shiraz
Kandahar
Siraf
R. Indus
Delhi
Ormuz
Persian Gulf
R. Ganges
BENGAL
Chittagong
HAINAN
Pagan
Muscat
Surat
South China Sea
INDIA
Vijaya
Arabian Sea
Mang-vu
Dhofar
MOLUCCAS
Calicut
Tani
Cochin
BORNEO
Quilon
CEYLON
Colombo
Baddegama
Galle
Malacca
Banda Sea
BANDA IS.
Malay Archipelago
SUMATRA
Palembang
TIMOR
Indian Ocean
JAVA
Majapahit
20°
0°
60°
80°
100°
120°

African states and empires, c.900-1800

By the end of the first millennium AD great changes had taken place in Africa. The rise of a culture based on iron-working (page 10) led to a large-scale displacement of Khoisan-speaking Bushmen and Hottentots by settled Bantu-speaking agriculturalists (map 3) and to the appearance of extensive states and empires based on trade. In the south, Zimbabwe, with its monumental stone buildings, exported gold and copper to the Orient via the port of Sofala, and the impressive Kongo state on the west coast had an important trade in ivory. Further north, the Arab conquest of the Maghreb and the rise of the Almoravid and Almohad empires (page 40) marked a watershed. The Arabs, great traders, developed and extended the trans-Saharan caravan routes, and there is no doubt that trade was an important factor in the development of the great empires which arose in the sub-Saharan savanna. The early history of Ghana (some 500 miles north-west of the modern state with the same name) precedes the Islamic era; but its successors, Mali and Songhay, owed much of their wealth and civilisation, described in glowing terms by Arab travellers, to the Islamic impact. So also did the Kanem-Borno empire around Lake Chad and, after the fifteenth century, the city states of Hausaland (map 1). Arab merchant colonies also spread far down the east coast from Mogadishu to Kilwa. The staples of trade in all cases were gold, ivory and slaves. According to a conservative estimate, the trans-Saharan slave trade before the coming of the Europeans amounted to almost 5 million.

The arrival of the Portuguese on the African coast and the building in 1448 of a first European fort and warehouse at Arguin, followed (1482) by a second at Elmina on the Gold Coast, had at first little impact on Africa. The immediate objective was to share directly in the gold trade, hitherto dominated by Muslim middlemen, and the slave trade was a secondary by-product. But with the development of sugar plantations in Brazil (page 68) and later in the West Indies, the slave trade became a major source of profit, particularly after Dutch and British traders ousted the Portuguese. Along the length of the Gold and Slave Coasts, from Axim to the Niger Delta, fortified trading stations (or 'factories') were set up as bases for this trade (map 2, inset), and the Portuguese continued to export slaves further south in Angola. Of some 15 million Africans shipped aboard between 1450 and 1870, some 90 per cent went to South America and the Caribbean, most of them between 1700 and 1800. The effects on Africa of this appalling trade in human beings are not easy to quantify, though the effects on the victims themselves need no description. Furthermore, the loss of population was not evenly divided and some areas suffered disproportionately. Others profited from the trade. After the invasion and destruction of the great Songhay empire by Morocco in 1591, the forest states of Asante, Dahomey and Benin, having direct access to the Atlantic and to European trade, increased in importance and political power (map 2). The Europeans remained largely ignorant of the African interior, and their influence was limited. In the far south the Dutch were established in the Cape Colony; but, in a continental perspective, its extent was still minimal. In the north-east Islam was spreading; but the Christian kingdom of Ethiopia, despite a serious setback in the 1520s, still held its own. By 1800, with the exception of the Ottomans in the north (and even their power was more nominal than real), Africa remained independent of foreign control. Nevertheless there is little sign that it was ready to meet the European challenge that developed in the nineteenth century (page 102). It was a world unto itself, but in no position to compete with the technological dynamism of the West.

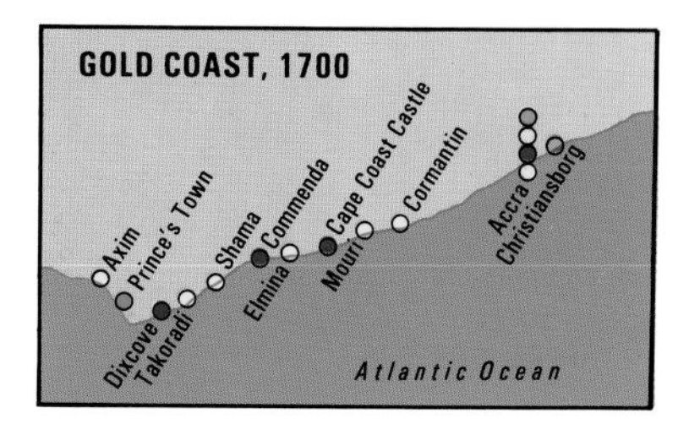

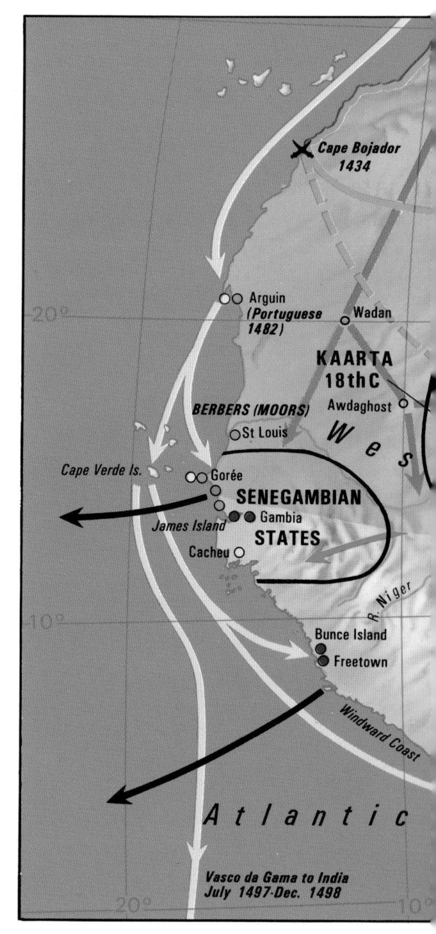

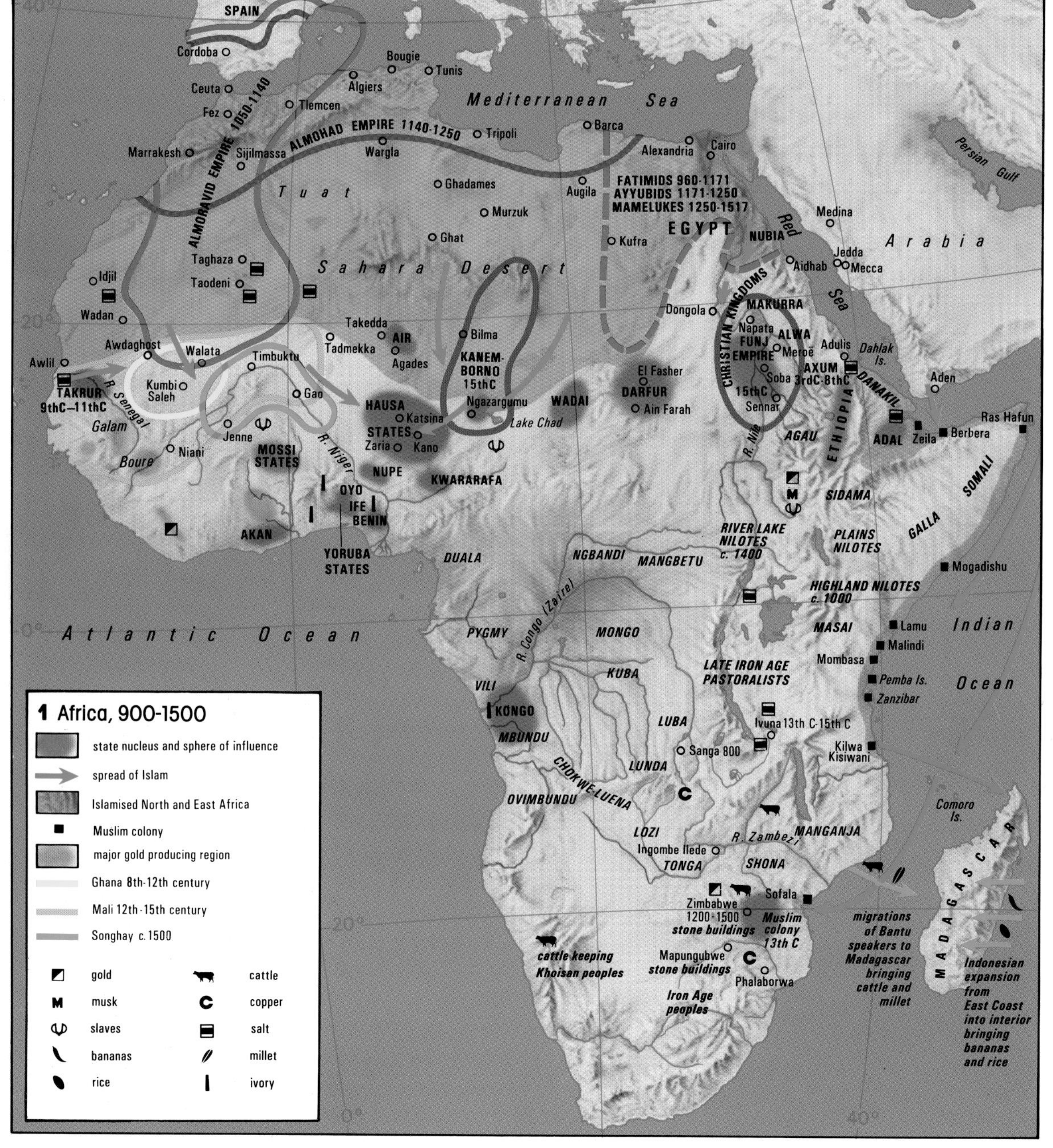

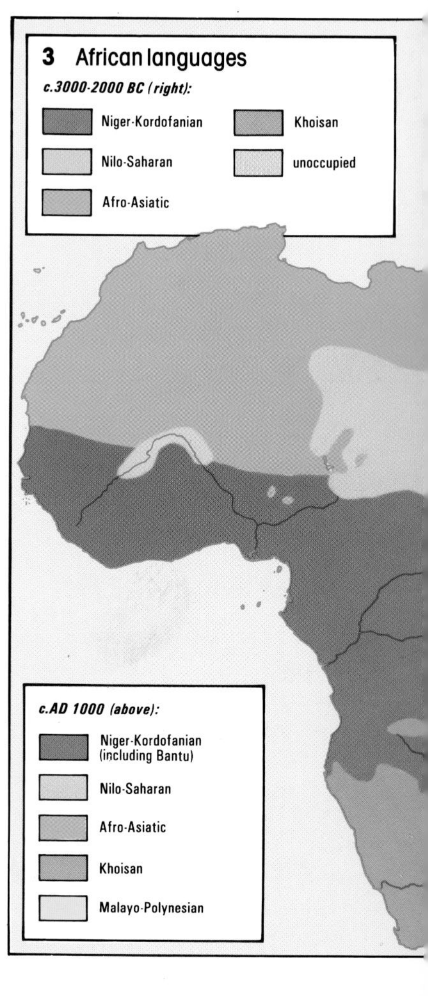

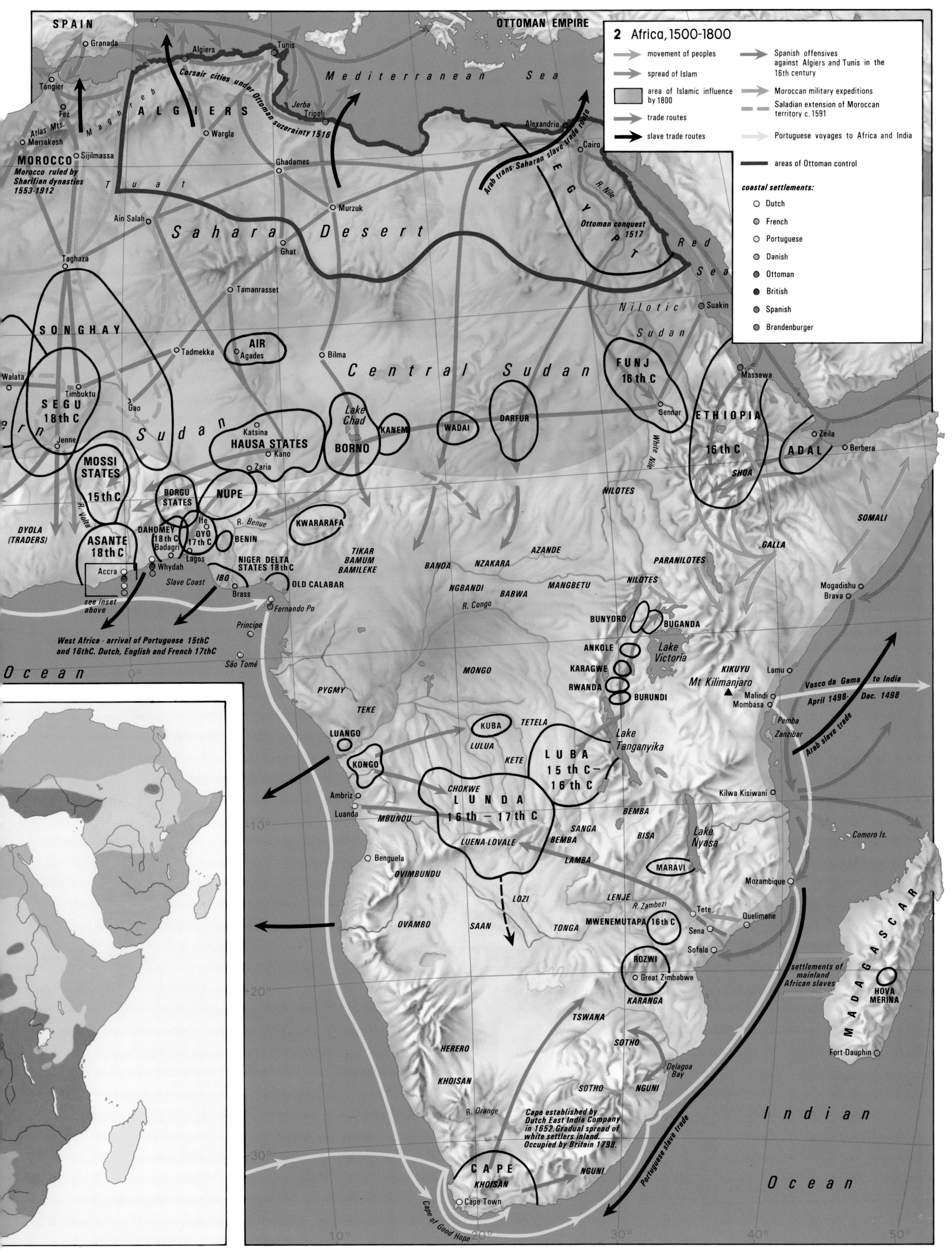

2 Africa, 1500-1800
movement of peoples
spread of Islam
area of Islamic influence by 1800
trade routes
slave trade routes
Spanish offensives against Algiers and Tunis in the 16th century
Moroccan military expeditions
Saladian extension of Moroccan territory c. 1591
Portuguese voyages to Africa and India
areas of Ottoman control
coastal settlements:
Dutch
French
Portuguese
Danish
Ottoman
British
Spanish
Brandenburger
SPAIN
OTTOMAN EMPIRE
Granada
Algiers
Tunis
Tangier
Fez
Atlas Mts.
Marrakesh
MOROCCO
Morocco ruled by Sharifian dynasties 1553-1912
Sijilmassa
ALGIERS
Maghreb
Corsair cities under Ottoman suzerainty 1516
Wargla
Mediterranean Sea
Jerba
Tripoli
Ghadames
Tuat
Alexandria
Cairo
Arab trans-Saharan slave trade route
EGYPT
R. Nile
Ottoman conquest 1517
Murzuk
Ain Salah
Sahara Desert
Ghat
Taghaza
Tamanrasset
Red Sea
Nilotic Sudan
Suakin
SONGHAY
AIR
Agades
Tadmekka
Bilma
Central Sudan
FUNJ 16th C
Massawa
Walata
Timbuktu
SEGU 18th C
Gao
Jenne
Sudan
Lake Chad
KANEM
WADAI
DARFUR
Sennar
ETHIOPIA 16th C
Zeila
ADAL
Berbera
Katsina
HAUSA STATES
Kano
BORNO
White Nile
SHOA
MOSSI STATES 15th C
Zaria
BORGU STATES
NUPE
NILOTES
R. Volta
Ife
R. Benue
KWARARAFA
SOMALI
DYOLA (TRADERS)
ASANTE 18th C
DAHOMEY 18th C
Badagri
OYO 17th C
BENIN
TIKAR
BAMUM
BAMILEKE
AZANDE
GALLA
Accra
Whydah
Lagos
NIGER DELTA STATES 18th C
BANDA
NZAKARA
PARANILOTES
Slave Coast
IBO
OLD CALABAR
MANGBETU
NILOTES
Mogadishu
Brava
see inset above
Brass
Fernando Po
NGBANDI
BABWA
R. Congo
BUNYORO
BUGANDA
Principe
West Africa - arrival of Portuguese 15thC and 16thC. Dutch, English and French 17thC
ANKOLE
Lake Victoria
São Tomé
KARAGWE
KIKUYU
Lamu
Ocean
MONGO
Mt Kilimanjaro
Vasco da Gama to India April 1498 - Dec. 1498
RWANDA
BURUNDI
Malindi
Mombasa
PYGMY
TEKE
Pemba
Zanzibar
Arab slave trade
LUANGO
KUBA
TETELA
Lake Tanganyika
LULUA
KONGO
KETE
LUBA 15th C - 16th C
CHOKWE
Ambriz
LUNDA 16th - 17th C
Kilwa Kisiwani
Luanda
MBUNDU
BEMBA
SANGA
BISA
Lake Nyasa
BEMBA
Comoro Is.
LUENA-LOVALE
Benguela
LAMBA
MARAVI
OVIMBUNDU
Mozambique
LOZI
LENJE
R. Zambezi
Tete
Quelimane
OVAMBO
SAAN
TONGA
MWENEMUTAPA 16th C
Sena
Sofala
ROZWI
MADAGASCAR
Great Zimbabwe
settlements of mainland African slaves
HOVA MERINA
KARANGA
TSWANA
HERERO
SOTHO
Fort-Dauphin
Delagoa Bay
KHOISAN
SOTHO
NGUNI
R. Orange
Cape established by Dutch East India Company in 1652. Gradual spread of white settlers inland. Occupied by Britain 1798.
Indian Ocean
Portuguese slave trade
CAPE
KHOISAN
NGUNI
Cape Town
Cape of Good Hope

America on the eve of European conquest

Two great and wealthy civilisations confronted the Spaniards when they arrived in America at the beginning of the sixteenth century: the Aztec empire in Mexico and the Inca empire in Peru. The former had a population of 10–12 millions, the latter 6 millions or possibly considerably more. A few other centres of civilisation existed, such as the Chibcha state in modern Colombia; but the remainder of the continent was sparsely inhabited (perhaps 1 million north of the Rio Grande and 1 million in the rest of South America) and divided among more than a thousand small tribal societies, with distinct, often unrelated languages (map 1). Few regions, particularly in the north, had reached the stage of settled agriculture (map 4).

The Aztec and Inca empires were different in character, and there is no evidence of any contact between them. The Aztecs, like the Toltecs who controlled much of Mexico in the eleventh and twelfth centuries, were raw warriors from the north who entered Mexico during the thirteenth century and settled on islands in Lake Texcoco, where c.1325 they founded the town of Tenochtitlán, which was to become their capital. The Inca empire was created by one of the numerous tribes of Quechua stock inhabiting the central Andes, which established itself in the Cuzco valley in the twelfth century. The expansion of both came late and only reached its full extent on the eve of the Spanish conquest. In the case of the Aztecs (map 2) the first step was to ally with the neighbouring tribes in Texcoco and Tlacopán against their overlords in Azcapotzalco, and then to turn against their allies. This aggressive policy began c.1427 under Itzcoatl and was continued by Montezuma I. It reached its peak under Montezuma II (1502–20), when the Aztecs, in control of the greater part of Mexico, were beginning to enter Maya territory in Yucatán. Inca expansion began under the eighth emperor, Viracocha, and his son Pachacuti (1438–63), whose son Topa subdued the coastal civilisation of Chimú (1470), and then, after his accession as emperor (1471), pushed south into Chile and northern Argentina (map 3). Huayna Capac (1493–1525) advanced north into modern Ecuador, where he founded a second capital at Quito. By now the Inca empire was some 200 miles wide and 2500 miles long, held together by an impressive system of highways and post-stations, with relays of runners who conveyed imperial orders to all parts of the empire.

The Incas created a genuine imperial system, with an hereditary dynasty, a Quechua aristocracy and a highly trained bureaucracy. All land was state-owned, and there was a complex system of irrigation. The ordinary Indian spent nine months of the year working for the state, but in return was protected from famine by large state-owned food repositories and provided for in sickness and old age. The Aztec empire, on the other hand, rather like that of the Mongols in Europe (page 46), was essentially a harsh military dominion over vassal peoples, who were left to rule themselves on condition that they paid heavy tribute to Tenochtitlán in food, textiles, pottery and other goods, but increasingly in human beings for sacrifice to the Aztec gods. The number of sacrificial victims rose from 10,000 a year to 50,000 a year at the time of the Spanish conquest. This was certainly one reason why the Totonacs and Tlaxcalans welcomed the Spanish invaders of Mexico (page 68), and resentment against Inca oppression probably played a similar role in Peru. Neither empire was as stable as it seemed. Nevertheless their collapse at the hands of small bands of adventurers (Cortés had only 600 men, a few small cannon, 13 muskets and 16 horses when he invaded Mexico in 1519, and Pizarro had only 180 men, 27 horses and 2 cannon when he attacked the Inca empire in 1531) is not easily explained.

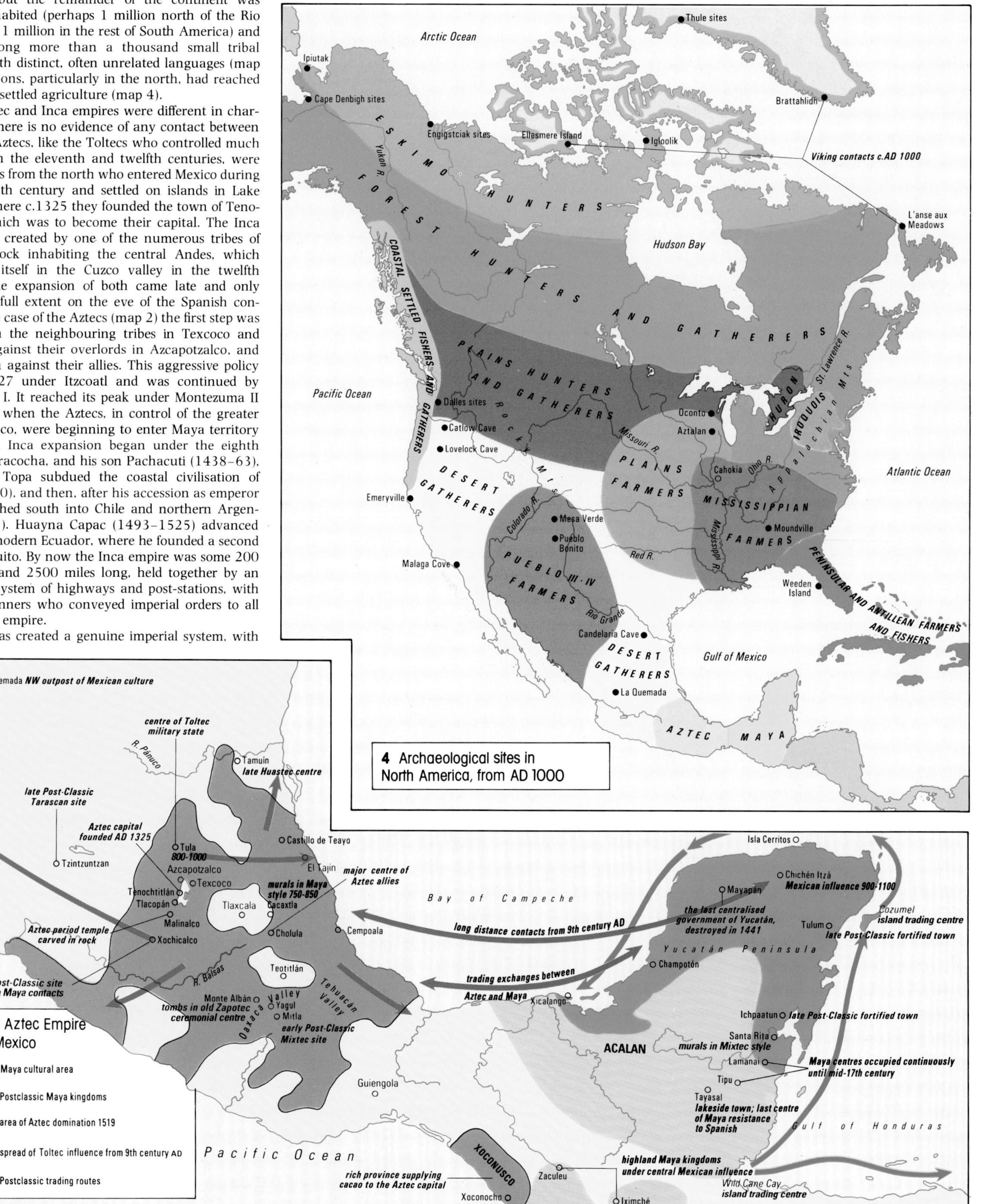

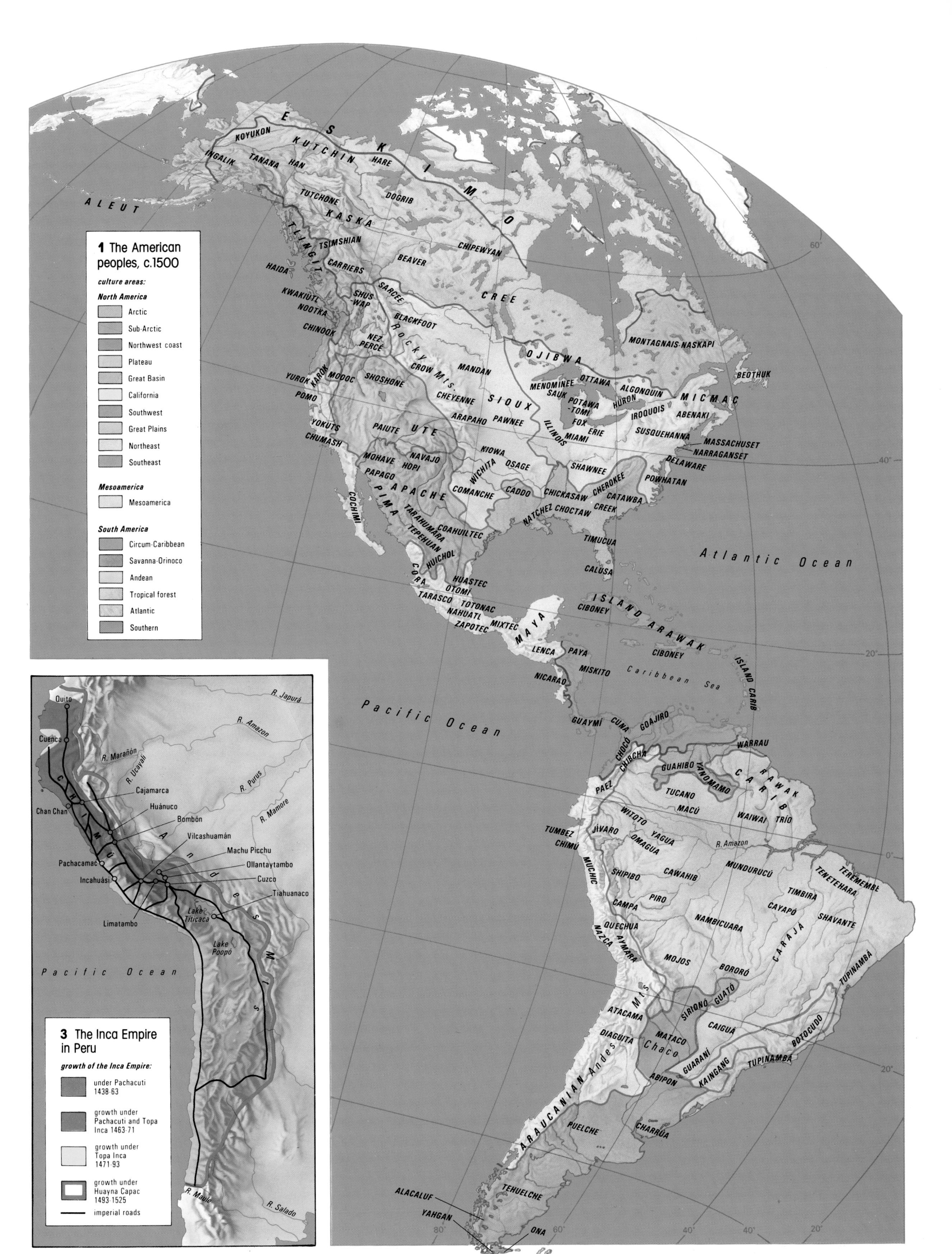
1 The American peoples, c.1500
culture areas:
North America
Arctic
Sub-Arctic
Northwest coast
Plateau
Great Basin
California
Southwest
Great Plains
Northeast
Southeast
Mesoamerica
Mesoamerica
South America
Circum-Caribbean
Savanna-Orinoco
Andean
Tropical forest
Atlantic
Southern
ESKIMO
KOYUKON
KUTCHIN
INGALIK
TANANA
HAN
HARE
ALEUT
TUTCHONE
DOGRIB
KASKA
TLINGIT
TSIMSHIAN
CHIPEWYAN
HAIDA
CARRIERS
BEAVER
KWAKIUTL
NOOTKA
SHUSWAP
SARCEE
CREE
CHINOOK
BLACKFOOT
NEZ PERCÉ
Rocky Mts.
MONTAGNAIS-NASKAPI
OJIBWA
CROW
MANDAN
BEOTHUK
YUROK
KAROK
MODOC
SHOSHONE
MENOMINEE
OTTAWA
ALGONQUIN
MICMAC
POMO
CHEYENNE
SIOUX
SAUK
POTAWATOMI
HURON
FOX
IROQUOIS
ABENAKI
ARAPAHO
PAWNEE
ILLINOIS
YOKUTS
PAIUTE
UTE
MIAMI
ERIE
SUSQUEHANNA
CHUMASH
MASSACHUSET
NARRAGANSET
KIOWA
MOHAVE
HOPI
NAVAJO
WICHITA
OSAGE
DELAWARE
SHAWNEE
PAPAGO
APACHE
POWHATAN
PIMA
COMANCHE
CADDO
CHICKASAW
CHEROKEE
CATAWBA
COCHIMI
TARAHUMARA
NATCHEZ
CHOCTAW
CREEK
TEPEHUAN
COAHUILTEC
TIMUCUA
HUICHOL
Atlantic Ocean
CALUSA
CORA
HUASTEC
OTOMÍ
TARASCO
TOTONAC
ISLAND ARAWAK
CIBONEY
NAHUATL
MIXTEC
ZAPOTEC
MAYA
LENCA
PAYA
CIBONEY
ISLAND CARIB
MISKITO
Caribbean Sea
NICARAO
Pacific Ocean
GUAYMÍ
CUNA
GOAJIRO
CHOCÓ
CHIBCHA
WARRAU
GUAHIBO
YANOMAMO
CARIB
ARAWAK
PAEZ
TUCANO
MACÚ
WAIWAI
TRÍO
WITOTO
TUMBEZ
CHIMÚ
JIVARO
YAGUA
OMAGUA
R. Amazon
MUNDURUCÚ
TEREMEMBÉ
TENETEHARA
MUCHIC
SHIPIBO
CAWAHIB
TIMBIRA
PIRO
CAYAPÓ
CAMPA
SHAVANTE
NAMBICUARA
QUECHUA
NAZCA
AYMARA
CARAJÁ
MOJOS
BORORÓ
TUPINAMBÁ
Mts
ATACAMA
SIRIONÓ
GUATÓ
MATACO
CAIGUÁ
DIAGUITA
Chaco
Andes
BOTOCUDO
GUARANÍ
KAINGANG
TUPINAMBÁ
ABIPON
ARAUCANIAN
PUELCHE
CHARRÚA
TEHUELCHE
ALACALUF
YAHGAN
ONA
60°
40°
20°
0°
80°
3 The Inca Empire in Peru
growth of the Inca Empire:
under Pachacuti 1438-63
growth under Pachacuti and Topa Inca 1463-71
growth under Topa Inca 1471-93
growth under Huayna Capac 1493-1525
imperial roads
Quito
R. Japurá
Cuenca
R. Amazon
R. Marañón
R. Ucayali
CHIMU
Cajamarca
R. Purus
Chan Chan
Huánuco
Bombón
R. Mamore
Vilcashuamán
Andes Mts
Machu Picchu
Pachacamac
Ollantaytambo
Incahuási
Cuzco
Tiahuanaco
Limatambo
Lake Titicaca
Lake Poopó
Pacific Ocean
R. Maule
R. Salado

European voyages of discovery
1487-1780

The European voyages of discovery opened a new era in world history. They began early in the fifteenth century when Portuguese navigators advanced southward, round the coast of Africa, in search of gold, slaves and spices, until in 1487 Dias and de Covilhã, brought them into the Indian Ocean (map 1). Thenceforth voyages of exploration multiplied, particularly after the resurgence of Islam made the old route to the east via Alexandria and the Red Sea precarious.

While the Portuguese explored the eastern route to Asia, the Spaniards sailed west. Once in the Indian Ocean the former quickly reached their goal: Malabar (1498), Malacca (1511), and the Moluccas (1512). The Spanish search for a western route to the Spice Islands was less successful. Its unintended but momentous result was Columbus' discovery of the New World in 1492 (map 2), followed by the Spanish conquest of America (page 68). But it was not until after 1524, when Verrazzano traced the coastline of North America as far north as Nova Scotia, that the existence of a new continent was generally accepted, and meanwhile the search for a western route to Asia continued, leading to extensive exploration of the Caribbean (map 3). Finally, in 1521, Magellan rounded South America, entered the Pacific, and reached the Philippines, but the route was too long and hazardous for commercial purposes. In 1557 the Portuguese occupied Macao, and after 1571 Spanish galleons traded between Manila and Acapulco in Mexico; but otherwise the exploration of the Pacific was delayed until the eighteenth century (map 4). This was the work of British, Dutch and Russians seeking a navigable passage via the Arctic between the Atlantic and the Pacific, and hoping also to locate a hypothetical southern continent. Both proved illusory; but the result was the charting of New Zealand and the eastern coast of Australia, both in a few years opened to European colonisation (page 112).

Meanwhile England and France, unwilling to recognise the monopoly claimed by Spain and Portugal in the Treaty of Tordesillas (1494), had embarked on a series of voyages intended to reach Asia by a northern route (map 2). All these proved abortive and were abandoned after 1632, but they resulted in the opening of North America to European settlement. The English, French and Dutch were also unwilling to abandon the profitable trade with South and South-East Asia to the Portuguese and Spaniards, and the later years of the sixteenth and first half of the seventeenth centuries saw a determined and ultimately successful effort to breach their privileged position (page 66). After 1500 direct sea contact was established between continents and regions which hitherto had gone their own way in isolation. It was necessarily a slow process, and for long the European footholds in Asia and Africa remained tenuous and precarious. But by the time of the death of the last great explorer, James Cook, in 1779, the worldwide network of relationships had been formed which characterises the modern era and differentiates it from all preceding times.

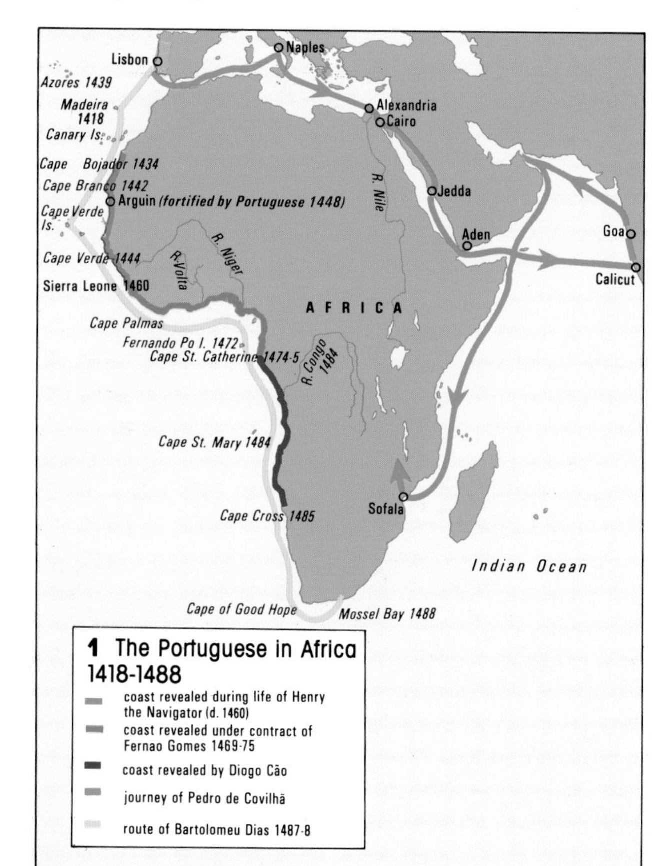

1 The Portuguese in Africa 1418-1488

Voyages intended for S. Asia by S.E. Route:
1/Dias 1487/88 (outward) discovered open water S. of Cape Agulhas; entered Indian Ocean; reached Great Fish River.
2/Vasco da Gama 1497–99 (outward) discovered best use of Atlantic winds on way to Cape of Good Hope; reached India, navigated by local pilot.
3/Cabral 1500 (outward) the second Portuguese voyage to India, sighted coast of Brazil at Monte Pascoal, probably accidentally.

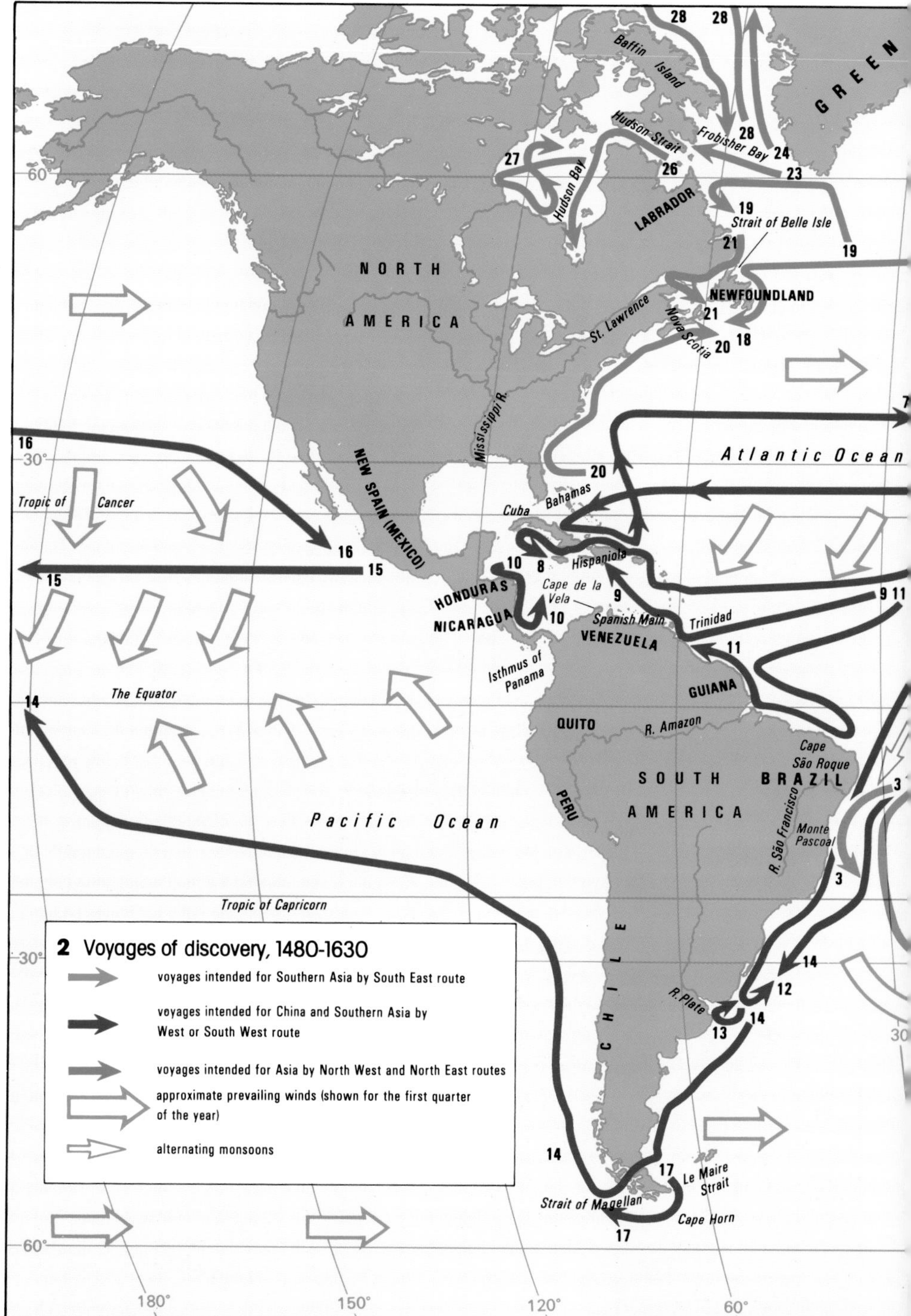

2 Voyages of discovery, 1480-1630

Voyages in the Caribbean:
29/Bastidas & La Cosa 1501–02 explored coast from Gulf of Maracaibo to Gulf of Urabá.
30/Pinzón & Solís 1508 sent from Spain to find strait to Asia, coasted E. coast of Yucatán.
31/Ponce de León 1512–13 sailed from Puerto Rico, explored coast of Florida from N. of Cape Canaveral to (possibly) Pensacola. May have sighted Yucatán on return. First explorer to note force of Gulf Stream.
32/Hernández de Córdoba 1516 sailed from Cuba, explored N. and W. coasts of Yucatán. First report of Mayan cities.
33/Grijalva 1517 followed S. and W. coasts of Gulf of Mexico as far as Pánuco River.
34/Pineda 1519 explored N. and W. coasts of Gulf of Mexico from Florida to Pánuco River. Finally ended hope of strait to Pacific in that region.

Voyages in the Pacific:
35/Roggeveen 1721–22 discovered Easter Island and some of the Samoan group. Circumnavigation.
36/Bering 1728 sailed from Kamchatka, discovered strait separating N.E. Asia from N.W. America.
37/Wallis 1766–68 discovered Society Islands (Tahiti), encouraged hope of habitable southern continent. Circumnavigation.
38/Cook 1768–71 charted coasts of New Zealand, explored E. coast of Australia, confirmed existence of Torres Strait. Circumnavigation.
39/Cook 1772–75 made circuit of southern oceans in high latitude, charted New Hebrides, ended hope of habitable southern continent. Circumnavigation.
40/Cook & Clerke 1776–80 discovered Sandwich Islands (Hawaii), explored coast of N. America from Vancouver to Unimak Pass, sailed through Bering Strait to edge of pack ice, ended hope of passage through Arctic to Atlantic.

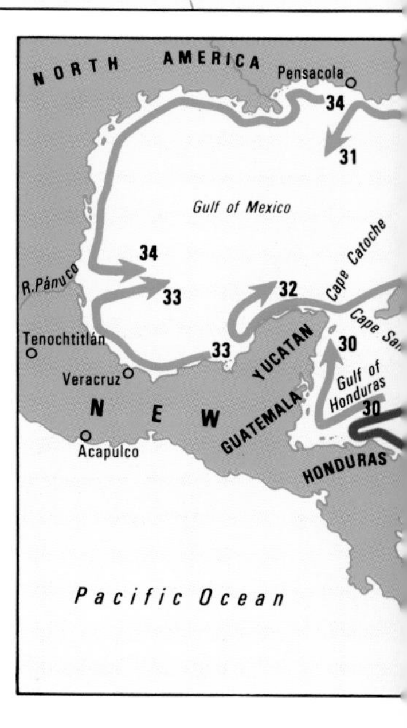

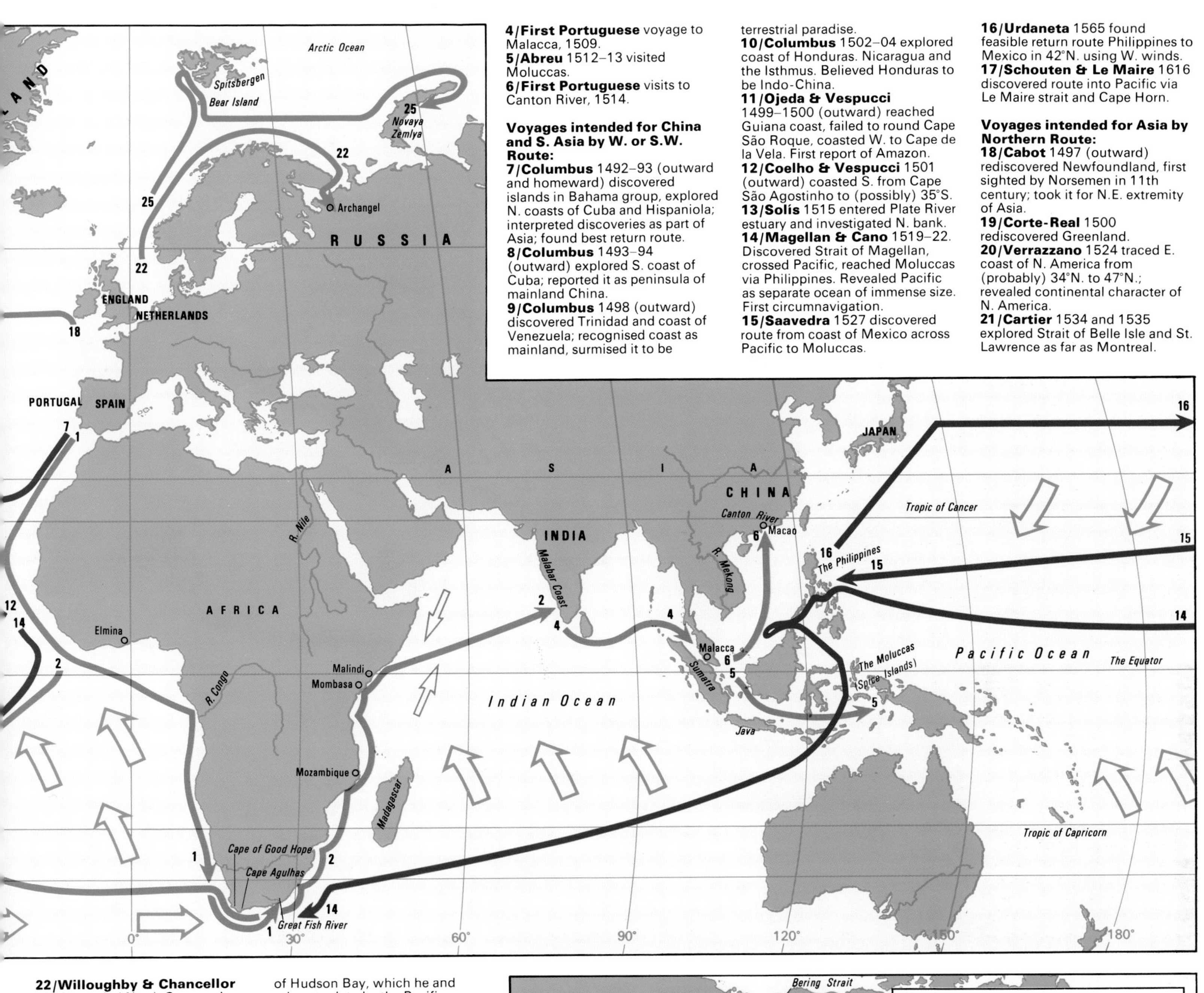

4/First Portuguese voyage to Malacca, 1509.
5/Abreu 1512–13 visited Moluccas.
6/First Portuguese visits to Canton River, 1514.

Voyages intended for China and S. Asia by W. or S.W. Route:
7/Columbus 1492–93 (outward and homeward) discovered islands in Bahama group, explored N. coasts of Cuba and Hispaniola; interpreted discoveries as part of Asia; found best return route.
8/Columbus 1493–94 (outward) explored S. coast of Cuba; reported it as peninsula of mainland China.
9/Columbus 1498 (outward) discovered Trinidad and coast of Venezuela; recognised coast as mainland, surmised it to be terrestrial paradise.
10/Columbus 1502–04 explored coast of Honduras. Nicaragua and the Isthmus. Believed Honduras to be Indo-China.
11/Ojeda & Vespucci 1499–1500 (outward) reached Guiana coast, failed to round Cape São Roque, coasted W. to Cape de la Vela. First report of Amazon.
12/Coelho & Vespucci 1501 (outward) coasted S. from Cape São Agostinho to (possibly) 35°S.
13/Solís 1515 entered Plate River estuary and investigated N. bank.
14/Magellan & Cano 1519–22. Discovered Strait of Magellan, crossed Pacific, reached Moluccas via Philippines. Revealed Pacific as separate ocean of immense size. First circumnavigation.
15/Saavedra 1527 discovered route from coast of Mexico across Pacific to Moluccas.
16/Urdaneta 1565 found feasible return route Philippines to Mexico in 42°N. using W. winds.
17/Schouten & Le Maire 1616 discovered route into Pacific via Le Maire strait and Cape Horn.

Voyages intended for Asia by Northern Route:
18/Cabot 1497 (outward) rediscovered Newfoundland, first sighted by Norsemen in 11th century; took it for N.E. extremity of Asia.
19/Corte-Real 1500 rediscovered Greenland.
20/Verrazzano 1524 traced E. coast of N. America from (probably) 34°N. to 47°N.; revealed continental character of N. America.
21/Cartier 1534 and 1535 explored Strait of Belle Isle and St. Lawrence as far as Montreal.
22/Willoughby & Chancellor 1553 rounded North Cape and reached Archangel.
23/Frobisher 1574 reached Frobisher Bay in Baffin Island, which he took for a 'strait'.
24/Davis 1587 explored W. coast of Greenland to the edge of the ice in 72°N.
25/Barents 1596–97 discovered Bear Island and Spitsbergen and wintered in Novaya Zemlya.
26/Hudson 1610 sailed through Hudson Strait to the S. extremity of Hudson Bay, which he and others took to be the Pacific.
27/Button 1612 explored W. coast of Hudson Bay, concluded Bay land-locked on the W.
28/Baffin & Bylot 1616 explored whole coastline of Baffin Bay and decided that no navigable N.W. passage existed in that area.

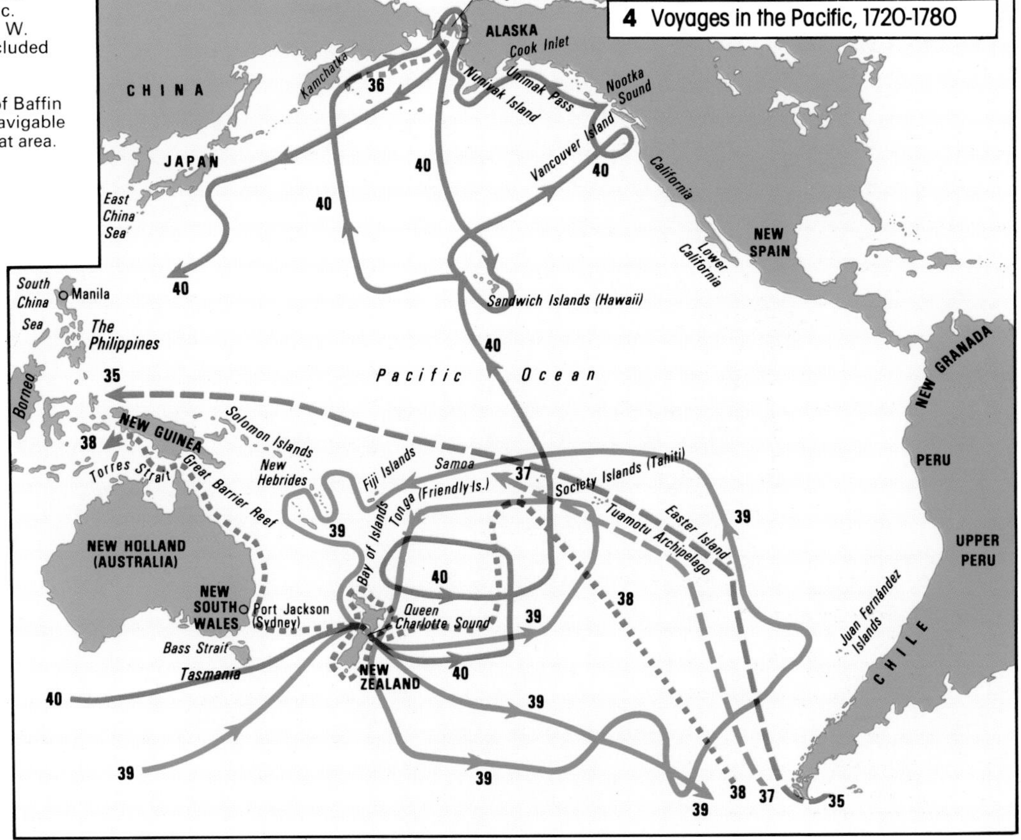

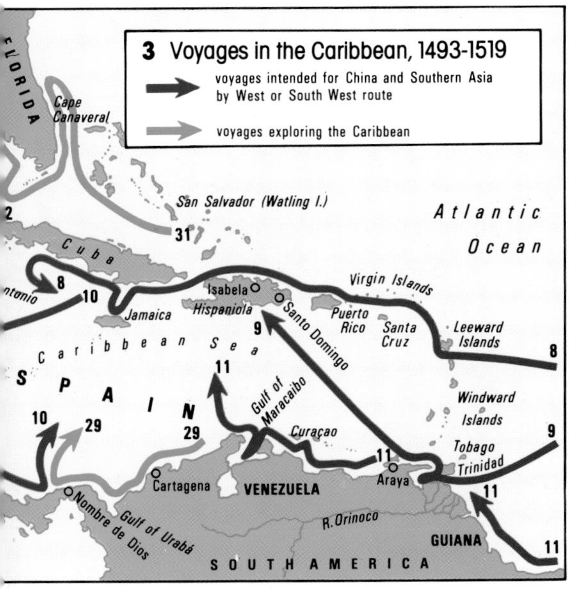

European expansion overseas, 1493-1713

The Portuguese were the first to exploit the European voyages of discovery. Theirs was essentially a trading empire, and by the middle of the sixteenth century they had more than fifty forts and factories reaching from Sofala on the Zambezi to Nagasaki in Japan (map 1). In 1557 they occupied Macao on the Chinese mainland. The Spaniards, on the other hand, set out on a deliberate policy of conquest and settlement, first in Hispaniola and, a decade or so later, in Mexico and Peru. The result was the foundation of the great Spanish colonial empire (page 68). But the Iberian preponderance did not go unchallenged. Particularly after the foundation of the English and Dutch East India Companies, in 1600 and 1602 respectively, Portuguese trade came under attack (map 2). With the acquisition of Batavia (1619) as an eastern headquarters and of the Cape of Good Hope (1652) as a station on the route to the east, Dutch commercial pre-eminence in Asian waters was assured.

While there was no direct attack on Spain's mainland empire the islands of the Caribbean, coveted as a prime source of sugar for the European market, became an object of intense rivalry and competition, in which all the leading powers engaged (map 4). Furthermore, whatever Spanish pretensions may have been, it was unable to make its presence felt much north of the Rio Grande. There was a slow advance in the west into California; but on the east coast Spanish power was limited to a tenuous foothold in Florida. Here the states of northern Europe, led by England and France, took the lead. France, in particular, advancing down the St. Lawrence estuary, penetrated deep into the interior, exploring the whole Mississippi valley (1682) and establishing fortified posts all the way to the Gulf of Mexico (map 3). The English, on the other hand, established a series of settlements along the eastern coast, beginning with Virginia in 1607. The clash of commercial and colonial interests which ensued ushered in the first age of imperial rivalry and conflict (page 86). Its prelude was the Anglo-Dutch wars of 1652–73 (page 80) which resulted in the British seizure (1664) of the Dutch settlement of New Amsterdam, subsequently renamed New York. It marked the decline of the Netherlands and the rise of England and France to the paramount position in the overseas world.

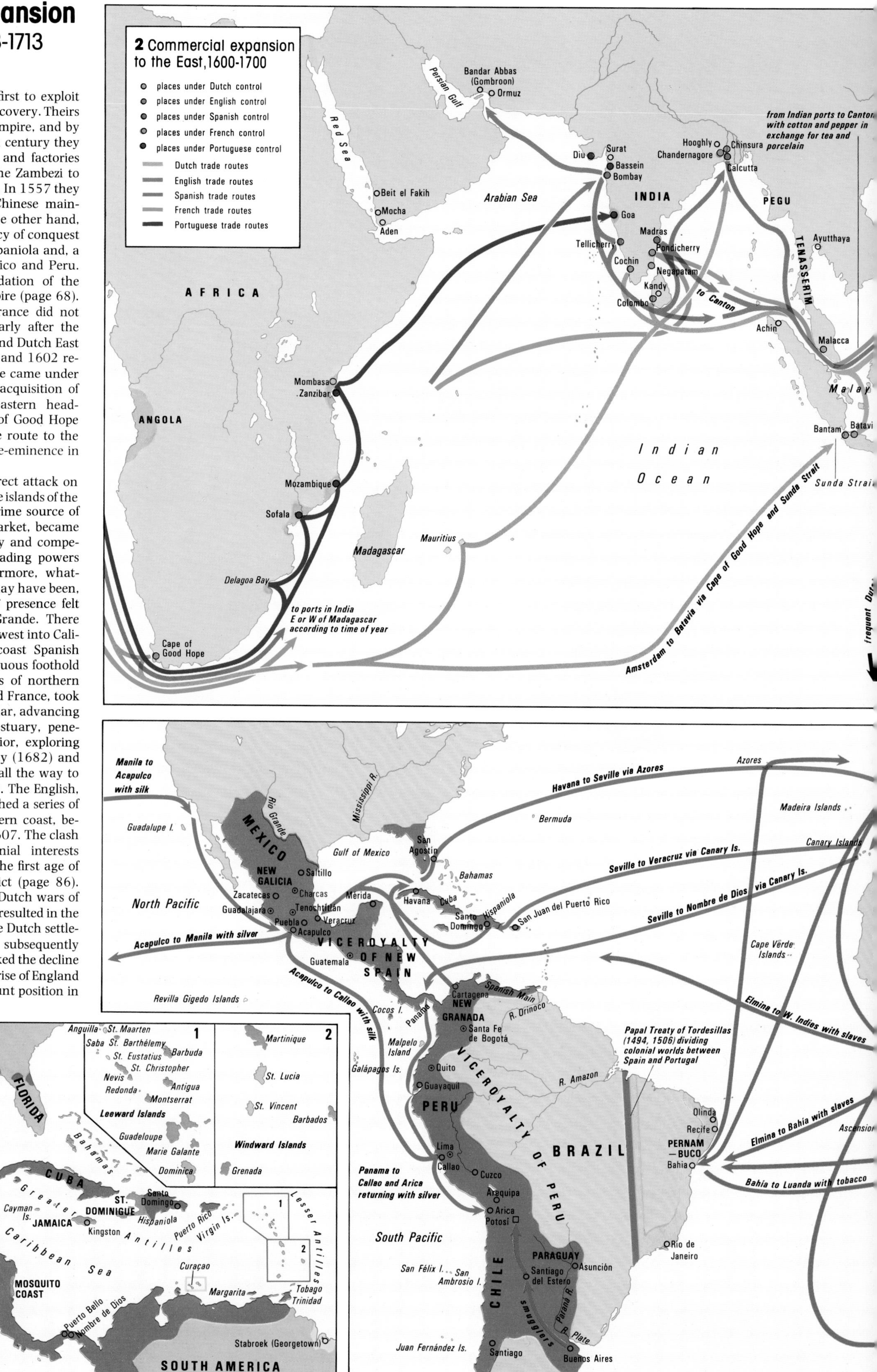

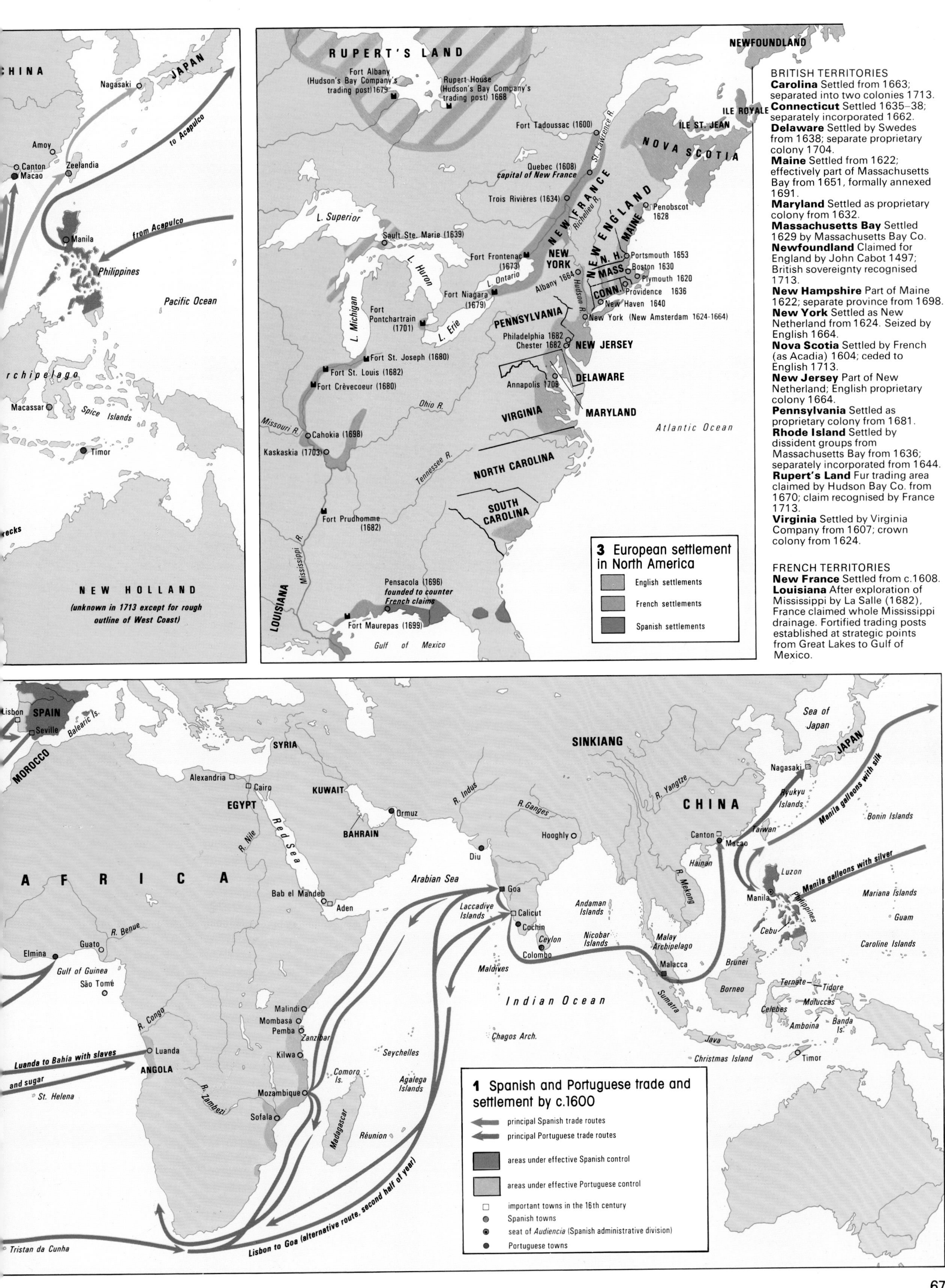

BRITISH TERRITORIES

Carolina Settled from 1663; separated into two colonies 1713.
Connecticut Settled 1635–38; separately incorporated 1662.
Delaware Settled by Swedes from 1638; separate proprietary colony 1704.
Maine Settled from 1622; effectively part of Massachusetts Bay from 1651, formally annexed 1691.
Maryland Settled as proprietary colony from 1632.
Massachusetts Bay Settled 1629 by Massachusetts Bay Co.
Newfoundland Claimed for England by John Cabot 1497; British sovereignty recognised 1713.
New Hampshire Part of Maine 1622; separate province from 1698.
New York Settled as New Netherland from 1624. Seized by English 1664.
Nova Scotia Settled by French (as Acadia) 1604; ceded to English 1713.
New Jersey Part of New Netherland; English proprietary colony 1664.
Pennsylvania Settled as proprietary colony from 1681.
Rhode Island Settled by dissident groups from Massachusetts Bay from 1636; separately incorporated from 1644.
Rupert's Land Fur trading area claimed by Hudson Bay Co. from 1670; claim recognised by France 1713.
Virginia Settled by Virginia Company from 1607; crown colony from 1624.

FRENCH TERRITORIES

New France Settled from c.1608.
Louisiana After exploration of Mississippi by La Salle (1682), France claimed whole Mississippi drainage. Fortified trading posts established at strategic points from Great Lakes to Gulf of Mexico.

Colonial America
1519-1783

The conquest of Mexico by Hernán Cortés in 1519–20 (map 1), and of Peru by Francisco Pizarro in 1531–33 (map 2), laid the foundations of the Spanish colonial empire in America. With the help of rebellious tribes, oppressed by their Aztec and Inca conquerors (page 62), both were amazingly successful. By 1535, when vice-regal government was set up in Mexico and Lima was founded as the capital of Peru, the first dramatic phase of conquest was over. By 1550 all the chief centres of settled population were in Spanish hands, though the task of pushing forward frontiers into unexplored territory continued until the end of the colonial period (map 3). New viceroyalties were set up in New Granada (1739) and Rio de la Plata (1776), and new military governments in Texas (1718) and California (1767). But none of the later, sparsely inhabited conquests compared with Mexico and Peru in wealth and importance. Potosí in Upper Peru and Zacatecas in Mexico became the biggest sources of silver in the world, and by 1560 silver was the chief export from the American colonies to Spain.

Elsewhere on the American mainland colonisation was slower to take effect. The Portuguese, on the eastern coast of South America, were only goaded into action by fear of the French. But in 1549 they founded Bahía as an administrative capital, and sugar plantations and mills, worked by slaves from Africa, were introduced. Between 1575 and 1600 coastal Brazil became the foremost sugar-producing territory in the western world, and attracted many land-hungry immigrants from Portugal and the Azores. But the vast Brazilian interior remained largely unexplored and in the hands of native Indian tribes (map 4). The same was true of the whole of North America at this date, beyond the frontier of New Spain. With its harsh climate and poor soil, the eastern seaboard of North America was uninviting territory, and for the first century after its discovery the great Newfoundland fisheries were its main attraction. There was also a fur trade with the natives, and by 1535 French explorers had penetrated far up the St. Lawrence river in the quest of skins and furs. When, after 1670, the English also built up a fur-trading empire, based on Hudson Bay (map 5), the result was a rivalry which erupted in the colonial wars of the eighteenth century (page 86). Nevertheless, fish and furs were the original staple of North America, and settlement, strongly opposed by fishing interests, only began in the seventeenth century, with the foundation of Acadia, or Nova Scotia, by the French in 1604, of Virginia (1607) and Massachusetts Bay (1629) by the English, and of New Netherland, later New York, by the Dutch in 1623. Even so, progress was slow. As late as the end of the seventeenth century, the total population of the twelve English colonies was a mere 250,000.

The pattern of settlement was also different in the north. The English colonists wanted land for farms and plantations, expelling or exterminating the native population. The history of the British colonies in the eighteenth century is punctuated by savage Indian wars. In Virginia, and later in the Carolinas, where tobacco was introduced as a cash-crop from Guiana, the plantations were worked by Negro slaves, numbering well over 100,000 by the time of the American War of Independence. The Spaniards, on the other hand, relied on Indian labour, both in ranching and mining, and readily intermarried; hence the extensive *mestizo* population, particularly in Mexico and Peru. At the same time, all the colonies were firmly administered in the interests of the mother country. This inevitably provoked resentment on the part of the colonial élites, and lay behind the demand for independence which erupted in the north in 1775 (page 92) and in Latin America in 1808 (page 96).

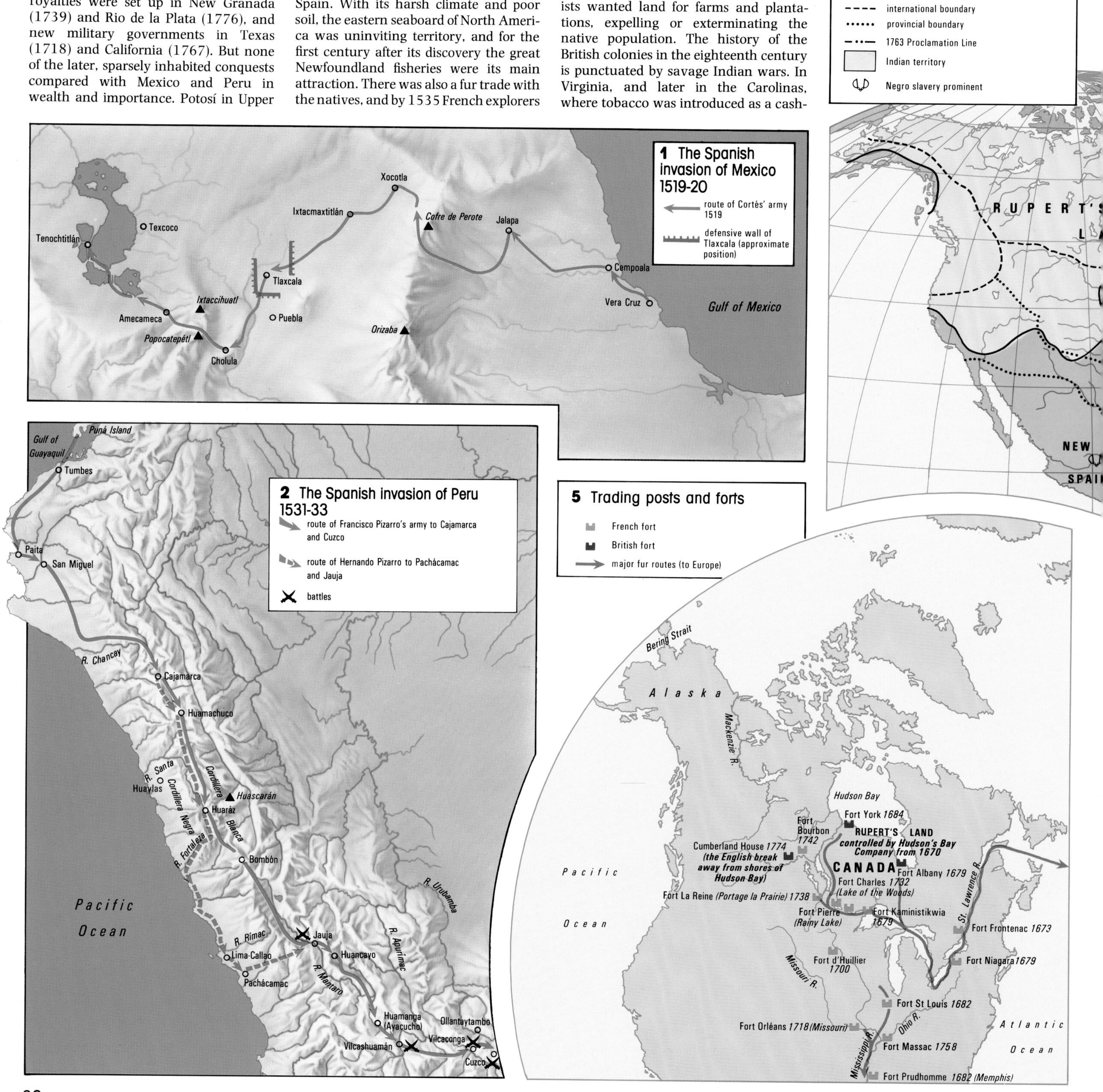

3 The development of colonial America
French territory
Spanish territory
Portuguese territory
Dutch territory
Russian territory
British by 1763
ceded by France to Britain 1763
ceded by France to Spain 1763
United States 1783
international boundary
provincial boundary
major exports
colonisation routes:
Spanish
Portuguese
British
Russian
French
Arctic Ocean
GREENLAND
unexplored
RUPERT'S LAND (Hudson's Bay Company)
Hudson Bay
disputed by Russia and Spain
furs
NEWFOUNDLAND
QUEBEC
St. Lawrence R.
ceded to Britain 1763
NOVA SCOTIA
whale products, fish
Quebec
Montreal
Boston
New York
Philadelphia
naval stores, furs, fish, grain
UNITED STATES OF AMERICA 1783
THE THIRTEEN COLONIES
Jamestown
Ohio R.
Mississippi R.
LOUISIANA
San Francisco
Los Angeles (1780)
INTERIOR PROVINCES
Rio Grande
North
tobacco, grain
WEST FLORIDA
New Orleans
skins
EAST FLORIDA (Br. 1763-83)
BAHAMA ISLANDS (Br. 1783)
sugar, tobacco
Gulf of Mexico
NEW SPAIN
Zacatecas
Mexico
silver
WEST INDIES
CUBA
Atlantic
SANTO DOMINGO
JAMAICA (Br. 1655)
SAINT-DOMINGUE
GUADELOUPE (Fr.)
MARTINIQUE (Fr.)
Belize (Br. 1683)
Caribbean Sea
CENTRAL AMERICA
cochineal, gold
gold
CURAÇAO (Dutch 1634)
Caracas
VENEZUELA
R. Orinoco
tobacco, cocoa beans, hides
Panama
Paramaribo
Cayenne
GUIANA
Pacific
Santa Fé de Bogotá
NEW GRANADA
drugs, rare plants
Ocean
Quito
gold, naval stores
R. Amazon
BRAZIL
Treaty of Tordesillas 1494, 1506
dyewoods, sugar, tobacco, cotton
Bahia
R. São Francisco
PERU
silver, drugs
Lima
Cuzco
UPPER PERU
Potosí
Paraguay R.
R. Paraná
gold, diamonds
Rio de Janeiro
copper, grain
beef
RIO DE LA PLATA 1776
CHILE
hides, silver
Buenos Aires
Indian frontier
South Atlantic Ocean
FALKLAND IS.
slave trade from Africa
Venezuela
NEW GRANADA
BRAZIL
PERU
RIO DE LA PLATA
CHILE
Spanish American population in 1800 (total 16.9 millions)
Whites 3.3
Negros 0.8
Indians 7.5
Mestizos 5.3
Population of the United States and Canada, 1820 (total 11.6 millions)
Whites 9.0
Mulattos 0.1
Negroes 1.9
Indians 0.6

South-East Asia, 1511-1826

When European traders and adventurers broke through into the Indian Ocean at the close of the fifteenth century (page 64), the great prize, drawing them forward, was the spices of South-East Asia. Here was untold wealth to be tapped. But here also, at one of the world's main crossroads, where cultural influences from China and India intermingled, they found themselves in a region of great complexity, divided in religion between Buddhism, Hinduism and Islam, and politically fragmented and unstable (map 1). On the mainland, rival peoples and dynasties competed for hegemony. In the Malayan archipelago the empires of Srivijaya and Majapahit (page 50) had disappeared, leaving behind scores of petty states, with little cohesion. This was the situation when Albuquerque conquered the great international emporium of Malacca for the king of Portugal in 1511.

The Portuguese presence changed little at first. Albuquerque and his successors were there to dominate the spice trade through a chain of fortified trading-stations, linked by naval power. Provided this was accepted, they had no wish to interfere with the native potentates. Far more important, after the arrival on the scene of the Dutch and English (page 66), was the challenge to their trading monopoly by their European rivals. For most of the seventeenth century this rivalry was the dominant factor (map 3). The Dutch, in particular, began a systematic conquest of the Portuguese settlements, capturing Malacca in 1641, and then turned against the British. But in doing so, they were inevitably drawn into local politics. After establishing a base at Batavia in 1619, they interfered in succession disputes among the neighbouring sultans, to ensure their own position, and in this way gradually extended control over Java, expelling the British from Bantam in 1682 (map 4). Already earlier they had driven them out of the Spice Islands by the 'massacre of Amboina' (1623) and the seizure of Macassar (1667), in this way forcing the English East India Company to turn instead to the China trade. With this in view the British acquired Penang on the west coast of Malaya in 1786, the first step in a process which was ultimately to make them masters of the Malay peninsula.

But this was still exceptional. European activities encroached on the outlying islands, but had little impact on the mainland monarchies, which had no direct interest in European trade and were mainly concerned with extending their power at the expense of their neighbours. This is a complicated story, because all the main centres were also under pressure from the hill peoples of the interior, always waiting to assert their independence; but the main lines of development are indicated on map 2. They include the advance of Annam at the expense of Cambodia, the rise of a new Burmese empire under Alaungpaya (1735–60), after a Mon rebellion in 1740, and successful Siamese resistance to Burmese encroachment, in spite of Burmese conquest in 1767. These events occurred for the most part without European involvement, but during the struggle for empire between England and France in the eighteenth century (page 86) some states were implicated. Already under Louis XIV France had intervened in Siam against the Dutch. During the Anglo-French war in India after 1746 it supported the Mon rebellion in Burma, and in reply the English East India Company seized the island of Negrais at the mouth of the Bassein river. Later, when the Burmese, foiled in their attempt to conquer Siam, switched their efforts to the north, the British, fearing for the security of Bengal, again intervened. The result was the first Anglo-Burmese war (1824–26) and the British annexation of Assam, Arakan and Tenasserim.

In Malaya there was similar encroachment on the independent rulers when the British, after acquiring Penang in 1786, established Singapore in 1819 as a free trade port after its acquisition by Raffles. This led to a conflict of interests with Holland which was only settled by the Anglo-Dutch treaty of 1824 when the British withdrew from Sumatra in return for Dutch withdrawal from Malacca (map 5). The future Dutch and British colonial empires in South-East Asia were taking shape. But their control was still loose and indirect. Only after the Industrial Revolution in Europe, and the expanding demand for raw materials and markets, were the lives and fortunes of the peoples of the region seriously affected.

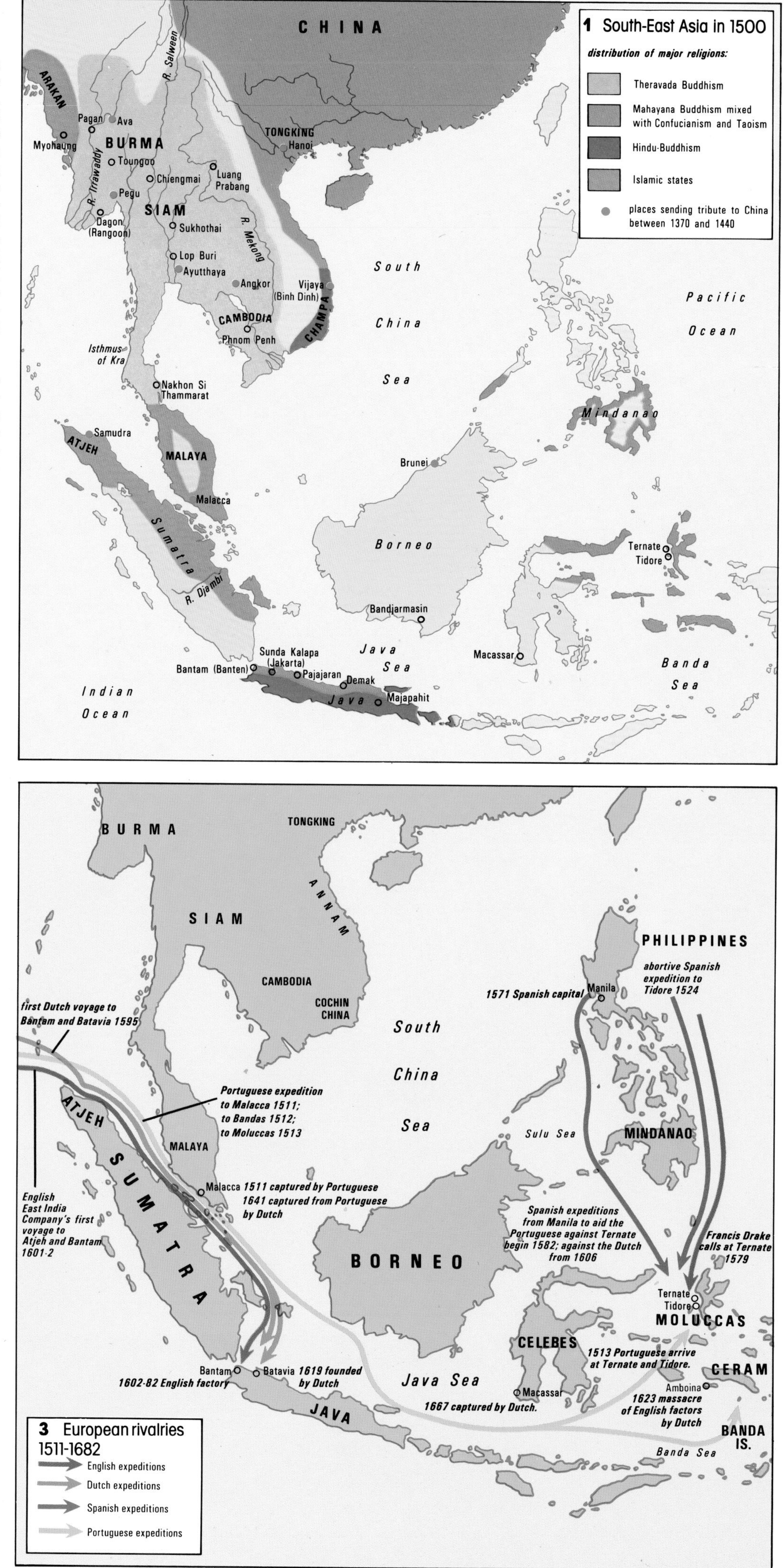

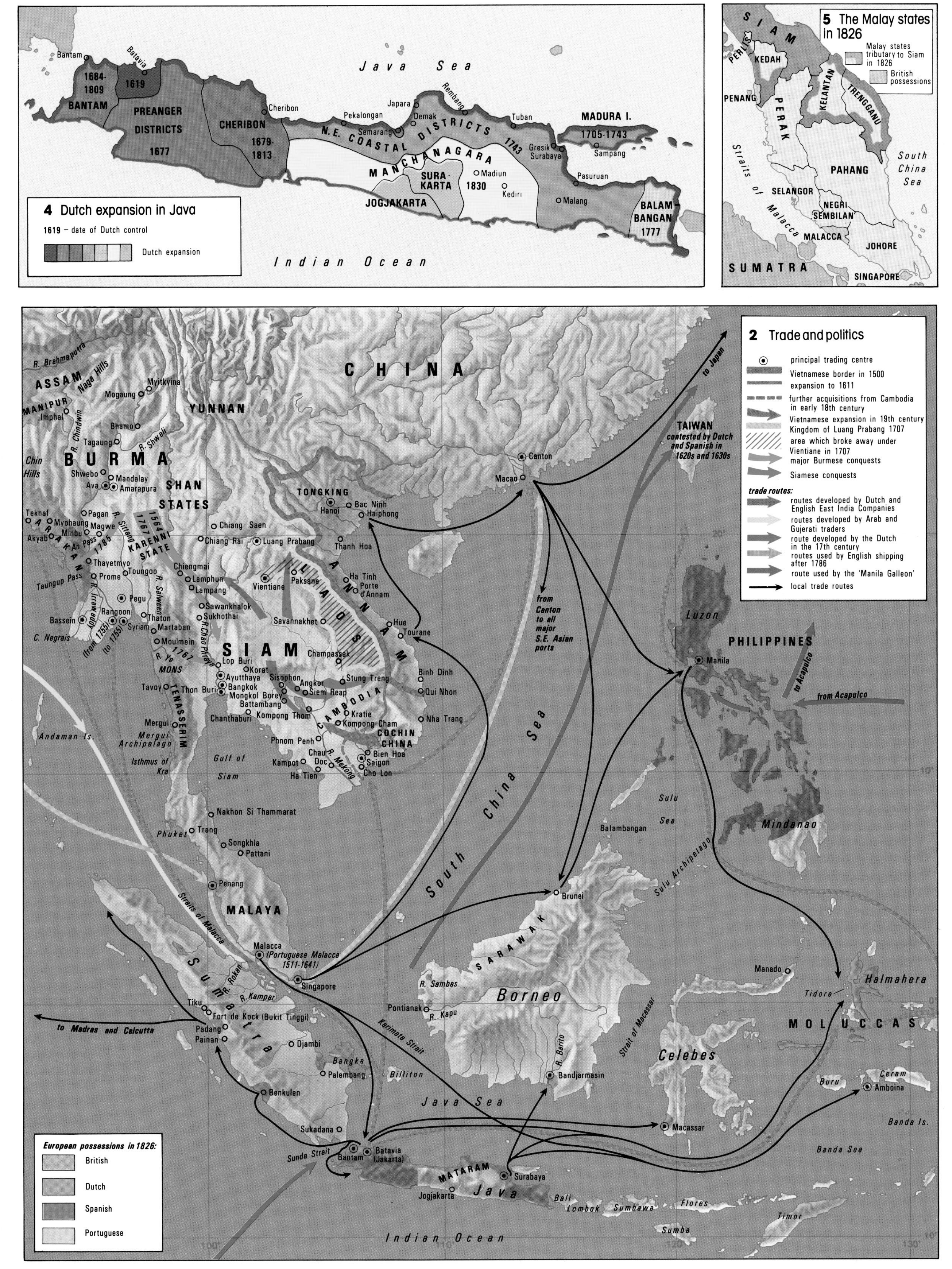

4 Dutch expansion in Java
1619 – date of Dutch control
Dutch expansion
Java Sea
Indian Ocean
Bantam
Batavia
1619
1684-1809
BANTAM
PREANGER DISTRICTS 1677
CHERIBON 1679-1813
Cheribon
Pekalongan
Japara
Rembang
Demak
Semarang
N.E. COASTAL DISTRICTS 1743
Tuban
MADURA I. 1705-1743
Sampang
Gresik
Surabaya
MANCHANAGARA
SURAKARTA
Madiun
1830
Kediri
JOGJAKARTA
Pasuruan
Malang
BALAMBANGAN 1777
5 The Malay states in 1826
Malay states tributary to Siam in 1826
British possessions
SIAM
PERLIS
KEDAH
KELANTAN
TRENGGANU
PENANG
PERAK
PAHANG
SELANGOR
NEGRI SEMBILAN
MALACCA
JOHORE
SINGAPORE
SUMATRA
Straits of Malacca
South China Sea
2 Trade and politics
principal trading centre
Vietnamese border in 1500
expansion to 1611
further acquisitions from Cambodia in early 18th century
Vietnamese expansion in 19th century
Kingdom of Luang Prabang 1707
area which broke away under Vientiane in 1707
major Burmese conquests
Siamese conquests
trade routes:
routes developed by Dutch and English East India Companies
routes developed by Arab and Gujerati traders
route developed by the Dutch in the 17th century
routes used by English shipping after 1786
route used by the 'Manila Galleon'
local trade routes
CHINA
YUNNAN
ASSAM
MANIPUR
BURMA
SHAN STATES
KARENNI STATE
ARAKAN
SIAM
LAOS
ANNAM
TONGKING
CAMBODIA
COCHIN CHINA
MONS
TENASSERIM
MALAYA
TAIWAN contested by Dutch and Spanish in 1620s and 1630s
PHILIPPINES
Luzon
Mindanao
Borneo
SARAWAK
Celebes
MOLUCCAS
Halmahera
Sumatra
Java
MATARAM
from Canton to all major S.E. Asian ports
to Japan
to Acapulco
from Acapulco
to Madras and Calcutta
South China Sea
Gulf of Siam
Sulu Sea
Java Sea
Banda Sea
Indian Ocean
Canton
Macao
Manila
Malacca (Portuguese Malacca 1511-1641)
Singapore
Batavia (Jakarta)
Bantam
Surabaya
Jogjakarta
Macassar
Amboina
Bandjarmasin
Brunei
Penang
Benkulen
Palembang
Hanoi
Luang Prabang
Vientiane
Ava
Amarapura
Mandalay
Pegu
Bassein
Rangoon
Syriam
Ayutthaya
Bangkok
Saigon
Bien Hoa
Cho Lon
European possessions in 1826:
British
Dutch
Spanish
Portuguese

New monarchy in Europe, 1453-1547

In Europe revival after the setbacks of the fourteenth century (page 56) began around 1450. The whole continent was affected. In the east Ivan III (1462–1505) profited from the decline of the Mongol khanates (page 46) to inaugurate a rapid expansion of the territory of Muscovy (page 84) and to attack the independence of Tver, Novgorod and the landowning aristocracy. In the west endemic civil war in Spain was ended after the union of Castile and Aragon in 1479. The ending of the Hundred Years' War between England and France (1453) and the expulsion of the English from French territory saw a rapid extension of the area controlled by the French monarchy (map 2), while in England Edward IV (1461–83) began a restoration of royal power which was carried further by the new Tudor dynasty after 1485. Through the Council in the North with its seat at York, and the Council in the March of Wales, with its seat at Ludlow, the turbulent outlying regions were brought under control, while Wales itself and the palatinates of Chester and Durham were integrated into the parliamentary and judicial systems from 1536 (map 4). But an attempt to integrate Ireland by Poynings' Law (1494) had little effect, and although Henry VIII was proclaimed King of Ireland (1541), English power was effectively limited to the Pale around Dublin. Scotland also resisted successfully.

Not all attempts at state-building were a success. The efforts of the dukes of Burgundy to erect an independent state in the rich lands between France and the Empire collapsed when the ambitious Charles the Bold was killed at Nancy in 1477 (map 3). The empire of Matthias Corvinus of Hungary (1458–90) also proved ephemeral. Italy remained divided, in spite of a marked strengthening of government under rulers such as Lorenzo de' Medici (1469–92) at Florence and Ludovico Sforza (1460–99) at Milan (map 5), and after the French invasion of 1494 internal divisions left Italy a prey to foreign intervention. The main legatee in all instances was the house of Habsburg, which succeeded to the Spanish possessions in 1516 and emerged, under Charles V (1519–56) as the preponderant power in western Europe (map 1). But the diversified Habsburg empire lacked cohesion, and when the Ottoman advance, halted on the middle Danube since 1456, was resumed after 1520 (page 48), and at the same time the emperor was involved in the religious wars in Germany (page 74), the strain was too great. In 1556 Charles V abdicated and the empire was divided between the Austrian and Spanish Habsburgs. Only ten years later the Dutch revolt began.

The Dutch revolt, although the most formidable uprising (page 76), was not exceptional. In England, from Henry VII to Elizabeth I, the Tudors were faced by repeated rebellions, and elsewhere, even in Russia, resistance to centralisation became a powerful force after 1550. The rise of the new monarchies was less a new beginning than the culmination of the long struggle of aristocracy and monarchy. Their financial and administrative machinery was not enough to raise a modern system of government in place of the feudal order, and the decisive change from the old to the new was not made until after another century of strife and turmoil.

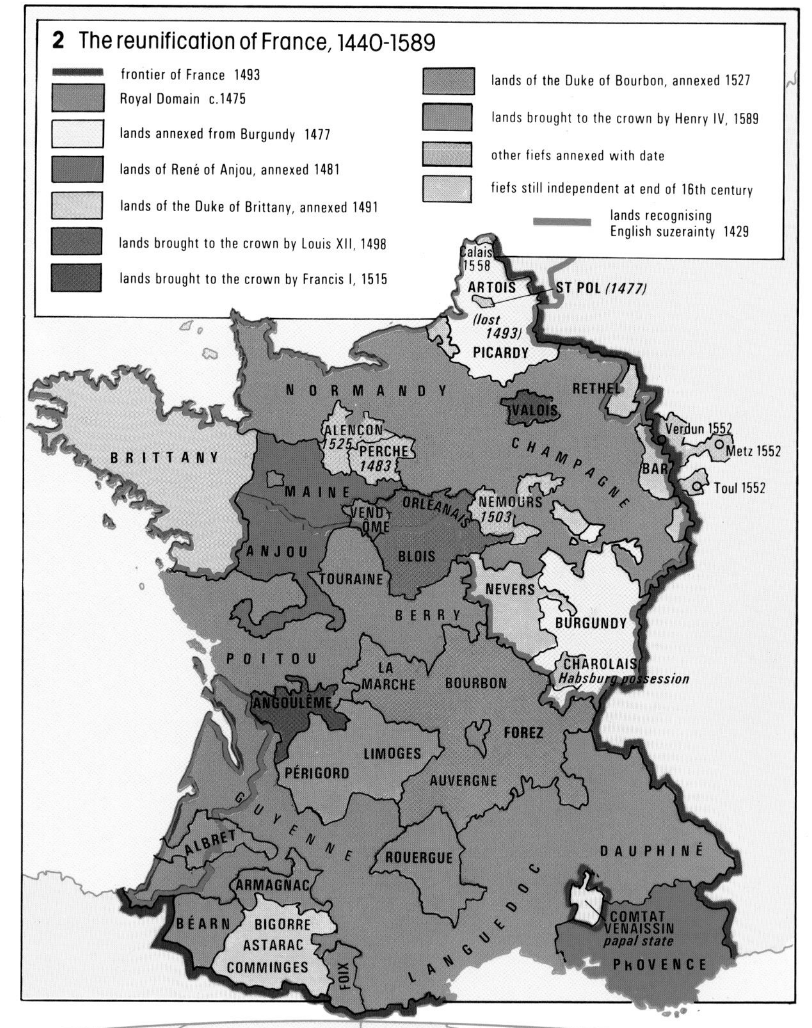

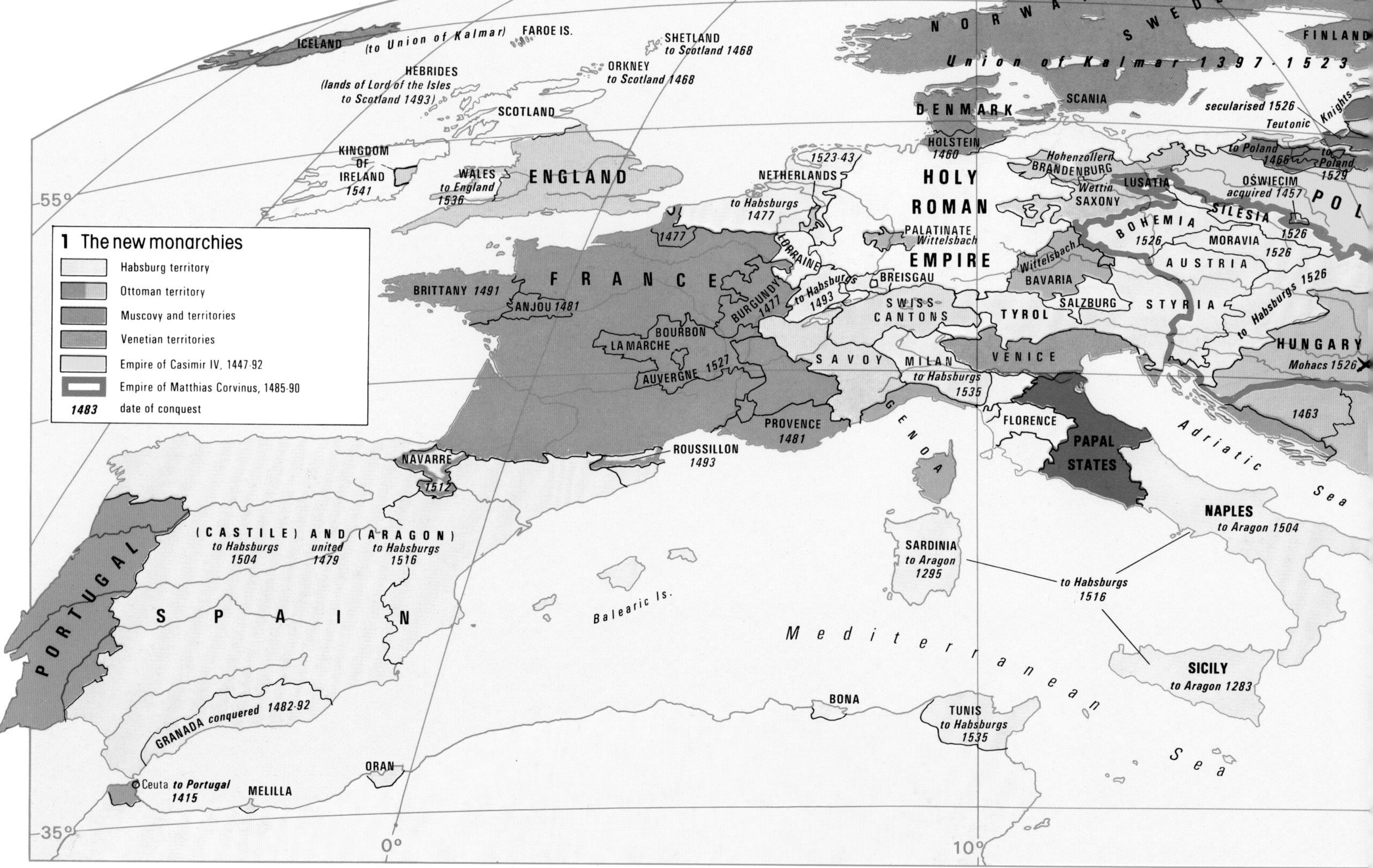

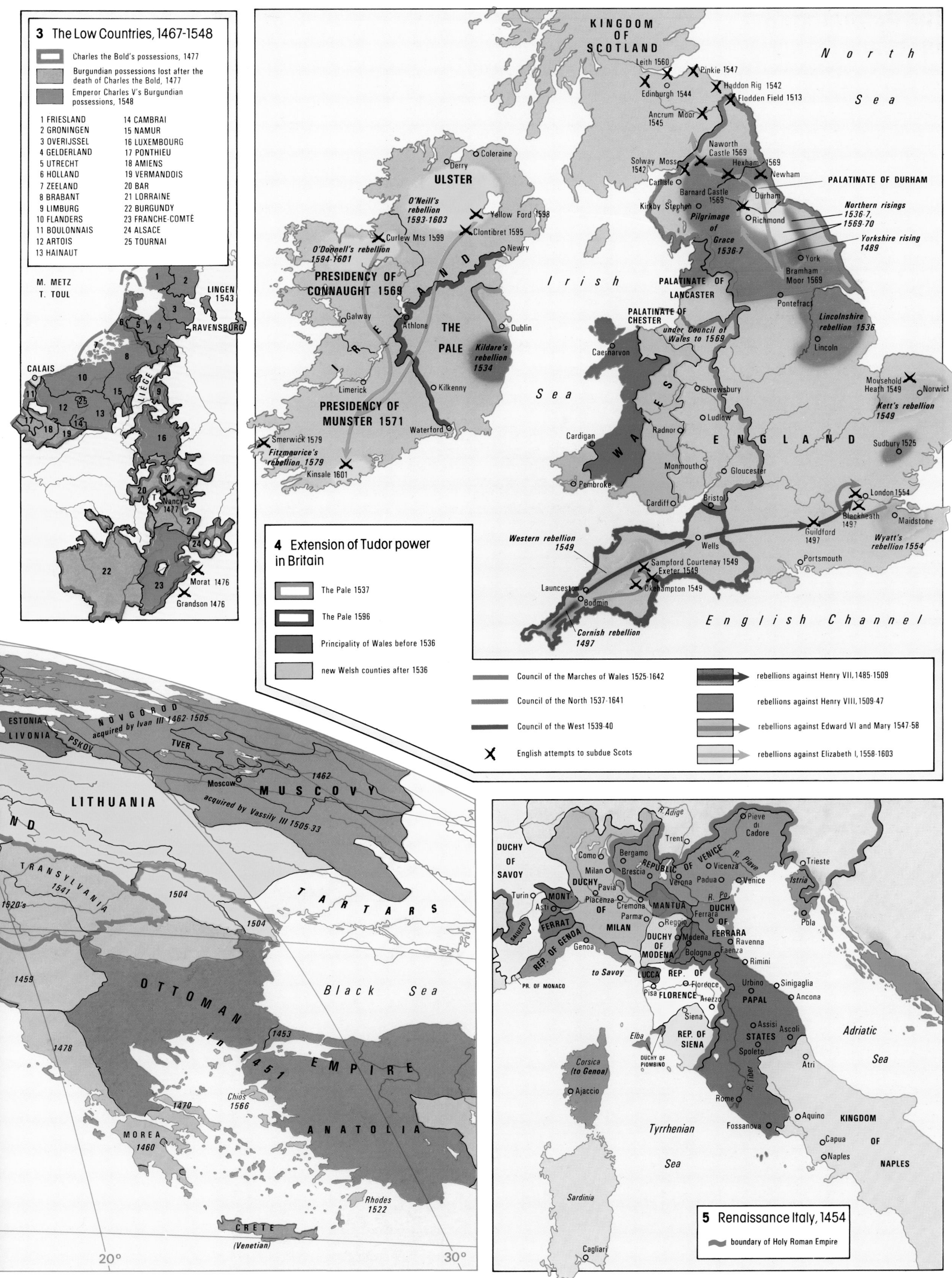
3 The Low Countries, 1467-1548
Charles the Bold's possessions, 1477
Burgundian possessions lost after the death of Charles the Bold, 1477
Emperor Charles V's Burgundian possessions, 1548
1 FRIESLAND
2 GRONINGEN
3 OVERIJSSEL
4 GELDERLAND
5 UTRECHT
6 HOLLAND
7 ZEELAND
8 BRABANT
9 LIMBURG
10 FLANDERS
11 BOULONNAIS
12 ARTOIS
13 HAINAUT
14 CAMBRAI
15 NAMUR
16 LUXEMBOURG
17 PONTHIEU
18 AMIENS
19 VERMANDOIS
20 BAR
21 LORRAINE
22 BURGUNDY
23 FRANCHE-COMTÉ
24 ALSACE
25 TOURNAI
M. METZ
T. TOUL
LINGEN 1543
RAVENSBURG
CALAIS
LIÈGE
Nancy 1477
Morat 1476
Grandson 1476
4 Extension of Tudor power in Britain
The Pale 1537
The Pale 1596
Principality of Wales before 1536
new Welsh counties after 1536
Council of the Marches of Wales 1525-1642
Council of the North 1537-1641
Council of the West 1539-40
English attempts to subdue Scots
rebellions against Henry VII, 1485-1509
rebellions against Henry VIII, 1509-47
rebellions against Edward VI and Mary 1547-58
rebellions against Elizabeth I, 1558-1603
KINGDOM OF SCOTLAND
North Sea
Irish Sea
English Channel
Leith 1560
Pinkie 1547
Haddon Rig 1542
Edinburgh 1544
Flodden Field 1513
Ancrum Moor 1545
Naworth Castle 1569
Solway Moss 1542
Hexham 1569
Newham
Carlisle
PALATINATE OF DURHAM
Barnard Castle 1569
Durham
Kirkby Stephen
Richmond
Pilgrimage of Grace 1536-7
Northern risings 1536-7, 1569-70
Yorkshire rising 1489
York
Bramham Moor 1569
PALATINATE OF LANCASTER
Pontefract
PALATINATE OF CHESTER
under Council of Wales to 1569
Lincolnshire rebellion 1536
Lincoln
Caernarvon
Shrewsbury
Mousehold Heath 1549
Norwich
Kett's rebellion 1549
Ludlow
WALES
ENGLAND
Cardigan
Radnor
Sudbury 1525
Monmouth
Gloucester
Pembroke
Cardiff
Bristol
London 1554
Blackheath 1497
Maidstone
Guildford 1497
Wyatt's rebellion 1554
Western rebellion 1549
Wells
Portsmouth
Sampford Courtenay 1549
Exeter 1549
Launceston
Bodmin
Okehampton 1549
Cornish rebellion 1497
Derry
Coleraine
ULSTER
O'Neill's rebellion 1593-1603
Yellow Ford 1598
Clontibret 1595
Curlew Mts 1599
O'Donnell's rebellion 1594-1601
Newry
PRESIDENCY OF CONNAUGHT 1569
Galway
Athlone
IRELAND
THE PALE
Dublin
Kildare's rebellion 1534
Limerick
Kilkenny
PRESIDENCY OF MUNSTER 1571
Waterford
Smerwick 1579
Fitzmaurice's rebellion 1579
Kinsale 1601
ESTONIA
LIVONIA
PSKOV
NOVGOROD acquired by Ivan III 1462-1505
TVER
1462
Moscow
MUSCOVY
acquired by Vassily III 1505-33
LITHUANIA
TRANSYLVANIA 1541
1520's
1504
TARTARS
1459
OTTOMAN EMPIRE in 1451
Black Sea
1453
1478
Chios 1566
1470
ANATOLIA
MOREA 1460
Rhodes 1522
CRETE (Venetian)
20°
30°
5 Renaissance Italy, 1454
boundary of Holy Roman Empire
R. Adige
Pieve di Cadore
Trent
DUCHY OF SAVOY
Como
Bergamo
REPUBLIC OF VENICE
R. Piave
Vicenza
Trieste
Milan
Brescia
Verona
Padua
Venice
Istria
Turin
DUCHY OF MILAN
Pavia
R. Po
Asti
MONTFERRAT
Piacenza
Cremona
MANTUA
DUCHY OF FERRARA
Parma
Ferrara
Pola
SALUZZO
Reggio
REP. OF GENOA
Genoa
DUCHY OF MODENA
Modena
Ravenna
Bologna
Faenza
Rimini
to Savoy
LUCCA
REP. OF FLORENCE
PR. OF MONACO
Florence
Urbino
Sinigaglia
Pisa
Arezzo
PAPAL STATES
Ancona
Siena
Elba
REP. OF SIENA
Assisi
Ascoli
Adriatic Sea
DUCHY OF PIOMBINO
Spoleto
Atri
Corsica (to Genoa)
R. Tiber
Ajaccio
Rome
Aquino
KINGDOM OF NAPLES
Fossanova
Tyrrhenian Sea
Capua
Naples
Sardinia
Cagliari

The Reformation in Europe, 1517-1648

The closing years of the fifteenth century saw a great revival of popular religion in Europe, but the established church, which never fully recovered from the effects of the schism of 1378–1417 (page 56), was ill equipped to satisfy its needs. Except in Bohemia and Moravia, where the Hussites comprised over half the population, and in England, where small groups of Lollards survived, heresy was virtually dead by 1500; but the materialism of the Renaissance popes and the self-seeking of the higher clergy discredited the hierarchy in the eyes of many laymen. Some, like Erasmus of Rotterdam (1466–1536) and Sir Thomas More (1478–1535), still pinned their hopes on spiritual renewal; but elsewhere, particularly in Germany and German-speaking Switzerland, financial and other abuses fired revolt. In 1517 Martin Luther (1483–1546) posted his 95 theses on the church door at Wittenberg. In 1520, under the impulse of Huldreich Zwingli (1484–1531), Zurich renounced allegiance to Rome. Their denunciations of the clergy and the supremacy of the pope and their demand for a return to the standards of early Christianity exercised a vast appeal. By 1560 (map 1) seven out of ten of the Emperor's subjects were Protestants, and the reformed faith prevailed in Scandinavia, Baltic Europe and England. Further impetus came from the teaching of John Calvin (1509–64). In France over one hundred Calvinist churches existed by 1559 and perhaps 700 by 1562, and Calvinism also made rapid progress in Poland, Hungary and Scotland, where it became the official religion in 1560. In addition, a number of more radical sects

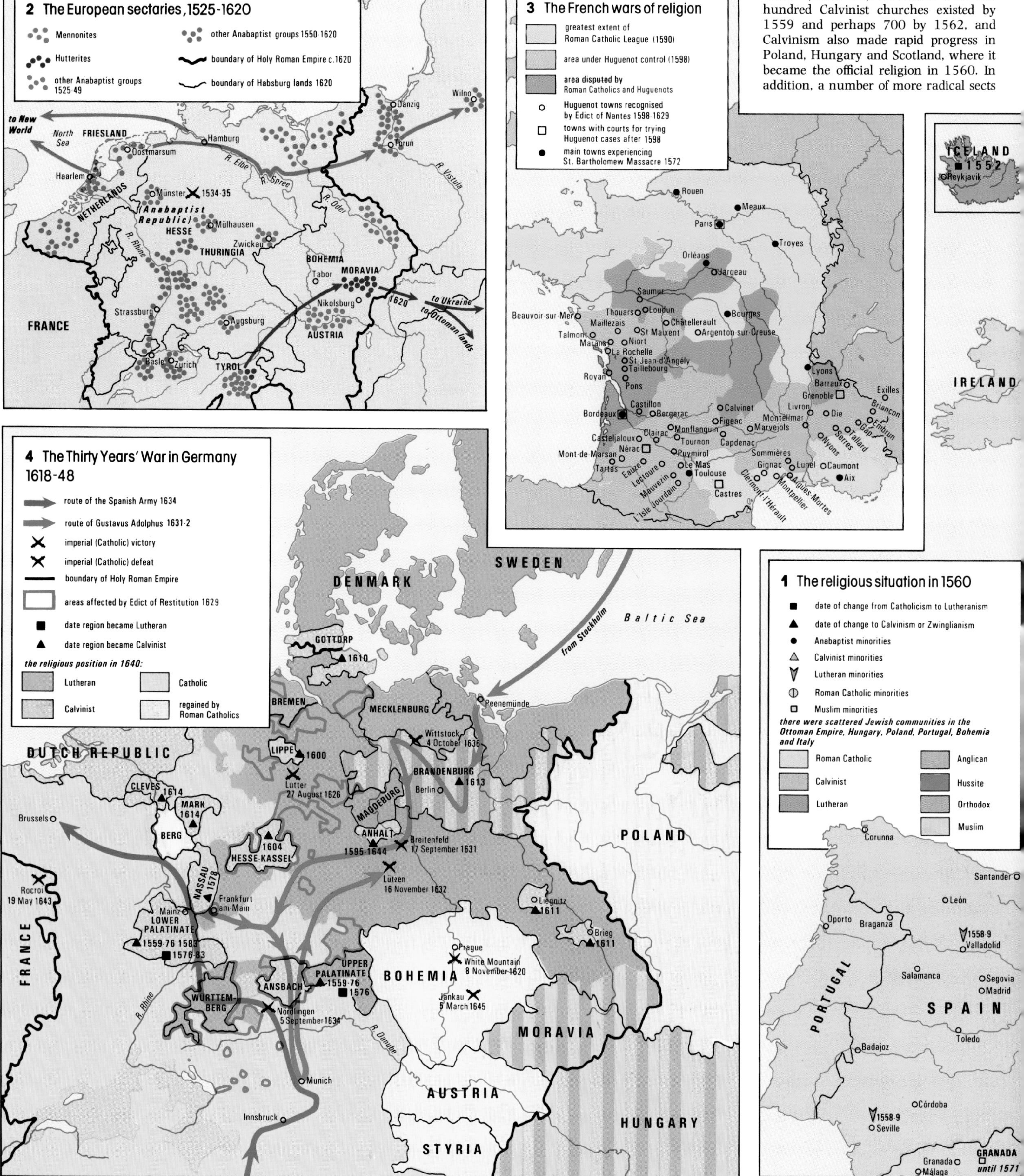

sprang up, Anabaptists, Mennonites and others (map 2), which rejected theology, ritual and clerical order in favour of Biblical simplicity and often combined evangelism with social protest. They even proclaimed an Anabaptist republic at Münster in 1534, but it was brutally suppressed the next year.

However, the Reformation was soon entangled in politics. Princes and kings, including Henry VIII of England, saw an opportunity to despoil the church of its wealth. Some German princes espoused Protestantism out of fear of imperial power. Luther himself, dependent on princely support, turned against the more radical sectaries and condemned the peasants' revolt of 1525. Foreign policy also played a part. The Valois kings of France, though combating the protestant Huguenots at home, supported the German Protestant princes against the Habsburg emperor. Although the French Huguenots won toleration by the Edict of Nantes (1598), their numbers were severely reduced during the religious wars between 1562 and 1598 (map 3), and elsewhere in Europe the second half of the sixteenth century saw a great Catholic revival, led by the Jesuit Order, founded in 1534 by St. Ignatius Loyola (1491–1556), and inspired by the reforms of the Council of Trent between 1545 and 1563. Using the Jesuits as their spearhead, Catholic rulers went over to the offensive. Protestants were expelled from Bavaria (1579) and Styria (1600), and in Poland the number of Protestant churches decreased from 560 in 1572 to 240 in 1650.

The decisive phase of the struggle between Protestants and Catholics, the Thirty Years' War, took place in the Holy Roman Empire (map 4). It began in 1618–21 when the emperor Ferdinand II defeated the Bohemian Protestants at the battle of the White Mountain (1620) and won back Bohemia and Moravia for Catholicism. When he turned against the Protestant princes of Germany, Denmark, England and the Dutch intervened on the Protestant side, but the imperial forces were initially successful and in 1629 an Edict of Restitution was promulgated which reclaimed large areas of church lands held by Protestant princes. Only the intervention of Gustavus Adolphus of Sweden saved the Protestant cause from collapse. But the Swedish victories at Breitenfeld (1631) and Lützen (1632) brought in Spain on the imperial side, while France allied with Sweden and declared war on Spain (1635). The war was now a struggle in which it seemed that neither side could hope for outright victory, until in 1648 the Peace of Westphalia brought a compromise solution. Lutherans and Calvinists retained the lands they held in 1624, and the wars of religion were over. But Germany, the scene of battle, suffered a lasting setback.

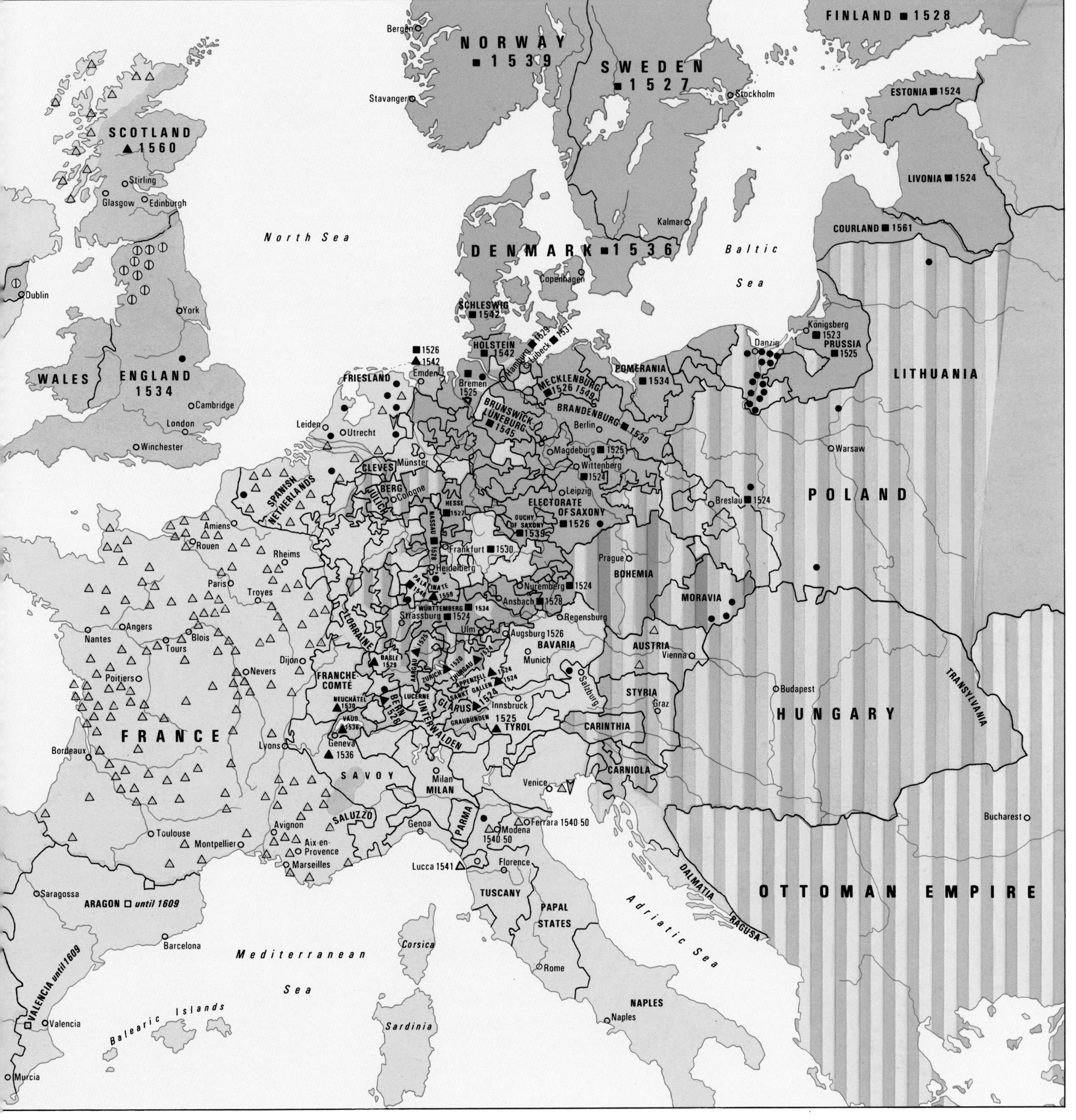

Western Europe, 1558-1648

The second half of the sixteenth and the first half of the seventeenth centuries were a time of turbulence throughout Europe. In Russia the 'time of troubles' after the death of Ivan the Terrible (1584) lasted until 1613. Northern Europe was embroiled in almost continuous war from 1561 to 1658, as Sweden, independent since the time of Gustavus Vasa (1523–60), struggled with Denmark, Russia, Poland and Brandenburg for control of the Baltic and its important trade. The rise of the Swedish empire (map 3), leading to Gustavus Adolphus' intervention in the Thirty Years' War (page 74) and the Swedish acquisition of western Pomerania, Wismar and the bishoprics of Bremen and Verden at the Peace of Westphalia, vitally affected the balance of power in Europe and was one of the most significant developments of the period. In western Europe developments were more confused. The new monarchies of the preceding period (page 72) had over-reached themselves, and from around 1530 reaction set in, particularly when rising prices, recession and widespread unemployment reinforced existing discontents. The Elizabethan Poor Law and other legislation of 1563 was no remedy; indeed, the reign of Elizabeth I (1558–1603), was less auspicious than often painted, and Elizabeth, whose relations with parliament deteriorated sharply at the end of her reign, left her Stuart successors on the English throne a legacy of unsolved problems with which they failed to cope.

From around 1530, sometimes earlier, the history of France and England was punctuated by revolts. As in Germany (page 74), they reflected a combination of religious, social and political grievances. In England the northern risings of 1536 and 1569 (page 72) were Catholic protests against the suppression of the old faith, but they also embodied the resistance of the northern gentry to centralisation and control from London. On the other wing the unrest of radical dissenters combined dissatisfaction with Henry VIII's and Elizabeth's conservative church settlements with resistance to the enclosure of common lands for the benefit of grasping landlords. A similar mixture of motives permeated the frequent uprisings, 500 in all, in France (map 2). These were largely revolts of the common people, driven to extremes by economic hardship; but in the end the most influential factor, visible in France in the revolt of the judges and nobility which drove the king from Paris in 1649, was resistance to autocracy, centralisation and taxation. The Dutch revolt, which began in the North Netherlands in 1572 and ended in 1648 (map 1), was inspired by fear that the central government, controlled from Spain, intended to override the traditional liberties of the Netherlands. Similar motives underlay the Catalan and Portuguese revolts against Castile (1640).

In the British Isles, united from 1603 under a single monarch, the efforts of Charles I (1625–49) to change the traditional religious and political structure resulted in rebellions in Scotland (1638) and Ireland (1641). The king's innovations were no more popular with many of England's political leaders, called to Parliament to vote the taxes required to restore royal control in the other two kingdoms: their refusal provoked a civil war in England (1642). In a complex sequence of political and military moves (map 4), a small Parliamentary faction not only contrived the defeat and execution of the king (1649), creating an English Republic under the Lord Protector Oliver Cromwell, but went on to establish London's direct control over the entire British Isles (1649–51). Even though the Monarchy was restored in 1660, power was now shared between the crown and Parliament (in constant existence from 1689).

In continental Europe the sequel was different. In France the failure of the Fronde broke the power of the aristocracy and cleared the way for the absolutism of Louis XIV (page 80). Only in Germany was the disarray caused by a century of religious and political conflict enduring. Here the devastation of the Thirty Years' War resulted in a decline of population from some 21 millions in 1618 to around 13 millions in 1648 (map 5), and though some regions were spared, the setback was undeniable. The outcome was a major shift in the European balance. The Habsburgs, who had dominated the previous period, were in retreat, and the future in the West was in the hands of a resurgent France and its rivals, the maritime powers.

The English Civil War (below)

1/Edinburgh 1638: National Covenant signed.

2/Newcastle 1640: Scottish Covenanters invade England and force Charles I to buy them off.

3/Kilkenny 1641: centre of rebellion by Irish Catholics (to 1649).

4/Antrim 1641: massacre of Catholics by Protestants.

5/Westminster 1642: English Parliament raises army against Charles I.

6/Edgehill 1642: first battle of English Civil War, indecisive.

7/Westminster 1643: alliance of English Parliament and Scottish Covenanters against Charles I (to 1648).

8/Nantwich 1644: Parliamentary army defeats Irish Catholic invasion in support of Charles I.

9/Marston Moor 1644: Scots and Parliamentary army defeat Charles I and occupy N. England.

10/Lostwithiel 1644: Parliamentary army loses control of SW England to King.

11/Tippermuir 1644: Montrose and Scottish royalists defeat Covenanters.

12/Philiphaugh 1645: Montrose defeated by Covenanters and forced to flee.

13/Naseby 1645: Parliamentary army defeats Charles I and wins control of all England.

14/Burford 1647: Oliver Cromwell suppresses mutiny of Parliamentary troops (the 'Levellers').

15/Preston 1648: Cromwell defeats Covenanters' invasion of England in support of Charles I.

16/Whitehall 1649: Parliament tries and executes Charles I.

17/Drogheda and Wexford 1649: Cromwell overruns Ireland and ends rebellion there; occupied to 1660.

18/Dunbar 1650: Cromwell defeats Covenanters and occupies Scotland (to 1660).

19/Scone 1651: Charles II crowned king of Scotland by Covenanters.

20/Worcester 1651: Cromwell defeats invasion of Covenanters in support of Charles II who is forced to flee abroad (to 1660).

21/Whitehall 1658: death of Oliver Cromwell (Head of State since 1654).

22/Westminster 1660: coronation of Charles II as king of England.

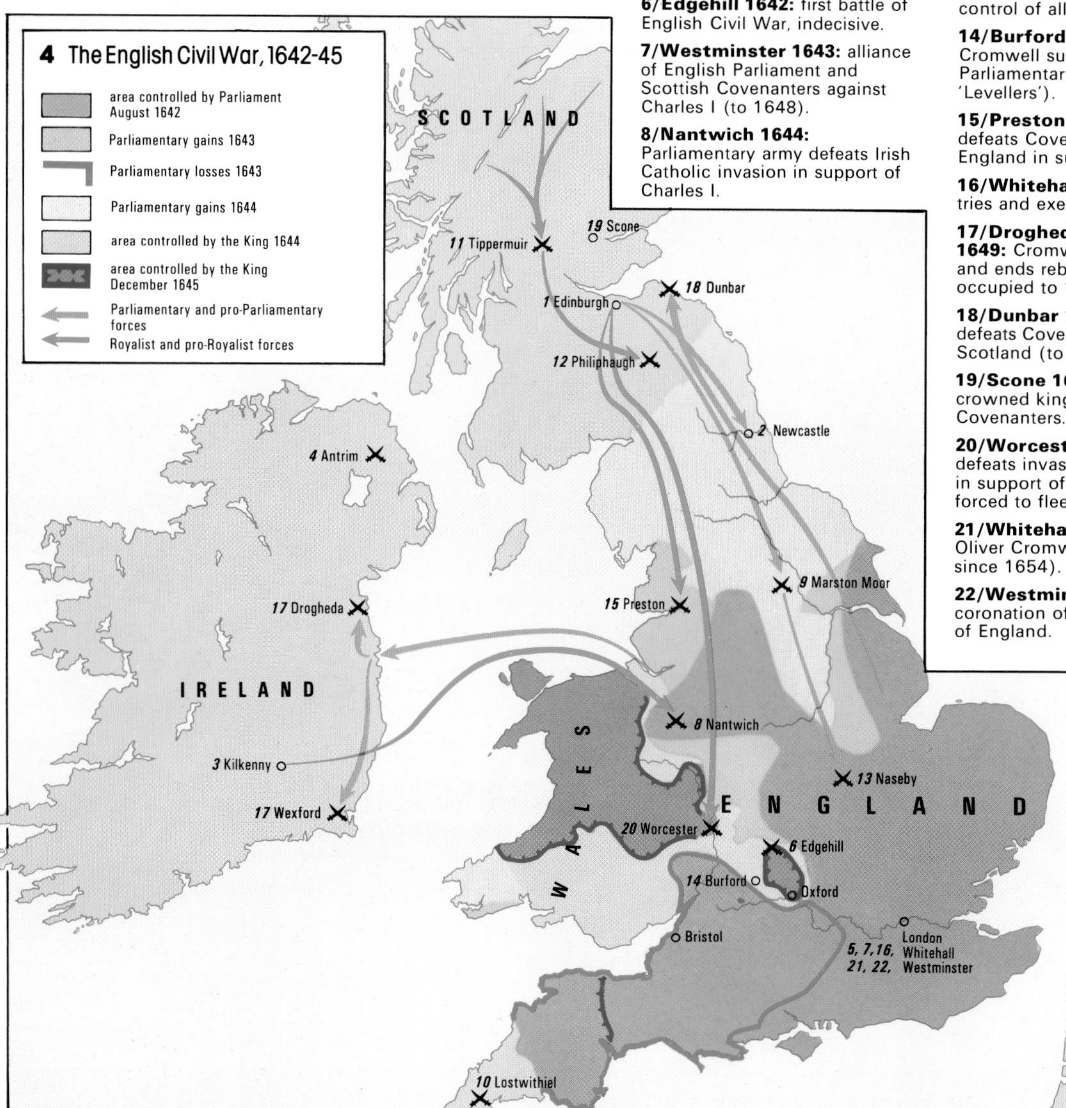

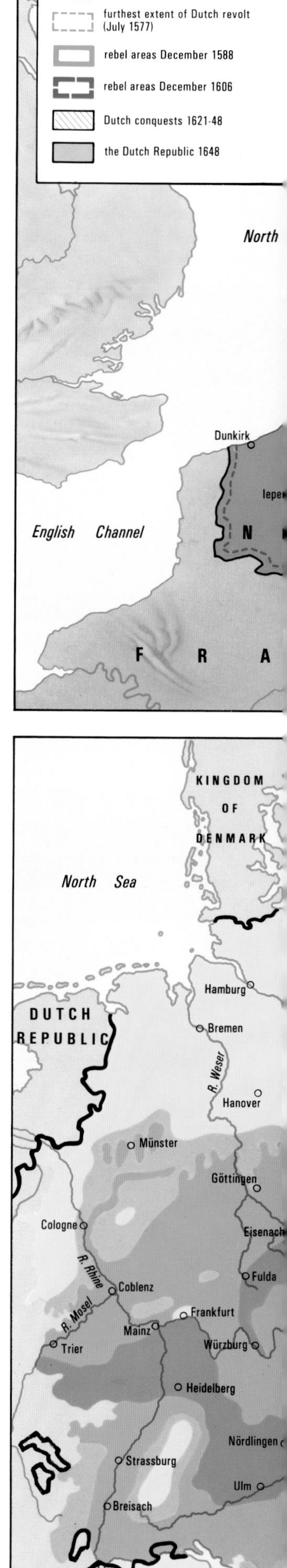

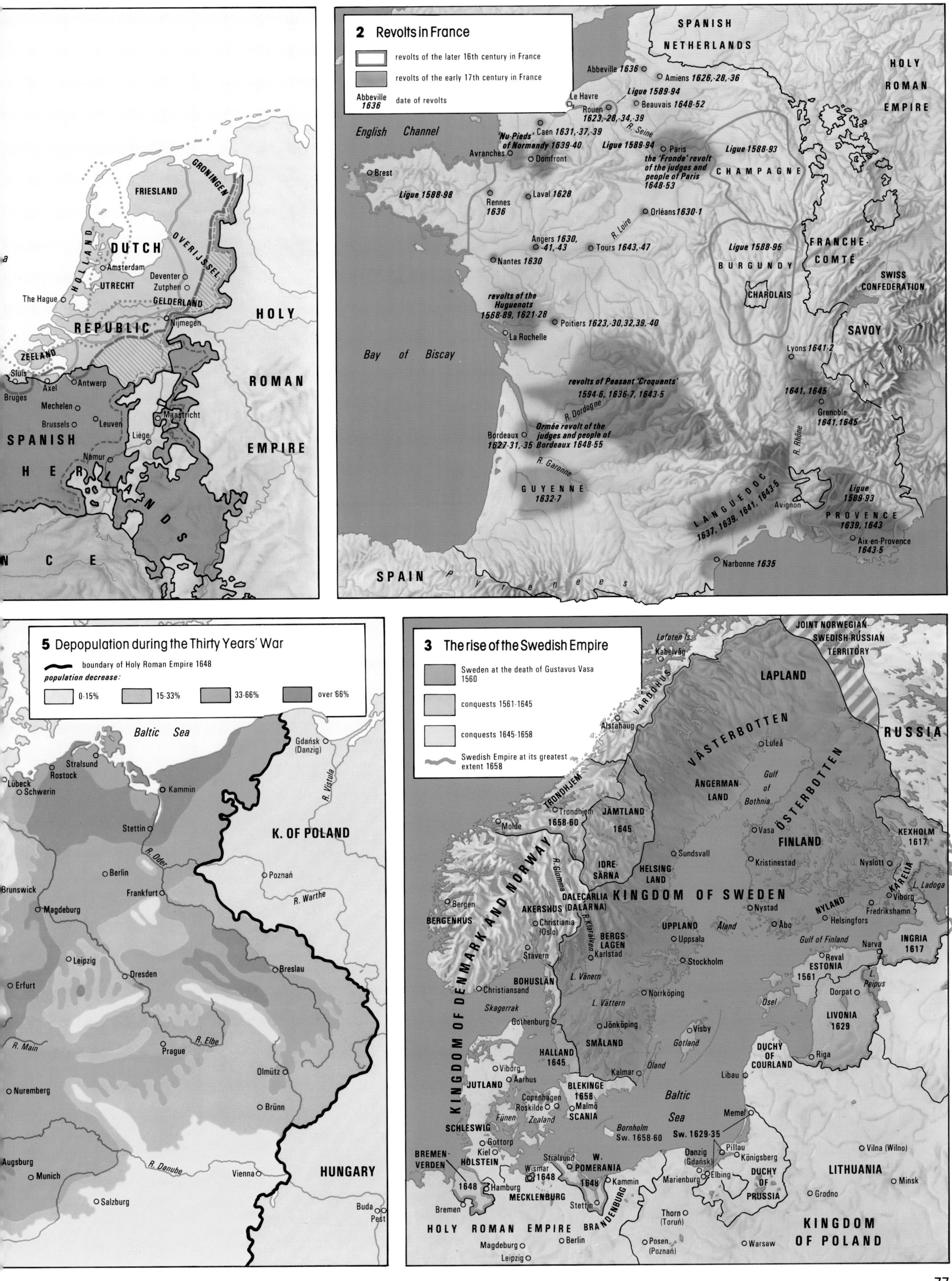

2 Revolts in France
revolts of the later 16th century in France
revolts of the early 17th century in France
Abbeville 1636 date of revolts
SPANISH NETHERLANDS
HOLY ROMAN EMPIRE
Abbeville 1636
Amiens 1626,-28,-36
Ligue 1589-94
Beauvais 1648-52
Le Havre
Rouen 1623,-28,-34,-39
English Channel
'Nu-Pieds' of Normandy 1639-40
Caen 1631,-37,-39
Avranches
Domfront
Ligue 1589-94
Paris
the 'Fronde' revolt of the judges and people of Paris 1648-53
Ligue 1588-93
CHAMPAGNE
Brest
Ligue 1588-98
Rennes 1636
Laval 1628
Orléans 1630-1
Angers 1630,-41,-43
Tours 1643,-47
Nantes 1630
Ligue 1588-95
BURGUNDY
FRANCHE-COMTÉ
CHAROLAIS
SWISS CONFEDERATION
revolts of the Huguenots 1568-89, 1621-28
Poitiers 1623,-30,32,39,-40
La Rochelle
SAVOY
Bay of Biscay
Lyons 1641-2
revolts of Peasant 'Croquants' 1594-6, 1636-7, 1643-5
1641, 1645
Grenoble 1641,1645
Bordeaux 1627-31,-35
Ormée revolt of the judges and people of Bordeaux 1648-55
GUYENNE 1632-7
LANGUEDOC 1637, 1639, 1641, 1643-5
Ligue 1589-93
Avignon
PROVENCE 1639, 1643
Aix-en-Provence 1643-5
Narbonne 1635
SPAIN
Pyrenees
5 Depopulation during the Thirty Years' War
boundary of Holy Roman Empire 1648
population decrease:
0-15%
15-33%
33-66%
over 66%
Baltic Sea
Gdańsk (Danzig)
Stralsund
Rostock
Lübeck
Schwerin
Kammin
Stettin
K. OF POLAND
Berlin
Poznań
Brunswick
Frankfurt
Magdeburg
Leipzig
Dresden
Breslau
Erfurt
Prague
Olmütz
Nuremberg
Brünn
Augsburg
Munich
Vienna
HUNGARY
Salzburg
Buda
Pest
3 The rise of the Swedish Empire
Sweden at the death of Gustavus Vasa 1560
conquests 1561-1645
conquests 1645-1658
Swedish Empire at its greatest extent 1658
JOINT NORWEGIAN-SWEDISH-RUSSIAN TERRITORY
Lofoten Is.
Kabelvåg
LAPLAND
RUSSIA
Alstahaug
VÄSTERBOTTEN
Luleå
ÖSTERBOTTEN
ÅNGERMANLAND
Gulf of Bothnia
TRONDHJEM
Trondhjem 1658-60
JÄMTLAND 1645
Molde
Vasa
FINLAND
KEXHOLM 1617
Sundsvall
Kristinestad
Nyslott
KARELIA
L. Ladoga
IDRE-SÄRNA
HELSINGLAND
Bergen
DALECARLIA (DALARNA)
KINGDOM OF SWEDEN
Viborg
BERGENHUS
AKERSHUS
Nystad
NYLAND
Helsingfors
Fredrikshamn
Christiania (Oslo)
UPPLAND
Åland
Åbo
Uppsala
BERGSLAGEN
Karlstad
Gulf of Finland
Narva
INGRIA 1617
Stavern
Stockholm
Reval
ESTONIA 1561
L. Peipus
BOHUSLÄN
L. Vänern
Christiansand
Norrköping
Skagerrak
L. Vättern
Ösel
Dorpat
Gothenburg
Jönköping
LIVONIA 1629
KINGDOM OF DENMARK AND NORWAY
Visby
SMÅLAND
Gotland
HALLAND 1645
DUCHY OF COURLAND
Riga
Viborg
Aarhus
Kalmar
Öland
Libau
JUTLAND
BLEKINGE 1658
Copenhagen
Roskilde
Malmö
SCANIA
Baltic Sea
Fünen
Zealand
Memel
SCHLESWIG
Bornholm Sw. 1658-60
Sw. 1629-35
Gottorp
Pillau
Kiel
Königsberg
BREMEN-VERDEN
HOLSTEIN
Stralsund
W. POMERANIA
Danzig (Gdańsk)
Vilna (Wilno)
Wismar 1648
DUCHY OF PRUSSIA
Elbing
LITHUANIA
1648
Hamburg
1648
Kammin
Marienburg
Minsk
MECKLENBURG
Grodno
Bremen
Stettin
BRANDENBURG
Thorn (Toruń)
KINGDOM OF POLAND
HOLY ROMAN EMPIRE
Berlin
Magdeburg
Posen (Poznań)
Warsaw
Leipzig
DUTCH REPUBLIC
FRIESLAND
GRONINGEN
OVERIJSSEL
HOLLAND
Amsterdam
Deventer
UTRECHT
Zutphen
The Hague
GELDERLAND
HOLY ROMAN EMPIRE
Nijmegen
ZEELAND
Sluis
Axel
Antwerp
Bruges
Mechelen
Brussels
Leuven
Maastricht
SPANISH NETHERLANDS
Liège
Namur

Germany and its neighbours
1648-1806

The Peace of Westphalia (1648), besides bringing to a close the wars of religion (page 74), was a milestone in German history. The failure of the emperor to impose his will on the Protestant princes confirmed the political fragmentation which had gathered pace since the fourteenth century (page 54). After 1648 Germany was a patchwork of some 300 small, petty states and free cities (map 1). In addition, the independence of Holland and Switzerland was formally recognised. Theoretically the rights of the princes were limited by the rights of the Holy Roman Empire, but in practice every prince was emperor in his own lands, with full sovereign powers including the laws to make foreign alliances. Political disruption was also compounded by a sharp economic setback, due partly to the devastation and depopulation resulting from the Thirty Years' War, but also to a long-term shift in the European economy. The great south German banking houses of Welser and Fugger went bankrupt in 1614 and 1627 respectively. The Hanseatic League, in disarray since the closing years of the sixteenth century, was dissolved in 1669. Everywhere the towns were in decline, particularly in Austria, Prussia and Bavaria, but even worse was the plight of the peasantry. In Bohemia and Moravia their legal rights were abolished; in the north and north-east they were ejected from their holdings to permit the consolidation of Junker estates, and reduced to serfdom (page 82). Impoverishment and stagnation were the result. A modest economic recovery occurred after 1750; but with its resources dissipated on ostentatious building and the upkeep of princely households Germany was an economic and social backwater. It was also a pawn in great power politics. Divided among themselves and fearful of Habsburg ambitions, the princes were clients of foreign powers, including Britain and Sweden, but particularly of France, which used its position to make inroads on German territories in the west (page 80), annexing the Franche-Comté of Burgundy (1678), Strassburg (1681), most of Alsace (1697) and Bar and Lorraine (1766).

After 1648, apart from Austria, only Saxony, Bavaria and Brandenburg could claim even the status of second-rate powers. Saxony, with the mineral resources of the Erzgebirge and its varied industries, was the most advanced, while Bavaria was falling behind; but Brandenburg-Prussia was beginning, under the Great Elector (1640–88) the long climb which made it by 1786 the second German power and the rival of Austria. The rise of Prussia (map 2) is a story of tenacity, unscrupulous diplomacy, but above all of single-

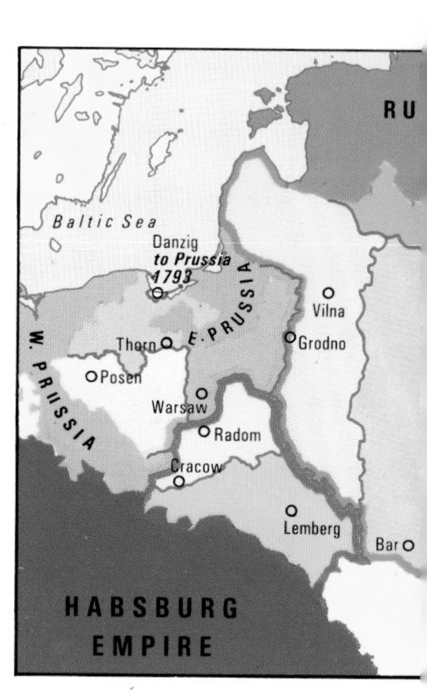

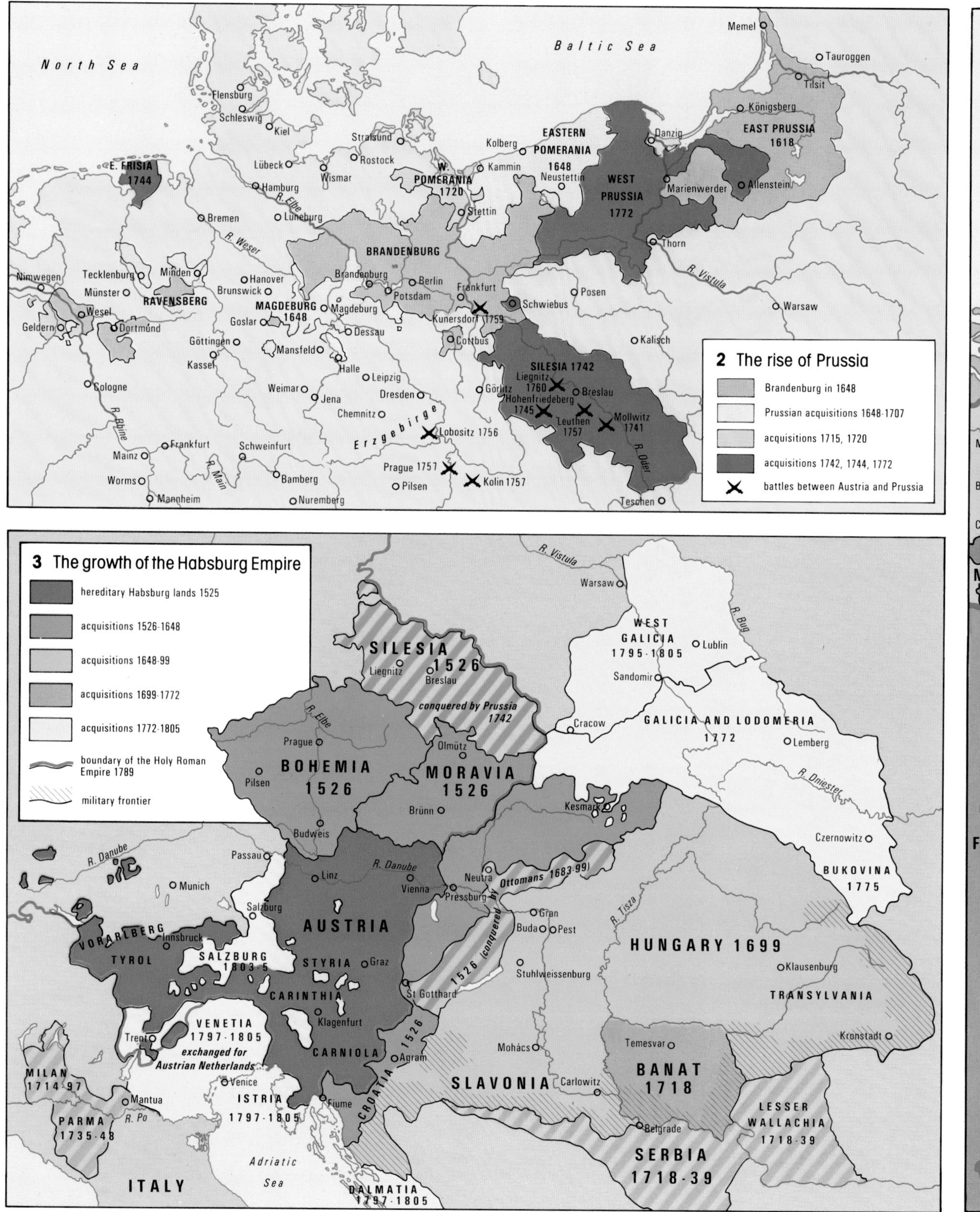

4 The partitions of Poland

Poland before the partitions

Russian, Prussian and Austrian acquisitions in the first partition 1772

Russian and Prussian acquisitions in the second partition 1793

Russian, Prussian and Austrian acquisitions in the third partition 1795

IAN

itebsk

EMPIRE

Targovitsa

alta

minded devotion to building a strong military and administrative apparatus to weld together the scattered territories stretching from the Vistula to the Rhine. The Hohenzollern domains lacked internal and external cohesion. Prussia itself was until 1657 a Polish fief; and it was only in 1772, after the first partition of Poland (map 4) that Frederick the Great (1740–86) succeeded in creating a continuous Prussian territory from Memel to Magdeburg. More impressive, and a cardinal fact in eighteenth-century history, was the recovery of Austria after its setbacks in the Thirty Years' War and the creation of a vast new Austrian empire (map 3). This was largely the work of the great field marshal, Prince Eugene of Savoy (1663–1736). As late as 1683 Vienna itself was besieged by Turkish armies. Eugene turned the tide and by 1699 they had been thrown back and the whole of Hungary brought under Habsburg rule. Austria was now a major power in eastern Europe, while in the west the peace settlement of 1714 brought it the Spanish Netherlands and the Spanish inheritance in Italy. But it was a giant with feet of clay, with weak finances and an inadequate army. Serbia and Belgrade, acquired in 1718, were lost again in 1739, Lombardy and southern Italy in 1734–5. When, on the death of Charles VI (1711–40) and the accession of Maria Theresa (1740–80), Frederick II of Prussia seized Silesia, Austria's inherent weaknesses were exposed. Although the struggle went on until 1763, it proved impossible to dislodge the Prussians. Later both Prussia and Austria took advantage of the disarray of Poland to enlarge their territories in the east. But in the three partitions (map 4) they had to share the spoils with Russia, and their mutual suspicions and rivalry left the west exposed to France. When the French revolutionary armies marched into Germany in 1793 the old order was doomed, and in 1806 the Holy Roman Empire passed unmourned from the map of Europe.

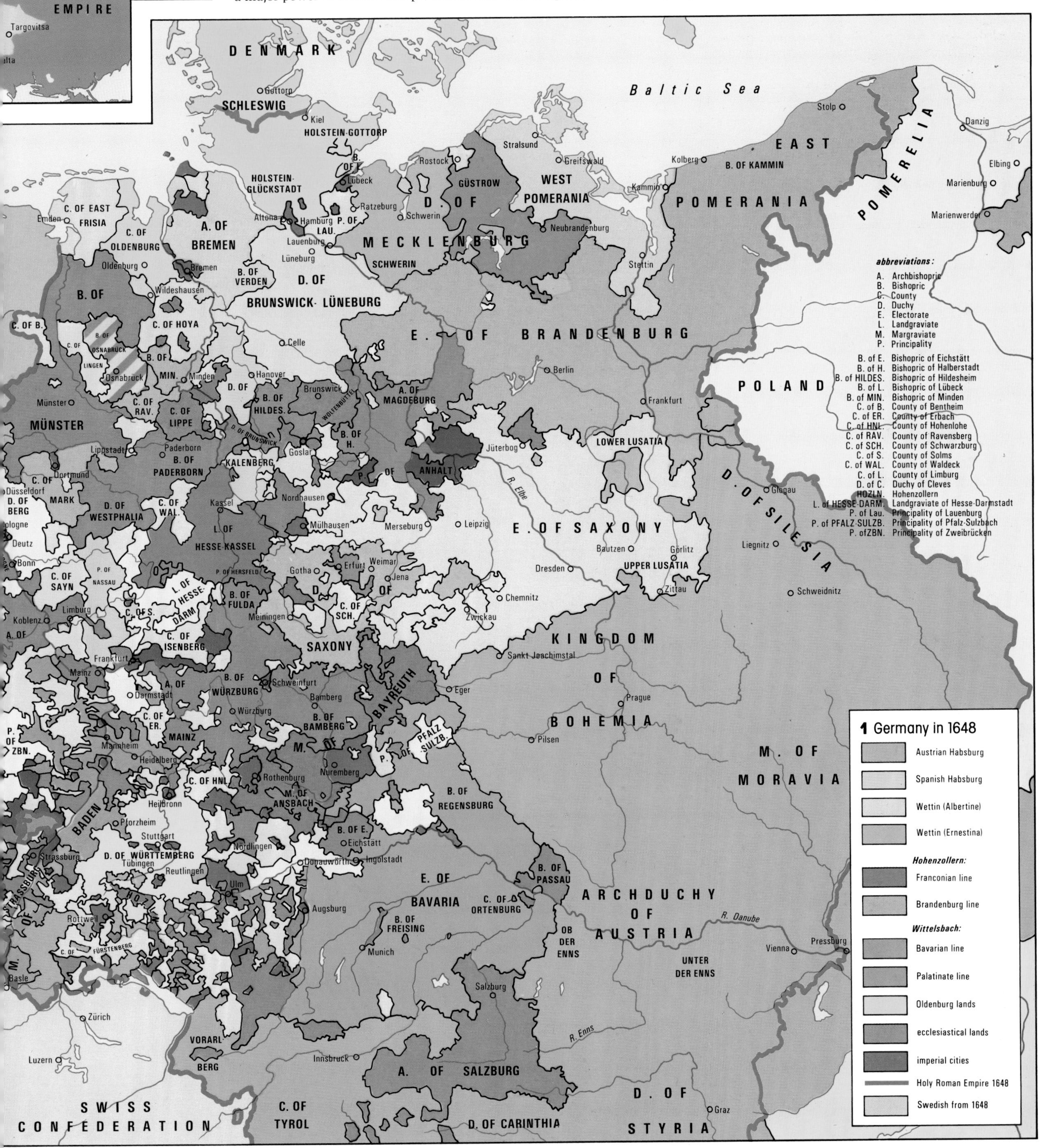

France and Europe
1648 – 1715

Under Louis XIV who succeeded to the throne in 1643, France became the leading country of Europe. His long minority, during Cardinal Mazarin's rule, saw the last major revolts of the aristocracy in defence of its prescriptive rights. When in 1661 Louis became effective ruler, the ground had been prepared for a new regime of centralisation and absolutism. This was the work of Mazarin, who had broken the aristocratic revolts and who turned the *intendants* into permanent representatives of the royal will in the provinces; of Louvois, who reformed the army; and particularly of Colbert's programme of financial reform. At the same time Vauban encircled France with a chain of defensive fortresses (map 1). All this was accompanied by great public works, including the Languedoc canal, connecting the Atlantic and the Mediterranean, the palace of Versailles, and much building in Paris which became the centre of the cosmopolitan civilisation of Europe.

But Louis XIV's wars, inspired by an almost neurotic fear of the revival of the empire of Charles V and the encirclement of France by Habsburg power, seriously damaged this solid achievement. Beginning with his attack on the Spanish Netherlands in 1667, they imposed a growing burden of taxation and gradually united Europe against him (map 4). England and Holland, maritime and colonial rivals since 1652 (map 3), settled their differences by the Treaty of Breda (1667) and in alliance with Sweden compelled Louis to make peace at Aix-la-Chapelle in 1668. Thereupon Louis detached England from the anti-French alliance by the Secret Treaty of Dover (1670), won over Sweden, and turned against Holland in 1672; but he was halted by an alliance between Austria, Spain and Brandenburg (which defeated his Swedish allies at Fehrbellin in 1675), and at the Peace of Nimwegen (1678) Holland emerged unscathed.

These inconclusive results convinced Louis that there was little hope of major territorial acquisitions by direct conquest, and after 1679 he turned to a policy of indirect aggression, nibbling away at German territory in the east, particularly in Alsace (map 2), the object being to absorb the remainder of the Burgundian territories which had been partitioned between France and Austria after the death of Charles the Bold in 1477 (page 72). Strasbourg was annexed in 1681, the Palatinate burnt and ravaged in 1689. But these provocative and often brutal actions united German opinion against him, and the revocation of the Edict of Nantes (1685) and the persecution of the French Huguenots incensed the Protestant powers. The result was the formation of the Grand Alliance (1689), led by William of Orange, who had succeeded to the English throne after the revolution

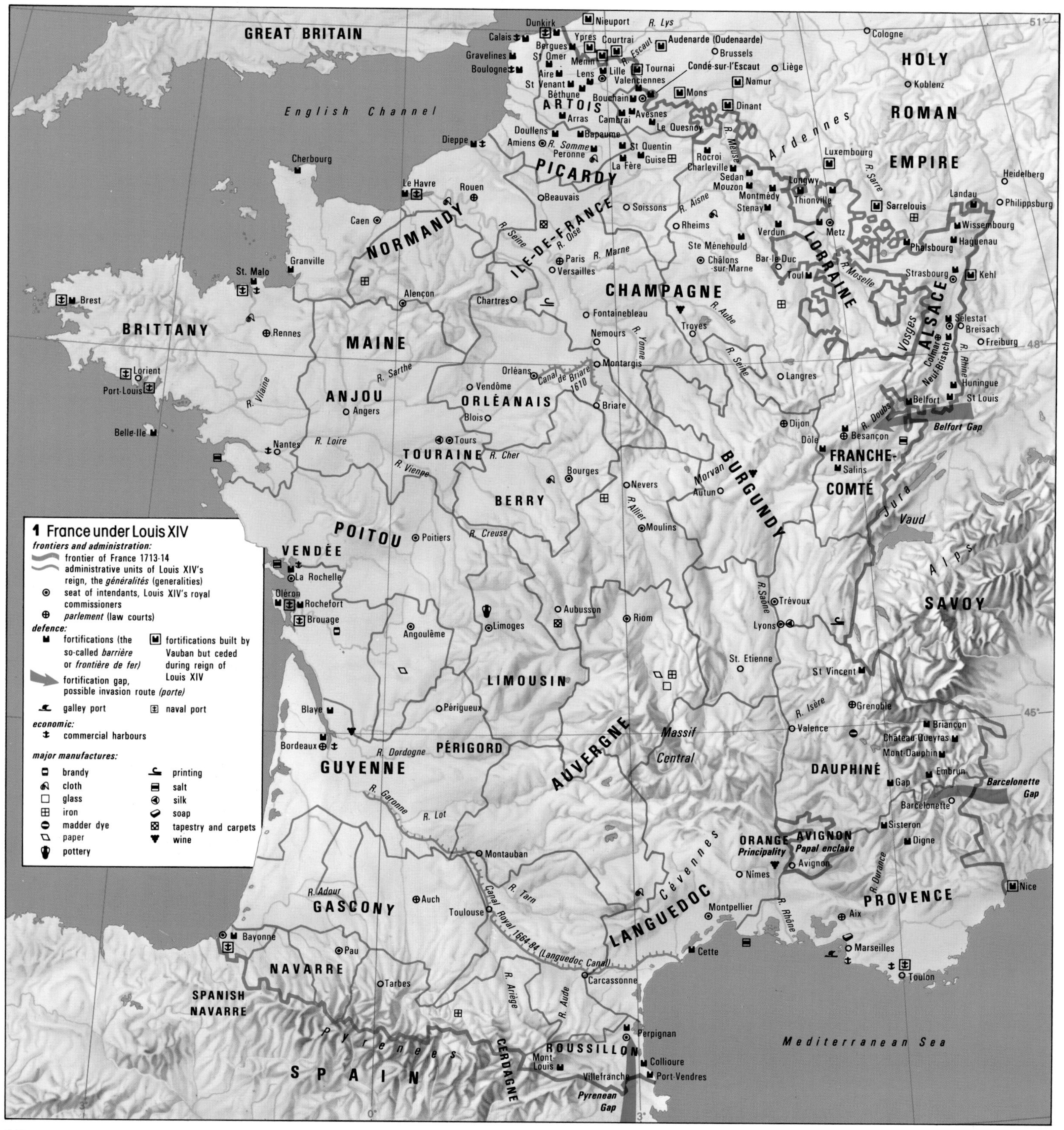

of 1688 and the deposition of James II. Louis' attempts to foment rebellion in Ireland failed after the defeat of the French navy at La Hogue (1692), but fighting continued inconclusively on the continent until 1697, when the Peace of Ryswick registered Louis' first serious setback.

A new phase opened with the death without heirs of Charles II of Spain in 1700. This event had long been anticipated, but plans to divide the Spanish dominions in such a way as to maintain the balance of power were thwarted not only by the rivalry of France and Austria, but also by the maritime powers (England and Holland), which feared French ascendancy in overseas trade if it acquired the Spanish overseas empire. The result was the long War of the Spanish Succession (map 5), ended, in spite of the victories of Prince Eugene of Savoy and the Duke of Marlborough, by the compromise Peace of Utrecht in 1713. The French candidate retained the Spanish throne as Philip V, and France kept most of its gains on its eastern frontier (map 2). But the ruinous expense of Louis' wars left France in a desperate situation, with a legacy of financial disorder and internal discontent from which his successors never fully recovered.

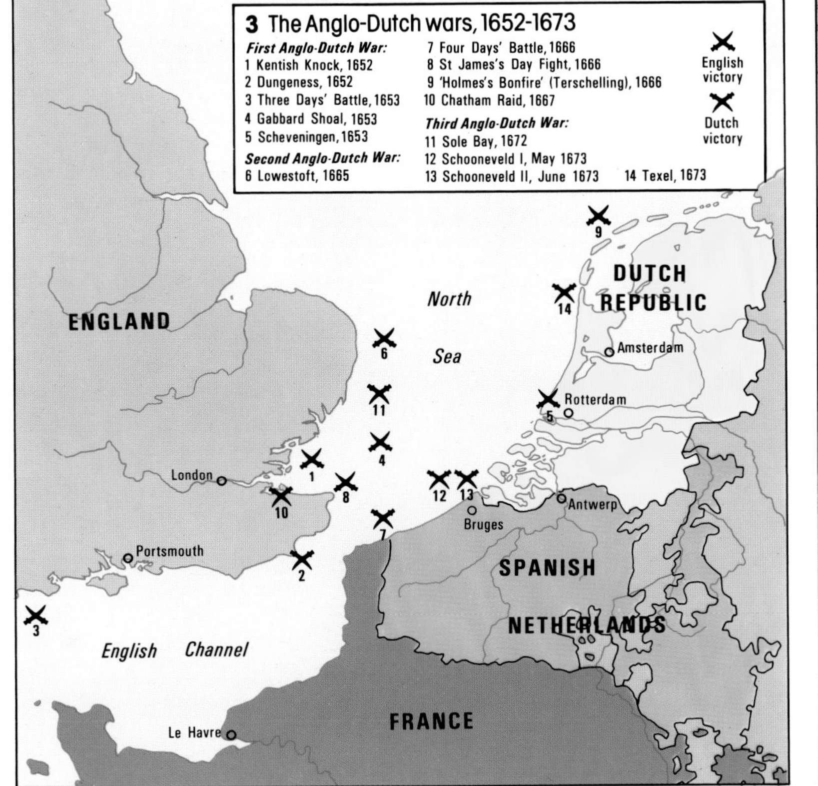

The European economy c.1500-1815

Recovery from the economic setbacks of the fourteenth century (page 56) began around 1450, and Europe's population expanded rapidly, though the fast growth of the sixteenth century was interrupted by war, rebellion, famine and plague in the seventeenth century and not resumed until the middle of the eighteenth century. Overall it increased from an estimated 69 million in 1500 to 188 million in 1800, but the increase was uneven and most marked in Britain and the Netherlands, by 1700 the greatest textile producers of Europe, the most active traders, with the largest merchant fleets and rapidly growing shipbuilding and metalware industries. The result was a shift in the economic axis. In 1500 industry was concentrated in the narrow corridor running north-south from Antwerp and Bruges through Ulm and Augsburg to Milan and Florence. By 1700 the axis ran west-east from England and Holland through the metal and woollen districts of the lower Rhine to the industrial concentrations of Saxony, Bohemia and Silesia, and thence to Russia, now beginning to build up an industrial base (map 4). The great expansion of overseas trade, particularly after 1700, also favoured the maritime powers (map 5). A consequence was the decline of the great trading cities of northern Italy, dominant two centuries earlier. In 1500 only four cities – Paris, Milan, Naples and Venice – had more than 100,000 inhabitants. By 1700 this number had trebled, and the majority of the rising urban centres lay west of the Rhine. London and Paris had already passed the half-million mark.

Significant as these developments were, agriculture was still Europe's most important industry. As late as 1815 three-quarters of its population were employed on the land, though here again there were sharp regional differences. In most of Europe farmers were subsistence peasants, whose smallholdings of 2–10 hectares produced only about 20 per cent more than their immediate needs. But in the west the need to feed growing urban populations led, first in Holland and then in Britain, to an agricultural revolution. The Dutch poured capital into land reclamation, recovering some 180,000 hectares between 1540 and 1715 (map 3), and developed intensive cultivation, eliminating the need to leave land fallow by means of a rotation of crops, which was later taken over in England. The growing population was also sustained by the introduction of new, more productive crops, mainly from America, including maize, which gave a far higher yield than the old regional cereals of southern Europe, and the potato, introduced in c.1565, which spread slowly until it became a key field crop after 1700 (map 2). Urban demand also stimulated specialisation (Holland was exporting 90 per cent of its cheese by 1700), and generated a massive demand in western Europe for wheat and rye from Pomerania, Prussia, Poland and Russia, greatly to the profit of Holland which virtually monopolised the Baltic carrying trade in the sixteenth and seventeenth centuries.

The profitable grain-export trade of eastern Europe adversely affected the position of the peasant population which had enjoyed relative freedom before 1500 but now was reduced to a state of abject serfdom on large commercial estates. Only on the frontiers (e.g. in Hungary and on the Volga) where they performed military service, did the peasants retain freedom. Otherwise emancipation (postponed in Russia until 1861) only came slowly after the French Revolution, and the same was true in western Germany where, following the savage repression of the great peasant revolt of 1525, feudal relationships persisted (map 1). A few rulers, notably the emperor Joseph II (1780–90), realised that improvement of productivity depended on breaking the old feudal relationships; but they were frustrated by landed interests. The position in north-west Europe was very different. Serfdom had disappeared in the Low Countries by 1300. In France and England feudal services had been replaced, even before 1500, by money rents; and although, when prices rose after 1700, French lords sought to recoup themselves by reviving ancient dues (only abolished in 1793), peasant ownership was protected by the courts. Rising prices led, in England, to enclosure of the common fields, a precondition for agricultural improvement. Rich peasants benefited, but poor peasants, driven off the land, flocked to the towns, where they provided the labour force for the new industries.

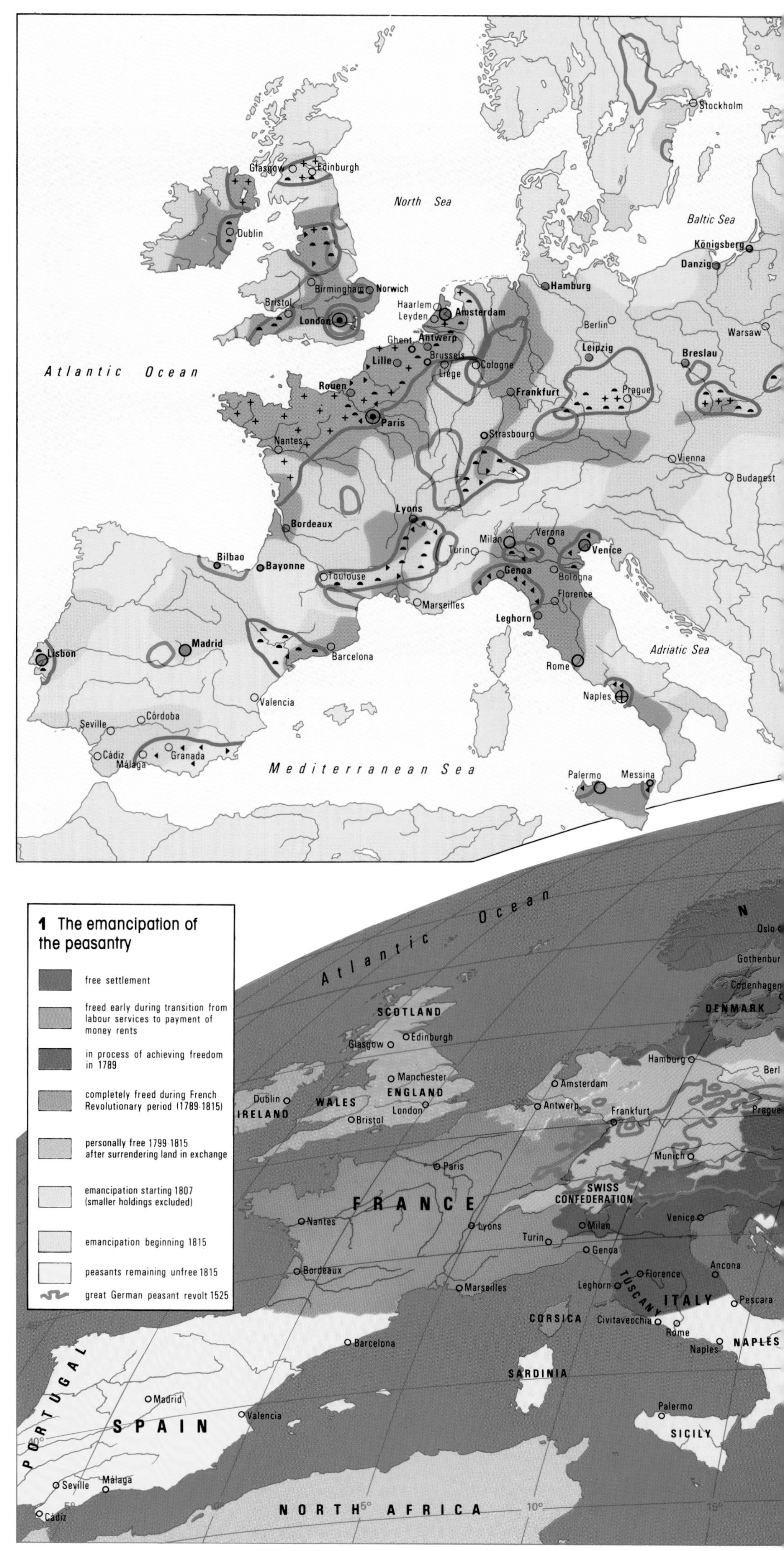

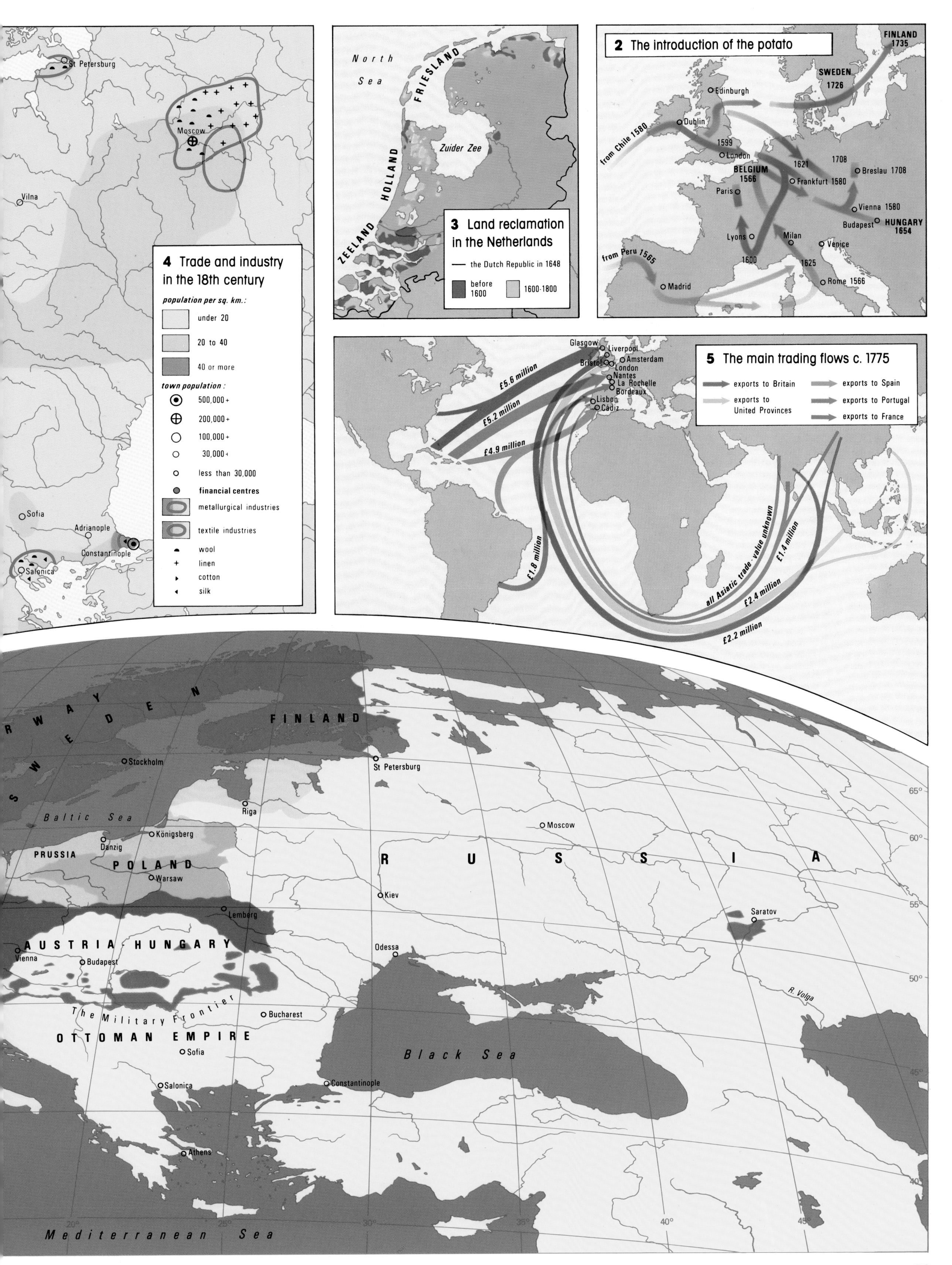

St Petersburg
Moscow
Vilna
4 Trade and industry in the 18th century
population per sq. km.:
under 20
20 to 40
40 or more
town population:
500,000+
200,000+
100,000+
30,000+
less than 30,000
financial centres
metallurgical industries
textile industries
wool
linen
cotton
silk
Sofia
Adrianople
Constantinople
Salonica
North Sea
FRIESLAND
Zuider Zee
HOLLAND
ZEELAND
3 Land reclamation in the Netherlands
the Dutch Republic in 1648
before 1600
1600-1800
2 The introduction of the potato
FINLAND 1735
SWEDEN 1726
Edinburgh
Dublin
from Chile 1580
1599
London
BELGIUM 1566
1621
1708
Breslau 1708
Frankfurt 1580
Paris
Vienna 1580
Budapest
HUNGARY 1654
Lyons
Milan
Venice
from Peru 1565
1600
1625
Madrid
Rome 1566
5 The main trading flows c. 1775
exports to Britain
exports to United Provinces
exports to Spain
exports to Portugal
exports to France
Glasgow
Liverpool
Bristol
Amsterdam
London
Nantes
La Rochelle
Bordeaux
Lisbon
Cádiz
£5.6 million
£5.2 million
£4.9 million
£1.8 million
all Asiatic trade: value unknown
£1.4 million
£2.4 million
£2.2 million
FINLAND
SWEDEN
Stockholm
St Petersburg
Riga
Baltic Sea
Königsberg
Danzig
PRUSSIA
POLAND
Warsaw
Moscow
RUSSIA
Kiev
Lemberg
AUSTRIA-HUNGARY
Vienna
Budapest
Odessa
Saratov
R. Volga
The Military Frontier
Bucharest
OTTOMAN EMPIRE
Sofia
Black Sea
Salonica
Constantinople
Athens
Mediterranean Sea
65°
60°
55°
50°
45°
40°
20°
25°
30°
35°
40°
45°

The expansion of Russia, 1462-1905

The rise of modern Russia dates from the reign of Ivan III (1462–1505). During the preceding century the principality of Moscow had expanded at the expense of its immediate neighbours; but it was still a tributary of the Mongols (page 46), and in the west it was hemmed in by the great Polish-Lithuanian state, which extended deep into the Ukraine (page 56). Ivan III threw off the Mongol overlordship (1480), and in the west his conquest of the ancient republic of Novgorod (1478) opened the way to Livonia and the White Sea. Under his son Vassily (1505–33) and his grandson Ivan IV (1533–84) the advance continued. The subjection of the Khanate of Kazan (1552) opened the way across the Urals into Siberia; the conquest of the Khanate of Astrakhan (1556) gave Moscow control of the Volga to the Caspian Sea. But in the west Lithuania and Poland, joined after 1560 by Sweden, fought back vigorously, and during the 'time of troubles' following the death of Ivan IV made substantial gains at Russian expense (map 1). This, on the other hand, was the time of the great Russian thrust across Siberia, which, beginning in 1582, reached the Sea of Okhotsk by 1639 (map 2).

Siberia, where the population in 1720 was only about 400,000, still counted for little. The axis of Russian expansion was in the west, its thrust symbolised by Peter the Great's foundation of the new capital, St. Petersburg (1703). His long Swedish wars, concluded by the Peace of Nystad (1721), brought him Estonia, Livonia and part of Karelia. Russia now had free access to the Baltic. Under Catherine II (1762–96) it won control of the northern shore of the Black Sea, where Odessa (founded 1794) became a main outlet for Russian exports. But the question of secure access from the Black Sea to the Mediterranean remained unsolved. It was to be a central concern of Russian policy in the nineteenth century, and when it was thwarted by the other European powers in 1856 and again in 1878 Russia turned from Europe to Asia, securing control of the Caucasus (1857–64) and then of the Khanates of Tashkent (1865), Samarkand (1868), Bukhara (1868), Khiva (1873) and Kokand (1876), while in the Far East it conquered the Amur and Ussuri regions at the expense of China (map 3). But defeat in the Crimean War (1854–56) convinced Russia of its backwardness, and in 1861, as a first step to modernisation, the serfs were liberated. Some went to Siberia, far more to the towns, where they provided a working force for industrialisation which began in the 1870s and was especially rapid 1893–1904 and 1909–13, when it exceeded the American growth rate. A metallurgical industry was developed in the Ukraine (map 4) producing mainly rails for the expanding railways. But the achievement was unstable. Russian ambitions in the Far East excited British and Japanese fears, and the result was the Anglo-Japanese alliance (1902) and the Russo-Japanese war of 1904–5 (page 126), which halted Russian expansion until 1945. At home the consequences were even more ominous. An urban proletariat had been formed which became the mainstay of the revolution of 1905 and more fatefully still in 1917.

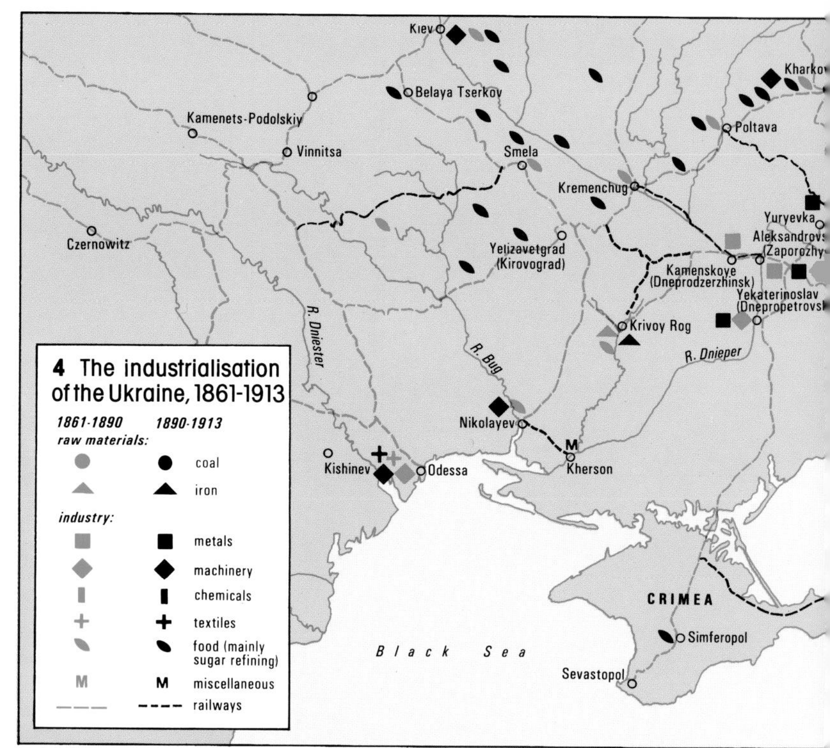

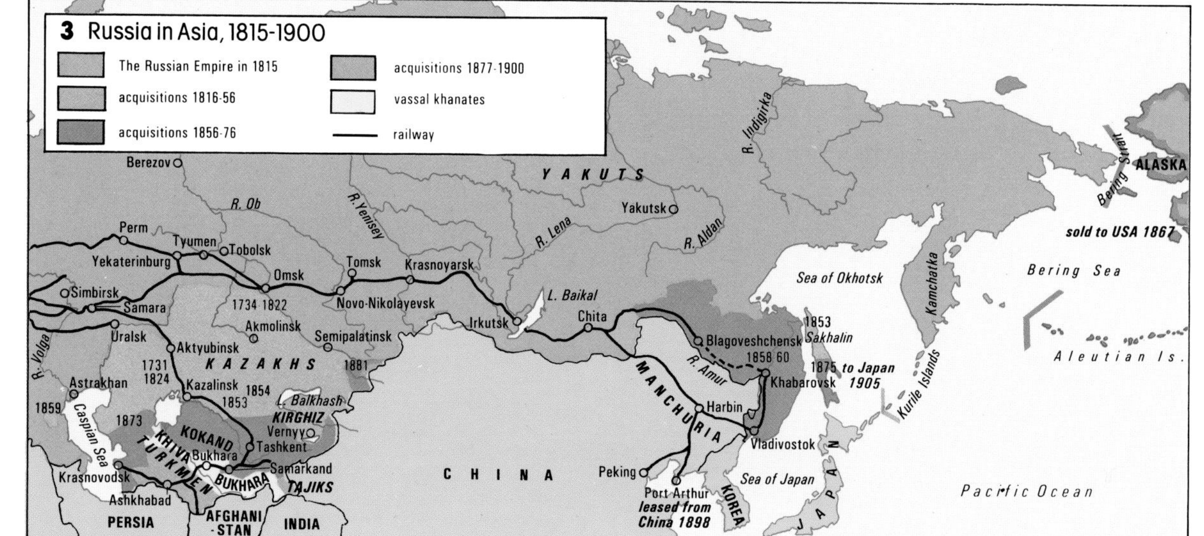

1 Muscovy and the Russian Empire, 1462-1815
boundary of Russian territories in 1462
boundary of Lithuania in 1462
the expansion of Muscovy :
Moscow territory at end of 13th century
1478 date of acquisition by Muscovy
acquisitions to 1462
acquisitions under Ivan III, 1462-1505
acquisitions during 16th century (1505-86)
acquisitions during 17th century
acquisitions during 18th century
acquisitions 1801-15
territory ceded to Sweden 1617 and Poland 1618
recovered from Poland 1634
recovered from Poland 1667
area affected by Pugachev uprising 1773-4
route of Pugachev rebels
Orel 1564 date of foundation of new town
Barents Sea
Baltic Sea
Black Sea
Caspian Sea
Sea of Azov
FINLAND
1809
ESTONIA
1721
LIVONIA
COURLAND
LITHUANIA
POLAND
AUSTRIA
MOLDAVIA
BESSARABIA
OTTOMAN EMPIRE
ZAPOROZHYE
DON COSSACKS
KUBAN COSSACKS
KALMUKS
NOGAI TARTARS
KHANATE OF ASTRAKHAN
KHANATE OF KAZAN
KHANATE OF CRIMEA
CHUVASHI
MORDVA
MESHCHERA
MARI
UDMURTY
BASHKIRS
SIBERIA
NOVGOROD TERRITORY
PECHORA
YUGRA
KARELIA
DAGHESTAN
GEORGIA
AZERBAIJAN
Ural Mts.
Kola Peninsula
White Sea
L. Ladoga
L. Onega
L. Peipus
L. Ilmen
Gulf of Finland
Obdorsk 1595
Berezov 1593
Archangel 1584
Kholmogory
Kargopol
Solvychegodsk
Ustyug
Solikamsk
Vologda
Soligalich
Galich
Kostroma
Yaroslavl
Tver
Dmitrov
Moscow
Vladimir
Murom
Arzamas
Nizhniy Novgorod
Kazan
Vyatka
Perm 1724
Kungur
Nizhniy Tagil 1724
Yekaterinburg 1725
Ufa 1586
Orenburg 1743
Simbirsk 1648
Samara 1586
Syzran 1683
Penza 1650
Tambov 1636
Saratov 1590
Kamyshin
Tsaritsyn 1589
Astrakhan
Guryev 1645
Voronezh 1586
Yelets 1592
Kursk 1586
Belgorod 1593
Kharkov 1654
Poltava
Orel 1564
Bryansk
Tula
Kaluga
Serpukhov
Kolomna
Ryazan
Mozhaysk
Vyazma
Smolensk
Velikiye Luki
Vitebsk
Polotsk
Mogilev
Gomel
Chernigov
Kiev
Pereyaslavl
Novgorod
Pskov
Narva
Kronstadt 1704
St. Petersburg 1703
Vyborg
Riga
Memel
Kovno
Vilna
Grodno
Minsk
Pinsk
Warsaw
Kalish
Lublin
Lemberg
Novograd-Volynskiy
Kamenets
Bratslav
Kishinev
Akkerman
Odessa 1794
Ochakov
Nikolayev 1789
Kherson 1774
Sech
Yekaterinoslav (Kodak) 1786
Taganrog
Azov
Cherkassk
Karasubazar
Kerch
Yevpatoriya
Feodosiya (Kaffa)
Simferopol 1784
Sevastopol 1783
Bakhchisaray
Yekaterinodar 1792
Stavropol
Pyatigorsk
Vladikavkaz 1806
Sukhum-Kale
Kutaisi
Poti
Tiflis
Derbent
Baku
ceded temporarily by Persia 1723-32
R. Pechora
R. Mezen
R. Onega
Northern Dvina
R. Vychegda
R. Sukhona
R. Kama
R. Vyatka
R. Ob
R. Belaya
R. Ural
R. Volga
R. Oka
R. Sura
R. Khoper
R. Don
R. Donets
R. Dnieper
R. Desna
R. Pripet
R. Dniester
R. Prut
R. Danube
R. Vistula
R. Niemen
Western Dvina
R. Lovat
R. Kuma
R. Terek
R. Kura
Chertkovo
Millerovo
Kramatorsk
Lisichansk
Druzhkovka
Lugansk
Kadiyevka
Gorlovka
Makiyevka (Makeyevka)
Yuzovka (Donetsk)
Aleksandrovsk-Grushevskiy
Novocherkassk
Rostov
Taganrog
Mariupol (Zhdanov)
Berdyansk
Kerch
Yekaterinodar (Krasnodar)
Novorossiysk

The struggle for empire
1713-1805

The Treaty of Utrecht (1713), which ended the War of Spanish Succession (page 80), sought to establish stability in Europe and overseas on the basis of a balance of power. But owing to commercial disputes and colonial rivalries, particularly in America, peace remained precarious. In 1739 war broke out between England and Spain; in 1740 Frederick II of Prussia, supported by France, seized Silesia (page 78); and when France, supporting Spain, declared war on England in 1744, the European and overseas wars were fused into a single global conflict. It also quickly turned into a duel between England and France, particularly when, after the inconclusive Treaty of Aix-la-Chapelle (1748), fighting again broke out in North America in 1754. Here the French, with their strategically situated forts, were initially successful. But the whole situation changed when William Pitt the Elder, later Earl of Chatham, became British prime minister in 1756. By allying with and subsidising Prussia, struggling to retain Silesia against an overwhelming French-Austrian-Russian coalition, Pitt compelled France to concentrate on the continental war. Naval victories at Quiberon Bay and Lagos in 1759 assured British control of the Atlantic and prevented reinforcements reaching Canada (map 1). The result was the loss of the French and, when Spain entered the war on the French side in 1761, of the

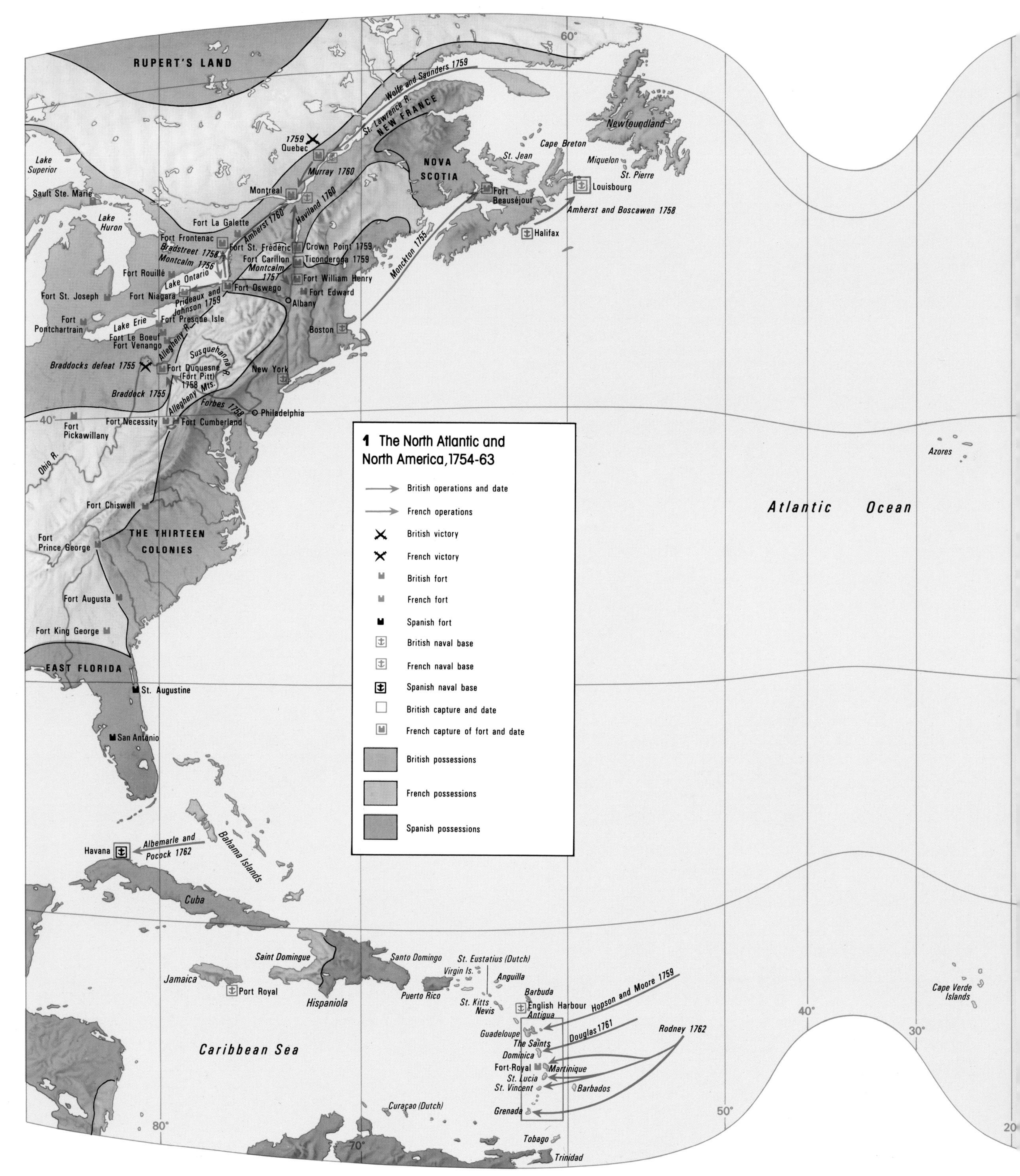

Spanish colonial empires in North America. At the Peace of Paris (1763) the French and Spanish possessions in the West Indies were restored, but England retained the North American mainland east of the Mississippi, including Florida which was ceded by Spain.

The British triumph was nevertheless short-lived. When the thirteen colonies rebelled in 1776 (page 92), France, which had rebuilt its navy, supported the rebels and by naval action compelled Great Britain to recognise American independence in the Treaty of Versailles (1783). In India, on the other hand, Britain built an empire which lasted until 1947. Here again, sea-power was decisive, enabling the English East India Company to checkmate the ambitions of the able French governor, Joseph Dupleix, to expand French influence in south India (map 2). By 1763 France was eliminated as a rival in India. An important determinant of the pace of British expansion was the decline of the Mughal Empire (page 48) after the death of Aurangzeb in 1707. Some states, the Marathas and the Sikh Punjab for example, asserted their independence, while former Mughal provinces, such as Oudh, Bengal and Hyderabad, achieved virtual autonomy. The British both feared, and profited from these developments. By the end of the governor-generalship of Richard Wellesley (1797–1805) British supremacy was an acknowledged fact. Revolutionary France attempted a comeback, and Napoleon planned an invasion of India (page 90). But once again sea-power was decisive, and in 1815 Great Britain occupied an unrivalled position in the colonial world.

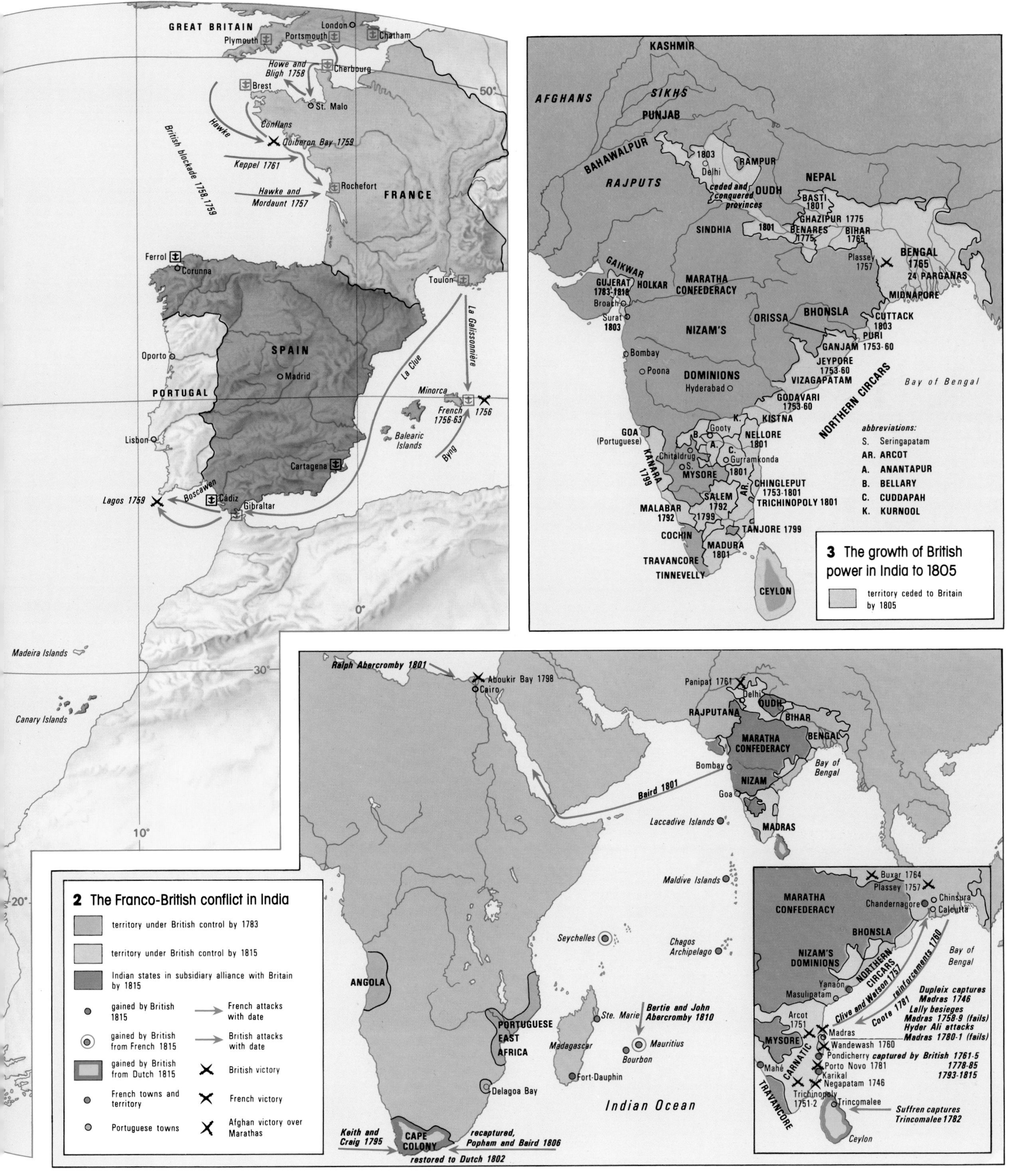

2 The Franco-British conflict in India

3 The growth of British power in India to 1805

The age of revolution
1773-1810

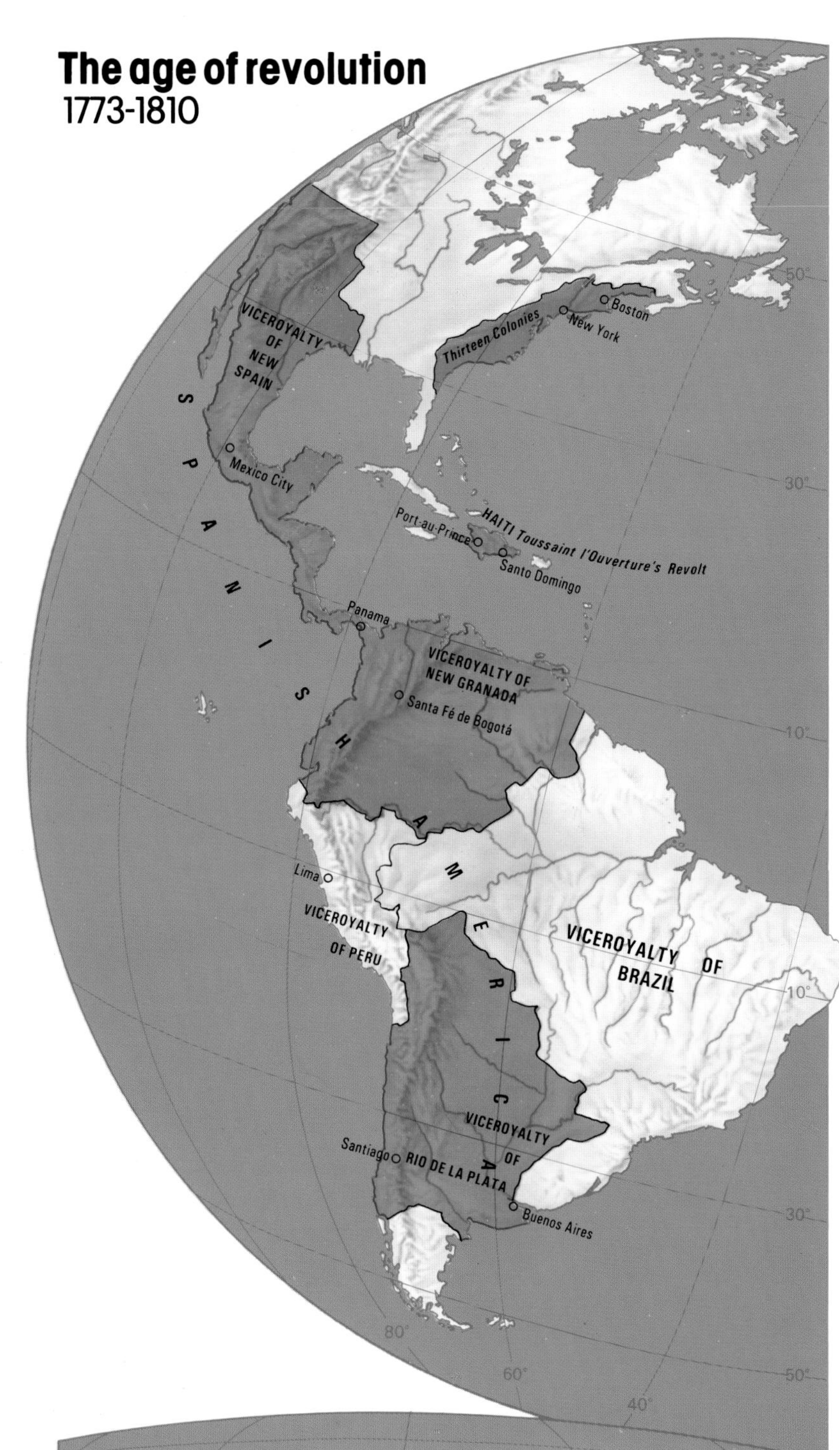

1755, 1793 Corsica Local clans led by Paoli rebelled against Genoese rule and established independent democratic government. France bought island from Genoa in 1768, crushed revolt. Second attempt by Paoli to secure independence from (revolutionary) France, 1793, resulted in brief British occupation; rise of Bonaparte, himself a Corsican, put an end to separatist movement.

1768 Geneva Middle-class citizens of small city-state rebelled against domination by few patrician families; with French support the latter stayed in control.

1773 South-East Russia Serfs, Cossacks and Asiatic tribes rebelled in Volga and Ural region under leadership of Pugachev, a Don Cossack. Russian army put down revolt in 1774.

1775 America Resistance by Britain's Thirteen Colonies to her financial policies resulted in open warfare and Declaration of Independence, 1776.

1784 Dutch Netherlands Three-cornered struggle for power between Stadtholder, patrician families who controlled Estates General, and middle class Patriot party which aimed to democratise government. In 1787 Prussian troops defeated Patriot army and restored Stadtholder with greater powers.

1787 Austrian Netherlands (Belgium) Revolt against centralising policy of Emperor Joseph II, leading to proclamation of the Republic of the United Belgian Provinces (1790). Fights broke out between aristocratic and middle-class rebels; Austrian Emperor reconquered area, 1790.

1789 France (See main text). Risings by peasantry and Parisians overthrew feudal social and political order; Louis XVI's opposition and attempted flight led to abolition of monarchy (1792). King and Queen were guillotined as traitors (1793). Threat of invasion led to Jacobin 'reign of terror', ended by fall and execution of Robespierre (1794). Following weak and corrupt rule of Directory (1795–99) power passed to Napoleon Bonaparte.

1789 Liège Middle-class citizens supported by workers and peasants expelled prince-bishop and abolished feudalism. Bishop restored by Austrian troops, 1790.

1790 Hungary Magyar nobles rejected edicts of Austrian emperor and demanded greater independence for Hungary within Habsburg Empire; later, frightened by peasant disturbances, accepted compromise with the monarchy.

1791 Poland King, supported by lesser nobles, adopted new constitution designed to strengthen Poland against Russian encroachment. Catherine II of Russia, at invitation of greater nobles, invaded, destroyed constitution and divided large areas of Polish territory between Russia and Prussia. Attempt by Kościuszko and lesser nobles to strengthen surviving Polish state (1794) crushed by Russia and Prussia; Poland partitioned and ceased to exist as a separate state.

1791 Haiti Slave rising in western (French) part of island (Saint Domingue) resulted in rise of black leader, Toussaint l'Ouverture; by 1801 had conquered rest of island from Spaniards and secured virtual independence. Island then seized by the French, rising suppressed, and independence not fully secured until 1825.

1793 Sardinia In return for expelling French revolutionary invaders, islanders demanded autonomy within combined kingdom of Piedmont-Sardinia. King reasserted his authority when French threat subsided in 1796.

1798 Ireland Rebellion of United Irishmen seeking independence from England, put down by British army. Suicide of Wolfe Tone.

1804 Serbia Peasant rising against local garrison developed into demand for autonomy within Ottoman Empire. Under Karageorge Serbs fought fiercely for three years before revolt crushed by Turks.

1808 Spain After Napoleon placed his own brother, Joseph, on throne, a peasant rebellion gave assistance to British expeditionary force under Wellington. Middle-class intellectuals proclaimed constitution, but it did not survive restoration of Bourbon king in 1814.

1809 Tyrol After Austria renewed war against Napoleon, the peasants of Tyrol, whose territory had been taken from Austria by Napoleon in 1805 and given to Bavaria, rebelled under Hofer against new rulers. Revolt was crushed by Bavarian and French troops.

1810 Spanish America (See page 96).

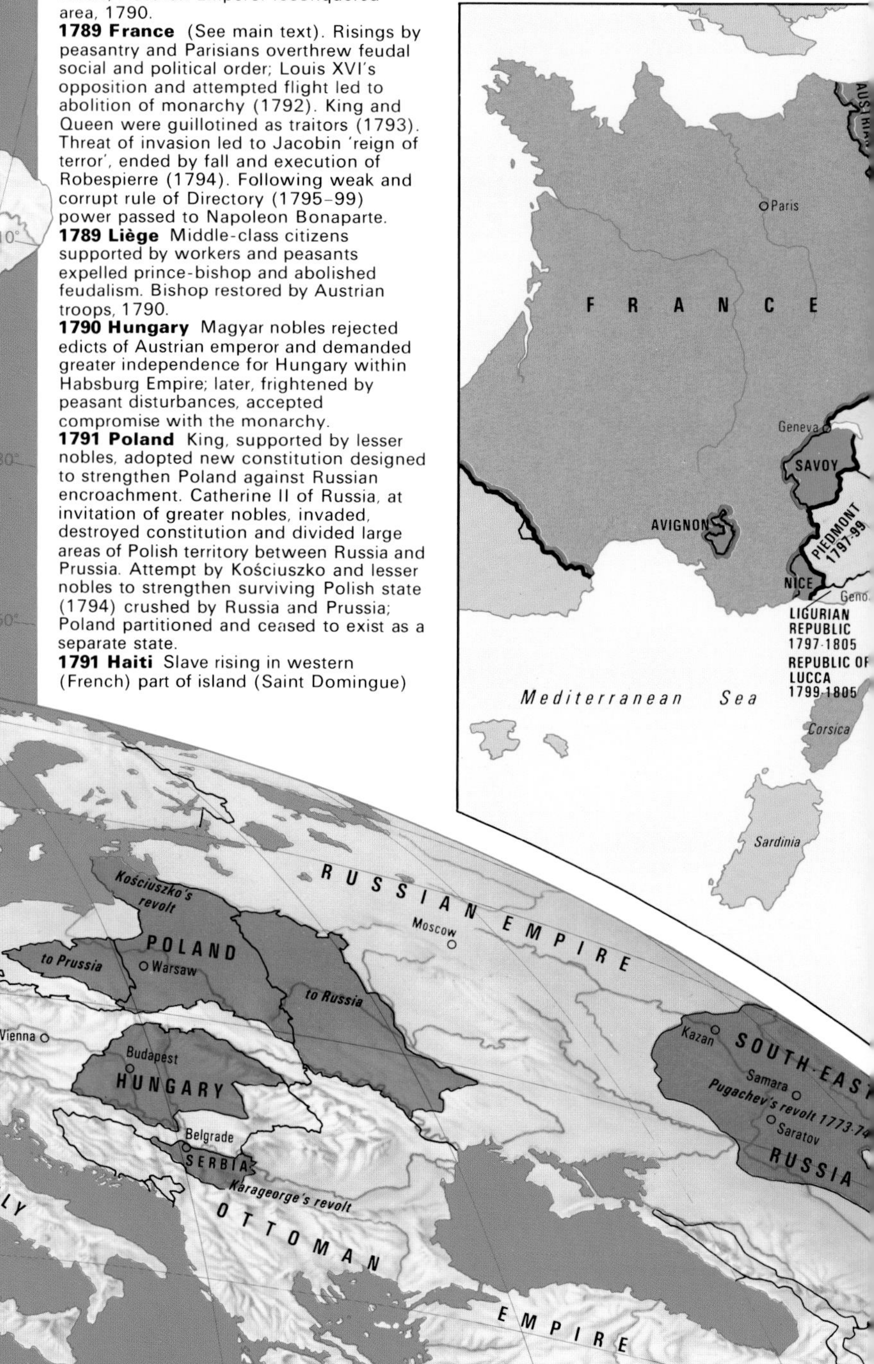

1 Revolts and revolutions in Europe and America

boundaries at 1789 — areas affected by revolution

The second half of the eighteenth century was a time of revolutionary ferment throughout the western hemisphere, from the Volga, where a great peasant insurrection under Pugachev in 1773 took Kazan and threatened Moscow, to Haiti, where the black population rose in rebellion in 1791 under Toussaint l'Ouverture and won control of the island by 1801. The character of the many rebellions of the period (map 1) was varied, but all derived, directly or indirectly, from the Enlightenment, with its assertion of the rights of man, its rationalism and rejection of traditional authority. Paradoxically, it was enlightened rulers, such as Catherine II of Russia (1762–96) and Joseph II of Austria (1780–90), searching for more modern and efficient foundations for government, who gave practical expression to the new ideas, thus provoking the opposition of vested interests, aristocratic and provincial. Provinces like the Austrian Netherlands (1787) and Hungary (1790) rose in rebellion against the centralising policies and reforming edicts of progressive rulers; colonial peoples resisted dictation by the home government and demanded autonomy or at least no taxation without consent, as in North America in 1775 (page 92) and in South America after 1808 (page 96). The demand for independence was the commonest motive for revolt, and lay behind the risings in Ireland (1798), Corsica (1755, 1793), Sardinia (1793), Spain (1808), Serbia (1804), and the Tyrol (1809). Sometimes they were underpinned by social unrest; but this was exceptional. Serfdom was abolished in Savoy (1771), Austria (1781), Baden (1783) and Denmark (1788), and peasants had more to hope for from reforming monarchs than from nobles who were their oppressors. Hence their failure to support the gentry in the Polish revolts of 1791 and 1794. Revolts against patrician oligarchies occurred in Geneva (1768) and the Netherlands (1784–87); but usually it was only when concerted aristocratic opposition to the monarchy opened the flood-gates that the peasants and the labouring class took a hand. This was what happened in France after 1787.

The immediate cause of the French revolution was the financial crisis arising from the American war (page 86). By 1786 the government was faced with bankruptcy, and after a vain attempt to persuade an Assembly of Notables to tax the privileged classes, Louis XVI was forced by a rebellious aristocracy to summon the Estates-General which had not met since 1614. When the Estates-General turned itself into a National Assembly on June 17, 1789, the revolution had begun, but it was still a middle-class revolution, and the constitution drawn up in 1791 showed their distrust of the masses by limiting the right to vote. But they counted without the workers, exasperated by a serious economic crisis and by fear of counter-revolution. In Paris, a popular rising stormed the Bastille (July 14, 1789); in the provinces peasants burned châteaux and murdered landlords. Matters now proceeded apace (map 2), particularly when Austria and Prussia threatened invasion. This sealed the fate of constitutional monarchy. In 1792 a republic was proclaimed; in 1793 Louis XVI was executed and a Committee of Public Safety set up, first under Danton and then under Robespierre, which instituted a reign of terror against enemies at home, while Carnot mobilised an army of 770,000 men against enemies abroad.

By 1795 the French armies were victorious and the revolution had spent itself. Spain and Prussia made peace; French troops held Belgium and the left bank of the Rhine, while William V of Holland was deposed and his country turned into a Batavian republic, closely bound to France, forerunner of other similar republics from Naples to Switzerland (map 3). French influence was spreading far and wide, a victory not simply for French arms but for the ideas and achievements of the revolution, equality before the law, the abolition of feudalism, and the 'rights of man' as defined in the famous declaration of October 2, 1789. When French troops entered the Rhineland in 1792 they were welcomed as liberators and 'brothers' by the educated middle classes. Except among the conservative peasantry, who fought the revolution in France itself from 1793 to 1802, the principles of the French revolution had immense appeal; and though their appeal was later dimmed, they lighted a torch which was never extinguished, even during the reaction which set in after 1815.

Amsterdam
BATAVIAN REPUBLIC 1795-1806
Brussels
NETHERLANDS
HELVETIC REPUBLIC 1798-1803
AUSTRIA
Campo Formio
Trieste
Venice
PARMA 1797-99
CISALPINE REPUBLIC 1797-1802
Adriatic Sea
Dalmatia
TUSCANY
ROMAN REPUBLIC 1798-99
Rome
Ragusa
Cattaro
Naples
PARTHENOPEAN REPUBLIC 1798-99
IONIAN ISLANDS 1797-99
Sicily

3 The expansion of revolutionary France, 1793-99

frontier of France 1789
frontier of France 1799
areas annexed by France
areas occupied by France
Venetian territory given by France to Austria 1797
states established by revolutionary France

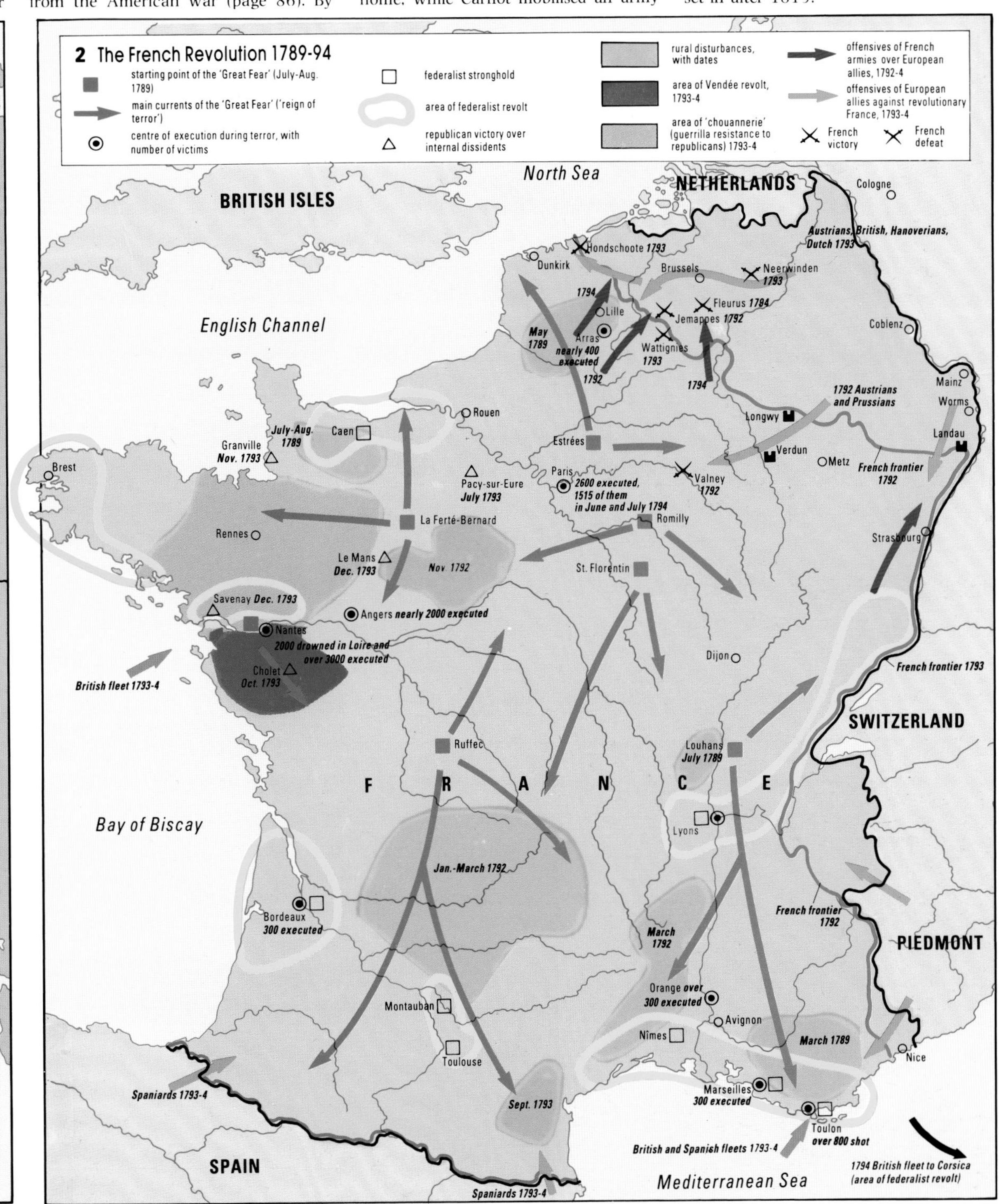

Napoleonic Europe

In 1799 the 31-year-old general Napoleon Bonaparte seized power in France and was to rule until 1814, first as First Consul and then, after 1804, as emperor. His reign was a watershed in the history not only of France but of the whole of Europe. Napoleon had won his reputation by his spectacular victories over Sardinia and Austria in the Italian campaign of 1796; but after 1799, particularly during the Consulate, he proved as brilliant a statesman and administrator as a general. In 1799 Frenchmen, particularly the urban and rural middle classes, wanted peace and security. Napoleon gave them both. The wars were ended by the treaties of Lunéville (1801) and Amiens (1802); for the first time in ten years there was general peace in Europe. At home he gave the citizens who had supported the 'Thermidorian reaction' of 1794 the stability which the Directory (1795–99) had failed to provide. But he was no reactionary. He made it his task to mould the essential achievements of the revolution into permanent institutions. In 1800 the 83 *départements* into which France had been divided in 1789 were reorganised under prefects responsible to the First Consul. The new civil code of 1804 confirmed the property rights created by the revolution and won him the lasting support of the peasant proprietors who were the backbone of the country. At the same time a career open to talents was provided for men of ability rising through the system of state schools and universities established in 1802.

These achievements outlived Napoleon himself, but peace proved elusive. A durable settlement might have been reached with the continental powers, Prussia and Austria; but the issues between France and England were too deep-seated for compromise, and in 1803 Great Britain declared war on France. Thereafter war continued almost without interruption until 1815. In essence it was a continuation of the Anglo-French conflict of the eighteenth century (page 86), complicated by the traditional British fear, ever since the French occupation of the Austrian Netherlands in 1792, of a hostile great power on the Scheldt. From that time Great Britain was the moving spirit behind the anti-French coalitions which it kept going, as in the Seven Years' War, by subsidies. France, on the other hand, had not abandoned the hope of recovering the overseas empire lost in 1763. Napoleon's expedition to Egypt (1798–99) was intended to open the back door to India, and there were other plans for recuperating France's position in the Caribbean and on the American mainland. They were foiled by British control of the sea. Nelson's destruction of the French fleet at Aboukir sealed the fate of the Egyptian expedition (map 2), and elsewhere the French navy was no match for the British, which thwarted French attempts to intervene in Ireland (1797–98) and a projected invasion of England in 1804 (map 3). After Nelson's victory at Trafalgar (1805), British control of the seas was assured, and Napoleon had no alternative except to turn against Britain's continental allies, hoping in this way to seal off Europe and bring Britain to heel by economic pressure.

Napoleon's campaigns against Austria, Prussia and Russia in 1806 and 1807 were brilliantly successful, and 1810 saw him at the peak of his power, directly controlling the whole of western Europe from Catalonia to Lübeck as well as Italy west of the Apennines, with satellite kingdoms and duchies in Spain, the remainder of Italy and Westphalia (map 1). But so long as Britain held out, Napoleon's position was insecure. Control of the sea enabled the British to land an expeditionary force under the future Duke of Wellington in Spain (1808). His at-

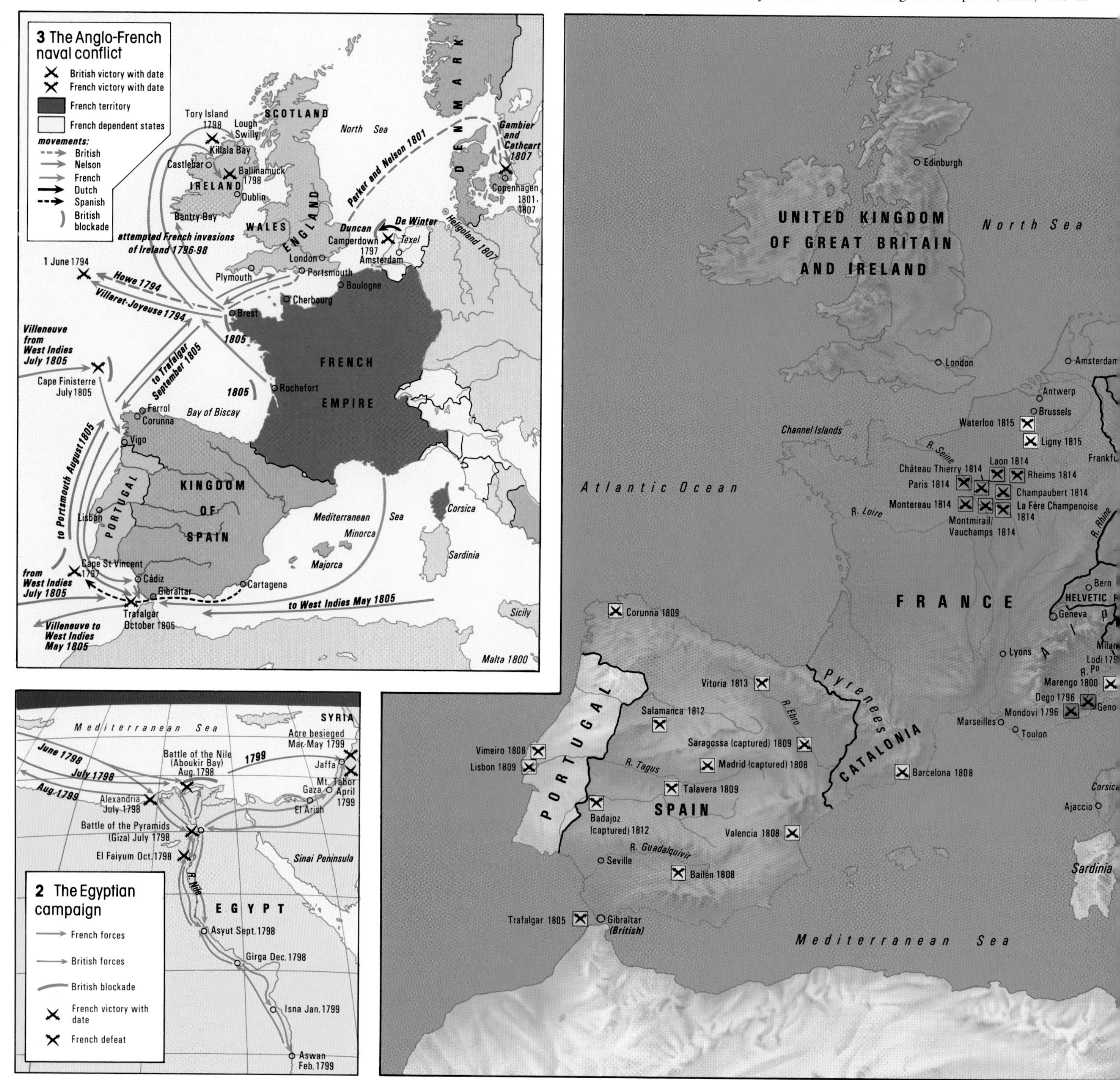

tempt to close the continent to British trade led to his breach with Russia. The invasion of Russia (1812) was an act of desperation, a gamble which failed, and after the retreat from Moscow and the battle of Leipzig (1813) Napoleon's fate was sealed. In the reaction which followed much, but not all, of his system perished. In Germany, in particular, the Napoleonic settlements of 1797–98 and 1803 reduced the 234 territories of the old empire to 40 (map 4), and after 1815 there was no going back. Equally important were the institutional changes introduced on the French model. A society based on wealth and merit rather than prescription and privilege was introduced in the Netherlands, the Rhinelands and north-east Italy, and even countries like Prussia reformed to meet the French challenge. The political geography of Europe was rationalised and the modern national state was born, fragile at first but destined to command the future.

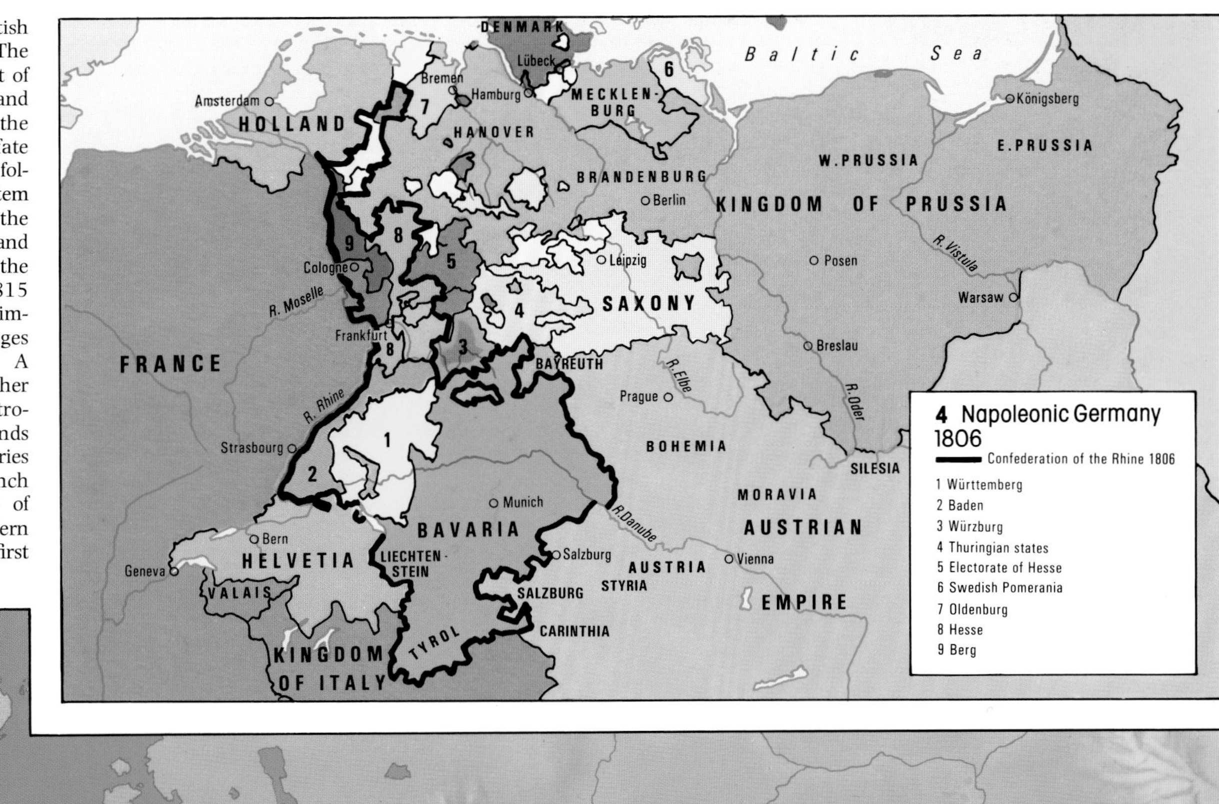

The United States
1783-1865

The disputes and difficulties leading to the American War of Independence and the foundation of the United States began almost immediately after the English victory over France and the acquisition of Canada at the Peace of Paris in 1763 (page 86). When the British government reorganised its vastly expanded North American possessions, establishing a huge Indian reserve west of the Alleghenies (1763) and extending the boundaries of Quebec to the Mississippi and Ohio rivers (1774), its measures were bitterly resented by the colonists in New England, Virginia and Pennsylvania as a check to westward expansion. This resentment, combined with resistance to English tax demands and trade controls, was one of the factors behind the revolt of the American colonies. The War of Independence (map 1) began at Lexington and Concord in Massachusetts in April 1775 and was ended, after the British surrender at Yorktown (October 1781), by the Treaty of Versailles (1783), which extended the frontiers of the newly independent United States to the Great Lakes in the north and the Mississippi in the west.

Once independence was achieved, expansion proceeded rapidly. In 1783 the new republic comprised some 800,000 square miles of territory. The purchase of Louisiana from France (1803) more than doubled its extent. Thereafter expansion in the south and west was largely by conquest at the expense of Mexico (map 2), though the Oregon question, finally settled in 1846, looked for a moment as though it might bring war with Great Britain. In the north settlers moved into the 'back country' in increasing numbers after 1800, but it was the arrival of a new wave of European immigrants, predominantly German and Irish, which populated the Midwest. By 1850 the frontier of settlement had reached the 100th meridian, the dividing line between sparse and adequate rainfall.

This vast territorial expansion, which raised the population from approximately 3,000,000 in 1783 to 31,000,000 on the eve of the Civil War, had important political consequences. By 1860 the original 13 states had increased to 34. The result was a deterioration in the relative position of the Southern states with their plantation economy and black slave population, as a result of which the plantation aristocracy saw itself being swamped by the industrialising North and the growing Midwest. This, rather than the simple issue of slavery, was the underlying cause of the American Civil War, but the issues were in fact inseparable because, with over 90 per cent of the black population living in the South (map 3), the moral question was also a regional question. Abraham Lincoln, elected President in 1860 by a northern vote, was right when he said that the nation could not permanently remain 'half-slave and half-free.'

The North fought at first to preserve the Union; but, significantly, it was over the question of whether slavery should be permitted in Kansas and Nebraska that the conflict came to a head. Soon after Lincoln's election South Carolina seceded from the Union and was quickly joined by ten other states (map 4) which came together as the Confederate States of America with their capital at Richmond, Virginia. The course of the war, which opened with an attack on Fort Sumter in April 1861, can be followed on map 5. Northern strategy was to deny the South vital resources by a naval blockade, to gain control of key river routes and forts in the west and to capture the Confederate capital of Richmond. In spite of the preponderance of the North in manpower and resources, the South held out for four years, a fact which heightened the bitterness and resentment during the subsequent period of Reconstruction. The outcome has been called 'the Second American Revolution'; by crippling the Southern ruling class and liberating its labour force, it determined that the thrusting, urban, industrialised North, with its creed of competitive capitalism, would stamp its pattern – for good or ill – on the entire post-bellum United States.

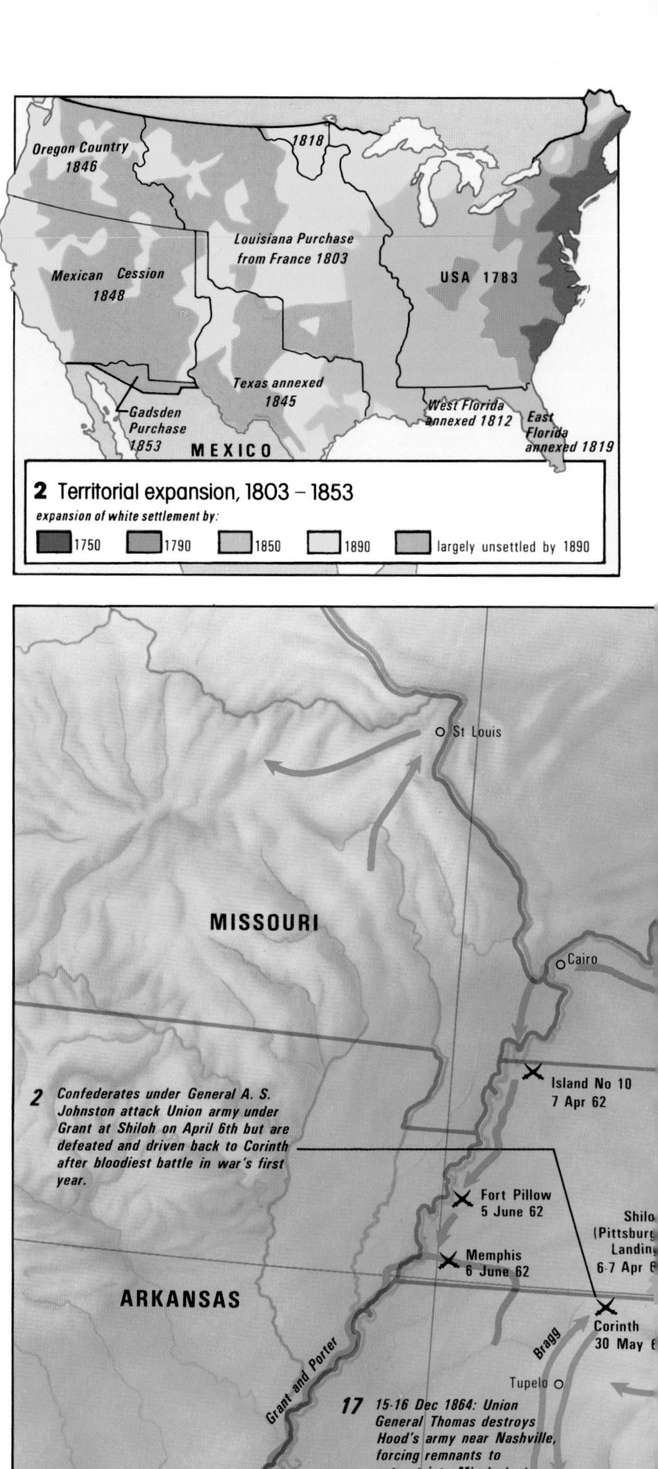

2 Territorial expansion, 1803 – 1853

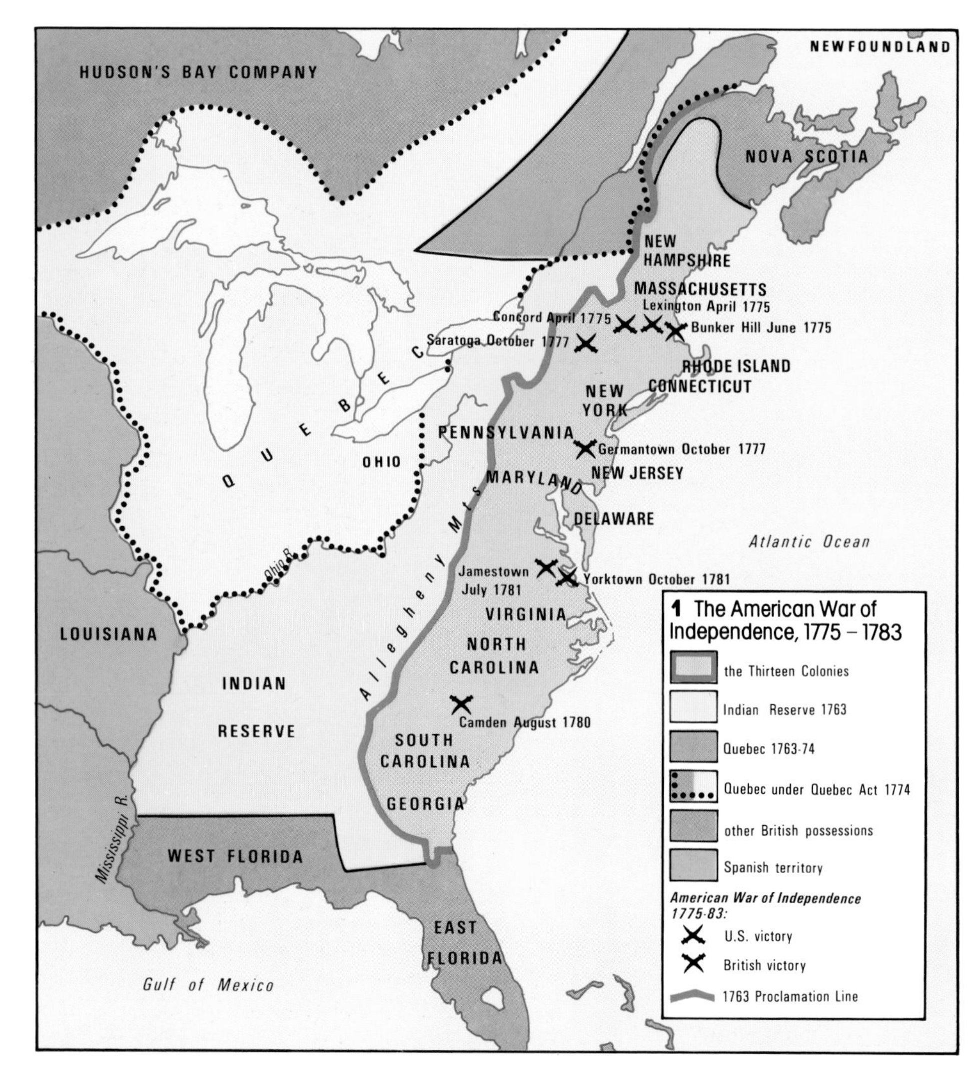

1 The American War of Independence, 1775 – 1783

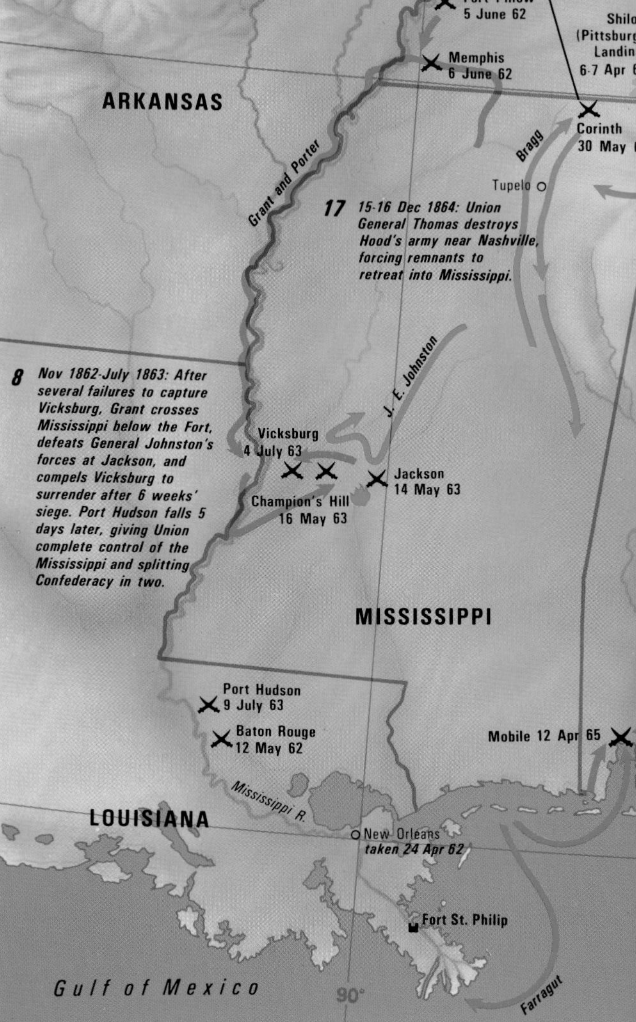

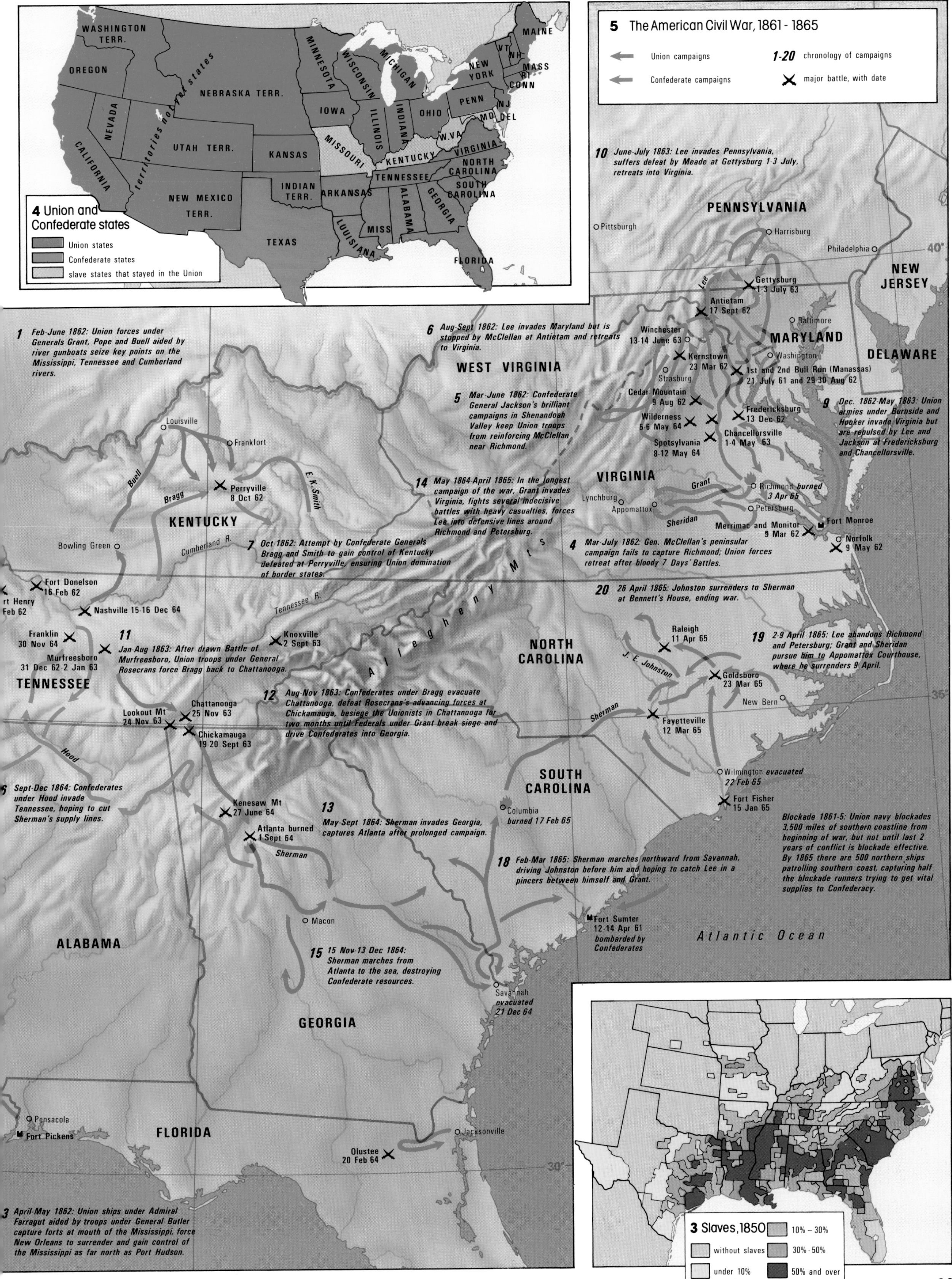
4 Union and Confederate states
Union states
Confederate states
slave states that stayed in the Union
WASHINGTON TERR.
OREGON
NEBRASKA TERR.
MINNESOTA
WISCONSIN
MICHIGAN
MAINE
VT
NH
MASS
RI
CONN
NEW YORK
PENN
NJ
MD
DEL
IOWA
ILLINOIS
INDIANA
OHIO
NEVADA
UTAH TERR.
KANSAS
MISSOURI
KENTUCKY
W.VA
VIRGINIA
NORTH CAROLINA
TENNESSEE
SOUTH CAROLINA
CALIFORNIA
territories not yet states
NEW MEXICO TERR.
INDIAN TERR.
ARKANSAS
ALABAMA
GEORGIA
MISS
TEXAS
LOUISIANA
FLORIDA
5 The American Civil War, 1861 - 1865
Union campaigns
Confederate campaigns
1-20 chronology of campaigns
major battle, with date
1 Feb-June 1862: Union forces under Generals Grant, Pope and Buell aided by river gunboats seize key points on the Mississippi, Tennessee and Cumberland rivers.
3 April-May 1862: Union ships under Admiral Farragut aided by troops under General Butler capture forts at mouth of the Mississippi, force New Orleans to surrender and gain control of the Mississippi as far north as Port Hudson.
4 Mar-July 1862: Gen. McClellan's peninsular campaign fails to capture Richmond; Union forces retreat after bloody 7 Days' Battles.
5 Mar-June 1862: Confederate General Jackson's brilliant campaigns in Shenandoah Valley keep Union troops from reinforcing McClellan near Richmond.
6 Aug-Sept 1862: Lee invades Maryland but is stopped by McClellan at Antietam and retreats to Virginia.
7 Oct 1862: Attempt by Confederate Generals Bragg and Smith to gain control of Kentucky defeated at Perryville, ensuring Union domination of border states.
9 Dec. 1862-May 1863: Union armies under Burnside and Hooker invade Virginia but are repulsed by Lee and Jackson at Fredericksburg and Chancellorsville.
10 June-July 1863: Lee invades Pennsylvania, suffers defeat by Meade at Gettysburg 1-3 July, retreats into Virginia.
11 Jan-Aug 1863: After drawn Battle of Murfreesboro, Union troops under General Rosecrans force Bragg back to Chattanooga.
12 Aug-Nov 1863: Confederates under Bragg evacuate Chattanooga, defeat Rosecrans's advancing forces at Chickamauga, besiege the Unionists in Chattanooga for two months until Federals under Grant break siege and drive Confederates into Georgia.
13 May-Sept 1864: Sherman invades Georgia, captures Atlanta after prolonged campaign.
14 May 1864-April 1865: In the longest campaign of the war, Grant invades Virginia, fights several indecisive battles with heavy casualties, forces Lee into defensive lines around Richmond and Petersburg.
15 15 Nov-13 Dec 1864: Sherman marches from Atlanta to the sea, destroying Confederate resources.
16 Sept-Dec 1864: Confederates under Hood invade Tennessee, hoping to cut Sherman's supply lines.
18 Feb-Mar 1865: Sherman marches northward from Savannah, driving Johnston before him and hoping to catch Lee in a pincers between himself and Grant.
19 2-9 April 1865: Lee abandons Richmond and Petersburg; Grant and Sheridan pursue him to Appomattox Courthouse, where he surrenders 9 April.
20 26 April 1865: Johnston surrenders to Sherman at Bennett's House, ending war.
Blockade 1861-5: Union navy blockades 3,500 miles of southern coastline from beginning of war, but not until last 2 years of conflict is blockade effective. By 1865 there are 500 northern ships patrolling southern coast, capturing half the blockade runners trying to get vital supplies to Confederacy.
PENNSYLVANIA
Pittsburgh
Harrisburg
Philadelphia
NEW JERSEY
Gettysburg 1-3 July 63
Antietam 17 Sept 62
Baltimore
MARYLAND
DELAWARE
Winchester 13-14 June 63
Kernstown 23 Mar 62
Washington
Strasburg
1st and 2nd Bull Run (Manassas) 21 July 61 and 29-30 Aug 62
Cedar Mountain 9 Aug 62
Wilderness 5-6 May 64
Fredericksburg 13 Dec 62
Chancellorsville 1-4 May 63
Spotsylvania 8-12 May 64
WEST VIRGINIA
VIRGINIA
Lynchburg
Appomattox
Richmond burned 3 Apr 65
Petersburg
Grant
Sheridan
Lee
Merrimac and Monitor 9 Mar 62
Fort Monroe
Norfolk 9 May 62
Louisville
Frankfort
Buell
Bragg
E. K. Smith
Perryville 8 Oct 62
KENTUCKY
Bowling Green
Cumberland R.
Fort Donelson 16 Feb 62
Fort Henry Feb 62
Nashville 15-16 Dec 64
Franklin 30 Nov 64
Murfreesboro 31 Dec 62-2 Jan 63
TENNESSEE
Tennessee R.
Knoxville 2 Sept 63
Allegheny Mts
NORTH CAROLINA
Raleigh 11 Apr 65
J. E. Johnston
Goldsboro 23 Mar 65
New Bern
Chattanooga 25 Nov 63
Lookout Mt 24 Nov 63
Chickamauga 19-20 Sept 63
Hood
Sherman
Fayetteville 12 Mar 65
SOUTH CAROLINA
Wilmington evacuated 22 Feb 65
Fort Fisher 15 Jan 65
Kenesaw Mt 27 June 64
Atlanta burned 1 Sept 64
Columbia burned 17 Feb 65
Macon
Fort Sumter 12-14 Apr 61 bombarded by Confederates
Atlantic Ocean
ALABAMA
Savannah evacuated 21 Dec 64
GEORGIA
Pensacola
Fort Pickens
FLORIDA
Jacksonville
Olustee 20 Feb 64
40°
35°
30°
3 Slaves, 1850
without slaves
under 10%
10% – 30%
30% - 50%
50% and over

The expansion of the United States
1803-1898

The dominant fact in the history of the United States during the nineteenth century was the opening of the continent. In 1783 the effective frontier of the new Republic was the Allegheny Mountains (page 92). The Louisiana Purchase (1803) opened vast new areas for explorers, led by the famous expedition of Lewis and Clark (1804–8), and for settlers who quickly followed in their wake (map 1). After the Mexican wars (1846–8) and the discovery of gold in California (1848) prospectors, miners, speculators and settlers pushed west across the mountain chains from Salt Lake City and Santa Fe or by the Overland Trail from San Antonio. The great westward movement, bolstered by a confident belief in America's 'manifest destiny', could not, however, proceed without brutal disregard for the native population. The destruction of the North American Indians had begun much earlier in New England in the Pequot war of 1636, and the Delaware Indians were uprooted and driven west before the end of the eighteenth century; but it was in the 1830s, when the land-hunger of the white planters and settlers became insatiable, that the expulsion of whole tribes, Cherokee, Chocktaw, Creek and Chickasaw, and their deportation to the Midwest (and later to Indian reservations) got underway. By 1850 the frontier had reached the 100th meridian, and it was here, in the Midwest and West, that the great battles of the 1860s and 1870s took place, which reduced the Indian population to scarcely more than 200,000 by the end of the nineteenth century (map 2).

In their place, and usurping their lands, poured in a flood of immigrants, mainly from Europe, which reached its peak in the last decade of the century (diagram 4). In the later phases most of the immigrants (from southern and eastern Europe) remained in the cities on the eastern seaboard, where they swelled the industrial proletariat; but by mid-century Germans and Scandinavians had formed a preponderant element on the farming frontier of Wisconsin, Iowa and Minnesota, and in the last quarter of the century British and Irish settlers, as well as native Americans, played an important part in the development of cattle ranching and stock raising in Texas, Wyoming and New Mexico. British capital and British land companies also contributed. But the most important area of European investment before 1914 was the financing of American railways, particularly the transcontinental lines. Railroads in operation in 1840 were confined to a few industrial regions in the east. British capital provided the finance to double the mileage between 1866 and 1873 and to carry it west, and this westward shift of transport and population was accompanied by a similar shift of agricultural production (map 3). The effects were dramatic. By 1890, when the rail network was larger than that of the whole of Europe, including the British Isles and Russia, a population moving onto virgin lands, with improved mechanisation, such as the steel plough, new strains of cotton, wheat and maize, and the ubiquitous barbed wire fence, had made the United States the world's leading agricultural producer.

By 1890 the frontier was closed, the prospect of indefinite opportunities within the boundaries of the United States becoming a thing of the past. West of the 100th meridian population was still sparse, and urban and industrial development negligible (page 110); the great upsurge in the colonisation and development of California and the Pacific seaboard was still to come. Nevertheless 1890 marked a turning point, registered in 1898 when the United States, denying its own past refusal to involve itself in other continents, turned from the American continent to the wider world of Asia. In 1898 American history merged into world history, with incalculable consequences for the future.

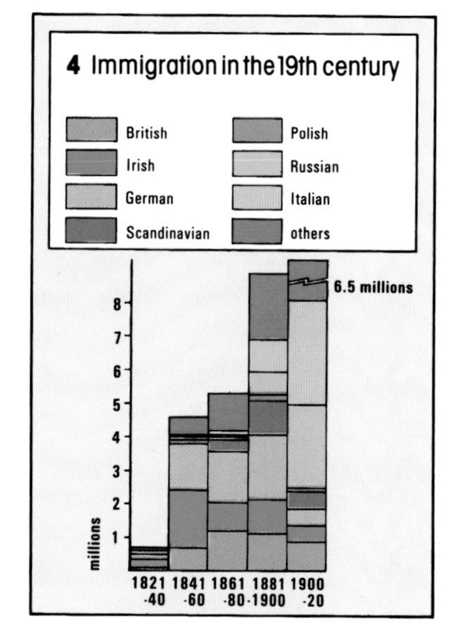

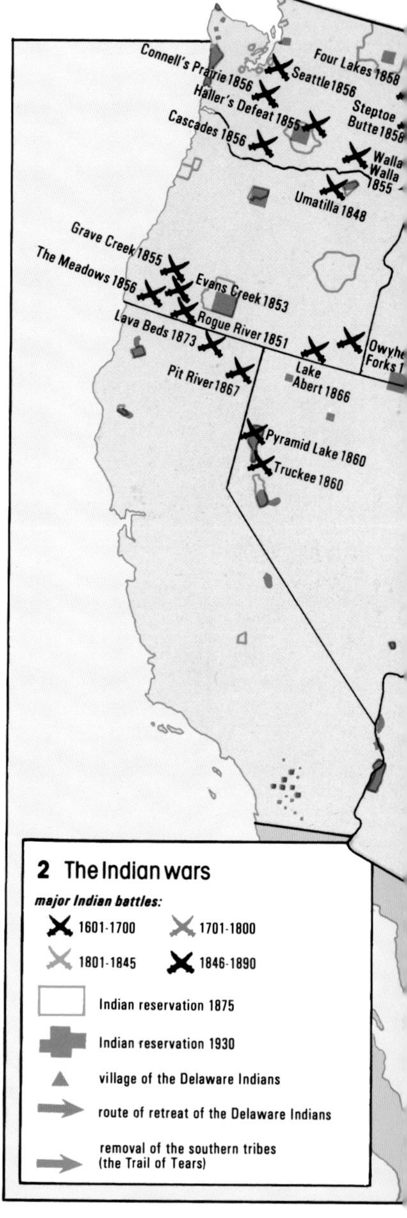

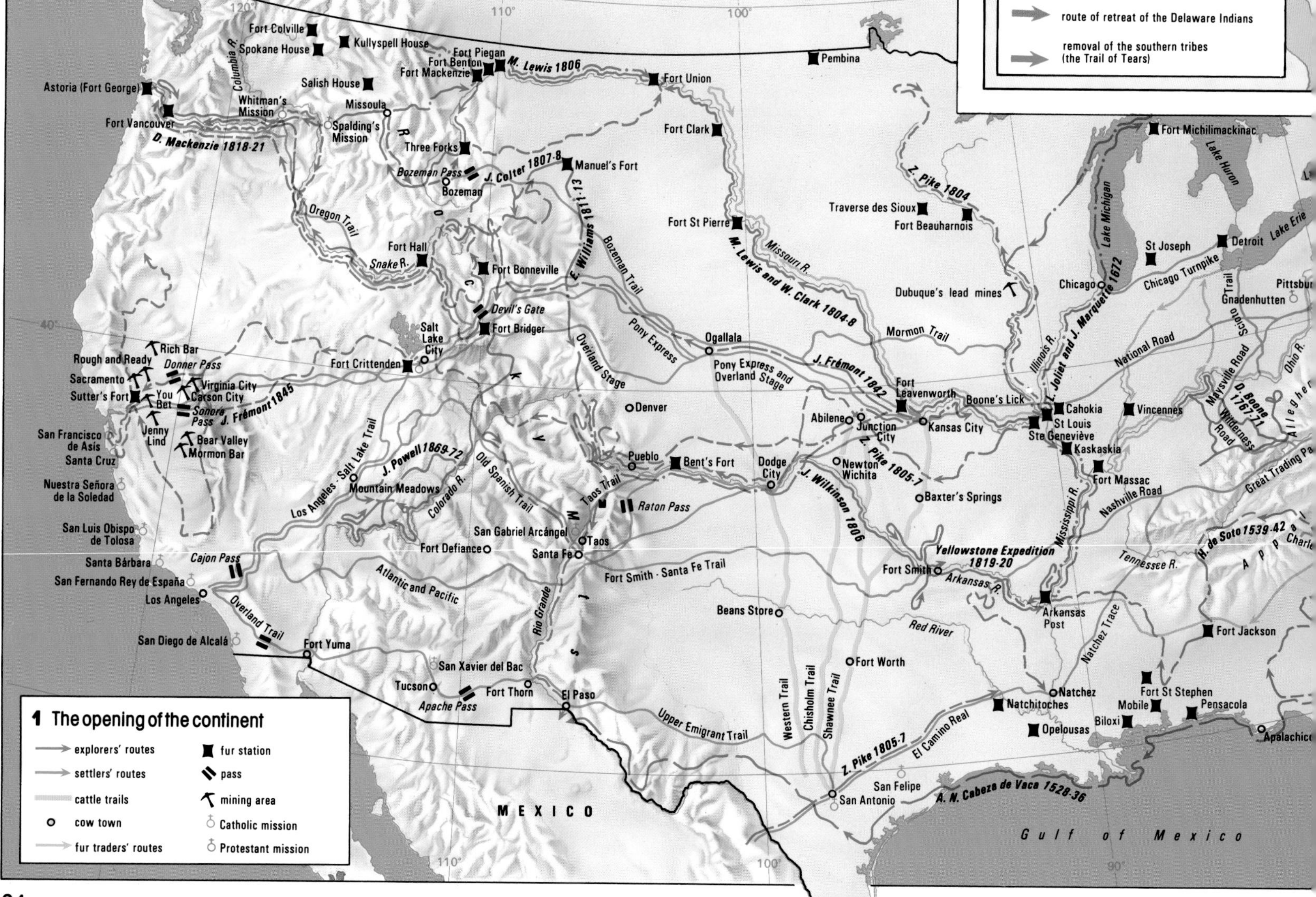

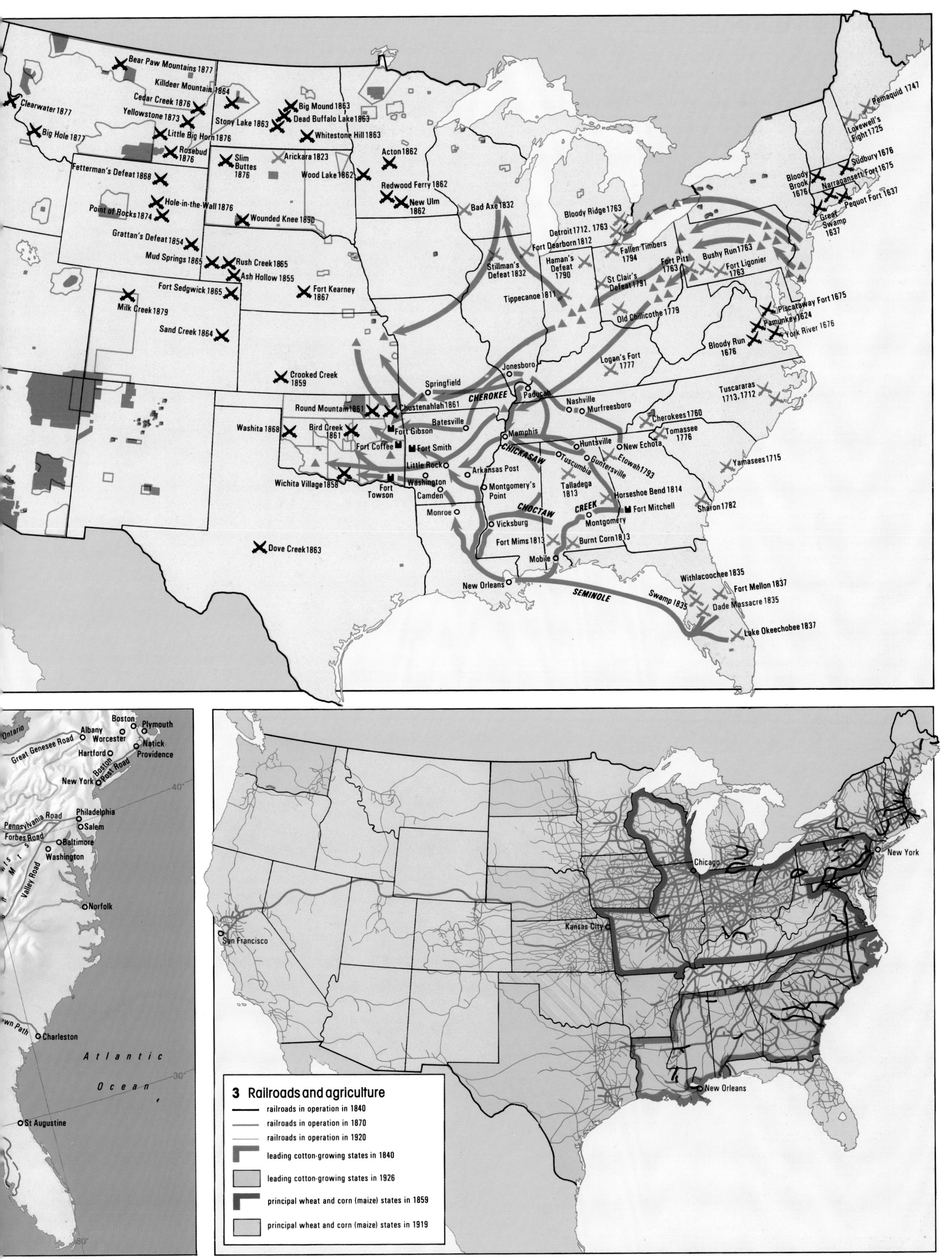
Bear Paw Mountains 1877
Killdeer Mountain 1864
Clearwater 1877
Cedar Creek 1876
Yellowstone 1873
Big Hole 1877
Little Big Horn 1876
Rosebud 1876
Big Mound 1863
Dead Buffalo Lake 1863
Stony Lake 1863
Whitestone Hill 1863
Slim Buttes 1876
Arickara 1823
Acton 1862
Wood Lake 1862
Redwood Ferry 1862
New Ulm 1862
Fetterman's Defeat 1868
Hole-in-the-Wall 1876
Point of Rocks 1874
Wounded Knee 1890
Grattan's Defeat 1854
Mud Springs 1865
Rush Creek 1865
Ash Hollow 1855
Fort Sedgwick 1865
Fort Kearney 1867
Milk Creek 1879
Sand Creek 1864
Crooked Creek 1859
Round Mountain 1861
Chustenahlah 1861
Washita 1868
Bird Creek 1861
Fort Gibson
Fort Coffee
Fort Smith
Wichita Village 1858
Fort Towson
Dove Creek 1863
Bad Axe 1832
Stillman's Defeat 1832
Fort Dearborn 1812
Detroit 1712, 1763
Bloody Ridge 1763
Haman's Defeat 1790
Fallen Timbers 1794
St Clair's Defeat 1791
Tippecanoe 1811
Old Chillicothe 1779
Fort Pitt 1763
Bushy Run 1763
Fort Ligonier 1763
Remaquid 1747
Lovewell's Fight 1725
Sudbury 1676
Bloody Brook 1676
Narragansett Fort 1675
Pequot Fort 1637
Great Swamp 1637
Piscataway Fort 1675
Pamunkey 1624
York River 1676
Bloody Run 1676
Logan's Fort 1777
Jonesboro
Springfield
Paducah
CHEROKEE
Nashville
Murfreesboro
Batesville
Memphis
CHICKASAW
Huntsville
New Echota
Tuscumbia
Guntersville
Etowah 1793
Tuscararas 1713, 1712
Cherokees 1760
Tomassee 1776
Yamasees 1715
Little Rock
Arkansas Post
Washington
Camden
Montgomery's Point
Talladega 1813
Horseshoe Bend 1814
Fort Mitchell
CHOCTAW
CREEK
Montgomery
Monroe
Vicksburg
Sharon 1782
Fort Mims 1813
Burnt Corn 1813
Mobile
New Orleans
SEMINOLE
Withlacoochee 1835
Fort Mellon 1837
Swamp 1835
Dade Massacre 1835
Lake Okeechobee 1837
Ontario
Boston
Plymouth
Albany
Worcester
Great Genesee Road
Natick
Hartford
Providence
Boston Post Road
New York
Philadelphia
Pennsylvania Road
Salem
Forbes Road
Baltimore
Washington
Valley Road
Norfolk
Charleston
Atlantic Ocean
St Augustine
Chicago
New York
Kansas City
San Francisco
New Orleans
3 Railroads and agriculture
railroads in operation in 1840
railroads in operation in 1870
railroads in operation in 1920
leading cotton-growing states in 1840
leading cotton-growing states in 1926
principal wheat and corn (maize) states in 1859
principal wheat and corn (maize) states in 1919

Independent Latin America
1808-1910

Napoleon's invasion of Spain and Portugal in 1808 (page 90) enabled their colonies to assert their independence. The revolt began in Argentina in 1810 and Venezuela in 1811, and was later helped by Great Britain and the United States which prevented intervention by the Iberian powers. After the fall of Lima (1821) and Bolívar's victory at Ayacucho (1824) Spain's fate in South America was sealed. In the north, early revolts in Mexico were suppressed, but in 1823 a republic was proclaimed, and a last Spanish attempt at reconquest in 1829 was defeated by Santa Ana. Only Brazil made the transition to nationhood peacefully. Here Portugal agreed to a constitution, and in 1822 the Portuguese king's eldest son became ruler of an independent Brazilian empire, as Pedro I. Only in 1889 when, following the abolition of slavery (1888), disgruntled plantation-owners rose in revolt, was the empire replaced by a federal republic.

Independence essentially was a political movement in the hands of the colonial aristocracy, who wanted a transfer of authority but a minimum of social upheaval. After 1826 the old colonial division between a privileged minority, monopolising land and office, and a barely subsisting mass of peasants, grew sharper. Though the period was rarely without civil strife, the *caudillos*, or military dictators, who dominated the scene during the 50 years following independence, ruled in the interests of the privileged classes, and there was only marginal reform before the Indian, Benito Juárez, took over in Mexico in 1861 (map 1). There were also repeated territorial disputes between the different republics, the fiercest being the War of the Pacific for control of the Atacama Desert nitrate deposits (map 4), to say nothing of the wars with the United States (page 92) which deprived Mexico of 40 per cent of its territory. Bolívar had plans for an all-encompassing South American Union, but they came to nothing at the Congress of Panama (1826). Instead, such federations as existed (e.g. Great Colombia, 1819–30) quickly fell apart into their constituent elements, usually representing former Spanish administrative units.

For most of the century there was virtually a subsistence economy in most republics. Brazil, with its coffee plantations based on slave labour, was an exception. Elsewhere the *hacendados* treated their estates more or less as self-supporting and self-sufficient, and had little interest in production for the market. Change only came after about 1880 when foreign investment, hitherto modest, increased rapidly (map 3). Even so, it was highly selective, concentrated mainly in Argentina, Brazil, Mexico and Chile. Except in Mexico, where the United States predominated, Britain had the lion's share, much of it in railways. The stimulus was undoubted, but it also shifted the economy sharply to the export of primary products. Argentina's 'revolution on the pampas' made it a main supplier of grain and meat; Chile was the world's leading producer of nitrates; Brazil exported coffee and rubber, and American food corporations invested heavily in the so-called 'banana republics.' The economic 'take off' also attracted a new wave of European, mainly Italian and Spanish, settlers, notably in Argentina, which greatly altered the population profile (map 2). Urbanisation increased apace, and with it came the beginning of a new urban and industrial proletariat and a middle class growing rich on the export trade. But unbalanced growth also produced new problems. The dictatorship of Porfirio Díaz (1877–1910) brought spectacular economic progress to Mexico, but the mass of the people were left in abject poverty. The result was the Mexican revolution of 1911, the harbinger of a new era in the history of Latin America.

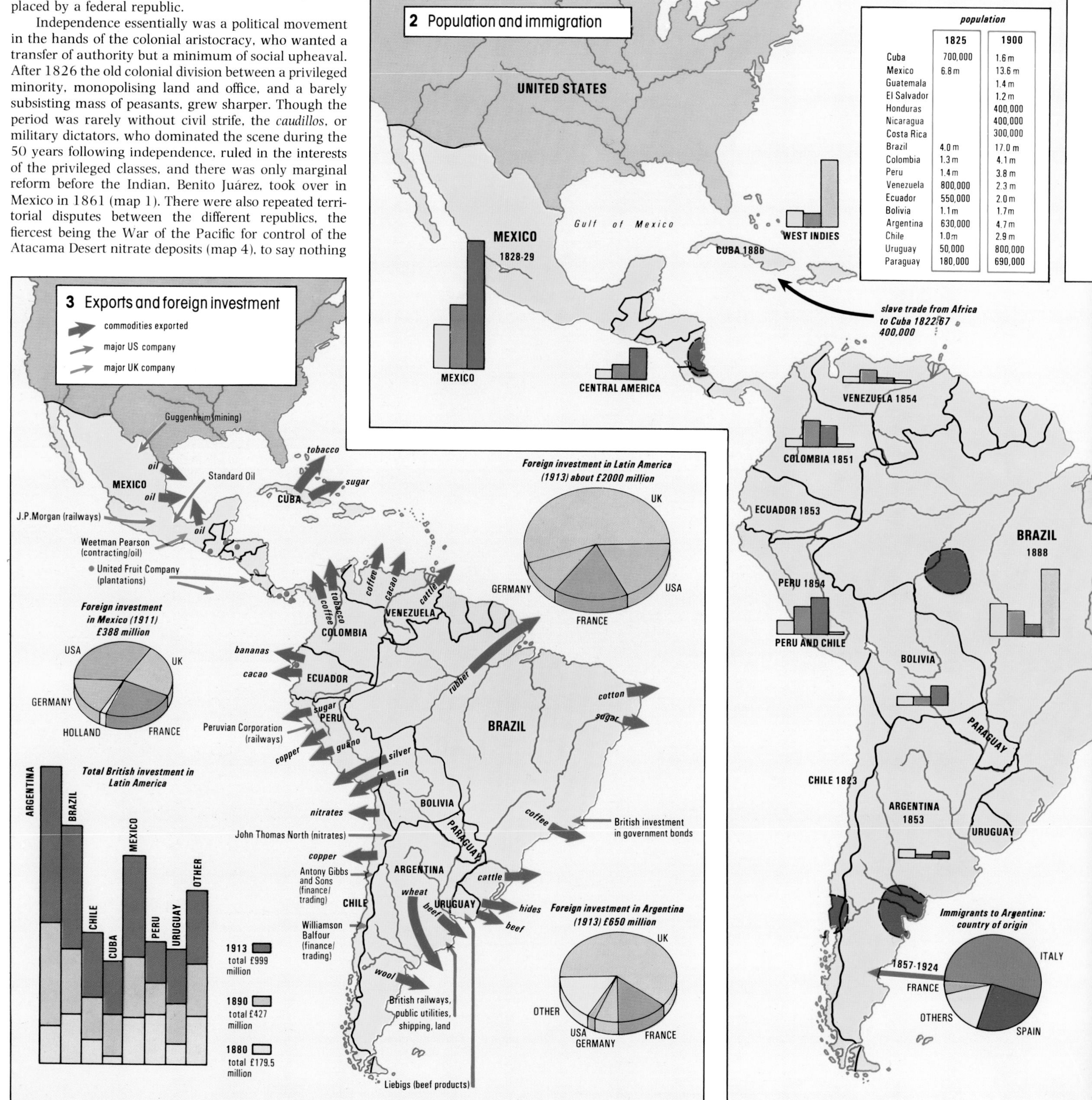

population	1825	1900
Cuba	700,000	1.6 m
Mexico	6.8 m	13.6 m
Guatemala		1.4 m
El Salvador		1.2 m
Honduras		400,000
Nicaragua		400,000
Costa Rica		300,000
Brazil	4.0 m	17.0 m
Colombia	1.3 m	4.1 m
Peru	1.4 m	3.8 m
Venezuela	800,000	2.3 m
Ecuador	550,000	2.0 m
Bolivia	1.1 m	1.7 m
Argentina	630,000	4.7 m
Chile	1.0 m	2.9 m
Uruguay	50,000	800,000
Paraguay	180,000	690,000

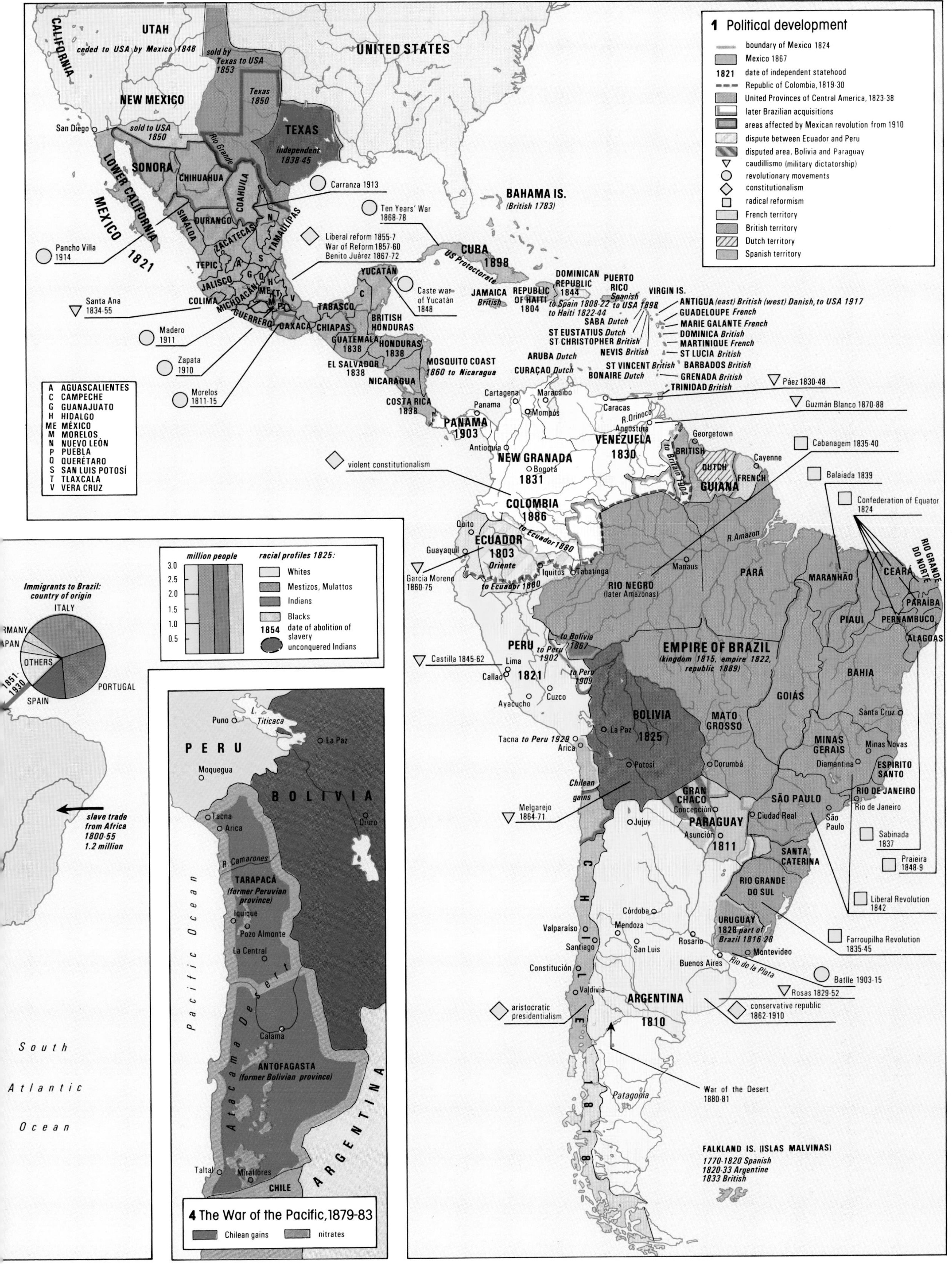
1 Political development
boundary of Mexico 1824
Mexico 1867
1821 date of independent statehood
Republic of Colombia, 1819-30
United Provinces of Central America, 1823-38
later Brazilian acquisitions
areas affected by Mexican revolution from 1910
dispute between Ecuador and Peru
disputed area, Bolivia and Paraguay
caudillismo (military dictatorship)
revolutionary movements
constitutionalism
radical reformism
French territory
British territory
Dutch territory
Spanish territory
UTAH
CALIFORNIA
ceded to USA by Mexico 1848
sold by Texas to USA 1853
UNITED STATES
Texas 1850
NEW MEXICO
San Diego
sold to USA 1850
TEXAS
independent 1838-45
Rio Grande
SONORA
CHIHUAHUA
COAHUILA
LOWER CALIFORNIA
MEXICO
1821
Carranza 1913
Ten Years' War 1868-78
BAHAMA IS.
(British 1783)
Liberal reform 1855-7
War of Reform 1857-60
Benito Juárez 1867-72
Pancho Villa 1914
SINALOA
DURANGO
ZACATECAS
TAMAULIPAS
CUBA 1898
US Protectorate
TEPIC
JALISCO
COLIMA
MICHOACÁN
GUERRERO
OAXACA
CHIAPAS
TABASCO
YUCATÁN
Caste war of Yucatán 1848
Santa Ana 1834-55
Madero 1911
Zapata 1910
Morelos 1811-15
BRITISH HONDURAS
GUATEMALA 1838
HONDURAS 1838
EL SALVADOR 1838
NICARAGUA
MOSQUITO COAST
1860 to Nicaragua
COSTA RICA 1838
PANAMA 1903
JAMAICA British
REPUBLIC OF HAITI 1804
DOMINICAN REPUBLIC 1844
to Spain 1808-22
to Haiti 1822-44
PUERTO RICO
Spanish to USA 1898
VIRGIN IS.
ANTIGUA (east) British (west) Danish, to USA 1917
GUADELOUPE French
MARIE GALANTE French
DOMINICA British
MARTINIQUE French
ST LUCIA British
BARBADOS British
GRENADA British
TRINIDAD British
SABA Dutch
ST EUSTATIUS Dutch
ST CHRISTOPHER British
NEVIS British
ST VINCENT British
ARUBA Dutch
CURAÇAO Dutch
BONAIRE Dutch
Páez 1830-48
Guzmán Blanco 1870-88
A AGUASCALIENTES
C CAMPECHE
G GUANAJUATO
H HIDALGO
ME MÉXICO
M MORELOS
N NUEVO LEÓN
P PUEBLA
Q QUERÉTARO
S SAN LUIS POTOSÍ
T TLAXCALA
V VERA CRUZ
Cartagena
Maracaibo
Panama
Mompós
Caracas
R. Orinoco
Angostura
VENEZUELA 1830
Georgetown
BRITISH
to Britain 1904
DUTCH
GUIANA
FRENCH
Cayenne
Cabanagem 1835-40
Balaiada 1839
Confederation of Equator 1824
Antioquia
NEW GRANADA
Bogotá
1831
violent constitutionalism
COLOMBIA 1886
Quito
ECUADOR 1803
Guayaquil
Oriente
to Ecuador 1880
García Moreno 1860-75
Iquitos
Tabatinga
Manaus
R. Amazon
RIO NEGRO (later Amazonas)
PARÁ
MARANHÃO
CEARÁ
RIO GRANDE DO NORTE
PARAÍBA
PIAUÍ
PERNAMBUCO
ALAGOAS
to Bolivia 1867
to Peru 1902
to Peru 1909
PERU
Lima
Callao
1821
Castilla 1845-62
Ayacucho
Cuzco
EMPIRE OF BRAZIL
(kingdom 1815, empire 1822, republic 1889)
BAHIA
GOIÁS
MATO GROSSO
BOLIVIA 1825
La Paz
Potosí
Tacna to Peru 1929
Arica
Corumbá
Santa Cruz
Minas Novas
MINAS GERAIS
Diamantina
ESPÍRITO SANTO
RIO DE JANEIRO
Rio de Janeiro
Chilean gains
Melgarejo 1864-71
GRAN CHACO
Concepción
PARAGUAY
Asunción
1811
Jujuy
SÃO PAULO
Ciudad Real
São Paulo
Sabinada 1837
Praieira 1848-9
SANTA CATERINA
RIO GRANDE DO SUL
Liberal Revolution 1842
Córdoba
Mendoza
Valparaíso
Santiago
San Luis
Rosario
URUGUAY
1828 part of Brazil 1816-28
Montevideo
Farroupilha Revolution 1835-45
Buenos Aires
Río de la Plata
Constitución
Valdivia
Batlle 1903-15
Rosas 1829-52
aristocratic presidentialism
ARGENTINA
1810
conservative republic 1862-1910
CHILE
1818
Patagonia
War of the Desert 1880-81
FALKLAND IS. (ISLAS MALVINAS)
1770-1820 Spanish
1820-33 Argentine
1833 British
million people
racial profiles 1825:
3.0
2.5
2.0
1.5
1.0
0.5
Whites
Mestizos, Mulattos
Indians
Blacks
1854 date of abolition of slavery
unconquered Indians
Immigrants to Brazil: country of origin
ITALY
PORTUGAL
SPAIN
OTHERS
1851-1930
slave trade from Africa 1800-55 1.2 million
South Atlantic Ocean
4 The War of the Pacific, 1879-83
Chilean gains
nitrates
Puno
L. Titicaca
La Paz
PERU
Moquegua
BOLIVIA
Oruro
Tacna
Arica
R. Camarones
TARAPACÁ
(former Peruvian province)
Iquique
Pozo Almonte
La Central
Pacific Ocean
Atacama Desert
Calama
ANTOFAGASTA
(former Bolivian province)
ARGENTINA
Taltal
Miraflores
CHILE

The Industrial Revolution in Europe, 1760-1914

The Industrial Revolution, which began in England in the reign of George III (1760–1820), was the catalyst of the modern world. Nevertheless the speed of change should not be exaggerated. Even in continental Europe its impact was limited before 1850 to a few industrial enclaves, and it was not until the last quarter of the nineteenth century – in the case of France, Italy and Russia only after 1890 – that the great surge forward occurred. Outside Europe, with the sole exception of the United States, its impact was delayed for much longer (page 108). Even in Germany 35 per cent of the population was engaged in agriculture in 1895, and most of eastern Europe (Poland, Romania, Bulgaria) and much of southern Europe (Spain, Greece, southern Italy) was virtually untouched by industry. Until 1900, when it began to be challenged by Germany and the United States, the United Kingdom was the workshop of the world, and its industrial strength, which enabled it to dominate world markets, accounts for its pre-eminence in the age of imperialism (page 100).

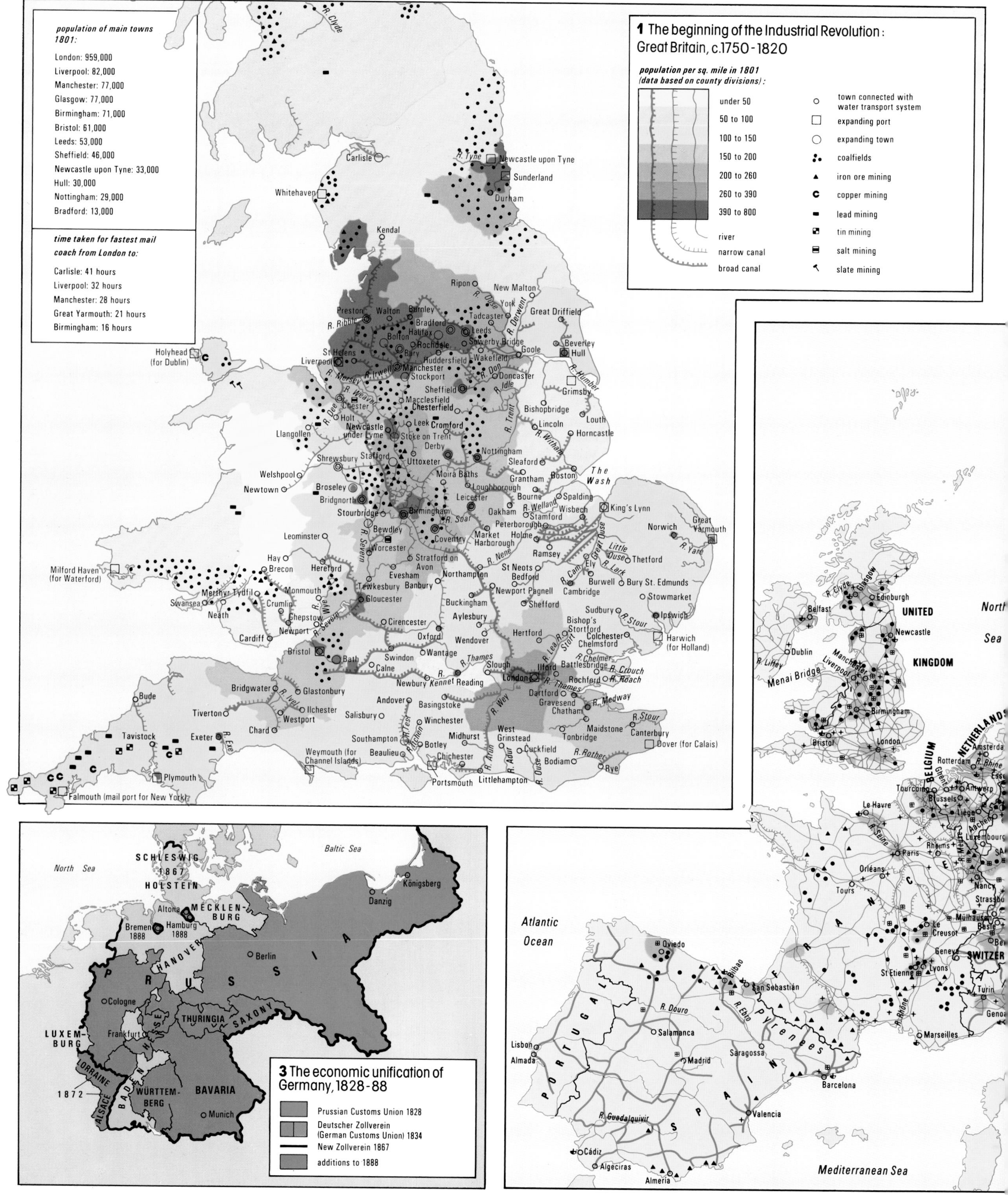

Many factors account for the precedence of Great Britain. It was not only that it was well endowed with coal, iron, and other basic materials; so were many other countries. It was also spared the ravaging effects of warfare on its own soil, unlike most of continental Europe during the revolutionary and Napoleonic wars (pages 88, 90). Unlike France and Germany, where markets and trade were limited by a multiplicity of customs barriers and internal and external frontiers, Great Britain after the union of England and Scotland in 1707 was a single economic unit, where men and goods moved freely. It also enjoyed an advantageous position in Atlantic trade, from which capital flowed into industry. In an age of sailing ships, ports like Liverpool, Glasgow and Bristol had obvious advantages over Hamburg and Bremen. The English social structure was also favourable. In contrast to continental Europe, where most peasants were still tied to the soil (page 82), the early disappearance of serfdom in England meant that the surplus labour released by the enclosure of common land during the eighteenth century could move, without legal obstacles, to the growing industrial centres. Finally, England had a unique network of navigable rivers and canals (map 1), which was of inestimable importance before the railway age for moving both raw materials and finished goods.

In its earliest phase English manufacture had relied on water power; hence the location of the early cotton and woollen mills on the slopes of the Pennines. But essentially the Industrial Revolution, in the century to 1870, was a revolution of coal and iron. Its basis was the application of steam power to machinery, and a series of technical innovations – Watt's rotative engine (1782) and Cartwright's power loom (1792) among others – quickly demonstrated the superiority of steam-power driven machines. In continental Europe, apart from Belgium, where industrialisation proceeded rapidly after 1820, the use of steam power came more slowly. The famous German steel firm of Krupp, later to be a giant of German industry, was founded in 1810 in green fields outside Essen, where a stream provided water power; it had only 7 employees in 1826 and 122 in 1846. Here, and elsewhere, large-scale industry was held back by political fragmentation, lack of capital, and, above all, by poor communications, which severely limited markets. What changed this, above all else, was railway development, beginning in the 1830s. By 1860 the railway networks of Britain, Belgium and Germany were virtually complete, although in Austria-Hungary and Russia large-scale construction was only beginning (map 2). With their demand for rails, sleepers, engines and carriages, railways also provided immense impetus to heavy industry. A second factor was the dismantling of obstructions to trade. In France internal tariffs had been demolished in 1790 as part of the revolutionary reorganisation. In 1818 Prussia followed suit, setting up free trade between its provinces, followed by a Prussian Customs Union (1828) including other smaller German territories, and finally (1834) the German Customs Union, or *Zollverein*, comprising 17 states and some 26 million people (map 3). Here was a solid basis for the development of German industry.

A new period, sometimes called the Second Industrial Revolution, opened after 1870. The new German Empire, founded in 1871, was in the forefront. Coal and iron were still basic, and here Germany forged ahead, increasing its coal output from 38 million tons in 1871 to 279 million tons in 1913 and its iron output from 1.5 million tons to 15 million tons. But it was in the new branches of industry – steel, electricity and chemicals – that Germany outpaced all other nations. German steel production leapt from 1.5 million tons in 1880 to over 13 million tons in 1910, by which time Krupps was employing 70,000 men. Steel, electricity and chemicals were the index of the new industrial society, and at a time of growing international tension (page 116) Germany's headstart was bound to produce a defensive reaction among its rivals. The intensive industrialisation which occurred in France after 1895 and in northern Italy after 1905 represented a deliberate national effort not to be left behind. The same was true of the great upsurge of Russian industry after 1890, particularly the massive development of the iron and steel industry of the Donets basin (page 84). By now much of heavy industry was keyed to armaments. Industrialisation had changed the face of Europe by 1914; but it had also made it more dangerous and more explosive.

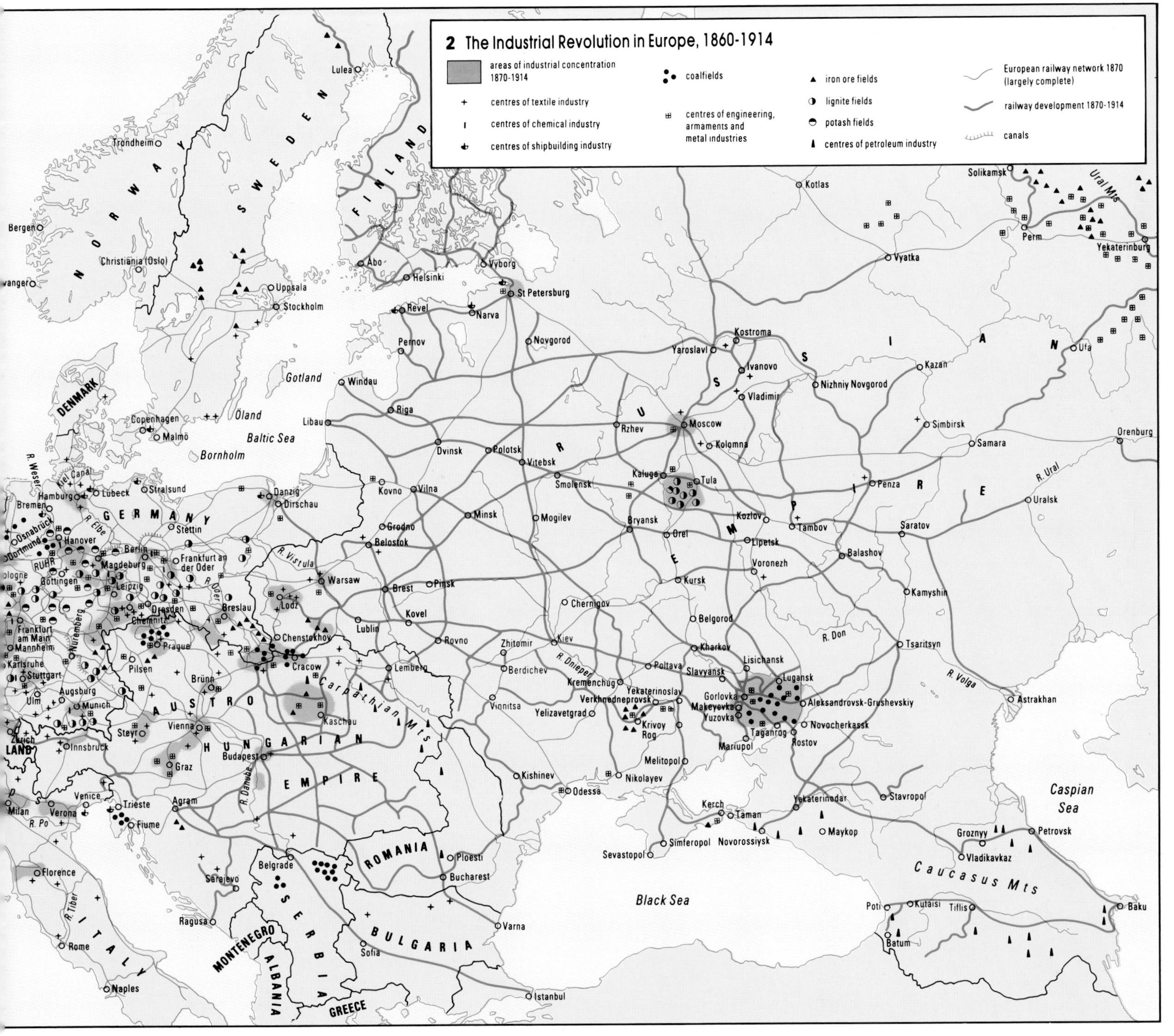

European imperialism 1815-1914

Between 1815 and 1914, under the impact of the Industrial Revolution, the character of European imperialism changed. Earlier the motivating force had been the search for the riches of the Orient, and the European stake in Asia and Africa was confined to trading stations and the strategic outposts necessary to protect the trade. In 1815, with the important exception of India, this was still the situation. But in the nineteenth century two new factors came into play. The first was the enforced opening of the world – Turkey and Egypt (1838), Persia (1841), China (1842), even Japan (1858) – to European, particularly British, commerce; in short, the breaking down of barriers to European penetration. The second, setting in around 1880, when a new phase of the Industrial Revolution got under way (page 98), was the search for the raw materials without which industry, in its new form, could not exist. Tin and rubber from Malaya, nickel from Canada, copper from Australia and South America were now the sinews of European industry; and so the scramble for natural resources began, providing a new impetus for colonial expansion. Between 1880 and 1914 Europe added over $8\frac{1}{2}$ million square miles, or one-fifth of the land area of the globe, to its overseas colonial possessions.

Nevertheless no clear line divides the period before and the period after 1880. Criticism of imperialism was certainly strong in the first half of the century. Free traders of the so-called 'Manchester School' argued cogently that empire was unnecessary, even detrimental, to commerce, and the burgeoning trade with the ex-colonial countries of North and South America seemed to prove their point. Nevertheless imperial expansion was continuous after 1815. Both Great Britain and France – particularly France, which had lost its first empire in 1815 and was determined to constitute a new empire – steadily advanced (map 1). The French conquered Algeria in the 1830s, annexed Tahiti and the Marquesas in the 1840s, expanded their colony in Senegal in the 1850s, and began the conquest of Indo-China in 1859. Great Britain, which had retained the Cape of Good Hope, the maritime provinces of Ceylon and other strategically important footholds (Malta, Mauritius, the Seychelles) in 1815, also continued to expand. Fearing a French challenge, it claimed sovereignty over Australia and New Zealand (page 112). It built up its power in India (page 104), acquired Singapore (1819), Malacca (1824), Hong Kong (1842), Natal (1843), Lower Burma (1852) and Lagos (1861). Many of these acquisitions were defensive reactions against France; most were intended to secure its position in India which, with its army of 150–200,000, made Britain the strongest territorial power in the east. Even so, except for India, imperialism still only touched the outer fringes of Asia and Africa. Even the Russian empire, which by 1886 was to engross much of central Asia (page 84), still only affected the periphery.

After 1880 a fundamental change came about. Its causes were partly economic, but still more important were the rivalries of the European powers, each of which feared that its competitors would steal a march on it. Comparison of maps 1 and 2 points out the difference. Even as late as 1870 colonial penetration was marginal. By 1914 the European powers had engrossed nine-tenths of Africa and a large part of Asia. Between 1871 and 1914 the French empire grew by nearly 4 million square miles and 47 million people, mainly in north and west Africa and Indo-China, but also in the Pacific islands and Madagascar. But a significant factor was the entry of new claimants, particularly Germany and Italy, challenging the old imperial powers. Germany acquired an empire of 1 million square miles and 14 million colonial subjects in South-West Africa, Togoland, the Cameroons, Tanganyika and the Pacific Islands. Italy obtained Tripoli and Libya, Eritrea and Italian Somaliland, but failed in 1896 to conquer Abyssinia. But the greatest gains of all were made by Great Britain, which secured control over Nigeria, Kenya, Uganda, Northern and Southern Rhodesia, Egypt and the Sudan, as well as areas in the Pacific including Fiji and parts of Borneo and New Guinea. The keystone of the British empire was India, and its acquisitions were made with a view to bolstering British control over access to India and the Indian Ocean via the Suez Canal and East Africa, but also via Singapore and the south Pacific (map 3). So long as it was assured of control of the Indian Ocean, the British imperial position was secure.

In retrospect, the fragility of the European empires so hastily assembled between 1884 and 1914, is obvious. None of the imperial powers had the resources to govern them adequately. European imperialism was more ephemeral than anyone, at the close of the nineteenth century, could have believed; and yet it left an indelible impression on the peoples of Asia and Africa, propelling them willingly or unwillingly into the twentieth century.

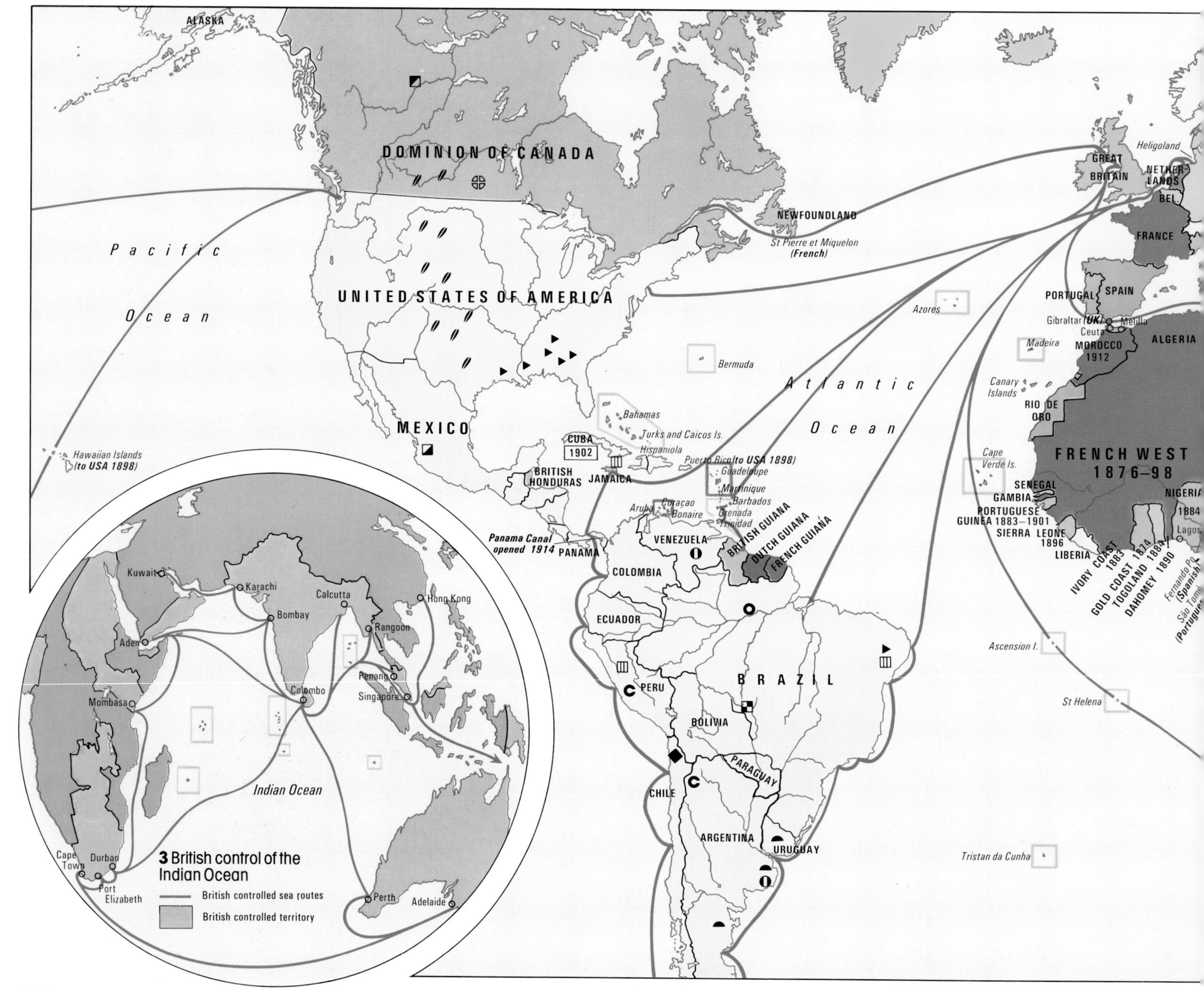

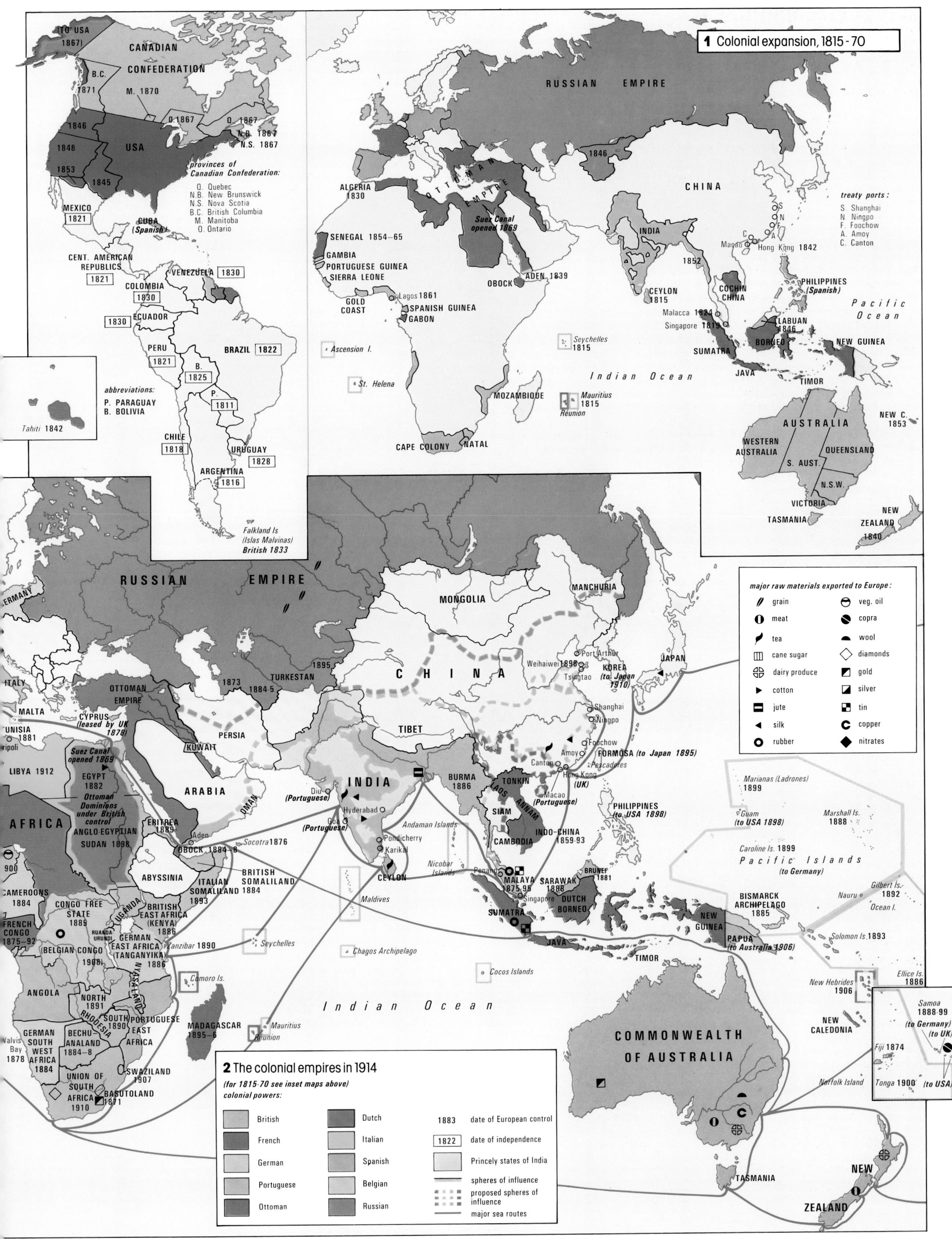

1 Colonial expansion, 1815-70
(to USA 1867)
CANADIAN CONFEDERATION
B.C. 1871
M. 1870
O. 1867
Q. 1867
N.B. 1867
N.S. 1867
1846
1848
USA
1853
1845
provinces of Canadian Confederation:
Q. Quebec
N.B. New Brunswick
N.S. Nova Scotia
B.C. British Columbia
M. Manitoba
O. Ontario
MEXICO 1821
CUBA (Spanish)
CENT. AMERICAN REPUBLICS 1821
VENEZUELA 1830
COLOMBIA 1830
ECUADOR 1830
PERU 1821
BRAZIL 1822
B. 1825
P. 1811
abbreviations:
P. PARAGUAY
B. BOLIVIA
Tahiti 1842
CHILE 1818
URUGUAY 1828
ARGENTINA 1816
Falkland Is (Islas Malvinas) British 1833
RUSSIAN EMPIRE
1846
OTTOMAN EMPIRE
ALGERIA 1830
Suez Canal opened 1869
SENEGAL 1854-65
GAMBIA
PORTUGUESE GUINEA
SIERRA LEONE
GOLD COAST
Lagos 1861
SPANISH GUINEA
GABON
OBOCK
ADEN 1839
Ascension I.
St. Helena
Seychelles 1815
MOZAMBIQUE
Mauritius 1815
Réunion
CAPE COLONY
NATAL
CHINA
INDIA
CEYLON 1815
1852
COCHIN CHINA
Macao
Hong Kong 1842
treaty ports:
S. Shanghai
N. Ningpo
F. Foochow
A. Amoy
C. Canton
PHILIPPINES (Spanish)
Malacca 1824
Singapore 1819
LABUAN 1846
BORNEO
SUMATRA
JAVA
NEW GUINEA
TIMOR
Pacific Ocean
Indian Ocean
AUSTRALIA
WESTERN AUSTRALIA
QUEENSLAND
S. AUST.
N.S.W.
VICTORIA
TASMANIA
NEW C. 1853
NEW ZEALAND 1840
RUSSIAN EMPIRE
MANCHURIA
MONGOLIA
CHINA
TURKESTAN
1895
1873
1884-5
Port Arthur
Weihaiwei 1898
Tsingtao
KOREA (to Japan 1910)
JAPAN
Shanghai
Ningpo
Foochow
Amoy
FORMOSA (to Japan 1895)
Canton
Hong Kong (UK)
Pescadores
Macao (Portuguese)
TIBET
PERSIA
KUWAIT
ITALY
MALTA
CYPRUS (leased by UK 1878)
TUNISIA 1881
LIBYA 1912
Suez Canal opened 1869
EGYPT 1882
Ottoman Dominions under British control
ANGLO-EGYPTIAN SUDAN 1898
OTTOMAN EMPIRE
ARABIA
OMAN
ERITREA 1889
Aden
OBOCK 1884-8
Socotra 1876
ABYSSINIA
ITALIAN SOMALILAND 1893
BRITISH SOMALILAND 1884
AFRICA
CAMEROONS 1884
CONGO FREE STATE 1885
FRENCH CONGO 1875-92
UGANDA
BRITISH EAST AFRICA (KENYA) 1886
RUANDA URUNDI
GERMAN EAST AFRICA (TANGANYIKA) 1886
Zanzibar 1890
(BELGIAN CONGO 1908)
ANGOLA
NYASALAND
NORTH 1891
SOUTH 1890
RHODESIA
PORTUGUESE EAST AFRICA
GERMAN SOUTH WEST AFRICA 1884
Walvis Bay 1878
BECHUANALAND 1884-8
SWAZILAND 1907
UNION OF SOUTH AFRICA 1910
BASUTOLAND 1871
MADAGASCAR 1895-6
Comoro Is.
Seychelles
Mauritius
Réunion
INDIA
Diu (Portuguese)
Hyderabad
Goa (Portuguese)
Pondicherry
Karikal
CEYLON
BURMA 1886
TONKIN
LAOS
ANNAM
SIAM
CAMBODIA
INDO-CHINA 1859-93
Andaman Islands
Nicobar Islands
Maldives
Chagos Archipelago
Cocos Islands
Indian Ocean
Penang
MALAYA 1875-95
SARAWAK 1888
BRUNEI 1881
DUTCH BORNEO
Singapore
SUMATRA
JAVA
NEW GUINEA
PAPUA (to Australia 1906)
TIMOR
PHILIPPINES (to USA 1898)
Marianas (Ladrones) 1899
Guam (to USA 1898)
Marshall Is. 1888
Caroline Is. 1899
Pacific Islands (to Germany)
BISMARCK ARCHIPELAGO 1885
Nauru
Gilbert Is. 1892
Ocean I.
Solomon Is. 1893
Ellice Is. 1886
New Hebrides 1906
NEW CALEDONIA
Samoa 1888-99 (to Germany) (to UK)
Fiji 1874
Tonga 1900 (to USA)
Norfolk Island
COMMONWEALTH OF AUSTRALIA
TASMANIA
NEW ZEALAND
major raw materials exported to Europe:
grain
meat
tea
cane sugar
dairy produce
cotton
jute
silk
rubber
veg. oil
copra
wool
diamonds
gold
silver
tin
copper
nitrates
2 The colonial empires in 1914
(for 1815-70 see inset maps above)
colonial powers:
British
French
German
Portuguese
Ottoman
Dutch
Italian
Spanish
Belgian
Russian
1883 date of European control
1822 date of independence
Princely states of India
spheres of influence
proposed spheres of influence
major sea routes

Nineteenth century Africa

Although European exploration began in the eighteenth century (map 1), its impact on Africa was limited until after 1870, except in the far south where Dutch settlers, or Boers, in Cape Colony, who had been brought under British rule in 1806, moved north in the Great Trek (1835) in search of land and freedom, and founded settlements which eventually became the republics of the Orange Free State and Transvaal (map 2). The only other area of European settlement was Algeria, conquered by France between 1830 and 1847 after fierce resistance under Abd al Kadir. Nevertheless this was a period of great change and instability in Africa. In the north-east the dominating fact was the advance of Egypt under Mohammed Ali, who conquered northern Sudan in 1820, founded Khartoum as its capital in 1830, and inaugurated the attempt to build a great Egyptian empire reaching the length of the Nile and east to the Horn of Africa. In the north-west a great Muslim religious revival, beginning around 1804 under Uthman dan Fodio, carried the Fulani south into Hausaland, where they founded the Sultanate of Sokoto. Later, another empire was carved out further west, between the Ivory Coast and the Upper Niger, by a Mandingo Muslim leader, Samory. In the south, the outstanding event was the rise of the Zulus, which resulted in a great political and demographic revolution (the so-called *Mfecane* or 'time of troubles'), as the local tribes were driven west and north into Rhodesia, Malawi and Zambia.

This was the situation when the European 'scramble for Africa' got under way after 1882 (page 100), and the countries named above were leaders of African resistance (map 3). The Zulus, hard pressed between British and Boers after the British annexation of Natal (1845), held out fiercely until the war of 1879–81, when their country was annexed (map 2). Resistance elsewhere was equally strong. Samory was only defeated by the French in 1898; Sokoto only fell to the British in 1903. In the north the British established a *de facto* protectorate over a bankrupt Egypt after 1882 (turned into a full-scale protectorate in 1914); but they were only able to secure control of the Sudan in 1898 after the slaughter of some 20,000 Sudanese. Nowhere was occupation unchallenged, as the great Herero and Maji-Maji revolts of 1904–6 against German colonialism showed. But the only lasting success was the Ethiopian defeat of Italy at Adowa in 1896. Morocco kept a precarious independence until 1912 before being divided between France and Spain, and Libya and Cyrenaica were occupied by Italy in the same year. By 1914 the European powers were in full control (map 5). Apart from Ethiopia, only Liberia could claim independence.

The position of the Boer republics in the south was different. Transvaal also had been annexed by Great Britain in 1877 and then restored to independence in 1881. But the discovery of diamonds at Kimberley and of gold on the Witwatersrand (1886) sealed their fate. The entry of foreign speculators (*Uitlanders*) sparked Boer hostility, and when an attempt by Cecil Rhodes (Prime Minister of Cape Colony, 1890–96) to stage a take-over failed dismally (Jameson Raid, 1895), the outcome was the Boer War (1899–1902), in which, after initial Boer successes, ruthless British suppression forced the Boers to capitulate (map 4). Nevertheless the Afrikaners secured favourable terms after the Peace of Vereeniging (May 31, 1902), including the use of their own language and the exclusion of blacks from the franchise, and this compromise made possible the formation (1910) of the Union of South Africa as a dominion of the British Commonwealth. It was nevertheless a betrayal of black Africans by Britain which led step by step to the policy of *Apartheid* (1948) and to the radical conflicts which bedevilled South Africa after the rest of the continent had won its independence.

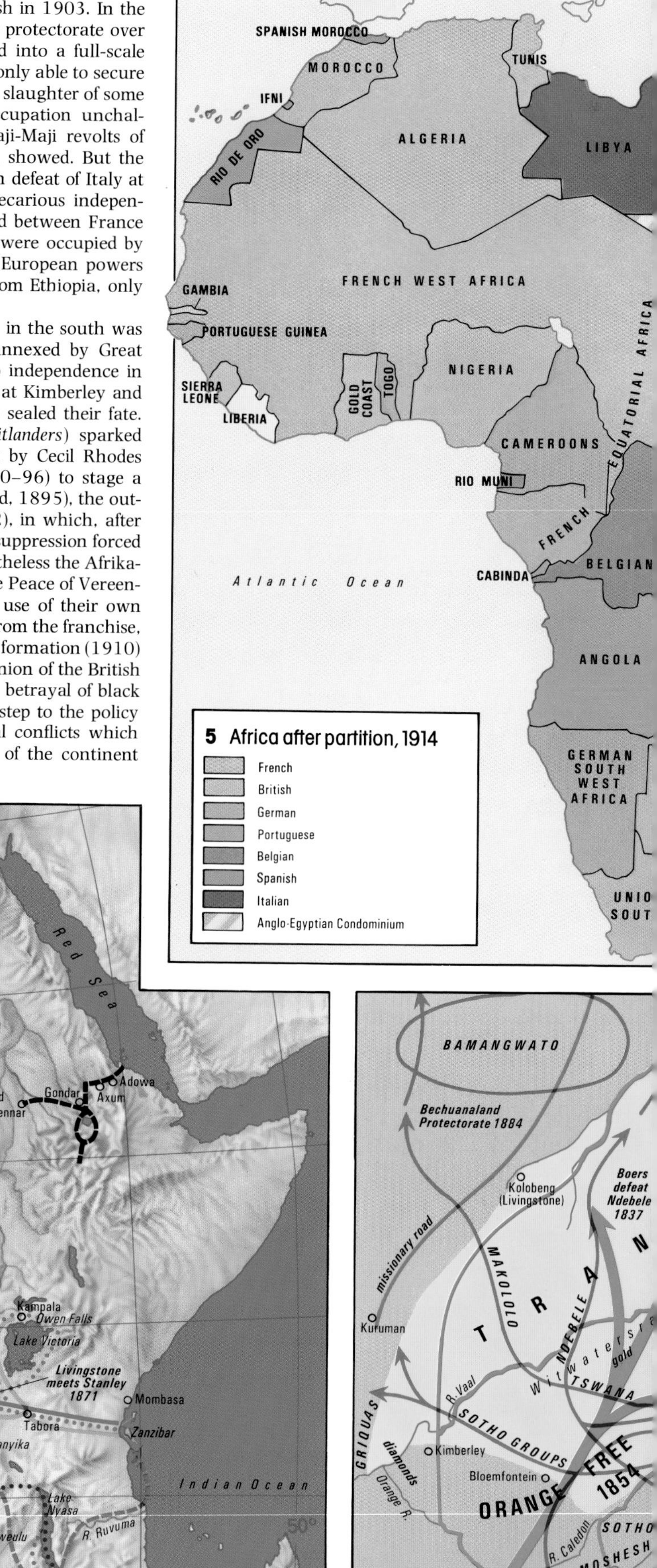

5 Africa after partition, 1914

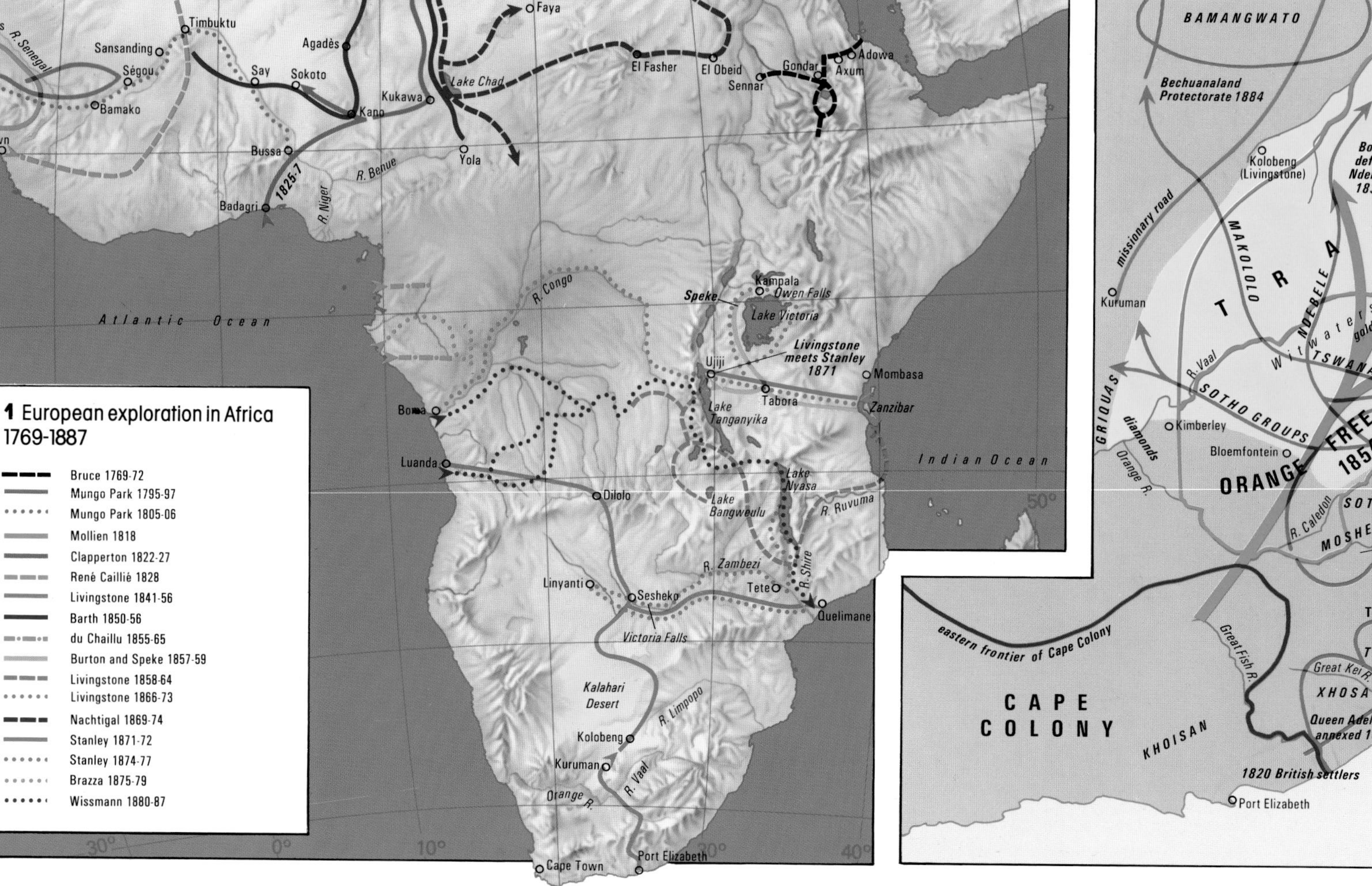

1 European exploration in Africa 1769-1887

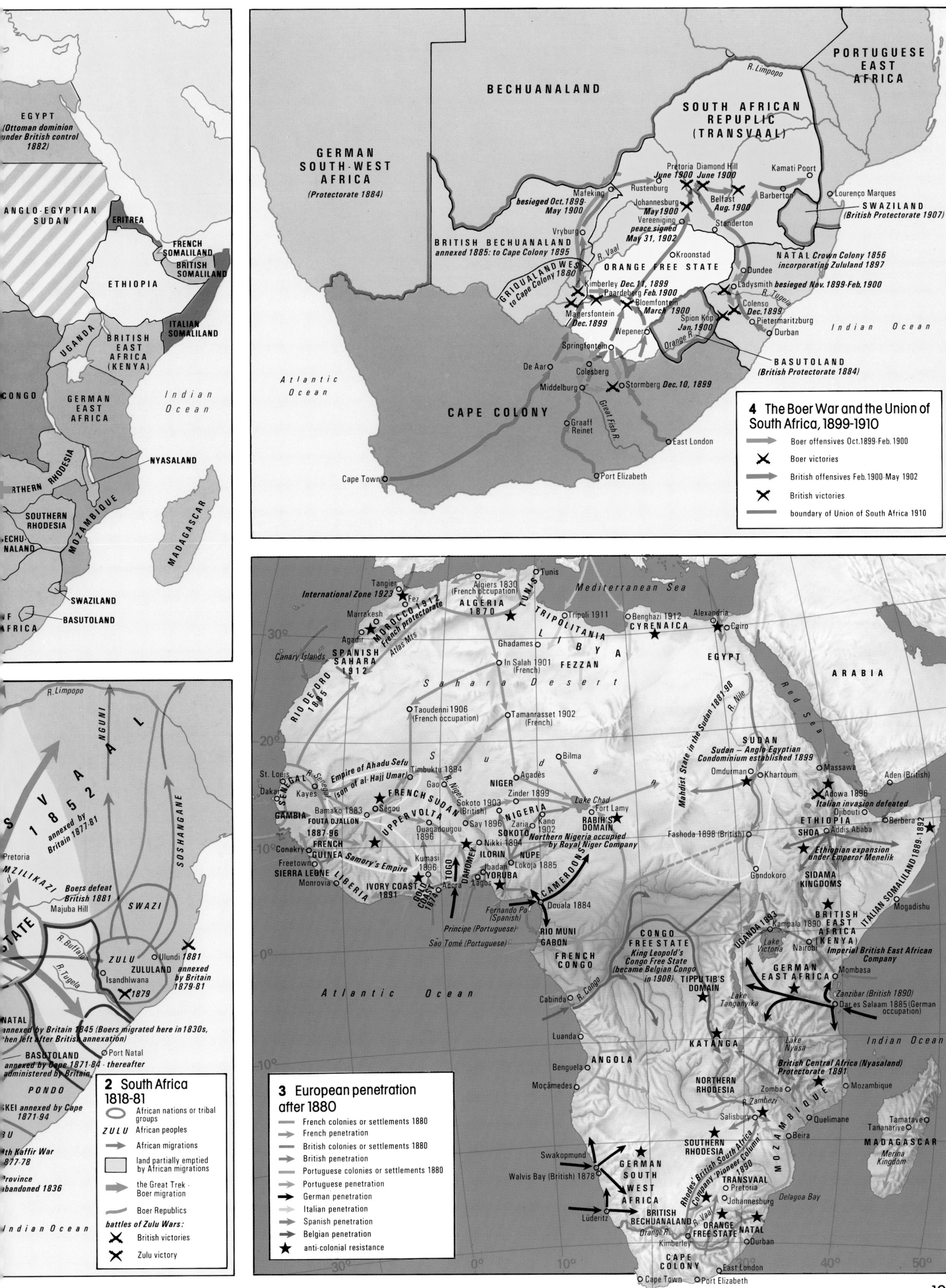
EGYPT
(Ottoman dominion under British control 1882)
ANGLO-EGYPTIAN SUDAN
ERITREA
FRENCH SOMALILAND
BRITISH SOMALILAND
ETHIOPIA
ITALIAN SOMALILAND
UGANDA
BRITISH EAST AFRICA (KENYA)
CONGO
GERMAN EAST AFRICA
Indian Ocean
NYASALAND
NORTHERN RHODESIA
SOUTHERN RHODESIA
MOZAMBIQUE
MADAGASCAR
SWAZILAND
BASUTOLAND
BECHUANALAND
PORTUGUESE EAST AFRICA
SOUTH AFRICAN REPUPLIC (TRANSVAAL)
GERMAN SOUTH-WEST AFRICA
(Protectorate 1884)
BRITISH BECHUANALAND
annexed 1885: to Cape Colony 1895
GRIQUALAND WEST to Cape Colony 1880
ORANGE FREE STATE
NATAL Crown Colony 1856 incorporating Zululand 1897
SWAZILAND (British Protectorate 1907)
BASUTOLAND (British Protectorate 1884)
CAPE COLONY
Atlantic Ocean
Mafeking besieged Oct.1899-May 1900
Pretoria June 1900
Diamond Hill June 1900
Johannesburg May 1900
Belfast Aug. 1900
Vereeniging peace signed May 31, 1902
Kimberley Dec. 11, 1899
Paardeberg Feb. 1900
Bloemfontein March 1900
Magersfontein Dec. 1899
Ladysmith besieged Nov. 1899-Feb. 1900
Colenso Dec. 1899
Spion Kop Jan. 1900
Stormberg Dec. 10, 1899
4 The Boer War and the Union of South Africa, 1899-1910
Boer offensives Oct.1899-Feb. 1900
Boer victories
British offensives Feb.1900-May 1902
British victories
boundary of Union of South Africa 1910
TRANSVAAL
1852
annexed by Britain 1877-81
Boers defeat British 1881
Majuba Hill
SWAZI
ZULU
ZULULAND
Ulundi 1881
annexed by Britain 1879-81
Isandhlwana 1879
NATAL
annexed by Britain 1845 (Boers migrated here in 1830s, then left after British annexation)
BASUTOLAND
annexed by Cape 1871-84 - thereafter administered by Britain
PONDO
2 South Africa 1818-81
African nations or tribal groups
ZULU African peoples
African migrations
land partially emptied by African migrations
the Great Trek - Boer migration
Boer Republics
battles of Zulu Wars:
British victories
Zulu victory
Mediterranean Sea
International Zone 1923
MOROCCO 1912 French protectorate
ALGERIA 1870
TUNIS
TRIPOLITANIA
LIBYA
CYRENAICA
EGYPT
SPANISH SAHARA 1912
RIO DE ORO 1885
FEZZAN
Sahara Desert
ARABIA
Red Sea
Mahdist State in the Sudan 1881-98
SUDAN
Sudan - Anglo-Egyptian Condominium established 1899
Empire of Ahadu Sefu (son of al-Hajj Umar)
FRENCH SUDAN
UPPER VOLTA
NIGER
NIGERIA
Northern Nigeria occupied by Royal Niger Company
RABIH'S DOMAIN
Adowa 1896 Italian invasion defeated
ETHIOPIA
Ethiopian expansion under Emperor Menelik
ITALIAN SOMALILAND 1889-1892
SIDAMA KINGDOMS
BRITISH EAST AFRICA (KENYA)
Imperial British East African Company
GAMBIA
SENEGAL
FOUTA DJALLON 1887-96
FRENCH GUINEA
SIERRA LEONE
LIBERIA
Samory's Empire
IVORY COAST 1891
GOLD COAST 1874
TOGO
DAHOMEY
CAMEROONS
RIO MUNI GABON
FRENCH CONGO
CONGO FREE STATE
King Leopold's Congo Free State (became Belgian Congo in 1908)
TIPPU TIB'S DOMAIN
UGANDA 1893
GERMAN EAST AFRICA
Zanzibar (British 1890)
Dar es Salaam 1885 (German occupation)
Atlantic Ocean
Indian Ocean
KATANGA
ANGOLA
British Central Africa (Nyasaland) Protectorate 1891
NORTHERN RHODESIA
SOUTHERN RHODESIA
MOZAMBIQUE
MADAGASCAR
Merina Kingdom
GERMAN SOUTH WEST AFRICA
Rhodes' British South Africa Company 'Pioneer Column' 1890
TRANSVAAL
BRITISH BECHUANALAND
ORANGE FREE STATE
NATAL
CAPE COLONY
3 European penetration after 1880
French colonies or settlements 1880
French penetration
British colonies or settlements 1880
British penetration
Portuguese colonies or settlements 1880
Portuguese penetration
German penetration
Italian penetration
Spanish penetration
Belgian penetration
anti-colonial resistance

India under British rule, 1805-1947

By 1805 the hegemony of the English East India Company in the Indian sub-continent was an established fact. With the conquest of Sind (1843) and the Sikh kingdom of the Punjab (1849) its dominion became co-terminous with the country's natural frontier in the north-west, while in the north a war with Nepal (1814–16) extended it to the Himalayan foothills (map 1). To the east the British clashed with the Burmese empire and in 1826 and 1852 annexed most of its territories, including Assam. Upper Burma itself was brought under British rule in 1886 (map 2). Within India Dalhousie's Doctrine of Lapse led to the absorption of several small kingdoms in central India, and in 1856 the kingdom of Oudh was annexed following charges of 'misgovernment'. Not surprisingly, this policy provoked disaffection which found a violent outlet in the rebellion of 1857. Beginning as a mutiny of the Company's Indian sepoys, the revolt soon involved princes, landlords and peasants throughout northern India, but the loyalty of the Sikhs and the passivity of southern India enabled the British to crush it after fourteen months of bitter fighting.

The mutiny was a watershed in the history of British India. It discredited the Company and in 1858 the British government assumed direct control, though the autonomy of the Indian princes was respected. The impetus to economic development was immediate. First-class roads were built, totalling 57,000 miles by 1927, but it was the railways which made possible the exploitation of raw materials and the profitable introduction of export crops, such as tea. Between 1869 and 1929 India's foreign trade increased sevenfold. How far this benefited the rural masses is a moot question; but modern industries brought into existence an Indian entrepreneurial class. After 1919, when protective tariffs were introduced, industrial expansion made further progress (map 3).

With the rise of a new middle class, partly through industry but more through the recruitment of educated Indians into the colonial administration, came a reawakened political consciousness. The Indian National Congress (1885) accepted British rule, though in 1905 there were periodic outbreaks of terrorist violence. But it was only after 1919 that Congress, under Gandhi's leadership, fought actively for Home Rule and, after 1929, for independence (map 4). Gandhi's civil disobedience campaigns galvanised the Indian masses; but Congress's claim to represent all Indians, Hindu and Muslim alike, alienated the Muslim minority and led to conflicts which resulted in 1947 in partition (map 5). Faced by mounting unrest and the naval mutiny of 1946, the Labour government in Britain realised that a transfer of power could not be delayed; but in 1946–7 the gradual breakdown of law and order, including communal riots, forced its hand. Plans for partition were hastily drawn up. But the boundary award in Kashmir, Punjab and Bengal resulted in large-scale disturbances in which some 500,000 lost their lives and many millions became refugees, leaving a tense situation which erupted in wars between India and Pakistan (1965, '71) and separatist violence in Kashmir since 1977.

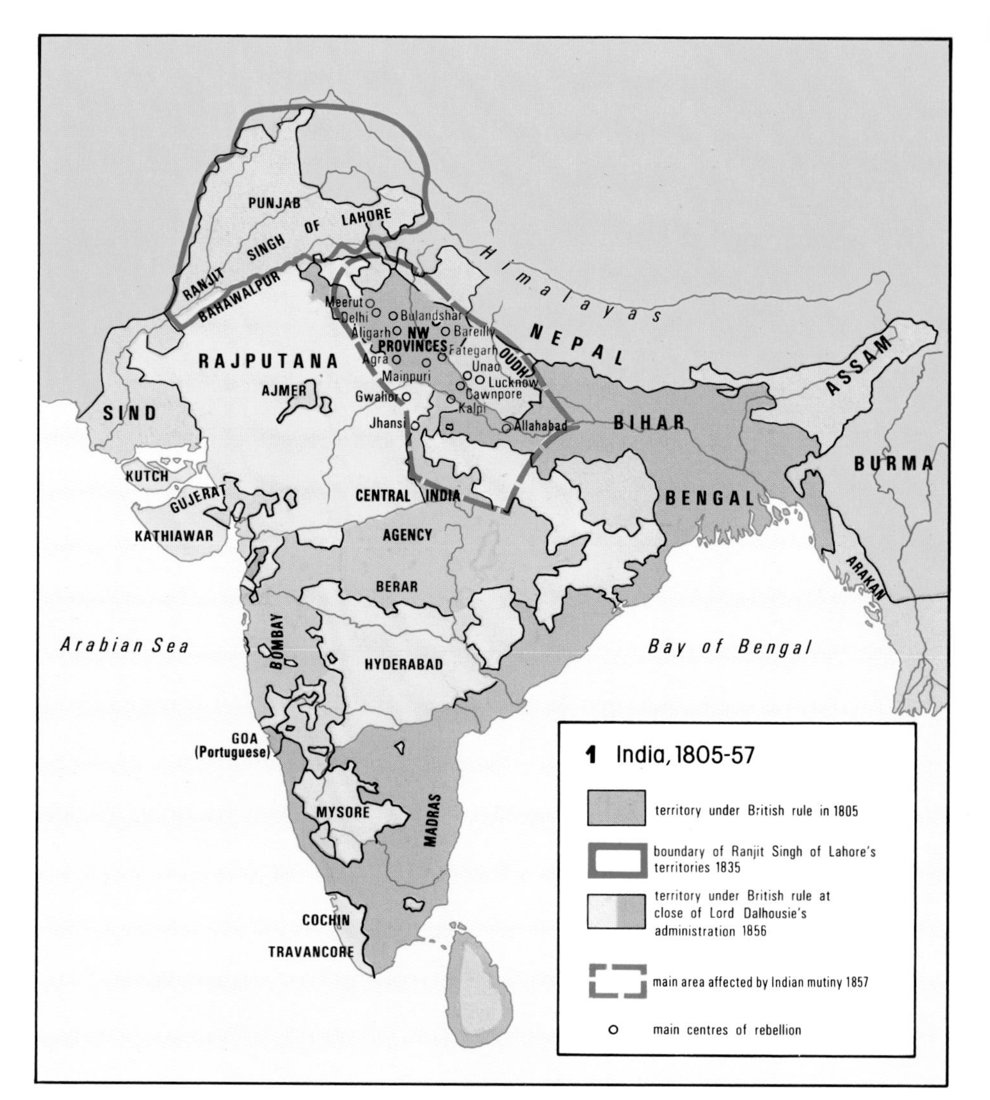

1 India, 1805-57

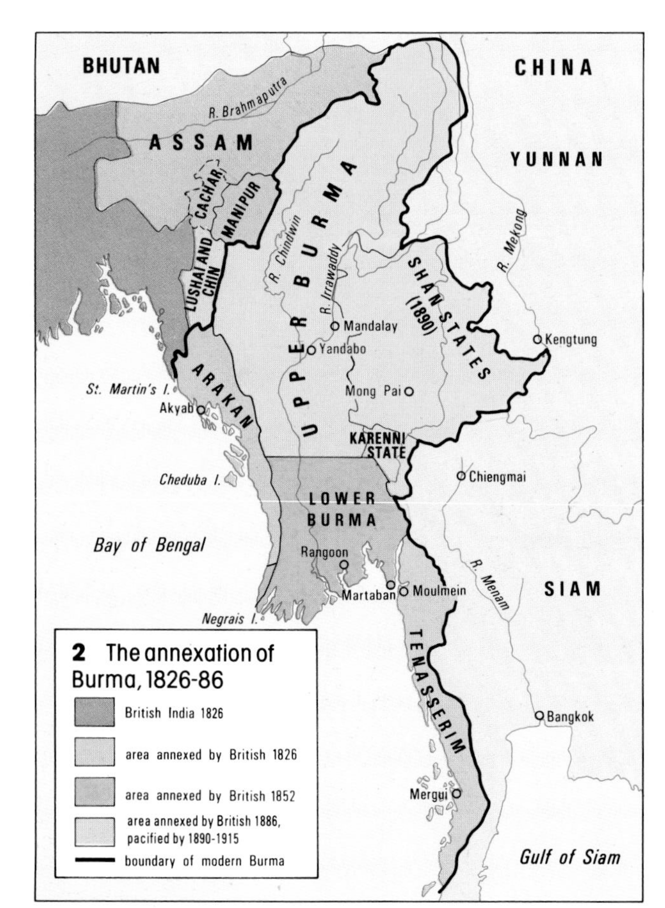

2 The annexation of Burma, 1826-86

India's Road to Independence (right)
1885 creation of Indian National Congress
1906 Muslim League formed
1915 Gandhi returns to India. Following death of Gokhale (1915) and Tilak (1920) emerges as leader of Congress
1916 Lucknow Pact: Congress and Muslim League agree to co-operate in demand for home rule (*swaraj*)
1917 Montagu Declaration: Britain's goal is 'responsible government for India as an integral part of the British Empire.' But
1919 Government of India Act: some Indian ministers, but central admin. and power in British hands
1919 Amritsar Massacre: troops fire on demonstrators and kill 379 Indians
1920 Khilafat Committee of Hindus and Muslims adopts Gandhi's programme of peaceful non-cooperation (*satyagraha*)
1920 First Civil Disobedience campaign
1922 after violence at Chauri Chaura and Moplah rising in South India
1922–29 Gandhi (in prison 1922–24) withdraws from active politics
1928 Revival of political activity; rise of Jawaharlal Nehru (President of Lahore Congress, 1929). Widening rift between Congress and Muslim League
1929 Lahore Congress demands immediate independence
1930 Gandhi's march to the sea opens Second Civil Disobedience campaign, 90,000 arrests
1930–32 Round Table Conference breaks down over question of separate electorates for Muslims, Sikhs and Untouchables
1935 Government of India Act. Denounced by Nehru as 'satanic', but main provisions accepted by Bombay Congress which agrees to participate in provincial elections
1937 Congress wins 8 out of 11 provinces in elections, but Muslim opinion alienated
1938 Jinnah reorganises Muslim League
1939 resignation of Congress ministries after Viceroy declares war without consulting Indian leaders
1940 Lahore resolution of Muslim League in favour of independent Pakistan
1942 Congress rejects British offer of Dominion Status after war. Gandhi launches 'Quit India' campaign. 'August Revolt' suppressed and Congress leaders imprisoned
1946 Second British Cabinet Mission fails. Communal violence in Calcutta, E. Bengal, Bihar and Punjab; half-million deaths
1947 partition and independence

4 The Indian Nationalist Movement, 1915-47

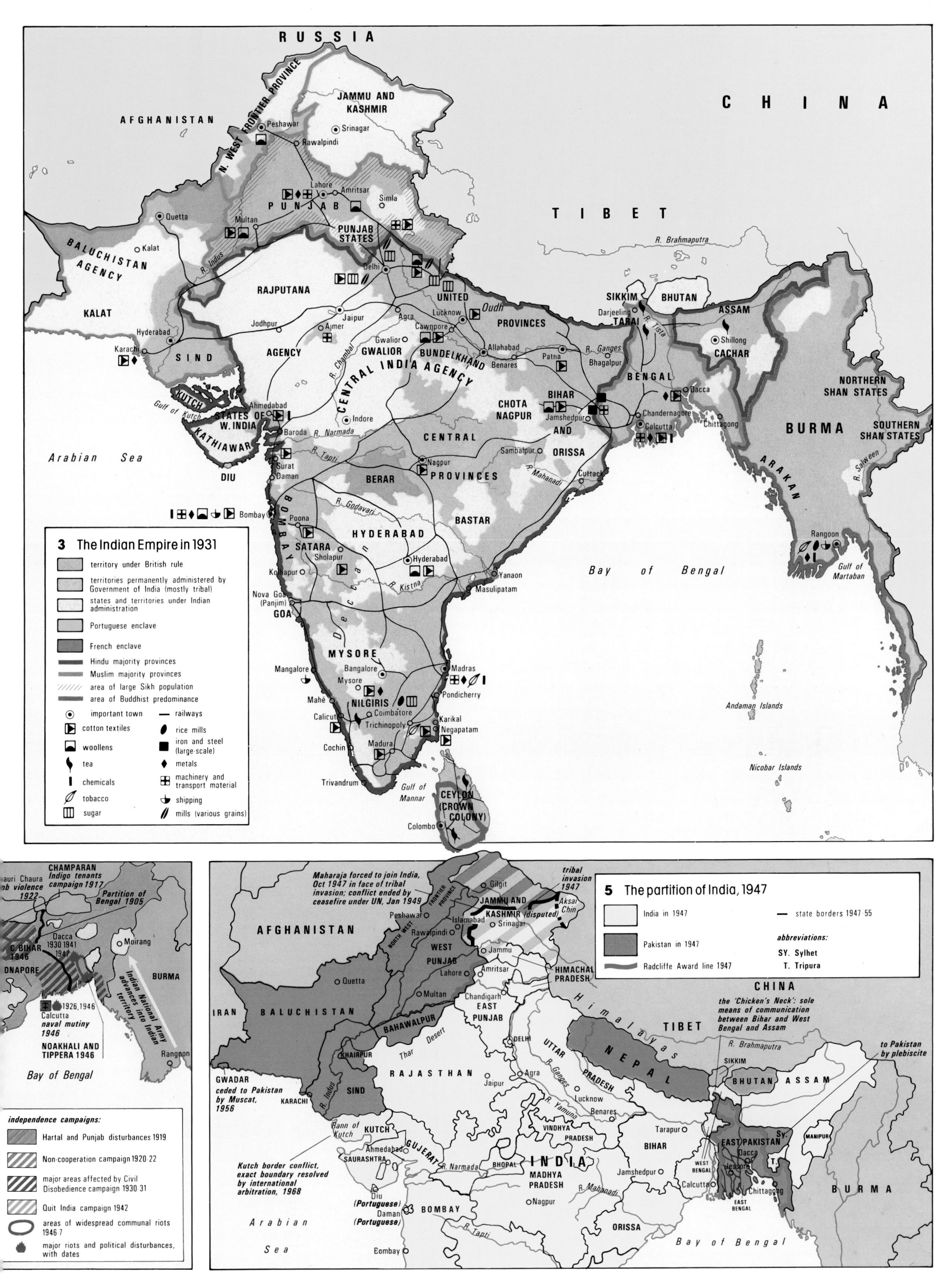

3 The Indian Empire in 1931
territory under British rule
territories permanently administered by Government of India (mostly tribal)
states and territories under Indian administration
Portuguese enclave
French enclave
Hindu majority provinces
Muslim majority provinces
area of large Sikh population
area of Buddhist predominance
important town
railways
cotton textiles
rice mills
woollens
iron and steel (large-scale)
tea
metals
chemicals
machinery and transport material
tobacco
shipping
sugar
mills (various grains)
RUSSIA
CHINA
AFGHANISTAN
TIBET
JAMMU AND KASHMIR
N. WEST FRONTIER PROVINCE
Peshawar
Srinagar
Rawalpindi
Lahore
Amritsar
Simla
PUNJAB
PUNJAB STATES
Multan
Quetta
Kalat
BALUCHISTAN AGENCY
KALAT
R. Indus
Delhi
RAJPUTANA
AGENCY
UNITED PROVINCES
Oudh
Lucknow
Cawnpore
Agra
Jaipur
Jodhpur
Ajmer
Gwalior
GWALIOR
BUNDELKHAND
Allahabad
Benares
Patna
Bhagalpur
R. Ganges
R. Chambal
CENTRAL INDIA AGENCY
Hyderabad
Karachi
SIND
KUTCH
Gulf of Kutch
STATES OF W. INDIA
KATHIAWAR
Ahmedabad
Baroda
R. Narmada
Indore
Arabian Sea
DIU
Surat
Daman
R. Tapti
Nagpur
BERAR
CENTRAL PROVINCES
BIHAR AND ORISSA
CHOTA NAGPUR
Jamshedpur
Sambalpur
R. Mahanadi
Cuttack
BASTAR
BOMBAY
Bombay
Poona
SATARA
Sholapur
HYDERABAD
R. Godavari
R. Kistna
Kolhapur
Yanaon
Masulipatam
Nova Goa (Panjim)
GOA
Deccan
MYSORE
Bangalore
Mysore
Mangalore
Madras
Mahé
NILGIRIS
Pondicherry
Calicut
Coimbatore
Karikal
Trichinopoly
Negapatam
Cochin
Madura
Trivandrum
Gulf of Mannar
CEYLON (CROWN COLONY)
Colombo
SIKKIM
BHUTAN
Darjeeling
TARAI
R. Tista
ASSAM
Shillong
CACHAR
R. Brahmaputra
BENGAL
Dacca
Chandernagore
Calcutta
Chittagong
BURMA
NORTHERN SHAN STATES
SOUTHERN SHAN STATES
ARAKAN
R. Salween
Rangoon
Gulf of Martaban
Bay of Bengal
Andaman Islands
Nicobar Islands
CHAMPARAN Indigo tenants campaign 1917
Chauri Chaura mob violence 1922
Partition of Bengal 1905
Dacca 1930 1941 1947
C. BIHAR 1946
DNAPORE
Moirang
BURMA
Indian National Army advances into Indian territory
1926, 1946
Calcutta naval mutiny 1946
NOAKHALI AND TIPPERA 1946
Rangoon
Bay of Bengal
independence campaigns:
Hartal and Punjab disturbances 1919
Non-cooperation campaign 1920-22
major areas affected by Civil Disobedience campaign 1930-31
Quit India campaign 1942
areas of widespread communal riots 1946-7
major riots and political disturbances, with dates
5 The partition of India, 1947
India in 1947
Pakistan in 1947
Radcliffe Award line 1947
state borders 1947-55
abbreviations:
SY. Sylhet
T. Tripura
Maharaja forced to join India, Oct 1947 in face of tribal invasion; conflict ended by ceasefire under UN, Jan 1949
tribal invasion 1947
Gilgit
JAMMU AND KASHMIR (disputed)
Aksai Chin
AFGHANISTAN
Peshawar
NORTH WEST FRONTIER PROVINCE
Islamabad
Rawalpindi
Srinagar
Jammu
WEST PUNJAB
Lahore
Amritsar
HIMACHAL PRADESH
Quetta
Multan
Chandigarh
EAST PUNJAB
IRAN
BALUCHISTAN
BAHAWALPUR
DELHI
Himalayas
TIBET
CHINA
the 'Chicken's Neck': sole means of communication between Bihar and West Bengal and Assam
NEPAL
R. Brahmaputra
SIKKIM
to Pakistan by plebiscite
BHUTAN
ASSAM
KHAIRPUR
Thar Desert
UTTAR PRADESH
R. Ganges
GWADAR ceded to Pakistan by Muscat, 1956
KARACHI
R. Indus
SIND
RAJASTHAN
Jaipur
Agra
Lucknow
Benares
R. Yamuna
Rann of Kutch
KUTCH
Ahmedabad
SAURASHTRA
GUJERAT
R. Narmada
BHOPAL
VINDHYA PRADESH
INDIA
MADHYA PRADESH
Tarapur
BIHAR
Jamshedpur
WEST BENGAL
Calcutta
EAST PAKISTAN
Dacca
Jessore
Sy.
T.
MANIPUR
Chittagong
EAST BENGAL
BURMA
Kutch border conflict, exact boundary resolved by international arbitration, 1968
Diu (Portuguese)
Daman (Portuguese)
BOMBAY
Nagpur
R. Mahanadi
R. Tapti
ORISSA
Arabian Sea
Bombay
Bay of Bengal

China under the Ch'ing Dynasty, 1644-1911

A new era in Chinese history opened in 1644 when the Ming dynasty, beset for a century by Mongol invasions, Japanese raids and civil war, was displaced by a line of foreign, Manchurian, emperors which ruled China until 1911. The Ch'ing, or Manchu, dynasty was resisted in south China for half a century but it quickly established good relations with the dominant Chinese gentry (*shen-chin*) and with its support began a successful policy of territorial expansion which went on until late in the eighteenth century (map 1).

At the same time there was a great economic upsurge (map 2) and a huge increase in population, from 100 million in 1650 to 300 million in 1820 and 420 million in 1850. There was also a considerable export trade in tea, silk and porcelain with the West from Canton and with Russia from Kyakhta. But the financial strain of the wars of expansion and the pressure of the growing population on the land imposed hardships which led to recurrent unrest and revolts, not only among the minority peoples who were harshly exploited by Chinese and Manchus alike, but also in the heart of China itself. Of these the most serious was the White Lotus rebellion between 1795 and 1804. Meanwhile the export surplus was converted after 1825 into a net outflow as a result of the opium trade. Manchu China was still the world's largest and most populous empire. But its growing economic difficulties, coupled with the failure to expand the administration to match the rapid growth of population, and the pressures of the Western powers, seeking to open the China market for their manufactures, resulted in a crisis which came to a head after Chinese attempts to halt the illicit opium trade were decisively defeated by the British in the Opium War of 1839–42.

The Opium War had two major consequences. First, it resulted in the cession of Hong Kong to the British and in the opening of the first five Treaty Ports (their number was thereafter steadily increased) in which foreigners enjoyed extra-territorial rights. Secondly, it weakened imperial authority and led to the great Taiping rebellion (1850–64), the most serious but only one of many rebellions which shook Manchu power to its foundations (map 3). The Taiping and Nien rebellions alone left 25 million dead and vast areas, including the wealthy region around Nanking, were devastated. They also convinced the Western powers that Ch'ing China was on the point of collapse and inaugurated a scramble for concessions (map 4).

The response of the Manchu court and bureaucracy was hesitant and half-hearted, more intent on maintaining traditional institutions and Confucian values than on modernisation. Foreign powers had taken advantage of the situation: the British and French occupied Peking in 1856 and forced open more treaty ports, the Russians occupied the Amur region in 1858 and the Maritime Province in 1860 and China was defeated by France in a war over Indo-China in 1884–85. But it was the overwhelming success of Japan in the war of 1894–95 that convinced a section of the Chinese intelligentsia that only a break with the past could save China, and they secured the support of the young emperor Kuang-su. But the reform movement of 1898 was defeated by the dowager empress Tzu-hsi whose reaction was to turn the popular discontent against the foreigners. The result was the Boxer Rising of 1900, an outburst of xenophobia savagely suppressed by the Western powers, who imposed a heavy indemnity and wrung still further concessions from China. By now even the imperial government realised that modernisation was imperative; but, in spite of a number of reforms, its attitude was still essentially conservative. Convinced that the imperial government was the main obstacle to change, revolutionary groups sprang up everywhere after 1901, and when in 1911 a small-scale army mutiny broke out in Wuchang, disaffection spread throughout the whole country (page 122). The imperial government fell, almost without fighting; but China had still to undergo more than forty years of tribulation before it finally made the transition to the modern world.

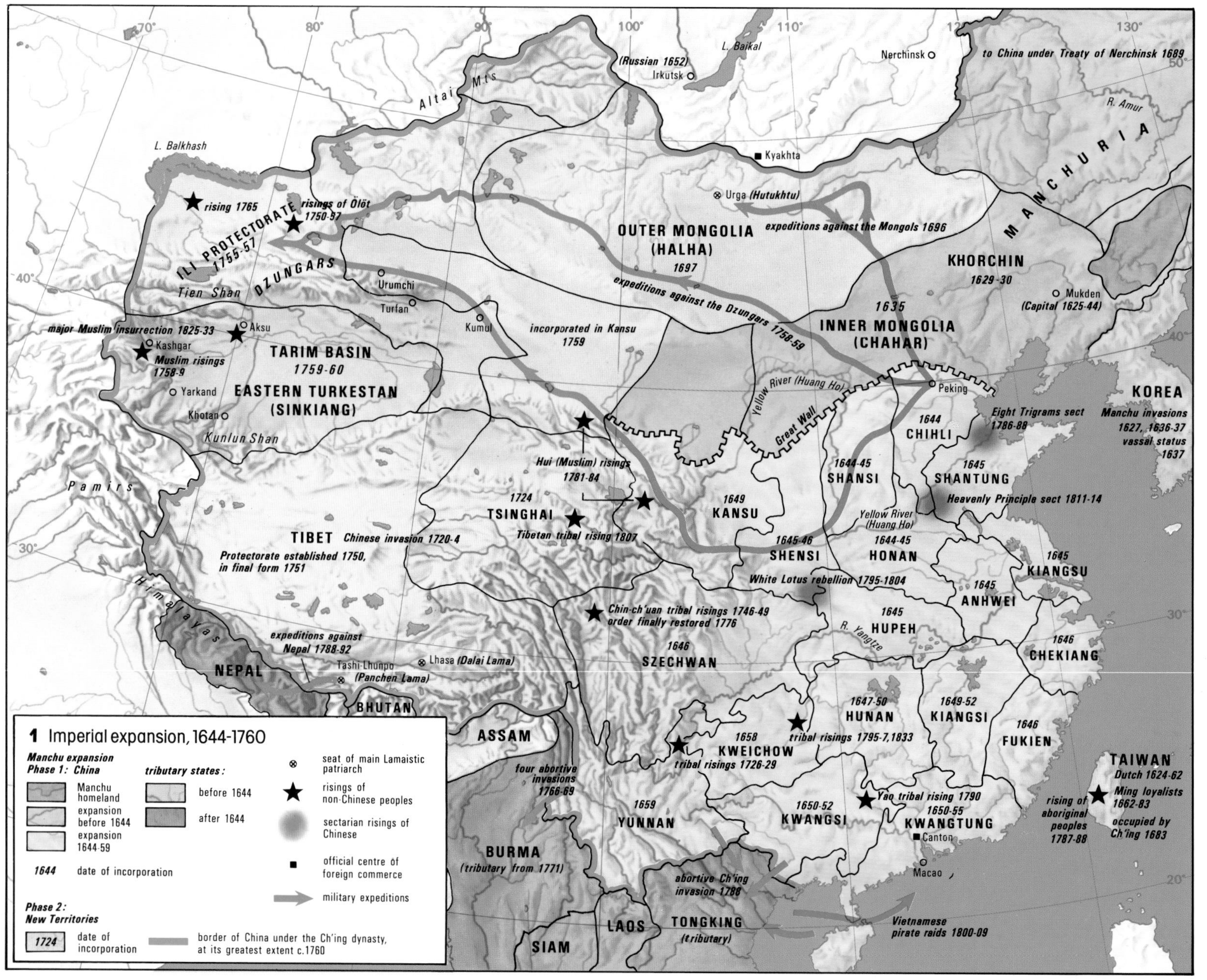

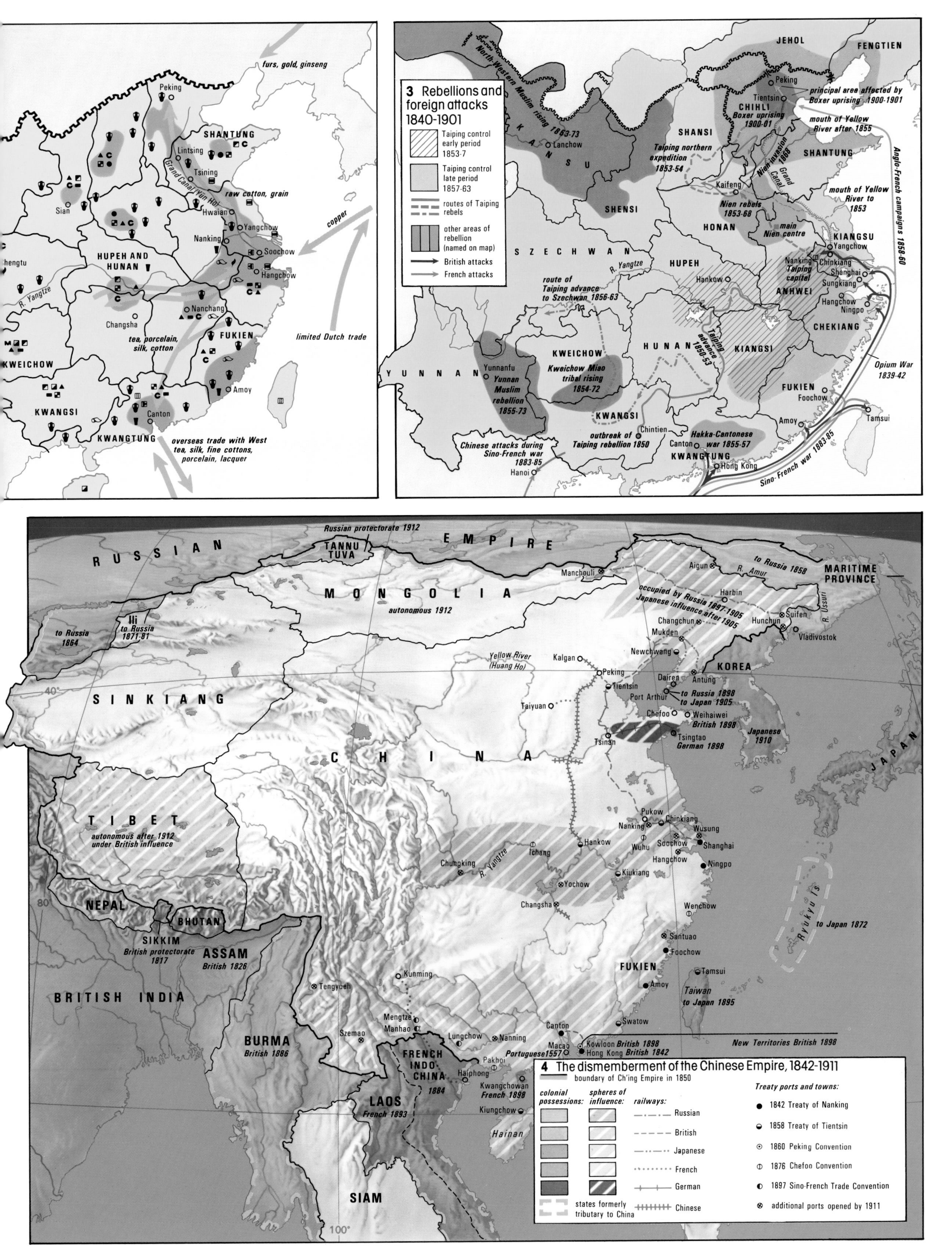

furs, gold, ginseng
Peking
SHANTUNG
Lintsing
Tsining
Grand Canal (Yun Ho)
raw cotton, grain
Hwaian
Sian
Yangchow
Nanking
copper
Soochow
HUPEH AND HUNAN
Hangchow
hengtu
R. Yangtze
Nanchang
Changsha
tea, porcelain, silk, cotton
FUKIEN
limited Dutch trade
KWEICHOW
Amoy
KWANGSI
Canton
KWANGTUNG
overseas trade with West tea, silk, fine cottons, porcelain, lacquer
3 Rebellions and foreign attacks 1840-1901
Taiping control early period 1853-7
Taiping control late period 1857-63
routes of Taiping rebels
other areas of rebellion (named on map)
British attacks
French attacks
North Western Muslim rising 1863-73
K A N S U
Lanchow
JEHOL
FENGTIEN
Peking
principal area affected by Boxer uprising 1900-1901
Tientsin
CHIHLI Boxer uprising 1900-01
mouth of Yellow River after 1855
SHANSI
Taiping northern expedition 1853-54
Nien invasion 1868
SHANTUNG
Grand Canal
Anglo-French campaigns 1858-60
Kaifeng
SHENSI
Nien rebels 1853-68
mouth of Yellow River to 1853
HONAN
main Nien centre
KIANGSU
Yangchow
S Z E C H W A N
R. Yangtze
HUPEH
Hankow
Nanking Taiping capital
Chinkiang
Shanghai
Sungkiang
route of Taiping advance to Szechwan 1856-63
ANHWEI
Hangchow
Ningpo
CHEKIANG
KWEICHOW
H U N A N
Taiping advance 1850-53
KIANGSI
Y U N N A N
Yunnanfu
Yunnan Muslim rebellion 1855-73
Kweichow Miao tribal rising 1854-72
Opium War 1839-42
FUKIEN
Foochow
KWANGSI
Amoy
Tamsui
Chintien
outbreak of Taiping rebellion 1850
Hakka-Cantonese war 1855-57
Canton
Chinese attacks during Sino-French war 1883-85
KWANGTUNG
Hong Kong
Sino-French war 1883-85
Hanoi
Russian protectorate 1912
R U S S I A N
TANNU TUVA
E M P I R E
Manchouli
Aigun
R. Amur
to Russia 1858
MARITIME PROVINCE
M O N G O L I A
autonomous 1912
Harbin
occupied by Russia 1897-1905 Japanese influence after 1905
Ili to Russia 1871-81
to Russia 1864
Changchun
Mukden
Suifen
Hunchun
R. Ussuri
Vladivostok
Newchwang
Yellow River (Huang Ho)
Kalgan
Peking
Dairen
Antung
KOREA
Tientsin
S I N K I A N G
Port Arthur
to Russia 1898 to Japan 1905
Taiyuan
Chefoo
Weihaiwei British 1898
Tsinan
Tsingtao German 1898
Japanese 1910
C H I N A
JAPAN
T I B E T
autonomous after 1912 under British influence
Pukow
Nanking
Chinkiang
Wusung
Hankow
Wuhu
Soochow
Shanghai
Ichang
Hangchow
Chungking
R. Yangtze
Kiukiang
Ningpo
Yochow
NEPAL
Changsha
Wenchow
BHUTAN
Ryukyu Is
to Japan 1872
SIKKIM British protectorate 1817
ASSAM British 1826
Santuao
Foochow
FUKIEN
Tamsui
Kunming
Tengyueh
Amoy
Taiwan to Japan 1895
B R I T I S H I N D I A
Mengtze
Manhao
Swatow
Szemao
BURMA British 1886
Lungchow
Nanning
Canton
Macao Portuguese 1557
Kowloon British 1898
Hong Kong British 1842
New Territories British 1898
FRENCH INDO CHINA 1884
Pakhoi
Haiphong
Kwangchowan French 1898
LAOS French 1893
Kiungchow
Hainan
SIAM
4 The dismemberment of the Chinese Empire, 1842-1911
boundary of Ch'ing Empire in 1850
colonial possessions:
spheres of influence:
railways:
Russian
British
Japanese
French
German
Chinese
states formerly tributary to China
Treaty ports and towns:
1842 Treaty of Nanking
1858 Treaty of Tientsin
1860 Peking Convention
1876 Chefoo Convention
1897 Sino-French Trade Convention
additional ports opened by 1911
40°
80
100°

The world economy, 1850-1929

After the middle of the nineteenth century the Industrial Revolution, which had radiated from Great Britain to north-west Europe and the eastern seaboard of the United States, spread to the rest of the world. The result, by 1914, was the formation of a single interdependent world economy. But the impact was extremely varied. Though the United States after 1890 was becoming an important subsidiary centre, the focus throughout was on Europe, and most of the development was keyed to the needs of European industry for raw materials and fed by European capital. In 1914 Great Britain was the largest source of foreign investment, with overseas assets totalling nearly £4,000 million, while the United States, like Russia, was still a net borrower (map 3); but in world trade it was losing the predominance it had enjoyed in 1860 to Germany and the United States (diagram 5).

One factor behind these developments was the vast, unprecedented flow of population, mainly from Europe to the New World, but also from China and India to South-East Asia and East Africa (map 2). Between 1850 and 1920 over 40 million Europeans emigrated overseas or to Siberia, carrying with them European institutions and skills which they used to exploit the vast overseas territories. Much foreign investment went into building the infrastructure of railways, ports and shipping and creating the network of communications upon which the functioning of the world economy depended. Outside Europe and the United States there were only 9,100 miles of railroad track in 1870. By 1911 it had increased to 175,000 miles. Equally important was the expansion of world shipping and the replacement of sailing ships by ocean-going steamships of large capacity. The opening of the Suez Canal (1869) and the Panama Canal (1914) gave a great fillip to world trade (diagram 4). Traffic via Suez rose from 437,000 tons in 1870 to over 20 million tons in 1913, and foreign trade increased threefold in volume during the same period.

Nevertheless the effects of industrialisation were distinctly one-sided. The main shipping routes (map 3) were between the advanced countries and the white dominions, or between them and the producers of raw materials. Even as late as 1929 the world was still a white man's world. A few countries such as India (page 104) and China had begun to develop their own industries; but, with the exception of Japan, they were small enclaves in a vast rural population. In 1914 there were still only 900,000 factory workers in the whole of India, and 69 per cent of cotton operatives in 1919 were in Bombay province. Nowhere outside the United States and Europe was the income produced by manufacturing substantial in 1930 (map 1) and in most cases it accrued to foreign investors. This was true of Malaya, which by 1900 was producing nearly half the world's tin and by 1910 was a major exporter of rubber, and of Katanga, where copper production rose from nothing in 1900 to 305,000 tons (including Northern Rhodesia) in 1930. Here, as elsewhere, the bulk of the population benefited only marginally, and per capita income in most countries seems actually to have declined. This was the situation which led, a generation later, to the conflict of rich nations and poor nations (page 150) and the demand for a New International Economic Order.

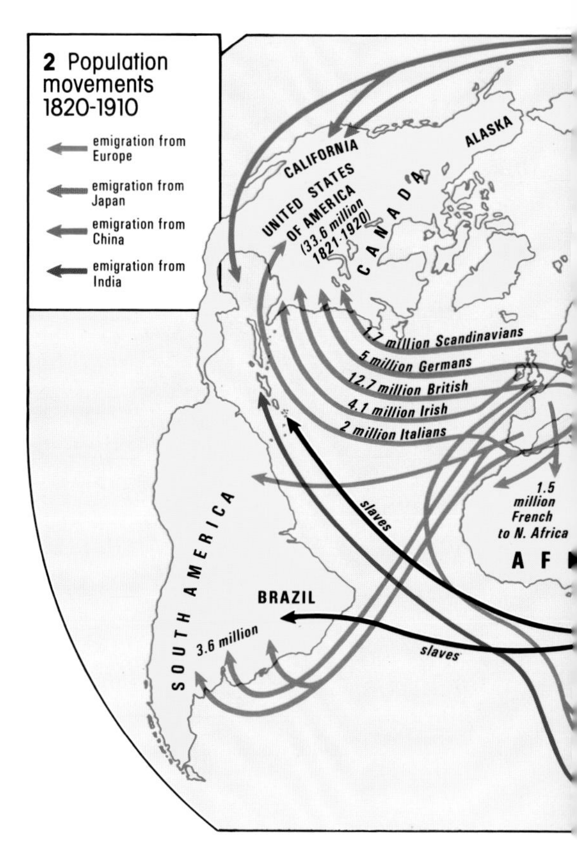

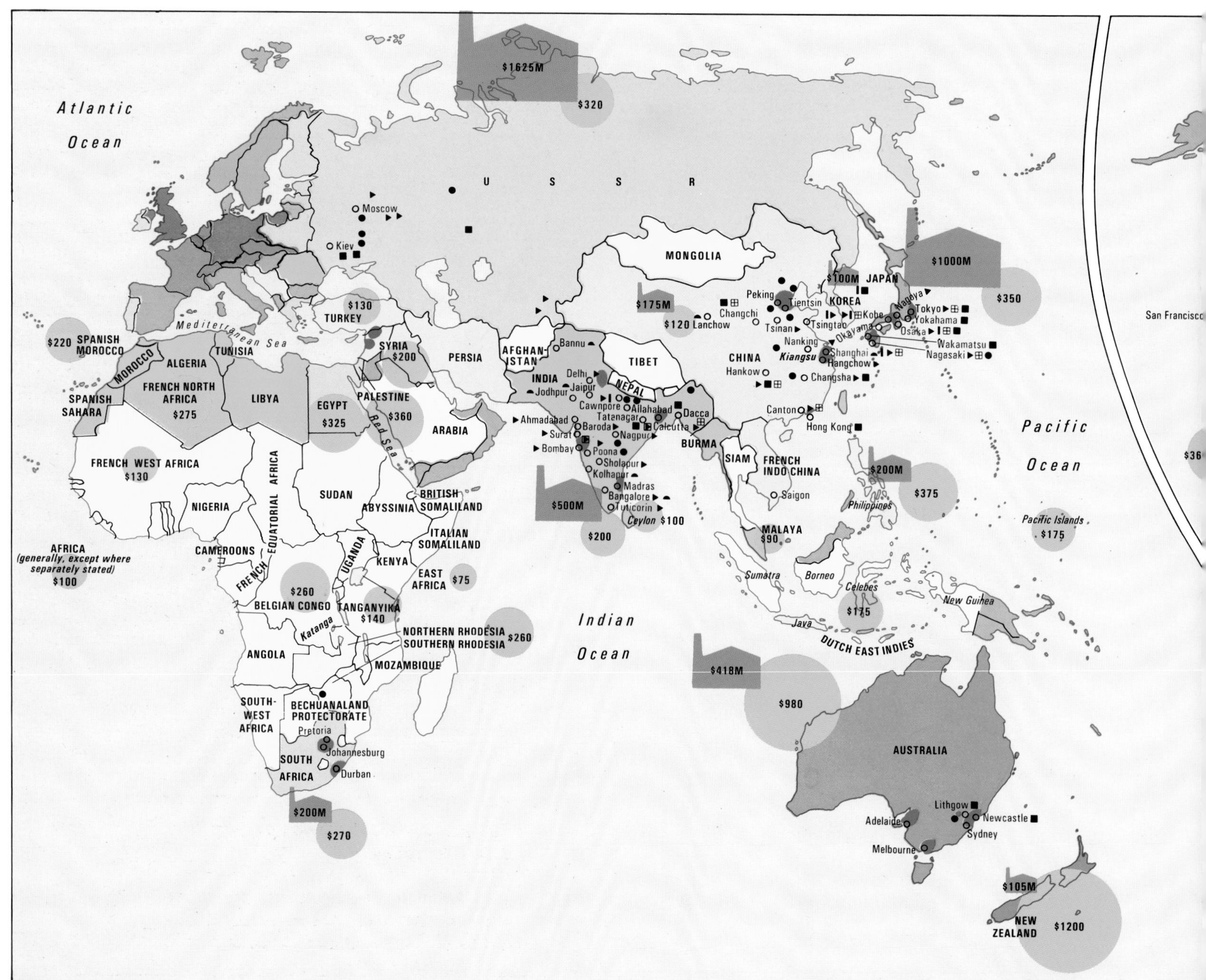

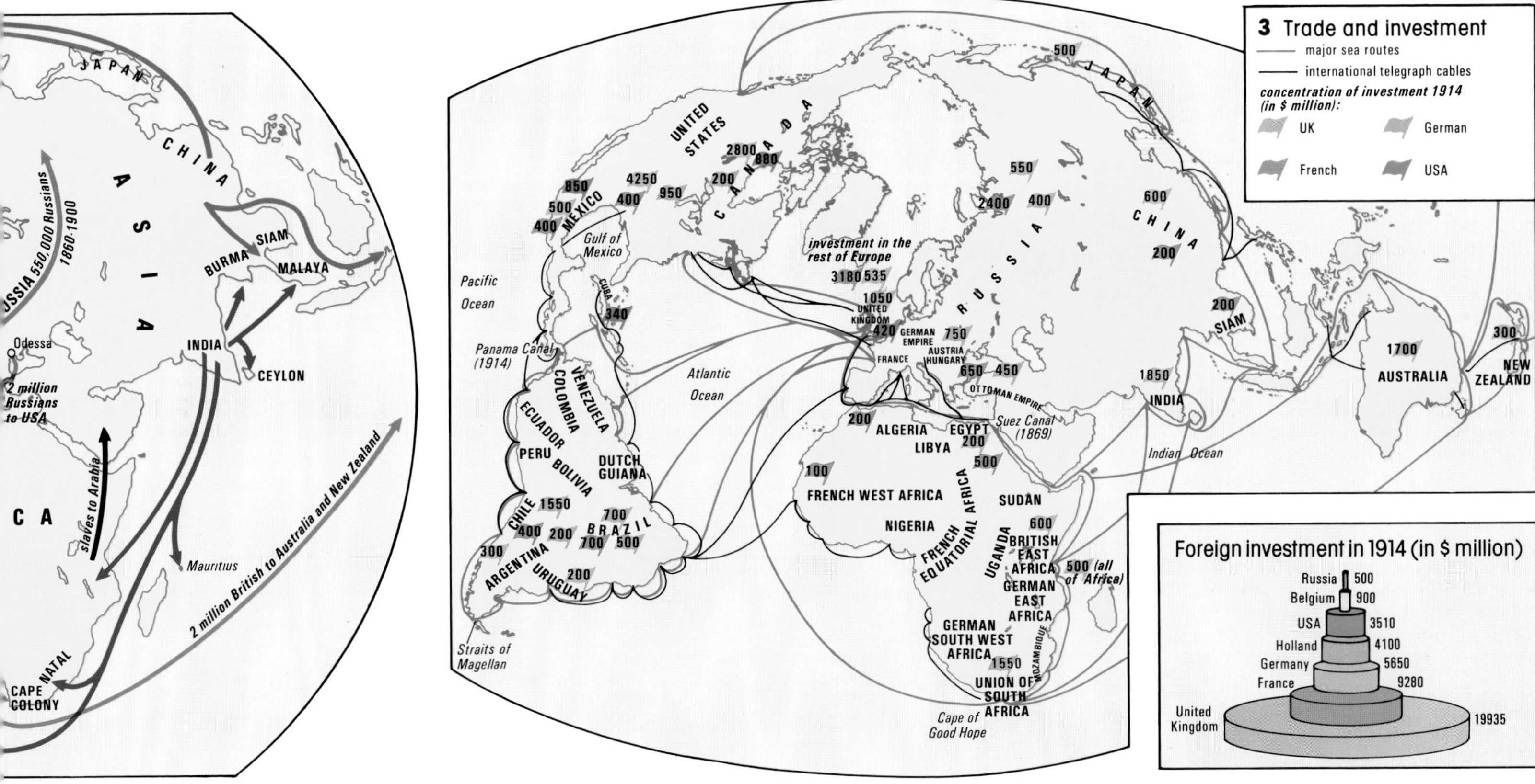

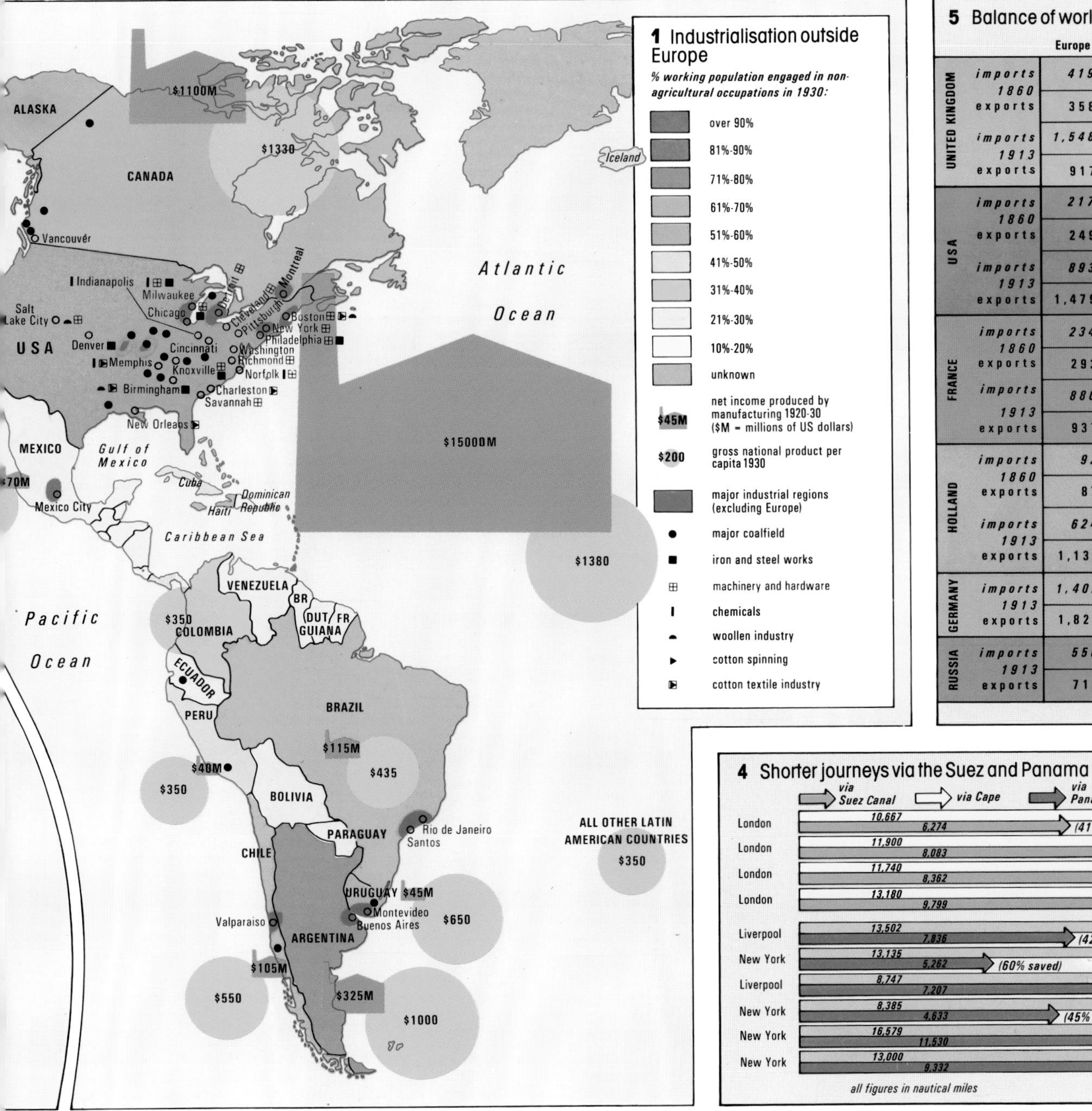

5 Balance of world trade, 1860 and 1913

			Europe	N. America	S. America	Asia	Africa
UNITED KINGDOM	1860	imports	419	252	96	143	80
		exports	358	132	74	139	36
	1913	imports	1,548	848	393	458	220
		exports	917	265	272	620	248
USA	1860	imports	217	–	80	29	–
		exports	249	–	46	11	–
	1913	imports	893	199	381	298	26
		exports	1,479	469	294	140	29
FRANCE	1860	imports	234	47	41	16	34
		exports	293	49	53	3	45
	1913	imports	880	187	183	192	148
		exports	937	89	94	36	181
HOLLAND	1860	imports	92	5	3	32	–
		exports	87	2	1	14	–
	1913	imports	624	190	87	274	14
		exports	1,131	57	9	73	14
GERMANY	1913	imports	1,402	423	290	250	118
		exports	1,828	184	183	130	50
RUSSIA	1913	imports	556	–	–	–	–
		exports	719	–	–	–	–

figures in million dollars US

4 Shorter journeys via the Suez and Panama Canals

via Suez Canal / via Cape / via Panama Canal / via Magellan

From	via Cape / via Magellan	via Suez / via Panama	Saving	To
London	10,667	6,274	(41% saved)	Bombay
London	11,900	8,083	(32% saved)	Calcutta
London	11,740	8,362	(29% saved)	Singapore
London	13,180	9,799	(26% saved)	Hong Kong
Liverpool	13,502	7,836	(42% saved)	San Francisco
New York	13,135	5,262	(60% saved)	San Francisco
Liverpool	8,747	7,207	(18% saved)	Valparaiso
New York	8,385	4,633	(45% saved)	Valparaiso
New York	16,579	11,530	(30% saved)	Hong Kong
New York	13,000	9,332	(29% saved)	Sydney

all figures in nautical miles

The United States and Canada, 1865-1920

The rise of the modern United States dates effectively from the Civil War, but development was very uneven. For the defeated South the period of Reconstruction (1865–77) was a bitter experience. South Carolina had ranked third in the nation in per capita wealth in 1860; ten years later it was fortieth, and Mississippi, Alabama and Georgia fared no better. Worst of all was the position of the 4 million liberated slaves, who found themselves (as the black leader Frederick Douglass said) without money, property or friends. The great upsurge in population, from 31 million in 1860 to 92 million in 1910, by-passed the South and concentrated wealth and power in the north-east where, with the exploitation of the rich ore reserves of the Mesabi Range in Minnesota and the vast coal reserves of the Appalachians, industry spread rapidly from the original manufacturing belt between Boston and New Jersey to Pittsburgh, Detroit and Chicago. Only around 1920 did cheap labour attract the textile industry from New England to the South (map 2).

The Civil War itself had stimulated Northern industry. After 1865 it forged ahead. But the most striking achievement of the immediate post-war period was the opening of the Great Plains, made possible by the railroad boom after 1870. In 1860 some 30,000 miles of railway were in operation, but few lines extended beyond the Great Lakes. By 1870 the mileage had reached 53,000, by 1880 93,000 and by 1890 163,000 miles (page 94). Land grants of more than 132 million acres encouraged railway promoters, and homestead grants of 285 million acres attracted settlers. The number of farms rose from 2 million in 1860 to 6 million in 1910, and grain exports, which the rail network made possible, were an important source of capital for industrial development. The population west of the Mississippi rose from 6 million in 1870 to 26 million in 1910. Nevertheless the bulk of the population was concentrated in the north-east (map 5), and most of the 25 million immigrants between 1870 and 1914 remained there, providing cheap labour for American industry. Their miserable conditions, and those of the southern blacks, lay behind the unrest which erupted in the 1890s (map 2).

In Canada railway development was even more important than in the United States. Hitherto the 'small and unimportant' eastern colonies (as Lord Durham described them in his famous Report of 1839) had gone their separate ways, more closely linked to the United States, which made no secret of its hope to absorb them, than with each other. After the acquisition of Alaska from Russia (map 4), United States' pressure grew, and to meet it the Canadian Federation was formed in 1867 and completed by the adhesion of Manitoba (1870) and British Columbia (1871). The great transcontinental railways – the Great Western and Canadian Pacific (completed 1885), followed by the Canadian Northern and Grand Trunk Pacific – were the lifeblood of the new Dominion and changed the axis of Canadian life. Railway development opened Manitoba and Saskatchewan, and made Canada into one of the world's leading wheat producers (map 1). It also led to the discovery of rich mineral deposits, particularly copper and nickel (1883). The other major industry in 1914 was lumber and the manufacture of paper and newsprint. In general, however, industrialisation was only beginning, though the value of Canada's industrial output increased from $190 million in 1890 to over $500 million in 1914.

In the United States, on the other hand, the 1880s and 1890s saw an astounding industrial upsurge. Output of coal and iron increased twenty times between 1870 and 1913, by which date steel production exceeded that of Britain and Germany combined. But the 'Gilded Age' was also a time of gross inequalities, and speculation and over-production caused serious economic setbacks, particularly in 1873 and 1893, which led not only to industrial unrest but also to a search for new markets, particularly in

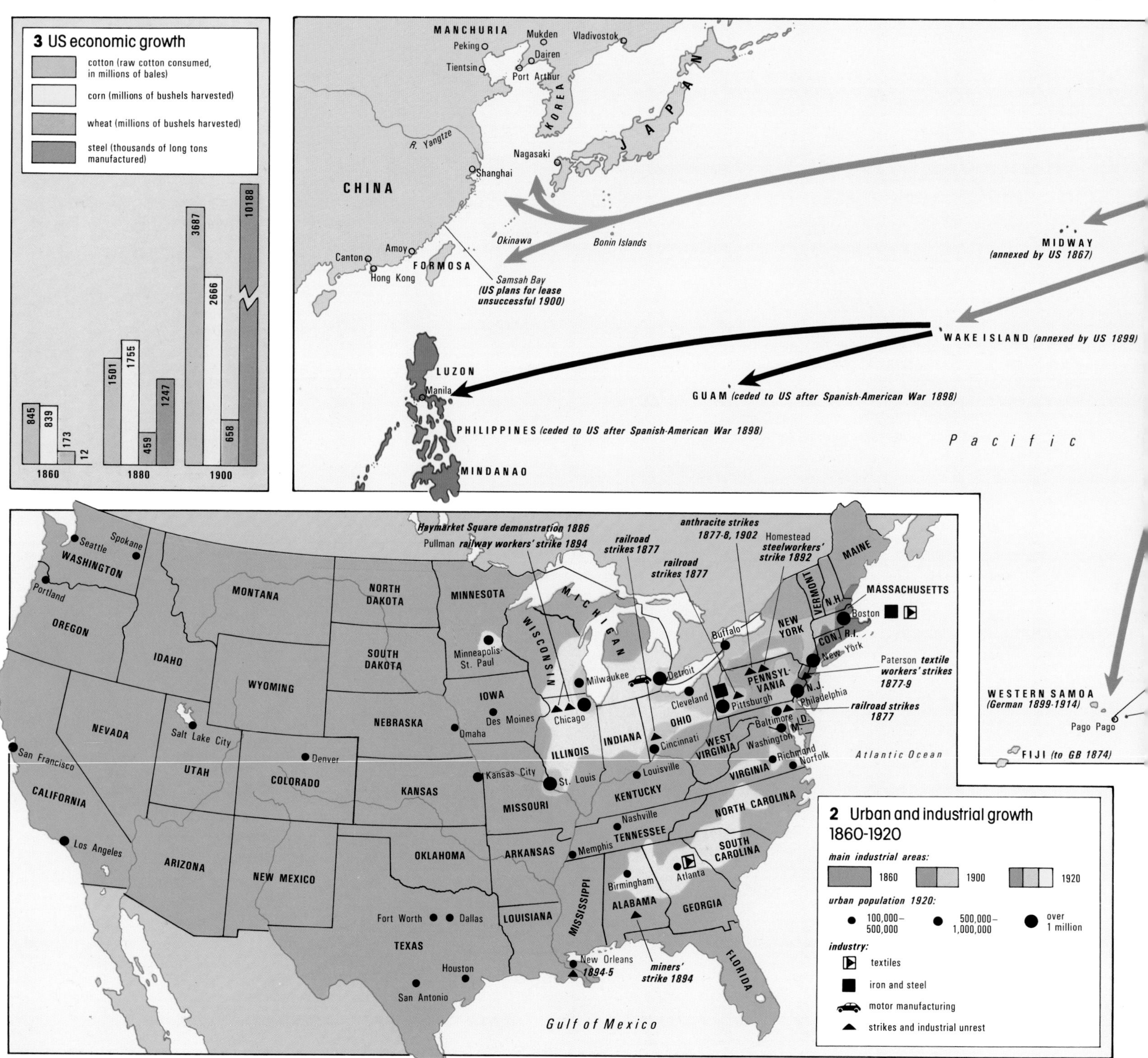

eastern Asia. Already in 1867 the United States had annexed Midway Island as a Pacific base; in 1887 it secured Pearl Harbor. The other area of advance was the Caribbean and Latin America, where, by the Hay-Pauncefote agreement of 1901, Great Britain gave the United States a free hand. But the turning point came with the Spanish-American war of 1898, which made Cuba into an American protectorate and brought the Philippines – 'a stepping-stone to China' – under American rule (map 4). By 1914, when the Panama Canal was opened, the United States was the world's greatest industrial power. It was also, without fully realising it, involved in world politics. The way was prepared for the United States' entry into the First World War.

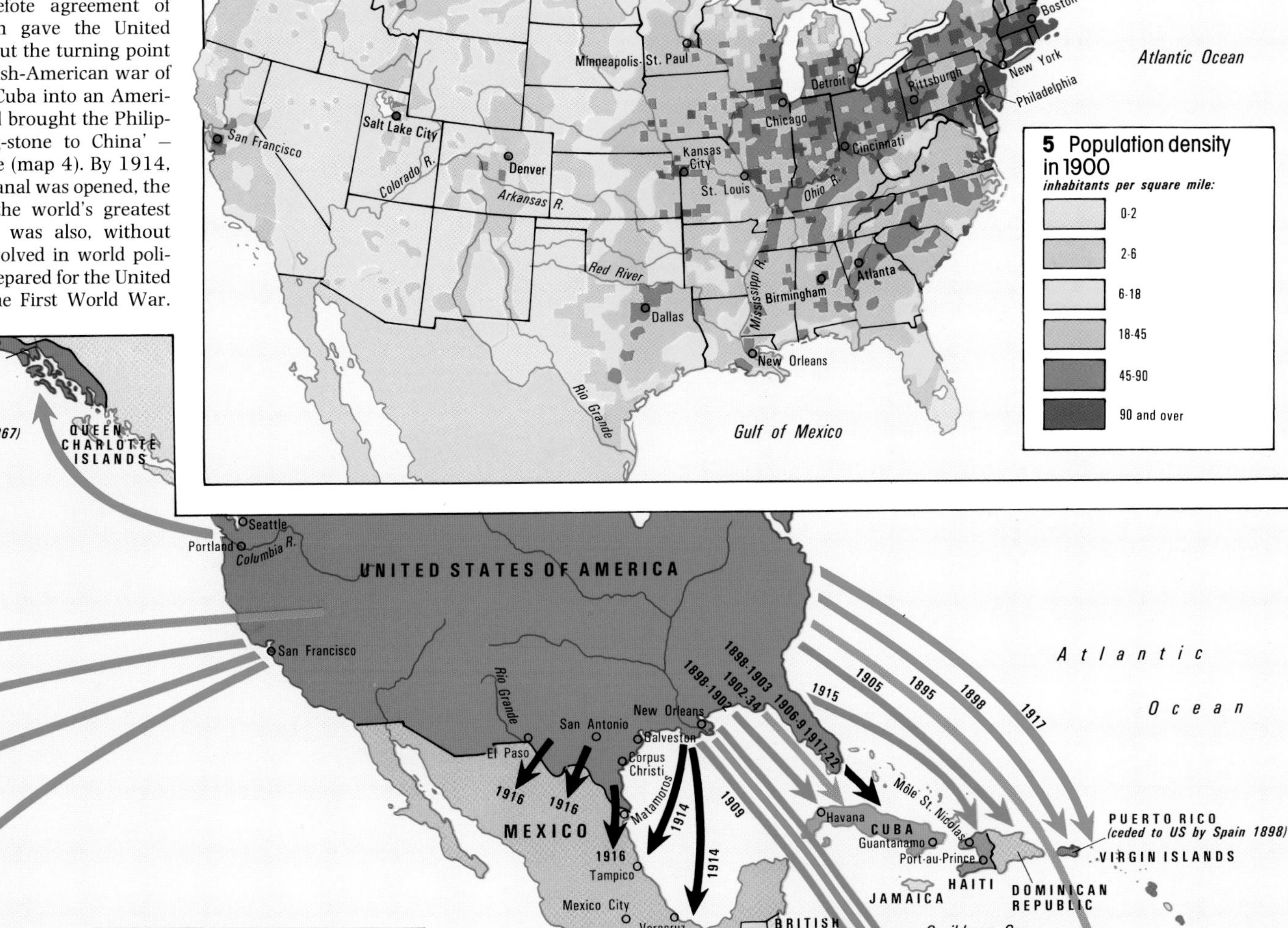

5 Population density in 1900

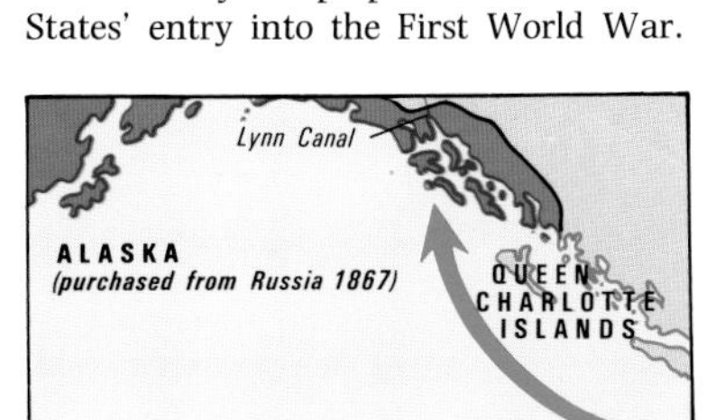

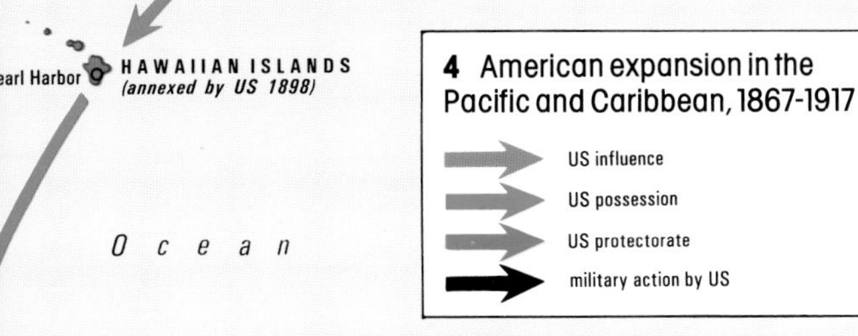

4 American expansion in the Pacific and Caribbean, 1867-1917

TUTUILA (annexed by US 1878)

SAMOA (annexed by US 1878)

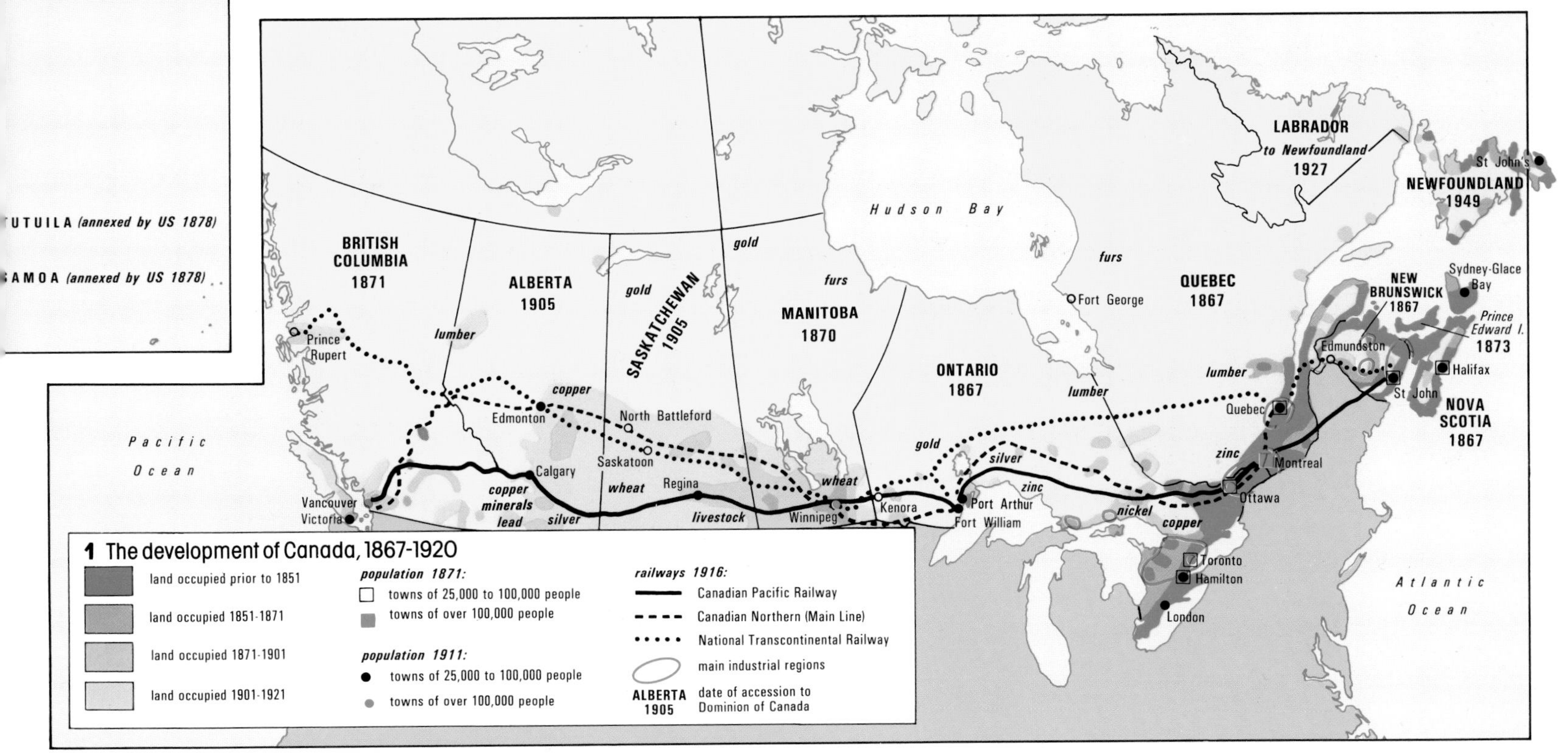

1 The development of Canada, 1867-1920

Australia and New Zealand from 1788

Although Australia and New Zealand were discovered by the Dutch explorer Tasman in 1642, colonisation only began after Cook hoisted the British flag at Botany Bay in 1770 (page 64). New South Wales served as a penal colony from 1788 to 1839, Van Diemen's Land (later Tasmania) from 1804 to 1853, and in 1829 the British government, fearing to be forestalled by the French, claimed the whole Australian continent. Fear of France also led to the annexation of New Zealand in 1840. But in both lands geographical obstacles, lack of exportable products, and, in the case of New Zealand, the bitter Maori wars between 1860 and 1871, made the early years of colonisation difficult. New South Wales was hemmed in by the Blue Mountains. Beyond the Great Dividing Range the country soon became arid and inhospitable. Coastal settlements at Perth (1829), Melbourne (1835), and Adelaide (1836) established bridgeheads for exploration in the west (map 5), but as late as 1850 the total white population was only around 350,000, while in New Zealand it was still below 100,000 in 1860. Inducements to settle were few. Neither country was self-supporting, and early trade (chiefly seal products and sandalwood) was insufficient to pay for imports (map 4), and was further hampered by the East India Company's monopoly in the area.

The discovery of gold in New South Wales and Victoria in 1851 and in Otago (South Island) in 1861 initiated a new phase. Even more important was the rapid growth of sheep farming. In 1850 Australia sent 39 million lb. of wool to Great Britain. By 1879 the quantity had increased to 300 million lb. In New Zealand, where wool was largely a South Island product, exports rose from £67,000 in value in 1853 to £2,700,000 twenty years later. The development of the North Island, held back by the Maori wars, came later, after the introduction of refrigeration. Refrigeration made possible the large-scale export of frozen lamb from the South Island, but it also lay behind the growth of dairy farming in the north, which now, stimulated by the exports trade in butter and cheese, drew ahead of the south in population.

Political development kept pace with economic growth. In 1855 New South Wales, Victoria, South Australia and Tasmania became self-governing colonies, followed by Queensland in 1859, and in 1901 joined together to form the Commonwealth of Australia. New Zealand, which had been divided in 1852 into six provinces, each with an elected council, became a united Dominion in 1876, after measures had been taken to safeguard the rights of the Maori population. Both dominions remained heavily dependent on primary exports. For long they enjoyed preferential treatment in the British market; but developments after 1945, particularly the British retreat from Asia, brought important changes. In 1952 both dominions joined for security with the United States in the ANZUS Pact, and when Great Britain entered the European Common Market (1973) and dismantled imperial preference, they were forced to diversify their economies and seek new markets. The process of reorientation is still continuing.

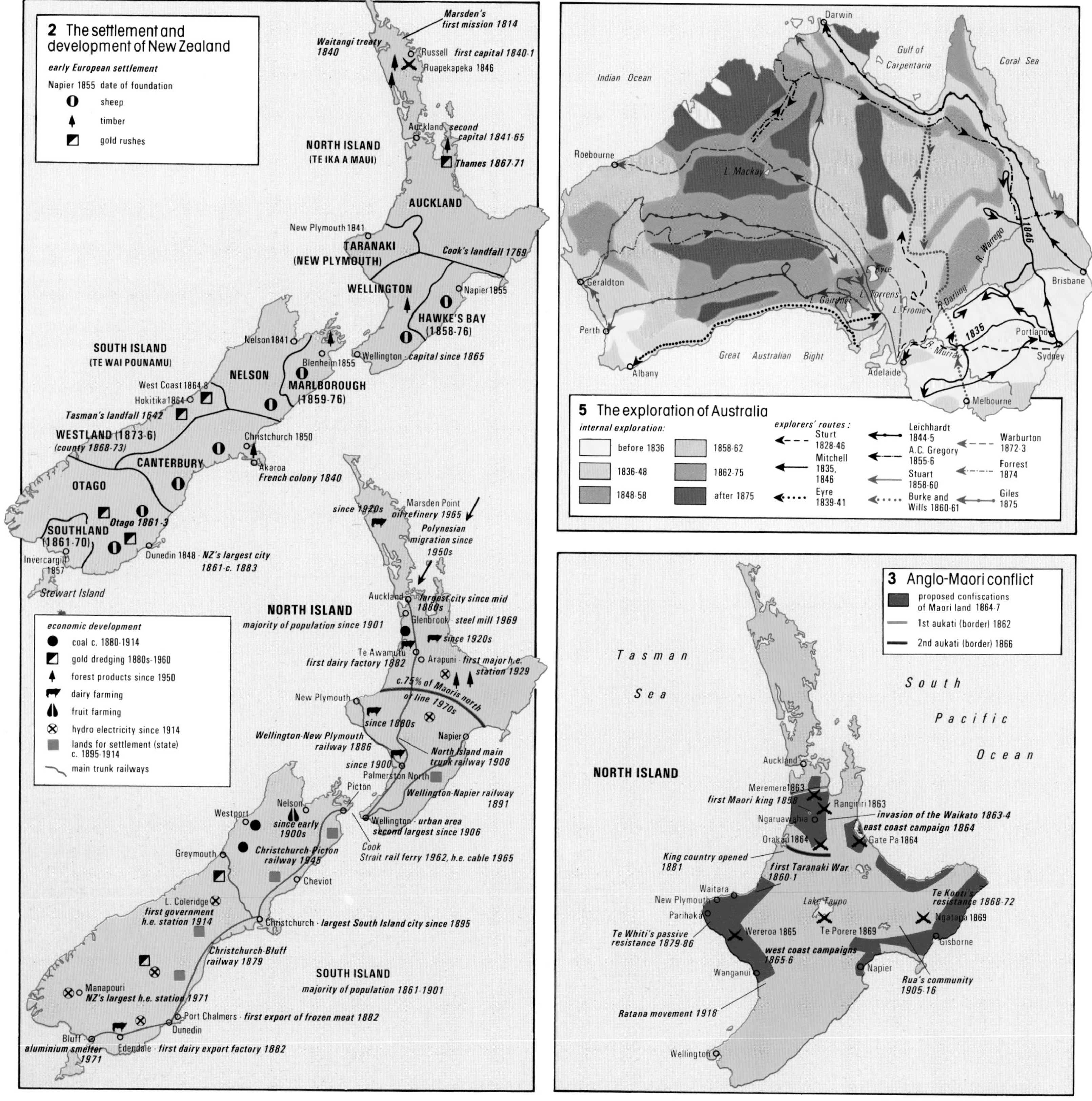

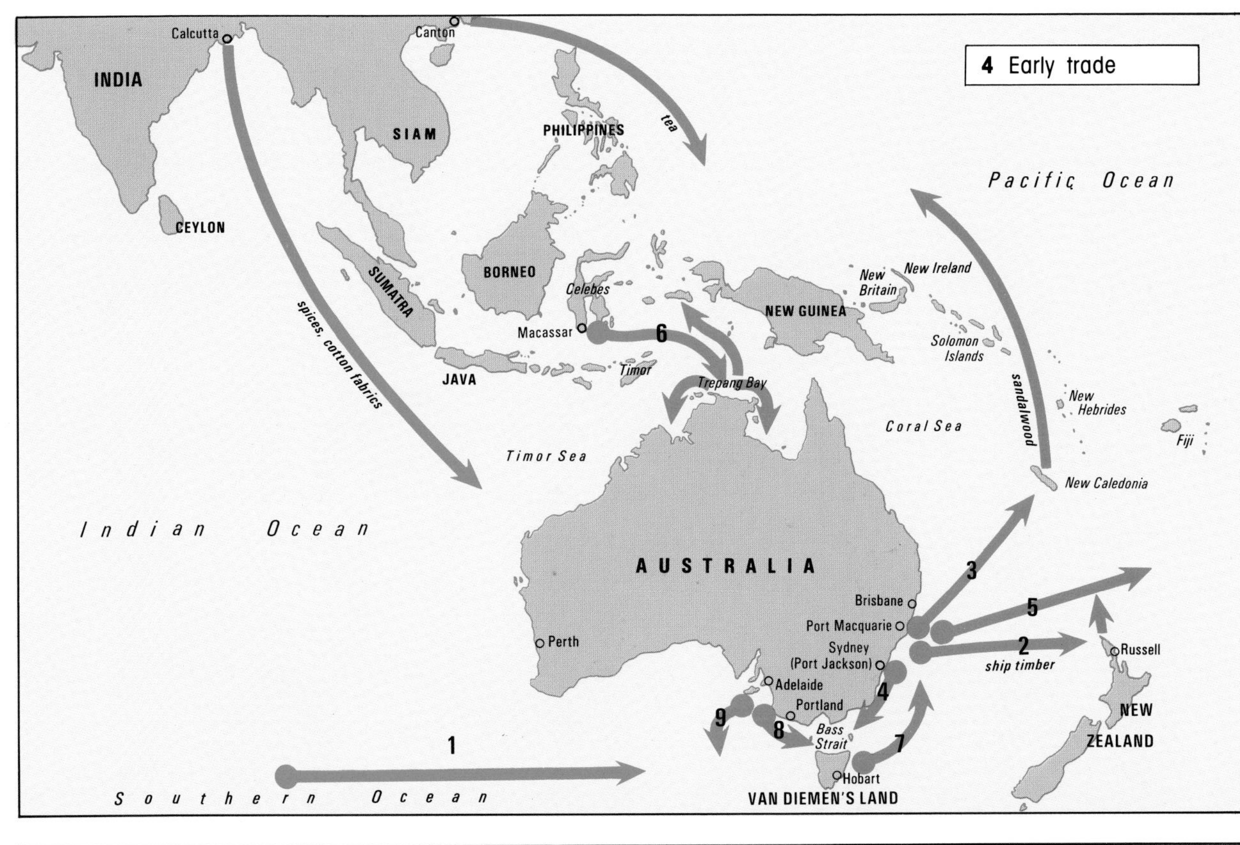

Early trade (left)

1/Main route from Europe via Cape of Good Hope. First colonisation fleet to New South Wales 1788, mainly convicts and marines. By 1790, with arrival of second fleet, it was clear that the colonies would be reliant upon regular supplies from Europe.

2/Convict transport ships return to U.K. via New Zealand for timber, and Canton for tea or Calcutta for oriental goods.

3/Sydney-based ships to Pacific islands for sandalwood to trade for tea at Canton.

4/Sydney-based ships to Bass Strait islands for seal skins and oil (first major exports to U.K.). Seal fields soon exhausted. Eastern colony ports used as bases for American and British whaling ships, an industry developed by colonists from 1820s.

5/Sydney to Tahiti for pork for provisioning convicts.

6/Macassan fishermen to northern Australian coast to collect trepang (sea cucumbers) to trade with Chinese merchants.

7/Van Diemen's land grain to Sydney.

8/South Australian grain to eastern colonies.

9/South Australian grain to Europe. From 1840s wool and minerals, the basis of late nineteenth century trade with Europe.

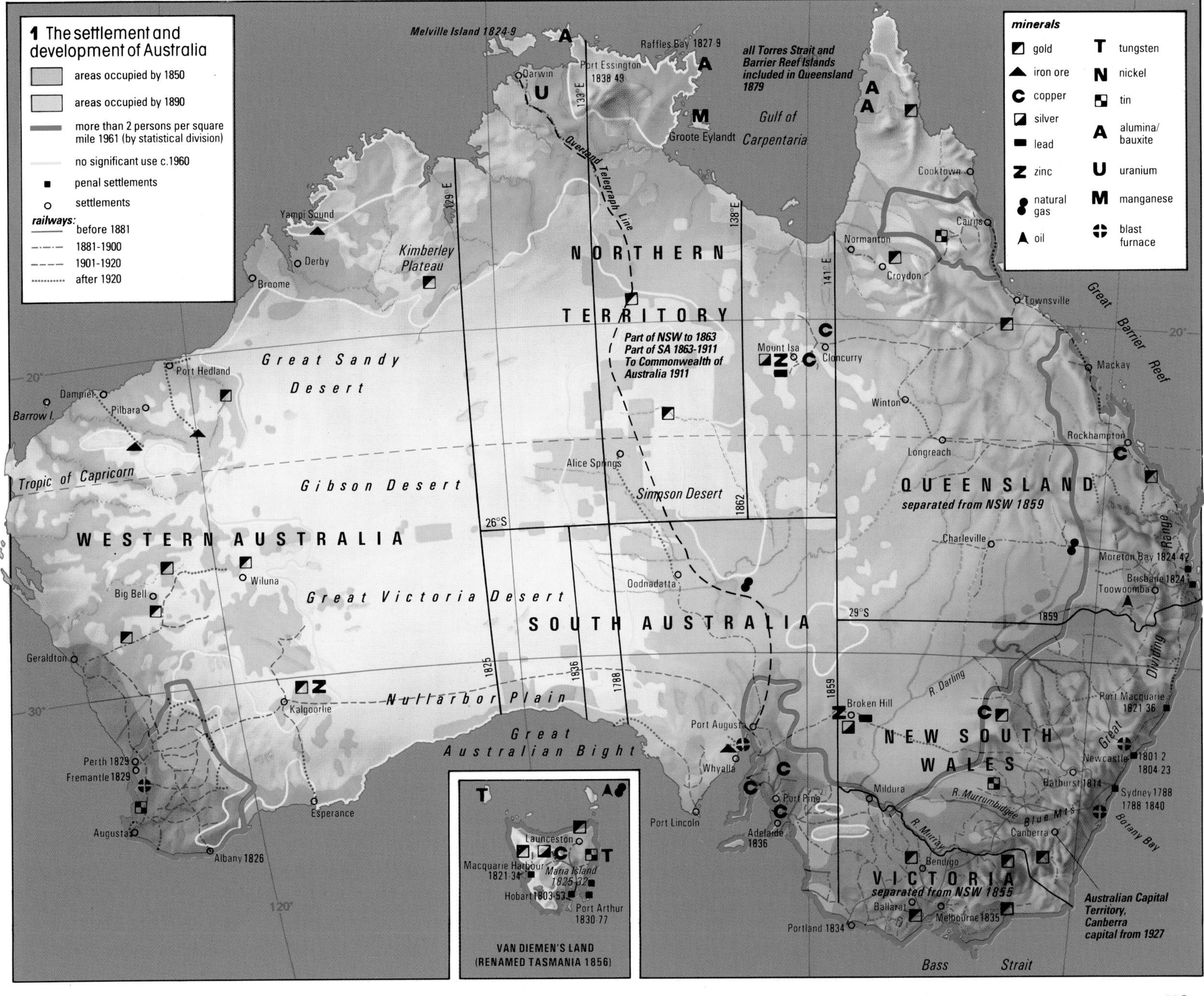

European nationalism
1815-1914

The flame of nationalism was kindled in Europe by the French revolution. In France itself the revolution forged a sense of national unity, and elsewhere, notably in Spain and Prussia, the humiliation of defeat and French occupation after 1807 produced a short-lived national reaction. For the most part, however, nationalism was confined to a narrow segment of the middle class. It was anathema to the ruling classes, and rarely touched working people. Polish peasants held aloof from the insurrections of 1831, 1846 and 1863; in Ireland only acute agrarian distress after 1877 lined them up behind the nationalists. Down to 1848 liberal and constitutional reform was the main demand, and it was against this, rather than nationalism, that the victorious powers set their faces after the fall of Napoleon at the Congress of Vienna in 1815. Their other main objective was to erect a barrier against a resurgence of revolutionary France. Hence their decision to transfer the Austrian Netherlands (later Belgium) to Holland, to install Prussia in Westphalia and most of the Rhineland, and to hand over the ancient republic of Genoa to Sardinia-Piedmont. As compensation for the loss of the Netherlands, Austria received the Venetian republic and the duchy of Milan, as well as indirect control of Parma, Modena and Tuscany. Sweden, which had to surrender Finland to Russia, was compensated with Norway.

The overriding objective of the great powers after 1815 was to uphold the Vienna settlement and to combat the threat of liberalism and nationalism, but by 1830, when a new wave of liberal and nationalist agitation broke out, the eastern and western powers were drawing apart. By destroying a common front, their divergence of interests enabled Greece (page 116) and Belgium to obtain independence, although in the latter case the territorial settlement, including the disposal of Limburg and Luxembourg was postponed until 1839 (map 5). In Norway the forced union with Sweden aroused resentment similar to that felt in Belgium towards Holland. There was friction, but little active resistance, and eventually a Norwegian declaration of independence was accepted by Sweden (map 4). The course of events in Poland (1831, 1846) and in Italy, Germany and Hungary in 1848–49 was more eventful. Here nationalist agitation erupted in full-scale war; but the solidarity of the conservative powers and divisions among the nationalists themselves brought all to nothing.

What changed this situation was the rise of a new generation of statesmen. Louis Napoleon, emperor of France since 1852, Cavour, who became prime minister of Sardinia-Piedmont in the same year, and Bismarck, minister-president of Prussia after 1862, all toyed with nationalism, confident of their ability to use it for their own ends. These were not the ends of the liberals who had led the nationalist movements of 1848–49. Cavour's purpose was to ensure that Italian unification was carried out by and in the interests of Sardinia; hence his opposition to the famous Sicilian expedition of the patriot Garibaldi (1807–82) in 1860. Bismarck was determined to ensure that Germany was merged in Prussia, not Prussia in Germany. Both also realised that their objectives could only be achieved by war and diplomacy. Hence Cavour's alliance with France against Austria (1858) and Bismarck's wars of 1864, 1866 and 1870. The result was the unification of Italy (except for Venetia and the Papal State) in 1861 (map 3) and the unification of Germany in 1871 (map 2). Both were retrospectively endorsed by liberal nationalists, but neither satisfied the nationalism they aroused. Italy still laid claim to the Alto Adige, Fiume and Trieste. Bismarck's 'small German' solution, excluding Austria, disappointed those who hankered after a Greater Germany. Indeed, it was after 1870, when the problems of the multi-national Austro-Hungarian state came to the fore, that nationalist claims became loudest. The confusion of peoples and languages in eastern Europe (map 1) defied easy solutions and exacerbated the conflicts which led, step by step, to war in 1914.

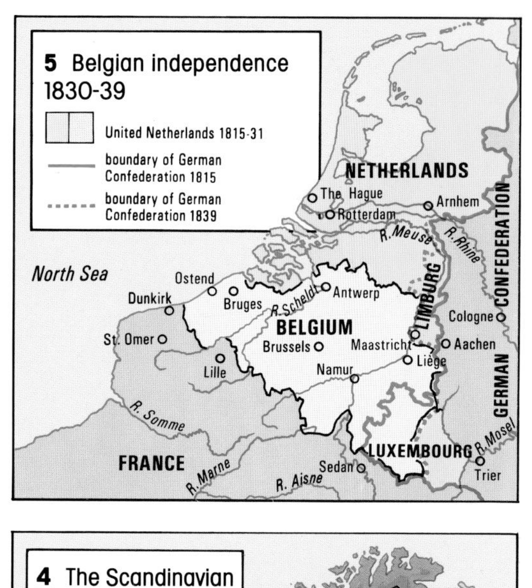

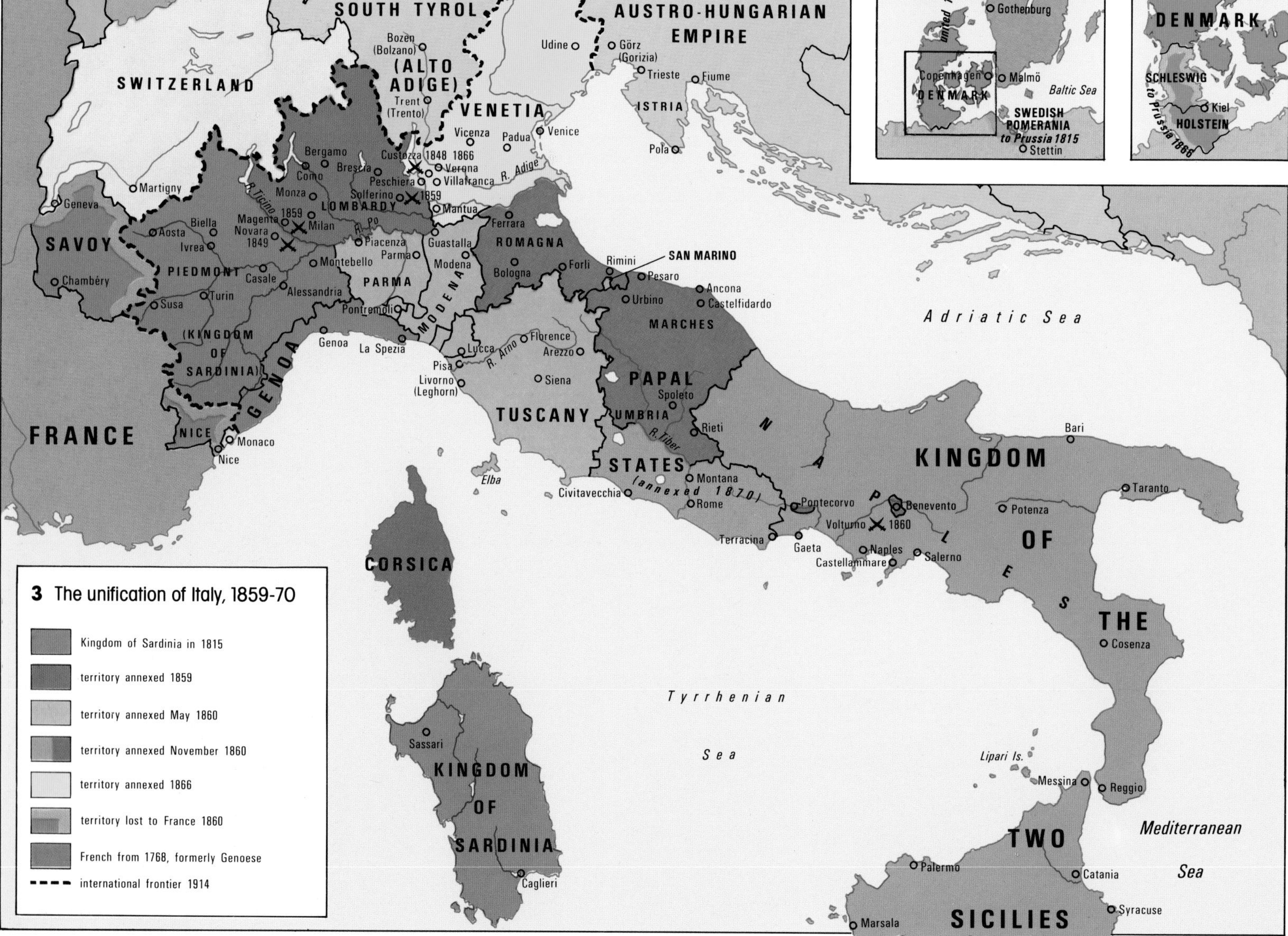

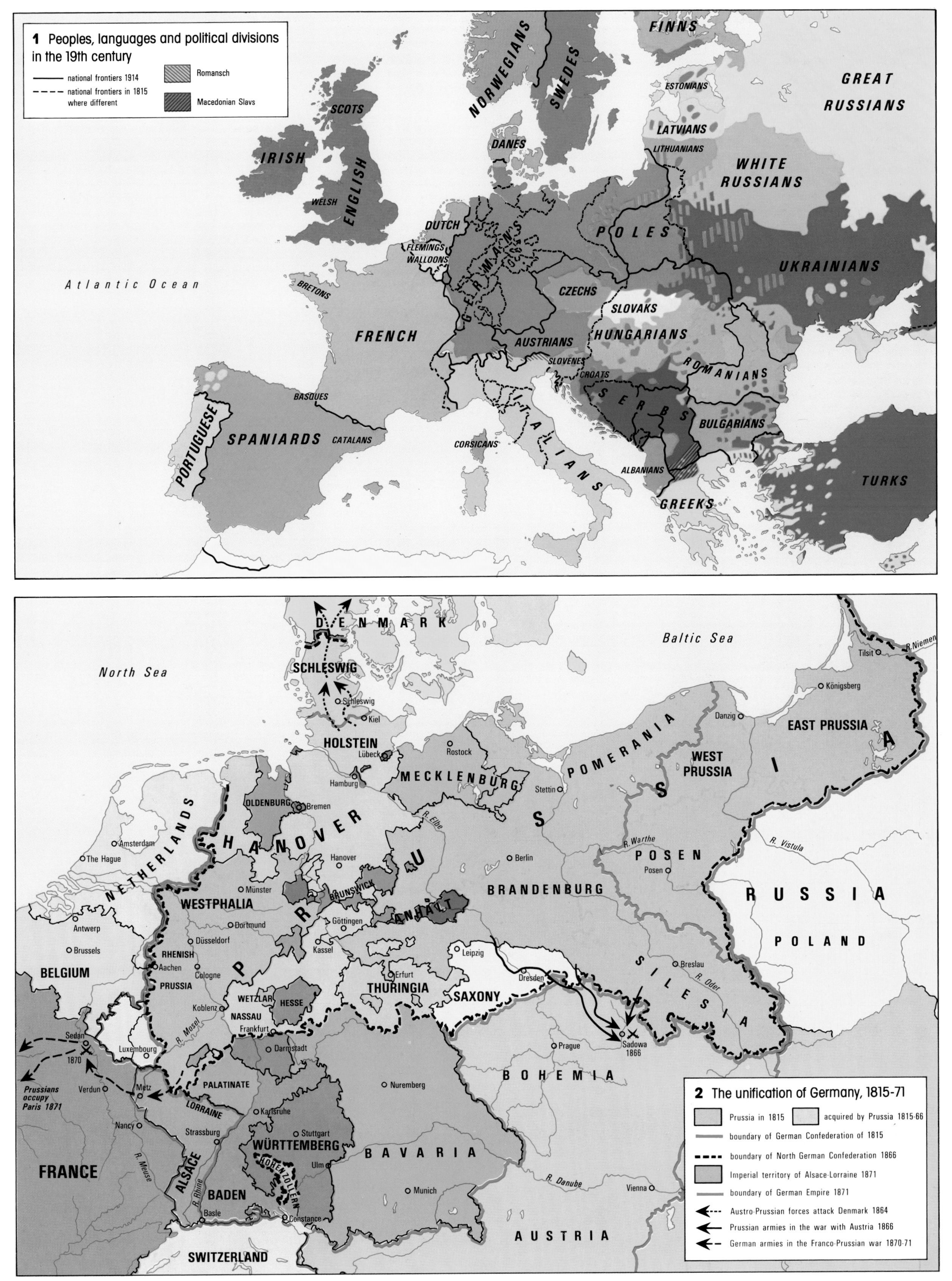
1 Peoples, languages and political divisions in the 19th century
national frontiers 1914
national frontiers in 1815 where different
Romansch
Macedonian Slavs
Atlantic Ocean
FINNS
NORWEGIANS
SWEDES
ESTONIANS
GREAT RUSSIANS
LATVIANS
LITHUANIANS
SCOTS
DANES
IRISH
ENGLISH
WELSH
WHITE RUSSIANS
DUTCH
FLEMINGS
WALLOONS
GERMANS
POLES
UKRAINIANS
BRETONS
CZECHS
SLOVAKS
FRENCH
AUSTRIANS
HUNGARIANS
SLOVENES
CROATS
ROMANIANS
BASQUES
SERBS
PORTUGUESE
SPANIARDS
CATALANS
CORSICANS
ITALIANS
BULGARIANS
ALBANIANS
GREEKS
TURKS
2 The unification of Germany, 1815-71
Prussia in 1815
acquired by Prussia 1815-66
boundary of German Confederation of 1815
boundary of North German Confederation 1866
Imperial territory of Alsace-Lorraine 1871
boundary of German Empire 1871
Austro-Prussian forces attack Denmark 1864
Prussian armies in the war with Austria 1866
German armies in the Franco-Prussian war 1870-71
North Sea
Baltic Sea
DENMARK
SCHLESWIG
Schleswig
Kiel
HOLSTEIN
Lübeck
Hamburg
Rostock
MECKLENBURG
Stettin
POMERANIA
Danzig
WEST PRUSSIA
EAST PRUSSIA
Königsberg
Tilsit
R. Niemen
PRUSSIA
OLDENBURG
Bremen
HANOVER
Hanover
NETHERLANDS
Amsterdam
The Hague
R. Elbe
Berlin
R. Warthe
POSEN
Posen
R. Vistula
RUSSIA
POLAND
BRANDENBURG
Münster
WESTPHALIA
Dortmund
Düsseldorf
BRUNSWICK
ANHALT
Göttingen
Kassel
Antwerp
Brussels
BELGIUM
RHENISH PRUSSIA
Aachen
Cologne
Leipzig
Erfurt
THURINGIA
SAXONY
Dresden
Breslau
R. Oder
SILESIA
WETZLAR
HESSE
NASSAU
Koblenz
R. Mosel
Frankfurt
Sedan
1870
Luxembourg
Darmstadt
Prague
Sadowa
1866
BOHEMIA
Prussians occupy Paris 1871
Verdun
Metz
PALATINATE
LORRAINE
Nuremberg
Nancy
Karlsruhe
Strassburg
Stuttgart
WÜRTTEMBERG
HOHENZOLLERN
BAVARIA
ALSACE
R. Meuse
FRANCE
R. Rhine
BADEN
Ulm
Munich
R. Danube
Vienna
Basle
Constance
AUSTRIA
SWITZERLAND

The European powers
1878-1914

After the unification of Germany and of Italy (page 114), it seemed for a time as though the major questions which had disturbed the peace of Europe since 1848 had been resolved. Bismarck, the architect of German unification, concentrated his efforts after 1871 upon building a system of alliances which would ensure the future of the new German Reich. The 'wild Junker' had become a conservative, anxious only to preserve what had been won; and his alliances were defensive. But the history of the next forty years is the story of how alliances, originally defensive and stabilising in intent, turned into an aggressive and destabilising system. Furthermore, the unification of Germany and of Italy, far from marking a halting place, opened up a hornet's nest of nationalist revindications. After 1870 the nationalist movement which had agitated western Europe for forty years, spilled over into the Balkans; and the struggles of the Balkan peoples for independence (map 1) inevitably involved the powers who were their supporters or adversaries, particularly Russia and Austria-Hungary, which, after its exclusion from Germany and Italy after 1866, was essentially an eastward-looking Balkan power.

The evolution of the relations between the great powers between 1879, when Bismarck tried to reconcile his sympathies with a conservative Russia with support for Austria-Hungary, and 1914, when the whole precarious balance fell apart, is indicated diagrammatically on maps 2(a) to 2(f). Until the beginning of the new century the system worked reasonably well. Revolts in the Balkans between 1875 and 1878, culminating in Russian intervention and war with Turkey, thoroughly alarmed the powers; and after the Congress of Berlin (1878) Balkan affairs took a secondary place. Checked in Europe, Russia turned to central Asia and the Far East, and during the first half of the period the dominant themes were Anglo-Russian rivalry in Asia and Anglo-French rivalry in Africa. What changed this situation was the decision of Germany under William II, particularly after Bülow became chancellor in 1900, to seek 'a place in the sun'. This was not unreasonable; but by now most places in the sun had been occupied, and German policy was seen as a threat by the established imperial powers. The result was the Anglo-French reconciliation (1904) and the Anglo-Russian reconciliation (1907). German 'world policy' also required a navy, resulting in the naval competition which soured Anglo-German relations between 1906 and 1912. After 1907 the Triple Entente with France and Russia became the lynch-pin of British policy, the only firm assurance against the German 'threat'. Germany, on the other hand, saw itself being 'encircled' by a hostile ring constructed by Great Britain.

The result was that the lines between the Triple Alliance and the Triple Entente were drawn tighter. Also

Germany was driven closer to its only dependable ally, Austria-Hungary. When Austria annexed Bosnia-Herzegovina in 1908, Bülow lent full support, and Austro-Russian antagonism in the Balkans, hitherto suppressed, was rekindled. The climax was postponed until the outbreak of the Balkan wars in 1912. The aggrandisement of Serbia which resulted was viewed by Austria as an intolerable threat. Russia, on the other hand, could not leave Serbia in the lurch without losing credibility. The result was the stupendous build-up of armaments (diagram 3) as the grinding logic of the system came into play. When in 1914 the murder of the Austrian archduke Franz Ferdinand brought matters to a head, the combustible material was piled up which exploded in the First World War.

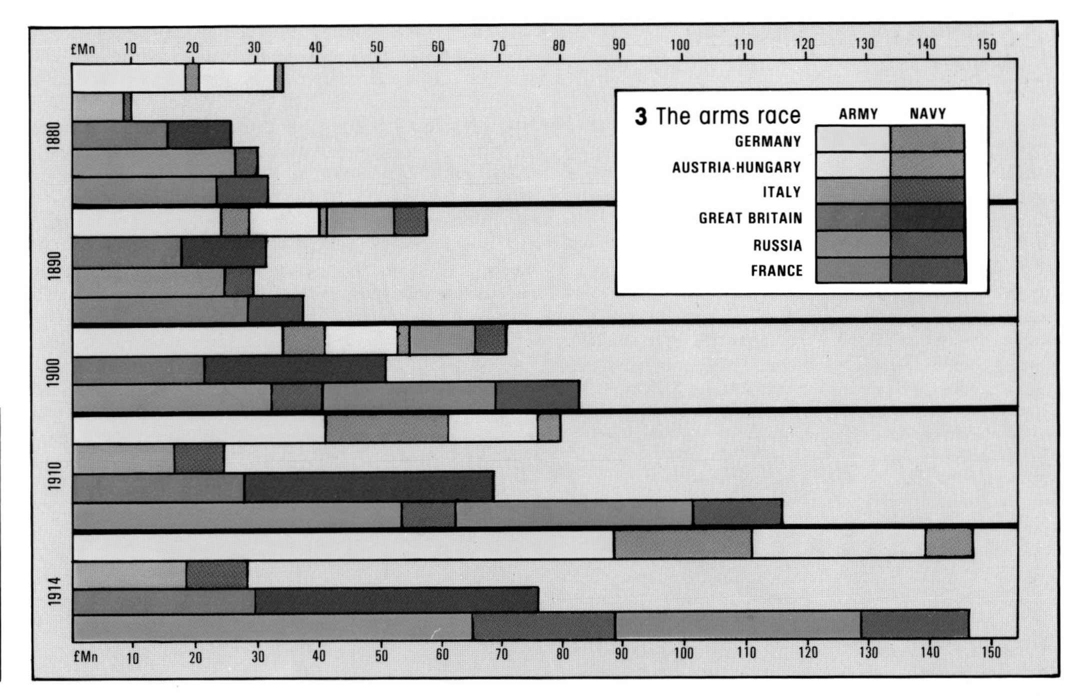

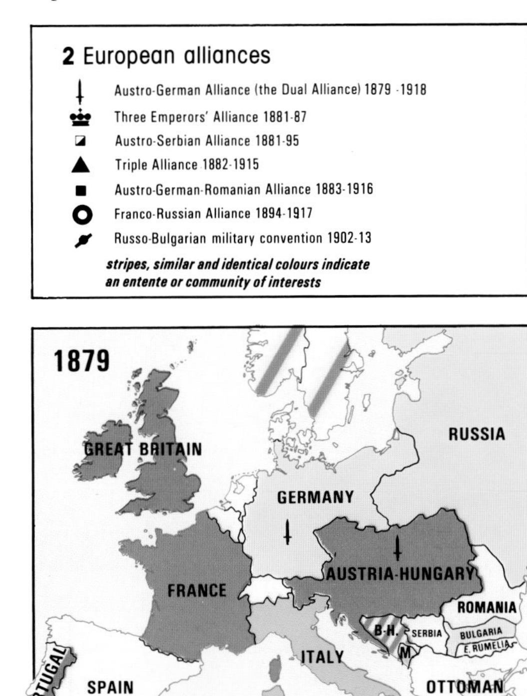

2a/The Dual Alliance: October 1879, resulted from the Balkan upheavals of 1875–8. When Russia attacked Turkey and imposed the Treaty of San Stefano, the Austro-Russian understanding of 1873 broke down. Bismarck's purpose in the Dual Alliance was to stabilise the situation. Germany could not afford to let Austria-Hungary succumb to a Russian attack; but the alliance was strictly defensive. It did not imply a common front against Russia, understanding with which was still a basic element in Bismarck's policy, still less a German commitment to underwrite Austrian ambitions in the Balkans. Nevertheless the Dual Alliance marked a turning point: the era of formal alliances had begun.

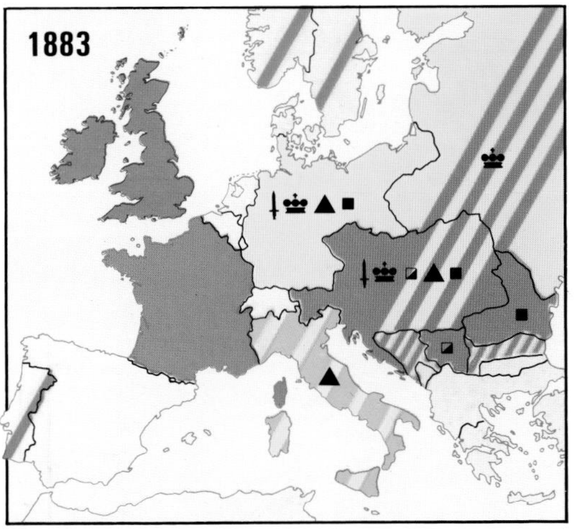

2b/Bismarck's system at its zenith: 1883. The formation of the Three Emperors' Alliance (1881) appeared to have restored stability in Eastern Europe. But the smouldering Austro-Russian antagonism continued, brought to a head again by the Bulgarian crisis of 1886–7. Alliances with Serbia (1881) and Romania (1883) sought to limit Russian influence in the Balkans. The Triple Alliance of Germany, Austria and Italy (1882) insured Austria against Italian attack in case of war with Russia. After the Three Emperors' Alliance broke down, Bismarck sought security by his Reinsurance Treaty with Russia (1887), while Austria joined in a 'Mediterranean agreement' with Britain, Italy and Spain against France and Russia.

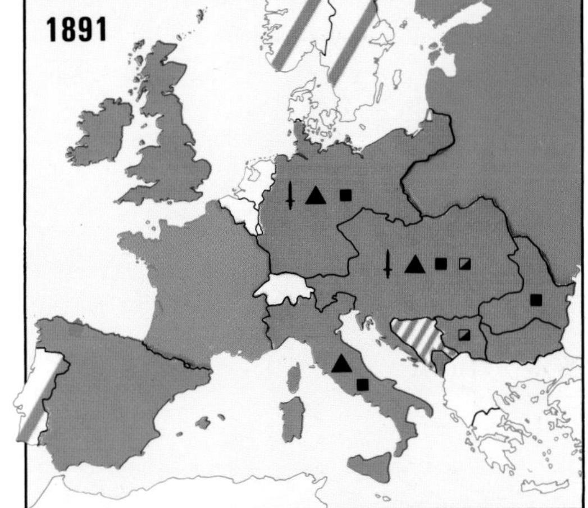

2c/The 'New Course' in Germany: 1891. Even before Bismarck's fall in 1890, it was evident that his complicated system of alliances was running into difficulties. Russo-German relations deteriorated sharply after 1887 as a result of tariff and loan disputes. When the new German chancellor, Caprivi, dropped Bismarck's Reinsurance Treaty, renewed the Triple Alliance, and lined up with the 'Mediterranean entente', Russia replied by a military convention and alliance with France (1894). But the 'new course' was short-lived. After 1895 Germany saw more profit in co-operation with France and Russia in the Far East, while Austria-Hungary and Russia agreed (1897) to put Balkan problems on ice.

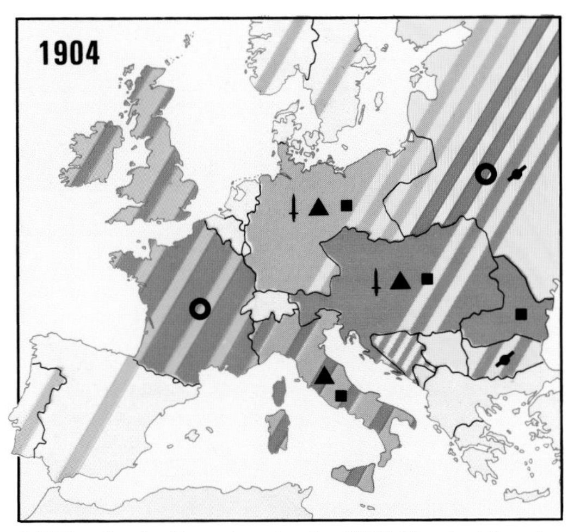

2d/The Anglo-French entente: 1904. The decision of William II and Bülow after 1897 to move from a continental, European to a 'world' policy challenged all three established imperial powers and brought about a major realignment. In 1902 France settled its long-standing dispute with Italy; in 1904 it reached a similar settlement with Great Britain. Germany's attempt to exploit Russia's weakness after the Russo-Japanese war and the 1905 revolution to prise apart the Franco-Russian alliance misfired. Franco-British ties were strengthened; Russia and England settled their colonial differences in 1907, and the three powers joined in the Triple Entente to counter and contain Germany.

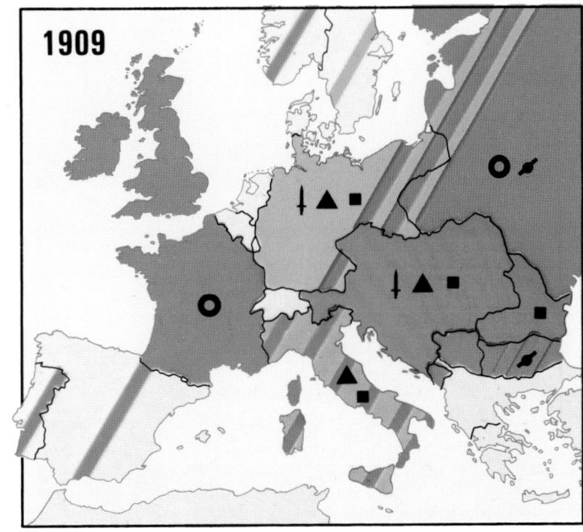

2e/Europe after the Bosnian crisis: 1909. The Austrian annexation of Bosnia and Herzegovina, a response to the Turkish revolution of 1908, ended the Austro-Russian Balkan entente of 1897 and caused a major crisis in international relations. When Russia protested, Germany gave Austria full support, reversing Bismarck's defensive interpretation of the Dual Alliance, and forced Russia to back down. Henceforward Austria-Hungary and Russia were at loggerheads in the Balkans. Anglo-German relations also were at their nadir, a consequence of growing naval rivalry. The result was to consolidate the Triple Entente, particularly after the second Morocco crisis (1911), when Britain took the lead in opposing Germany.

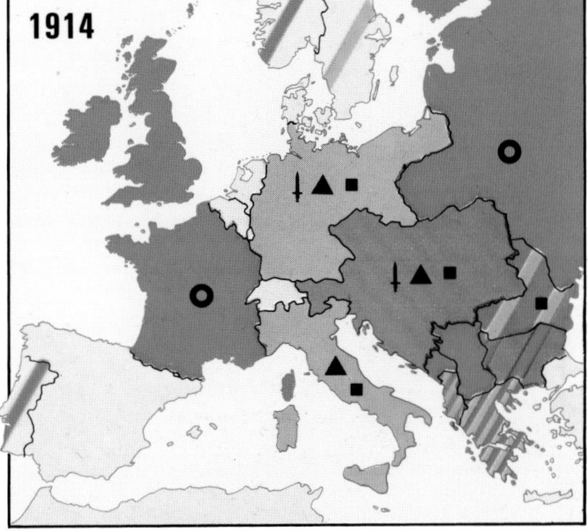

2f/Europe on the eve of war: 1914. Between 1911 and 1914 the front between the Triple Alliance and the Triple Entente hardened. During the Balkan wars (1912–13), when Serbia, Greece and Bulgaria combined to drive Turkey out of Europe, the two groups still co-operated. But Austria was aghast at the consequent enlargement of Serbia and feared pro-Serb irredentism in its Slav provinces, and Germany was haunted by the spectre of encirclement. When, after the assassination of Franz Ferdinand at Sarajevo on 28 June 1914, Austria decided to punish Serbia and Berlin threw itself unreservedly behind Vienna, the system of alliances almost automatically led to general war.

The First World War
1914-1918

When the assassination of the Austrian heir-presumptive, Archduke Franz Ferdinand, by Bosnian terrorists at Sarajevo on June 28, 1914, sparked off the immediate sequence of events that led to the First World War, the European powers were already divided into heavily armed camps (page 116), and neither was prepared to risk diplomatic defeat. Germany already had its battle plan prepared: the famous Schlieffen Plan, drawn up in 1905, to trap and annihilate the French army by a great encircling movement through Belgium before France's Russian ally had time to mobilise. The expectation everywhere was for a short war, over by Christmas 1914, and only after this expectation proved false did the search for allies begin in earnest. Germany and Austria were joined by the Ottoman Empire and Bulgaria, the Entente powers by Italy, Romania and Greece, and eventually by the United States (map 1).

The German strategy was very nearly successful and brought the German armies within 40 miles of Paris (map 2). It was frustrated by the unexpectedly rapid mobilisation of Russia, which invaded East Prussia and defeated the German 8th Army at Gumbinnen (August 20, 1914). Although the Russians were repulsed at Tannenberg (August 26–29), their offensive drew off German reserves, which helped the French and British armies in the west to halt the German advance in the battle of the Marne (September 5–8), while the Russians simultaneously inflicted a crushing defeat on Austria at Lemberg. The Schlieffen Plan had failed, Germany was forced to despatch troops to the east to prop up the Austrian front, and in the west the war became a war of trenches, artillery, barbed wire and machine guns. Each side launched offensives, with sickening casualties, but without succeeding in advancing more than a few thousand yards. Railways could bring up reinforcements to the front before slow-moving advancing troops could make good any advantage they might have created. The question for both, by the end of 1915, was how to break the stalemate. The answer of the Entente, sponsored by Winston Churchill, was to attack Germany from the rear by campaigns in the Dardanelles and Mesopotamia (page 124), at Salonika, and, after Italy entered the war on May 23, 1915, against Austria on the Isonzo. All were failures. The German answer was to bring Great Britain to its knees by crippling losses at sea. The submarine campaign, initiated on February 1, 1917, was nearly successful, and only defeated when Lloyd George introduced the convoy system in May. But its result was to bring the United States into the war on the Entente side on April 6, 1917.

Even so, the German position was not hopeless. Huge losses in the Brusilov offensive of 1916 and economic chaos at home had broken the Russian fighting spirit, and the Russian revolutions of March and October 1917 (page 120) enabled Germany to transfer troops from the Eastern to the Western Front in the hope of victory before the United States could mobilise. On March 21, 1918,

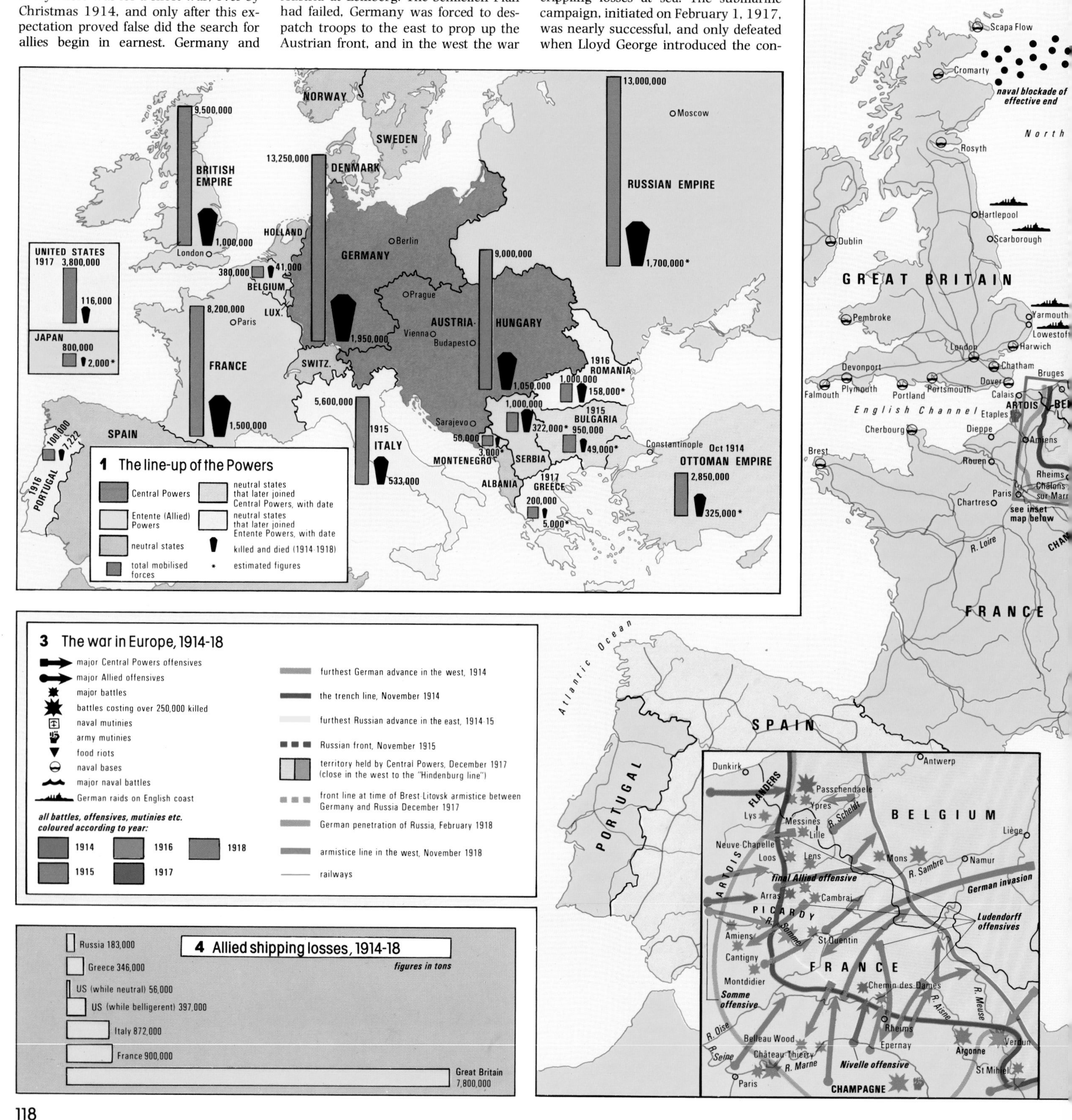

Hindenburg and Ludendorff launched their great offensive in the west (map 3). Once again it was a near success, but the Allied line held, and on July 18 the French commander Foch launched the counter-offensive which was to be the decisive compaign of the war. On September 29 Ludendorff acknowledged defeat. By now war weariness was rampant. Austria and Bulgaria were near to collapse; the British blockade had brought Germany to the edge of starvation; and the German government, fearful of a Bolshevik revolution, sued for an armistice. On November 11, 1918, fighting ceased. Over 8 million men had perished, as had three empires, the Tsarist, the Austro-Hungarian and the Ottoman. In retrospect the war of 1914–18 was the great European civil war, which destroyed the old European order, squandered Europe's human and material resources, and jeopardised its future. Few people realised in 1918 what had happened; but the age of European predominance was over and a new age of global politics had begun.

The Russian Revolution
1905-1925

Revolution came to Russia suddenly, but not unexpectedly, in the wake of the unsuccessful Russo-Japanese war of 1904–05 (page 126). Intensive industrialisation since 1890 had created a large, profoundly discontented urban proletariat, and it was they who spearheaded the revolution of 1905, although their revolt sparked off widespread unrest in the countryside (map 1). The Tsar was forced to grant a constitution, including a *duma*, or parliament, but by 1907 the government was back in full control. Nevertheless the 1905 revolution irreparably weakened the old order, and after 1912, following the shooting of strikers in the Lena goldfields in Siberia, a great new wave of social unrest swept the empire. Internally, Russia was in no position in 1914 to meet the challenge of the First World War; and when in the winter of 1916–17 economic dislocation, hunger and sheer incompetence brought the crisis to a head, the government capitulated almost without resistance. This was the February revolution of 1917, which placed power in the hands of liberal Duma politicians. But the Provisional Government's authority was circumscribed by the powerful Petrograd Council (or Soviet) of Soldiers' and Workers' Deputies, and it was also compromised by its commitment to continue the war. When, in April, Lenin returned from exile in Switzerland, promising peace, land and bread, and demanding all power for the Soviets, its days were numbered. An attempt in September by the Commander-in-Chief, General Kornilov, to seize the capital miscarried when his troops rebelled, and on November 7 (October 25 by the old calendar) the Bolsheviks struck, arrested the Provisional Government, and assumed power in the name of the Soviets. This was the October, or Bolshevik, revolution.

The odds were weighted heavily against the new government. The overriding need was peace, and Lenin insisted, against strong opposition, on accepting the onerous terms imposed by Germany in the Treaty of Brest-Litovsk (March 1918). But immediately the Bolsheviks were faced with civil war and foreign intervention, as White Russian armies with British, French, Czech and other support, attacked the new republic (map 2). Lenin pinned his hope on war-weariness and revolution in the west (map 3) and on uprisings among subject peoples in the east (map 4), but to little avail. In Europe, particularly in Germany, revolutionary currents were strong between 1919 and 1923, but they were met by counter-revolutionary forces, including Hitler's National Socialists. However, foreign intervention and the threat of a White Tsarist restoration rallied support for the Reds, and by 1920 the civil war had been won. But the devastation was immense. Industrial production in 1920 was down to one-seventh of the 1913 level, and shortages provoked a wave of strikes and riots, culminating in the Kronstadt naval mutiny (February 1921). Lenin's answer was the 'New Economic Policy' (NEP), in effect a relaxation of requisitioning and controls. The new policy worked: by the end of 1925 industrial production had regained its pre-war level. Furthermore, the overt hostility of the West relaxed. War with Poland, which had invaded Russia in 1920, was ended by the Treaty of Riga (March 1921), and at the same time a treaty of friendship was signed with Turkey. It was followed by the Rapallo Treaty with Germany (1922) and in 1924 by diplomatic recognition from Britain, France and other European countries.

After Lenin's death in 1924 and a period of disputed succession Lenin's eventual successor, Stalin, ousted Trotsky, with his policy of 'permanent revolution'. Stalin's policy of 'socialism in one country', implying large-scale industrialisation and a re-shaping of inefficient agriculture, placed Russia, at a terrible human cost, in the first rank of industrial and international powers. Inaugurated by the first Five Year Plan of 1928, in many respects it marked a sharp break with the revolution of 1917. But it was also a fulfilment of Lenin's work. Even at the time of Lenin's death Russia was backward and under-developed. By 1939, as Lenin foresaw, Bolshevism had become 'a world force', changing the course of history.

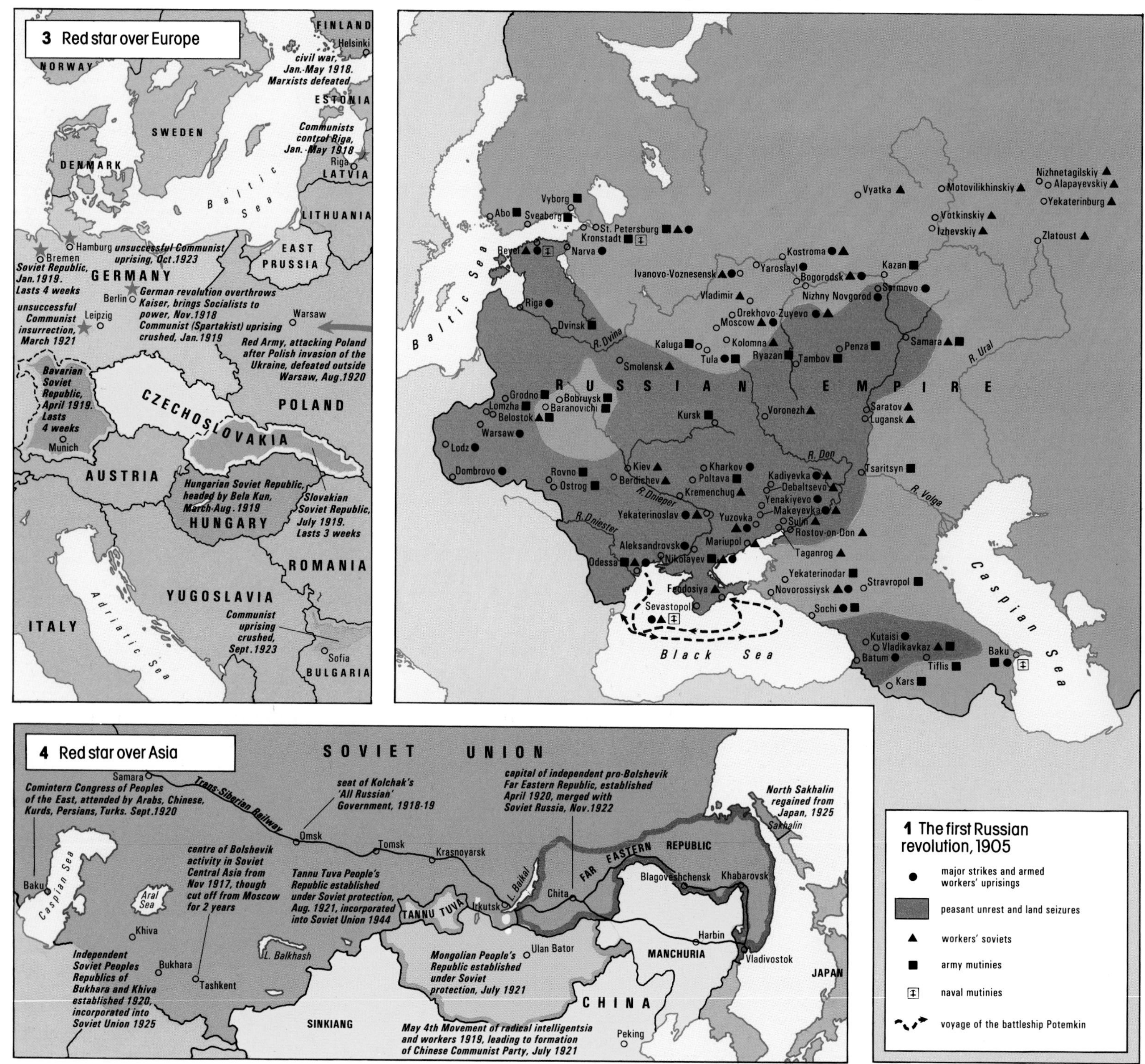

2 Russia in war and revolution
boundary of the Russian Empire, 1914
front between Russia and Central Powers, March 1917
principal towns where Bolsheviks took power, Nov. 1917-Feb. 1918 (dates in new calendar)
boundary of Russian territory occupied by Central Powers following the Treaty of Brest-Litovsk, March 1918
boundary of area controlled by the Bolsheviks, August 1918
eastern boundary of area controlled by the Bolsheviks, April 1919
area controlled by the Bolsheviks, October 1919
boundary of Soviet Territory, March 1921
boundary of areas controlled by anti-Bolshevik forces, May 1920
White Russian armies
non-Russian anti-Bolshevik forces
Entente fleet
Barents Sea
Murmansk
BRITISH FRENCH CANADIANS ITALIANS SERBS
White Sea
CANADIANS AMERICANS
Archangel 17 Feb 1918
BRITISH FRENCH
FINNS
NORWAY
SWEDEN
FINLAND
independence of Finland recognised December 1917
Petrozavodsk 17 Jan 1918
L. Onega
L. Ladoga
Helsinki
Kronstadt
Petrograd (Lenigrad) 7 Nov 1917
Kornilov's attack on Petrograd September 1917
Revel (Tallinn) 8 Nov 1917
Yudenich
British fleet
ESTONIA
Baltic Sea
Riga
LETTS
BALTIC GERMANS
LATVIA
LITHUANIA
GERMANY (E.PRUSSIA)
Pskov 15 Nov 1917
Novgorod 27 Nov 1917
Vologda 8 Feb 1918
BOLSHEVIK RUSSIA
Vyatka 8 Dec 1917
Perm 14 Nov 1917
Nicholas II and family shot by Bolsheviks July 1918
Yekaterinburg (Sverdlovsk) 8 Nov 1917
Kostroma 15 Dec 1917
Yaroslavl 9 Nov 1917
Ivanovo 7 Nov 1917
Tver (Kalinin) 10 Nov 1917
Nizhny Novgorod (Gorkiy) 10 Nov 1917
Izhevsk 9 Nov 1917
Kolchak 1918-19
Kazan 8 Nov 1917
Ufa 8 Nov 1917
CZECHS
Moscow 15 Nov 1917
Vitebsk 9 Nov 1917
Smolensk 12 Nov 1917
Kaluga 11 Dec 1917
Tula 20 Dec 1917
Trans-Siberian Railway
Minsk 7 Nov 1917
Mogilev 1 Dec 1917
Warsaw
Brest-Litovsk
POLAND
POLES
Gomel 12 Nov 1917
Orel 14 Nov 1917
Tambov 13 Feb 1918
Penza 4 Jan 1918
Samara 9 Nov 1917
Orenburg 31 Jan 1918
Saratov 9 Nov 1917
Voronezh 12 Nov 1917
Zhitomir 22 Jan 1918
Kiev 8 Feb 1918
Denikin 1919
Poltava 19 Jan 1918
Kharkov 24 Dec 1917
Don Cossacks 1917-19
R. Don
Tsaritsyn (Stalingrad) (Volgograd) 27 Nov 1917
Ural Cossack Army 1918-20
CZECHOSLOVAKIA
HUNGARY
ROMANIANS
BESSARABIA
Yekaterinoslva (Dnepropetrovsk) 11 Jan 1918
Novocherkassk 25 Feb 1918
R. Volga
Kishinev 10 Dec 1917
Nikolayev 27 Jan 1918
Rostov-on-Don 10 Nov 1917
ROMANIA
Odessa 31 Jan 1918
Wrangel 1920
Cossacks
Astrakhan 7 Feb 1918
Caspian Sea
Sevastopol 29 Dec 1917
Simferopol 26 Jan 1918
Novorossiysk 14 Dec 1917
FRENCH
BRITISH
BULGARIA
Black Sea
Georgians 1919-20
Mensheviks
Entente fleet
BRITISH
Batum
Tiflis (Tbilisi)
Kars
Baku 15 Nov 1917
Krasnovodsk
BRITISH
BRITISH
TURKEY
Tabriz
1918-19
PERSIA
12°
24°
36°
48°
60°
68°
60°
52°
44°

The Chinese Revolution 1911-1949

By 1911 the imperial government of China was thoroughly discredited, and it only needed an army mutiny at Wuchang to repudiate its authority (map 1). But the republic proclaimed in 1912, with Sun Yat-sen as its first president, was overwhelmed by its inherited problems, and within weeks Sun was displaced by Yuan Shih-k'ai, the most powerful general of the old regime. After Yuan's death in 1916 the government in Peking lost control and power passed into the hands of provincial warlords, whose armies caused untold damage and millions of casualties. Compounding this misery were the expansionist policies of Japan, which had secured control of Shantung and Manchuria in 1915 (page 126), as well as the presence of foreign powers, based in the Treaty Ports, who interfered in Chinese politics and exploited the struggling Chinese economy.

In 1919, when the Paris Peace Conference refused to abrogate Japanese and other foreign privileges, this desperate situation exploded in a massive upsurge of Chinese nationalism, which found vent in the 4 May Movement of 1919, a spontaneous uprising of students and urban workers, which was the real starting point of the Chinese revolution. It provided a new constituency for Sun Yat-sen, who had taken refuge at Canton, and in 1923 Sun reorganised his Nationalist (Kuomintang, KMT) Party, allied with the Chinese Communist Party (CCP, founded in 1921), and prepared to reunite the country. But Sun died in 1925, and it was Chiang Kai-shek, the Moscow-trained general of the KMT army, who led the great Northern Expedition of 1926 which aimed at the elimination of the warlords and the unification of the country (map 2). Helped by peasant and workers' uprisings along its route, it was astonishingly successful, and by April 1927 Chiang established his capital at Nanking. But the uneasy alliance of KMT and CCP could not hold, and in 1927 Chiang turned on his allies, massacring the Communists in Shanghai. Furthermore, the warlords were not entirely eliminated, and

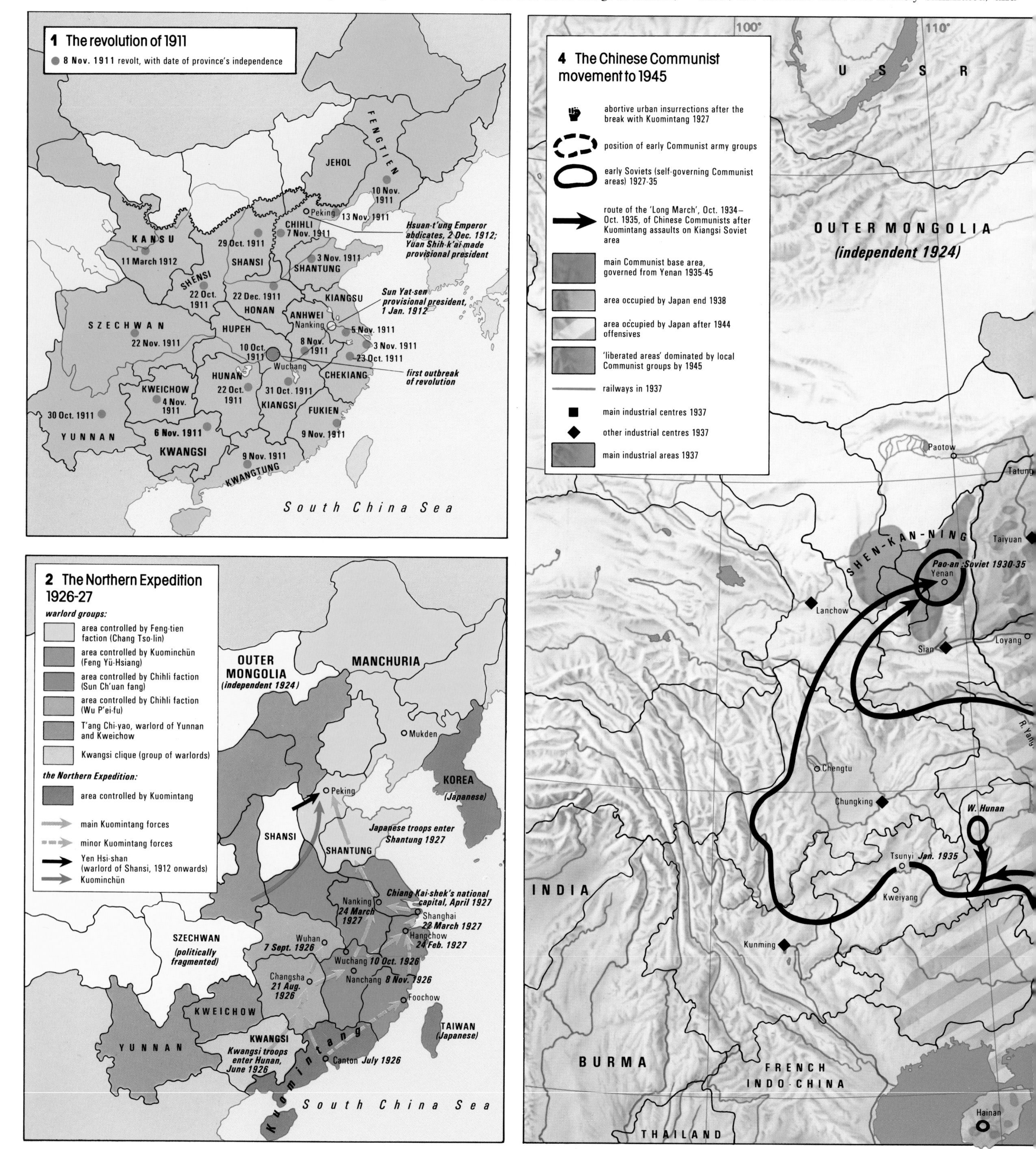

Chiang's direct rule was limited effectively to the lower Yangtze (map 3). Finally, the Japanese, fearing the potential challenge from a reunited China, decided to reinforce their hold in the north. After 1931, when Japan overran Manchuria, Chiang had to meet simultaneously the Japanese threat from without and the Communist threat at home.

Chiang's purge had virtually eliminated the Communists in the cities, but peasant disaffection, arising from his failure to carry out land reform, provided them with new possibilities in the countryside. It was Mao Tse-tung who realised this, and his base at Chingkang Shan in a remote mountainous area was the main, though not the only, seedbed of the revitalised Communist movement. KMT attacks drove Mao to Kiangsi where the most important Soviet was established and where the Communists ruled an area of several million people developing reform programmes as a peasant-based party rather than an urban, proletarian party on the Russian model. Further KMT attacks forced the Communists to abandon Kiangsi and it was on the famous Long March, to Yenan (map 4), where Mao gathered widespread support by his reform programmes and by spearheading resistance to the Japanese invasion, that his peasant-based wing of the party gained ascendancy. The result was that large areas of China passed under Communist control, while Chiang's government, which had withdrawn under Japanese pressure to the remote fastness of Chungking, was unpopular and out of touch. This was the situation in 1945 after the defeat of Japan, though other factors, particularly the growing Soviet-American involvement, played a part. Negotiations for a political settlement broke down and in 1947 open civil war broke out. The Communists defeated the Nationalists in Manchuria and took Peking in January 1949 (map 5). The great battle around Suchow (November 1948–January 1949) opened the way south. On October 1, 1949, the People's Republic was proclaimed, and the Nationalists fled to Taiwan. But the civil war compounded the devastation of the previous decades and China's new rulers were left with a formidable task of reconstruction.

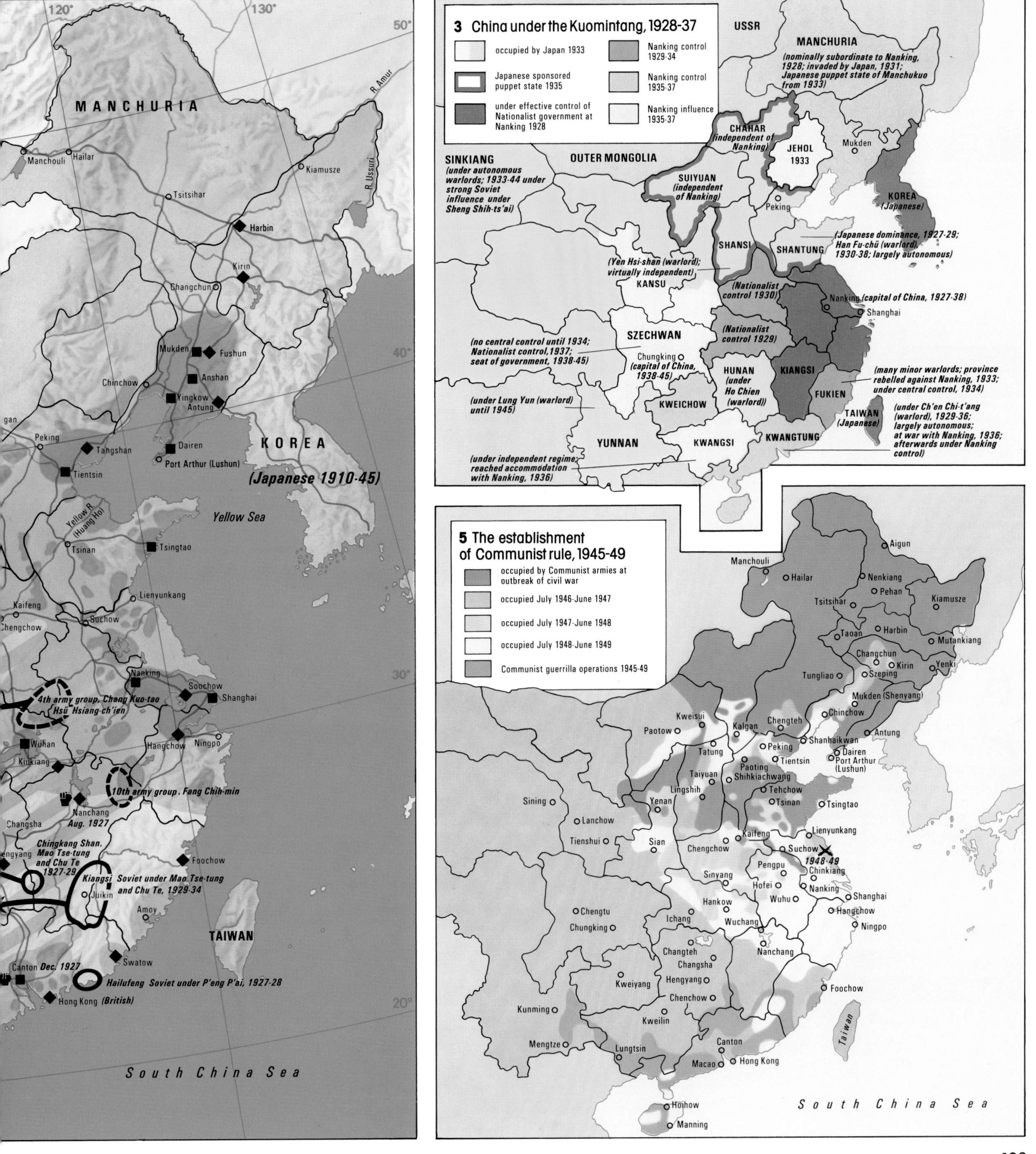

The Ottoman Empire
1800-1923

The Ottoman Empire gradually disintegrated between the beginning of the nineteenth century and the end of the First World War. Steady European economic and colonial penetration weakened the economy, and the success of the nationalist movements in the latter part of the century caused large areas either to break away or to fall effectively under foreign control.

Austria and Russia had been making inroads into the empire throughout the last decades of the eighteenth century; they were joined by France, whose expedition to Egypt in 1798 eventually resulted in the end of effective control from Constantinople and the creation of a dynasty by the Ottoman viceroy, Mohammed Ali Pasha, which lasted from 1805 to 1952. His son, Ibrahim Pasha, led expeditions to subdue the Wahabi rulers of Nejd, inaugurated a period of Egyptian rule over the Sudan, and conquered the whole area between what is now Turkey and Egypt between 1831 and 1839.

In the face of this and other challenges, the empire began a series of major reforms, first of its military establishment and then in the fields of law, education and administration. Two major edicts in 1839 and 1856 stressed the subjects' rights to equality and security of life and property. However, especially in the Balkans, the Powers' claims to be able to intervene on behalf of their protegés had the effect of encouraging the nascent nationalist movements; southern Greece, Bulgaria, Montenegro, Romania, and Serbia had all become independent by 1878.

At the same time France was making substantial inroads into North Africa, while Italy invaded Libya in 1911. There were also stirrings of discontent in other Arab provinces, particularly during the long and oppressive reign of Abdul-Hamid II (1876–1909), when ideas of autonomy gradually gained currency, encouraged by the revival of Arabic literature and campaigns to reform the Arab language. Opposition to Abdul-Hamid's rule culminated in the Young Turk revolution of 1908–09, but the policies pursued by the Young Turks alienated much of the Arab population, and contributed substantially to the Arabs' willingness to seek accommodation with Britain in the course of the war. They were to be disappointed, since the peace settlement put most of the Middle East firmly under British and French control. After Turkey's defeat the caliphate was abolished and a secular republic established.

Similar developments took place in Iran, where the Qajar dynasty (1779–1924) had faced constant Russian and British interference in their internal affairs, culminating in an agreement to divide the country into the spheres of influence of the two powers in 1907. However, the combination of foreign pressures and movements for reform within the country helped to arouse national consciousness and political awareness, and the Constitutional Revolution of 1905–1911 marked a major advance in political self-confidence and maturity.

The Middle East and North Africa 1800–1923 (*below*)

Afghanistan Independent state under Durrani dynasty to 1842; remained independent despite Russian invasions and wars with Britain 1839–42, 1878–90, 1919.
Albania Ottoman province since 14th century; independent principality 1912; kingdom 1928–39.
Armenia Western part in Ottoman Empire, eastern part in Persia until Russian occupation 1804; independent republic 1918–1920; subsequently absorbed into Turkey and USSR.
Azerbaijan Part of Persia until early 19th century; partly under Russian occupation 1803–28; northern part independent republic 1918–1920; northern part incorporated into USSR after 1920.
Bahrain Independent sheikdom under al-Khalifa family since 1783; under British protection since 1820, formalised in 1892.
Bessarabia Ottoman province; Russian 1812–56; ceded to [Ottoman] Moldavia 1856; Russian 1878; Romanian since 1918.
Bosnia-Herzegovina Ottoman province since 15th century; Austrian administration after 1878; part of Yugoslavia since 1918.
Bukhara Independent khanate; Russian protectorate 1868; part of USSR since 1924.
Bulgaria Ottoman province since 14th century; given autonomy but partitioned 1878; independent kingdom 1908; present (1991) boundaries since 1919.
Daghestan Part of Iran; incorporated into Russia/USSR since 1859.
Dodecanese Ottoman since 16th century; occupied by Italy 1912; to Greece 1947.
Eastern Rumelia Ottoman province since 14th century; part of Bulgaria since 1885.
Georgia Independent kingdom under intermittent Persian control; incorporated into Russia 1801; independent republic 1918–20; part of USSR since 1920.
Greece Ottoman rule since 14th century; independent since 1833; enlarged by additions of Crete and Macedonia in 1913.
Hejaz Under Ottoman suzerainty since early 16th century but generally autonomous under Sharifs of Mecca until 1916; independent 1916–24; absorbed into Saudi Arabia 1925.
Iraq Formed from Ottoman provinces of Basra, Baghdad and Mosul 1920; under Hashemite monarchy 1921–58; British mandate 1920–32.
Kars and Ardahan Ottoman provinces since 16th century; to Russia 1878; in Armenian republic 1918–20; part of Turkey since 1920.
Khiva Independent khanate; Russian occupation 1873.
Kokand Independent khanate; Russian occupation 1876.
Kuwait Ottoman province under hereditary rule of Al Sabah family since c.1756; treaty of protection with Britain 1899–1961.
Lebanon Ottoman conquest 1516–17; Mount Lebanon ruled by independent dynasties to 1840; given special status within the Ottoman Empire after civil war of 1860; under Ottoman Christian governors 1861–1915; enlarged and made a republic under French mandate 1920–1946.
Macedonia Ottoman province since 14th century; divided between Bulgaria, Greece and Serbia (later Yugoslavia) 1913.
Montenegro Ottoman province since 14th century but generally under autonomous rule; independent 1878; incorporated into Yugoslavia 1918.
Nejd Under Saudi family from 1746; occupied by Egypt for the Ottomans 1818–1822; Saudis regain control 1902; Kingdom of Saudi Arabia incorporating Hasa, Hejaz, Nejd, 1932; Asir added 1934.
Palestine Ottoman province since 16th century; British occupation 1917; assigned to Britain as mandate 1920–1947 with British obligation to facilitate creation of Jewish National Home.
Persia (Iran) Independent kingdom under Qajar Shahs 1779–1924; partition into British and Russian spheres of influence 1907; under Pehlevi dynasty 1924–79.
Qatar Autonomous sheikdom under al-Thani family; British protection 1916–1971.
Romania Formerly Ottoman provinces of Moldavia and Wallachia (since 14th century); united 1861, independent 1878; enlarged to present (1991) boundaries with the addition of Bessarabia 1918.
Serbia Ottoman province since 14/15th century; autonomous since 1817; separate kingdom 1878; part of Yugoslavia since 1918.
Syria (Name formerly applied to whole area of modern Jordan-Lebanon-Palestine/Israel-Syria.) Ottoman province since 1516; British occupation 1917; Arab kingdom of Damascus 1918–20; French occupation and mandate 1920–1946; sanjak of Alexandretta ceded to Turkey 1939.
Transjordan Part of Ottoman province of Damascus; emirate under British mandate 1923–1946.
Tunisia Ottoman conquest 1574; virtually independent under Husainid dynasty 1705–1881; French conquest 1881; French protectorate 1881–1956.
Turkey Core of Ottoman Empire (early 14th century to 1923); Turkish Republic created 1924.
Yemen Local rulers belonging to Za'idi (Shi'i) sect; nominally part of Ottoman Empire since 1517; Aden occupied by Britain 1839; parts of south in treaty relations with Britain 1886–1954; independent state in north 1918.

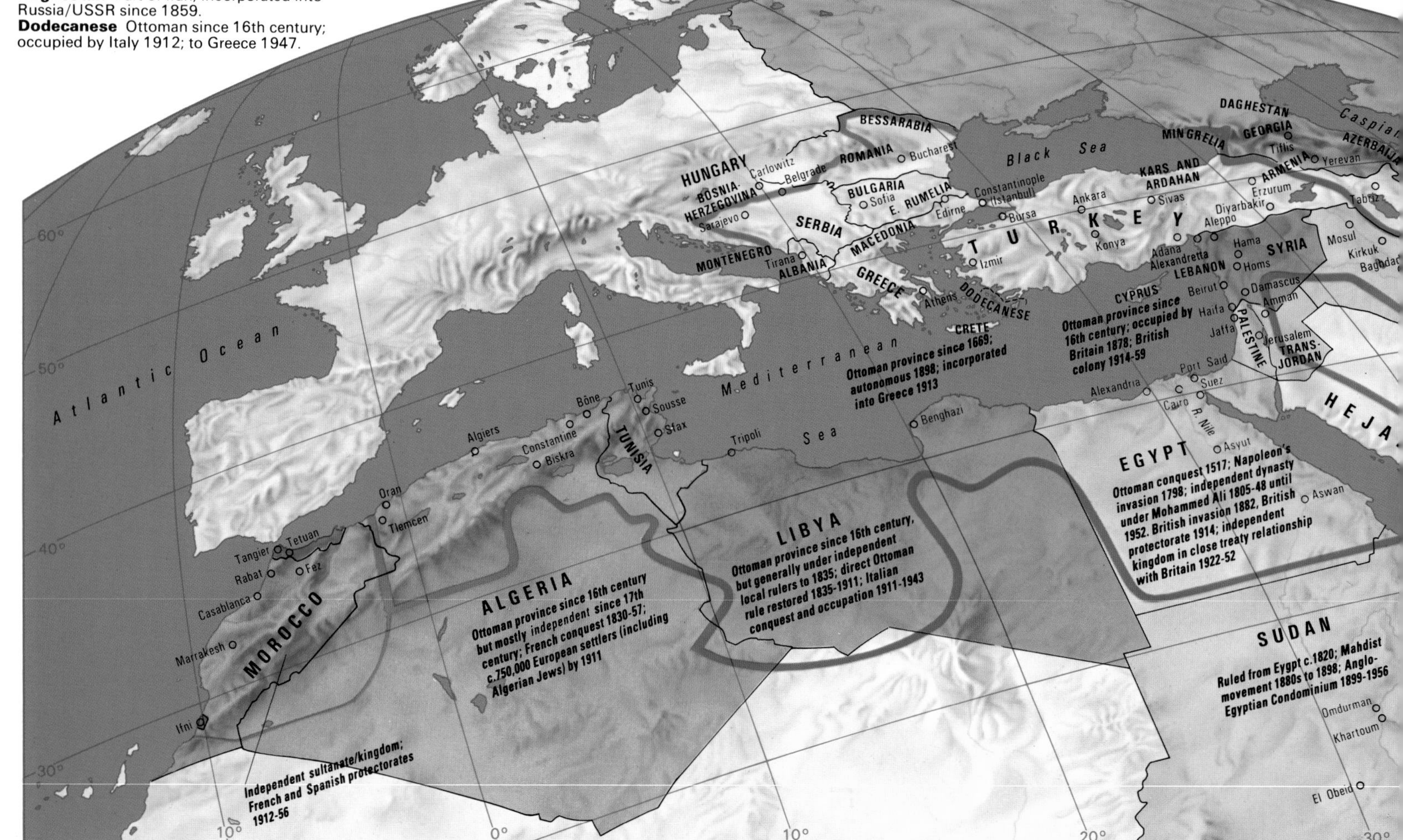

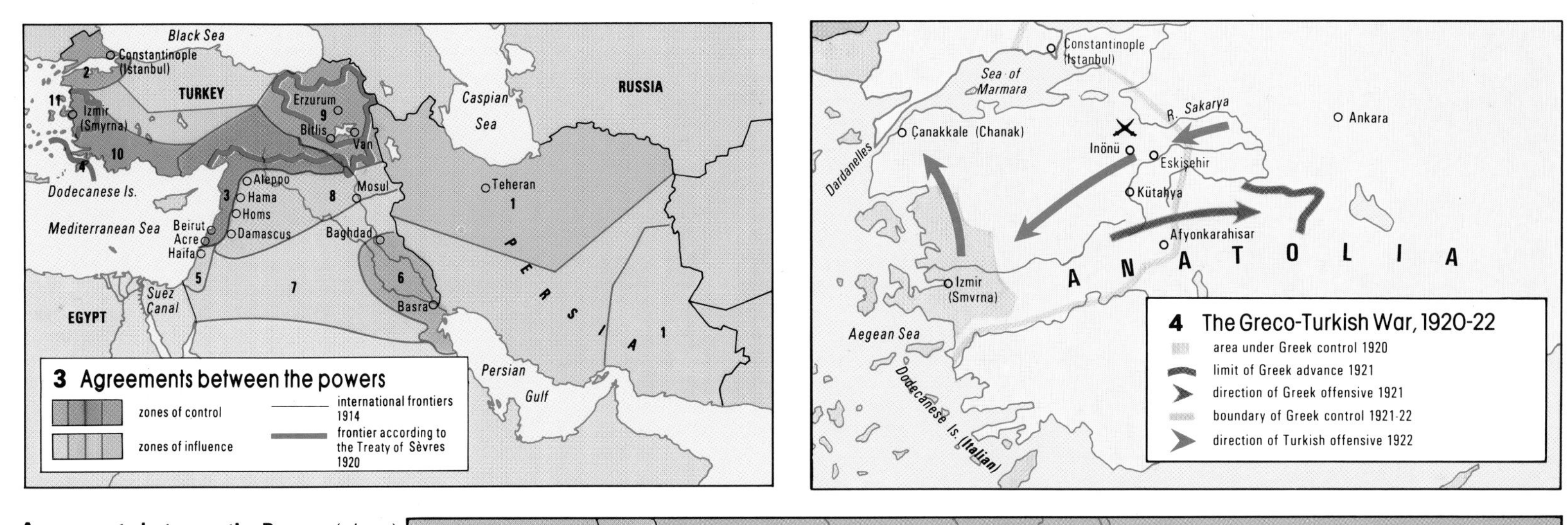

Agreements between the Powers *(above)*
In 1907 parts of Persia became British and Russian spheres of influence (**1**). During the First World War, Britain, France, Italy and Russia made provisional arrangements to divide the Ottoman Empire; in 1915 Russia was given Constantinople, the Straits and the Dardanelles (**2**), France a sphere of influence in Syria and Cilicia (**3**) and Italy in south-west Turkey and the Dodecanese islands (**4**). Under the Sykes-Picot agreement (1916) Palestine was to be internationalised (**5**), Britain was to be given Mesopotamia (**6**), Haifa and Acre on the Mediterranean coast, and the area between (**7**); France gained Aleppo, Damascus, Mosul and their hinterlands (**8**); Russia gained north-west Anatolia, and parts of Kurdistan and Armenia (**9**); subsequently the Italians were promised most of south-west Anatolia (**10**). The British, seeking Arab support, promised Sharif Husain of Mecca a state extending over most of the Arab provinces of the Ottoman Empire. Finally, the Balfour Declaration of 1917 stated that Britain favoured 'the establishment of a national home in Palestine for the Jewish people.' In 1920, the Treaty of Sèvres gave Smyrna (Izmir) and its hinterland to Greece (**11**) and created autonomous states in Armenia and Kurdistan, although the rise of the Turkish Republic meant that the Treaty was never ratified. Most of the present boundaries of the area were agreed at the Lausanne Conference (1923)

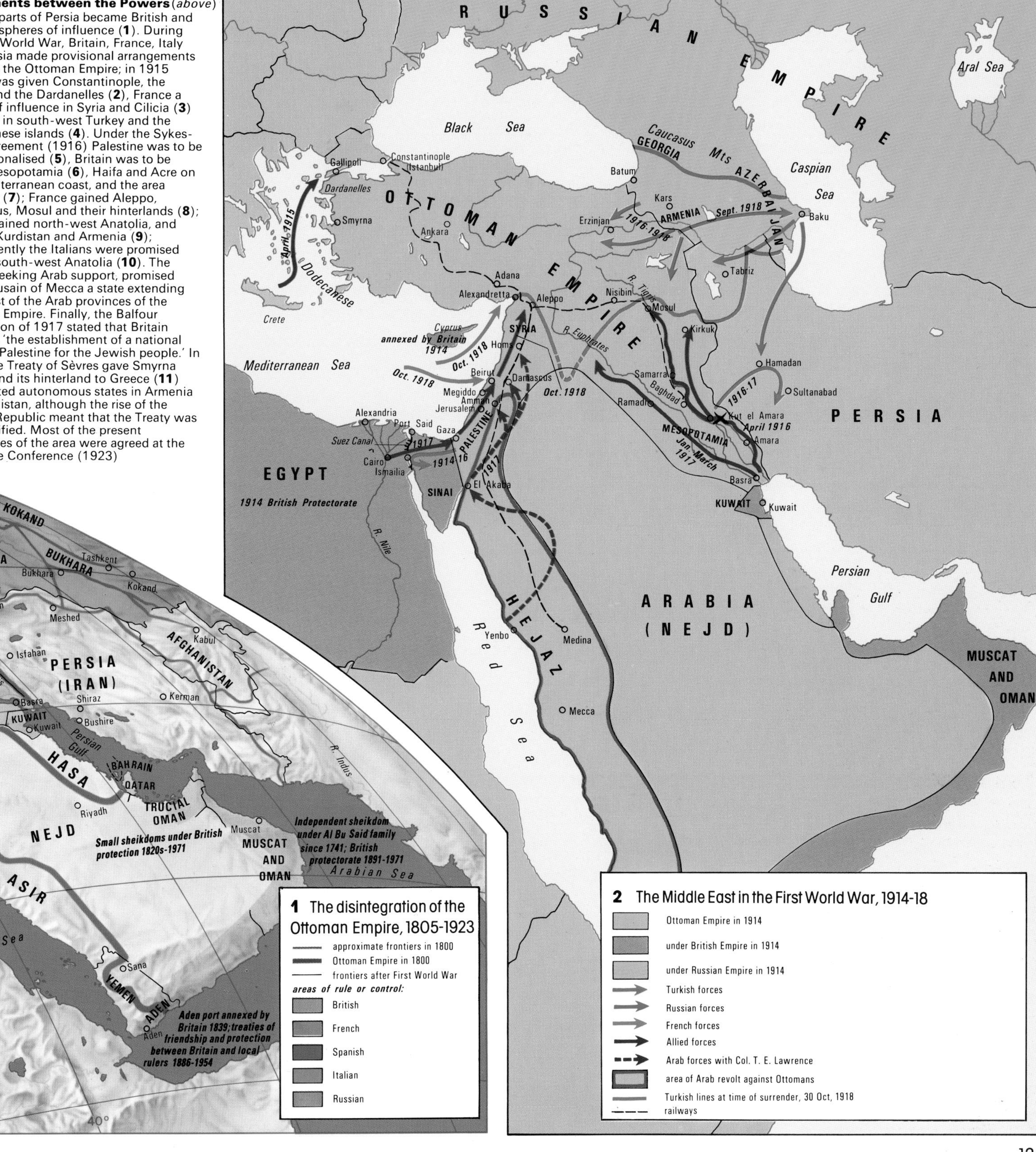

Modern Japan, 1868-1941

The Tokugawa shogunate, established in 1609 (page 50), gave Japan two hundred years of peace and prosperity. But a generation before 1868 it was evident that internal tensions were building up and that the *bakufu* (or Shogun's government) in Edo was losing control. Peasant unrest and discontent among impoverished *samurai*, whose position had been undermined by the growth of a money economy, was compounded by British, Russian, French and American pressure for the opening of Japan to foreign trade. A period of complicated manoeuvring ensued, in which the four western feudal domains (*han*), Satsuma, Choshu, Tosa and Hizen, took the lead (map 1). The outcome was the so-called Meiji restoration, when the emperor, supported by dissident elements, moved from Kyoto to Edo, now re-named Tokyo (or eastern capital), displaced the Shogun, and took direct control of government.

The Meiji restoration of 1868 was in reality a revolution, carried out with the definite aim of modernisation and westernisation. The old feudal structure was replaced in 1871 by a modern system of prefectures. Samurai privileges were abolished (1873), though samurai from Choshu had a leading place in the new conscript army. A western style peerage (1884), cabinet government (1885) and a two-chamber parliament (1889) laid the foundations of political stability; a national education system was instituted (1872) providing teaching for 90 per cent of children by 1900. At the same time economic development was taken in hand (map 2). The first railway was opened in 1872, and by 1906 the main network was completed. Industrialisation proceeded more slowly, beginning effectively only at the end of the 1800s. By 1889 the number of cotton mills had risen from 3 in 1877 to 83, and by 1913 Japanese production dominated the home market and had a substantial foothold abroad, particularly in China. Nevertheless agriculture remained the main employment until after the First World War. The number employed in agriculture fell from 70 per cent of the population in the 1870s to 57 per cent in 1914, but still provided almost all the foodstuffs for a population which rose from 39 million in 1868 to 56 million in 1918.

International recognition of Japan's new status was nevertheless slow in coming. It had been forced in the 1850s to negotiate unequal treaties with the western powers, and it was not until 1894 that foreign consular jurisdiction was abolished and only in 1911 that Tokyo regained tariff autonomy. These concessions were a tribute to Japan's military successes, seen above all in the war with China (1894–95) and in the Russo-Japanese war (map 4). The first overseas ventures, in the Bonin and Ryukyu islands and in Taiwan, were undertaken primarily to still unrest at home, but in 1894 Japan embarked on a full-scale imperialist policy (map 3). Even so, it was forced by the European powers to return all its conquests except Taiwan; but the Anglo-Japanese treaty of 1902, inspired by mutual fear of Russia, was a turning point. In the war with Russia (1904–05), Japan's forces achieved a series of victories culminating in the fall of Port Arthur (January 1905), the battle of Mukden (February–March), and the destruction of the Russian Baltic fleet in the Tsushima Straits (May). After the war the two combatants rapidly reached agreement over a division of spheres of interest, which allowed Japan to annex Korea in 1910. It had embarked on the creation of a Japanese empire on the Asian mainland, and the war of 1914–18 and the Russian revolution (page 120) enabled it to gain a foothold in Shantung and Manchuria. Although once again western pressure compelled it to withdraw, Japan was recognised at the Peace Conference in 1919 as a major power with a permanent seat on the Council of the League of Nations.

During the 1920s Japanese policy veered between cooperation with the west and an inherent anti-foreign feeling, fed by a sense of discrimination. Until 1932 cooperation prevailed, but the impact of the Great Depression (page 130) swung the balance in the opposite direction, and, beginning with the advance into Manchuria in 1931, Japan set out to carve out an empire in East Asia. After the Japanese attack on the Chinese mainland in 1937, tension grew with the United States. The lines of the Second World War were already being drawn. When Germany defeated France and Holland in 1940, Japan's moment seemed to have arrived, and the advance into South-East Asia began (map 5). In spite of astounding initial successes (page 134), it was a gamble that failed. But paradoxically the failure, and the subsequent American occupation, propelled Japan even more decisively into the modern world than the Meiji restoration, socially authoritarian and backward-looking, had done.

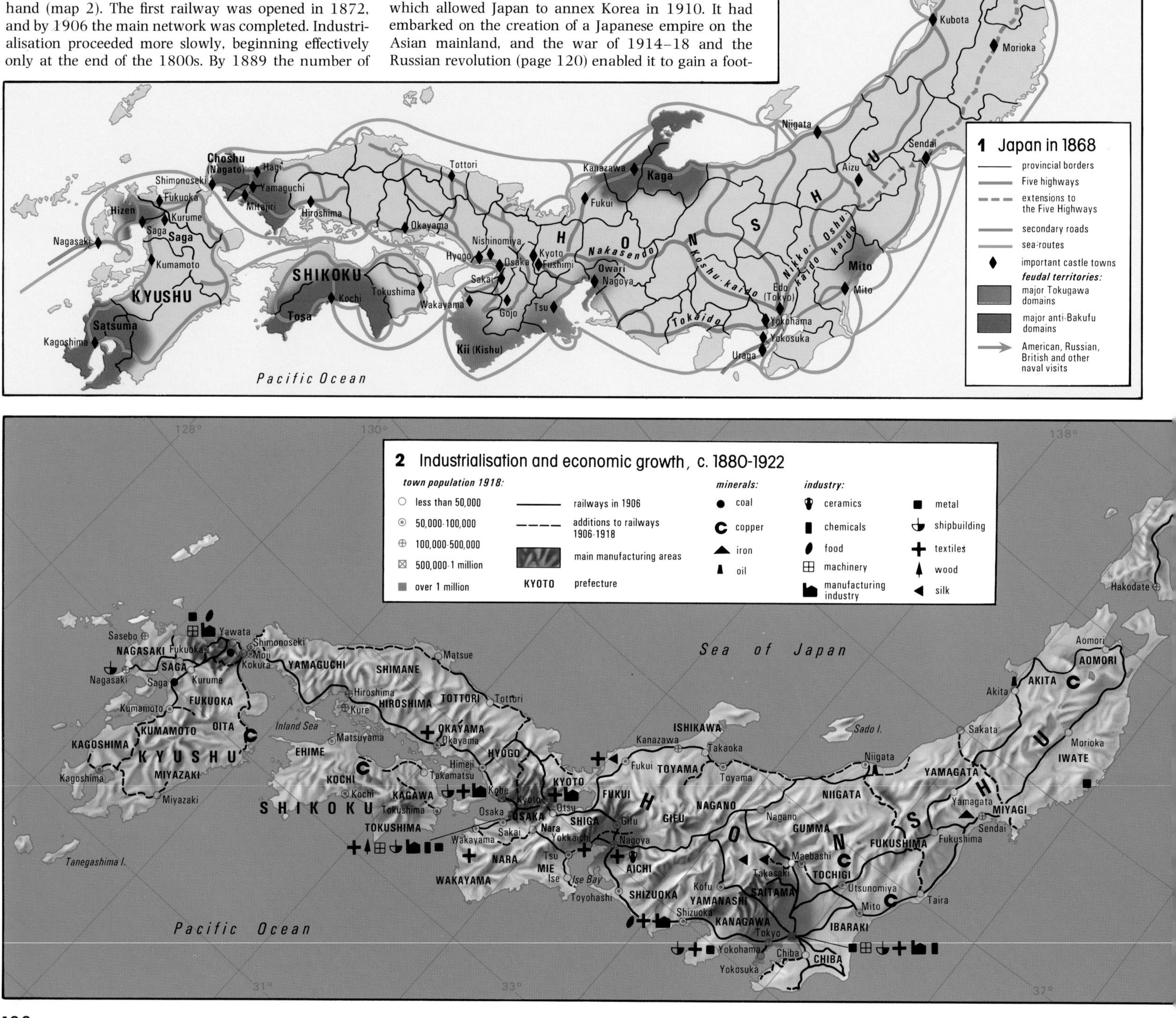

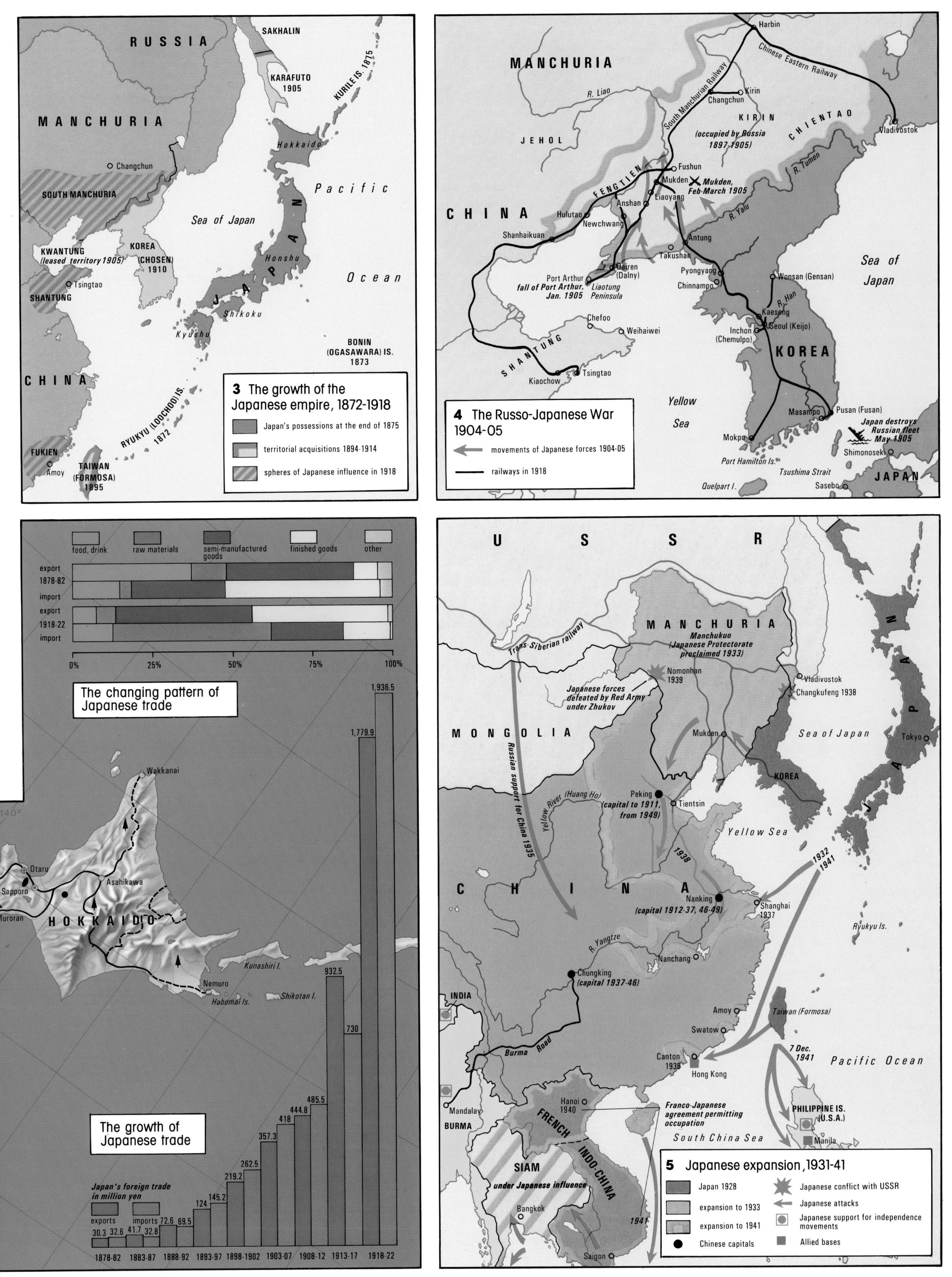

3 The growth of the Japanese empire, 1872-1918
Japan's possessions at the end of 1875
territorial acquisitions 1894-1914
spheres of Japanese influence in 1918
RUSSIA
SAKHALIN
KARAFUTO 1905
KURILE IS. 1875
MANCHURIA
Hokkaido
Changchun
SOUTH MANCHURIA
Pacific
Sea of Japan
JAPAN
KWANTUNG (leased territory 1905)
KOREA (CHOSEN) 1910
Honshu
Ocean
Tsingtao
SHANTUNG
Shikoku
Kyushu
BONIN (OGASAWARA) IS. 1873
CHINA
RYUKYU (LOOCHOO) IS. 1872
FUKIEN
Amoy
TAIWAN (FORMOSA) 1895
4 The Russo-Japanese War 1904-05
movements of Japanese forces 1904-05
railways in 1918
Harbin
MANCHURIA
Chinese Eastern Railway
South Manchurian Railway
R. Liao
Kirin
Changchun
KIRIN
(occupied by Russia 1897-1905)
CHIENTAO
Vladivostok
JEHOL
Fushun
FENGTIEN
Mukden
Mukden, Feb-March 1905
Liaoyang
Anshan
R. Tumen
CHINA
Hulutao
Newchwang
R. Yalu
Shanhaikuan
Antung
Takushan
Sea of Japan
Dairen (Dalny)
Port Arthur
fall of Port Arthur, Jan. 1905
Liaotung Peninsula
Pyongyang
Chinnampo
Wonsan (Gensan)
R. Han
Kaesong
Chefoo
Weihaiwei
Inchon (Chemulpo)
Seoul (Keijo)
SHANTUNG
KOREA
Kiaochow
Tsingtao
Yellow Sea
Masampo
Pusan (Fusan)
Japan destroys Russian fleet May 1905
Mokpo
Shimonoseki
Port Hamilton Is.
Tsushima Strait
Quelpart I.
Sasebo
JAPAN
The changing pattern of Japanese trade
food, drink
raw materials
semi-manufactured goods
finished goods
other
export
1878-82
import
export
1918-22
import
0%
25%
50%
75%
100%
The growth of Japanese trade
Japan's foreign trade in million yen
exports
imports
30.3
32.6
41.7
32.8
72.6
69.5
124
145.2
219.2
262.5
357.3
418
444.8
485.5
932.5
730
1,779.9
1,936.5
1878-82
1883-87
1888-92
1893-97
1898-1902
1903-07
1908-12
1913-17
1918-22
Wakkanai
Otaru
Asahikawa
Sapporo
Muroran
HOKKAIDO
Kunashiri I.
Nemuro
Shikotan I.
Habomai Is.
USSR
MANCHURIA
Manchukuo (Japanese Protectorate proclaimed 1933)
Trans-Siberian railway
Nomonhan 1939
Japanese forces defeated by Red Army under Zhukov
Vladivostok
Changkufeng 1938
MONGOLIA
Mukden
Sea of Japan
Tokyo
Russian support for China 1935
KOREA
JAPAN
Peking (capital to 1911, from 1949)
Tientsin
Yellow River (Huang Ho)
Yellow Sea
1938
1932
1941
CHINA
Nanking (capital 1912-37, 46-49)
Shanghai 1937
Ryukyu Is.
R. Yangtze
Nanchang
Chungking (capital 1937-46)
INDIA
Amoy
Taiwan (Formosa)
Swatow
Burma Road
7 Dec. 1941
Canton 1938
Hong Kong
Pacific Ocean
Mandalay
BURMA
Hanoi 1940
FRENCH INDO-CHINA
Franco-Japanese agreement permitting occupation
PHILIPPINE IS. (U.S.A.)
Manila
South China Sea
SIAM under Japanese influence
Bangkok
1941
Saigon
5 Japanese expansion, 1931-41
Japan 1928
expansion to 1933
expansion to 1941
Chinese capitals
Japanese conflict with USSR
Japanese attacks
Japanese support for independence movements
Allied bases

European political problems, 1919-1939

The First World War shattered the equipoise of 1914. The long-term goal after 1918 was a return to 'normalcy', but it was always an illusion. Not merely had the collapse of the Habsburg Empire, the defeat of Germany, and the Bolshevik Revolution completely altered the balance of power in Europe, but the pre-war economic equilibrium also was destroyed. All the victorious powers were in debt to the United States, and Great Britain, which had largely financed its allies, never fully recovered. These facts weighed heavily at the Paris Peace Conference in 1919, but the dominant fact was probably fear of the spread of revolution from Russia. This accounts for the relatively lenient treatment of Germany, which suffered only minor territorial losses, except for the restoration to the newly independent Poland of the lands seized in the partitions at the end of the eighteenth century. The real problem facing the peacemakers was the tangle of nationalities in Europe. Finland, Estonia, Latvia and Lithuania were detached as independent republics from Russia, which was not represented at the Conference, and Russia also lost Bessarabia to Romania and a large part of White Russia to Poland after the Russo-Polish war of 1920. However, the independent republics of White Russia, Georgia, Armenia and Azerbaijan were brought back into the Soviet Union in 1921 (map 2). The main beneficiary of the peace settlement was Romania, which, in addition to Bessarabia, acquired the Dobruja from Bulgaria and Transylvania from Hungary. But the projected dismemberment of Turkey was thwarted by the national revival under Mustapha Kemal Atatürk (page 124), and in 1923 the new republic was recognised by the Treaty of Lausanne.

The peace treaties left dissatisfied minorities everywhere, and there were widespread movements of refugees, the most extreme case being the wholesale exchange of populations negotiated after the Greco-Turkish war of 1920–22 (map 3). More important politically, they also created a lasting sense of injustice and discrimination. It was inconceivable that either Germany or Russia, once they recovered their strength, would accept a position of inferiority. In addition, there was the irredentism of Hungary, the country which had suffered most from the peace settlement, which was exploited, after 1927, by Mussolini's Fascist Italy, which hoped in this way to build up for itself a dominant position in the Danubian basin. Thus Europe was divided between revisionists and anti-revisionists, and the only hope for the latter was to support the status quo by a system of military pacts. France, with its alliances with Poland (1921) and Czechoslovakia (1924), underpinning the 'Little Entente' between Czechoslovakia, Yugoslavia and Romania (1921), was the heart and soul of this security system (map 1). It operated effectively until the Great Depression (page 130) and the instability it engendered in France, which undercut France's credibility among its East European clients. When Poland signed a Neutrality Pact with Germany in 1934, it marked the beginning of the collapse of the French security system.

The Locarno treaties (1925), whereby Germany recognised the post-war frontier settlements with France and Belgium, marked the end of the long years of frustration, civil disorder and conflict which had bedevilled Europe since 1918. Germany was welcomed back into the community of nations; so also, after 1925, was Soviet Russia. But the stabilisation of 1925–29 was more apparent than real. With the exception of Czechoslovakia, none of the new states of eastern Europe was economically viable, and the onset of the Depression exposed their weaknesses and left them a prey to German infiltration. Spain also, where the monarchy had been superseded by a republic in 1931, was caught up in its repercussions, which brought a confrontation of left and right and undermined the republican government. The result, in 1936, was civil war (map 4), in which eventually the rebels under General Franco, supported by Italy and Germany, were successful. The failure of France and England to aid the republic discredited them in the eyes of their allies and encouraged Italian and German aggression. Hitler's repudiation of the Locarno treaties, followed by the annexation of Austria (1938) was a clear sign of his intentions; but the destruction of Czechoslovakia, abetted by Poland and Hungary, and the Italian annexation of Albania (1939), further exposed the ambivalence of the western powers (map 5). Whether an alliance with the Soviet Union would have halted the aggressors is a matter of dispute. However, when negotiations between the Soviet Union and the Western powers broke down in 1939, and the Russians, fearing a war of two fronts with Germany and Japan, signed the notorious Nazi-Soviet Non-Aggression Pact, the collapse of the unstable European balance of 1919–39 was inevitable.

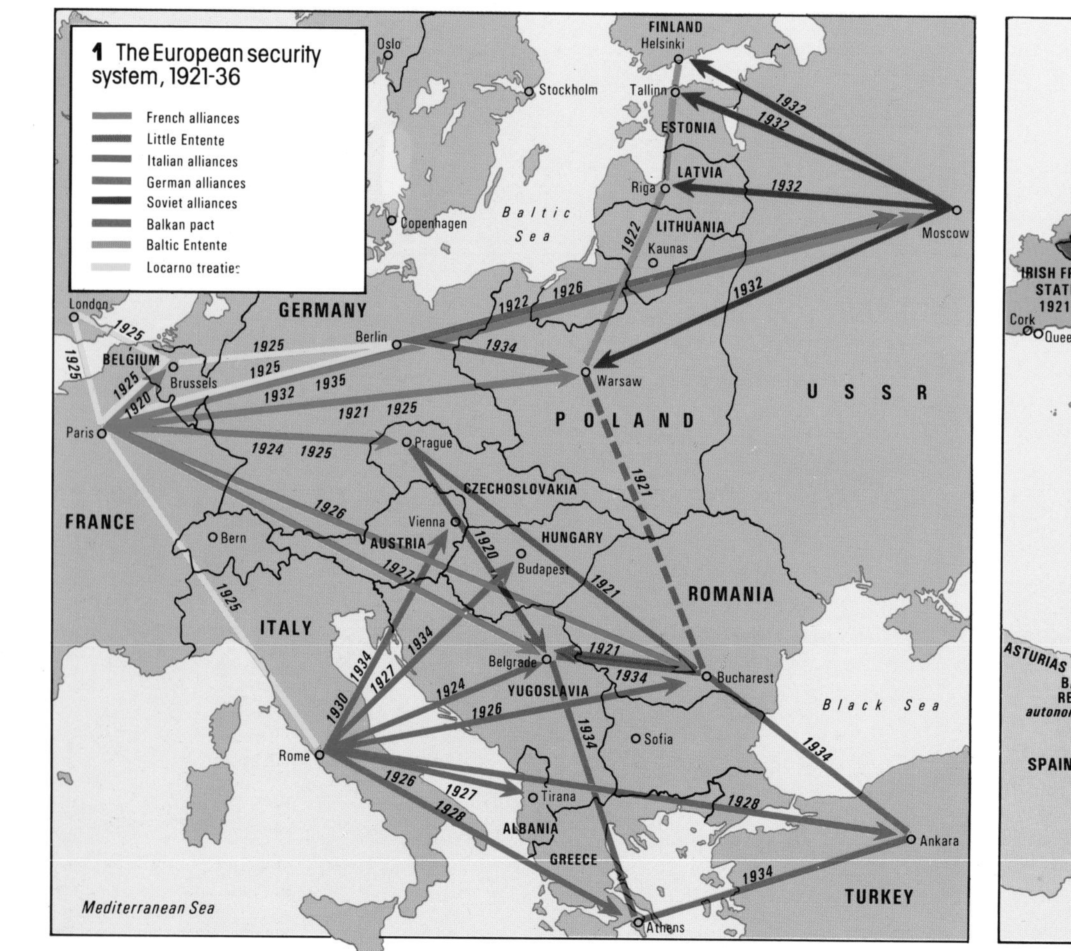

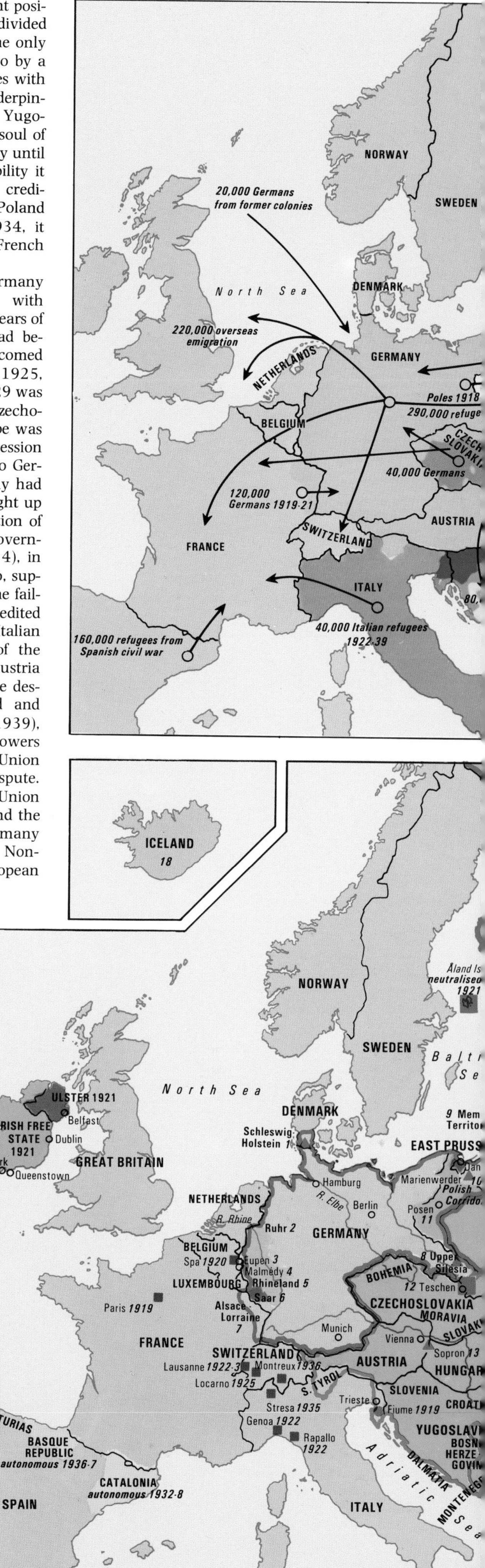

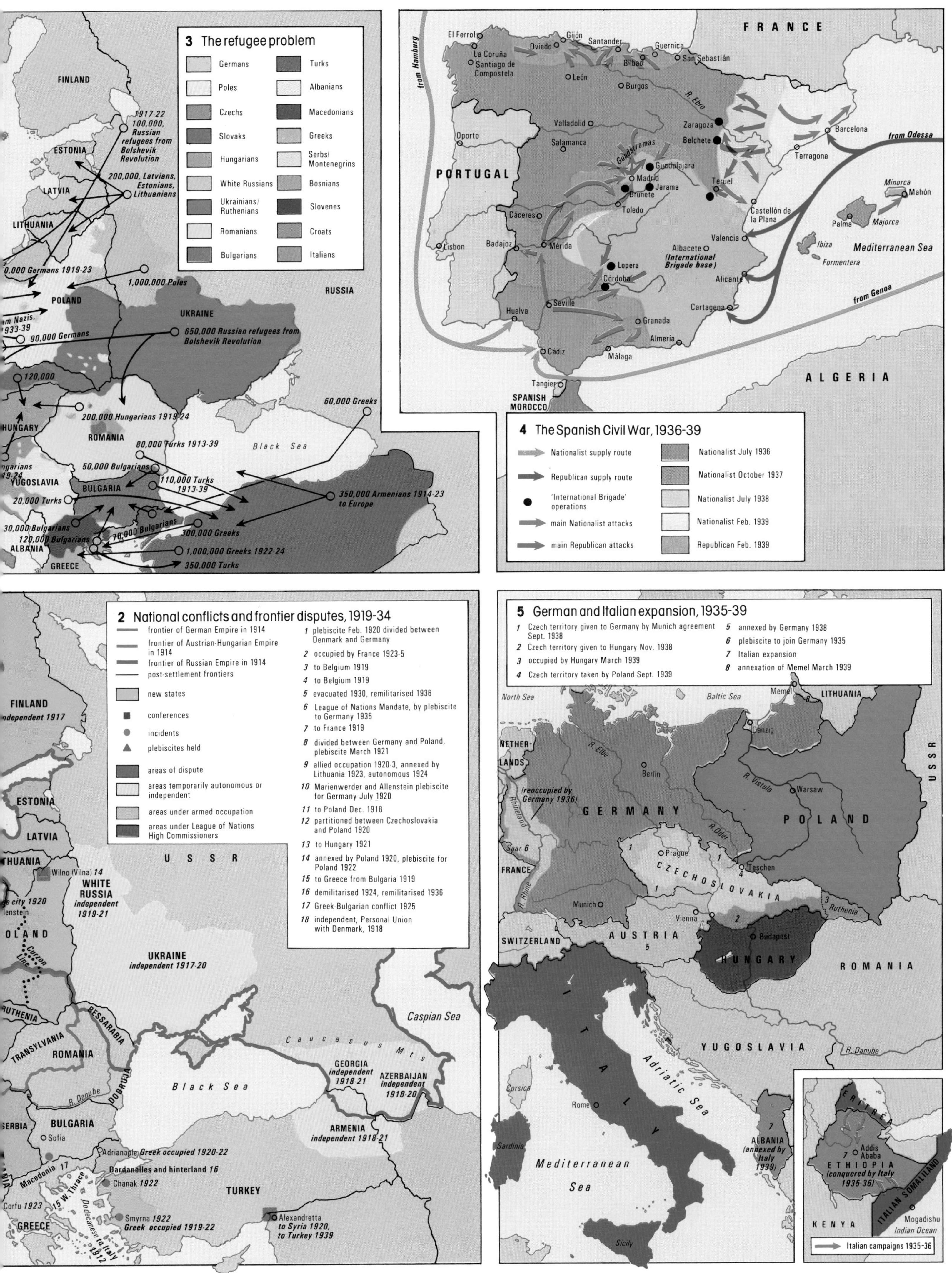

3 The refugee problem
Germans
Poles
Czechs
Slovaks
Hungarians
White Russians
Ukrainians/ Ruthenians
Romanians
Bulgarians
Turks
Albanians
Macedonians
Greeks
Serbs/ Montenegrins
Bosnians
Slovenes
Croats
Italians
FINLAND
ESTONIA
LATVIA
LITHUANIA
POLAND
UKRAINE
RUSSIA
HUNGARY
ROMANIA
YUGOSLAVIA
BULGARIA
ALBANIA
GREECE
Black Sea
1917-22 100,000, Russian refugees from Bolshevik Revolution
200,000, Latvians, Estonians, Lithuanians
1,000,000 Poles
90,000 Germans
650,000 Russian refugees from Bolshevik Revolution
120,000
200,000 Hungarians 1919-24
80,000 Turks 1913-39
60,000 Greeks
50,000 Bulgarians
110,000 Turks 1913-39
350,000 Armenians 1914-23 to Europe
20,000 Turks
30,000 Bulgarians
120,000 Bulgarians
70,000 Bulgarians
300,000 Greeks
1,000,000 Greeks 1922-24
350,000 Turks
4 The Spanish Civil War, 1936-39
Nationalist supply route
Republican supply route
'International Brigade' operations
main Nationalist attacks
main Republican attacks
Nationalist July 1936
Nationalist October 1937
Nationalist July 1938
Nationalist Feb. 1939
Republican Feb. 1939
FRANCE
PORTUGAL
ALGERIA
SPANISH MOROCCO
Mediterranean Sea
from Hamburg
from Odessa
from Genoa
El Ferrol
La Coruña
Santiago de Compostela
Oviedo
Gijón
Santander
Guernica
San Sebastián
Bilbao
León
Burgos
R. Ebro
Zaragoza
Belchete
Barcelona
Valladolid
Salamanca
Oporto
Guadarramas
Guadalajara
Madrid
Jarama
Brunete
Toledo
Teruel
Tarragona
Castellón de la Plana
Cáceres
Mérida
Badajoz
Lisbon
Valencia
Albacete (International Brigade base)
Lopera
Córdoba
Alicante
Seville
Huelva
Granada
Cartagena
Almería
Cádiz
Málaga
Tangier
Minorca
Mahón
Majorca
Palma
Ibiza
Formentera
2 National conflicts and frontier disputes, 1919-34
frontier of German Empire in 1914
frontier of Austrian-Hungarian Empire in 1914
frontier of Russian Empire in 1914
post-settlement frontiers
new states
conferences
incidents
plebiscites held
areas of dispute
areas temporarily autonomous or independent
areas under armed occupation
areas under League of Nations High Commissioners
1 plebiscite Feb. 1920 divided between Denmark and Germany
2 occupied by France 1923-5
3 to Belgium 1919
4 to Belgium 1919
5 evacuated 1930, remilitarised 1936
6 League of Nations Mandate, by plebiscite to Germany 1935
7 to France 1919
8 divided between Germany and Poland, plebiscite March 1921
9 allied occupation 1920-3, annexed by Lithuania 1923, autonomous 1924
10 Marienwerder and Allenstein plebiscite for Germany July 1920
11 to Poland Dec. 1918
12 partitioned between Czechoslovakia and Poland 1920
13 to Hungary 1921
14 annexed by Poland 1920, plebiscite for Poland 1922
15 to Greece from Bulgaria 1919
16 demilitarised 1924, remilitarised 1936
17 Greek-Bulgarian conflict 1925
18 independent, Personal Union with Denmark, 1918
FINLAND independent 1917
ESTONIA
LATVIA
LITHUANIA
Wilno (Vilna) 14
WHITE RUSSIA independent 1919-21
USSR
UKRAINE independent 1917-20
Curzon Line
RUTHENIA
BESSARABIA
TRANSYLVANIA
ROMANIA
DOBRUJA
R. Danube
Black Sea
Caucasus Mts
Caspian Sea
GEORGIA independent 1918-21
AZERBAIJAN independent 1918-20
ARMENIA independent 1918-21
SERBIA
BULGARIA
Sofia
Adrianople Greek occupied 1920-22
Dardanelles and hinterland 16
Chanak 1922
Macedonia 17
W. Thrace 15
Corfu 1923
GREECE
Dodecanese to Italy 1912
Smyrna 1922 Greek occupied 1919-22
TURKEY
Alexandretta to Syria 1920, to Turkey 1939
5 German and Italian expansion, 1935-39
1 Czech territory given to Germany by Munich agreement Sept. 1938
2 Czech territory given to Hungary Nov. 1938
3 occupied by Hungary March 1939
4 Czech territory taken by Poland Sept. 1939
5 annexed by Germany 1938
6 plebiscite to join Germany 1935
7 Italian expansion
8 annexation of Memel March 1939
North Sea
Baltic Sea
Memel
LITHUANIA
Danzig
NETHERLANDS
R. Elbe
Berlin
USSR
R. Vistula
Warsaw
(reoccupied by Germany 1936)
Rhineland
GERMANY
POLAND
R. Oder
Saar 6
FRANCE
Prague
CZECHOSLOVAKIA
Teschen
Ruthenia
R. Rhine
Munich
Vienna
SWITZERLAND
AUSTRIA
Budapest
HUNGARY
ROMANIA
ITALY
Adriatic Sea
YUGOSLAVIA
R. Danube
Corsica
Rome
Sardinia
Mediterranean Sea
Sicily
ALBANIA (annexed by Italy 1939)
ERITREA
Addis Ababa
ETHIOPIA (conquered by Italy 1935-36)
ITALIAN SOMALILAND
KENYA
Mogadishu
Indian Ocean
Italian campaigns 1935-36

The Great Depression
1929-1939

After 1925 it appeared that the disorders of the post-war world had been overcome and a period of relative stability and prosperity had begun. The Great Depression quickly dispelled this illusion. Conventionally its starting point was the financial crash on Wall Street in October 1929; but this was only the manifestation of deeper weaknesses in the world economy. In the United States business was in trouble long before the crash. Worldwide, commodity prices had been falling since 1926, impairing the capacity of exporters such as Australia to buy products from Europe and the United States. The German economy also was faltering by 1928. However, more important than the causes of the depression were its consequences. These were almost instantaneous, although it was only after 1930 that dislocation reached its peak. Its most arresting manifestation was unemployment which reached record heights in 1932. In many industrial countries over a quarter of the labour force was thrown out of work. Industrial production fell to 53 per cent of its 1929 level in Germany and the United States, and world trade sank to 35 per cent of its 1929 value. Attempts to solve the problem only made things worse. As early as 1930 the United States imposed the Hawley-Smoot Tariff, the highest in its history. The United Kingdom responded in 1932 by negotiating the Ottawa Agreements, a series of preferential tariffs for the Commonwealth. Another expedient was competitive devaluation. After England left the Gold Standard in 1931, country after country followed suit and the result was the development of closed currency blocs (map 1), which inhibited international trade still further.

Economic nationalism fostered political nationalism, just as unemployment and the erosion of middle-class living standards fostered political extremism. The fall of the Hamaguchi government in Japan in 1931 marked the end of constitutional democracy and the beginning of Japanese aggression in Manchuria (page 126). In Germany, Brüning's deflationary policies, raising unemployment from under 3 million in 1930 to 6 million two years later, paved the way for Hitler. Hitler's accession to power in January 1933 was followed by Dollfuss's dictatorship in Austria, and eastern Europe, with the exception of Czechoslovakia, quickly followed suit (map 3). France remained precariously democratic until 1940, and in the United Kingdom, where a right-wing 'national' government won a huge majority in 1931, Mosley's fascist movement made little headway. But even here and in the United States, where F. D. Roosevelt was elected president in 1932 with a promise of a 'New Deal', fascist movements exercised considerable pressure (map 2). Only the Soviet Union, isolated from the world economy, was able to sustain economic growth (map 1) – a fact which was to be of cardinal importance after 1941. Roosevelt's New Deal made initial progress, but faltered after 1936 when a new phase of economic down-turn began. By 1939 the United States had not regained the level of industrial output of 1929, and only the Second World War, and the boost it gave to production pulled it out of depression.

The effects of the depression also hit the primary producing countries of Asia, Africa and Latin America. Here, as the crisis radicalised peasants and workers, nationalist and revolutionary movements gained new bases of support. In this respect, as in many others, the Great Depression was the catalyst of the modern world.

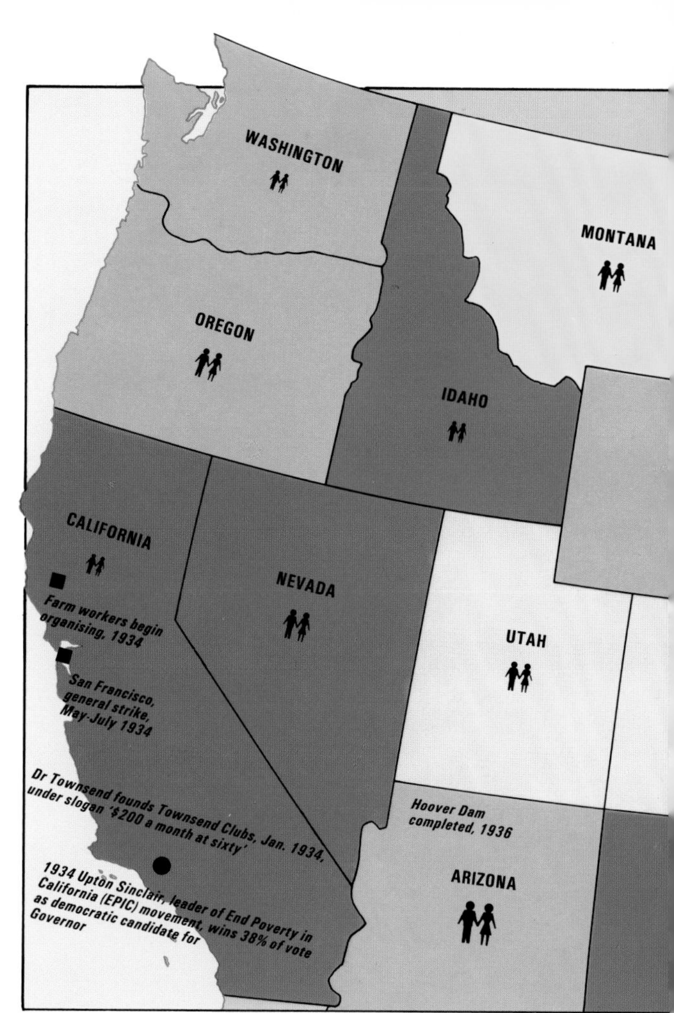

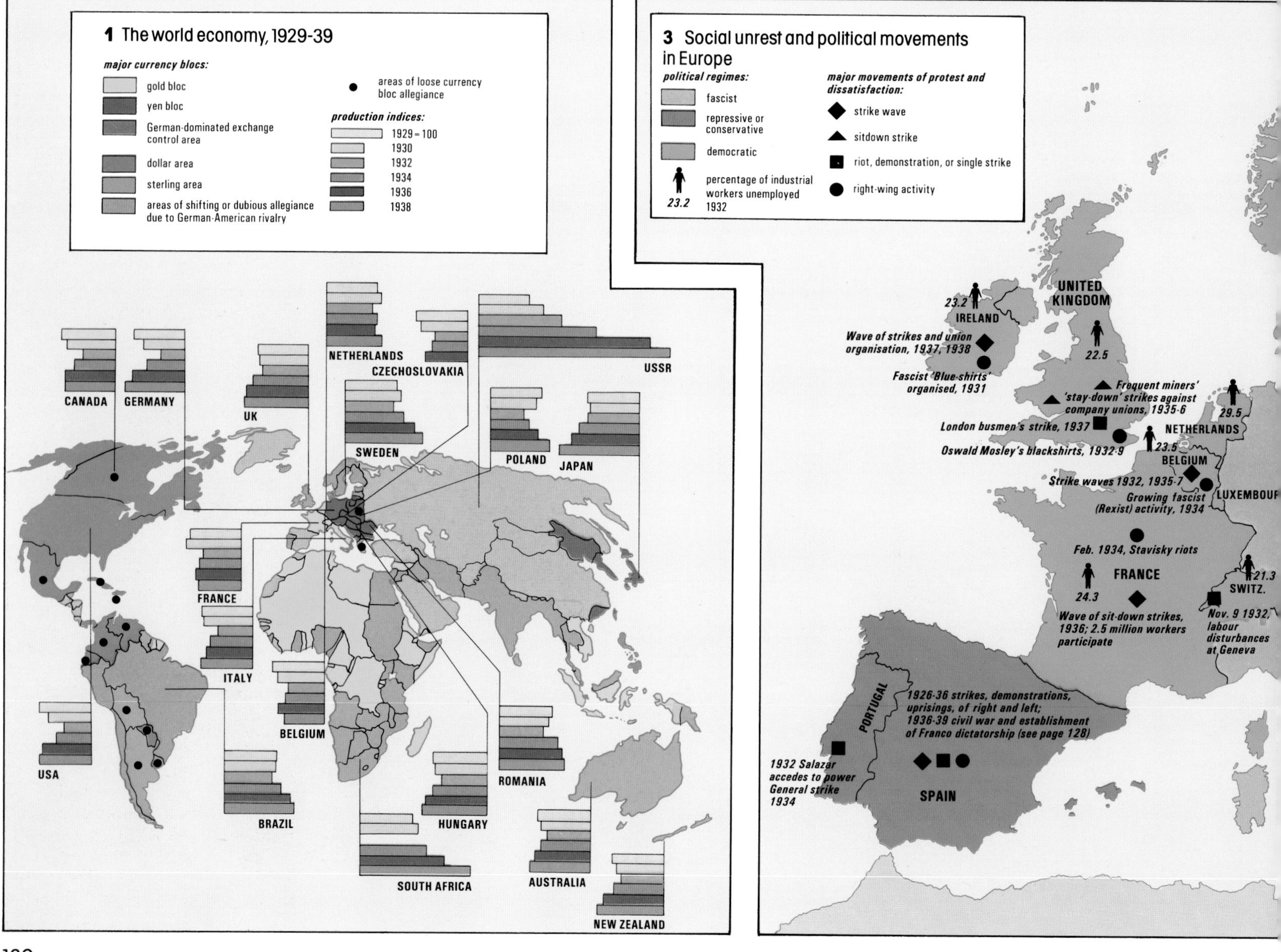

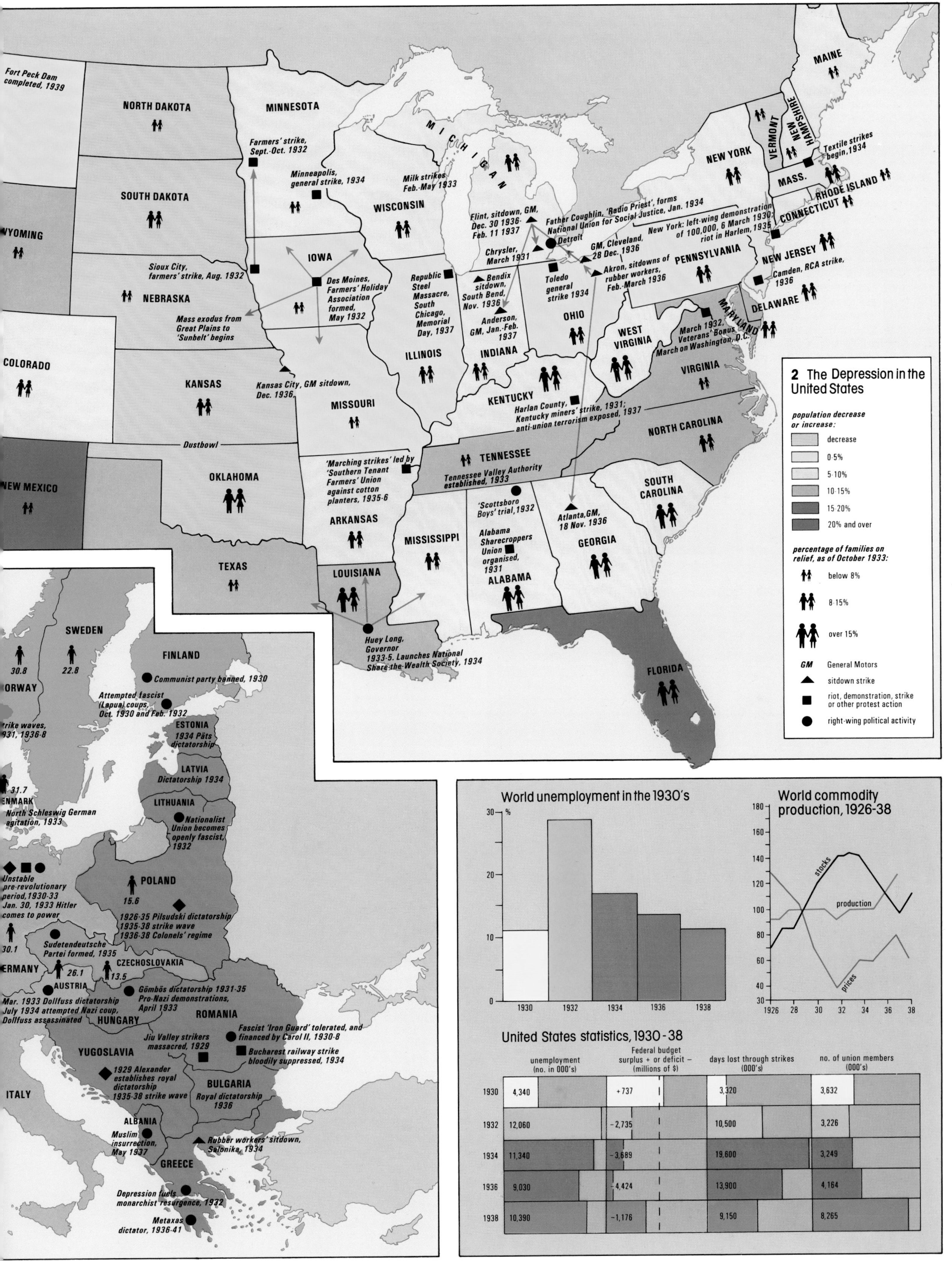

	unemployment (no. in 000's)	Federal budget surplus + or deficit − (millions of $)	days lost through strikes (000's)	no. of union members (000's)
1930	4,340	+737	3,320	3,632
1932	12,060	−2,735	10,500	3,226
1934	11,340	−3,689	19,600	3,249
1936	9,030	−4,424	13,900	4,164
1938	10,390	−1,176	9,150	8,265

The War in the West
1939-1945

Hitler's accession to power in 1933 added a new dimension to international politics. He was held back at first by Germany's diplomatic isolation and by the need to put the shattered economy back on its feet. But by 1936 this phase was over. The re-occupation of the Rhineland, the denunciation of the Locarno treaties (page 128), the Rome-Berlin axis, and the anti-Comintern Pact with Japan, demonstrated the new thrust of German policy. Nevertheless Hitler hoped to get his way by threats and bluster rather than by war, and the unopposed annexation of Austria and the dismemberment of Czechoslovakia in 1938 seemed to prove him right. When in the following year he turned against Poland he expected that England and France would once again give way, and believed that the notorious Nazi-Soviet pact of August 23, 1939, would deter the Western powers from intervention. But this time Hitler miscalculated. When German troops invaded Poland (September 1, 1939), England and France declared war, though they did nothing to aid the Poles.

For the first three years the German armies, with their *Blitzkrieg* strategy, were extraordinarily successful (map 1). After the fall of Poland Hitler halted, hoping that the Western powers would negotiate a compromise peace. Then, in April 1940, he launched his attack in the west, overran Denmark and Norway, and turned against France, which was knocked out of the war before the end of June. But the new Churchill government in London refused to concede defeat, and Hitler launched a major air offensive, intended to prepare the way for invasion. The victory of the Royal Air Force in the Battle of Britain forced him on September 17, 1940, to call off the projected invasion. Instead, Hitler decided to attack Soviet Russia. The directive for 'Operation Barbarossa' was issued in December 1940, the invasion of Russia launched on June 22, 1941. It nearly succeeded. Before the tide turned, German armies were outside Moscow and Leningrad and had overrun southern Russia to the Black Sea and the Caucasus.

Meanwhile two other events intervened. One was the lack of success of Italy, which had entered the war in 1940, which forced Hitler, in 1941, to divert troops to conquer Yugoslavia and Greece and to reinforce the African front. Secondly the United States, entering the war in 1941 (page 134), supplied Britain and Russia with much needed arms and equipment, and also helped to defeat the German submarine campaign in the Atlantic (map 3). The British victory at El Alamein (October 1942), the subsequent capitulation of the Italian and German armies in Africa (May 1943), the Anglo-American invasion of Sicily and then Italy, and the fall of Mussolini (July 1943), were major Allied successes. But it was the great Russian victory at Stalingrad (January 1943) that was decisive. The Germans' last major offensive in the east at Kursk failed in July 1943. Thereafter they fought a stubborn defensive war (map 2), but after the Anglo-American landings in northern France (June 1944) and the opening of the Second Front, the ring was closed, and the bases were lost for the 'secret weapons' which Hitler hoped would force the British to capitulate. The Ardennes offensive (December 1944) was a final attempt to break out in the west; but by now the Allies held the initiative. A major Soviet offensive against East Prussia opened in January 1945, and by April Berlin was under assault. On April 30 Hitler committed suicide, and on May 7 his successor, Admiral Doenitz, surrendered unconditionally. The costs were appalling: 15 million military and 35 million civilians had perished, 20 million of whom were Soviet citizens. Some 6 million Jews were exterminated in concentration camps or otherwise. Anglo-American saturation bombing reduced many German cities to rubble, and 25 million Russians were left homeless. Europe was in ruins, and already the differences between the victorious powers, which were to darken the post-war years (page 136), were visible.

3 The battle of the Atlantic, 1941-45
Allied shipping sunk by U-Boats:
3 Sept. 1939-6 Dec. 1941
7 Dec. 1941-18 Sept. 1943
19 Sept. 1943-8 May 1945
Allied shore-based air cover by 1941
Allied shore-based air cover by 1945
USA
CANADA
SOUTH AMERICA
Atlantic Ocean
AFRICA
EUROPE
2 The defeat of Germany, 1943-45
'Grossdeutsches Reich' 1942
Axis attacks
Axis withdrawal
cities under heavy air attack
major battles with date
Allied attacks
commando raids
airborne landings
partisan/resistance movements
V1 launching sites
V2 launching sites
NORWAY
SWEDEN
FINLAND
DENMARK
ESTONIA
LATVIA
LITHUANIA
E. PRUSSIA
POLAND
GERMANY
HOLLAND
SWITZERLAND
AUSTRIA
SLOVAKIA
HUNGARY
ROMANIA
CROATIA
SERBIA
MONTENEGRO
ALBANIA
BULGARIA
GREECE
ITALY
TURKEY
USSR
UKRAINE
Transnistria
SYRIA
IRAQ
IRAN
LEBANON
PALESTINE
TRANSJORDAN
SAUDI ARABIA
EGYPT
LIBYA
TUNISIA
Cyrenaica
North Sea
Baltic Sea
Black Sea
Caspian Sea
Mediterranean Sea
Caucasus Mts.
Carpathian Mts.
Petsamo
Murmansk
Archangel
Oslo
Stockholm
Helsinki
Vyborg
Leningrad
Lake Ladoga
Narva
Novgorod
Riga
Kaunas
Copenhagen
Flensburg
Lübeck
Hamburg
Bremen
Stettin
Königsberg
Minsk
Mogilev
Bryansk
Orel
Tula
Moscow
Rzhev
Velikiye Luki
Vyazma
Voronezh
Kursk
Gomel
Bialystok
Warsaw
Berlin
Hanover
Torgau
Dresden
Prague
Rotterdam
Arnhem
Antwerp
Brussels
Dusseldorf
Cologne
Ardennes
Frankfurt
Mannheim
Metz
Stuttgart
Munich
Vienna
Budapest
Debrecen
Lemberg
Tarnopol
Kiev
Karkhov
Stalino
Rostov
Stalingrad
Astrakhan
Krivoy Rog
Jassy
Odessa
Kerch
Crimea
Sebastopol
Ordzhonikidze
Batum
Ploesti
Bucharest
Belgrade
Sofia
Istanbul
Ankara
Milan
Trieste
Zagreb
Genoa
Rimini
Livorno
Florence
Zara
Sarajevo
Kotor
Rome
Anzio
Cassino
Naples
Salerno
Bari
Taranto
Salonika
Athens
Corsica
Sardinia
Sicily
Messina
Malta
Pantelleria
Bizerta
Tunis
Crete
Rhodes
Cyprus
Tripoli
Benghazi
El Agheila
Tobruk
Bardia
El Alamein
Alexandria
Cairo
R. Elbe
R. Vistula
R. Oder
R. Bug
R. Rhine
R. Po
R. Danube
R. Pruth
R. Dniester
R. Dnieper
R. Don
R. Donets
R. Volga
1940-44
1941-42
1942-43
1943-44
1943-45
1944-45
1941-44
1941-45
Feb.-April 1945
June-Aug. 1944
June-Aug. 1943
Dec. 1941
Sept. 1944
Dec. 1944
May 1945
Sept.-Oct. 1943
Nov. 1942-Feb. 1943
April 1945
taken June 1944
Jan.-March 1944
July 1943
April-May 1943
Feb.-May 1943
British offensive 23 Oct. 1942
Oct.-Nov. 1942
Jan.-June 1942

The War in Asia and the Pacific
1941-1945

Japanese expansionism in the 1930s was the product of a desire to achieve economic self-sufficiency, military security and a self-imposed leadership of eastern Asia (page 126). Japan after September 1931 overran Manchuria and then set about the reduction of its neighbouring provinces by overrunning much of China north of the Yangtze and sponsoring puppet regimes in its area of conquest. By 1941, Japan, with no possibility of militarily or politically ending the Chinese war, found its ambitions widening to include the European colonial empires in South-East Asia. These offered the raw materials and markets that would free Japan from an economic dependence upon an increasingly unfriendly United States. The latter's re-armament programmes were scheduled to near completion by 1944–1945; the prospect of future naval inferiority and the economic blockade imposed upon Japan after its occupation of Indo-China in 1940 prompted Japanese action. The attack upon the US Pacific Fleet at Pearl Harbor in December 1940 was an attempt to forestall American military preparation and thereby buy the time needed to secure and develop South-East Asia.

In challenging the United States Japan sought to fight the world's greatest industrialised power to a stalemate that would result in a negotiated peace which would recognise Japanese hegemony in eastern Asia. Within six months of the start of the Pacific war Japanese forces had conquered American, British and Dutch possessions throughout South-East Asia and had carried the war to the borders of India, to the waters that washed Australia and into the south-west Pacific (map 1). Yet in those months Japan failed to inflict a naval defeat sufficient to impair US military capacity and morale: indeed, in attempting to do so the Imperial Navy suffered a reverse in the Coral Sea in May 1942, the devastation of its front-line carrier force off Midway in June and crippling losses in the protracted Guadalcanal campaign of August 1942-February 1943. Thereafter, without the means to end the war that it had initiated, Japanese strategic mobility was rapidly eroded as the Imperial forces became obliged to fight defensively on widely separated fronts against a number of enemies (map 2). The United States no less slowly grew into a force that was able to sustain four major efforts: a devastatingly successful campaign against Japanese naval and merchant shipping; an 'island-hopping' strategy with amphibious forces that bypassed the major centres of Japanese resistance; an ultimately overwhelming carrier offensive that was to carry the war to the Japanese Home Islands; and a strategic air offensive, based upon the

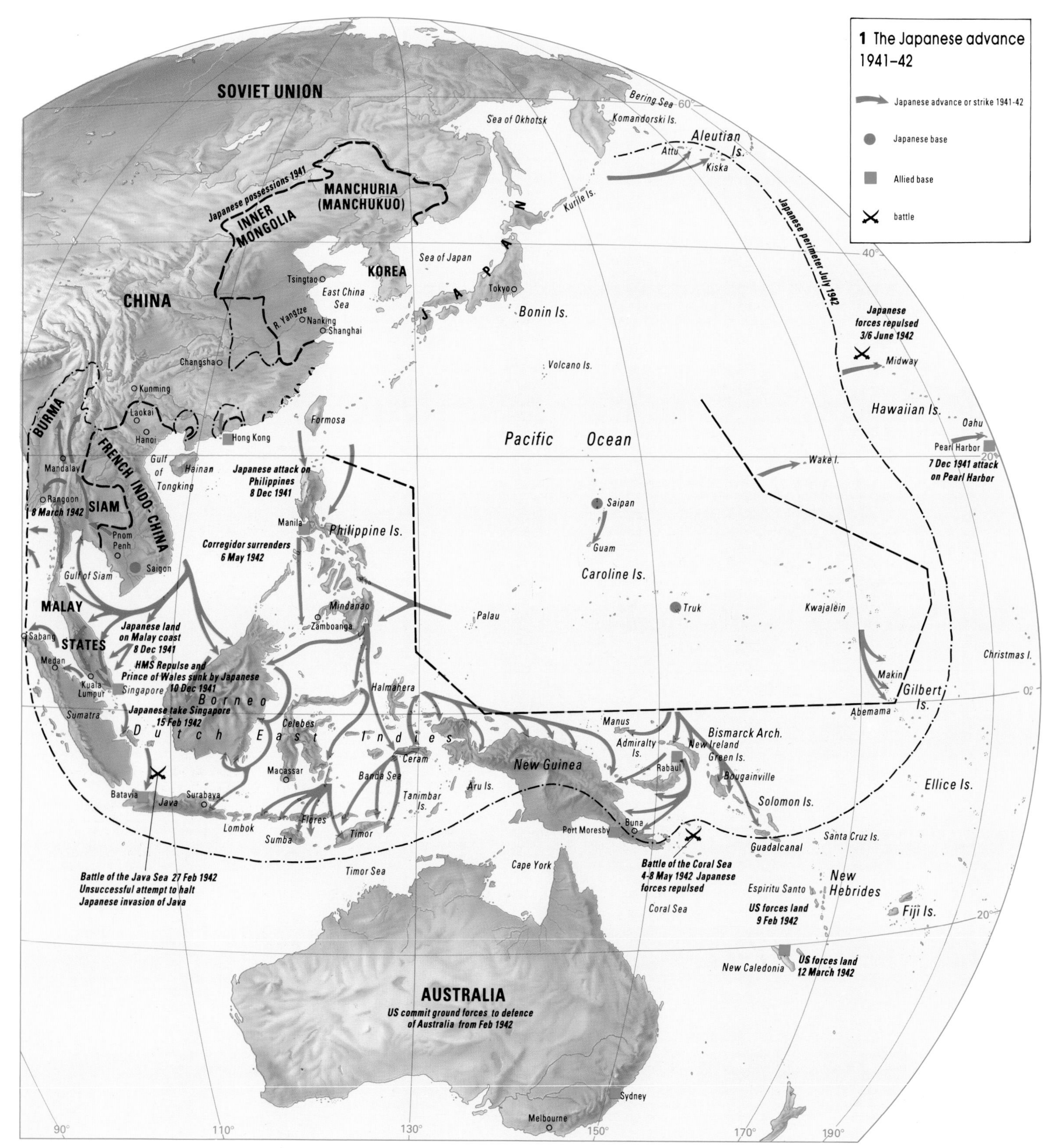

Marianas, that was to shatter Japanese urban areas in the last six months of the war (map 3). By August 1945, when the US atomic bomb attacks upon Hiroshima and Nagasaki and the Soviet offensive in Manchuria enforced their surrender, the Japanese had been utterly exhausted and defeated. However, the brief Japanese colonial adventure had unleashed forces of revolutionary nationalism that were to shape events throughout eastern and South-East Asia over the next three decades.

3 The bombardment of Japan, 1945

2 The Allied counter-offensive

Europe after 1945

Europe emerged from the war of 1939–45 devastated and politically divided. Major territorial changes in the east, where Soviet frontiers were advanced approximately to the former Tsarist boundary and Poland was compensated with German territory up to the Oder-Neisse line, were accompanied by a vast movement of displaced persons, including over 12 million Germans (map 1). Germany and Austria were divided into occupation zones and placed under four-power control. But growing Soviet-American conflict after the abortive Potsdam conference (July–August 1945) undermined four-power co-operation, and the consolidation of the Soviet hold in eastern Europe (map 4) accelerated the division of the continent into two armed camps, completed by the establishment of the North Atlantic Treaty Organisation (1949) and the Warsaw Pact Organisation (1955) (map 3). In 1949 the three western zones of Germany became the German Federal Republic, while Moscow established the German Democratic Republic in the east. (map 5).

Economic recovery in the West was stimulated by American aid under the Marshall Plan (1947), and after 1950 western Europe experienced an unprecedented economic boom (diagram 2). Simultaneously, the process of economic integration was initiated which led in 1957 to the creation of the European Economic Community (EEC), though at first Great Britain remained outside, founding a rival organisation, EFTA (European Free Trade Association), and only joining the EEC with Denmark and Ireland in 1973 (map 3). In eastern Europe economic growth was slower but continuous, thanks to Stalinist methods of industrial and agricultural development. Harsh conditions led to widespread strikes and demonstrations in eastern Germany in 1953 (map 5) and to national uprisings in Poland and Hungary in 1956, the latter, like the experiment in national communism in Czechoslovakia in 1968, brutally suppressed by Soviet troops. Nevertheless, after 1957 there was considerable economic progress. East Germany and Romania forged ahead. Elsewhere, progress was sluggish and uneven, notably in Poland where the formation, in 1979, of an active trade union movement, Solidarity, resulted in the imposition of martial law by 1981.

Steady economic growth helped to stabilise Europe politically. Parliamentary democracy flourished in most of western Europe. In 1954 West Germany was integrated into the western bloc, becoming a member of NATO. Austrian sovereignty was restored a year later. By the 1970s links between eastern and western Europe were much improved. At the European Security Conference in Helsinki in 1975 the post-war settlement of Germany and Poland was formally recognised, and a period of détente inaugurated. In the 1970s democracy finally triumphed in Spain, Portugal and Greece, paving the way for their eventual entry into the Common Market. During the 1980s ties between EEC members grew closer. In 1985 it was agreed that by 1992 a single market would be created for goods and services throughout the Community. In 1991 at the Dutch city of Maastricht it was further agreed that the Community would work towards full monetary union and a pooling of foreign and defence policies, paving the way for far-reaching plans for political union.

While western Europe drew closer together, the eastern bloc rapidly disintegrated (map 4). Popular protest against economic stagnation and political repression, encouraged by the reform programme of Soviet leader Gorbachev, gathered momentum throughout eastern Europe. In 1989 one Communist regime after another crumbled, to be replaced by freely elected multi-party parliaments. East Germany was reunited with West Germany in October 1990. The following year, the Soviet Union collapsed as its western regions voted for independence, with the Baltic States, the Ukraine and Belorussia all gaining independence that year. The remaining republics, plus the Ukraine and Belorussia, agreed in December 1991 to establish a loose Confederation of Independent States (CIS). New links were forged between western and eastern Europe as the continent once again became a single entity.

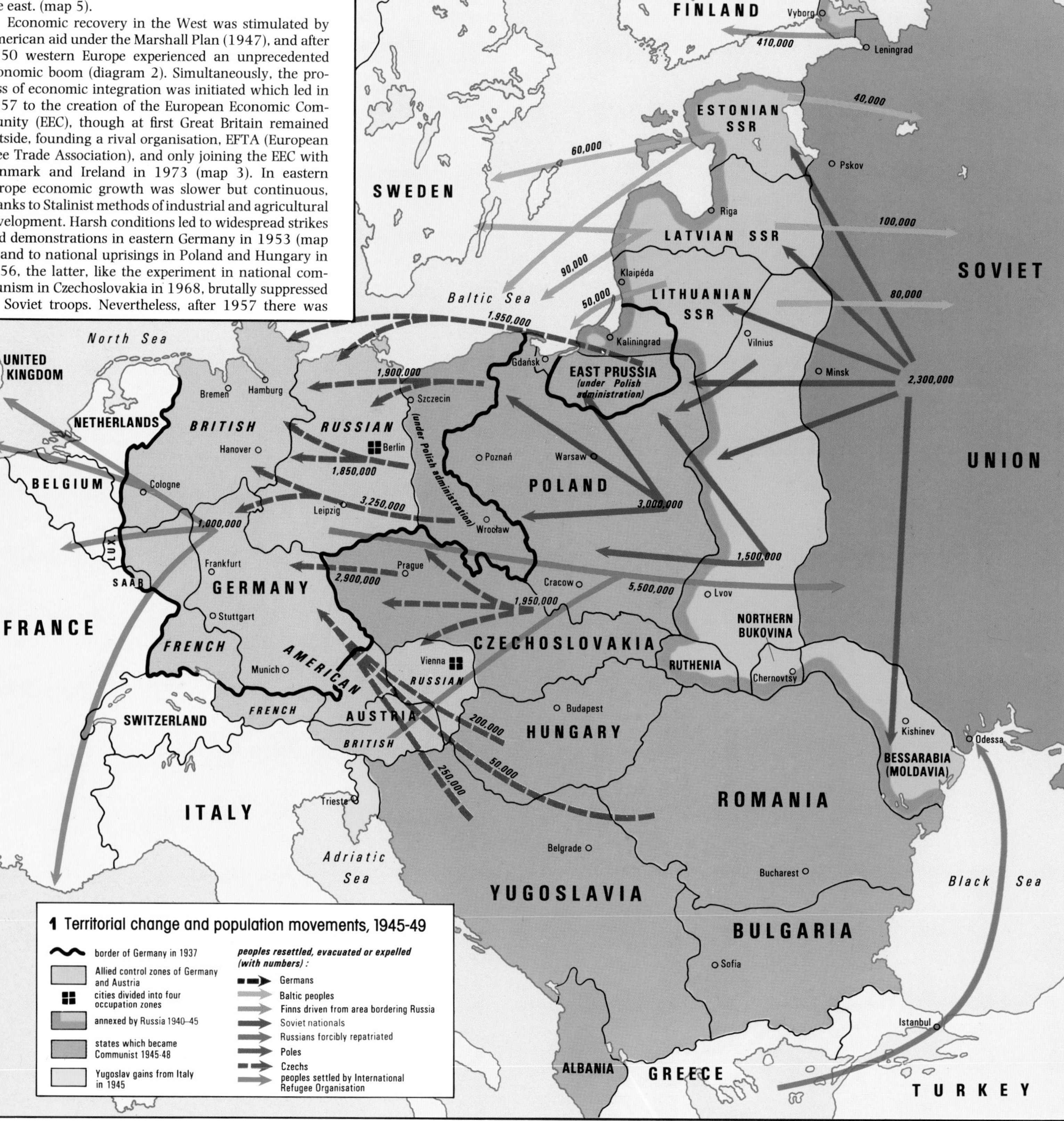

The collapse of Communism brought both political freedom and political instability. Efforts to reform state-run economies produced high inflation and unemployment in eastern Europe, and created sharp social divisions and a revival of ethnic tensions. In Yugoslavia, which had once enjoyed the highest living standards of the Communist world, the coming of democracy created complete fragmentation and civil war. Attempts by the Serbian people to hold the old Yugoslav federation together ended when Croatia and Slovenia won their independence in 1991. The crisis in Yugoslavia was symptomatic of a wider drift towards nationalist extremism elsewhere in Europe. In France, Italy and Austria semi-fascist parties made substantial gains at the polls. In eastern Europe extreme nationalist movements gained in popularity as the new states struggled with severe economic difficulties.

In the European Community there developed strong hostility to the plans for political union from nationalists anxious about the loss of sovereignty. Recession added to the climate of uncertainty. The European monetary union collapsed with the failure of the Exchange Rate mechanism (ERM) in 1992 and the withdrawal of Britain and Italy from the scheme. Nor did the Community agree on its response to foreign policy issues, particularly the Yugoslav civil war. The new Europe represented a profound paradox: on the one hand a general movement towards greater internationalism, on the other mounting evidence of renewed nationalism and political disintegration.

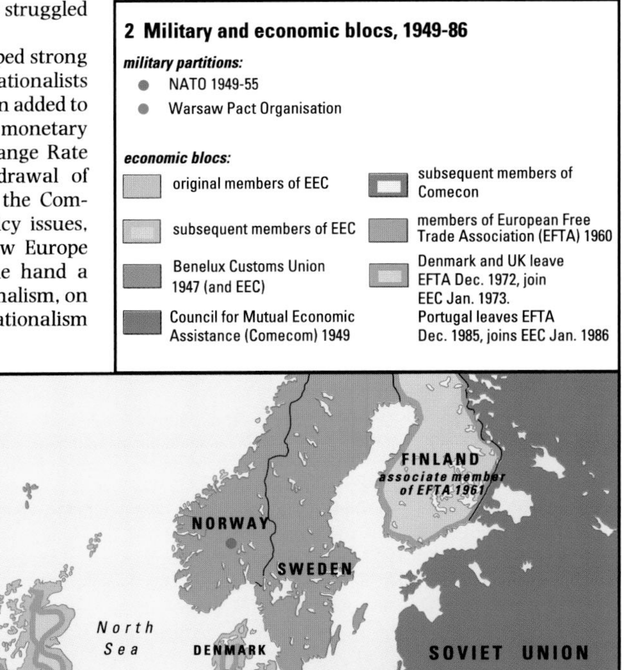

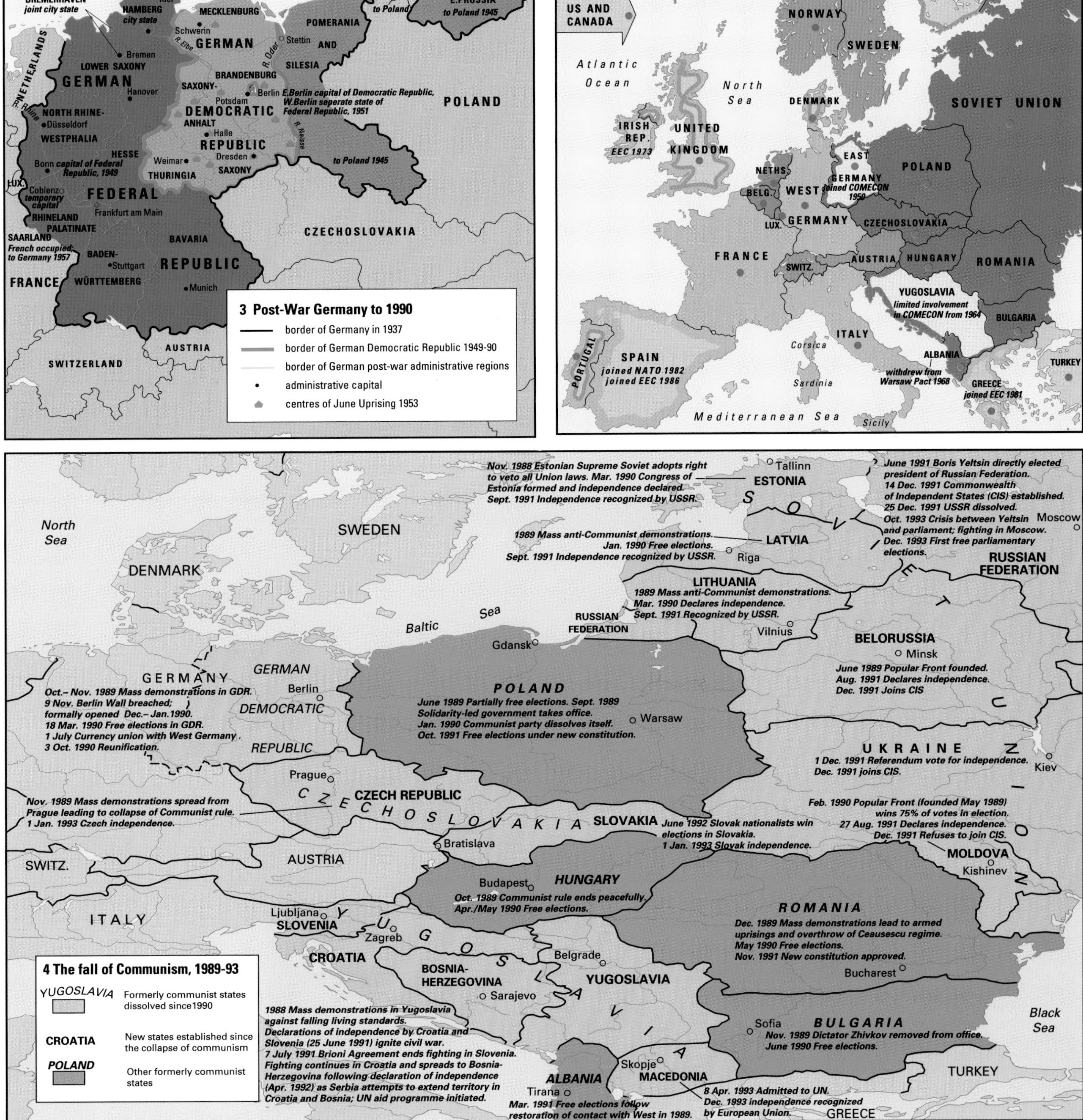

Retreat from empire
after 1947

The European empires of the nineteenth century (page 100) were still intact in 1939, though most German and Ottoman possessions had passed as League of Nations mandates to Britain, France and Japan. Nationalist unrest in the Middle East and Asia exposed the growing fragility of the empires in the 1930s. By the 1950s the demands for independence were irresistible.

None of the European powers surrendered its colonies voluntarily. France fought stubbornly to maintain control in Indo-China, and the Netherlands struggled to contain the nationalists in Java, who had proclaimed an Indonesian republic in 1945. Neither was successful. Vietnamese victory at Dien Bien Phu (1954) forced France to give way (page 148). In Indonesia the nationalists advanced step by step into Kalimantan, Celebes and the Moluccas, until by 1956 they controlled the whole of the former Dutch East Indies except West Irian, which they annexed in 1963 (map 2). The British, also, had no intention of abdicating their imperial position, but continual unrest forced their hand and in 1947 India and Pakistan became independent (page 104), followed by Burma and Ceylon. Nevertheless Britain still clung to its base at Singapore, fought a long war against Malayan insurgents and resisted Indonesian attempts to annex Sarawak and Brunei. Only after 1967, when Aden was evacuated, did Britain abandon its presence east of Suez, except in Hong Kong, to be retained until 1997, its economic success being of great benefit to China.

Resistance to independence was strongest in colonies with a white settler population, or where there was substantial European investment. This was the situation in the Belgian Congo (Zaire) where, within days of independence, the province of Katanga, with its rich copper and uranium resources, seceded, resulting in prolonged civil war, only halted in 1965 when a government favourable to Western mining interests was set up (map 4). In Algeria, with a white population of one million, the bloodiest war of liberation was fought between 1954 and 1962, first in the countryside and then in the cities (map 3). But conflict was scarcely less bitter in Rhodesia, Kenya and the Portuguese colonies of Angola, Mozambique and Guinea-Bissau. The British attempted to save the situation in the Rhodesias and Nyasaland by creating a Central African Federation (1953); but when Zambia and Malawi rejected this compromise (1964), Southern Rhodesia declared unilateral independence (1965) in order to ensure white predominance. But the collapse of the Portuguese empire in 1974 forced the Rhodesian government, now surrounded by black states, to cede control to the black majority and Zimbabwe was born in 1980.

By now the formal structures of European imperialism had been dismantled (map 1). In their place came different forms of association, the British Commonwealth and a special relationship between France and its ex-colonies. Britain showed in the Falklands War in 1982 that she was still prepared to fight on behalf of the few islands still directly ruled from London. Only in southern Africa did the white minority try to maintain traditional white rule. But even here pressure from popular democratic movements compelled change. Namibia won independence in 1990 and in South Africa the government abandoned 'apartheid' and in 1993 agreed to hold the first free multi-racial elections the following April.

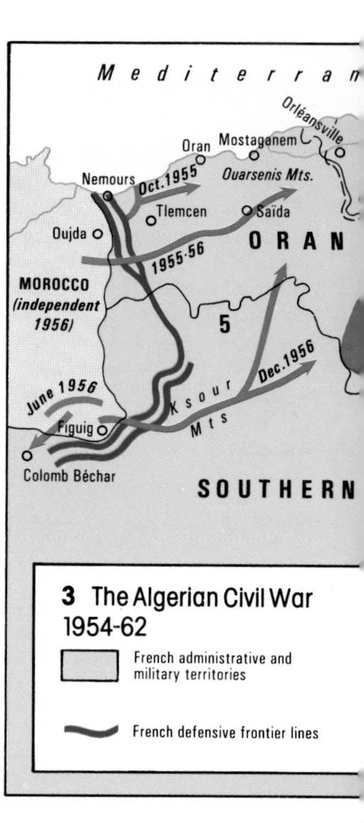

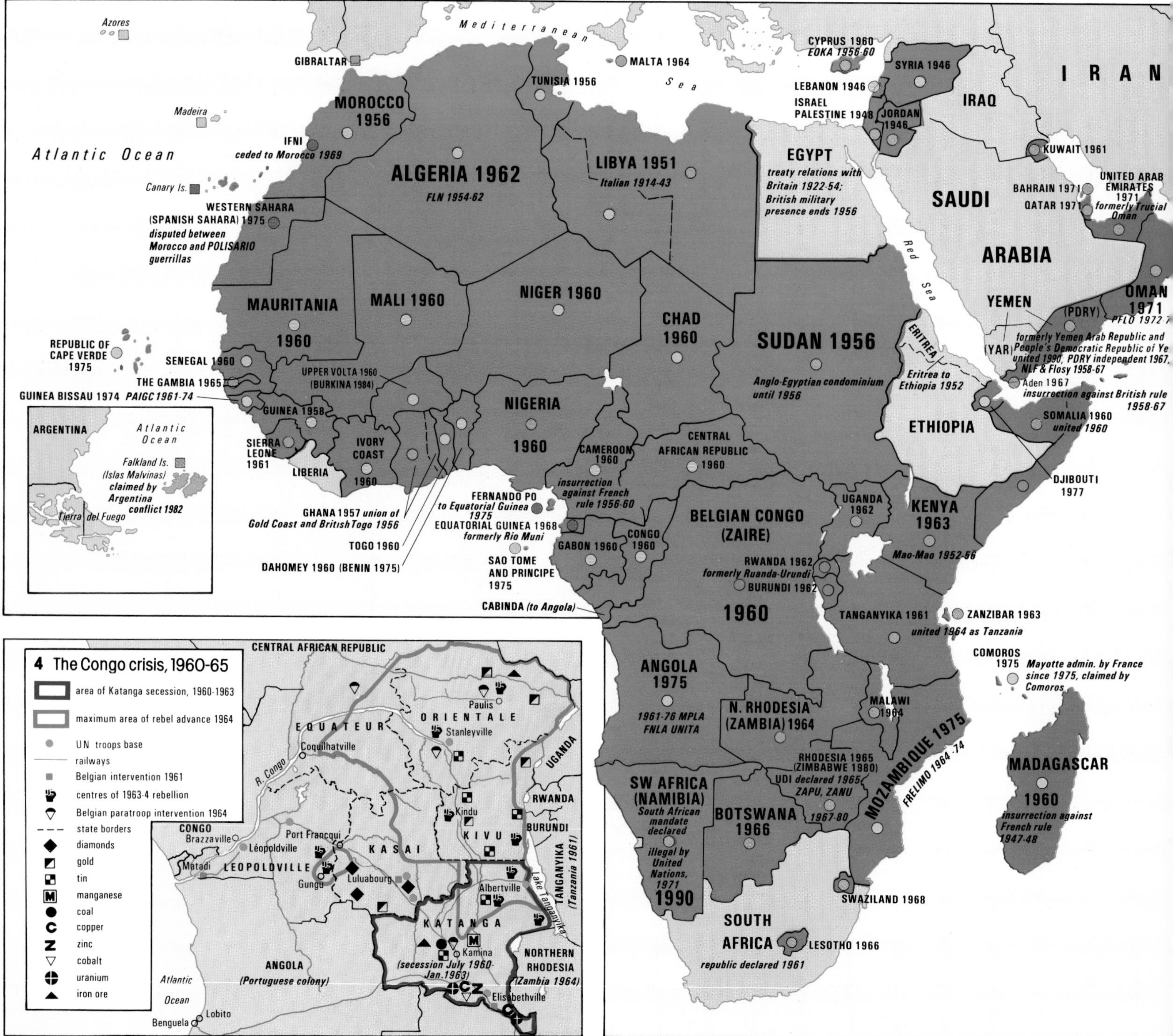

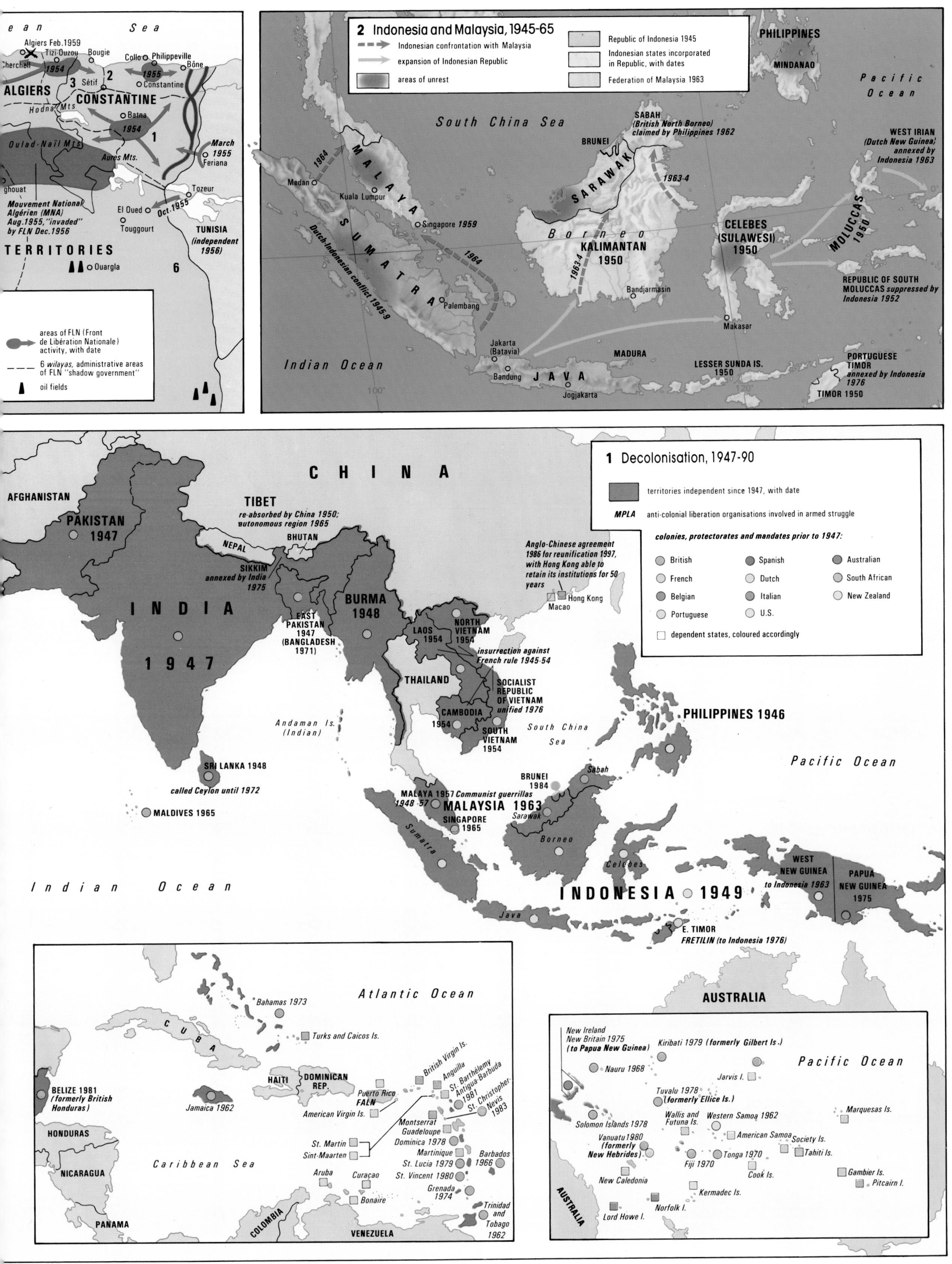

2 Indonesia and Malaysia, 1945-65
Indonesian confrontation with Malaysia
expansion of Indonesian Republic
areas of unrest
Republic of Indonesia 1945
Indonesian states incorporated in Republic, with dates
Federation of Malaysia 1963
PHILIPPINES
MINDANAO
Pacific Ocean
South China Sea
SABAH (British North Borneo) claimed by Philippines 1962
BRUNEI
SARAWAK
WEST IRIAN (Dutch New Guinea) annexed by Indonesia 1963
MALAYA
Medan
Kuala Lumpur
Singapore 1959
SUMATRA
Dutch-Indonesian conflict 1945-9
Palembang
Borneo
KALIMANTAN 1950
Bandjarmasin
CELEBES (SULAWESI) 1950
MOLUCCAS 1950
REPUBLIC OF SOUTH MOLUCCAS suppressed by Indonesia 1952
Makasar
Jakarta (Batavia)
Bandung
JAVA
Jogjakarta
MADURA
LESSER SUNDA IS. 1950
PORTUGUESE TIMOR annexed by Indonesia 1976
TIMOR 1950
Indian Ocean
Algiers Feb.1959
Tizi-Ouzou
Bougie
Collo
Philippeville
Bône
Cherchell
Sétif
Constantine
ALGIERS
CONSTANTINE
Hodna Mts
Batna
Oulad-Naïl Mts
Aures Mts.
March 1955
Feriana
Tozeur
Mouvement National Algérien (MNA) Aug.1955, "invaded" by FLN Dec.1956
El Oued
Oct.1955
Touggourt
TUNISIA (independent 1956)
TERRITORIES
Ouargla
areas of FLN (Front de Libération Nationale) activity, with date
6 wilayas, administrative areas of FLN "shadow government"
oil fields
1 Decolonisation, 1947-90
territories independent since 1947, with date
MPLA anti-colonial liberation organisations involved in armed struggle
colonies, protectorates and mandates prior to 1947:
British
Spanish
Australian
French
Dutch
South African
Belgian
Italian
New Zealand
Portuguese
U.S.
dependent states, coloured accordingly
CHINA
AFGHANISTAN
PAKISTAN 1947
TIBET re-absorbed by China 1950; autonomous region 1965
NEPAL
BHUTAN
SIKKIM annexed by India 1975
INDIA 1947
EAST PAKISTAN 1947 (BANGLADESH 1971)
BURMA 1948
Anglo-Chinese agreement 1986 for reunification 1997, with Hong Kong able to retain its institutions for 50 years
Hong Kong
Macao
LAOS 1954
NORTH VIETNAM 1954
insurrection against French rule 1945-54
THAILAND
SOCIALIST REPUBLIC OF VIETNAM unified 1976
CAMBODIA 1954
SOUTH VIETNAM 1954
Andaman Is. (Indian)
South China Sea
PHILIPPINES 1946
SRI LANKA 1948
called Ceylon until 1972
MALDIVES 1965
BRUNEI 1984
Sabah
MALAYA 1957 Communist guerrillas 1948-57
MALAYSIA 1963
Sarawak
SINGAPORE 1965
Pacific Ocean
Sumatra
Borneo
Celebes
WEST NEW GUINEA to Indonesia 1963
PAPUA NEW GUINEA 1975
Indian Ocean
INDONESIA 1949
Java
E. TIMOR FRETILIN (to Indonesia 1976)
AUSTRALIA
Atlantic Ocean
Bahamas 1973
CUBA
Turks and Caicos Is.
British Virgin Is.
Anguilla
St. Barthélemy
Antigua-Barbuda 1981
St. Christopher-Nevis 1983
HAITI
DOMINICAN REP.
Puerto Rico FALN
American Virgin Is.
BELIZE 1981 (formerly British Honduras)
Jamaica 1962
Montserrat
Guadeloupe
Dominica 1978
Martinique
St. Martin
Sint-Maarten
HONDURAS
Barbados 1966
St. Lucia 1979
St. Vincent 1980
Caribbean Sea
NICARAGUA
Aruba
Curaçao
Bonaire
Grenada 1974
Trinidad and Tobago 1962
PANAMA
COLOMBIA
VENEZUELA
New Ireland
New Britain 1975 (to Papua New Guinea)
Kiribati 1979 (formerly Gilbert Is.)
Nauru 1968
Pacific Ocean
Jarvis I.
Tuvalu 1978 (formerly Ellice Is.)
Solomon Islands 1978
Wallis and Futuna Is.
Western Samoa 1962
Marquesas Is.
American Samoa
Vanuatu 1980 (formerly New Hebrides)
Fiji 1970
Tonga 1970
Society Is.
Tahiti Is.
New Caledonia
Cook Is.
Gambier Is.
Pitcairn I.
AUSTRALIA
Kermadec Is.
Norfolk I.
Lord Howe I.

Asia and Africa after independence

The history of Asia and Africa since independence is one of chronic instability. Three factors stand out: first, the seizure of power by military leaders (Egypt 1952, Pakistan 1958, Ghana 1966, Indonesia 1967), with the aim (rarely successful) of abolishing corruption and stabilising the economy; second, the resurgence of long-standing regional, tribal and religious conflicts (Naga unrest in India, Kurdish revolts in northern Iraq, Turkey and Iran, nationalist uprisings among the Kachins, Mons, Shans and other 'hill peoples' in Thailand and Burma); finally persistent intervention by the great powers, particularly in the Middle East. Sino-Soviet rivalry lay behind the Vietnamese invasion of Cambodia and the Chinese invasion of Vietnam (1979). In Africa the United States and the Soviet Union intervened in the Somali-Ethiopian war (1976–78), and France sent troops to Chad, and, with other Western powers, helped to quell the insurrection in Zaire in 1978. The attempted secession of Biafra (map 2), essentially a revolt of the Ibo people in eastern Nigeria against northern domination, was defeated by the federal government, with broad international backing. On the other hand, the secession of Bangladesh from Pakistan (1971) was successful, though only achieved with massive Indian military support.

Two countries alone were exceptions from the general pattern. Japan's progress, after the recovery of independence in 1951, was phenomenal. Maintaining close relations with the United States, successive governments concentrated on industrial development and new technology until in the 1970s Japan emerged as the world's third industrial nation (diagram 4). The case of China is more equivocal. Reconstruction after the Revolution (page 122) proceeded apace; but the 'Great Leap Forward' (1958–60) and the 'Cultural Revolution' (1966–68) brought not only political strife but also severe economic disruption and widespread massacre. After the death of Mao Tse-tung (1976) stability returned and there was wide-ranging economic reform, particularly in agriculture; China also became an industrial power. Countries around the Pacific Rim – South Korea, Taiwan, Singapore – made significant economic progress in the 1970s and 1980s based on the cheap production of high-technology goods for the West. Elsewhere poverty remained endemic. In 1985 only 6 out of 47 African countries had an average annual income above $750 a head; only 10 out of 80 states in the whole region had an average annual income above $2,500.

Faced by the threat of internal disruption, governments everywhere looked

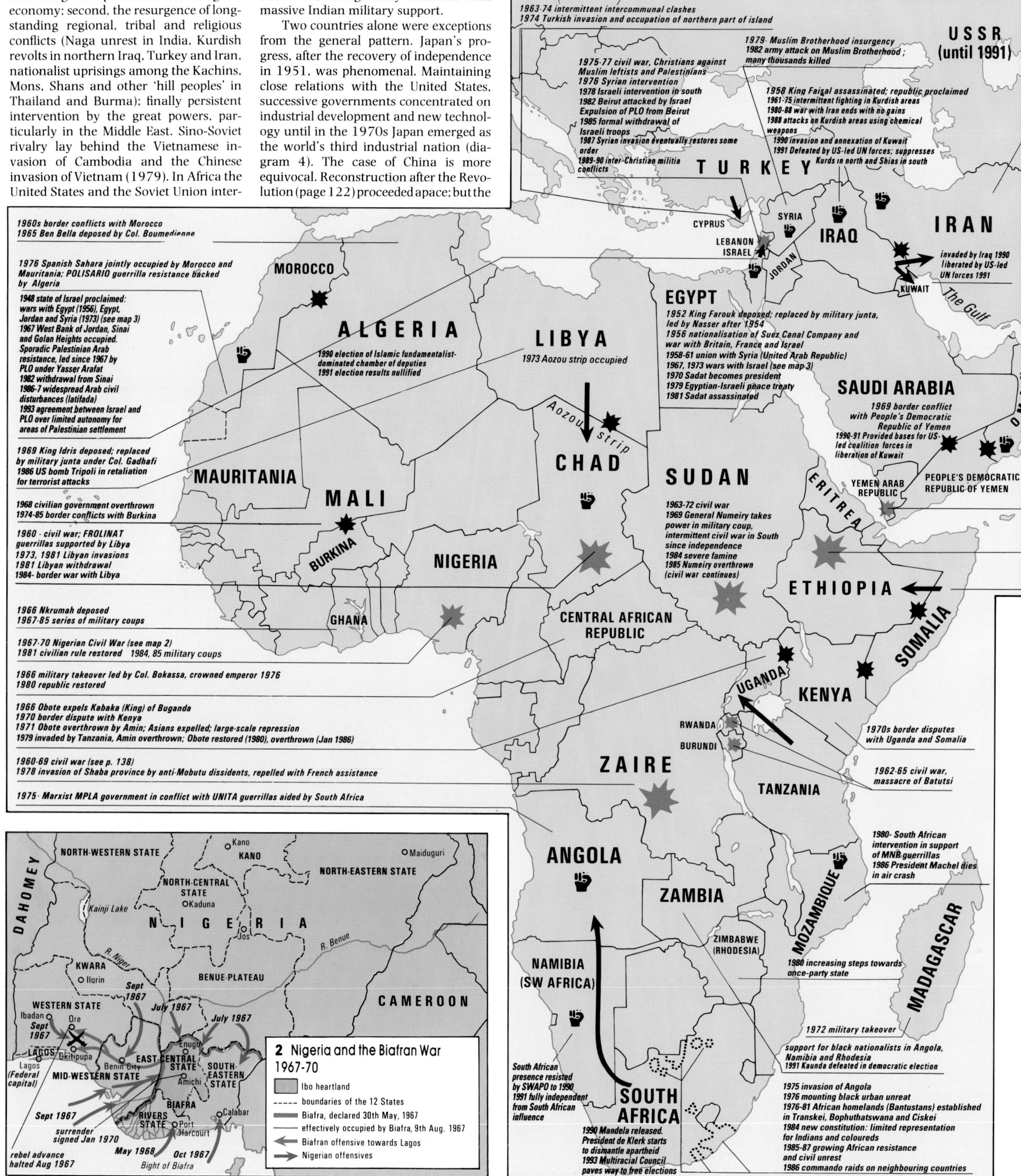

to the great powers for support. Inevitably they were drawn into great-power politics. Iran, where the United States covertly helped the Shah's supporters to oust the nationalist Mossadeq in 1953, was one bastion of American influence in the Middle East until 1979 when Ayatollah Khomeini introduced revolutionary Islamic fundamentalism and a long war with Iraq ensued. The Jewish state of Israel, at war with its Arab neighbours ever since its foundation in 1948 (map 3) received US support. The Soviet Union supported Syria and Egypt until the latter, after the Egyptian-Israeli war of 1973, turned to the United States for financial backing. This diplomatic revolution inaugurated a new phase. At Camp David in 1978 Egypt and Israel came to terms, but the rest of the Middle East remained in a constant state of crisis. From 1980 Iraq and Iran were at war for eight years; Lebanon collapsed in civil war; in 1990 Iraq invaded Kuwait and was driven out by UN forces early the following year.

Democracy made significant gains in the whole area during the 1980s and 1990s (notably in Pakistan, the Philippines, Namibia, South Africa and Zambia) but elsewhere single party or military regimes were still the rule. Prospects for stability and an end to violence and political coercion remained uncertain.

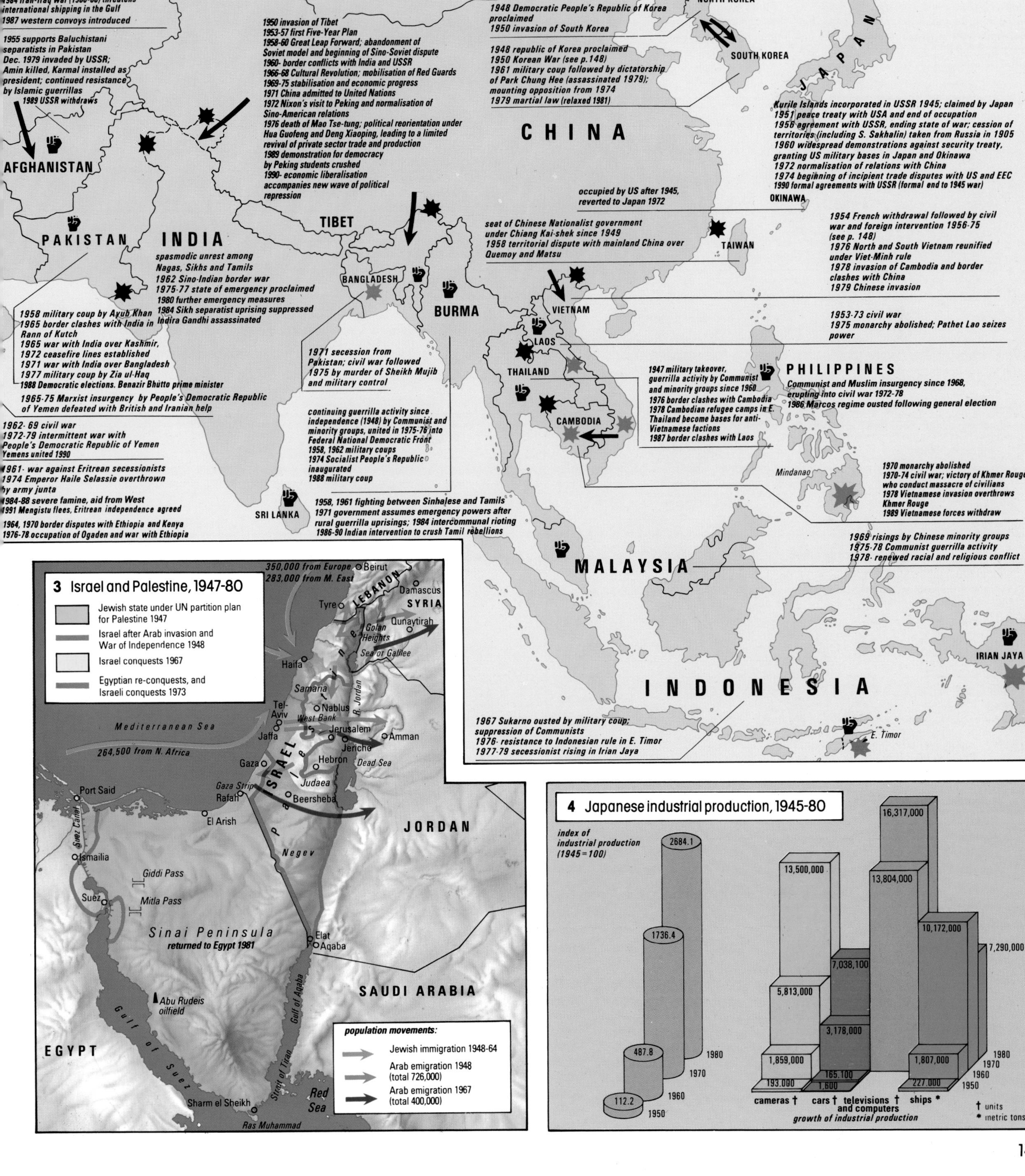

Latin America since 1930

The world depression of 1930 (page 130) was a watershed in the history of Latin America. Heavily dependent on primary exports (map 2), all the republics were hit by the drop in world trade. Chile's exports fell by over 80 per cent between 1929 and 1933; those of Bolivia and Peru by 75 per cent. In Brazil coffee was burnt. Only oil-exporting Venezuela more or less weathered the storm. The result was widespread disillusion with the middle-class liberal or radical parties, themselves apparently helpless. In 1930 and 1931, 11 of the 20 republics south of the Rio Grande experienced revolutionary changes of government. In Mexico, where Cárdenas (1934–40) revived the land distribution policies of 1911, the shift was to the left, but the swing was mainly to the right, though not back to nineteenth century *caudillismo* (page 96), the social bases of which were being eroded by urbanisation and population movements (map 3). The new dictators were populists, appealing directly to the masses and cooperating with organised labour and the trade unions. They also introduced programmes of industrialisation, following Soviet or, more often, fascist models, to reduce dependence on overseas markets and hasten economic development.

Manufacturing industry was given a further boost by the Second World War, which cut off imported consumer goods and stimulated the industrial sector. But industrialisation made Latin America dependent upon imported capital goods, raw materials, technology and finance, creating enormous foreign debts. Multinational corporations exploited the cheap labour markets of Latin America without stimulating economic development. Social tensions arose from income concentration, unemployment, lack of opportunities and the presence of foreign interests. Social revolutions were attempted but frustrated in Guatemala, Bolivia and Chile (map 1), and this underlined the obstacles to change when economies are too narrowly based to sustain welfare programmes and when local élites are prepared to collaborate with the United States. Cuba from 1959 attempted to achieve social change, economic growth and freedom from the United States simultaneously. The revolution led to greater social equality and an improvement in the prospects of rural workers but it also involved a commitment to a repressive government and a dependence on the Soviet Union.

In the face of revolutionary change, many governments closed their ranks. With some support from the upper and middle classes, military governments in the south combined political repression with economic liberalisation. But by the late 1980s their policies had largely failed, and in the face of economic recession and popular protest the grip of the military was gradually eroded. Democracy made ground, even if generally under the watchful eye of the military and, especially in Peru, in the face of violent far-left revolutionary movements. Yet foreign debt, civil conflict, enormous poverty and widespread crime remained perennial barriers to effective stabilization.

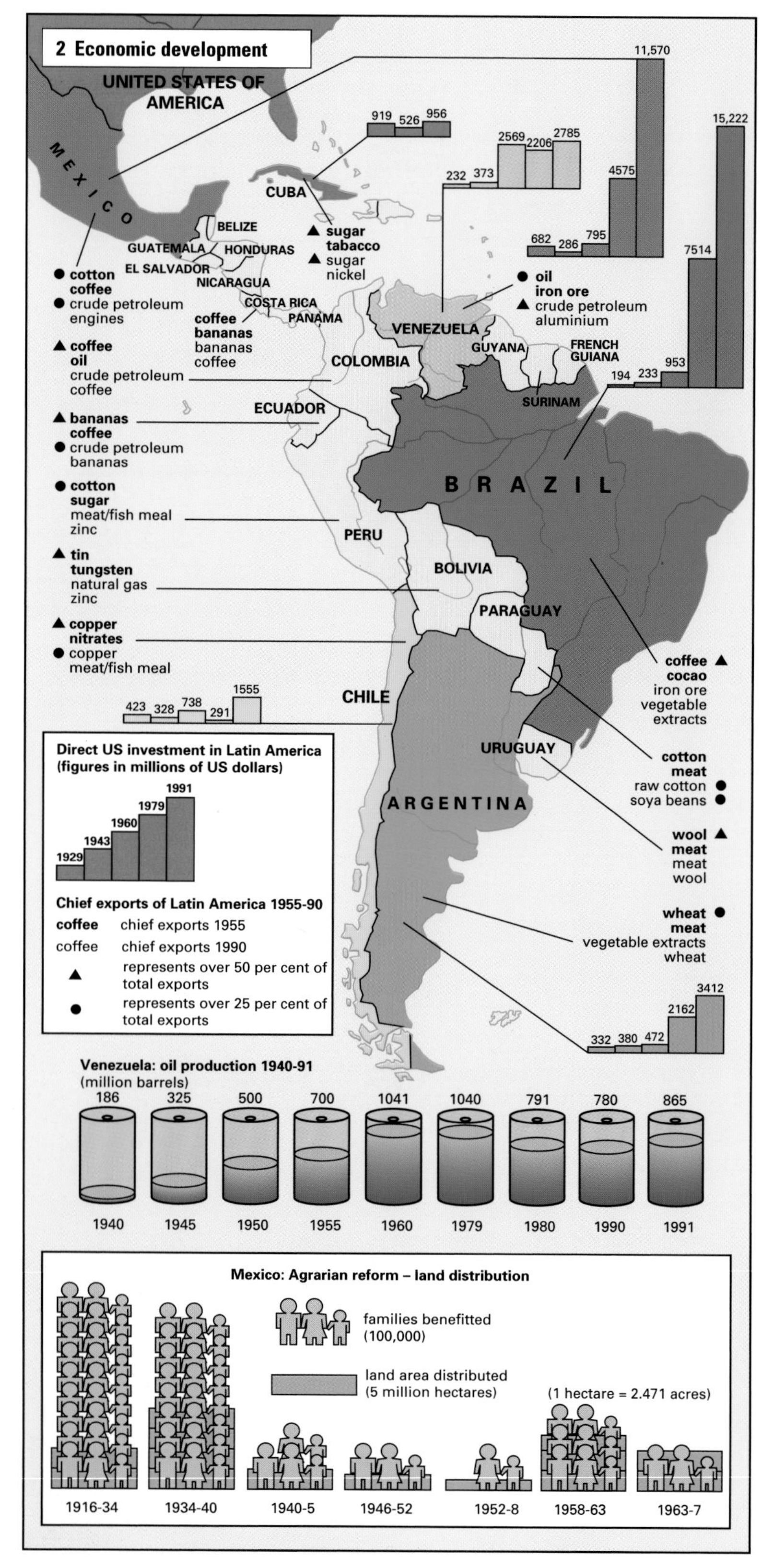

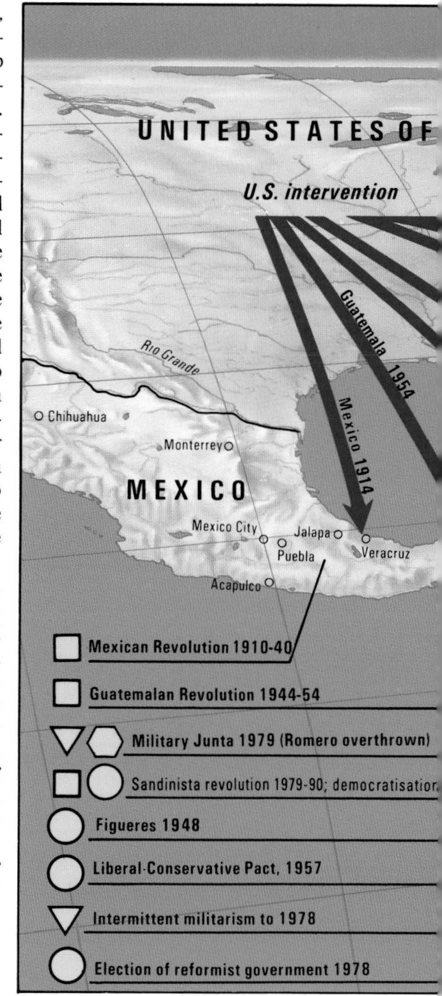

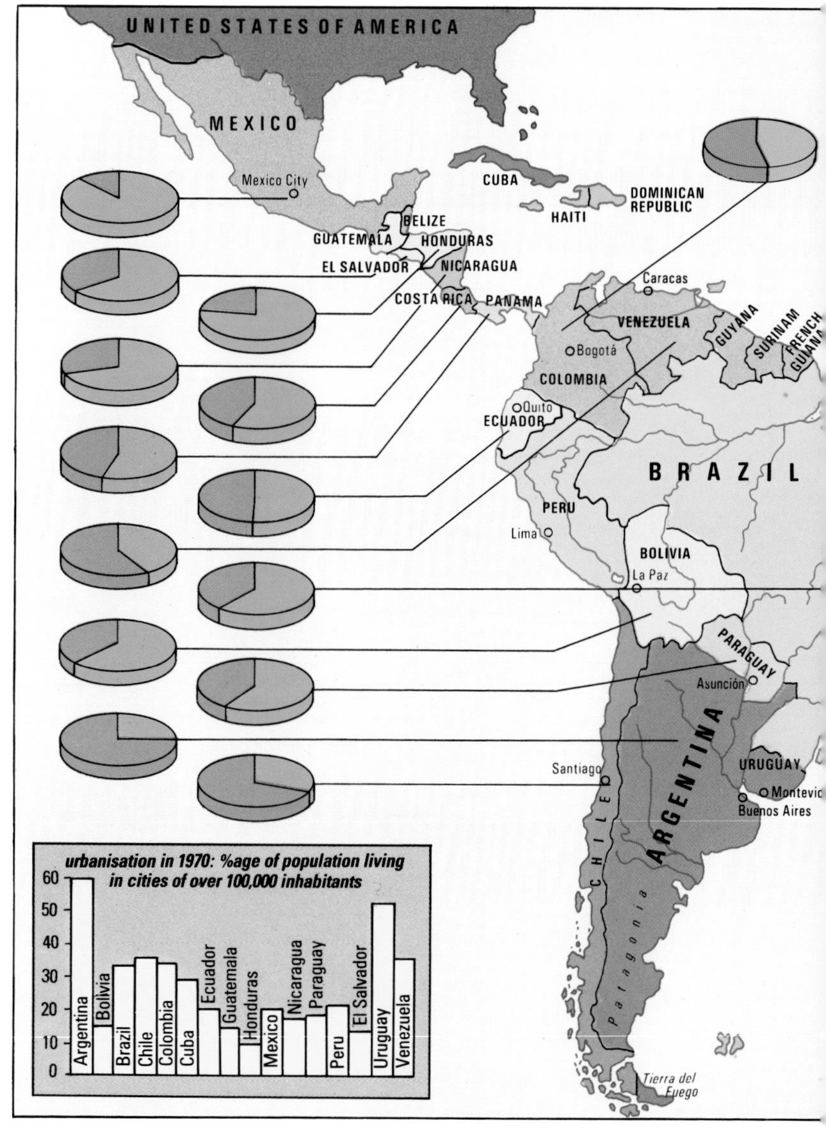

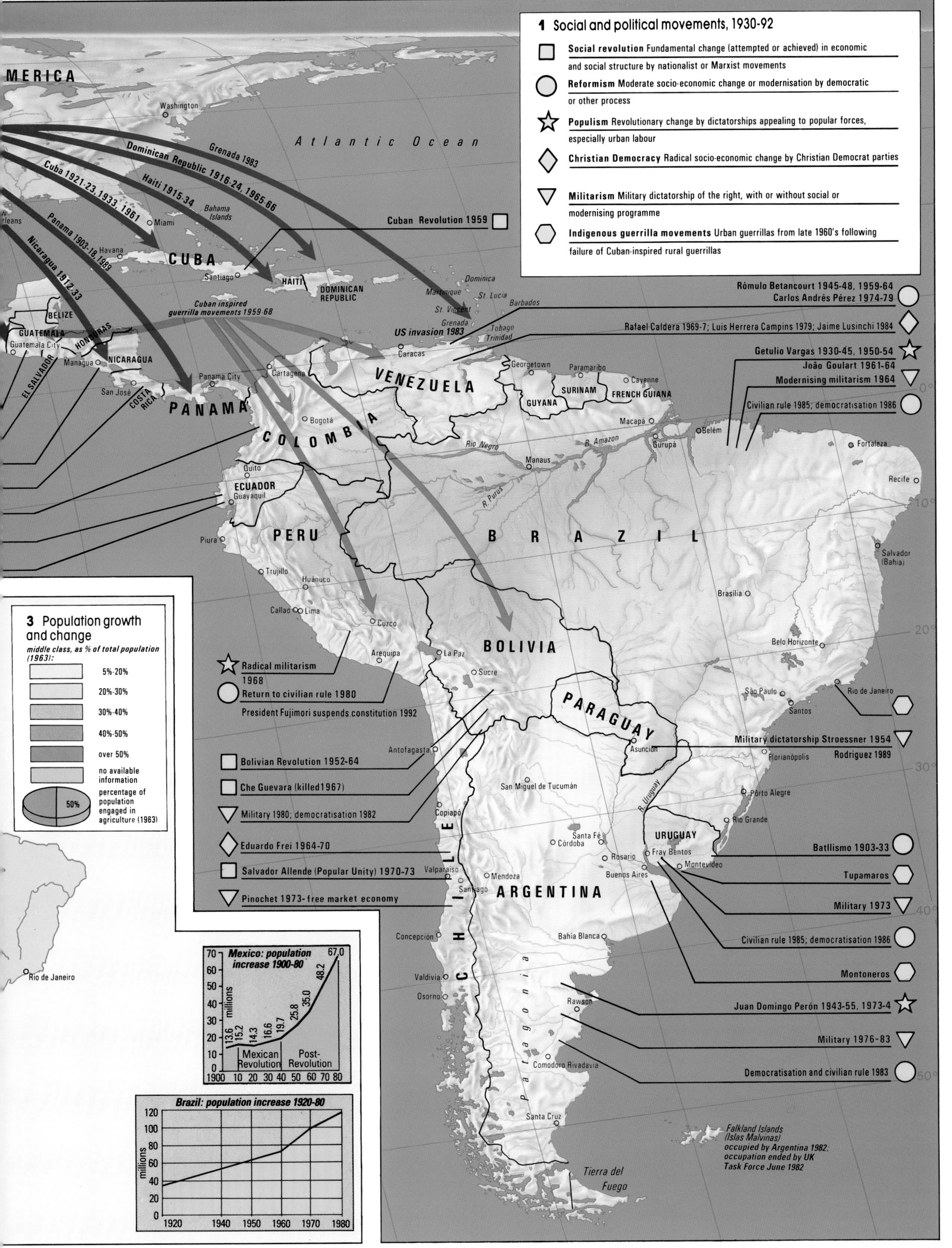
1 Social and political movements, 1930-92
Social revolution Fundamental change (attempted or achieved) in economic and social structure by nationalist or Marxist movements
Reformism Moderate socio-economic change or modernisation by democratic or other process
Populism Revolutionary change by dictatorships appealing to popular forces, especially urban labour
Christian Democracy Radical socio-economic change by Christian Democrat parties
Militarism Military dictatorship of the right, with or without social or modernising programme
Indigenous guerrilla movements Urban guerrillas from late 1960's following failure of Cuban-inspired rural guerrillas
Atlantic Ocean
Grenada 1983
Dominican Republic 1916-24, 1965-66
Haiti 1915-34
Cuba 1921-23, 1933, 1961
Panama 1903-18, 1989
Nicaragua 1912-33
Cuban Revolution 1959
Cuban inspired guerrilla movements 1959-68
US invasion 1983
Rómulo Betancourt 1945-48, 1959-64
Carlos Andrés Pérez 1974-79
Rafael Caldera 1969-7; Luis Herrera Campins 1979; Jaime Lusinchi 1984
Getulio Vargas 1930-45, 1950-54
João Goulart 1961-64
Modernising militarism 1964
Civilian rule 1985; democratisation 1986
Radical militarism 1968
Return to civilian rule 1980
President Fujimori suspends constitution 1992
Bolivian Revolution 1952-64
Che Guevara (killed 1967)
Military 1980; democratisation 1982
Eduardo Frei 1964-70
Salvador Allende (Popular Unity) 1970-73
Pinochet 1973- free market economy
Military dictatorship Stroessner 1954
Rodriguez 1989
Batllismo 1903-33
Tupamaros
Military 1973
Civilian rule 1985; democratisation 1986
Montoneros
Juan Domingo Perón 1943-55, 1973-4
Military 1976-83
Democratisation and civilian rule 1983
Falkland Islands (Islas Malvinas) occupied by Argentina 1982; occupation ended by UK Task Force June 1982
MERICA
CUBA
HAITI
DOMINICAN REPUBLIC
BELIZE
GUATEMALA
HONDURAS
NICARAGUA
EL SALVADOR
COSTA RICA
PANAMA
VENEZUELA
GUYANA
SURINAM
FRENCH GUIANA
COLOMBIA
ECUADOR
PERU
BRAZIL
BOLIVIA
PARAGUAY
URUGUAY
CHILE
ARGENTINA
Patagonia
Tierra del Fuego
3 Population growth and change
middle class, as % of total population (1963):
5%-20%
20%-30%
30%-40%
40%-50%
over 50%
no available information
percentage of population engaged in agriculture (1963)
50%
Mexico: population increase 1900-80
millions
13.6 15.2 14.3 16.6 19.7 25.8 35.0 48.2 67.0
Mexican Revolution
Post-Revolution
1900 10 20 30 40 50 60 70 80
Brazil: population increase 1920-80
millions
1920 1940 1950 1960 1970 1980

The United States from 1945

The years from 1940 to 1980 saw economic, demographic, and social changes in the United States that transformed the lives of its people. The agricultural, industrial, and service sectors of the economy reached unprecedented levels of productivity. Fewer farmers provided not only for a population which, by 1980, was overwhelmingly urban, but also a significant proportion of the world's production of major staples such as wheat, corn, and soya beans (diagram 5, A–C). Mechanisation (under 10 per cent of the cotton crop was harvested by machine in 1949, 96 per cent in 1969), greater yields from improved seed and fertilisers, and an intensely market-oriented and government subsidised system of sales and distribution made this possible. The economy at large grew at a comparable pace until the 1970s. The gross national product (in constant 1958 dollars) was $227.2 billion in 1940, $722.5 billion in 1970. The service sector expanded more rapidly than did manufacturing, and cities such as Atlanta and Houston in the South and South-west, and Los Angeles, San Francisco, and Denver in the West, became major centres of economic activity (map 4).

This economic growth was accompanied by massive flows of people both within and into the country. With the end of large-scale immigration in the 1920s and the relative immobility of the 1930s, it seemed as though the mobility of American life was over. But the armament build-up during the Second World War attracted many people to the old industrial centres of the Northeast and the Midwest, and to new plants elsewhere. Economic expansion after the war sustained these flows. Millions of blacks and whites left the Southern countryside for the East, the Midwest, and the far West: many more agricultural, industrial, and professional families moved to the West, the Sun Belt of the South and Southwest, and to burgeoning cities around the nation (map 1). An interstate system of highways totalling about 40,000 miles by 1980 facilitated the long-distance movement of people, and the rise of complex networks of residence and work (map 2). By 1980 only a third of the population lived in non-metropolitan areas.

About 10 million immigrants arrived in the US between 1950 and 1980 (map 1), plus millions more illegally. Perhaps the most dramatic social change was in the realm of race relations. Between 1940 and 1980 a centuries-old structure of formal, explicit racial discrimination against blacks and Asians all but disappeared. Minorities made major gains in education, income and social acceptance. But this revolution in race relations was not without strains. The massive black and Hispanic migration to American cities exploded in substantial urban riots during the troubled years of the 1960s (map 3). A further strain was imposed by the war in Vietnam, where US ground-troops were committed in large numbers from 1965 to 1973 (page 148). The war polarized American society and brought strong protests from abroad.

Vietnam also imposed serious strains on the American economy. From the late 1960s inflation and unemployment rose and in 1971 the dollar was devalued. High state spending also led to growing deficits. But during the 1980s, American confidence largely returned, taking its lead from President Reagan's promise to reverse economic decline and restore the country's world role. Military intervention in Grenada, Panama, Nicaragua (page 143) and the Middle East (page 141), coupled with the successful ending of the Cold War with the Soviet Union (page 148), provoked renewed national pride. A new consumer boom also produced economic revival, though at the cost of hugely increased deficits. Whatever the structural problems of the US economy, by the 1990s many Americans were persuaded that their country's liberal capitalism was still viable.

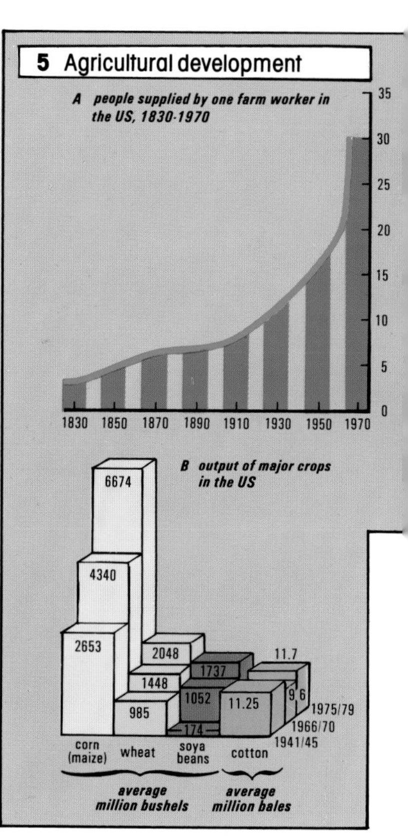

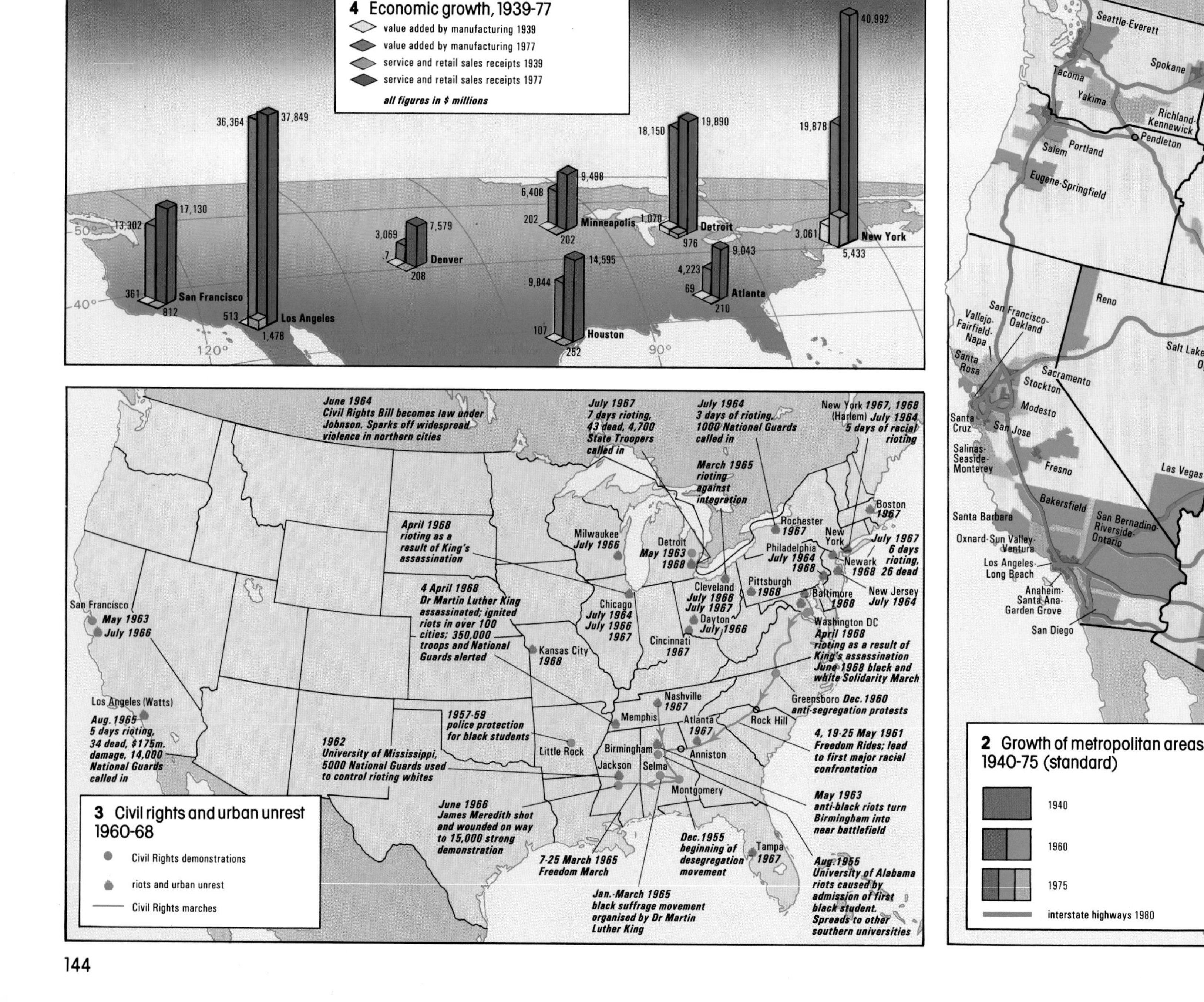

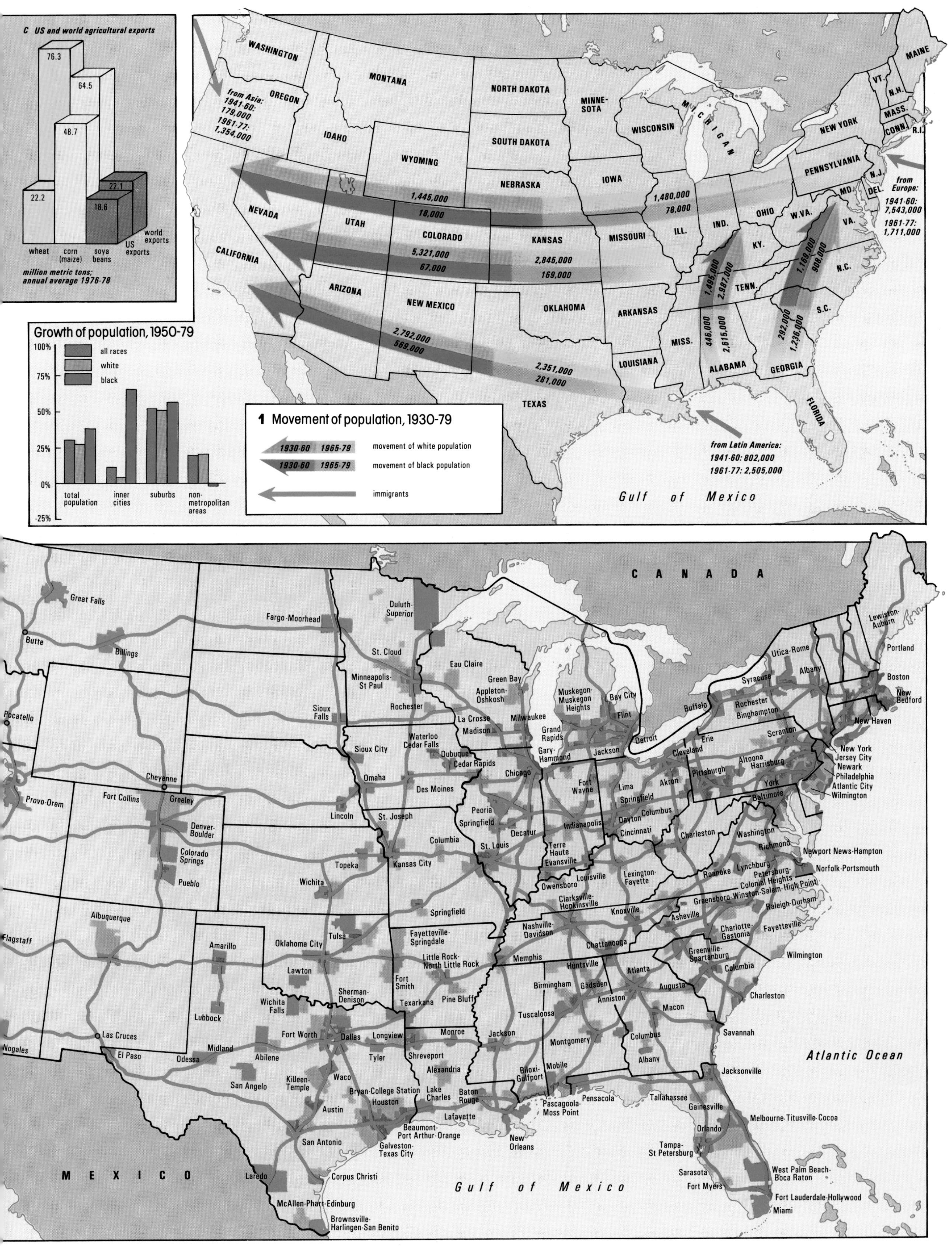

C US and world agricultural exports
76.3
64.5
48.7
22.2
22.1
18.6
wheat
corn (maize)
soya beans
world exports
US exports
million metric tons; annual average 1976-78
Growth of population, 1950-79
100%
75%
50%
25%
0%
-25%
all races
white
black
total population
inner cities
suburbs
non-metropolitan areas
1 Movement of population, 1930-79
1930-60
1965-79
movement of white population
movement of black population
immigrants
WASHINGTON
OREGON
MONTANA
IDAHO
WYOMING
NORTH DAKOTA
SOUTH DAKOTA
NEBRASKA
MINNESOTA
WISCONSIN
MICHIGAN
IOWA
NEW YORK
PENNSYLVANIA
MAINE
VT.
N.H.
MASS.
CONN.
R.I.
N.J.
DEL.
MD.
NEVADA
UTAH
COLORADO
KANSAS
MISSOURI
ILL.
IND.
OHIO
W.VA.
VA.
KY.
CALIFORNIA
ARIZONA
NEW MEXICO
OKLAHOMA
ARKANSAS
TENN.
N.C.
S.C.
MISS.
ALABAMA
GEORGIA
LOUISIANA
TEXAS
FLORIDA
from Asia: 1941-60: 179,000 1961-77: 1,354,000
from Europe: 1941-60: 7,543,000 1961-77: 1,711,000
from Latin America: 1941-60: 802,000 1961-77: 2,505,000
1,445,000
18,000
1,480,000
78,000
5,321,000
67,000
2,845,000
169,000
2,792,000
569,000
2,351,000
281,000
1,495,000
2,997,000
446,000
2,615,000
1,189,000
908,000
292,000
1,236,000
Gulf of Mexico
CANADA
Great Falls
Butte
Billings
Pocatello
Fargo-Moorhead
Duluth-Superior
St. Cloud
Minneapolis-St Paul
Eau Claire
Green Bay
Appleton-Oshkosh
Rochester
Sioux Falls
La Crosse
Madison
Milwaukee
Muskegon-Muskegon Heights
Bay City
Flint
Grand Rapids
Detroit
Buffalo
Syracuse
Utica-Rome
Albany
Lewiston-Auburn
Portland
Boston
New Bedford
Rochester
Binghampton
New Haven
Erie
Scranton
Cleveland
Sioux City
Waterloo Cedar Falls
Dubuque
Cedar Rapids
Chicago
Gary-Hammond
Jackson
Toledo
Pittsburgh
Altoona
Harrisburg
New York
Jersey City
Newark
Philadelphia
Atlantic City
Wilmington
Cheyenne
Provo-Orem
Fort Collins
Greeley
Omaha
Des Moines
Fort Wayne
Lima
Akron
York
Baltimore
Denver-Boulder
Lincoln
St. Joseph
Peoria
Springfield
Springfield
Dayton
Columbus
Indianapolis
Washington
Colorado Springs
Decatur
Terre Haute
Cincinnati
Charleston
Richmond
Newport News-Hampton
Pueblo
Topeka
Kansas City
Columbia
St. Louis
Evansville
Owensboro
Louisville
Lexington-Fayette
Roanoke
Lynchburg
Petersburg-Colonial Heights
Norfolk-Portsmouth
Wichita
Greensboro-Winston-Salem-High Point
Raleigh-Durham
Clarksville-Hopkinsville
Knoxville
Asheville
Springfield
Albuquerque
Tulsa
Fayetteville-Springdale
Nashville-Davidson
Charlotte-Gastonia
Fayetteville
Flagstaff
Amarillo
Oklahoma City
Little Rock-North Little Rock
Chattanooga
Memphis
Greenville-Spartanburg
Wilmington
Lawton
Fort Smith
Huntsville
Atlanta
Columbia
Birmingham
Gadsden
Augusta
Sherman-Denison
Texarkana
Pine Bluff
Anniston
Charleston
Wichita Falls
Lubbock
Tuscaloosa
Macon
Las Cruces
Fort Worth
Dallas
Longview
Monroe
Jackson
Savannah
Nogales
El Paso
Odessa
Midland
Abilene
Tyler
Shreveport
Montgomery
Columbus
Albany
Atlantic Ocean
Alexandria
Mobile
Biloxi-Gulfport
Jacksonville
San Angelo
Killeen-Temple
Waco
Bryan-College Station
Lake Charles
Baton Rouge
Pensacola
Tallahassee
Pascagoola-Moss Point
Gainesville
Austin
Houston
Lafayette
Melbourne-Titusville-Cocoa
Beaumont-Port Arthur-Orange
Orlando
San Antonio
Galveston-Texas City
New Orleans
Tampa-St Petersburg
MEXICO
Laredo
Corpus Christi
Sarasota
Fort Myers
West Palm Beach-Boca Raton
Gulf of Mexico
McAllen-Pharr-Edinburg
Fort Lauderdale-Hollywood
Miami
Brownsville-Harlingen-San Benito

The Soviet Union

1926-1991

By the time of Lenin's death in 1924 the new Bolshevik state had survived the perils of civil war and foreign intervention (page 120). The future character of the Soviet Union was decided principally by the policies introduced by Stalin after 1928: the first Five Year Plan and the forced collectivisation of agriculture, both implemented with massive brutality. Collective farming claimed at least 2–3 million victims. Nevertheless, by 1939 a much reduced agricultural population was tilling a larger area than in 1929 and getting a harvest 20 per cent bigger. The surplus population moved into industry. Between 1926 and 1940 the industrial labour force grew by 30 million, and output increased enormously, providing the Soviet Union with the industrial basis to withstand the German onslaught in 1941.

The war against Germany (page 132), in which some 20 million Russians perished, caused immense devastation; 1,700 towns and 70,000 villages were destroyed. But major new industrial centres, such as Magnitogorsk in the southern Urals and Stalinsk (Novokuznetsk) on the Kuzbass coalfield (map 1), were beyond the reach of the German armies, and during the war more than 1,000 important factories were evacuated from western Russia to the Urals and beyond. Nevertheless the setback was undeniable. Industrial production was down by over 30 per cent in 1946 as compared with 1940. What was remarkable was the speed of recovery. By 1953 the pre-war level was passed, but at immense human cost. Massive reparations, particularly from eastern Germany, accounted in part for the recovery, but more important was the large-scale use of forced labour, drafted into the hitherto barren north and north-east. The result was a shift in the centre of economic gravity and the foundation of towns far from the old industrial centres. But the onset of the Cold War (page 148) necessitated a diversion of productive capacity to armaments and, as in the pre-war period, heavy industry was the priority. The improvement of living standards lagged far behind. Agriculture was neglected. In 1953, grain production still hovered around its 1913 level.

Stalin's death in 1953 brought an immediate reaction against his heavy-handed rule, even more marked after Khrushchev's denunciation of Stalinism at the 20th Party Congress in 1956. Under Khrushchev (1955–64) there was genuine relaxation, both abroad, where the reduction of Cold War tension seemed to open new prospects, and at home. At the 21st and 22nd Party Congresses (1959, 1961) Khrushchev held out glowing promises of a future of plenty. In fact, Khrushchev's crash programme to open up the 'virgin lands' of Siberia and Kazakhstan failed to live up to expectations, and in 1963 it was necessary to import grain from Canada. Simultaneously, renewed tension with the United States, culminating in the Cuban missile crisis (page 148), enforced a further shift of productive capacity back to armaments. In addition, Soviet industrial growth slowed significantly. These setbacks sealed Khrushchev's fate. Under Kosygin (1964–80) and Brezhnev (1964–82) there was no abrupt reversal of direction. The Soviet economy continued to expand: between 1960 and 1980 oil production quadrupled; steel output doubled; grain harvests trebled. Nonetheless, increasingly the Soviet Union abandoned its role as the centre of world revolution to face its mounting economic problems.

By Brezhnev's death popular pressure for reform was growing. A cautious start was made under his successors, notably Andropov (1982–84). Under Gorbachev (1985–91) the pace quickened dramatically. Paradoxically, reform tended only to highlight the country's economic weaknesses and, by allowing greater freedoms, to encourage nationalist disturbances. The subsequent eclipse of the Communist Party, accompanied by what had now become a massive economic crisis and the imminent break-up of the union, prompted a conservative backlash in August 1991. Quickly put down, the attempted coup sparked the final disintegration of the Soviet Union as republic after republic, taking their cues principally from Russia itself and the now-independent Baltic republics, declared independence and allegiance to democracy. By Christmas 1991 Gorbachev was forced to resign. Lenin's revolution was over.

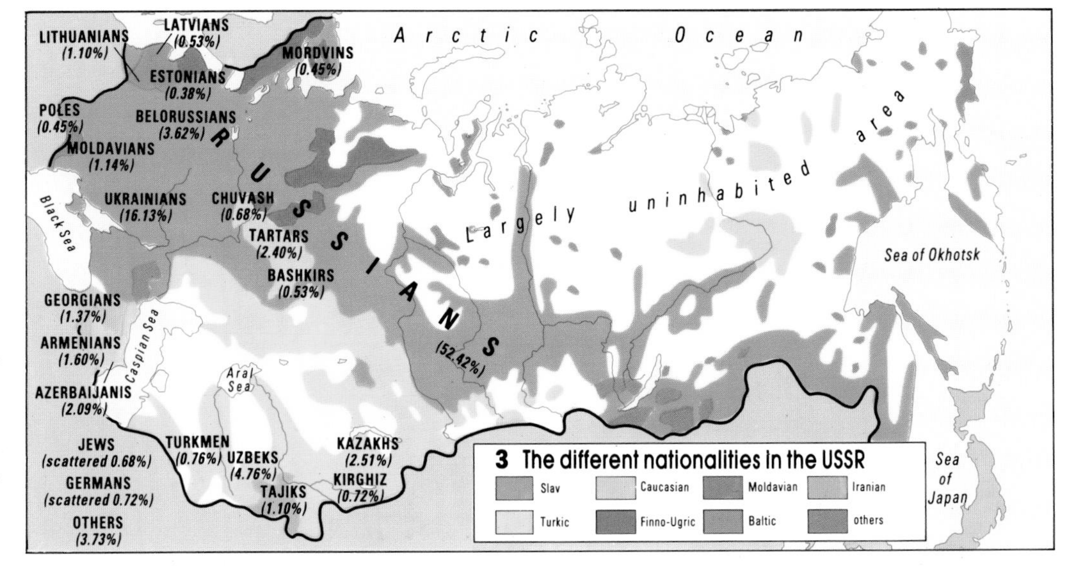

3 The different nationalities in the USSR

2 The constituent republics

1 Industrial expansion 1926-80
coal mining
lignite mining
petroleum extraction
natural gas extraction
oil shale mining
iron ore mining
electricity generation
integrated iron and steel industry
steel making
non-ferrous metal industry
metal working and machine building industry
chemical industry
periods of industrial expansion:
1926-1940
1941-1945
1946-1980
S I B E R I A
R U S S I A
K A Z A K H S T A N
UKRAINE
BELORUSSIA
BALTIC REGION
DONBASS
KUZBASS
W. SIBERIAN OILFIELD
LOWER OB GASFIELD
VOLGA-URAL OILFIELD
CENTRAL ASIAN GASFIELD
forced labour camps operated in Siberia during Stalin's rule 1928-1953
Arctic Ocean
Arctic Circle
MONGOLIA
CHINA
KOREA
JAPAN
IRAN
AFGHANISTAN
TURKEY
FINLAND
POLAND
CZECHOSLOVAKIA
ROMANIA
BULGARIA
Caspian Sea
Black Sea
Aral Sea
Baltic Sea
Sea of Azov
White Sea
Ural Mts
Caucasus Mts
Moscow
Leningrad
Sverdlovsk
Magnitogorsk
Novokuznetsk
Novosibirsk
Kiev
Baku
Vladivostok
Tokyo
Peking
Istanbul

The Cold War from 1947

With the elimination of Germany, Japan and Italy and the weakening of Great Britain and France in the Second World War, the USA and the USSR emerged as the two 'super-powers'. The Cold War was the expression of their political and ideological confrontation. Conflict was already visible before the end of the war. In view of the US monopoly of the atom-bomb and the potential threat it implied for the USSR, Stalin decided, after the failure of the Potsdam Conference (July–Aug. 1945), to consolidate Soviet control in eastern Europe (page 136). In reply, the USA built up the defence of western Europe, with the formation of the North Atlantic Treaty Organisation (NATO) in 1949.

Starting as a conflict over central Europe and divided Germany, the Cold War soon developed into a global confrontation. For the United States the Korean War (1950) was evidence of a world-wide Communist conspiracy, although, in fact, the Chinese only intervened when the American advance to the Yalu river seemed to threaten their security (map 2); but American policy hereafter was to 'contain' the Communist powers by a series of encircling alliances. NATO was followed by SEATO (South-East Asia Treaty Organisation, 1954) and the Baghdad Pact (1955), converted into CENTO (Central Treaty Organisation) in 1959. By this time the USA had over 1400 foreign bases, including 275 bases for nuclear bombers, in 31 countries around the Soviet perimeter (map 1). Meanwhile the USSR had acquired nuclear weapons (A-bomb 1949, H-bomb 1953), and when it launched the first space satellite (Sputnik) in 1957, a new dimension was added. Although the intercontinental ballistic missile (ICBM) did not make the American bases obsolete, it meant that, in the event of nuclear war, each of the two super-powers could attack the other's cities directly. The resulting 'nuclear stalemate' enforced a gradual reappraisal.

There were other contributory factors. The monolithic blocs were showing signs of strain, evidenced on the Soviet side by Polish and Hungarian uprisings (1956) and growing signs of a Sino-Soviet rift. In western Europe, France under General de Gaulle rejected American political leadership after 1958. Furthermore, the Baghdad Pact, far from increasing security in the Middle East, divided it into hostile camps, opening it, after America declined to finance the Aswan high dam and after the Suez War (1956), to Soviet influence (map 4). For the USA the Cuban revolution (1959) posed more immediate problems. When, after an unsuccessful attempt by US-supported dissidents to unseat Fidel Castro, the USSR sent nuclear missiles to Cuba, war seemed imminent, until Khrushchev agreed (Oct. 26, 1962) to their removal (map 5). But in Indo-China, where the US had refused in 1954 to endorse the settlement of the long anti-colonial war against France (page 138) and had set up a counter-revolutionary regime in Saigon, the situation remained tense. In the end the US was forced to intervene directly, and by 1968 some 543,000 American ground troops, as well as substantial naval and air forces, were committed. But this failed to defeat the guerrilla tactics of the Vietnamese National Liberation Front (map 3), and in 1973, with the US economy under severe pressure, President Nixon called a halt. In 1972 Nixon signed the first SALT treaty limiting nuclear armaments, but after the Soviet invasion of Afghanistan (1979) a new arms race began, culminating in the controversial US 'Star Wars' programme. A new era of super-power co-operation began under Reagan and Gorbachev, which led to agreement to reduce nuclear arsenals. Soviet withdrawal from Afghanistan and from eastern Europe, and joint agreement on a re-unification of Germany in 1990 brought the 'classical' Cold War to an end.

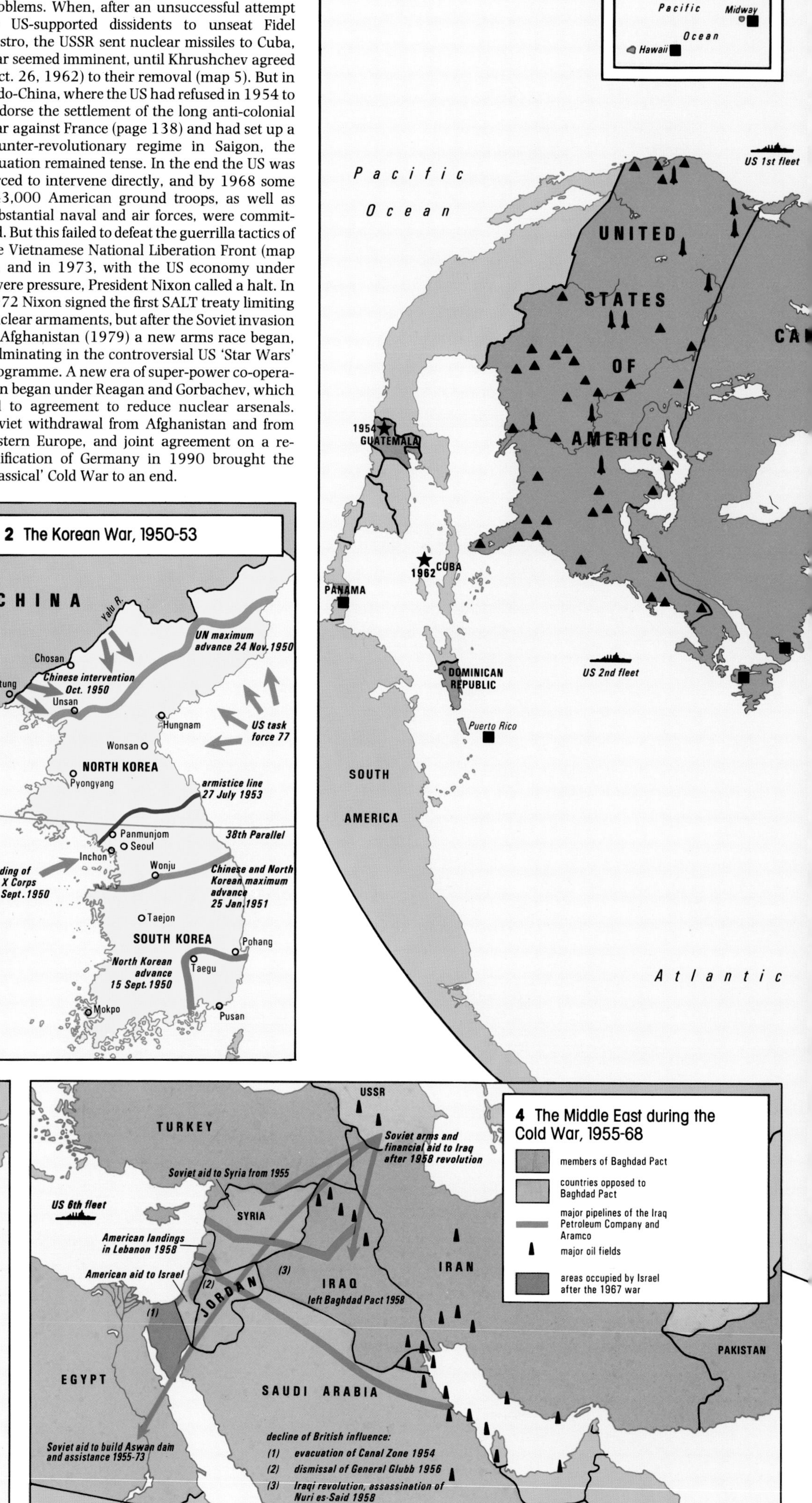

2 The Korean War, 1950-53

4 The Middle East during the Cold War, 1955-68

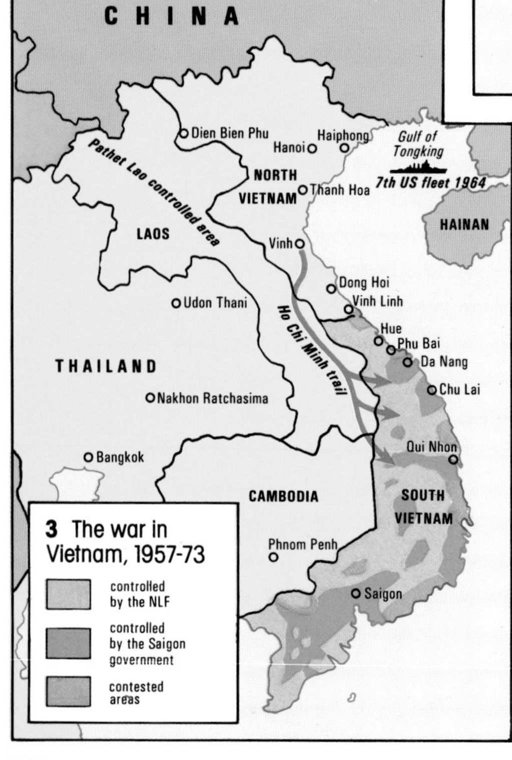

3 The war in Vietnam, 1957-73

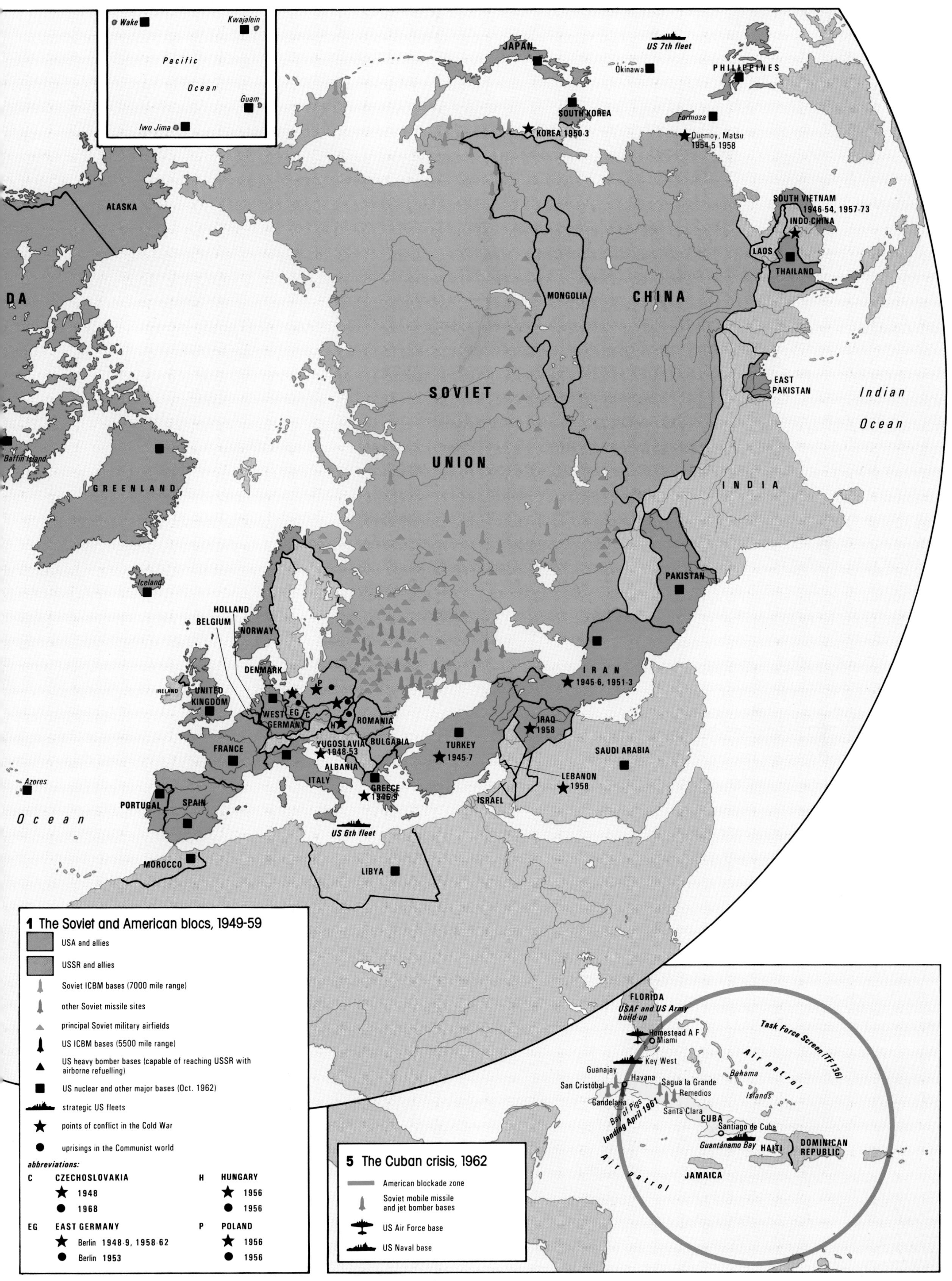

Wake
Kwajalein
Pacific
Ocean
Guam
Iwo Jima
JAPAN
US 7th fleet
Okinawa
PHILIPPINES
SOUTH KOREA
Formosa
KOREA 1950-3
Quemoy, Matsu 1954-5 1958
ALASKA
SOUTH VIETNAM 1946-54, 1957-73
INDO-CHINA
LAOS
THAILAND
MONGOLIA
CHINA
DA
EAST PAKISTAN
Indian Ocean
SOVIET UNION
Baffin Island
GREENLAND
INDIA
Iceland
PAKISTAN
HOLLAND
BELGIUM
NORWAY
IRAN 1945-6, 1951-3
DENMARK
IRELAND
UNITED KINGDOM
P
WEST GERMANY
EG
C
H
ROMANIA
IRAQ 1958
YUGOSLAVIA 1948-53
BULGARIA
TURKEY 1945-7
FRANCE
SAUDI ARABIA
ALBANIA
LEBANON 1958
Azores
ITALY
GREECE 1946-9
PORTUGAL
SPAIN
ISRAEL
Ocean
US 6th fleet
MOROCCO
LIBYA
1 The Soviet and American blocs, 1949-59
USA and allies
USSR and allies
Soviet ICBM bases (7000 mile range)
other Soviet missile sites
principal Soviet military airfields
US ICBM bases (5500 mile range)
US heavy bomber bases (capable of reaching USSR with airborne refuelling)
US nuclear and other major bases (Oct. 1962)
strategic US fleets
points of conflict in the Cold War
uprisings in the Communist world
abbreviations:
C CZECHOSLOVAKIA
1948
1968
H HUNGARY
1956
1956
EG EAST GERMANY
Berlin 1948-9, 1958-62
Berlin 1953
P POLAND
1956
1956
FLORIDA
USAF and US Army build-up
Homestead A F
Miami
Task Force Screen (TF 136)
Key West
Air patrol
Guanajay
Bahama
Havana
Sagua la Grande
San Cristóbal
Remedios
Islands
Candelaria
Bay of Pigs landing April 1961
Santa Clara
CUBA
Santiago de Cuba
Guantánamo Bay
HAITI
DOMINICAN REPUBLIC
JAMAICA
Air patrol
5 The Cuban crisis, 1962
American blockade zone
Soviet mobile missile and jet bomber bases
US Air Force base
US Naval base

The world in the 1990s

For forty years after 1945 the world was dominated by the rival blocs headed by the United States and the Soviet Union and by confident expectations of increasing economic growth. From the mid-1980s, both collapsed. The fall of the USSR and prolonged recession transformed the world.

The collapse of the Soviet system and ending of the Cold War at the end of the 1980s were initially welcomed as an end to tyranny. Hopes that east and west would converge and democracy and economic liberalism triumph worldwide were widespread. These expectations were soon dashed. The global economy, in part adversely affected by the economic ruin of the former Soviet bloc, grew fitfully. Massive international debts, especially in the developing world, and high unemployment became commonplace. The gap between rich and poor nations widened further, prompting discontent and instability in the latter (map 1).

The stability of much of Africa, Latin America and Asia was also threatened by rapid population growth, with 90 million added to their populations every year (chart 3). Coupled with economic mismanagement, this produced persistent famine in Africa and even faster destruction of forested areas in an attempt to increase agricultural land. In tandem with high levels of industrial pollution in the developed world, the loss of areas such as these led to further damage to the environment.

Failures to tackle global problems effectively contributed to another feature of the 1990s: declining confidence in the state and established political institutions. If the disintegration of state power in the Soviet bloc demonstrated this most clearly (map 4), even in the west there was a growing sense that governments were helpless in the face of worldwide problems. With confidence in the rule of law undermined further by evidence of institutionalised political corruption in countries such as Japan and Italy, voters almost everywhere drifted towards more radical parties.

One result of this crisis of confidence was a move towards political fragmentation. In Europe, Czechoslovakia broke up along ethnic lines and Yugoslavia disintegrated into half-a-dozen republics (pages 136–7). In the former Soviet Union small separatist movements sprang up throughout the new states. Ethnic conflict also continued in the Middle East, India and southern Africa.

The crisis of legitimacy was also evident in the spread of organised crime and 'warlordism'. The most striking example was the spread of the illicit trade in drugs (map 1). By 1992 this was worth an estimated $500 billion, and provided relative prosperity in countries such as Bolivia and Colombia, where prospects for more normal trade development were poor. In Peru, a coca farmer could earn ten times more from an acre of land than a coffee farmer. In the former Soviet Union, it was estimated that three million acres were devoted to marijuana. In turn, the drug trade provoked further layers of criminality in the laundering of drug earnings and in rising crime rates in the developed world.

Elsewhere, warlords emerged in areas where legitimate central government had broken down or where corruption on a vast scale came to replace the more normal operation of the market. In Somalia, in former Yugoslavia, in Lebanon, in Afghanistan and in much of Central Asia the rule of law disintegrated amid violent conflict between rival gangs using terror to gain economic advantage. The spread of violence of this kind also helped fuel a growing refugee problem. In 1992 there were an estimated 38 million refugees across the world, most living in makeshift camps with little food or medical aid. Much of the progress made in the 1980s in the promotion of human rights was reversed. State terror, private corruption and local brigandage were still the lot of a large fraction of the world's population.

The international order inevitably altered in this climate of uncertainty. Despite the ending of the Cold War and subsequent scaling down of their nuclear arsenals by the US and the states of the former Soviet Union (page 148), the spread of nuclear weapons remained an acute concern. The struggle for control of the former Soviet arsenal was a source of continuing tension while other states, notably Pakistan and North Korea, already possessed or were poised to develop nuclear weapons. China, meanwhile, which had weathered the collapse of the Soviet Union with apparent impunity, found itself the new super-power of Asia. With vast military resources and an economy growing faster than that of any other industrial power's, its elevation underlined the rapidly increasing might of east Asia, an apparently decisive tilt in the balance of world power.

But if the world in the 1990s was in a critical state of transition, there were hopeful signs. The position of the United Nations, for example, was enhanced by its greater willingness to take initiatives, notably in the Gulf War even if interventions in Somalia and Bosnia were less successful. International cooperation was successfully demonstrated, too, in the 'Earth Summit' in Rio de Janiero in 1992, in which 185 nations assembled to tackle the problems of global pollution. And in December 1993, after years of negotiation, agreement was reached through GATT on a liberalization of world trade designed to end the period of economic stagnation. Nonetheless, the world remained poised between economic stabilisation and political cooperation on the one hand and nationalism, state decline and economic crisis on the other.

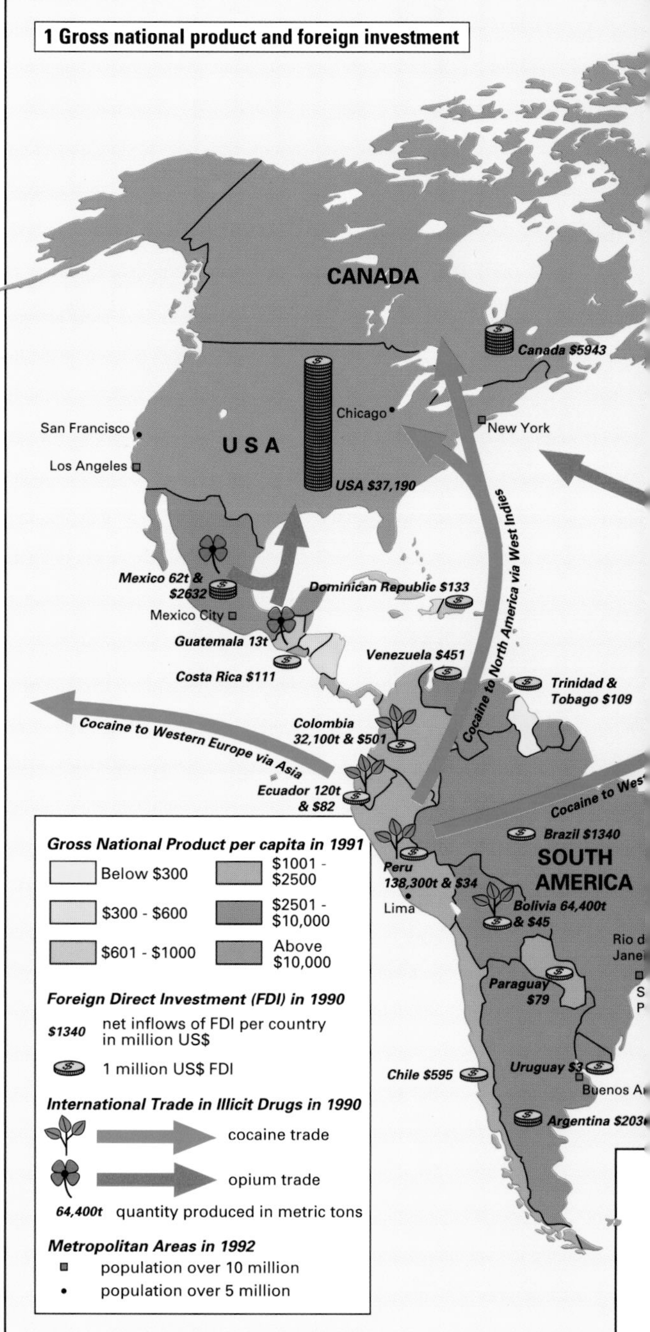

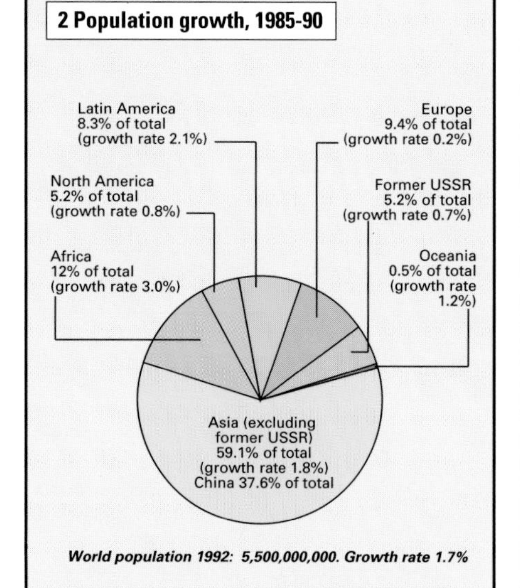

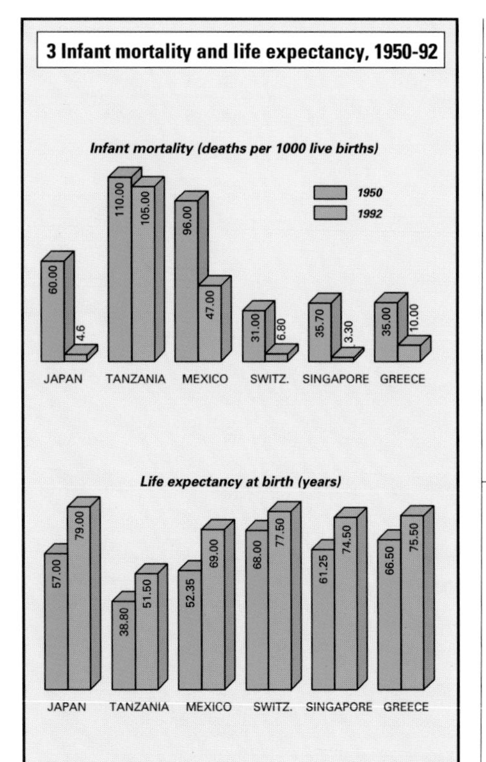

Republic	Date of Independence	GDP per head (US$)	Form of Government (1992)
Armenia	September 1991	2,000	democracy
Azerbaijan	October 1991	2,300	democratic coalition (Popular Front)
Belorussia	August 1991	4,763	reformed communism
Estonia	August 1991	5,209	democratic coalition
Georgia	April 1991	2,000	democracy rules by State Council
Kazakhstan	December 1991	3,786	reformed communism
Kyrgyzstan	August 1991	2,062	democratic coalition
Latvia	September 1991	4,500	democratic coalition
Lithuania	August 1991	3,759	reformed communism
Moldova	August 1991	2,762	democracy under Popular Front
Russia		4,325	Presidential democracy
Tajikistan	August 1991	1,220	reformed communism
Turkmenistan	October 1991	2,509	reformed communism
Ukraine	August 1991	3,560	democratic nationalist
Uzbekistan	August 1991	1,925	authoritarian communism

Distribution of population by ethnic origin

Armenia	Armenians 93.3% Azeris 5% Russians 1.5%
Azerbaijan	Azeris 82.7% Russians 6%
Belorussia	Belorussians 78% Russians 13%
Estonia	Estonians 61.2% Russians 30.3%
Georgia	Georgians 70% Armenians 8.1% Russians 6.3%
Kazakhstan	Kazakhs 39.7% Russians 37.8% Germans 5.8% Ukrainians 5.4%
Kyrgyzstan	Kyrgyz 52% Russians 21% Uzbeks 13%
Latvia	Latvians 51.8% Russians 34%
Lithuania	Lithuanians 82% Russians 9%
Moldova	Moldovans 64.5% Ukrainians 13.8% Russians 13% Gagauz 3.5%
Russia	Russians 82% Tartars 3.8% Ukrainians 3%
Tajikistan	Tajiks 58% Uzbeks 23% Russians 8%
Turkmenistan	Turkmen 72% Russians 9.5%
Ukraine	Ukrainians 72% Russians 22%
Uzbekistan	Uzbeks 71.4% Russians 8.3% Tajiks & Karakalpak nomads 20.3%

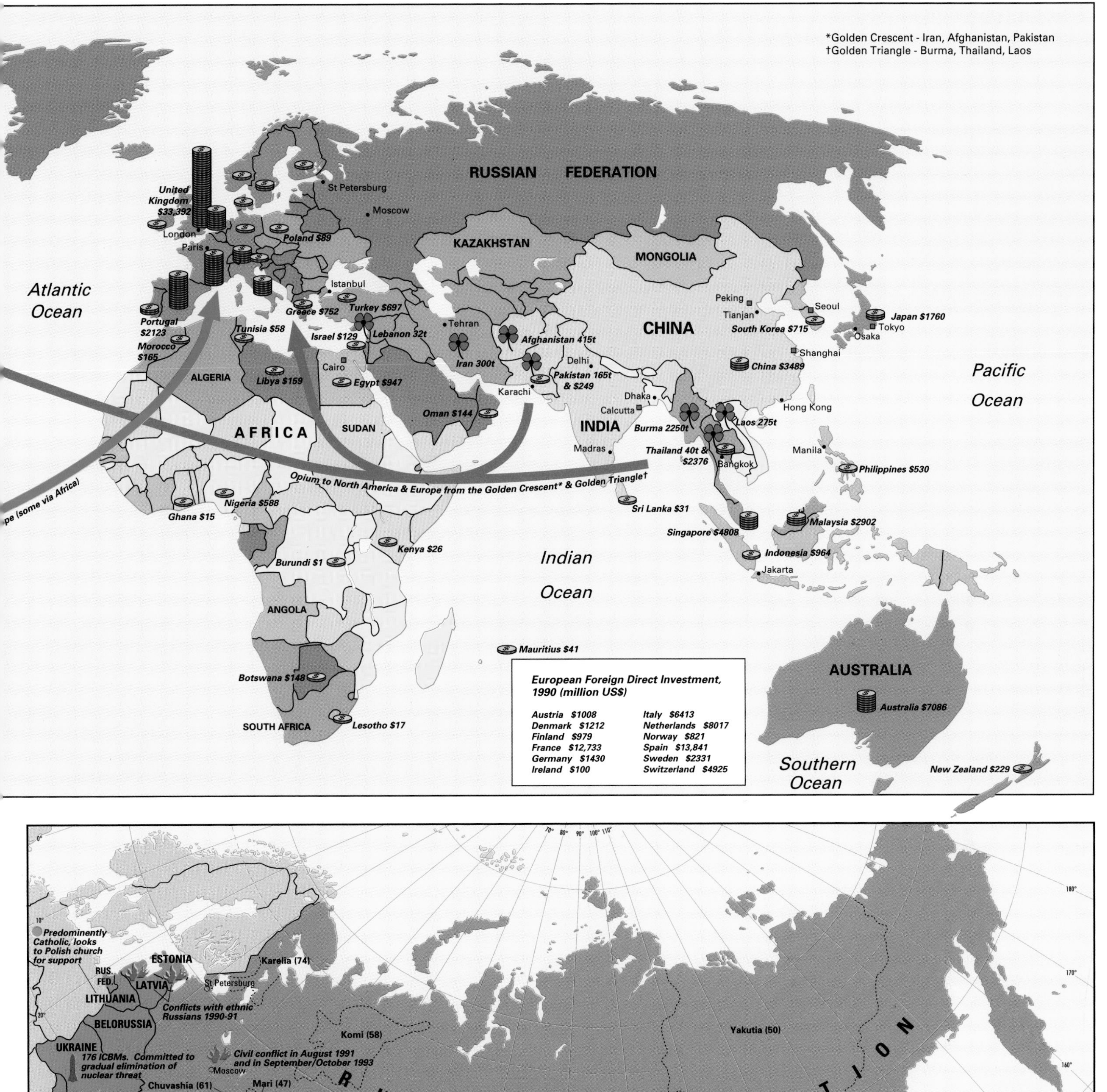
*Golden Crescent - Iran, Afghanistan, Pakistan
†Golden Triangle - Burma, Thailand, Laos
RUSSIAN FEDERATION
St Petersburg
Moscow
United Kingdom $33,392
London
Paris
Poland $89
KAZAKHSTAN
MONGOLIA
Atlantic Ocean
Istanbul
Greece $752
Turkey $697
Portugal $2123
Morocco $165
Tunisia $58
Israel $129
Lebanon 32t
Tehran
Iran 300t
Afghanistan 415t
CHINA
Peking
Tianjan
Seoul
South Korea $715
Japan $1760
Tokyo
Osaka
Shanghai
China $3489
Pacific Ocean
Cairo
Egypt $947
ALGERIA
Libya $159
Delhi
Pakistan 165t & $249
Karachi
Dhaka
Calcutta
Hong Kong
Oman $144
INDIA
Burma 2250t
Laos 275t
AFRICA
SUDAN
Madras
Thailand 40t & $2376
Bangkok
Manila
Philippines $530
Opium to North America & Europe from the Golden Crescent* & Golden Triangle†
pe (some via Africa)
Nigeria $588
Ghana $15
Sri Lanka $31
Singapore $4808
Malaysia $2902
Kenya $26
Burundi $1
Indian Ocean
Indonesia $964
Jakarta
ANGOLA
Mauritius $41
Botswana $148
AUSTRALIA
Australia $7086
SOUTH AFRICA
Lesotho $17
Southern Ocean
New Zealand $229
European Foreign Direct Investment, 1990 (million US$)
Austria $1008
Denmark $1212
Finland $979
France $12,733
Germany $1430
Ireland $100
Italy $6413
Netherlands $8017
Norway $821
Spain $13,841
Sweden $2331
Switzerland $4925

Predominently Catholic, looks to Polish church for support
ESTONIA
RUS. FED.
LATVIA
LITHUANIA
Karelia (74)
St Petersburg
Conflicts with ethnic Russians 1990-91
BELORUSSIA
UKRAINE
176 ICBMs. Committed to gradual elimination of nuclear threat
Komi (58)
Yakutia (50)
Civil conflict in August 1991 and in September/October 1993
Moscow
MOLDOVA
Chuvashia (61)
Mari (47)
Udmurtia (59)
Mordovia (61)
Tatarstan (43)
RUSSIAN FEDERATION
Racial conflict between Moldavians and Russians/Ukrainians in Transdniestr 1990-92; separatist movements in Transdniestr and in Comrat where Gagauz seek separate state
Bashkiria (39)
Adygei (68)
Kalmykia (38)
Muslim separatist movement in Abkhazia
Karachai-Circassia (42)
Violent conflict between nationalists and democrats 1991/92; separatist movements in South Ossetia and Abkhazia
Karbardino-Balkaria (32)
Chechnya-Ingushia (23)
N.Ossetia (30)
GEORGIA
Dagestan (9)
ARMENIA
KAZAKHSTAN
140 ICBMs, 40 strategic bombers. Co-operates on defence with Russia
Violent racial clashes from 1988 with Armenians; domestic civil conflict 1992
AZERBAIJAN
Khakassia (79)
Buryatia (70)
Gorno-Altai (60)
Tuva (32)
Violent racial clashes from 1988 with Azeris
Armenian Apostolic Church opposed to Islamic revival
UZBEKISTAN
TURKMENISTAN
Violent racial conflict between Kyrgyz and Uzbeks from 1990
KYRGYZSTAN
TAJIKISTAN
Political conflict between pro-communists and Islamic revivalists from 1991; racial conflict between Tajiks and Uzbeks from 1992; separatist movement in Gorno-Badakhstan
Islamic Renaissance Party led civil violence against ex-Communist regime
4 The successor states of the Soviet Union
former non-Russian Soviet socialist republics
Komi autonomous republics within the Russian Federation
75 percentage of Russians within autonomous republics
regional conflicts
religious conflicts
former Soviet-controlled nuclear weapons outside Russia

Acknowledgements

ACKNOWLEDGEMENTS AND BIBLIOGRAPHY

We have pleasure in acknowledging the following:

Map 5, page 76, is based, with kind permission, on map 2, page 107 in *Grosser Atlas Zur Weltgeschichte*, Westermann

Map 5, page 111, is based, with the kind permission of George Philip & Son Ltd, on page 215 of *The New Cambridge Modern History Atlas* H.C. Darby, H. Fullard (eds.)

Among the large number of works consulted by contributors, the following contain valuable maps and other data that have been particularly useful:

I. History Atlases

Atlas zur Geschichte 2 vols. Leipzig 1976
Bazilevsky, K.V., Golubtsov, A., Zinoviev, M.A. *Atlas Istorii SSR*, Moscow 1952
Beckingham, C.F. *Atlas of the Arab World and the Middle East*, London 1960
Bertin, J. (et al) *Atlas of Food Crops*, Paris 1971
Bjørklund, O., Holmboe, H., Røhr, A. *Historical Atlas of the World*, Edinburgh 1970
Cappon, L. (et al) *Atlas of Early American History*, Chicago 1976
Darby, H. C., Fullard, H. (eds.) *The New Cambridge Modern History* vol. XIV: Atlas, Cambridge 1970
Davies, C.C. *An Historical Atlas of the Indian Peninsula*, London 1959
Engel, J. (ed.) *Grosser Historischer Weltatlas* 3 vols. Munich 1953–81
Fage, J.D. *An Atlas of African History*, London 1958
Gilbert, M. *Russian History Atlas*, London 1972
Gilbert, M. *Recent History Atlas 1860–1960*, London 1966
Gilbert, M. *First World War Atlas*, London 1970
Gilbert, M. *Jewish History Atlas*, London 1969
Hazard, H.W. *Atlas of Islamic History*, Princeton 1952
Herrmann, A. *Historical and Commercial Atlas of China*, Havard 1935
Herrmann, A. *An Historical Atlas of China*, Edinburgh 1966
Jedin, H., Latourette, K.S., Martin, J. *Atlas zur Kirchengeschichte*, Freiburg 1970
Joppen, C., Garrett, H.L.O. *Historical Atlas of India*, London 1938
Kinder, H., Hilgermann, W. *DTV Atlas zur Weltgeschichte* 2 vols. Stuttgart 1964
Matsui and Mori *Ajiarekishi chizu*, Tokyo 1965
May, H.G. (ed.) *Oxford Bible Atlas*, Oxford 1974
Nelson's Atlas of the Early Christian World, London 1959
Nelson's Atlas of World History, London 1965
Nihon rekishi jiten Atlas vol., Tokyo 1959
Palmer, R.R. (ed.) *Atlas of World History*, Chicago 1965
Paullin, C.O. *Atlas of the Historical Geography of the United States*, Washington 1932
Ragi al Faruqi, I. *Historical Atlas of the Religions of the World*, New York 1974
Roolvink, R. *Historical Atlas of the Muslim Peoples*, London 1957
Schwartzberg, J.E. (ed.) *A Historical Atlas of South Asia* Chicago 1978
Shepherd, W.R. *Historical Atlas*, New York 1964
Toynbee, A.J., Myers, E.D. *A Study of History, Historical Atlas and Gazetteer*, Oxford 1959
Treharne, R.F., Fullard, H. (eds.) *Muir's Historical Atlas*, London 1966
Van der Heyden, A.M., Scullard, H.H. *Atlas of the Classical World*, London 1959
Wesley, E.B. *Our United States .... its History in Maps*, Chicago 1977
Westermann *Grosser Atlas zur Weltgeschichte*, Brunswick 1978
Whitehouse, D. & R. *Archaeological Atlas of the World*, London 1975
Wilgus, A.C. *Latin America in Maps*, New York 1943

II. General Works

Ahzweiler, H. *L'Asie Mineure et les Invasions Arabes*, Revue Historique 1962
Ajayi, J.F.A., Crowder, M. *History of West Africa* vols. 1 & 2 London 1974
Allchin, B. & R. *The Birth of Indian Civilisation*, London 1968
Australia, Commonwealth of, Department of National Development, *Atlas of Australian Resources*
Barraclough, G. *Medieval Germany*, Oxford 1938
Basham, A.L. *The Wonder that was India*, London 1967
Beresford, M. *New Towns of the Middle Ages*, London 1967
Berney, M. (ed.) *Australia*, Sydney 1965
Bloch, M. *Les Caractères Originaux de l'Histoire Rurale Française*, Oslo 1931
Boisselier, J. *La Statuaire du Champa*, Paris 1963
Bury, J.B., Cook, S.A., Adcock, F.E. (eds.) *The Cambridge Ancient History*, Cambridge 1923–
Bury, J.B., Gwatkin, H.M., Whitney, J.P. (eds.) *The Cambridge Medieval History*, Cambridge 1911
Chang, K.C. *The Archaeology of Ancient China*, New Haven & London 1968
Cheng Te-k'un *Archaeology in China*, Cambridge 1959
Churchill, Winston S. *The Second World War*, London 1948–53
Coedès, G. *Les Etats Hindouisés de l'Indochine et d'Indonésie*, Paris 1964
Cook, M.A. (ed.) *A History of the Ottoman Empire to 1730*, Cambridge 1974
Cresswell, K.A.C. *A Short Account of Early Muslim Architecture*, Oxford 1958
Crowder, M. *West Africa under Colonial Rule*, London 1968
Cumberland, K.B. *Aotearoa Maori: New Zealand about 1780*, Geographical Review no. 39
Curtin, P. de A. *The Atlantic Slave Trade*, Wisconsin 1969
Dalton, B.J. *War and Politics in New Zealand 1855–1870*, Sydney 1967
Darby, H.C. (ed.) *An Historical Geography of England before AD 1800*, Cambridge 1936 & 1960
Despois, J., Raynal, R. *Géographie de l'Afrique du Nord*, Paris 1967
Dyos, H.J., Aldcroft, D.H. *British Transport*, Leicester 1969
East, W.G. *The Geography behind History*, London 1965
East, W.G. *An Historical Geography of Europe*, London 1966
Edwardes, M. *A History of India*, London 1961
Evans, B.L. *Agricultural and Pastoral Statistics of New Zealand 1861–1954*, Wellington 1956
Ferguson, J. *The Heritage of Hellenism*, London 1973
Fisher, C.A. *South-East Asia*, London 1964
Fletcher, A. *Tudor Rebellions*, London 1968
Fowler, K. *The Age of Plantagenet and Valois*, New York 1967
Fourquin, G. *Histoire Economique de l'Occident Médiéval*, Paris 1969
Ganshof, F.L. *Etude sur le Développement des Villes entre Loire et Rhin au Moyen Age*, Paris–Brussels 1943
Geelan, P.J.M., Twitchett, D.C. (eds.) *The Times Atlas of China*, London 1974
Gernet, J. *Le Monde Chinois*, Paris 1969
Grousset, R. *The Empire of the Steppes: A History of Central Asia*, New Brunswick N.J. 1970
Guillermaz, J. *Histoire du Parti Communiste Chinois*, Paris 1968
Hall, D.G.E. *A History of South-East Asia*, London 1968
Harlan, J.R. *The Plants and Animals that Nourish Man*, Scientific American 1976
Harlan, J.R., Zohary, D. *The Distribution of Wild Wheats and Barleys*, Science 1966
Hatton, R.M. *Europe in the age of Louis XIV*, London 1969
Henderson, W.O. *Britain and Industrial Europe 1750–1870*, Liverpool 1954
Hopkins, A.G. *Economic History of West Africa*, London 1973
Inalcik, H. *The Ottoman Empire: The Classical Age 1300–1600*, London 1973
Jeans, D.N. *An Historical Geography of New South Wales to 1901*, Sydney 1972
Kennedy, J. *A History of Malaya 1400–1959*, London 1962
Kjölstad, T., Rystad, G. *5000 år: Epoker och utvecklingslinjer*, Lund 1973
Konigsberger, H., Mosse, G.L. *Europe in the sixteenth century*, London 1968
Langer, W.L. *An Encyclopedia of World History*, London 1972
La Roncière (et al) *L'Europe au Moyen Age*, Paris 1969
Lattimore, O. *Inner Asian Frontiers of China*, New York 1951
Lyashchenko, P.I. *History of the National Economy of Russia to the 1917 Revolution*, New York 1949
Majumdar, R.C. *The Vedic Age*, Bombay 1951
Majumdar, R.C. *History and Culture of the Indian People, Age of Imperial Unity*, Bombay 1954
Macmillan's Atlas of South-East Asia, London 1964
McBurney, C.B.M. *Proceedings of the British Academy LXI* 1975
McIntyre, W.D., Gardner, W.J. *Speeches and Documents on New Zealand History*, Oxford 1970
McNeill, W.H. *A World History*, New York 1971
Meinig, D.W. *On the Margins of the Good Earth*, New York 1962, London 1963
Mellaart, J. *The Neolithic of the Near East*, London 1975
Ministry of Works *A Survey of New Zealand Population*, Wellington 1960
Miquel, A. *L'Islam et sa Civilisation*, Paris 1968
Morrell, W.P., Hall, D.O.W. *A History of New Zealand Life*, Christchurch 1957
Moss, H. St. L.B. *The Birth of the Middle Ages*, Oxford 1935
Mulvaney, D.J. *The Prehistory of Australia*, London 1975
Mussett, L *Les Invasions: Les Vagues Germaniques*, Paris 1965
Musset, L. *Les Invasions: Le Second Assaut contre l'Europe Chrétienne*, Paris 1971
The National Atlas of the United States of America, Washington DC 1970
Neatby, H. *Quebec, The Revolutionary Age 1760–1791*, London 1966
New Zealand Official Yearbook, Wellington 1893–
Ogot, B.A. (ed.) *Zamani, A Survey of East African History*, London 1974–1976
Oliver, R., Fagan, B. *Africa in the Iron Age c.500 BC–AD 1400*, Cambridge 1975
Oliver, R., Atmore, A. *Africa since 1800*, Cambridge 1972
Ostrogorsky, G. *History of the Byzantine State*, Oxford 1956
Parker, W.H. *An Historical Geography of Russia*, London 1968
Piggott, S. *Prehistoric India to 1000 BC*, London 1962
Pitcher, D.E. *An Historical Geography of the Ottoman Empire*, Leiden 1973
Sanders, W.T., Marino, J. *New World Prehistory: Archaeology of the American Indian*, Englewood Cliffs, N.J. 1970
Saum, L.O. *The Fur Trader and the Indian*, London 1965
Seltzer, L.E. (ed.) *The Columbia Lippincott Gazetteer of the World*, New York 1952
Simkin, C.F. *The Traditional Trade of Asia*, Oxford 1968
Smith, C.T. *An Historical Geography of Western Europe before 1800*, London & New York 1960
Smith, W.S. *The Art and Architecture of Ancient Egypt*, London 1965
Snow, D. *The American Indians: their Archaeology and Prehistory*, London 1976
Stavrianos, L.S. *The World to 1500*, Englewood Cliffs, N.J. 1975
Stein, Sir Aurel *Travels in Central Asia*, London 1935
Stratos, A.N. *Byzantium in the seventh century*, Athens 1965
Tarn, W.W. *Alexander the Great*, Cambridge 1948
Tate, D.J.M. *The Making of South-East Asia*, Kuala Lumpur 1971
Thapar, R. *A History of India*, London 1967
The Times Atlas of the World, Comprehensive Edition, London 1980
Toynbee, A.J. (ed.) *Cities of Destiny*, London 1967
Toynbee, A.J. *Mankind and Mother Earth*, Oxford 1976
U.S. Strategic Bombing Survey, Summary Report (Pacific War), Washington 1946
Van Alstyne, R.W. *The Rising American Empire*, Oxford 1960
Van Heekeren, H.R. *The Stone Age of Indonesia*, The Hague 1957
Wadham, S., Wilson, R.K., Wood, J. *Land Utilization in Australia*, Melbourne 1964
Watters, R.F. *Land and Society in New Zealand*, Wellington 1965
Wheatley, P. *The Golden Khersonese*, Kuala Lumpur 1961
Wheeler, M. *Early India and Pakistan to Ashoka*, London 1968
Willey, G. *An Introduction to American Archaeology* vols. 1 & 2 Englewood Cliffs, N.J. 1970
Williams, M. *The Making of the South Australian Landscape*, London 1974
Wilson, M., Thompson, L. *Oxford History of South Africa* vols. 1 & 2 Oxford 1969, 1971

INDEX

1 HISTORICAL PLACE NAMES

Geographical names vary with time and with language, and there is some difficulty in treating them consistently in an historical atlas, especially for individual maps within whose time span the same place has been known by different names. We have aimed at the simplest possible approach to the names on the maps, using the index to weld together the variations.

On the maps forms of names will be found in the following hierarchy of preference:
a English conventional names or spellings, in the widest sense, for all principal places and features, e.g., Moscow, Vienna, Munich, Danube (including those that today might be considered obsolete when these are appropriate to the context, e.g., Leghorn)

b Names that are contemporary in terms of the maps concerned. There are here three broad categories:
i names in the ancient world, where the forms used are classical, e.g., Latin or latinized Greek, but extending also to Persian, Sanskrit, etc.
ii names in the post-medieval modern world, which are given in the form (though not necessarily the spelling) current at the time of the map (e.g., St. Petersburg before 1914, not Leningrad).
iii modern names where the spelling generally follows that of *The Times Atlas of the World*, though in the interests of simplicity there has been a general omission of diacritics in spellings derived by transliteration from non-roman scripts, e.g., Sana rather than Ṣana‘ā’.

2 THE INDEX

The index does not include every name shown on the maps. In general only those names are indexed which are of places, features, regions or countries where ‘something happens’, i.e., which carry a date or symbol or colour explained in the key, or which are mentioned in the text.

Where a place is referred to by two or more different names in the course of the atlas, there will be a corresponding number of main entries in the index. The variant names in each case are given in brackets at the beginning of the entry, their different forms and origins being distinguished by such words as *now*, *later*, *formerly* and others included in the list of abbreviations (*right*).

‘Istanbul (*form.* Constantinople, *anc.* Byzantium)’ means that the page references to that city on maps dealing with periods when it was known as Istanbul follow that entry, but the page references pertaining to it when it had other names will be found under those other names.

Places are located generally by reference to the country in which they lie (exceptionally by reference to island groups or sea areas), this being narrowed down where necessary by location as E(ast), N(orth), C(entral), etc. The reference will normally be to the modern state in which the place now falls unless (a) there is a conventional or historical name which conveniently avoids the inevitably anachronistic ring of some modern names, e.g., Anatolia rather than Turkey, Mesopotamia rather than Iraq, or (b) the modern state is little known or not delineated on the map concerned, e.g., many places on the Africa plates can only be located as W., E., Africa, etc.

Reference is generally to page number/map numbers (e.g., 118/1) unless the subject is dealt with over the plate as a whole, when the reference occurs as 118-19 (i.e., pages 118 and 119). All entries with two or more references have been given sub-headings where possible, e.g., Civil War 129/4. Battles are indicated by the symbol ⚔. References to names of persons, treaties, etc., occurring in the text are followed by the abbreviation T. e.g. ‘Alexander the Great 22T’.

Though page references are generally kept in numerical order, since this corresponds for the most part with chronological order, they have been rearranged occasionally where the chronological sequence would be obviously wrong, or in the interests of grouping appropriate references under a single sub-heading.

All variant names and spellings are cross-referenced in the form ‘Bourgogne (Burgundy)’, except those which would immediately precede or follow the main entries to which they refer. The bracketed form has been chosen so that such entries may also serve as quick visual indications of equivalence. Thus Bourgogne (Burgundy) means not only ‘see under Burgundy’ but also that Burgundy is another name for Bourgogne.

3 ABBREVIATIONS

a/c also called
AD Autonomous District
Alb. Albanian
anc. ancient
AR Autonomous Region
Ar. Arabic
a/s also spelled
ASSR Autonomous Soviet Socialist Republic
Bibl. Biblical
Bulg. Bulgarian
C Century (when preceded by 17, 18 etc.)
C Central
Cat. Catalan
Chin. Chinese
Cz. Czech
Dan. Danish
Dut. Dutch
E East(ern)
Eng. English
Est. Estonian
f/c formerly called
Finn. Finnish
form. former(ly)
Fr. French
f/s formerly spelled
Ger. German
Gr. Greek
Heb. Hebrew
Hung. Hungarian
Indon. Indonesian
Ir. Irish
Is. Island
It. Italian
Jap. Japanese
Kor. Korean
Lat. Latin
Latv. Latvian
Lith. Lithuanian
Mal. Malay
med. medieval
mod. modern
Mong. Mongolian
N North(ern)
n/c now called
Nor. Norwegian
n/s now spelled
NT New Testament
obs. obsolete
OT Old Testament
Pers. Persian
Pol. Polish
Port. Portuguese
Rom. Romanian
Russ. Russian
S South(ern)
s/c sometimes called
Som. Somali
Sp. Spanish
S. Cr. Serbo-Croat
SSR Soviet Socialist Republic
Sw. Swedish
T text
Turk. Turkish
Ukr. Ukrainian
US(A) United States (of America)
var. variant
W West(ern)
Wel. Welsh
WW1 The First World War
WW2 The Second World War

Aachen (*Fr.* Aix-la-Chapelle *anc.* Aquisgranum) W Germany Frankish royal residence 34/4; industrial development 98/2; WW1 119/3
Aargau Switzerland Reformation 75/1
Aarhus (*n/s* Århus) Denmark bishopric 38/2; archbishopric 52/3
Abal Takalik E Mexico Mayan centre 12/2
Abasgia region of Caucasus 43/1
Abbasid Caliphate 40/2
Abbasids Muslim dynasty 40/2,3
Abbeville N France 17C revolt 77/2
Abd al Kadir Algerian leader 102T
Abdera NE Greece Greek colony 19/4
Abemama Gilbert Is captured by Japanese 134/1; retaken by US 135/2
Abenaki NE Canada Indian tribe 63/1
Abhisara NW India kingdom 23/3
Abilene C USA cow town 94/1
Abipon Argentina Indian tribe 63/1
Abkhaz ASSR Caucasus 146/2
Abodrites Germany tribe 33/5, 34/4, 54/2
Aboukir Bay Egypt⚔87/2, 90/2
Abreu Portuguese explorer 65/2
Abr Nahr Syria province of Achaemenid Empire 20/5
Abrotonum (Sabrata)
Abu Bakr First Caliph 41/1
Abu Rawash Lower Egypt pyramid 17/3
Abu Salabikh C Mesopotamia Sumerian site 16/2
Abu Simbel Upper Egypt New Kingdom temple 21/1
Abu Sir Lower Egypt pyramid 17/3
Abydus W Turkey Persian War 23/1; Dorian colony 19/4; Byzantine Empire 43/1
Abydus Upper Egypt 17/3; 21/1
Abyssinia (*now* Ethiopia) 101/2
Acadia (Nova Scotia)
Acancéh E Mexico Mayan site 12/2
Acapulco Mexico early trade 66/1
Acarnania country of ancient Greece 18/3
Accho (Acre)
Accra Ghana early European settlement 61/2
Aceh (Atjeh)
Achaea (*a/s* Achaia) early Greek state 18/3; 19/4; 22/1; Roman province 31/3
Achaemenid Empire Persia 24T, 20/5
Achaia (Achaea)
Açores (Azores)
Acragas (*Lat.* Agrigentum, *mod.* Agrigento) Sicily Dorian colony 19/4
Acre (*OT* Accho *NT* Ptolemais *Fr.* St. Jean-d'Acre *Heb.* Akko) Palestine 21/4; Levantine city 21/1; Muslim reconquest 40/3; early trade 58/3
Actium W Greece⚔31/3
Acton SE USA⚔95/2
Adab Mesopotamia Sumerian site 16/2
Adal E Africa early state 60-61
Adamgarh C India site 9/1
Adana W Turkey Byzantine Empire 42/2, 43/1; revolt against Ottoman rule 48/2; Ottoman Empire 124/1
Ad Dawhah (Doha)
Addis Ababa Ethiopia Italian penetration 103/3
Adelaide S Australia founded 113/1; industry 108/1
Aden S Arabia early trading centre 25/1; Muslim trade 58/3; early trade with China 58/3; early church 38/1; Portuguese in 64/1; early town 67/1; Ottoman Empire 125/1; taken by British 101/2; British base 138/1
Aden Protectorate (*successively renamed* Protectorate of South Arabia, Federation of South Arabia, People's Republic of South Yemen, People's Democratic Republic of Yemen; now part of United Yemen)
Adichanallur S India site 9/1
Admiralty Islands S Pacific Japanese attack 135/1
Adowa N Ethiopia⚔103/3
Adramyttium (*mod.* Edremit) W Turkey 43/3
Adrar W Africa rock painting 10/1
Adrar Bous SE Algeria early site 11/1
Adrar Tiouiyne SE Algeria early site 11/1
Adrianople (*anc.* Adrianopolis *mod.* Edirne) W Turkey Byzantine Empire 43/1, 3; Ottoman centre 49/1; occupied by Greece 129/2
Adrianopolis (*mod.* Edirne *Eng.* Adrianople) W Turkey archbishopric 27/2
Adriatic Sea Mycenaean trade 18/2
Adulis Red Sea Iron Age site 11/1; early port 25/1, 60/1
Adyge AR Caucasus 146/2
Adzhar ASSR Caucasus 146/2
Aegates *islands* S Italy⚔31/2
Aegean Mycenaean settlement 19/1
Aegospotami (*Turk.* Karaova Suyu) NW Turkey⚔23/2
Aegyptus (*mod.* Egypt) Roman province 31/3
Aelana (*a/c* Aela, *mod.* Aqaba) Roman Empire 25/2
Aelia Capitolina (*mod.* Jerusalem) Judaea Roman city 25/2
Aenus (*mod.* Enez) W Turkey Aeolian colony 19/4
Aeolians early people of N Greece 18/3
Aequii early people of C Italy 30/1
Aesernia (*mod.* Isernia) C Italy Latin colony 30/1
Aethelred II of England 36T
Aetolia ancient country of C Greece 18/3; 22/1, 3
Afars and Issas, French Territory of (*form.* French Somaliland *now* Republic of Djibouti)
Afghanistan under Abbasid sovereignty 41/2; independent sultanate 125/1; invaded by USSR 141/1
Africa early man 3/3; agricultural origins 6/2, 11/1; early cultures 11/1; Portuguese exploration 64/1; early trade 58/3; early European voyages of discovery 65/2; European expansion and trade 66/2, 67/1; early empires 60-61; European penetration 103/3; slave trade 60-61; colonial empires 100/2; anti-colonial resistance 138/1; modern political developments 140/1; economy 151/1
Africa (*mod.* Tunisia and Libya) Roman province 31/3, 4; conversion to Christianity 26/1; Byzantine province 42/1
Afrikaners 102T
Aga-Buryat Mongol AD E USSR 146/2
Agade Mesopotamia early city 17/4
Agadès (*var.* Agadez) W Africa early site 11/1; 58/3, 60-61
Agathe (*mod.* Agde) SW France Ionian colony 19/4
Agde (Agathe)
Aggersborg N Denmark circular fortification 52/3
Aghlabids Muslim dynasty of Tunisia 40/2
Agincourt (*mod.* Azincourt) N France⚔56/5
Aglar (Aquileia)
Agra N India Mutiny 104/1
Agram (Zagreb)
Agrigentum (*Gr.* Acragas *mod.* Agrigento) Sicily Roman Empire 24/2, 31/3
Agrippa II Kingdom of 26/3
Aguascalientes state of C Mexico 97/1
Aguntum (*mod.* San Candido) N Italy bishopric 26/2
Ahar NW India site 9/1
Ahicchatra N India 9/1; 29/4
Ahmadabad (Ahmedabad)
Ahmedabad (*n/s* Ahmadabad) W India industry 105/3
Ahvenanmaa (Åland Islands)
Aichi prefecture of C Japan 126/2
Aidan, St. 38/3
Aigues-Mortes S France Mediterranean trade 59/2; Huguenots 74/3
Aigun NE China treaty port 107/4
Ain Jalut Palestine⚔40/2, 46/1
Air W Africa rock painting 11/1
Aire NW France fort 80/1
Aisne *river* NE France WW1 118/3
Aistulf Lombard ruler 32T
Aix (*or* Aix-en-Provence *anc.* Aquae Sextiae) S France archbishopric 34/4; St Bartholomew Massacre 74/3; parlement 80/1
Aix-la-Chapelle (Aachen)
Aix-la-Chapelle, Treaty of 86T
Aizu N Japan 126/1
Ajanta C India Buddhist site 27/1
Ajayameru (*mod.* Ajmer) C India 29/4
Ajmer (*form.* Ajayameru) N India British rule 104/1; industry 105/3
Ajnadain Palestine⚔41/1
Akan W Africa early state 60/1
Akaroa S Island, New Zealand early French colony 112/2
Akhisar (Thyatira)
Akhtiar (Sevastopol)
Akita town and prefecture of N Japan 126/2
Akjoujt W Africa early site 10/1
Akkad Mesopotamia 17/3
Akkerman (*from 1946* Belgorod-Dnestrovskiy *anc.* Tyras *Rom.* Cetatea Alba) S Russia Ottoman conquest 49/1
'Akko (Acre)
Akkoyunlu Muslim dynasty of Anatolia 49/1
Ak-Mechet (Simferopol)
Akmolinsk (Tselinograd)
Akrotiri S Aegean early settlement 19/1
Aksai-Chin district of N Kashmir territorial dispute with China 105/5
Akşehir (Philomelium)
Aksu (*a/s* Aqsu) Sinkiang trade 25/1; Muslim insurrection against China 106/1
Aktyubinsk Kazakhstan 84/3
Alabama state of SE USA Civil War 93/5; Depression 131/2; population 145/1
Alaca Hüyük C Anatolia Hittite city 21/1
Alacaluf Indian tribe of S Chile 63/1
Alagoas state of E Brazil 97/1
Alalakh (*a/c* Atchana) Syria Mycenaean trade 18/2; Mitannian city 21/1
Alalia (*or* Aleria) Corsica Ionian colony 19/4
Alamgirpur India stone age and Harappan site, 9/1, 5
Åland Islands (*Finn.* Ahvenanmaa) SW Finland neutralised 128/2
Alans (*Lat.* Alani) E and W Europe, Africa tribal movements 32/2
Alarcos S Spain⚔37/4
Alaric I King of Visigoths 32/2
Alaşehir (Philadelphia)
Alashiya (*mod.* Cyprus) under Hittite Empire 20/2
Alaska state of USA purchase from Russia 84/3, 111/4
Alaungpaya King of Burma 70T
Alba Fucens C Italy 30/1
Alba Iulia (*anc.* Apulum *Hung.* Gyulafehérvár *Ger.* Karlsburg) Romania Mithraic site 26/1
Albania Black Death 57/1; principality 116/1; Ottoman province 124/1; Muslim insurrection 130/3; inter-war alliances 128/1; annexed by Italy 129/5; WW2 132-3; Cold War 149/1; free elections 137/4
Albania ancient country of Caucasus 31/3
Albany (*form.* Fort Orange) NE USA seized by English 67/3
Albany W Australia founded 113/1
Albazinsk SE Siberia founded 84/2
Alberta province of Canada 111/1
Albertville (*now* Kalémié) E Belgian Congo 138/4
Ålborg N Denmark megalithic flint mine 15/3
Albret region of SW France 72/2
Albuquerque Portuguese empire-builder 70T
Alcalá S Portugal Megalithic tomb 14/3
Alcibiades Athenian leader 23/2
Alkeksandropol (Leninakan)
Alemanni tribe of C Europe 32/2, 34/1
Alemannia SW Germany part of Frankish Empire 34/4, 35/2
Alençon N France fief annexed by France 72/2; provincial capital 80/1
Alep (Aleppo)
Aleppo (*anc.* Beroea *a/c* Yamkhad *Fr.* Alep *Ar.* Halab) Syria Mitannian city 21/1; bishopric 39/1; Byzantine Empire 43/1; early trade 58/3; conquest by Ottomans 49/1; French occupation 125/3
Aleria (Alalia)
Alessandria N Italy Lombard League 55/3; Signorial domain 56/3
Aleut tribe of Alaska 63/1
Aleutian Islands W Alaska to USA 84/3; attacked by Japanese 134/1; retaken by Americans 135/2
Alexander's Empire 22/3
Alexander the Great 22T
Alexandreschata (Alexandria Eschata)
Alexandretta (*mod.* Iskenderun) E Turkey Achaemenid Empire 21/5; ceded to Turkey 129/2
Alexandria (*Ar.* Al Iskandariyah) Egypt spread of Christianity 26/1; Alexander's route 22/3; Roman Empire 25/2, 31/3; Christian centre 27/2, 39/1, 4; trade 58/3, 61/2; Arab conquest 41/1; conquered by Ottomans 49/1
Alexandria NW India Alexander's route 23/3
Alexandria (*mod.* Gulashkird) S Persia Alexander's route 23/3
Alexandria (*mod.* Ghazni) Afghanistan Alexander's route 23/3
Alexandria (*later* Merv *since 1937* Mary) C Asia 23/3
Alexandria ad Caucasum Afghanistan Alexander's route 23/3
Alexandria Arachoton (*mod.* Qandahar *Eng.* Kandahar) Afghanistan Alexander's route 23/3
Alexandria Areion (*mod.* Herat) Afghanistan Alexander's route 23/3
Alexandria Eschata (*a/c* Alexandreschata) C Asia Alexander's route 23/3
Alexandria Prophthasia (*mod.* Farah) Afghanistan Alexander's route 23/3
Alexandria Sogdiana NW India Alexander's route 23/3
Alexandria Troas W Anatolia Roman Empire 31/3
Alexios I Byzantine Emperor 42T
Al Fas (Fez)
Alfonso VI of León and Castile 36T
Alger (Algiers)
Algeria economy under French rule 108/1; Ottoman province 124/1; French invasion 103/3; French colonisation 101/1, 103/3, 102/5; immigration from France 108/2; civil war 138/3; under Vichy control 132/1; independence 138/1; political development 140/1
Algiers (*Fr.* Alger *Sp.* Argel *Ar.* Al Jaza'ir *anc.* Icosium) N Algeria Mediterranean trade 58/3; Corsair city 61/2; Ottoman rule 48/2; Allied landing WW2 132/2
Algonquin Indian tribe of C Canada 63/1
Al Hadhr (Hatra)
Al Hudaydah (Hodeida)
Ali fourth Caliph 41/1
Alice Springs C Australia 113/1
Aligarh N India Mutiny 104/1
Ali Kosh W Persia early farming site 7/4
Ali Murad NW India Harappan site 9/5
Alişar Hüyük C Anatolia Hittite city 21/1
Al Iskandariyah (Alexandria)
Al Jaza'ir (Algiers)
Aljubarrota Portugal⚔56/1
Al Khalil (Hebron)
Allahabad NE India Indian Mutiny 104/1; industry 105/3
Allahdino NW India pre-Harappan site 9/5
Allenstein (*Pol.* Olsztyn) W Poland acquired by Germany after plebiscite 129/2
Alma-Ata (*until 1921* Vernyy) C Asia industry 147/1
Al Madinah (Medina)
Al Makkah (Mecca)
Almalyk Mongolia bishopric 39/1
Almanza Spain⚔/81/5
Al Mawsil (Mosul)
Almería S Spain early agriculture 6/2; Mediterranean trade 36/2
Almohads Muslim dynasty and empire of North Africa 40/2; 60/1
Almoravids Muslim dynasty of Morocco 40/2. North African empire 36/2
Alpes Cottiae Roman province, France/Italy 30/3
Alpes Maritimae Roman province, France/Italy 30/3
Alpes Poeninae Roman province, France/Italy 30/3
Al Qahirah (Cairo)

Al Quds (Jerusalem)
Al Raydaniyya N Egypt⚔49/1
Alsace (*anc.* Alsatia *Ger.* Elsass) in German Empire 55/3; acquired by Habsburgs 78/3; acquired by French 80-81; customs union 98/3; WW1 119/2
Alsace-Lorraine *Ger.* Elsass-Lothringen) region of E France annexed by German Empire 115/2; ceded to France 128/2
Alsatia (Alsace)
Altaich S Germany monastery 34/4
Altamira N Spain Palaeolithic art 5/3
Altan Khan Mongol Chieftain 46T
Altendorf N Germany megalithic tomb 15/3
Altmark region of E Germany 53/3
Alto Adige (South Tyrol)
Altona N Germany customs union 98/3
Altun Ha E Mexico Mayan site 12/2
Altxerri N Spain Palaeolithic art 5/3
Alwa early Christian kingdom of the Sudan 60/1
Alwar district of N India communal riots 104/4
Amalfi S Italy Byzantine port 36/2
Amara Upper Egypt fortress 21/1
Amara NW India pre-Harappan site 9/5
Amarapura C Burma Neolithic site 8/3; early trade centre 71/2
Amaravati E India early trading centre 25/1
Amasia (*mod.* Amasya) E Anatolia archbishopric 27/2; Roman Empire 31/3
Amastris (*earlier* Sesamus) N Anatolia Byzantine Empire 42/2
Amasya (*anc.* Amasia) C Turkey Ottoman town 49/1
Amathus Cyprus ancient Greek colony 19/4
Ambianum (Amiens)
Amboina C Indonesia massacre of English 70/3; trade centre 71/2
Ambriz Angola Portuguese settlement 61/2
Amchitka Aleutian Is. Alaska retaken from Japanese 135/2
Amecameca Mexico on Cortés' route 68/1
America, Central (*a/c Mesoamerica*) early peoples 12-13; agricultural origins 6/4; early civilisations 13/1; Aztec Empire 62/2; Indian tribes 63/1; early voyages of discovery 65/3; colonial expansion 66/1, 68/1
America, North Colonisation 5/2; agricultural origins 6/4; early cultures 12-13, 62/4; Indian tribes 63/1; early voyages of discovery 64/2; colonial expansion 67/3, 69/3; European colonial rivalry 86/1; immigration from Europe 108/2; industrialisation 144/4. See also Canada, United States
America, South Colonisation 5/2; early peoples 12-13; agricultural origins 6/4; early civilisations 13/1; Indian tribes 13/5; Inca Empire 63/3; early voyages of discovery 64/2; colonial expansion 66/1, 68/2, 69/3; industrialisation 96/2; independence 97/1; immigration from Europe 108/2; economic development 96/3; modern politics 97/1; population 97/2
American Samoa S Pacific 139/1 (inset)
Amida (*mod.* Diyarbakir) E Anatolia 31/3; archbishopric and monastery 27/2
Amiens (*anc.* Samarobriva *later* Ambianum) N France 17C revolt 77/2; provincial capital 80/1; WW1 118/3
Amisea N Anatolia Byzantine Empire 43/2
Amisus (*mod.* Samsun) N Anatolia Ionian colony 19/4; early archbishopric 27/2; Byzantine Empire 42/2
Amiternum C Italy 30/1
Amman (*Bibl.* Rabbath Ammon *anc.* Philadelphia) Jordan Levantine city 21/1; 125/2
Ammon ancient country of Palestine 21/2
Ammon, Sanctuary of Egypt Alexander's route 22/3
Amnisos Crete Mycenaean settlement 19/1
Amol N Persia Alexander's route 23/3
Amöneburg W Germany monastery 38/3
Amorium C Anatolia Byzantine Empire 42/2, 43/3
Amoy S China early trade 106/2; treaty port 107/4; Anglo-French attacks 107/3; Japanese influence 107/4; occupied by Japanese 127/5
Amphipolis N Greece⚔23/2; Roman Empire 24/2; early church 27/2
Amir NW India Harappan site 9/5
Amritsar N India political disturbances under British rule 104/4
Amselfeld (Kosovo)
Amsterdam Netherlands trading port 83/5; 18C financial centre 82/4
Amud Palestine site of early man 3/3
Amur River Russia/China border 84/2
Anabaptists 74/2, 75/1, T
Anadyrsk E Siberia founded 84/2
Anagnia (*mod.* Anagni) C Italy early town 30/1
Anantapur S India ceded to Britain 87/3
Anatolia early settlement 7/2; early agriculture 7/4; Mycenaean trade 18/2; Hittite cities 21/1; Muslim conquest 42/4; Ottoman conquest 49/1; Black Death 57/1; Italian and Russian spheres of influence 125/3. See also Asia Minor
Anatolic Theme Anatolia district of Byzantine Empire 42/2
Anazarbus SW Anatolia early archbishopric 27/2; Byzantine Empire 42/2
Ancona N Italy Roman Empire 24/2, 30/1, 3; medieval city 56/3
Ancrum Moor Scotland⚔73/4
Ancyra (*mod.* Ankara *obs. Eng.* Angora) W Anatolia Alexander's route 22/3; Roman Empire 24/2; 31/3; early archbishopric 27/2; Byzantine Empire 43/1, 3
Åndalsnes C Norway WW2 132/1
Andalusia (*Sp.* Andalucia) region of S Spain reconquest by Castile 37/4
Andaman Islands Indian territory of Bay of Bengal 101/2, 139/1
Andegavum (*earlier.* Juliomagus *mod.* Angers) W France early bishopric 26/2
Andernach (*anc.* Antunnacum) W Germany Palaeolithic art 5/3⚔55/3
Andover S England Industrial Revolution 98/1
Andredescester S England⚔33/3
Andredesweald S England 33/3
Anegray E France early monastery 38/3
Anga region of NE India 29/4
Angarsk S Siberia industry 147/1
Angers (*anc.* Juliomagus *med.* Andegavum) W France 17C revolt 77/2; centre of French Revolution 89/2
Angevin Empire France 52T, 52/2
Anghelu Ruju N Sardinia burial site 14/2
Angkor Cambodia Buddhist site 27/1, 51/2
Angkor Borei S Cambodia Hindu-Buddhist remains 51/2
Angles tribe of NW Europe, migrations 32/1, 2; 33/3; 34/1
Angles-sur-l'Anglin SW France Palaeolithic art 5/3
Anglo-Dutch Wars 81/3
Anglo-Egyptian Sudan Ottoman territory under British control 101/2; condominium 102/5
Angola SW Africa Portuguese discovery 64/1; early Portuguese trade 67/1; source of slaves 67/1; Portuguese colonisation 100/2, 102/5, 103/3; independence 138/1; political development 140/1
Angora (*anc.* Ancyra *mod.* Ankara) W Anatolia⚔47/4
Angoulême (*anc.* Iculisma) C France region annexed to France 72/2; provincial capital 80/1
Anguilla island of West Indies settled by English 66/4; independence 139/1 (inset)
Anhalt C Germany principality and duchy 79/1, 114/1; Reformation 75/1
Anhui (Anhwei)
Anhwei (*a/s* Anhui) province of E China Manchu expansion 106/1
Ani Persia Byzantine Empire 43/1
Aniane S France monastery 34/4
Aniba Upper Egypt fortress 21/1
Anjira NW India pre-Harappan site 9/5
Anjou region of NW France annexed by France 52/2; province of France 80/1
Ankara (*anc.* Ancyra *obs. Eng.* Angora) W Turkey⚔49/1; revolt against Ottoman rule 48/2; Ottoman Empire 124/1
Ankole Uganda kingdom 61/2
Annaba (Bône, Hippo Regius)
Annam N Indo-China under T'ang control 50/1; under Mongol control 47/1; expansion and early trade 71/2
Annapolis (*until 1694* Anne Arundel Town *earlier* Providence) NE USA 67/3
Ansbach S Germany Reformation 75/1, 74/4; margraviate 79/1
Anshan Manchuria Russo-Japanese War 127/4; industry 123/4
Ansi N China trade 25/1
Anta dos Gorgions S Portugal megalithic tomb 14/3
Antakya (Antioch)
Antalya (Attalia)
Antananarivo (Tananarive)
Antibes (Antipolis)
Antietam (*a/c Sharpsburg) NE USA*⚔92/5
Antigonid Kingdom Mediterranean 22/4
Antigua island of West Indies settlement by British 66/4; colony 97/1; independence 139/1 (inset)
Anting NW China Han commanderie 29/3
Antioch (*Lat.* Antiochia *mod.* Antakya) NW Syria Mediterranean trade 25/1, 37/2, 58/3; spread of Christianity 27/2; Roman Empire 25/2, 31/3; archbishopric 38/2, 39/1; Byzantine rule 43/1, 3; principality 40/3
Antiochia (Antioch, Antakya)
Antipolis (*mod.* Antibes) SE France Ionian colony 19/4
Antium (*mod.* Anzio) C Italy Roman colony 30/1
Antofagasta region of N Chile dispute with Peru and Bolivia 97/4
Antonine Plague 25/3
Antrim N Ireland massacre of Catholics 76/4
Antung (*now* Dandong) Manchuria treaty port 107/4; Russo-Japanese war 127/4
Antunnacum (Andernach)
Antwerp (*Fr.* Anvers *Dut.* Antwerpen) Belgium Hansa city 59/2; trade 59/2; 18C financial centre 82/4; town of Spanish Netherlands 76/1; industrial development 98/2; WW1 118/3; WW2 132/2
Anuradhapura Ceylon Buddhist site 27/1
Anvers (Antwerp)
Anxur (Terracina)
An-yang N China early urban settlement 8/4
Anyer Lor W Java site 8/3
Anzio (*anc.* Antium) C Italy WW2 133/2
Aomori N Japan town and prefecture 126/2
Aornos (*mod.* Tash-Kurghan) Afghanistan Alexander's route 23/3
Apache Indian tribe of SW USA 63/1
Apache Pass SW USA on trail west 94/1
Apamea Syria Roman Empire 25/2, 31/3; early archbishopric 27/2
Aphrodisias SW France Ionian colony 19/4
Apollonia NE Greece Dorian colony 19/4; early church 27/2
Apollonia NW Greece Dorian colony 19/4; Roman Empire 24/2
Apollonia (*mod.* Sozopol) Bulgaria Ionian colony 19/4
Apollonia Libya Greek colony 19/4; Roma Empire 24/2; Byzantine Empire 43/1
Apollinopolis (Edfu)
Appenzell Switzerland Reformation 75/1
Appian Way (Via Appia)
Appomattox SE USA Confederates surrender 93/5
Apulia region of SE Italy unification with Naples 56/3
Apulum (*mod.* Alba Iulia) Romania Roman Empire 24/2, 31/3
Aqaba (Aelana)
Aqsu (Aksu)
Aquileia (*med.* Aglar) N Italy Latin colony 30/1; Roman Empire 24/2; early archbishopric 26/2, 35/4; Byzantine Empire 43/1, 3
Aquincum (*mod.* Budapest) Hungary Chinese finds 24/1; Roman Empire 24/2, 31/3
Aquisgranum (Aachen)
Aquitaine (*anc.* Aquitania *mod.* Guyenne) region of SW France English possession 52/2; Black Death 57/1
Aquitania (*mod.* Aquitaine *later* Guyenne) Roman province of Gaul 30/3; Visigothic territory conquered by Franks 34/4, 35/2
Arabaya Arabia satrapy of Achaemenid Empire 21/5
Arabia early trade 59/3; spread of Judaism 26/1; early Christian activity 39/1; centre of Islam 41/1
Arabian Gulf (Persian Gulf)
Arabia Petraea Roman province of N Arabia 31/3
Arabissos E Anatolia Byzantine Empire 43/1
Arabs territorial losses to Byzantine Empire 43/1; independence from Ottomans 124-125; emigration from Israel 141/3
Arachosia (*a/c* Harauvatish) Afghanistan ancient province of Persian and Alexander's Empires 29/4
Aradus (*Bibl.* Arvad *later* Arward *Fr.* Rouad) Syria Phoenician city 19/4; Alexander's route 22/3
Arago S France site of early man 3/3
Aragon (*sp.* Aragón) region of E Spain at time of Reconquista 37/4; Muslim minorities 75/1; rural uprisings 57/1; acquired by Habsburgs 72/1
Arakan diistrict of SW Burma Islamic states 51/2, 70/1; British control 71/2; annexed by British 104/2
Aralsk C Asia 147/1
Aram ancient country of Middle East 21/2
Arapaho C USA Plains Indian tribe 63/1
Araucanian S America Andean Indian tribe 63/1
Arausio (*mod.* Orange) S France 26/2
Arawak S America Indian tribe 63/1
Arbailu (*a/c Arbela mod.* Arbil) Mesopotamia 17/3, 21/1
Arbela (*a/c* Arbailu *mod.* Arbil) Mesopotamia Alexander's route 22/3; early archbishopric 27/2, 39/1
Arcadia country of Ancient Greece 18/3
Arcadiopolis Bulgaria Byzantine Empire 43/1
Archangel (*Russ.* Arkhangelsk) N Russia founded 85/1; Allied occupation 121/2; industry 147/1
Arcole N Italy⚔91/1
Arcot S India ceded to British 87/3;⚔7/2
Arcy-sur-Cure C France site of early man 3/3
Ardabil Azerbaijan early trade 58/3
Ardales S Portugal Palaeolithic art 5/3
Ardea N Italy ancient town 30/1
Ardennes *forest* Belgium/France WW1 119/3; WW2⚔132/2
Ardmore Ireland early bishopric 26/2
Arelate (*mod.* Arles) S France Roman Empire 24/2, 30/3; archbishopric 26/2
Arene Candide NW Italy site 15/1
Arequipa Peru early Spanish city 66/1
Arezzo (*anc.* Arretium) C Italy medieval city 56/3
Argel (Algiers)
Argentina independence from Spain 97/1; exports and foreign investment 96/3; population 96/2; industrialisation and economy 142/2, 3; 150/1; political developments 143/1
Argentoratum (*mod.* Strasbourg) E France Mithraic site 26/1
Arginusae islands of the Aegean⚔23/2
Argissa Greece site 15/1
Argolis country of Ancient Greece 18/3
Argos S Greece 22/1
Arguin island off NW Africa Portuguese settlement 60/2, 64/1; French port 60/2
Århus (*a/s Aarhus)* C Denmark archbishopric 52/3
Aria (*a/c* Haraiva) ancient region of Afghanistan 23/3
Arica Peru trading post 66/1
Arickara E USA⚔95/2
Ariha (Jericho)
Ariminium (*mod.* Rimini) N Italy Latin colony 30/1; archbishopric 26/2
Arizona state of USA Depression 130/2; population 145/1
Arjunayanas tribe of N India 29/5

Arkansas state of C USA Depression 131/2; population 145/1

Arkhanes Crete Mycenaean settlement and palace 19/1

Arkhangelsk (Archangel)

Arles (*anc.* Arelate *or* Arelas) S France early archbishopric 34/4; medieval trade 55/3

Arlit SE Algeria early site 11/1

Armagh N Ireland archbishopric 26/2; monastery 38/3

Armagnac region of SW France under English rule 52/2; annexed to France 72/2

Armenia (*anc.* Uratu) country of Caucasus spread of Christianity 26/1; Alexander's Empire 22/3; Roman province 31/3; Muslim conquest 41/1; Ottoman Empire 124/1; independence after WW1 125/3, 129/2; SSR 146/2; independence 151/4

Armenia, Lesser region of Asia Minor 40/3

Armeniac Theme Anatolia Byzantine Empire 42/2

Armenians emigration from Turkey 129/3

Arpachiyah N Mesopotamia early farming village 7/4

Arpi C Italy early town 30/1

Arpino (Arpinum)

Arpinum (*mod.* Arpino) C Italy early town 30/1

Arrapkha Mesopotamia trading town 17/4

Arras (*anc.* Nemetocenna) N France fort 80/1; French Revolution 89/2; WW1 118/3

Arretium (*mod.* Arezzo) C Italy Etruscan city 19/4, 30/1; Roman Empire 24/2

Arsinoe Libya ancient town 31/3

Artacoana Afghanistan Alexander's route 23/3

Artajona NE Spain megalithic tomb 14/3

Artaphernes Persian general 23/1

Artashat Caucasus patriarchate 27/2

Artaxata Armenia Roman Empire 31/3

Artemision (Cape Artemisium)

Artois region of NE France Burgundian possession 72/2; province of France 80/1

Aruba island of Dutch West Indies 97/1, 139/1 (inset)

Arvad (Arwad)

Arwad (*anc.* Aradus *Bibl.* Arvad *Fr.* Rouad) Syria Assyrian Empire 20/3; Crusader states 40/3

Asahikawa N Japan 126/2

Asante W Africa early state 61/2

Ascalon (*mod.* Ashqelon) S Palestine Philistine city 19/4; Venetian naval victory 37/2

Ascension Island S Atlantic British colony 100-101

Ascoli Piceno (Asculum)

Ascoli Satriano (Ausculum)

Asculum (*a/c* Asculum Picenum *mod.* Ascoli Piceno) N Italy 30/1

Ashdod (*Lat.* Azotus) Palestine Philistine city 19/4, Levantine city 21/1

Ash Hollow C USA ⚔95/2

Ashkenazi N European Jews 39/4

Ashkhabad (*from 1919*⚔*27* Poltoratsk) SW Central Asia industry 147/1

Ashqelon (Ascalon)

Ash Sham (Damascus)

Ash Shariqah (Sharjah)

Ashtaroth ancient Israel 21/4

Ashur (*mod.* Sharqat) Mesopotamia early urban centre 16/1, 17/4; Assyrian Empire 20/3; Mitannian city 21/1

Asia early man 3/3, 4/1, 5/2, 6/7; agricultural origins 7/2, 5; early trade routes 59/3; tribal movements 32/3; expansion of Christianity 39/1; Chinese expansion 28/2; Mongol expansion 46/7; early voyages of discovery 65/2, 67/1; Russian expansion 84/2, 3; industrialisation 108/1; colonial empires 100/101; anti-colonial resistance 139/1

Asia (*Byzantine name* Asiana) Roman province of Anatolia 31/3, 4

Asiago N Italy WW1 119/3

Asia Minor spread of civilisation 16/1; conversion to Christianity 27/1; Ottoman control 49/1. See also Anatolia

Asiana (Asia)

Asir SW Arabia Ottoman Empire 125/1

Asoka's Empire India 28T; 29/4

Aspendus SW Anatolia Dorian colony 19/4

Aspern/Essling Austria ⚔91/1

Assam state of NE India Mongol control 47/1; British control 71/2, 104-5

Assus W Anatolia Aeolian colony 19/4

Assyria Empire 20/3; Roman province 31/3

Astacus (*mod.* Izmit) NW Anatolia Dorian colony 19/4

Astarac SW France independent fief 72/2

Asti N Italy Lombard League 55/3

Astorga (Asturica Augusta)

Astoria NW USA fur station 94/1

Astrakhan S Russia occupied by Mongols 47/4; Tartar khanate 85/1; Bolshevik seizure 121/2; WW2 133/2

Asturias region of N Spain kingdom 34/4; part of Castile 37/4

Asturica Augusta (*mod.* Astorga) N Spain Roman Empire 31/3; bishopric 26/2

Asunción Paraguay early Spanish settlement 66/1; 97/1

Aswan (Syene)

Asyut (*anc.* Lycopolis) S Egypt trade 58/3

Atacama (*Sp.* Atacameño) S America Andean Indian tribe 63/1

Atacama Desert Chile/Peru War of the Pacific 97/4

Atacameño S America early cultural centre 13/4

Atapuerca N Spain site of early man 3/3

Atchana (Alalakh)

Athenae (*Eng.* Athens *mod. Gr.* Athinai) Greece Roman Empire 24/2, 31/3

Athenopolis SE France Ionian colony 19/4

Athens (*Lat.* Athenae *mod. Gr.* Athinai) Greece Mycenaean palace 19/1; Greek parent state 19/4; Persian wars 20/5, 22/1; war with Sparta 23/2; Chinese finds 24/1; bishopric 27/2; invaded by Huns 32/1; Byzantine Empire 43/1, 3; WW2 133/2

Athinai (Athens)

Athura Mesopotamia satrapy of Achaemenid Empire 21/5

Atjeh (*n/s* Aceh) N Sumatra Islamic state 70/1

Atlanta SE USA ⚔93/5; industry 110/2; strike 130/2

Atlantic Ocean U-Boat warfare WW2 133/3

Atranji Khera N India site 9/1

Atropatene (Azerbaijan)

Attalia (*mod.* Antalya) S Anatolia early church 27/2; Byzantine Empire 43/1, 3

Attica ancient state of SE Greece 18/3, 22/1, 23/2

Attigny NE France Frankish royal residence 34/4

Attila ruler of the Huns 32/2

Attirampakkan and Gudiyam Cave S India Stone Age site 9/1

Attu Island Aleutians, W Alaska Japanese attack 134/1

Atwetwebooso W Africa Iron Age site 11/1

Auckland N Island, New Zealand province and second capital 112/2

Audenarde (*Dut.* Oudenaarde) Belgium fort 80/1

Augila (*n/s* Awjilah) Libya early trade 60/1

Augsburg (*anc.* Augusta Vindelicorum) S Germany town of Swabia 55/1; medieval trade centre 59/2

Augusta W Australia early settlement 113/1

Augusta Argentorate (*mod.* Strasbourg) E France Roman Empire 24/2

Augusta Rauricorum (*mod.* Augst) W Germany Roman Empire 24/2, 30/3

Augusta Taurinorum (*mod.* Turin) N Italy early bishopric 26/2

Augusta Treverorum (*mod.* Trier *Eng.* Treves) W Germany Mithraic site 26/1; Roman Empire 24/2, 30/3; archbishopric 26/2

Augusta Vindelicorum (*mod.* Augsburg) S Germany Roman Empire 24/2, 30/3

Augustodunum (*mod.* Autun) C France Roman Empire 24/2, 30/3; early bishopric 26/2

Augustów NE Poland WW1 119/3

Augustus Roman Emperor 30T

Auliye-Ata (Dzhambul)

Aulon (*later* Avlona *mod.* Vlorë) Albania Dorian colony 19/4

Aurangzeb Mughal emperor 87T

Auranitis region of Judaea 26/3

Auschwitz-Birkenau (*Pol.* Oświęcim) concentration camp 132/1

Ausculum (*a/c* Ausculum Apulum *mod.* Ascoli Satriano) C Italy early town 30/1

Austerlitz (*mod.* Slavkov) Czechoslovakia ⚔91/1

Australia (*originally called* New Holland) early man 3/3; before the Europeans 10/2; early voyages of discovery and exploration 112/5; early trade 113/4; settlement and development 113/1; emergence of Commonwealth 101/1, 2; economy and industrialisation 108/1; WW2 134-135

Austrasia the eastern Frankish Empire, 34/4

Austria (*Ger.* Österreich) German settlement 55/3; Black Death 57/1; acquired by Habsburgs 56/2, 78/3, 78-9T; War of the Spanish Succession 81/5; attacked by Ottomans 48/2; archduchy 79/1; opposition to Napoleon 91/1; inter-war alliances 128/1; socio-political change 130/3; annexed by Germany 129/5; Allied occupation zones 136/1; EFTA 137/4

Austro-Hungarian Empire agriculture and peasant emancipation 83/1; Military Frontier with Ottoman Empire 78/3; industrial revolution 99/2; ethnic composition 115/1; European alliances 117/2; overseas trade 109/3; WW1 118-9; dismantled 128/2

Autun (Augustodunum)

Auvergne region of C France English possession 52/5; annexed to France 72/2; French province 80/1

Auvernier E Switzerland early settlement 14/2

Auximum E Italy Roman colony 30/1

Ava C Burma political centre 70/1, 71/2

Avanti region of C India 29/4

Avaricum (Bourges)

Avaris (*a/c* Tanis) Lower Egypt Hyksos capital 21/1

Avars (*Chin.* Juan-juan) ancient people of Asia and Europe 31/4; 33/1, 5; 35/4

Avdeyevo E Russia Palaeolithic art 5/3

Avenio (Avignon)

Avesnes N France megalithic flint mine 15/3; fort 80/1

Avignon (*anc.* Avenio) S France in Great Schism 57/1; Papal enclave 80/1; annexed by France 88/3

Ávila C Spain expulsion of Jews 38/4

Avlona (*Gr.* Aulon *mod.* Vlorë *It.* Valona) Albania Byzantine Empire 43/1, 3; Ottoman conquest 48/1

Avranches NW France 17C revolt 77/2

Awdaghost W Africa trans-Saharan trade 61/2

Awjilah (Augila)

Axel S Netherlands town of Dutch Republic 77/1

Axim Ghana early Dutch settlement 61/1 (inset)

Axum ancient kingdom of NE Africa 11/1, 25/1, 60/1

Aydhab Sudan early trade 58/3

Aydin W Anatolia emirate 49/1

Ayia Irini SW Aegean Mycenaean settlement 19/1

Ayia Triadha (*a/s* Hagia Triada) Crete Mycenaean village and palace 19/1

Aylesbury S England Industrial Revolution 98/1

Aymará Andean Indian tribe of S America 63/1

Ayodhya (*earlier* Saketa) NC India town of Kosala 29/4

Ayutthaya (*a/s* Ayuthia *properly* Phra Nakhon Si Ayutthaya) S Thailand early political centre 70/1; early trade 71/2

Ayyubids Muslim dynasty, Egypt 60/1

Azak (*mod.* Azov) S Russia Ottoman conquest 49/1

Azerbaijan (*anc.* Atropatene) country of the Caucasus Muslim conquest 41/1; Ottoman conquest 48/2; acquired by Russia 85/1, 124/1; independence after WW1 129/2; SSR 146/2

Azincourt (Agincourt)

Azores (*Port.* Acores) islands of N Atlantic Portuguese discovery 64/1; trade 66/1; Portuguese colony 100/2

Azotus (*mod.* Ashdod) Palestine bishopric 27/2; in Judaea 26/3

Azov (*Turk.* Azak) S Russia Ottoman town 49/1

Aztalan C USA Hopewell site 12/3

Aztec Empire Mexico 62/2; conquest by Spain 68/1

Baalbek (Heliopolis)

Bab el Mandeb S Arabia land bridge 5/2

Babirush Mesopotamia satrapy of Achaemenid Empire 21/5

Babylon Mesopotamia early urban settlement 16/1; Sumerian city 17/4; Alexander's route 22/3

Babylonia ancient country of Mesopotamia Kingdom 20/4; under Alexander 22/3

Baçain (Bassein)

Bactra (*a/c* Zariaspa *mod.* Balkh) Afghanistan silk route 25/1; Alexander's route 23/3

Bactria (*a/c* Bactriana *Pers.* Bakhtrish) ancient country of Afghanistan 22T, 23/3

Badajoz SW Spain ⚔90/1

Bad Axe N USA ⚔95/2

Badegoule SW France Palaeolithic art 5/3

Baden S Germany margraviate 79/1; Confederation of the Rhine 91/4; state 115/2; German customs union 98/3

Badr W Arabia ⚔41/1

Badra (Der)

Bad-tibira Mesopotamia Sumerian site 16/2

Baecula SW Spain ⚔30/2

Baetica S Spain Roman province 30/3

Baffin, William explorer 65/1

Baffin Island N Canada discovery 64/2

Baghdad Mesopotamia early archbishopric 39/1; Mongol conquest 46/1, 47/4; early trade 58/3; under Ottoman rule 49/1; WW1 125/3

Baghdad Pact 148/4, T

Bagneux NW France megalithic tomb 14/3

Bagram (Begram)

Bagrationovsk (Eylau)

Bahadarabad NW India site 9/1

Bahamas islands of N Caribbean discovery 64/2; British colony 66/4, 69/3, 86/1, 97/1, 100/2; independence 139/1 (inset)

Bahawalpur native state of NW India under British rule 104/1; joins Pakistan at Partition 105/5

Bahçesaray (Bakhchesaray)

Bahia E Brazil Portuguese control 66/1; province 97/1

Bahrain (*f/s* Bahrein *Ar.* Al Bahrayn) island of Persian Gulf Ottoman siege 48/2; independent sheikhdom 125/1; independence 138/1

Baile Átha Cliath (Dublin)

Bailén S Spain ⚔90/1

Baiovarii tribe of S Germany 32/2

Bairat (*a/c* Bhabra) N India site 9/1

Bakhchesaray (*Turk.* Bahçesaray) Crimea Ottoman Empire 49/1

Bakhtrish (a/c Bactria) Afghanistan Achaemenid province 21/5

Baku Azerbaijan Muslim trade 59/3; conquered by Ottomans 48/2; Congress of Peoples of the East 120/4; British occupation 121/2; industry 147/1

Balagansk SC Siberia founded 84/2

Bala-Kot NW India Harappan site 9/5

Balambangan district of Java Dutch control 71/4

Bâle (Basle)

Balearic Islands W Mediterranean Byzantine Empire 42/1; attacked by Saracens 37/1; conquest by Pisa 36/2; reconquered by Aragon 37/4; to Spain 81/5

Balikpapan E Borneo recaptured from Japanese 135/2

Balkans rise of nationalism 116/1; alliances 117/2

Balkh (*anc.* Bactra *a/c* Zariaspa) Afghanistan early bishopric 39/1; Muslim conquest 41/1; early trade 59/3

Balkhash C Asia 147/1

Ballarat SE Australia goldfield 113/1

Ballinamuck Ireland ⚔90/3

Ballynagilly Ireland site 15/1

Baltic Viking trade 37/1

Baltic Entente 128/1

Baltic States (Estonia, Latvia, Lithuania)

Baltimore E USA industry 110/2

Baluchistan region of NW India tribal agency 105/3; joins Pakistan after Partition 105/5

Bamako W Africa reached by Mungo Park 102/1; occupied by French 103/3
Bamangwato tribe of S Africa 102/2
Bamberg S Germany bishopric 38/2, 79/1; medieval trade 58/1, 59/2
Bamburgh NE England⚔33/3
Banat region of Hungary/Romania/Yugoslavia conquered by Habsburgs 78/3
Banbury C England Industrial Revolution 98/1
Ban Chiang N Thialand early site 7/2, 8/3
Ban Chiang Hiang C Thailand Neolithic site 8/3
Bancorna Wales early bishopric 26/2
Banda Islands East Indies early trade 70/3
Bandar Abbas (*form.* Gombroon) SW Persia Ottoman siege 48/2
Bandarawela Bridge Ceylon site 9/1
Bandjarmasin (*n/s Banjarmasin) S Borneo* trade centre 71/2
Bangalore S India industry 105/3
Banghazi (Benghazi)
Bangka island off E Sumatra Dutch settlement 71/2
Bangkok (*Thai.* Krung Thep) S Thailand early trade centre 71/2; captured by Japanese 135/1
Bangladesh (*form.* East Pakistan *or* East Bengal) 141/1
Bangor N Ireland monastery 38/2, 3
Bangor-is-y-coed Wales monastery 38/3
Banjarmasin (Bandjarmasin)
Banjul (Bathurst)
Ban Kao SW Thailand early site 8/3
Ban Na Di N Thailand Neolithic siite 8/3
Bannockburn C Scotland⚔53/6, 56/4
Bannu (*form.* Edwardesabad) NW Pakistan industry 108/1
Bañolas N Spain site of early man 3/3
Banpo (Pan-p'o)
Ban Prasat N Thailand Neolithic site 8/3
Bantam (*form.* Banten) Java Islamic town 40/5; early trade 70/1, 3; sultanate under Dutch control 71/4
Banten (Bantam)
Bantu peoples of Africa early movements 10T, 60T
Banzart (Bizerta)
Bapaume NW France fort 80/1
Bar region of NE France/W Germany Burgundian possession 72/2; duchy 78/1
Bara-Bahau SW France Palaeolithic art 5/3
Baragunda C India site 9/1
Baranovichi (*Pol.* Baranowicze) W Russia WW1 119/3
Barbados island of West Indies settled by English 66/4; British colony 86/1, 97/1; independence 139/1 (inset)
Barbuda island of West Indies settled by English 66/4
Barca Libya Dorian colony 19/4;⚔20/5
Barcelona (*anc.* Barcino) NE Spain Mediterranean trade 36/2, 59/2, 3; urban revolt 57/1; 18C urban development 82/4;⚔90/1; Civil War 129/4
Barcelonette SE France fort 80/1
Barcino (*mod.* Barcelona) NE Spain early bishopric 26/2
Bardaa NW Persia early archbishopric 39/1
Bardia (*n/s* Bardiyah) Libya WW2 133/2
Barduli (Barletta)
Bareilly N India Mutiny 104/1
Barents, Willem explorer 65/2
Barguzinsk (*now* Barguzin) SC Siberia founded 84/2
Bari (*anc.* Barium) S Italy Magyar occupation 37/1; captured by Normans 36/2
Barium (Bari)
Barletta (*anc.* Barduli) S Italy medieval city 55/3
Barmen-Elberfeld (*since 1930* Wuppertal) W Germany industrial development 99/2
Barnard Castle N England⚔73/4
Barnaul C Asia founded 84/2; industry 147/1
Barnsley C England Industrial Revolution 98/1
Baroda C India industry 108/1
Bar-sur-Aube C France medieval fair 58/1
Barygaza (*mod.* Broach *n/s Bharuch) NW India* trading centre 25/1
Basel (Basle)
Bashkirs Turkic people of C Russia 85/1; ASSR 146/2
Basingstoke S England Industrial Revolution 98/1
Basle (*Fr.* Bâle *Ger.* Basel) Switzerland medieval trade 58/1; Reformation 75/1; bishopric 78/1
Basque Provinces N Spain reconquest by Castile 37/4
Basque Republic N Spain autonomy 128/2
Basques people of N Spain and SW France 34/1; 35/2, 115/1
Basra (*Ar.* Al Basrah) Mesopotamia early archbishopric 39/1;⚔41/1; trade 59/3; Ottoman conquest 48/2; British control 125/3; WW1 125/2
Bassano N Italy⚔91/1
Bassein Burma early trade centre 71/2
Bassein (*Port.* Baçain) W India Portuguese settlement 66/2
Bassia NE India site 9/1
Bass Strait SE Australia land bridge 5/2; early trade 113/4
Bastar former state of C India 105/3
Basti district of N India ceded to Britain 87/3
Bastidas, Rodrigo explorer 64/3
Basutoland (*now* Lesotho) S Africa British protectorate 102/2, 4, 5
Batanea district of Judaea 26/3
Batavi tribe of the Netherlands 30/3
Batavia (*form.* Sunda Kalapa, *since 1949* Jakarta *f/s* Djakarta) Java early trade 66/2; Dutch control 71/4; occupied by Japanese 134/1
Batavian Republic (*mod.* Netherlands) state established by French Revolution 89/3
Bath W England Industrial Revolution 98/1
Bathurst SE Australia founded 113/1
Bathurst (*now* Banjul) Gambia, W Africa 102/1
Bato Caves C Philippines early site 8/3
Baton Rouge S USA⚔93/5
Batu Buruk E Malaya Neolithic site 8/3
Batu Khan Mongol leader 46T
Batum (*n/s Batumi) Caucasus* British occupation 121/2
Bautzen E Germany⚔91/1
Bavaria (*Ger.* Bayern) conversion to Christianity 38/3; part of Frankish Empire 35/2, 4, 55/3; Wittelsbach territory 72/1; Reformation 75/1; Electorate 79/1; German Empire 115/2; customs union 98/3; Confederation of the Rhine 91/4; short-lived soviet republic 120/3
Bawit Egypt monastery 38/1
Baxter Springs C USA cow town 94/1
Bayern (Bavaria)
Bayonne (*anc.* Lapurdum) SW France 18C financial centre 82/4; 80/1
Bayreuth S Germany margraviate 79/1
Bayrut (Beirut)
Beachy Head S England Dutch naval victory 81/4
Beans Store C USA cow town 94/1
Bear Island Spitsbergen discovered 65/2
Béarn region of SW France under English rule 52/2; acquired by France 72/2
Bear Paw Mountains C USA⚔95/2
Bear Valley W USA mining site 94/1
Beas Valley NW India site 9/1
Beaucaire S France medieval fair 59/2
Beaulieu S England Industrial Revolution 98/1
Beaumaris N Wales castle 53/7
Beauvais N France 17C revolt 77/2
Beaver NW Canada sub-arctic Indian tribe 63/1
Beç (Vienna)
Beacan E Mexico Mayan site 12/2
Bechuanaland (*now* Botswana) country of S Africa British protectorate 102/5, 103/5
Bedcanford S England⚔33/3
Bédeilhac SW France Palaeolithic art 5/3
Bedford S England Industrial Revolution 98/1
Begram (*a/s* Bagram, *anc.* Kapisa) Afghanistan early trading 25/1
Beidha NW Arabia early farming site 7/4
Beira SE Africa Portuguese occupation 103/3
Beirut (*anc.* Berytus *Fr.* Beyrouth *Ar.* Bayrut) Lebanon Mediterranean trade 58/3
Belfast N Ireland IRA 137/6
Belfast S Africa⚔103/4
Belfort E France fort 80/1
Belgian Congo *form.* Congo Free State *now* Zaire) colony 100/2, 102/5; independence 138/1
Belgica Roman province of NE France 30/3
Belgium *form.* Spanish Netherlands *or* Southern Netherlands) independence 114/5; industrial revolution 99/2; colonial empire 100/2; WW1 118-9; acquisition of Eupen and Malmédy 128/2; economic and social development 1929-39, 130/1; inter-war alliances 128/1; WW2-132/1, 2; EEC and NATO 137/3, 149/1
Belgorod S Russia founded 85/1; early bishopric 38/2
Belgorod-Dnestrovski (Akkerman)
Belgrade (*anc.* Singidunum *S. Cr.* Beograd) C Yugoslavia⚔46/1; Ottoman conquest 48/2; WW1 119/3; WW2 132-3
Belize city of C America founded by British 66/3, 69/3
Belize (form. *British Honduras)* 142/1, 2, 3; independence 139/1 (inset)
Bellary district of S India ceded to Britain 87/3
Belleau Wood NE France WW1 118/3 (inset)
Belorussia (*a/s Byelorussia, f/c* White Russia) independence after WW1 129/2; SSR 146/2; industry 147/1; independence 137/4, 151/4
Beloye Ozero N Russia monastery 38/2
Belzec S Poland concentration camp 132/1
Bemba tribe of Rhodesia 61/2
Benares (*anc.* Kasi *now* Varanasi) N India 87/3
Bender (*mod.* Bendery *Rom.* Tighina) S Russia Ottoman conquest 48/2
Bendigo SE Australia goldfield 113/1
Benevento *anc.* Beneventum) C Italy dukedom under Byzantine Empire 42/1
Beneventum (*mod.* Benevento) C Italy Roman Empire 30/1, 3
Bengal country of E India spread of Islam 41/4; under Mughal Empire 48/2; medieval trade 59/3; under British rule 87/3, 104/1, 105/3; partition between India and Pakistan 105/5
Benghazi (*anc.* Berenice *Ar.* Banghazi) Libya Italian occupation 103/3; WW2 132/1
Benguela Angola Portuguese settlement 61/2
Benin early state of Nigeria 60-61
Benin (*form.* Dahomey) country of W Africa independence 138/1
Benkulen Sumatra trading post 71/2
Bensington S England⚔35/3
Bentheim W Germany county 79/1
Bent's Fort C USA fur station 94/1
Beograd (Belgrade)
Beothuk Newfoundland Indian tribe 63/1
Berar C India tribal territory 105/3
Berbera (*anc.* Malao) Somalia Muslim colony 60/1; British occupation 103/3
Berbers people of NW Africa 45/1; attack Roman Africa 32/1
Bere Welsh stronghold 53/7
Bernice Red Sea early trading port 24/1
Berenice (*mod.* Benghazi) Libya city of Roman Empire 24/2, 31/3; early bishopric 26/2
Berezina *river* W Russia⚔91/1
Berezov (*now* Berezovo) W Siberia founded 84/2, 85/1
Berg W Germany Reformation 74/4, 75/1; duchy 79/1
Bergama (Pergamum)
Bergamo (*anc.* Bergomum) N Italy medieval city 55/3
Bergen Norway bishopric 38/2; Hanseatic trading post 59/2; WW2 132/1
Bergen (Mons)
Bergen-Belsen N Germany concentration camp 132/1
Bergues NE France fort 80/1
Bering, Vitus explorer 65/4
Beringia N Pacific landbridge 4/1
Bering Strait N Pacific European discovery 65/4
Berlin Germany Hanseatic city 59/2; WW1 119/3; Communist uprising 120/3; WW2 132/2; Cold War 149/1
Bermuda British colony in W Atlantic 100/2
Bern (*Fr.* Berne) Switzerland early canton 54/5; Reformation 75/1
Bernicia ancient kingdom of NE England 33/3, 35/3
Bernifal SW France Palaeolithic art 5/3
Beroea (*mod.* Veroia) N Greece bishopric 27/2
Beroea (Aleppo)
Berry region of C France French Royal domain 52/2, 72/2; province 80/1
Bersham N England Industrial Revolution 98/1
Berytus (*mod.* Beirut) Lebanon Roman Empire 25/2, 31/3; early bishopric 26/2
Besançon (*anc.* Vesontio) E France archbishopric 34/4; medieval fair 59/2; gained by France 81/4; fort 80/1
Beshbalik W Mongolia 47/1, 3
Besigheim W Germany Mithraic site 26/1
Bessarabia region of Romania/Russia acquired by Russia 85/1; Ottoman province 124/1; lost to Romania 128/2; regained by Russia 121/2
Beth Katraye SE Arabia early bishopric 39/1
Bethlehem Palestine bishopric 26/2
Beth-shan Palestine Levantine city 21/1
Béthune N France fort 80/1
Beverley NE England Industrial Revolution 98/1
Bewdley W England Industrial Revolution 98/1
Beyrouth (Beirut)
Bhabra (Bairat)
Bhagatrav NW India Harappan site 9/5
Bhagrapir E India site 9/1
Bharatpur district of N India communal riots 104/4
Bharuch (Broach)
Bhongir C India site 9/1
Bhonsla state of C India 87/3; alliance with Britain 87/2 (inset)
Bhota (*mod.* Tibet) 29/4
Bhutan Himalayan kingdom 105/3, 107/4, 139/1
Biache-Saint-Vaast NE France site of early man 3/3
Biafra E Nigeria civil war 140/2
Biak island of NW New Guinea captured by Allies 135/2
Big Bell W Australia gold town 113/1
Big Hole NW USA⚔95/2
Big Mound N USA⚔95/2
Bigorre region of SW France under English rule 52/2; independent fief 72/2
Bihar state of E India under British control 104/1, 105/3; civil disobedience 104/4
Bílá Hora (White Mountain)
Bilbao N Spain 18C financial centre 82/4; Civil War 129/4
Billungmark district of N Germany 55/1
Bilma W Africa early trade 60-61
Biloxi S USA fur station 94/1
Bilston C England Industrial Revolution 98/1
Bilzingsleben E Germany site of early man 3/3
Bindon S England⚔33/3
Bingen W Germany Mithraic site 26/1
Binh Dinh (Vijaya)
Birbhanpur E India site 9/1
Bird Creek C USA⚔95/2
Birkenhead N England Industrial Revolution 98/1
Birmingham C England 18C industry 82/4; Industrial Revolution 98/1; bombed in WW2 132/1
Birmingham SE USA industry 109/1; civil unrest 144/3
Bisa tribe of C Africa 61/2
Bishopbridge E England Industrial Revolution 98/1
Bishop's Stortford S England Industrial Revolution 98/1
Bismarck, Prince von 114T, 116T
Biterrae S France bishopric 26/2
Bithynia ancient country of NW Anatolia 19/4, 22/3, 4; Byzantine Empire 43/1
Bithynia and Pontus Anatolia Roman province 31/3
Bitlis E Anatolia Byzantine Empire 43/1

Bitolj (*n/s Bitola Turk.* Monastir) S Yugoslavia Ottoman control 48/1
Bituricae C France archbishopric 26/2
Biysk Russ. C Asia founded 84/2
Bizerta (*anc.* Hippo Zarytus *Fr.* Bizerte *Ar.* Banzart) Tunisia under Abbasids 40/2; WW2 132/2
Bjerre N Denmark megalithic flint mine 15/3
Blackburn NE England Industrial Revolution 98/1
Blackburn S Africa Iron Age site 11/1
Black Death 57/1
Blackfoot W Canada Plains Indian tribe 63/1
Blackheath S England ⚔ 73/4
Black Patch SE England megalithic flint mine 14/3
Blagoveshchensk Russ. Far East 84/3; industry 147/1
Blaye W France fort 80/1
Blekinge region of S Sweden under Danish rule 53/3; acquired by Sweden 77/3
Blenheim (*Ger.* Blindheim) W Germany ⚔ (called Höchstädt by French and Germans) 81/5
Blenheim S Island, New Zealand founded 112/2
Bloemfontein S Africa ⚔ 103/4
Blois region of N France 72/2
Bloody Brook NE USA ⚔ 95/2
Bloody Ridge NE USA ⚔ 95/2
Bloody Run NE USA ⚔ 95/2
Bloody Sunday N Ireland 137/6
Bluefish Cave Alaska early site 5/2
Blue Turks tribe of Mongolia 33/1
Bluff S Island, New Zealand aluminium 112/2
Bobbio N Italy monastery 34/4, 38/3
Bodh Gaya NE India Buddhist site 27/1
Bodiam SE England Industrial Revolution 98/1
Bodrum (Halicarnassus)
Boeotia ancient country of C Greece 18/3; Persian influence 22/1
Boer War 102T, 103/4
Boğazköy (*anc.* Hattushash *Gr.* Pteria) C Anatolia Hittite city 21/1
Boğdan (Moldavia)
Bohemia (*Ger.* Böhmen) W part of mod. Czechoslovakia Bronze Age 14/2; occupied by Poland 52/1; medieval German Empire 55/1; expansion 56/2; Black Death 57/1; acquired by Habsburgs 72/1, 78/3, 79/1; Reformation 74/4, 75/1; kingdom within Holy Roman Empire 55/3; Austro-Hungarian Empire 129/2
Bohemians Slav tribe of C Europe 33/5
Boii early people of N Italy 30/1
Bojador, Cape W Africa Portuguese exploration 64/1
Boleslav II of Bohemia 52T
Boleslav Chrobry King of Poland 52T
Bolgar (*a/c* Bulgar) C Russia city of the Volga Bulgars 44-45, 46/1
Bolívar, Simon soldier-statesmen 96T
Bolivia country of S America independence 97/1; War of the Pacific 97/4; exports and foreign investment 96/3; population 96/2; 20C revolutions 143/1; economy 142/2, 3
Bologna (*anc.* Felsina *later* Bononia) N Italy Mithraic site 26/1; medieval city 55/3, 56/3
Bolsheretsk Russ. Far East founded 84/2
Bolton N England Industrial Revolution 98/1
Bombay W India British settlement 66/2; British rule 104/1; naval mutiny 104/4; industry 105/3
Bona (*mod.* Annaba *Fr.* Bône) N Algeria acquired by Habsburgs 73/1
Bonaire island of Dutch West Indies 97/1, 139/1 (inset)
Bonampak E Mexico Mayan site 12/2
Bône (*mod.* Annaba *Sp.* Bona *anc.* Hippo Regius) N Algeria Pisan raids 37/2
Boniface, St. 38/3
Bonin Islands (*a/c* Ogasawara Islands) N Pacific annexed by Japan 127/3; attacked by US forces 134/1
Bonna (*mod.* Bonn) W Germany Roman Empire 24/2
Bononia (*earlier* Felsina *mod.* Bologna) N Italy Roman Empire 30/1, 3
Bonteberg S Africa Stone Age site 11/1
Bordeaux (*anc.* Burdigala) SW France early archbishopric 34/4; occupied by English 56/5; medieval fair 59/2; trading port 83/5; 18C financial centre 82/4; St Bartholomew Massacre 74/3; French Revolution 89/2; industry 80/1
Border Cave SE Africa site of early man 3/3
Borneo (*Indon.* Kalimantan) island of East Indies Muslim expansion 40/5; Dutch trade 71/2; Dutch and British colonisation 101/1, 2; occupied by Japanese 134/1; retaken by Allies 135/2
Bornhöved N Germany ⚔ 55/3
Bornu Nigeria early state 61/2
Borobudur C Java Buddhist site 27/1, 51/2
Borodino W Russia ⚔ 91/1
Bororo forest Indian tribe of S Brazil 63/1
Bosnia country of C Yugoslavia vassal state of Ottoman Empire 48/1; under Hungarian Kingdom 56/2; Black Death 57/1
Bosnia-Herzegovina (*S. Cr.* Bosna i Hercegovina) part of Austria-Hungary 116/1; under Ottoman rule 124/1; Balkan alliances 116-117; after WW1 128/2; independence and civil war 137/4
Bosporan Kingdom S Russia 31/3
Boston E England medieval trade 59/2; Industrial Revolution 98/1
Boston NE USA founded 67/3; British naval base 86/1; trade and industry 110/2
Bostra S Syria Roman fort 25/2; early archbishopric 26/2
Botany Bay SE Australia penal settlement 113/1
Botocudo Indian tribe of S Brazil 63/1
Botswana (*form.* Bechuanaland) S Africa independence 138/1
Bouchain N France fort 80/1
Bougainville one of Solomon Islands, W Pacific recaptured from Japanese 135/2
Bougie (*anc.* Saldae *Sp.* Bugia *mod.* Bejaia) N Algeria Genoese raids 36/2
Bougon W France megalithic tomb 14/3
Boulogne (*anc.* Gesoriacum) N France fort 80/1
Bourbon (*now* Réunion) island of Indian Ocean French possession 87/2
Bourbon (Bourbonnais)
Bourbonnais (*a/c* Bourbon) region of C France Royal domain 52/2; annexed to France 72/2
Boure early state of W Africa, 60/1
Bourges (*anc.* Avaricum) C France archbishopric 34/4; St Bartholomew Massacre 74/3; 80/1
Bourgogne (Burgundy)
Bourg-St. Andéol S France Mithraic site 26/1
Bourne E England Industrial Revolution 98/1
Boussargues S France early settlement 14/2
Bouvines NE France ⚔ 52/2
Boyne, Battle of the 81/4
Bozeman Trail and Pass NW USA 94/1
Brabant region of Belgium/Holland medieval German Empire 52/2, 55/3; Burgundian possession 72/3
Bracara (*mod.* Braga) Portugal archbishopric 26/2
Braddock, Edward English general 86/1
Bradford N England Industrial Revolution 98/1
Braga (Bracara)
Brahmagiri S India site 9/1
Branč E Czechoslovakia burial site 14/2
Branco, Cape W Africa Portuguese exploration 64/1
Brandenburg region of E Germany under Bohemian rule 56/2; Black Death 57/1; Hohenzollern territory 72/1; Reformation 74/4, 75/1; Electorate 79/1; part of Prussia 78/2, 115/2
Brass Nigeria early European settlement 61/2
Brassempouy SW France Palaeolithic art 5/3
Bratislava (Pressburg)
Bratsk SC Siberia founded 84/2; industry 147/1
Braunschweig (Brunswick)
Brava Somalia trade 61/2
Brazil discovered 64/2; early trade 66/1; Portuguese colony 69/3, 4, 88/1; independent empire 97/1; exports and foreign investment 96/3; population 97/2; economy and political development 142-3, 150/1
Brecon S Wales Industrial Revolution 98/1
Breda, Treaty of 80T
Breitenfeld E Germany ⚔ 74/4
Bremen N Germany bishopric 38/2; archbishopric 79/1; Hanseatic city 59/2; Reformation 74/4, 75/1; German customs union 98/3; WW1 119/3; short-lived Soviet Republic 120/3; WW2 132/2
Bremen and Verden region of N Germany acquired by Sweden 77/3
Bremerhaven N Germany WW1 119/3
Brescia (*anc.* Brixia) N Italy medieval city 55/3, 56/3
Breslau (*now* Wrocław) W Poland Hanseatic city 59/2; 18C financial centre 82/4; Reformation 75/1; WW1 119/3
Brest NW France English base for 100 Years War 56/5; fort and naval base 80/1, 87/1; French Revolution 89/2
Brest (*a/c* Brest-Litovsk *Pol.* Brześć nad Bugiem) W Russia WW1 119/3
Bretagne (Brittany)
Brétigny, Peace of 56/3
Breton March NW France 34/4
Bretons Celtic people of NW France 35/2, 115/1
Bretteville-le-Rabet NW France megalithic flint mine 14/3
Brezhnev, Leonid 146T
Briançon SE France fort 80/1
Bridgnorth W England Industrial Revolution 98/1
Bridgwater W England Industrial Revolution 98/1
Brieg (*Pol.* Brzeg) W Poland Reformation 74/4
Brigantes Britain early tribe 30/3
Brigetio Hungary Mithraic site 26/1; Roman Empire 24/2
Brihuega C Spain ⚔ 81/5
Brindisi (*anc.* Brundisium) S Italy captured by Normans 36/2; WW1 119/3
Brisbane E Australia founded 113/1
Bristol W England textile industry 82/4; trading port 83/5; bombed in WW2 132/1
Britain conversion to Christianity 38/3; Anglo Saxon invasions 32/3; invasion by Germanic tribes 34/1; 13C 53/6; Tudor power 73/4. See also England, United Kingdom
Britannia Inferior Roman province of N England 30/3
Britannia Superior Roman province of S England 30/3
British Bechuanaland S Africa 103/3, 4
British Cameroons (*now part of* Cameroon)
British Central Africa (*later* Nyasaland) protectorate 103/3
British Columbia province of W Canada joins Confederation 101/1, 111/1
British East Africa (*now* Kenya) colony 103/3, 5
British Empire 100/1
British Guiana (*now* Guyana) S America colony 97/1
British Honduras (*now* Belize) C America colony 97/1
British North Borneo (*now* Sabah)
British Somaliland (*now part of* Somalia) E Africa protectorate 103/5
Britons tribe of SW England, movement to Britanny 32/2
Brittany (*Fr.* Bretagne) NW France on borders of Frankish Empire 34/4; conquered by Normans 52/2; Hundred Years War 56/5; Black Death 57/1; annexed to France 72/2
Brixia (Brescia)
Brno (*Ger.* Brünn) Moravia Palaeolithic art 5/3; WW1 119/3
Broach (*anc.* Barygaza *mod.* Bharuch) NW India ceded to Britain 87/2
Brody SE Poland WW1 119/3
Broken Hill SE Australia mining 113/1
Broome W Australia early settlement 113/1
Broseley C England Industrial Revolution 98/1
Brouage W France port 80/1
Bruges (*Dut.* Brugge) Belgium medieval city 55/3; urban revolt 57/1; Hanseatic city 59/2, 3
Brundisium (*mod.* Brindisi) S Italy Latin colony 30/1, Roman Empire 24/2, 31/2, 3; Byzantine Empire 42/1
Brunei sultanate of N Borneo spread of Islam 40/5, recaptured from Japanese 135/2; independence 139/1
Brunete C Spain Civil War 129/4
Bruniquel SW France Palaeolithic art 5/3
Brünn (*Cz.* Brno) Czechoslovakia Industrial Revolution 99/2
Brunswick (*Ger.* Braunschweig) N Germany urban revolt 57/1; Hanseatic city 59/1; German state 115/2, WW1 119/3
Brunswick-Lüneburg duchy of N Germany Reformation 75/1; 79/1
Brunswick-Wolfenburg duchy of N Germany 79/1
Brusa (Bursa)
Brussels (*Fr.* Bruxelles, *Dut.* Brussel) Belgium 18C 82/4
Bruttii ancient tribe of S Italy 30/1
Bruttium ancient district of S Italy 31/2
Bruxelles (Brussels)
Bryansk W Russia bishopric 38/2; town of Novgorod Seversk 45/2; WW2 133/2; industry 147/1
Brycheiniog dist. of Wales 33/3
Brzeg (Brieg)
Brześć Kujawski Poland farming site 15/1
Bubastis Lower Egypt 21/1
Bucellarian Theme Byzantine province of C Anatolia 42/2
Bucephala NW India on Alexander's route 23/3
Bucharest (*Rom.* Bucureşti *Turk.* Bükreş) Romania in Ottoman Empire 124/1; WW2 133/2
Buchenwald W Germany concentration camp 132/1
Buckingham S England Industrial Revolution 98/1
Bucureşti (Bucharest)
Buda Hungary Ottoman conquest 48/2
Budapest Hungary WW2 133/2
Buddhism 27/1, 28T, 39/1
Buenos Aires Argentina colonised 66/1
Buganda state of E Africa 61/2
Buhen Upper Egypt Old Kingdom city 17/3; fortress 21/1
Builth S Wales castle 53/7
Bujak vassal state of Ottoman Empire in SW Russia, 49/1
Bukhara city and province of C Asia early bishopric 39/1; Muslim conquest 41/1; in Timur's empire 47/4; trade 59/3; khanate 84/3, 124/1; People's Republic incorporated into USSR 120/4; industry 147/1
Bukit Tengku Lembu N Malaya Iron Age site 8/3
Bukit Tinggi (Fort de Kock)
Bukovina region of Romania acquired by Habsburgs 78/3; WW1 119/3
Bükreş (*Eng.* Bucharest *Rom.* Bucureşti) Romania Ottoman control 49/1
Bulandshar N India Indian Mutiny 104/1
Bulgar (Bolgar)
Bulgaria conversion to Christianity 38/2; Slav settlement 44/1; Mongol invasion 46/2; Black Death 57/1; under Ottoman rule 49/1, 124/1; independence 116/1, 230/4; Balkan alliances 116-117; WW1 118-9; conflict with Greece 129/2; socio-political change 1929-39 120/3; WW2 133/2; Warsaw Pact and Comecon 137/2; end of Communist rule 137/4. See also Rumelia
Bulgarians emigration from Greece and Turkey 129/3
Bulgars tribe of E Europe 31/4, 33/5
Bull Run (*a/c* Manassas) SE USA ⚔ 93/5
Buna SE New Guinea recaptured by Allies 135/2
Bunce Island Sierra Leone British settlement 61/2
Bundelkhand district of Central India Agency 105/3
Bunker Hill NE USA ⚔ 92/1
Bunyoro early state of E Africa 61/2
Buqayq (Abqaiq)
Burdigala (*mod.* Bordeaux) SW France Roman Empire 24/2, 30/3; early archbishopric 26/2
Buret' E Siberia Palaeolithic art 5/3
Burford C England mutiny of Parliamentary forces 76/4
Burgondiones (*Eng.* Burgundians) early tribe of Germany 30/3; invade France 32/2
Burgos N Spain Civil War 129/4
Burgundy (*Fr.* Bourgogne) region of E France kingdom conquered by Franks 34/1, 4, 35/2; province of medieval German Empire 55/1, 3; French Royal domain 52/2; acquisitions 14C and 15C 56/5; possessions in Low

Countries 73/3; annexed to France 72/2; province of France 80/1
Burkina (Faso) see Upper Volta
Burma spread of Buddhism 70/1; Mongol invasion 47/1; early state 51/2, 71/2; tributary state of Chinese Empire 106/1; annexed by Britain 104/2; under British rule 101/2, 105/3; Indian National Army 105/4; Japanese support for independence movements 127/5; Japanese occupation 134/1; retaken by Allies 135/2; independence 139/1; political development 141/1
Burnley N England Industrial Revolution 98/1
Burnt Corn SE USA ⚔95/2
Bursa (*anc.* Prusa *later* Brusa) W Anatolia Byzantine Empire 42/4; centre of Ottoman state 49/1
Burundi (*form.* Urundi) country of C Africa native state 61/2; independence 138/1; political development 140/1. See also Ruanda-Urundi
Burwell E England Industrial Revolution 98/1
Bury N England Industrial Revolution 98/1
Buryat-Mongol ASSR E USSR 146/2
Buryats Mongolian tribe 47/1
Bury St. Edmunds E England Industrial Revolution 98/1
Bushy Run NE USA⚔95/2
Bussa W Africa reached by Mungo Park 102/1
Buto Egypt early urban centre 16/1
Button, Sir Thomas explorer 64/1
Buxar NE India site 9/1;⚔87/2 (inset)
Buxentum (*Gr.* Pyxous, *a/s* Pyxus) S Italy Roman colony 30/1
Byblos (*mod.* Jubail) Syria early trade 17/4; Mycenaean trade 18/2; Phoenician city 19/4; Levantine city 21/1; Alexander's route 22/3
Byelorussia (Belorussia)
Bylany Czechoslovakia site 15/1
Bylot, Robert explorer 64/1
Byzantine Empire (*a/c* East Roman Empire) 30T; 36/2, 37/1, 40/2, 41/1, 42-43; conflict with Seljuks 41/2
Byzantium (*Eng.* Constantinople *mod.* Istanbul) E Thrace Dorian colony 19/4; Peloponnesian War 23/2; Roman Empire 24/1, 2; Achaemenid Empire 20/5

Cabeço da Arruda C Portugal megalithic tomb 14/1
Cabinda coastal district of SW Africa occupied by Portuguese 103/3
Cabral, Opero Portuguese explorer 64/2
Cacaxtla C Mexico early site 12/2
Cáceres W Spain Civil War 129/4
Cachar district of E India annexed by British 104/2, 105/3
Cacheu W Africa Portuguese settlement 60/2
Caddo S USA Indian tribe 63/1
Cádiz (*anc.* Gades) SW Spain reconquered from Muslims 37/4; trading port 82/4; naval base 87/2; Civil War 129/4
Caen N France 80/1; French Revolution 89/2; WW2 132/1, 2
Caere (*mod.* Cerveteri) C Italy Etruscan city 19/4
Caerleon (Isca)
Caernarvon (*Wel.* Caernarfon *anc.* Segontium) N Wales castle 53/7
Caesaraugusta (*mod.* Zaragoza *Eng.* Saragossa) N Spain Roman Empire 24/2, 30/3; early archbishopric 26/2
Caesarea C Israel Roman Empire 25/2, 31/3; early archbishopric 27/2; town of Judaea 26/3
Caesarea (*mod.* Cherchell) N Algeria Roman Empire 30/3
Caesarea (a/c Caesarea Cappadociae, *mod.* Kayseri) C Anatolia early archbishopric 27/2; Roman Empire 31/3; Byzantine Empire 43/1
Caesarodunum (Tours)
Caesaromagus (Chelmsford)
Cagliari (Carales)
Cahokia C USA early site 12/3; French post 67/3; fur station 94/1
Caiguá forest Indian tribe of S Brazil 63/1
Cairns E Australia early settlement 113/1
Cairo (*Fr.* Le Caire *Ar.* Al Qahirah and Al Fustat – Old Cairo) Egypt Muslim conquest 41/1; early trade 58/3, 61/2; captured by Ottomans 49/1; Ottoman Empire 48/2
Cajamarca C Andes site 12/4, 5
Cajamarqilla C Andes site 12/5
Cajon Pass SW USA 94/1
Calabria region of S Italy part of Kingdom of Naples 56/3
Calagurris (*mod.* Calahorra) N Spain Roman Empire 30/3
Calais N France 100 Years War 56/5; WW1 118/3; WW2 132/2
Calcutta E India trade 67/2; British settlement 66/2; industry 105/3; naval mutiny 105/4
Çaldıran (*a/s* Chaldiran) E Turkey⚔49/1
Caldy Island S Wales monastery 38/3
Caledonia (Scotland)
Cales C Italy Latin colony 30/1
Calgary W Canada growth 111/1
Calico Hills W USA early site 5/2
Calicut (*a/c* Kozhikode) SW India trade 59/3, 67/1; industry 105/3
California state of SW USA ceded by Mexico 97/1; Depression 130/2; population 145/1
Callao Peru trade 66/1
Callatis Bulgaria Ionian colony 19/4
Calleva (*mod.* Silchester) S England Roman Empire 30/3
Callipolis (*mod.* Gallipoli) S Italy Greek colony 19/4
Calne SW England Industrial Revolution 98/1
Calusa Indian tribe of SE USA 63/1
Camarina Sicily Dorian colony 19/4, 23/2
Cambaluc Mongolia early bishopric 39/1
Cambodia (*known formally as* Democratic Kampuchea *earlier* Khmer Republic) early sites 8/3; temple kingdoms 51/2; invaded by Siam and Vietnam 71/2; French protectorate 101/2; independence 139/1; Vietnamese war 148/3; political development 141/1
Cambous S France early settlement 14/2
Cambrai N France Burgundian possession 73/3; WW1 118/3 (inset)
Cambria (*mod.* Wales) expansion of Christianity 38/3
Cambridge E England castle 36/3; Industrial Revolution 98/1
Camden SE USA⚔92/1
Cameroon (*f/s* Cameroons, Cameroun *Ger.* Kamerun) country of W Africa German colony 100/1, 102-103, independence 138/1; economy 151/1
Campa forest Indian tribe of S America 63/1
Campania region of C Italy Roman Empire 30/1
Camp David Agreement 140T
Campeche province of S Mexico 97/1
Camulodunum (*mod* Colchester) S England Roman Empire 24/2, 30/3
Cana (*a/s* Cane) S Arabia early port 24/1
Canada early trade 68/5; Confederation 101/1; development 110-111; NATO 149/1; economy 109/1, 150/1
Canadian Pacific Railway 111/1
Çanakkale (*f/s* Chanak) W Turkey Greco-Turkish War 125/4
Çanakkale Boğazi (Dardanelles]
Canal de Briare N France 80/1
Canal Royal S France 80/1
Canary Islands Portuguese exploration 64/1; on early trade routes 66/1; Spanish sovereignty 87/1, 138/1
Canaveral, Cape (*for a short time called* Cape Kennedy) SE USA 65/3
Canberra SE Australia capital territory 113/1
Candamo N Spain Palaeolithic art 5/3
Çandar (*a/c* Kastamonu) early emirate of N Anatolia 49/1
Candelaria W Cuba Soviet missile site 149/5
Candida Casa S Scotland monastery 38/3
Çankırı (Gangra)
Cannae S Italy⚔31/2
Canterbury (*anc.* Durovernum *ecclesiastical Lat.* Cantuaria) S England monastery 38/3; Industrial Revolution 98/1
Canterbury S Island, New Zealand 112/2
Cantigny NE France WW1 118/3 (inset)
Canton S China trade 25/1, 59/3; treaty port 107/4; captured by Japanese 127/5
Canton River S China first European visit 65/2
Cantuaria (*mod.* Canterbury) archbishopric 26/1
Canusium (*mod.* Canosa di Puglia) S Italy Roman Empire 30/1
Canute the Great 38/2, 53/4
Caparcotna Palestine Roman Empire 25/2
Cap Blanc SW France Palaeolithic art 5/3
Cape Artemisium (*mod. Gr.* Artemision) E Greece⚔22/1
Cape Bojador NW Africa⚔60/2
Cape Breton Island E Canada French possession 86/1
Cape Coast Castle (*a/c* Cape Coast) Ghana early British settlement 60/2 (inset)
Cape Colony S Africa early settlement 60T; captured by British from Dutch 87/2; British colony 102-103 (inset)
Cape Finisterre NW Spain⚔90/3
Capeletti N Algeria cattle domestication 11/1
Cape of Good Hope S Africa first European voyage 65/2; Dutch settlement 61/2
Cape Province S Africa established by Dutch East India Co. 61/2
Cape St. Vincent S Portugal⚔90/3
Cape Town South Africa Dutch settlement 61/2
Cape Verde Islands W Africa Portuguese exploration 60/2; Portuguese sovereignty 100/2; independence 138/1
Capitanata region of C Italy part of Kingdom of Naples 56/3
Caporetto N Italy WW1⚔119/3
Cappadocia (*Pers.* Katpatuka) county of E Anatolia Alexander's Empire 22/3; independent state 22/4; Roman province 31/3; Byzantine province 42/2, 43/1
Capsa (*mod.* Gafsa) Tunisia Roman Empire 30/3
Capua S Italy Mithraic site 26/1; Roman Empire 24/2, 31/3
Caracas Venezuela colonised 69/3
Carajá forest Indian tribe of C Brazil 63/1
Carales (*mod.* Cagliari) Sardinia Roman Empire 30/3; archbishopric 26/2
Carapito N Portugal megalithic tomb 14/3
Carchemish (*Turk.* Karkamiş) E Anatolia 20/2, 21/1
Cardiff S Wales Industrial Revolution 98/1
Caria (*Pers.* Karka) country of W Asia Minor Persian province 23/1
Carib Indian tribe of Caribbean 63/1
Caribbean early voyages of discovery 65/3; European settlement 66/1; colonial expansion 69/3; US involvement 111/4, 142/1
Carinthia (*Ger.* Kärnten) province of S Austria Frankish duchy 54/1; medieval German Empire 55/3; acquired by Habsburgs 56/2, 78/3; Habsburgs duchy 79/1
Carlisle N England rebellion against Henry VIII 73/4; Industrial Revolution 98/1
Carmana (Kirman)
Carmania county of E Persia 23/3, 29/4
Carnatic (*a/c* Karnataka) coastal region of SE India 87/2
Carniola (*Ger.* Krain) region of Austria/Yugoslavia medieval Germany 55/3; acquired by Habsburgs 56/2, 78/3; Habsburg duchy 79/1
Carnuntum ancient town of Austria Mithraic site 26/1; Roman Empire 24/2, 31/3
Carolina N America British settlement 67/3
Caroline Islands C Pacific German sovereignty 101/2; captured by US from Japanese 135/2
Carolingian Empire (Frankish Kingdom)
Carpathos (*It.* Scarpanto) island of E Mediterranean colonisation 19/1
Carpi N Italy⚔81/5
Carreg Cennen S Wales castle 53/7
Carrier sub-arctic Indian tribe of NW Canada 63/1
Carson City W USA mining site 94/1
Cartagena (*anc.* Carthago Nova) SE Spain naval base 87/1, Civil War 129/4
Carteia S Spain Roman Empire 30/3
Carthage (*Lat.* Carthago) Tunisia Stone Age site 11/1; Phoenician colony 19/4; Roman Empire 24/2, 30/2, 3; early archbishopric 27/2; Byzantine reconquest 32/1; Muslim conquest 40/1
Carthago Nova (*mod.* Cartagena) SE Spain Roman Empire 24/2, 30/2, 3, 32/3; archbishopric 26/2
Cartier, Jacques French explorer 64/2
Cascades NW USA⚔95/2
Cashel Ireland bishopric 26/2
Casimir I king of Poland 72/1
Caspian Gates N Persia Alexander's route 23/3
Cassano N Italy⚔81/5
Cassel N France⚔81/4
Cassino C Italy WW2 133/2
Castellón de la Plana E Spain Civil War 129/4
Castiglione N Italy⚔91/1
Castile region of Spain at time of Reconquista 36/2; acquired by Habsburgs 72/1
Castillo N Spain Palaeolithic art 5/3
Castillo de Teayo Mexico Aztec town 62/2
Castle Cavern S Africa Iron Age site 11/1
Castoria N Greece Byzantine Empire 43/3
Castra Regina (*mod.* Regensburg *form. Eng.* Ratisbon) C Germany Roman fort 24/2
Castulo (*mod.* Cazlona) S Spain Roman Empire 30/3
Catalans people of NE Spain 115/1
Catalonia (*Sp.* Cataluña *Cat.* Catalunya) region of NE Spain reconquest by Aragon 37/4; under French rule 90/1; autonomous 128/2
Catana (*mod.* Catania) Sicily ally of Athens 23/2; Roman Empire 31/3; medieval German Empire 55/3
Catanzaro S Italy WW1 119/3
Catawba Indian tribe of SE USA 63/1
Cattaro (*mod.* Kotor) E Adriatic WW1 119/3
Caucasus early urban settlement 16/1; Muslim expansion 41/1
Cawahib forest Indian tribe of W Brazil 63/1
Cawnpore (*n/s* Kanpur) N India Indian Mutiny 104/1; civil unrest 104/4
Cayapó forest Indian tribe of C Brazil 63/1
Cayenne French Guiana colonisation 69/3
Çayönü E Anatolia early farming site 7/4
Cazlona (Castulo)
Ceará NE Brazil Confederation of the Equator 97/1
Cebu island of C Philippines Spanish control 67/1
Cedar Creek C USA⚔95/2
Cedar Mountain SE USA⚔93/5
Cefalù (*anc.* Cephaloedium) Sicily medieval German Empire 55/3
Celebes (*Indon.* Sulawesi) island of East Indies Muslim expansion 40/5; occupied by Japanese 134/1; state of Indonesia 139/2
Celenderis S Anatolia Ionian colony 19/4
Celts tribe of W Europe, France 19/4; expansion 15/5
Cempoala Mexico Aztec town 62/2; on Cortés' route 68/1
Cenomani early people of N Italy 30/1
CENTO treaty organisation 148T
Central African Federation (Northern Rhodesia, Southern Rhodesia, Nyasaland)
Central African Republic (*form.* Central African Empire *form.* Ubangi-Shari) independence 138/1; political development 140/1
Central Asian Gasfield USSR 147/1
Central India Agency Indian states under British control 104/1, 105/3
Central Provinces (*now* Madhya Pradesh) state of central India 105/3
Ceos (*mod.* Kea) island of the Aegean colonisation 19/1
Cephaloedium (Cefalù)
Cephalonia (*mod.* Kefallinia) island of the Ionian Byzantine Empire 43/3; Venetian territory 48/1
Cerdagne (*Sp.* Cerdaña) region of France and Spain Habsburg territory 80/1
Cerdicesford S England⚔33/2
Ceredigion district of Wales 53/7
Cerebon (Cheribon)

Cerigo (*anc.* Cythera, *mod.* Kithira) island of S Greece Venetian territory 48/1
Cerkes (Circassia)
Cernăuţi (Czernowitz)
Cerro de Trinidad C Andes early site 12/4
Cerveteri (Caere)
Cēsis (Wenden)
Ceský Těšín (Teschen)
Cetatea Alba (Akkerman)
Ceuta (*Ar.* Sebta) Spanish enclave in N Morocco Spanish occupation 100/2
Ceylon (*anc.* Taprobane, Sinhala *or* Lanka *a/c* Saylan, Sarandib) Graeco-Roman finds 25/1; 29/4; under British rule 87/3; Buddhism 105/3; independence 139/1; adopted title Republic of Sri Lanka 139/1; political developments 141/1
Chad (*Fr.* Tchad) country of C Africa independence from French 138/1; political development 140/1; economy 151/1
Chad, Lake C Africa European exploration 103/3
Chaeronea C Greece 23/2
Chagar Bazar (*a/c* Shubat-Enlil) Mesopotamia 16/1; Mitannian city 21/1
Chagatai Khanate C Asia 47/3, 4
Chagos Archipelago Indian Ocean British control 101/2
Chahar former province of N China 106/1; independent of Nanking 123/3
Chaiya S Thailand Hindu-Buddhist remains 51/2
Chakipampa C Andes early site 12/5
Chak Purbane Syal NW India early settlement 9/5
Chalcedon (*mod.* Kadiköy) NW Anatolia centre of early Christianity 26/1; Dorian colony 19/4; Council 38T
Chalcidice (*mod.* Khalkidhiki) region of N Greece Persian War 22/1
Chalcis C Greece parent state 19/4
Chaldian Theme Byzantine province of E Anatolia 42/2
Chaldiran (Çaldiran)
Chalon-sur-Saône S France medieval fair 59/2
Châlons-sur-Marne N France bishopric 117/1; seat of intendant 80/1; WW1 118/3; WW2 132/1
Chambéry SE France medieval fair 59/2
Champa Hindu-Buddhist kingdom of Indo-China 50/1, 51/2, 70/1; under Mongol control 47/1
Champagne region of NE France French Royal domain 52/2
Champaran district of N India civil disobedience 105/4
Champaubert NE France 90/1
Champion's Hill S USA✕93/5
Chanak (*Turk.* Çanakkale) W Turkey 1922 incident 129/2
Chancellorsville SE USA✕93/5
Chandernagore E India French settlement 67/2, 87/2
Chandoli W India site 9/1
Chandragupta I Indian king 29/5
Chandragupta II Indian king 29/5
Chandragupta Maurya Indian emperor 28T, 29/4
Changan N China Han capital on Silk Road 25/1; 29/3; T'ang city 50/1
Changchou E China T'ang prefecture 50/1
Changchun Manchuria treaty port 107/4; railway 127/4
Changi NW China Han commanderie 29/3
Changkufeng Manchuria Russo-Japanese conflict 127/5
Changsha C China Han principality 29/3; treaty town 107/4; captured by Kuomintang 122/2; captured by Japanese 135/1
Chang Tso-lin Chinese warlord 122/2
Changyeh NW China conquered by Han 28/2
Chanhu-Daro N India Harappan site 9/1, 5
Chansen N Thailand Iron Age site 8/3
Chao early state of N China 28/1
Chard SW England Industrial Revolution 98/1
Chardzhou (*until 1940* Chardzhuy) Russ. C. Asia industry 147/1
Charlemagne Frankish king 34T
Charles the Bold, of Burgundy, 35/5, 6; 72T
Charles Martel King of Franks 34T
Charles Town Path SE USA settlers' route 94/1
Charles V Holy Roman Emperor 72T
Charolais region of E France Habsburg possession 72/2
Charrúa Indian tribe of Argentina 63/1
Charsadda (*a/s Charsada) NW India* early trading centre 25/1
Charsinian Theme Byzantine province of C Anatolia 42/2
Charsinianum C Anatolia Byzantine Empire 42/2
Chassey E France farming site 15/1
Château-Thierry N France✕90/1; WW1 118/3 (inset)
Chatham SE England Dutch naval raid 81/3; naval base 87/1; Industrial Revolution 98/1; WW1 119/3
Chattanooga SE USA✕93/5
Chatti Germanic tribe of Roman Empire 30/3
Chauci Germanic tribe of Roman Empire 30/3
Chavín C Andes site 13/1
Chechen-Ingush ASSR Caucasus 146/2
Chedi early kingdom of N India 29/4
Chekiang province of E China Ming economy 51/4; Manchu expansion 106/1; Taiping control 107/3
Chełm (Kholm)
Chelmno Poland concentration camp 132/1
Chelmsford (*anc.* Caesaromagus) E England Industrial Revolution 98/1
Chelyabinsk C Russia industry 147/1
Chemin des Dames NE France WW1 118/3 (inset)
Chemnitz (*since 1953* Karl-Marx-Stadt) E Germany WW1 119/3
Chemulpo (Inchon)
Ch'en N China Chou domain 9/6
Cheng-chou N China Shang site 8/4; on railway 123/4
Cheng-ho early Chinese navigator 59/3
Chengtu W China on trade route 59/3; Ming provincial capital 51/4
Chepstow W England Industrial Revolution 98/1
Chera (*mod.* Kerala) region of S India 29/4
Cherbourg N France English base in 100 Years' War 56/5; French naval base 80/1, 87/1; WW2 132/2
Cherchell (Caesarea)
Cherchen Chin. C Asia silk route 28/2
Cheremkhovo S Siberia industry 147/1
Cherepovets NW Russia industry 147/1
Cheribon (*Dut.* Tjeribon *n/s* Ceribon) District of Java Dutch control 70/4
Chernigov Ukraine bishopric 38/2; principality 45/2
Chernovtsy (Czernowitz)
Cherokee Indian tribe of SE USA 63/1
Cherokees SE USA✕95/2
Chersonesus Crimea Ionian colony 19/4; bishopric 27/2
Cherusci Germanic tribe of Roman Empire 30/3
Chesowanja E Africa site of early man 3/3
Chester (*anc.* Deva) C England castle 36/3;✕33/3; county palatine 73/4; Industrial Revolution 98/1
Cheyenne plains Indian tribe of C USA 63/1
Ch'i NE China Chou domain 9/6; state 28/1
Chia NW China Western Chou domain 9/6
Chiang-hsi-an (*a/s Jiangxi'an) S China* early settlement 8/2
Chiang Kai-shek Chinese statesman 122T
Chiangling C China Western Chou site 9/6
Chiang Mai (Chiengmai)
Chiangnan Hsitao S China T'ang province 50/1
Chiangnan Tung E China Sung province 50/1
Chiangnan Tungtao SE China T'ang province 50/1
Chiao N China Western Chou domain 9/6
Chiaochih China/Vietnam Han commanderie 29/3
Chiaoho Chin. C Asia Han expansion 28/2
Chiapa de Corzo C Mexico early site 12/2
Chiapas province of S Mexico 97/1
Chiba C Japan city and prefecture 126/2
Chibcha Andean Indian tribe 63/1
Chicago N USA industry 109/1, 110/2; population 111/5; civil unrest 144/3
Chichén Itzá Mexico Mayan centre 12/2; Toltec domination 62/2
Chichester S England castle 36/3; Industrial Revolution 98/1
Chichou NE China T'ang prefecture 50/1
Chichun C China Western Chou site 9/6
Chickamauga SE USA✕93/5
Chickasaw Indian tribe of SE USA 95/2
Chienchou NE China Ming military post 51/4
Chienchung SW China T'ang province 50/1
Chiengmai (*n/s* Chiang Mai) N Thailand early political centre 51/2
Chiennan W China T'ang province 50/1
Chientao district of Manchuria occupied by Russia 127/4
Chienwei W China Han commanderie 29/3
Chieti (Teate)
Chihli former province of N China Boxer uprising 107/3
Chihuahua province of N Mexico 97/1; US military action 111/4
Chile Spanish colony 69/4; independence from Spain 97/1; War of the Pacific 97/4; exports and foreign investment 96/3; population 96/2; economy 142/2, 3; political development 143/1
Chilia-Nouă (Kilia)
Chimkent Russ. C Asia industry 147/1
Chimú Andean Indian tribe 63/1, 2
Chin district of W Burma annexed by British 104/2
Chin N China Chou domain 9/6; empire conquered by Mongols 46/1
Ch'in NW China Chou domain 9/6; empire 28/1, 2; 47/1
China early man 3/3; agricultural origins 7/2, 5; early agriculture 8/2; Shang dynasty 8/4; Chou dynasty 9/6; Silk Road 25/1; Buddhism 27/1; unification 28/1; Han expansion 28/2, 29/3; early Christianity 39/1; T'ang Empire 50/1; Mongol conquests 47/1; Ming Empire 51/4; early trade 51/4, 59/3; Ch'ing 106-107; Manchu expansion 106/1; Manchu Empire 107/4; Russo-Japanese war 127/4; European spheres of influence 107/4; Boxer rebellion 107/3; Empire overthrown 122/1; Communist Party founded 123/4, 5; Japanese occupation 127/3, 5; WW2 134-135; Cold War 149/1; political development 141/1
Chingchi N China T'ang province 50/1
Chinghai (Tsinghai)
Chingkang Shan SE China early Communist soviet 123/4
Chingleput SE India ceded to Britain 87/3
Chinkiang E China treaty port 107/4
Chinkultic E Mexico Mayan centre 12/2
Chinnampo N Korea Russo-Japanese war 127/4
Chinook coast Indian tribe of W Canada 63/1
Chinsura Bengal Dutch settlement 66/2; 87/2
Chios (*mod. Gk.* Khios) island of E Aegean in Mycenaean world 18/2; bishopric 27/2; to Genoa 48/1; ceded to Greece 116/1
Chiozza N Italy Palaeolithic art 5/3
Chipewyan sub-arctic Indian tribe of N Canada 63/1
Chirand NE India site 9/1
Ch'i-shan (*a/s Qishan) W China* oracle bones 8/4
Chishima-retto (Kurile Islands)
Chisholm Trail C USA cattle trail 94/1
Chişinău (Kishinev)
Chita E Siberia Trans-Siberian railway 84/3; capital of Far Eastern Republic 120/4; industry 147/1
Chittagong SE Bangladesh trade 59/3
Chiuchang E China Han commanderie 29/3
Chiuchen N Indo-China Han commanderie 29/3
Chiuhua Shan mountain of E China Buddhist site 27/1
Chiusi (Clusium)
Chkalov (Orenburg)
Chocó Indian tribe of S America 63/1
Choctaw Indian tribe of S USA 95/2
Choga Mami Mesopotamia farming village 7/4
Choga Mish W Persia early city 16/2
Chola ancient country of S India 29/4
Cholet NW France French Revolution 89/2
Cholula C Mexico early site 12/2; on Cortés' route 68/1
Chorasmii people of C Asia 23/3
Chosen (Korea)
Chota Nagpur region of N India 105/3
Chotin (Khotin)
Chou NC China Western Chou domain 9/6; warring state 28/1
Chou-k'ou-tien N China site 3/3, 5/2
Christchurch S Island, New Zealand founded 112/2
Christiania (Oslo)
Christianity, spread of 26-27, 38-9
Christiansborg Gold Coast early Danish settlement 60/2 (inset)
Chu N China Western Chou domain 9/6
Ch'u C China Chou domain 9/6; warring state 28/1
Ch'u NE China Western Chou domain 9/6
Chud (*a/c* Chudi) early tribe of N Russia 45/2
Chudskoye Ozero (Lake Peipus)
Chufin N Spain Palaeolithic art 5/3
Chukchi tribe of NE Siberia 84/2; AD 146/2
Chumash Indian tribe of W USA 63/1
Chün C China Western Chou domain 9/6
Chün N China Western Chou site 9/6
Chungking C China treaty town 107/4; capital during WW2 127/5
Chustenahlah C USA✕95/2
Chuvashi tribe of C Russia, conquered 85/1; ASSR 146/2
Chuyen NW China administrative centre of later Han 28/2
Ciboney Indian tribe of the Caribbean 63/1
Cibyrrhaeot Theme Byzantine province of S Anatolia 42/2
Cieszyn (Teschen)
Cilicia (*Hittite name* Kizzuwadna) region of S Anatolia 19/4, 20/4; Alexander's Empire 22/3; Achaemenid Empire 20/5; Roman province 31/3, Byzantine Empire 43/1; French sphere of influence 125/3
Cincinnati N USA industry 109/1, 110/2; civil unrest 144/3
Circassia (*Turk.* Çerkes) region of Caucasus 49/1
Circeii C Italy Latin colony 30/1
Cirencester (*anc.* Corinium) W England Industrial Revolution 98/1
Cirene (Cyrene)
Cirrha C Greece early site 19/1
Cirta (*mod.* Constantine) N Algeria Roman Empire 24/2, 30/2, 3; early bishopric 26/2
Cisalpine Republic N Italy state established by French Revolution 89/2
Cishan (Tz'u-shan)
Cissbury SE England megalithic flint mine 14/3
Citium (*OT* Kittim) Cyprus Phoenician colony 19/4; Levantine port 21/1
Ciudad de México (Mexico City)
Civil War England 76/4
Civil War Spain 129/4
Civil War USA 92/5
Civita Castellana (Falerii)
Claudy N Ireland IRA 136/6
Clava N Scotland megalithic tomb 14/3
Clearwater NW USA✕95/2
Cleveland N USA industry 109/1, 110/2; civil unrest 144/3
Cleves (*Ger.* Kleve) NW Germany Reformation 75/1; duchy 79/1
Clonard Ireland monastery 38/3
Cloncurry N Australia copper mining 113/1
Clonfert Ireland monastery 38/3
Clonmacnoise Ireland monastery 38/3
Clontibret N Ireland✕73/4
Clovis S USA early site 5/2
Clovis King of Franks 34T
Cloyne Ireland bishopric 26/2
Clusium (*mod.* Chiusi) N Italy Etruscan city 30/1
Clyde-Carlingford Cairns Scotland 15/4
Clysma Red Sea early port 25/1; Roman Empire 25/2
Cnossus (*Gr.* Knossos) Crete Roman Empire 24/2, 31/3

Coahuila province of N Mexico 97/1; US military action 111/4
Coahuiltec Indian tribe of N Mexico 63/1
Coalbrookdale C England Industrial Revolution 98/1
Cobá E Mexico Mayan centre 12/2
Coblenz *(n/s Koblenz) W Germany* WW1 119/3; administrative centre 137/5
Cochimi Indian tribe of W Mexico 63/1
Cochin region of S India early trade 59/3; Portuguese rule 66/2, 67/1; Dutch settlement 67/1; British rule 104/1
Cochin-China region of S Indo-China expansion into Cambodia 71/2; French control 101/1
Cocos Islands *(now* under Australian administration *called* Cocos-Keeling islands) Indian Ocean British control 101/2
Coele Roman province of SE Anatolia 31/3
Coelho, Duarte Portuguese soldier 64/2
Coimbatore district of S India civil unrest 104/4
Colchester (Camulodunum)
Colchis ancient country of the Caucasus, Ionian colonisation 19/4; 22/3, 31/3
Coldizzi Slav tribe of SE Germany 54/2
Cold War 148-9
Colenso S Africa✕103/4
Colima province of C Mexico 97/1
Cologne *anc.* Colonia Agrippina *Ger.* Köln) W Germany medieval city 54/1, 55/3; Hanseatic city 59/2; archbishopric 34/4; WW1 119/3; WW2 133/2
Colombia independence from Spain 97/1; exports and foreign investment 96/3; population 96/2; political development 143/1; economy 142/2, 3; 150/1
Colombo Ceylon early trade 59/3; Portuguese trade 67/1; Dutch trade 66/2; capital of British colony 105/3
Colón Panama Canal Zone 111/4
Colonia Agrippina *(a/c* Colonia Agrippinesis *mod* Köln *Eng* Cologne) NW Germany Mithraic site 26/1; Roman Empire 24/2, 30/3; bishopric 26/2
Colonian Theme Byzantine province of E Anatolia 42/2
Colorado state of W USA Depression 130/2; population 145/1
Colossae W Anatolia town of Achaemenid Empire 20/5
Columba, St. 38/3
Columban, St. 38/3
Columbia SE USA burned 93/5
Columbus, Christopher 64-65
Comacchio N Italy captured by Venice 36/2
Comalcalco E Mexico early site 12/2
Comanche plains Indian tribe of S USA 63/1
Combarelles SW France Palaeolithic art 5/3
COMECON 137/3
Commagene region of SE Anatolia Roman province 31/3
Commenda W Africa early British settlement 60/2 (inset)
Comminges independent fief of SW France 72/2
Como N Italy Lombard League 55/3
Comoro Islands E Africa spread of Islam 61/2; French colonisation 101/2; independence 138/1
Compiègne NE France WW1 119/2
Comtat Venaissin S France Papal state 72/2
Conakry W Africa occupied by French 103/3
Concord NE USA✕92/1
Condatomagus *(mod.* La Graufesenque) S France Roman Empire 24/2
Confederate States of America 93/4
Confederation of the Rhine 91/1
Confucius Chinese philospher 26T
Congo *(form.* Middle Congo *or* French Congo) region of Africa independence 138/1; economy 151/1
Congo Free State *(later* Belgian Congo *now* Zaire) 101/2, 103/3
Connaught *(a/s* Connacht) region of W Ireland Norman-Angevin overlordship 53/6; Presidency 73/4
Connecticut NE USA colony 67/3; Depression 131/2; population 145/1
Connell's Prairie NW USA✕95/2
Consentia *(mod.* Cosenza) S Italy Roman Empire 30/1
Constance *(anc.* Constantia *Ger.* Konstanz) S Germany Frankish kingdom 55/3
Constanța *(Turk.* Küstence) E Romania WW1 119/3
Constantia (Salamis)
Constantinople *(anc.* Byzantium *mod.* Istanbul) NW Turkey centre of early Christianity 26/1; Avar attack 32/1; patriarchate 38/2; Arab attacks 41/1; Byzantine Empire 42/4; trade 58/3; WW1 119/3; Russian sphere of influence 125/3
Conway Castle N Wales 53/7
Cook, Capt. James 64-65
Cook Islands S Pacific early Polynesian settlement 10/2; New Zealand possession 139/1 (inset)
Cook Strait New Zealand rail ferry 112/2
Cooktown E Australia early settlement 113/1
Copán E Mexico Mayan site 12/2
Copenhagen *(Dan.* København) Denmark✕90/3; WW2 133/2
Copts Christian people of Egypt and Ethiopia 38/1
Coptus Lower Egypt Roman Empire 25/2, 31/3; bishopric 27/2
Coquilhatville *(now* Mbandaka) NW Belgian Congo 138/4
Cora Indian tribe of C Mexico 63/1
Coracesium S Anatolia 19/4
Coral Sea S Pacific✕134/1, 135/2
Corbie N France monastery 34/4
Corcyra *(mod.* Corfu *Gr.* Kerkira) island of NW Greece Donan colony 19/4
Córdoba *(anc.* Corduba) S Spain Muslim conquest 40/1; Umayyad Caliphate and Muslim city 36/2, 37/1; reconquered from Muslims 37/4; Mediterranean trade 58/3; Civil War 129/4
Corduba *(mod.* Córdoba) S Spain Roman Empire 24/2, 30/3; bishopric 26/2
Corfe Castle S England 36/3
Corfu *(anc.* Corcyra *mod. Gr.* Kerkira) island of W Greece Byzantine Empire 42/3; under Venetian rule 48/1; Ottoman siege 48/2
Corinium (Cirencester)
Corinth *(Lat.* Corinthus *Gr.* Korinthos) C Greece parent state 19/4; archbishopric 27/2; Byzantine Empire 43/1
Corinth SE USA✕93/5
Corinthus *(Gr.* Korinthos *eng.* Corinth) C Greece town of Roman Empire 24/2, 31/3
Cork S Ireland Viking settlement 37/1; monastery 38/3
Cormantin W Africa early Dutch settlement 60/2 (inset)
Corneto (Tarquinii)
Cornwall county of SW England early tin source 14/2; rebellion 73/4
Corregidor C Philippines surrender to Japanese 134/1
Corsica island of W Mediterranean Muslim conquest 40/1; Saracen attack 37/1; Byzantine Empire 42/1; Pisan conquest 36/2; Genoese rule 73/5; annexed by France 114/3
Corte-Real, Gaspar and Miguel Portuguese explorers 54/2
Cortés, Hernando conqueror of Mexico 68T/1
Cortona N Italy Etruscan city 19/4, 30/1
Corunna *(Sp.* La Coruña) NW Spain✕90/1
Cos island of E Aegean bishopric 27/2
Cosa N Italy Roman Empire 30/1
Cosenza (Cosentia)
Cossacks S Russia attacked by Ottomans 85/1; anti-Bolshevik activity 121/2
Cossaei tribe of W Persia 22/3
Costa Rica country of C America independence 97/1; political development 143/1; economy 142/2, 3; 150/1
Costoboci early tribe of SE Europe 31/3
Cotyora *(mod.* Ordu) N Anatolia Ionian colony 19/4
Cougnac SW France Palaeolithic art 5/3
Courland *(Ger.* Kurland) region of W Russia occupied by Teutonic Knights 54/4; Reformation 75/1
Courtrai *(Dut.* Kortrijk) Belgium✕52/2
Cova Negra SE Spain site of early man 3/3
Coventry C England Industrial Revolution 98/1; WW2 132/1
Coveta de l'Or SE Spain farming site 15/1
Cracow *(Pol.* Kraków) SE Poland bishopric 38/2, 53/1; Hanseatic city 59/2
Craigavon N Ireland IRA 137/6
Crécy N France✕56/5
Cree sub-arctic Indian tribe of N Canada 63/1
Creek Indian tribe of SE USA 95/2
Crema N Italy Lombard League 55/3
Cremona N Italy Latin colony 30/1; Lombard League 55/3; Signorial domination 56/3
Crescent Island E Africa early site 11/1
Crete *(Lat.* Creta *mod. Gr.* Kriti) migrations to Greece and Aegean 18-19; Muslim conquest 41/1; Byzantine Empire 36/2, 43/1; Venetian territory 73/1; Ottoman province 124/1; cession to Greece 116/1; German capture 133/2
Criccieth N Wales castle 57/7
Crimea *(Russ.* Krym) S Russia conquered by Mongols 46/1; acquired by Russia 85/1; Ottoman vassal khanate 49/1
Crna Gora Montenegro)
Croatia *(S. Cr.* Hrvatska) conversion to Christianity 38/2; Mongol invasion 46/2; under Hungarian Kingdom 56/2; forms part of Yugoslavia 128/2; WW2 133/2; independence and civil war 137/4
Croats Slav people of SE Europe 32/2
Cro-Magnon France site of early man 3/3
Cromarty N Scotland WW1 118/3
Cromna N Anatolia Ionian colony 19/4
Crooked Creek C USA✕95/2
Cross, Cape SW Africa Portuguese discovery 64/1
Crossmaglen N Ireland IRA 137/6
Croton *(mod.* Crotone) S Italy Achaean colony 19/4; Roman colony 30/1, 31/2, 3
Crow plains Indian tribe of W Canada 63/1
Crown Point *(Fr.* Fort St. Frédéric) Quebec capture by British 86/1
Croydon NE Australia early settlement 113/1
Crumlin S Wales Industrial Revolution 98/1
Cruni Bulgaria Ionian colony 19/4
Crusades 36T, 38T, 40/3, 43/3
Ctesiphon *(a/c* Tayspun) Mesopotamia early trade 25/1; Roman Empire 31/3
Cuba discovered 64/2; Spanish colony 66/1, 4; 69/3, 86/1; independence 97/1; exports and investment 96/3; US Protectorate 143/1; Cold War crisis 149/5
Cuddapah S India ceded to Britain 87/3
Cueva de la Menga S Spain megalithic tomb 14/3
Cuiry-lès-Chaudardes NE France farming site 15/1
Cullalvera N Spain Palaeolithic art 5/3
Cultural Revolution China 140T
Cumae C Italy Ionian colony 19/4, 23/2; Roman Empire 30/1
Cumberland House C Canada fort 68/5
Cuna Indian tribe of C America 63/1
Cunaxa Mesopotamia✕21/5
Curaçao island of S West Indies captured by Dutch from Spanish 69/3; Dutch settlement and colonisation 97/1, 139/1 (inset)
Curium Cyprus Greek colony 19/4
Curlew Mts NW Ireland✕73/4
Custozza N Italy✕114/3
Cutch (Kutch)
Cuttack E India ceded to Britain 87/3
Cuxhaven N Germany WW 119/3
Cuzco Peru Inca Empire 68/2
Cymru (Wales)
Cynoscephalae C Greece✕22/4
Cynossema W Anatolia✕23/2
Cyprus *Gr.* Kypros *Turk.* Kibris *anc.* Alashiya) Mycenaean trade 18/2; Greek and Phoenician colonisation 19/4; Muslim expansion 41/1; Byzantine Empire 37/2, 40/3, 43/1; Venetian territory 49/1; acquired by Turks 48/2; annexed by Britain 125/2; independence 138/1; invaded by Turkey 140/1
Cyrenaica region of N Africa Roman province 31/3; Muslim conquest 41/1; Ottoman rule 61/2; Italian conquest 103/3
Cyrene *(It.* Cirene) N Libya Iron Age site 11/1; Dorian colony 19/4; spread of Christianity and Judaism 26/1; Achaemenid Empire 20/5; centre of Roman province 24/2, 31/3; early bishopric 27/2
Cyropolis *a/c* Krukath) C Asia Alexander's route 23/3; Achaemenid Empire 21/5
Cyrus King of Persia 21/5
Cythera *(a/c* Cerigo *mod. Gr* Kithira) *island* S Greece colonisation 19/1; captured by Athens 23/2
Cytorus N Anatolia Ionian colony 19/4
Cyzicus NW Anatolia✕23/2; Ionian colony 19/4; early archbishopric 27/2
Czechoslovakia created 128/2; inter-war alliances 128/1; socio-political development 131/3; territory lost to Germany and Hungary 129/5, 132-3; Comecon and Warsaw Pact 137/2; end of Communist rule 137/4
Czech Republic independence 137/4
Czechs post-War migration to West 136/1
Czernowitz *(now Russ.* Chernovtsy *Rom.* Cernăuţi) E Austro-Hungarian Empire WW1 119/3

Dabarkot NW India Harappan site 9/5
Dabromierz (Hohenfriedeberg)
Da But N Vietnam Neolithic site 8/3
Dacca Bangladesh anti-British riots 105/4; industry 105/3
Dachau S Germany concentration camp 132/1
Dacia *(mod.* Romania) province of Roman Empire 31/3; Byzantine Empire 43/1
Dade Massacre SE USA✕95/2
Dagestan ASSR Caucasus 146/2
Daghestan region of Caucasus acquired by Russia 125/1
Dagobert I King of Franks 34T
Dagon *(mod.* Rangoon) S Burma Buddhism 70/1
Dahae early tribe of C Asia 23/3
Dahomey *(n/c* Benin) country of W Africa early state 61/2; French colony 100/2, 103/3; independence 138/1
Dahshur Lower Egypt pyramid and royal tomb 17/3
Daima NW Africa Iron Age site 11/1
Daimabad S India site 9/1
Daimyo Japanese military class 50T, 51/3
Dairen *(Russ.* Dalny) Manchuria ceded to Russia and Japan 107/4; Russo-Japanese war 127/4
Dai Viet kingdom of N Indo-China 51/2
Dakar Senegal, W Africa French settlement 103/3
Daleminzi Slav tribe of C Germany 54/2, 55/1
Dalmatia region of E Adriatic Byzantine Empire 43/3; acquired by Habsburgs 78/3
Dalny (Dairen)
Daman *(Port.* Damão) NW India Portuguese settlement 105/3
Damascus *(Fr.* Damas *Ar.* Ash Sham *or* Dimashq) Syria Levantine city 21/1; Roman Empire 25/2; early trade 25/1, 58/3; archbishopric 38/1; Muslim conquest 41/1; Byzantine Empire 43/1; revolt against Ottoman rule 48/2; Ottoman Empire 49/1; WW1 125/2; French occupation 125/3
Damb Buthi N India early site 9/5
Damietta *(Ar.* Dumyat) N Egypt Byzantine Empire 43/1
Danakil tribe of NE Africa 60/1
Da Nang *(Fr.* Tourane) C Indo-China Vietnamese war 148/3
Danelaw England under Scandinavian control 36T
Danes people of N Europe 37/1, 3; 115/1
Danzig *(Pol.* Gdańsk) N Poland to Prussia 78/4; Hanseatic city 59/2; Baltic trade 58/3; 18C financial centre 82/4; Free City 128/2
Dara C Egypt pyramid 17/3
Dardanelles *(Turk.* Çanakkale Boğazi *anc.* Hellespont) straits, NW Turkey Russian sphere of influence 125/3; demilitarised and remilitarised 128/2
Dardani early people of the Balkans 22/3
Dar es Salaam E Africa occupied by the Germans 103/3
Dar-Es-Sultan N Morocco site of early man 3/3

Darfur region of W Sudan stone age culture 11/1; early state 60/1, 61/2
Darius I, of Persia 22/1
Dartford SE England Industrial Revolution 98/1
Darwin N Australia early settlement 113/1; Allied base in WW2 135/2
Dascylium NW Anatolia Greek colony 19/4
Daugavpils (Dünaburg)
Dauphiné region of SE France French Royal domain 52/5, 56/5; province of France 80/1
David King of Israelites 21/4
Davis, John English explorer 64-65
Dawenkou (Ta-wen-k'ou)
Dead Buffalo Lake E USA⚔95/2
Debre Birhan Ethiopia monastery 38/1
Debre Markos Ethiopia monastery 38/1
Decapolis Judaea 26/3
Deccan region of C India Sultanates 48/2
Dego N Italy⚔90/1
Deheubarth dist. of Wales 36/3
Deira ancient kingdom of N England 33/3, 35/3
Delagoa Bay SE Africa early trade 61/2; Portuguese settlement 87/2
Delaware state of E USA settled by Swedes 67/3; British colony 92/1; Depression 131/2; population 145/1
Delaware Indian tribe of NE USA 63/1
Delhi city and region of N India⚔41/4; Mongol invasion 47/1; Mughal Empire 48/2, 47/1, 3; medieval trade 59/3; Indian Mutiny 104/1
Delhi Sultanate N India 41/4, 48T
Delian League Greece 23/2
Delium E Greece⚔/23/2
Delphi C Greece early settlement 15/5
Demetrias E Greece Byzantine Empire 43/1
Denain N France⚔81/5
Denbigh N Wales⚔53/7
Denizli (Laodicea)
Denmark conversion to Christianity 38/2; rise of 52/3; union with Norway and Sweden 72/1, 114/4; Reformation 75/1; emancipation of peasantry 82/1; loss of Schleswig-Holstein 114/4; war with Prussia and Austria 115/2; WW1 118-9; N Holstein acquired by plebiscite 128/2; socio-political change 130/3; WW2 132-3; EEC and NATO 137/3, 149/1
Denver W USA industry 109/1
Deorham S England⚔33/3
Deoti N India early site 9/1
Der (*n/c* Badra) E Mesopotamia early city 16/2, 17/4
Derbe S Anatolia early bishopric 27/2
Derbent Caucasus 23/3, 48/2
Derby C England Danish Viking base 37/1; Industrial Revolution 98/1
Derby W Australia early settlement 113/1
Derry *(a/c Londonderry) N Ireland* castle 53/6
Derrynahinch S Ireland megalithic tomb 14/3
Dertona (*mod.* Tortona) NW Italy Roman colony 30/1
Desalpur NW India Harappan site 9/5
Desert, War of the Argentina 97/1
Desmond dist. of SW Ireland 53/6
Detroit *form.* Fort Pontchartrain) C USA fur station 94/1;⚔95/2; industry 109/1; civil unrest 144/3
Deutscher Zollverein German Customs Union 98/3
Deva (*mod.* Chester) C England Mithraic site 26/1; Roman Empire 24/2, 30/3
Deventer Netherlands Hanseatic town 59/2
Devil's Gate W USA pass 94/1
Devonport SW England WW1 118/3
Dhal N India early site 9/5
Dhali (Idalium)
Dharwar district of W India civil unrest 104/4
Dhodhekanisos (Dodecanese)
Dhofar S Arabia early trade 59/3
Dhu'l-Kadr early emirate of SE Anatolia 49/1
Diaguita Andean Indian tribe of S America 63/1
Dibse (Thapsacus)
Diedenhofen (*now* Thionville) NE France Frankish royal residence 34/4
Die Kelders S Africa Stone Age site 11/1
Dien Bien Phu N Vietnam French defeat 148/3
Dieppe N France fortification 80/1; WW1 118-119; WW2 132/1
Dijon E France parlement 80/1; French Revolution 89/2
Dilmun Persian Gulf early urban centre 16/1
Dilolo C Africa Livingstone's route 102/1
Dimashq Damascus)
Dimolit N Philippines Neolithic site 8/3
Dinefwr (*a/c* Dinevor) S Wales castle 53/7
Diocaesarea Palestine early archbishopric 27/2
Diocletian Roman emperor 30T
Dioscurias (*mod.* Sukhumi) Caucasus Ionian colony 19/4; Roman Empire 25/2
Diospolis Magna (Thebes)
Diu NW India Portuguese settlement 66/2, 67/1, 100/2; Ottoman siege 48/2
Divostin C Yugoslavia farming site 15/1
Dixcove Ghana early British settlement 60/2 (inset)
Diyarbakir SE Anatolia revolt against Ottoman rule 48/2
Djakarta (Jakarta)
Djenné (Jenne)
Djerba *island* Tunisia⚔48/2
Djibouti *(s/s Jibuti) NE Africa* occupied by French 103/3
Djibouti (French Territory of the Afars and Issas. French Somaliland)
Dmitrov W Russia town of Vladimir-Suzdal 45/2
Dnepropetrovsk (*until 1926* Yekaterinoslav) S Russia industry 84/4, 147/1
Dobruja (*a/s* Dobrudja) region of Romania/Bulgaria Ottoman Empire 49/1, 116/1, 128/2
Dodecanese (*Gr.* Dhodhekanisos) islands of SE Aegean occupied by Italy, ceded to Turkey 116/1; ceded to Italy 124/3
Dodge City C USA cow town 94/1
Dogrib sub-arctic Indian tribe of NW Canada 63/1
Dôle Switzerland occupied by France 81/4
Dolmen de Soto SW Spain megalithic tomb 14/3
Dolní Věstonice Czechoslovakia site of early man 3/3; Palaeolithic art 5/3
Domfront NE France 17C revolts 77/2
Dominica island of West Indies disputed by England and France 86/1; British colony 97/1; independence 139/1 (inset)
Dominican Republic Caribbean independence 97/1; US intervention 143/1
Donbass industrial region of S Russia 147/1
Doncaster N England Industrial Revolution 98/1
Donets S Russia town of Pereyaslavl 45/2
Donetsk (*until 1924 called* Yuzovka *until 1961* Stalino) S Russia industry 147/1
Dong Dau N Vietnam Neolithic site 8/3
Dong Duong C Indo-China Hindu-Buddhist temple 51/2
Dong Son N Indo-China early site 8/3
Donner Pass W USA 94/1
Dorchester-on-Thames S England⚔35/3
Dorestad *(a/c Duurstede) Netherlands* Viking invasion and settlement 37/1
Dorginarti island of Upper Nile Egyptian fortress 21/1
Dorians early Greeks 18-19
Dorpat (*form. Russ.* Yuryev *mod.* Tartu) W Russia founded by Teutonic Knights 54/4; Hanseatic city 59/2
Dortmund W Germany Hanseatic city 59/2
Dorylaeum (*mod.* Eskişehir) W Anatolia Byzantine Empire 42/2
Dos Pilas E Mexico Mayan centre 12/2
Douai NE France medieval fair 58/1
Douala Cameroon W Africa German occupation 103/3
Dove Creek C USA⚔95/2
Dover (*anc.* Dubris) SE England Industrial Revolution 98/1; WW1 118/3
Dowlais S Wales Industrial Revolution 98/1
Down N Ireland bishopric 26/2
Dowth E Ireland megalithic tomb 14/3
Doxanii Slav tribe of E Europe 54/2
Drangiana (*Pers.* Zranka) Afghanistan province of Alexander's Empire 23/3
Drapsaca (*mod.* Kunduz) Afghanistan Alexander's Empire 23/3
Dregovichi Slav tribe of W Russia 44/1
Dresden E Germany⚔90/1; WW1 119/3; WW2 133/2
Drevlyane Slav tribe of Russia 44/1
Dristov Romania⚔44/1
Drobetae (*mod.* Turnu-Severin) Roman Empire 31/3
Drogheda E Ireland⚔76/4
Drogochin W Russia town of Vladimir-Volynsk 45/2
Dublin (*Ir.* Baile Atha Cliath) Ireland Scandinavian settlement and control 37/1; taken by England 73/4; 18C urban development 82/4; WW1 118/3
Dubris (*mod.* Dover) SE England Roman Empire 24/2
Dubrovnik (Ragusa)
Duisburg W Germany WW1 118/3
Dumfries county of S Scotland acquired by Edward III 56/4
Dumyat (Damietta)
Dünaburg (*Russ.* Dvinsk *n/c* Daugavpils) W Russia occupied by Teutonic Knights 54/4
Dunbar S Scotland⚔53/6, 56/4, 76/4
Dunedin S Island, New Zealand 112/2
Dungannon N Ireland IRA 137/6
Dungeness S England Dutch naval victory 81/3
Dunkirk (*Fr.* Dunkerque) N France fortification 80/1; WW2 132/1
Dupleix, Joseph French administrator in India 87T/2
Dura-Europos (*mod.* Salahiyeh) Syria early trade 25/1; Mithraic site 26/1; Roman Empire 25/2, 31/3; early church 27/2
Durango province of N Mexico 97/1
Durazzo (*anc.* Epidamnus *later* Dyrrhachium *mod.* Durrës) Albania captured by Mormons 36/2; WW1 119/3
Durban S Africa Boer War 103/4
Durham N England castle 36/3; bishopric 56/4; palatinate 73/4
Durocortorum (*mod.* Rheims) N France Roman Empire 30/3
Durostorum (*mod.* Silistra) Bulgaria Roman Empire 24/2, 31/3
Durrës (Dyrrhachium)
Dushanbe *(1929-1961 Stalinabad) Russ. C Asia* industry 147/1
Düsseldorf W Germany WW1 118/3; WW2 132/1
Dutch East Indies (*now* Indonesia) early Dutch trade 67/2; early Dutch possessions 71/2; occupied by Japanese 134/1; independence 139/1 (inset)
Dutch Guiana (*now* Surinam) S America 69/3, 100/2
Dutch New Guinea (*later* West Irian *n/c* Irian Jaya) East Indies transferred to Indonesia 139/1
Dutch Republic (*or* United Provinces *or* Holland) revolt against Spain 76/1; wars with England 81/3; in War of Spanish Succession 81/5
Dutch West Indies (Netherlands Antilles)
Duurstede (Dorestad)
Dvaravati W Thailand early Mon kingdom 51/2
Dvin Caucasus early archbishopric 27/2
Dyfed early kingdom of Wales 33/3, 35/3, 53/7
Dyola trading people of W Africa 61/2
Dyrrhachium (*earlier* Epidamnus *mod.* Durrës/*t.* Durazzo) Albania Roman Empire 24/2, 31/3; Byzantine Empire 43/1, 3
Dzaudzhikau (Ordzhonikidze)
Dzhambul (*from 1936-8 called Mirzoyan earlier* Auliye-Ata) Russ. C Asia industry 147/1
Dzhruchula Caucasus site of early man 3/3
Dzibilchaltún E Mexico Mayan site 12/2
Dzungaria region of C Asia occupied by Chinese 50/1
Dzungars people of NW China 106/1

East Anglia region of E England conversion to Christianity 38/3; Scandinavian settlement 37/1
East Bengal (*later* East Pakistan *now* Bangladesh) separation from India 105/5
Easter Island E Pacific Polynesian settlement 10/2
Eastern Rumelia region of Balkans Ottoman province 124/1; ceded to Bulgaria 116/1
Eastern Turkestan C Asia Chinese protectorate 106/1
East Frisia county of N Germany 78/2, 79/1
East India Company 70-71, 104T
East Indies agricultural origins 7/4; spread of Islam 40/5; early kingdoms 51/2; early trade 71/2; European rivalries 70/3. See also Dutch East Indies, Indonesia
East Pakistan (Bangladesh)
East Prussia (*Ger.* Ostpreussen) region of E Germany unification with Germany 78/2; WW2 132/1; divided between Poland and Russia 137/4
East Roman Empire (Byzantine Empire)
Ebbou SW France Palaeolithic art 5/3
Ebbsfleet SE England⚔33/3
Ebla Syria early urban settlement 16/1, 17/4
Eburacum (*mod.* York) N England Mithraic site 26/1; Roman Empire 24/2, 30/3; archbishopric 26/2
Eburodunum (Embrun)
Ecbatana (*mod.* Hamadan) W Persia 20/2; Alexander's route 22/3
Echmiadzin (Vagarshapat)
Echternach W Germanyy monastery 34/4
Eckmühl/Ebersberg S Germany⚔91/1
Ecnomus Sicily⚔31/2
Ecuador independence 97/1, 143/1; political development 143/1; economy 96/3, 142/2, 3, 150/1
Edessa (*mod.* Urfa) SE Anatolia Roman Empire 25/1, 2; early archbishopric 27/2; First Crusade 43/3; Crusader state 40/3
Edfu (*a/s Idfu anc.* Apollinopolis) Upper Egypt 17/3
Edgehill C England⚔76/4
Edinburgh S Scotland medieval trade 59/2;⚔73/4; National Covenant 76/4; 18C textile industry 82/4; industrial development 98/1
Edirne (*Eng.* Adrianople) SE Europe Ottoman Empire 49/1
Edjek S Philippines Neolithic site 8/3
Edmonton W Canada growth 111/1
Edmundston E Canada growth 111/1
Edo (*mod.* Tokyo) C Japan under Tokugawa Shogunate 126/1
Edom Palestine 21/2
Edremit (Adramyttium)
Edward I King of England 52T, 53/6, 7, 56/4
Edwardesabad (Bannu)
EEC 136T, 137/3
Efes (Ephesus)
Eflâk (Wallachia)
EFTA 136T, 137/3
Egypt (*officially* Arab Republic of Egypt *form.* United Arab Republic *Lat.* Aegyptus *Ar.* Misr) agricultural origins 6/2, 7/5; early settlement 11/1; Old Kingdom 17/3; Mycenaean trade 18/2; ancient 21/1; Alexander's Empire 22/3, 4; early trade 24/1; spread of Christianity and Judaism 26/1; Arab conquest 43/1; Byzantine Empire 43/1; Fatimid Caliphate 60/1; conquered by Turks 61/2; French attack 90/2; Ottoman province 124/1; expansion into Sudan 103/3; British control 102-103; WW2 132-3; independence 138/1; political development 140/1; Anglo-French attack (Suez War) 140/1; wars with Israel 141/3, 148/4; economy 150/1
Ehime S Japan prefecture 126/2
Eichstätt SE Germany bishopric 79/1
Eilat (Elat)
Eire (Ireland)
Ekain N Spain Palaeolithic art 5/3
El Agheila Libya WW2 133/2
El Alamein Egypt⚔WW2 133/2
Elam (*a/c* Susiana *or* Uvja *mod.* Khuzistan) state of ancient Middle East 20/4
El Amarna C Egypt 21/1
El Arish Sinar Egyptian-Israeli war 141/3

Elat *(f/s Eilat) S Israel* port 141/3
Elba (Ilva)
El Barranquete SE Spain megalithic tomb 14/3
Elbasan Albania Ottoman Empire 49/1
El Baúl E Mexico Mayan site 12/2
Elbing (*Pol.* Elbląg) W Poland founded by Teutonic Knights 54/4; Hanseatic city 59/2
El Camino Real S USA settlers' route 94/1
Elea (*a/c* Velia) S Italy Ionian colony 19/4
Elephantine Upper Egypt Old Kingdom city 17/3
El Fasher Sudan early trade 60/1
El Ferrol NW Spain Civil War 129/4
Elis ancient country of W Greece 18/3
Elisabethville (*now* Lubumbashi) S Belgian Congo 138/4
Elizabeth I Queen of England 73/4
El-Kab (*a/c Eleithyiaspolis) Upper Egypt* Old Kingdom city 17/3
El-Kula Upper Egypt pyramid 17/3
Ellasar (Larsa)
Ellice Islands (*now* Tuvalu) W Pacific British colony 139/1 (inset)
Elmedsaete (*a/c* Elmet) ancient people of C England 33/3
Elmenteita E Africa site of early man 11/1
Elmina (*Port.* Sào Jorge da Mina) Ghana early trade 60T, 66/1; Dutch settlement 60/2 (inset)
El Mries N Morocco megalithic tomb 14/3
Elne (Illiberris)
El Paso SW USA on trail west 94/1
El Reguerillo C Spain Palaeolithic art 5/3
El Salvador country of C America 97/1, 142/1, 2, 3
Elsass (Alsace)
Elsloo S Holland farming site 15/1
El Tajin Mexico site 13/1
Ely E England Industrial Revolution 98/1
Emar N Syria Mitannian city 21/1
Embrun (*anc.* Eburodunum) S France archbishopric 34/4; fort 80/1
Emerita Augusta (*mod.* Mérida) SW Spain Mithraic site 26/1; Roman Empire 24/2, 31/3
Emesa (*mod.* Homs) Syria Roman Empire 31/3
Emmaus Palestine town of Judaea 26/3
Emmen N Germany megalithic tomb 15/3
Emona (*mod.* Ljubljana) NW Yugoslavia Roman Empire 31/3
Emporiae NE Spain Ionian colony 18/4, 30/2
Enez (Aenus)
Engels (*till 1932* Pokrovsk) SE Russia industry 147/1
England Scandinavian settlement 37/1; Norman kingdom 53/6; expansion of Christianity 38/2,3; expulsion of Jews 39/4; Black Death and religious unrest 57/1; Anglo-Scottish wars 56/4; war with France 56/5; possessions in France 72/2; Reformation 75/1; Civil War 76/4; rebellions 73/4; Industrial Revolution 98/1; WW1 118-9; WW2 132-3. See also Britain, Great Britain, United Kingdom
English Harbour Antigua, West Indies British naval base 86/1
Eniwetok Marshall Is, C Pacific US Base 135/2
Enkomi E Cyprus Levantine port 21/1
Ennedi Chad rock painting 11/1
Enniskillen N Ireland IRA 137/6
EOKA Cyprus guerrilla movement 138/1
Epernay NE France WW1 118/3 (inset)
Ephesus (*Turk.* Efes) W Anatolia early trade 17/4; Roman Empire 24/2, Byzantine Empire 43/1; centre of early Christianity 27/2; archbishopric 27/2
Epidamnus (*later* Dyrrhachium *It.* Durazzo *mod.* Durrës) Albania Dorian colony 19/4
Epidaurum NW Greece Mithraic site 26/1
Epinal E France WW1 119/3
Epirus ancient country of NW Greece 19/4; independent state 22/3; Roman province 31/3; Byzantine Empire 43/1; to Greece 116/1
Equateur province of NW Belgian Congo 138/4
Equator, Confederation of the E Brazil 97/1
Equatorial Guinea (*form.* Spanish Guinea *a/c* Rio Muni) country of W Africa independence 138/1; economy 150/1
Erbach county of S Germany 79/1
Erech (Uruk)
Ereg (Heraclea Pontica)
Eretria E Greece parent state 19/4
Erfurt E Germany bishopric 38/3; Hanseatic city 59/2
Erh-li-t'ou (*a/s* Erlitou) N China Shang city 8/4
Eridu Mesopotamia early farming village 7/4; early city 17/2, 4
Erie Indian tribe of NE USA 63/1
Eritrea region of NE Ethiopia Italian colony 103/5, 129/5; political development 138/1
Ermeland region of E Germany and Poland occupied by Teutonic Knights 54/4
Erzerum (Erzurum)
Erzurum (*a/s* Erzerum) conquered by Suleiman I 49/1
Escoural S Portugal Palaeolithic art 5/3
Esfahan (Isfahan)
Eshnunna (*mod.* Tell Asmar) N Mesopotamia early city 16/2, 17/4
Eskimo Indian tribe of Arctic America 63/1
Eskisehir (*anc.* Dorylaeum) W Turkey Ottoman centre 49/1; Greco-Turkish war 125/4
Esperance W Australia early settlement 113/1
Espirito Santo province of Brazil 97/1
Espiritu Santo New Hebrides, W Pacific US base 135/1
Essaouira (Mogador)
Essex E England conversion to Christianity 38/3
Es-Skhul Israel site of early man 3/3
Essling (Aspern)
Estonia country of the Baltic occupied by Teutonic Knights 54/4, 73/1; acquired by Russia 85/1; Reformation 75/1; under Swedish rule 77/3; independence from Russia 128/2; inter-war alliances 128/1; WW2 132-3; constituted SSR 136/1, 146/2; independence 137/4, 151/4
Estrées N France French Revolution 89/2
Estremadura region of W Spain reconquered by Castile 37/4
Ests people of Estonia 45/2
Etaples NE France mutiny WW1 118/3
Ethiopia early agriculture 6/2; expansion of Christianity 26/1; 16C state 61/2; Italian invasion 103/3, 129/5; independence regained 138/1; economy 150/1
Etowah SE USA ⚔Mississippian site 12/3; 92/2
Etruria ancient country of C Italy 30/1, 31/2
Etruscans ancient people of Italy 19/4, 30/1
Etzná E Mexico Mayan centre 12/2
Euboea (*It.* Negroponte *mod. Gr.* Evvoia) island of E. Greece war with Persia 22/1
Eugene of Savoy, Prince 79T
Euhesperides Libya Dorian colony 19/4
Eupen E Belgium ceded by Germany 128/2
Europe early man 3/3; Palaeolithic art 5/3; agricultural origins 6/2, 7/5; early settlement 6-7, 14-15; amber trade 14/1; introduction of metallurgy 14/2; megalithic monuments 14/3; agricultural settlement 15/1; Hun and Avar invasions 32/1; Germanic and Slavonic invasions 32/1; expansion of Christianity 38/2, 3; Jewish migrations 39/4; Viking, Magyar and Saracen invasions 37/1; Mongol invasion 46/2; Black Death 57/1; Great Schism 57/6 (inset); new monarchies 72/1; Ottoman expansion 48-49; peasant emancipation 82/1; Reformation 74-5; trade and industry 16-18C 82-83; industrial revolution 99/2; rise of nationalism 115/1; 19-20C alliances 117/2; WW1 118-9; 20C socio-political changes 128-9, 130-31; WW2 132-3; post-war territorial changes 136/1; economic blocs (EEC, EFTA, Comecon) 137/2; collapse of Communist power 137/4
Europus (Rai)
Eurymedon River (*mod.* Köprüirmaği) W Anatolia ⚔21/5
Evans Creek W USA ⚔95/2
Evenki people of E Siberia 84/2; AD 146/2
Evesham W England ⚔53/6; Industrial Revolution 98/1
Evtresis C Greece Mycenaean settlement 19/1
Evvoia (Euboea)
Exeter SW England Norman castle 36/3; Industrial Revolution 98/1
Exloo N Holland burial site 14/2
Eylau (*a/c* Preussisch-Eylau *now* Bagrationovsk) E Prussia ⚔91/1
Eynsham S England burial site 14/2

Faenza N Italy Lombard League 55/3
Faeroe Islands (*a/s* Faroes) Norse settlement 37/1
Faesulae (*mod.* Fiesole) N Italy Roman Empire 30/1
Falerii (*mod.* Civita Castellana) N Italy Etruscan city 30/1
Falkirk C Scotland ⚔56/4
Falkland Islands (*Span.* Islas Malvinas) islands of S Atlantic 97/1; claimed by Argentina 138/1; war 138T, 143/1
Fallen Timbers NE USA ⚔95/2
Falmouth SW England WW1 118/3
Fang C China Western Chou domain 9/6
Fanning Island C Pacific British possession 139/1 (inset)
Fara (Shuruppak)
Farah (Alexandria Prophthasia)
Faras Upper Egypt fortress 21/1
Far Eastern Republic E Siberia merged with USSR 120/4
Faroe Islands (*a/s* Faeroes) Norse settlement 37/1
Fars (*a/c* Persis, Parsa) Persia Muslim conquest 41/1
Fashoda S Sudan British/French confrontation 103/3
Fategarh N India Indian Mutiny 104/1
Fatimids Muslim dynasty of Egypt 36/2, 40/2, 60/1
Fayetteville SE USA ⚔93/5
Fayum Egypt early site 11/1
Federated Malay States (*now* Malaysia) independence 139/1
Fehrbellin N Germany ⚔81/4
Feng NC China Western Chou capital 9/6
Feng-pi-t'ou Taiwan early settlement 8/2
Fengtien former province of Manchuria Hsin-hai revolution 107/3; Russo-Japanese war 127/4
Feodosiya (*a/c* Kefe, Kaffa *anc* Theodosia) Crimea acquired by Russia 85/1
Ferghana region of C Asia Han finds 25/1; Muslim expansion 41/1; Chinese protectorate 50/1
Fermanagh county of N Ireland 137/6
Fermo (Firmum)
Fernando Po (*Sp.* Fernando Poó *form.* Macias Nguema Biyogo) island of Equatorial Guinea Portuguese exploration 64/1; Dutch and Spanish settlement 61/2; Spanish colony 100/2; 138/1
Ferrara N Italy Lombard League 55/3; Signorial domination 56/3; Duchy 73/3
Ferrol (*now* El Ferrol del Caudillo) NW Spain naval base 87/1
Fès (Al Fas, Fez)
Fetterman's Defeat SE USA ⚔95/2
Fez (*Fr.* Fès *Ar.* Al Fas) Morroco early trade 58/3, 61/2; occupied by French 103/3
Fezzan (*anc.* Phazania) region of C Libya occupied by Italians 103/3
Fiesole (Faesulae)
Fihl Palestine ⚔41/1
Fiji S Pacific Melanesian settlement 10/2; British colony 101/2; independence 139/1 (inset)
Filibe (*Eng.* Philippopolis *now* Plovdiv) Bulgaria Ottoman Empire 49/1
Finland Union of Kalmar 72/1; Reformation 75/1; under Swedish rule 77/3; under Russian rule 114/4; railway development 99/2; WW1 119/3; independence 121/2; socio-political change 131/3; WW2 132-3; EFTA 137/4
Finno-Ugrians people of N Russia 7/3
Finns post-war migration from Karelia 136/1
Firenze (Florence)
Firmum (*a/c* Firmum Picenum *mod.* Fermo) N Italy Latin colony 30/1
Fitzmaurice's rebellion Ireland 73/4
Fiume (*S. Cr.* Rijeka) N Yugoslavia WW1 119/3; 1919 incident 129/2
Five-Year Plan, First USSR 146T
Flaminian Way (Via Flaminia)
Flanders (*Fr.* Flandre *Dut.* Vlaanderen) region of N Belgium medieval trade 58/1; French Royal domain 52/2; acquired by Burgundy 73/3; Black Death 57/1; WW1 118/3 (inset)
Flemings Dutch-speaking people of Flanders 115/1
Flensburg N Germany WW2 133/2
Fleurus Belgium ⚔81/4
Flint N Wales castle 53/7
FLN Algeria guerrilla movement 138/1, 139/3
Flodden Field N England ⚔73/4
Florence (*anc.* Florentia *It.* Firenze) N Italy early bishopric 26/2; medieval city 55/3, 56/3; Renaissance republic 73/5; WW2 133/2
Flores island of C East Indies occupied by Japanese 134/1
Florida seaborne exploration 65/3; British rule 69/3, 92/1; Spanish rule 86/1; annexed by USA 92/2; Civil War 93/5; Depression 131/2; population 145/1; base for invasion of Cuba 149/5
Flossenbürg S Germany concentration camp 132/1
Foix region of S France English possession 52/2; acquired by France 72/2
Fondi (Fundi)
Fontanaccia Corsica megalithic tomb 15/3
Font de Gaume SW France Palaeolithic art 5/3
Fontéchevade W France early site 3/3
Foochow SE China early trade 59/3; treaty port 107/4; French attack 107/3
Forbe's Quarry S Spain site 3/3
Forbes Road NE USA settlers' route 94/1
Forez region of C France annexed to France 72/2
Formentera island of Balaerics Spanish Civil War 129/4
Formosa (*n/c* Taiwan) cession to Japan 127/3; air attack by US 135/1; US bases 149/1
Fort Albany N Canada Hudson Bay Co. post 67/3; British fort 68/5
Fort Amsterdam (*later* New Amsterdam *now* New York) Dutch post 67/3
Fort Augusta SE USA British fort 86/1
Fort Beauharnais C USA fur station 97/1
Fort Beauséjour Nova Scotia French fort captured by British 86/1
Fort Benton NW USA fur station 94/1
Fort Bonneville N USA fur station 97/1
Fort Bourbon N Canada French fort 68/5
Fort Bridger W USA fur station 94/1
Fort Carillon (*later* Fort Ticonderoga) Quebec captured from French 86/1
Fort Charles (*a/c* Lake of the Woods) N Canada French fort 68/5
Fort Chiswell E USA British fort 86/1
Fort Clark SE USA fur station 94/1
Fort Coffee C USA 95/2
Fort Colville NW USA fur station 94/1
Fort Crèvecoeur N USA French fort 67/3
Fort Crittenden W USA fur station 94/1
Fort Cumberland E USA British fort 86/1
Fort Dauphin Madagascar French settlement 61/2, 87/2
Fort Dearborn N USA ⚔95/1
Fort de Kock (*Indon.* Bukitt Tinggi) W Sumatra Dutch trade 71/2
Fort Donelson SE USA ⚔93/5
Fort Duquesne (*later* Fort Pitt) E USA French fort captured by British 86/1
Fort Edward NE USA British fort 86/1
Fort Fisher SE USA ⚔93/5
Fort Frontenac Quebec French fort 67/3, 68/5; captured by British 86/1
Fort Gibson C USA 95/2
Fort Hall NW USA fur station 94/1
Fort Henry SE USA ⚔93/5
Fort Jackson S USA fur station 94/1
Fort Kamininistikwia N Canada French fort 68/5
Fort Kearney C USA ⚔95/2
Fort King George SE USA British fort 86/1
Fort La Galette Quebec French fort 86/1

Fort Lamy (*now* N'Djamena) C Africa occupied by French 103/3
Fort La Reine (*a/c* Portage la Prairie) C Canada French fort 68/5
Fort Leavenworth C USA fur station 94/1
Fort Le Boeuf E USA French fort 86/1
Fort Ligonier NE USA ⚔95/2
Fort Mackenzie NW USA fur station 94/1
Fort Massac C USA fur station 94/1
Fort Maurepas S USA French fort 67/3
Fort Mellon SE USA ⚔95/2
Fort Michilimackinac NE USA fur station 94/1
Fort Mimms SE USA ⚔95/2
Fort Mitchell SE USA 95/2
Fort Monroe E USA 93/5
Fort Necessity E USA British fort 86/1
Fort Niagara C Canada French fort 67/3, 68/5; captured by British 86/1
Fort Orange (Albany)
Fort Orléans N Canada French fort 68/5
Fort Oswego NE USA British fort captured by French 86/1
Fort Pickawillany N USA British fort 86/1
Fort Pickens SE USA 93/5
Fort Piegan NW USA fur station 94/1
Fort Pierre (*a/c* Rainy Lake) N Canada French fort 68/5
Fort Pillow SE USA ⚔93/5
Fort Pitt (*form. Fr.* Fort Duquesne) E USA British fort captured from French 86/1; ⚔95/2
Fort Pontchartrain (*now* Detroit) N USA French post 67/3, 86/1
Fort Presque Isle E USA French fort 86/1
Fort Prince George SE USA British fort 86/1
Fort Prudhomme C USA French fort 67/3, 68/5
Fort Rouillé C Canada French fort 86/1
Fort Royal Martinique, W Indies French fort 86/1
Fort St. Frédéric (*later* Crown Point) Quebec captured by British 86/1
Fort St. Joseph C USA French fort 67/3, 86/1
Fort St. Louis N USA French post 67/3
Fort St. Louis N Canada French fort 68/5
Fort St. Pierre NW USA fur station 94/1
Fort Sedgwick C USA ⚔95/2
Fort Smith C USA 95/2
Fort Smith-Santa Fe Trail C USA settler's route to west 94/1
Fort Sumter SE USA 93/5
Fort Tadoussac Quebec French post 67/3
Fort Towson C USA 95/2
Fort Union N USA fur station 94/1
Fort Vancouver NW USA fur station 94/1
Fort Venango E USA British fort 86/1
Fort William (*n/c* Thunder Bay) C Canada growth 111/1
Fort William Henry NE USA British fort captured by French 86/1
Fort York N Canada British fort 68/5
Fort Yuma SW USA on trail west 94/1
Forum Iulii (*mod.* Fréjus) S France Roman Empire 24/2
Four Days' Battle English Channel Dutch naval victory 81/3
Four Lakes NW USA⚔95/2
Fourneau de Diable SW France Palaeolithic art 5/3
Fouta Djallon (*a/s* Futa Jallon) W Africa early state 103/3
Fox Indian tribe of C USA 63/1
Frainet (Fraxinetum)
France (*anc.* Gaul *Lat.* Gallia) Palaeolithic art 5/3; conversion to Christianity 27/1, 32/2; Jewish immigration 39/4; Viking and Saracen invasions 37/1; Arab invasion 40/1; Scandinavian settlement 37/1; expansion of monarchy 52/2; war with England 56/5; Black Death 57/1; 15C-16C reunification 72/2; peasant emancipation 83/1; trade and industry 82/4; Huguenot-Catholic conflict 74/3; 16-17C rebellions 77/2; NE Frontier 81/2; War of Spanish Succession 81/5; administrative system under Louix XIV 80/1; Vauban fortresses 80/1; British blockade 87/1; seaborne trade 83/5; French Revolution 88-89; expansion of Revolutionary France 89/3; expansion under Napoleon 90-91; industrial revolution 98/2; colonial empire 100-101; growth in armaments 117/3; European alliances 117/2; WW 1 118-9; overseas trade and investment 109/3; socio-political development 130/3; inter-war alliances 128/1; WW 2 132-3; EEC, NATO 137/4, 149/1; economy 150/1
Franche-Comté region of E France acquired by Habsburgs 79/1; Burgundian possession 73/3; provinces of Germany 78/1; gained by France 81/2
Francia (Frankish Kingdom)
Franconia (*Ger.* Franken) state of German Empire 55/1, 3
Frankfurt-am-Main W Germany medieval fair 59/2; 18C financial centre 82/4; Reformation 75/1; WW 1 119/3; WW 2 133/2
Frankfurt-an-der-Oder E Germany Hanseatic city 59/2
Frankish Kingdom (*a/c* Francia, Carolingian Empire) France/Germany 34-35, 54/1; Irish missionaries 38/3
Franklin SE USA⚔935
Franks tribe of NW Europe, movement into France 32/2
Fraxinetum (*mod.* Frainet) S France Saracen base 37/1
Frederick I medieval king of Germany 54T
Frederick II medieval king of Germany 54T
Fredericksburg E USA⚔93/5
Frederick the Great King of Prussia 79T
Freetown Sierra Leone, W Africa British settlement 60/2, 103/3
Fregellae C Italy Latin colony 30/1
Freising S Germany bishopric 79/1
Fréjus (Forum Iulii)
FRELIMO Mozambique guerrilla movement 138/1
Fremantle W Australia founded 113/1
French Cameroons (*now part of* Cameroon) W Africa independence 138/1
French Congo (*a/c* Middle Congo *now* People's Republic of the Congo) W Africa colony 101/2, 103/3
French Equatorial Africa union of French colonies 102/5
French Guiana S America 97/1, 142-3
French Guinea (*now* Guinea) W Africa colony 103/3
French Indochina (*now* Cambodia, Laos and Vietnam) colonised 107/4; occupied by Japanese 127/5, 134/1; independence 139/1
French Somaliland (*Fr.* Côte Française des Somalis *later* French Territory of the Afars and Issas *now* Republic of Djibouti) NE Africa 103/3
French Sudan (*now* Mali) W Africa colony 103/3
French Territory of Afars and Issas (Djibouti)
French West Africa former union of French colonies 101/2, 102/5
FRETILIN East Timor guerrilla movement 139/1
Fribourg (*Ger.* Freiburg) C Switzerland early canton 54/5
Friedberg W Germany medieval fair 59/2
Friedland (*now* Pravdinsk) E Prussia⚔91/1
Friedlingen W Germany⚔81/5
Friesland region of northern Netherlands Burgundian possession 73/3; province of Dutch Republic 77/1
Frisia (*mod.* Netherlands) part of Frankish Empire 34/4
Frisians (*Lat.* Frisii) tribe of NW Europe 32/2, 34/1
Friuli region of NE Italy under medieval German Empire 34/4, 55/3
Frobisher, Sir Martin English explorer 64/2
Frunze (*until 1926* Pishpek, n/c Bishek) Russ. C Asia industry 147/1
Fufeng W China Western Chou site 9/6
Fukien province of SE China Ming province 51/4; Manchu expansion 106/2; Japanese influence 107/4, 127/3, under Nanking control 123/3
Fukui city and prefecture of C Japan 126/1, 2
Fukuoka a city and prefecture of W Japan 126/1, 2
Fukushima city and prefecture of NE Japan 126/1, 2
Fulda N Germany monastery 34/4; bishopric 79/1
Funa River C Africa Iron Age site 11/1
Fundi (*mod.* Fondi) C Italy Roman Empire 30/1
Funj Sudan early state 61/2
Fürstenberg S Germany Duchy 79/1
Fusan (Pusan)
Fushun Manchuria on railway 127/4
Fustat (Old Cairo) Egypt 41/1
Fyrkat N Denmark circular fortification 52/3

Gabae W Persia Alexander's route 22/3
Gabbard Shoal S North Sea English naval victory 81/3
Gabon W Africa French colony 103/3; independence 138/1
Gades (*mod.* Cádiz) SW Spain Phoenician city 18/4; Roman Empire 24/2, 30/3
Gaeta C Italy Mediterranean trade 36/2
Gafsa (Capsa)
Gagarino E Russia Palaeolithic art 5/3
Gaikwar Maratha state of W India 87/3
Galam early state of W Africa 60/1
Galatia country of C Anatolia 15/5; Roman province 31/3
Galich (*mod.* Galicia) region of SW Russia Kievan principality 45/2
Galicia (*Russ.* Galich) region of E Europe acquired by Habsburgs 78/3; in Austria-Hungary during WW 1 119/3
Galicia region of NW Spain invaded by Suebi 32/2; part of Castile 37/4
Galla people of S Ethiopia 60-61
Galle Ceylon early trade 59/3
Gallia (*Eng.* Gaul *mod.* France) Roman province 30/2
Gallipoli (*anc.* Callipolis *Turk.* Gelibolu) W Turkey Ottoman centre 49/1; WW 1 119/3
Galloway region of SW Scotland acquired by Edward III 56/4
Gambia country of W Africa British settlement 61/2; British colony 102-103; independence 138/1
Gand (Ghent)
Gandara (*a/s* Gandhara) region of E Afghanistan satrapy of Achaemenid Empire 21/5; Indian kingdom 29/4
Gangra (*mod.* Çankin) N Anatolia early archbishopric 27/2
Ganja N Caucasus conquered by Ottomans 48/2
Ganjam region of E India ceded to Britain 87/3
Ganties-Montespan SW France Palaeolithic art 5/3
Gao W Africa Iron Age site 11/1; capital of Songhay 60/1; early trade 61/2
Gargas SW France Palaeolithic art 5/3
Gascony (*Fr.* Gascogne) region of SW France part of Frankish Empire 34/4; English possession 52/2; province of France 80/1
Gath Palestine Philistine city 19/4
Gaugamela Mesopotamia⚔21/5, 22/3
Gaul (*Lat.* Gallia *mod.* France) conversion to Christianity 26/2; invasion by German and Slav tribes 32/2
Gaulanitis district of N Judaea 26/3
Gavrinis NW France megalithic tomb 14/3
Gaza Palestine Philistine city 19/4; Levantine city 21/1; Alexander's route 22/3; 23/1, 2; Roman Empire 25/2, 43/1; Byzantine Empire 31/3; WW 1 125/2
Gaza Strip Palestine occupied by Israel 141/3
Gdańsk (*Ger.* Danzig) N Poland founded 53/1
Gebel Barkal Upper Egypt New Kingdom temple 21/1
Gedrosia region of SE Persia Alexander's Empire 23/3
Gela (*later* Terranova de Sicilia *mod.* Gela) Sicily Pelopponesian War 23/2; Dorian colony 19/4
Gelderland region of C Netherlands Burgundian possession 73/3; province of Dutch Republic 77/1
Gelibolu (Gallipoli)
Geneva (*Fr.* Genève *Ger.* Genf) Switzerland medieval fair 59/2; Reformation 75/1; middle-class revolt 88T
Genf (Geneva)
Genghis Khan Mongol ruler 46T/1
Genoa (*anc.* Genua *It.* Genova) N Italy medieval city 55/3, 56/3; city-state 73/5; trade 58/3; 18C financial centre 82/4
Gensan (Wonsan)
Gent (Ghent)
Genua (Genoa, Genova)
Georgetown (Stabroek)
Georgia state of S USA colony 92/1; Civil War 93/5; Depression 131/2; industry 110/2; population 111/5, 145/1
Georgia country of the Caucasus acquired by Russia 85/1; kingdom 124/1; independent after WW 1 129/2; SSR 146/2; independence 151/4
Gepidae ancient tribe of C Europe 31/4
Geraldton W Australia early settlement 113/1
Gerar Palestine Philistine city 19/4
German East Africa (*later* Tanganyika *now* Tanzania) 102-103
Germania Inferior province of Roman Empire 31/3
Germania Superior province of Roman Empire 31/3
Germaniceia E Anatolia Byzantine base 42/2
Germans early movements 54/2; post-war migration to west 136/1; migration after WW 1 129/3
German South-West Africa (Namibia)
Germantown E USA⚔92/1
Germany (*Lat.* Germania *Ger.* Deutschland *now* Federal Republic of Germany *and* German Democratic Republic) conversion to Christianity 38/2; Jewish migrations 39/4; Magyar invasion 37/1; medieval Empire 55/1, 3; agriculture and the peasant revolt 82/1; Thirty Years War 74/4; Reformation 75/1; fragmentation 79/1, 91/1; industrial revolution 99/2; unification 115/2; customs union 98/3; expansion in Africa 102/3; colonial empire 101/2; growth in armaments 117/3; 19C alliances 117/2; overseas trade and investment 109/3; WW 1 118-9; territorial changes after WW 1 129/2, 5; inter-war alliances 128/1; expansion 1934-41 129/5; WW 2 132-3; Allied control zones 136/1; territorial losses to Poland 137/3; East and West reunited 137/4
Germany, East (German Democratic Republic *or* DDR) 137/3; Warsaw Pact 137/2, 149/1
Germany, West (German Democratic Republic *or* FDR) 137/5; EEC 137/3; NATO 149/1
Germiyan Turkoman principality of W Anatolia 49/1
Gesoriacum (*mod.* Boulogne) N France Roman Empire 24/2, 30/3
Getae ancient tribe of the Balkans 22/3
Gettysburg E USA⚔93/5
Ghadamès (*n/s* Ghudamis) W Libya early trade route 58/3, 60-61
Ghana (*form.* Gold Coast) W Africa early kingdom 10/1; early empire 60T/1; independence 138/1, 140/1
Ghat SW Libya trade 58/3, 60-61
Ghazipur district of N India ceded to Britain 87/3
Ghaznavids Muslim dynasty of Afghanistan 41/2
Ghazni (Alexandria)
Ghent (*Dut.* Gent *Fr.* Gand) Belgium medieval city 55/3; trade 58/1; urban revolt 57/1
Ghudamis (Ghadamès)
Gibraltar 90/1, 100/2; dependent state 138/1
Gifu C Japan city and prefecture 126/2
Gijón N Spain Civil War 129/4
Gilbert Islands (*n/c* Kiribati) C Pacific British colony 101/2; captured by Japanese 134/1; retaken by US 135/2; independence 139/1 (inset)
Gilimanuk E Java early site 8/3
Giurgiu (Yergoğu)
Giza Lower Egypt pyramid 17/3
Gla C Greece palace site 19/1
Glace Bay Nova Scotia growth 111/1
Glarus C Switzerland early canton 54/5
Glasgow S Scotland 18C textile industry 82/4
Glastonbury W England Industrial Revolution 98/1
Glenbrook N Island, New Zealand steel 112/2
Glevum (*mod.* Gloucester) W England Roman Empire 30/3
Gloucester (*anc.* Glevum) W England Norman castle 36/3; Industrial Revolution 98/1
Gnadenhütten NE USA Protestant mission 94/1
Gnesen (Gniezno)
Gnewitz N Germany megalithic tomb 15/3
Gniezno *Ger.* Gnesen) medieval fair 59/2

Goa district of W India early trade 66/2, 67/1; Portuguese settlement 48/2, 87/3, 105/3
Godavari district of E India ceded to Britain 87/3, 104/4
Goias province of Brazil 97/1
Gokomere S Africa early site 11/1
Golan Heights Syria occupied by Israel 141/3
Gold Coast (*now* Ghana) early European settlement 103/3 (inset); British colony 100/2, 103/3
Golden Bull 54/T
Golden Horde Khanate of C Asia 47/3, 4
Goldsboro SE USA⚔93/5
Gombroon (Bandar Abbas)
Gomel WC Russia WW1 119/3; industry 147/1
Go Mun N Vietnam Neolithic site 8/3
Gondeshapur Persia early archbishopric 27/2
Gönnersdorf W Germany Palaeolithic art 5/3
Go Oc Eo Indo-China trade 25/1
Good Hope, Cape of S Africa Portuguese discovery 64/1
Goole N England Industrial Revolution 98/1
Gophna Israel city of Judaea 26/3
Gordium C Anatolia early city 16/1; Alexander's route 22/3; Achaemenid Empire 21/5
Gorée W Africa French settlement 61/2
Gorgan (Gurgan)
Gorkiy (*until 1932* Nizhniy Novgorod) C Russia industry 147/1
Gorlice SE Poland⚔119/3
Gornja Tuzla N Yugoslavia early settlement 14/2
Gorno-Altai AR C Asia 146/2
Gorno-Badakhshan AR C Asia 146/2
Gorodets SW Russia town of Pereyaslavl 45/2
Gortyna Crete Roman Empire 24/2; archbishopric 27/2
Goslar C Germany Hanseatic city 59/2
Gothenburg (*Sw.* Göteborg) W Sweden 77/3
Goths invasions 32/1
Gotland island of Baltic occupied by Teutonic Knights 54/4; transferred to Sweden 77/3
Gottorp NW Germany Reformation 74/4
Gough's Cave S England site of early man 3/3; Palaeolithic art 5/3
Gournia Crete palace site 19/1
Gouy N France Palaeolithic art 5/3
Goyet Belgium Palaeolithic art 5/3
Grado N Italy bishopric 26/2
Graeco-Bactrian Kingdom Afghanistan 22/4
Graig Llwyd N Wales megalithic axe factory 14/3
Gran (*Hung.* Esztergom) Hungary bishopric 38/2; Ottoman conquest 48/2
Granada city and region of Spain Muslim kingdom 37/4; acquired by Habsburgs 72/1; 18C urban development 82/4; Muslim minority 74/1; Civil War 129/4
Grand Pressigny W France megalithic flint mine 14/3
Grandson Switzerland⚔73/3
Granicus W Anatolia⚔20/5, 22/3
Grantham C England Industrial Revolution 98/1
Granville NW France French Revolution 89/2
Grattan's Defeat C USA⚔95/2
Grave Creek W USA⚔95/2
Gravesend SE England Industrial Revolution 98/1
Great Britain agriculture and peasant emancipation 82/1; trade and industry 82/4; colonisation of North America 86/1; opposition to Napoleon 90-91; colonial empire 100-101; growth in armaments 117/3; 19C European alliances 117/2; WW1 118-9; WW2 132-3. See also England
Great Driffield NE England Industrial Revolution 98/1
Great Genesee Road NE USA 94/1
Great Khan, Empire of the E Asia 47/3
Great Langdale NW England megalithic axe factory 14/3
Great Leap Forward China 140T
Great St. Bernard *pass* Switzerland/Italy 58/1
Great Swamp NE USA⚔95/2
Great Trading Path E USA settlers' route 94/1
Great Yarmouth (*a/c* Yarmouth) E England Industrial Revolution 98/1
Great Zimbabwe early city of SE Africa 61/2
Greco-Turkish War 125/4
Greece (*anc. Gr.* Hellas *mod. Gr.* Ellas) Ancient Greece 18-19, 20-21; Levantine ports 21/1; arrival of Christianity 26-7; invaded by Visigoths 32/1; Black Death 57/1; independent kingdom 116/1; WW1 118/9; conflict with Bulgaria and Turkey 124/1; inter-war alliances 128/1; socio-political change 131/3; WW2 133/2; Cold War 149/1
Greeks migration after WW1 129/3
Greenland rediscovered 64/2; US bases 149/1
Grenada island of W Indies British colony 97/1; self-government 139/1 (inset); US invasion 143/1
Grenoble SE France *parlement* 80/1
Grijalva, Juan de Spanish explorer 64/3
Grimaldi N Italy site of early man 3/3
Grimes Graves E England megalithic flint mine 14/3
Grimsby N England Industrial Revolution 98/1
Griqualand West S Africa 103/4
Griquas tribe of S Africa 102/2
Grønhøj C Denmark megalithic tomb 15/3
Groningen N Netherlands Hanseatic town 59/2; Burgundian possession 73/3
Gross Rosen (*now Pol.* Rogoźnica) SE Germany concentration camp 132/1
Grotte des Fées SE France burial site 14/2
Groznyy Caucasus industry 147/1
Gruta de Furninha C Portugal farming site 15/1
Gua Cha Malaya early site 8/3
Guadalajara C Spain Civil War 129/4
Guadalajara C Mexico capital of New Spain 66/1
Guadalcanal island of Solomons, S Pacific⚔135/2
Guadeloupe island of W Indies French settlement 66/4, 69/3; attacked by British 87/1; French territory 97/1, 139/1 (inset)
Guahibo Indian tribe of S America 63/1
Gua Kechil Malaya early site 8/3
Gua Kepah W Malaya Iron Age site 8/3
Guam island of W Pacific occupied by US 110/1; occupied by Japanese 134/1; recaptured by US 135/2; US base 149/1 (inset)
Guanajay W Cuba Soviet missile site 149/5
Guanajuato province of C Mexico 97/1
Guantánamo Bay E Cuba US naval base 149/5
Guaraní forest Indian tribe of Paraguay 63/1
Guatemala country and city of C America founded 66/1; independence 97/1; US involvement 149/1
Guató Indian tribe of C Brazil 63/1
Guayaquil port of Ecuador 66/1
Guaymí Indian tribe of C America 63/1
Guernica N Spain Civil War 129/4
Guerrero province of S Mexico 97/1
Guiana region of S America discovered 65/3; colonised by Dutch and French 69/3. See also Surinam, French Guiana, Guyana
Guibray NW France medieval fair 59/2
Guildford S England⚔73/4
Guinea (*form.* French Guinea) independence 138/1
Guinea-Bissau (*form.* Portuguese Guinea) W Africa independence 138/1
Gujerat (*n/s Gujarat) region of W India* under British rule 87/3, 104/1; Partition 105/5
Gulbarga S India political disturbance 104/4
Gumbinnen E Prussia⚔WW1 119/3
Gumma prefecture of C Japan 126/2
Güns (*Hung.* Köszeg) Hungary Ottoman siege 48/2
Guntur district of S India civil unrest 104/4
Günük (Xanthus)
Gupta Empire India 29/5; destroyed by White Huns 33/1
Gurgan (*a/s* Gorgan *anc.* Hyrcania) city and region of N Persia Muslim conquest 41/1
Gurgaon district of N India communal riots 104/4
Guryev Russ. C Asia founded 85/1; industry 147/1
Gusev (Gumbinnen)
Gustavus Adolphus King of Sweden 74/1
Guyana (*form.* British Guiana) S America 142-3, 150/1
Guyenne (*a/c Aquitaine anc.* Aquitania) region of SW France English possession 52/2; French Royal domain 72/2; province of France 80/1
Gwadar (*f/s* Gwador) Pakistan Alexander's route 23/3; ceded by Muscat 105/5
Gwalior former state of C India 104/1
Gwynedd early Welsh principality 33/3, 35/3, 53/7
Gwynllwg early district of S Wales 33/3
Gyulafehérvár (Alba Iulia)

Habsburg Lands 56/2, 57/1
Hacilar N Turkey site 7/4
Hadar Ethiopia site of early man 5/3
Hadhramaut region of S Arabia Muslim expansion 41/1
Hadrumetum (*mod.* Sousse) Tunisia Phoenician city 19/4; Roman Empire 30/3
Haervej Denmark Land route of Jutland 53/3
Haestingas people of S England 33/3
Hafrsfjord S Norway⚔53/5
Hafsids Muslim dynasty of Tunisia 40/2
Haga S Sweden megalithic tomb 15/3
Hagi W Japan 126/1
Hagia Triada (Ayia Triadha)
Hagmatana (*a/c Ecbatana) Persia* 21/5
Haida coast Indian tribe of NW Canada 63/1
Hailar Manchuria on railway 122/4
Hainan *island* S China early soviet 122/4
Hainaut (*Dut.* Henegouwen) district of Belgium under medieval German Empire 55/3; Burgundian possession 73/3
Haiphong N Vietnam early trade 71/2; railway 107/4; Vietnamese war 148/3
Haiti Toussaint l'Ouverture's revolt 88/1; independence 97/1; US intervention 142/1, 2; political development 143/1. See alsoo Hispaniola
Hakka-Cantonese War S China 107/3
Hakodate city of N Japan 126/1
Halab (Aleppo)
Hala Sultan Tekke E Cyprus Levantine port 21/1
Halberstadt N Germany bishopric 79/1
Halicarnassus (*mod.* Bodrum) W Anatolia Byzantine Empire 43/1
Halidon Hill SE Scotland⚔56/4
Halifax N England Industrial Revolution 98/1
Halifax E Canada British naval base 86/1; growth 111/1
Halin N Burma Hindu-Buddhist remains 51/2
Halland province of SW Sweden under Danish rule 53/3; regained from Denmark 77/3
Halle C Germany WW1 119/2
Haller's Defeat NW USA⚔95/2
Halwan Mesopotamia early archbishopric 39/1
Halys River C Anatolia⚔20/5
Hama (*anc.* Hamath) W Syria occupied by French 125/3
Hamadan (*anc.* Ecbatana) W Persia Mongol conquest 47/4; Ottoman control 48/2
Haman's Defeat NE USA⚔95/2
Hamath (*mod.* Hama) Syria Mitannian city 21/1
Hamburg N Germany bishopric 38/2; Hanseatic city 59/2; 18C financial centre 82/4; industrial development 99/3; German customs union 98/3; WW1 119/2; Communist uprising 120/3; WW2 132-3; post-war 137/5
Hami (Kumul)
Hamid early Ottoman principality of SW Anatolia 49/1
Hamilton C Canada growth 111/1
Hammurabi, Empire of 17/4
Han NW China Western Chou domain 9/6; warring state 28/1; expansion 106/1; Empire 107/4
Han sub-Arctic Indian tribe of Alaska 63/1
Hanau W Germany⚔90/1
Hanchung C China Han commanderie 29/3
Hangchow C China early agriculture 7/2; provincial capital 51/4; early trade 59/3, 107/2; captured by Kuomintang 123/3; industry 108/1, 123/4
Hang Gon S Vietnam Iron Age Site 8/3
Hankow C China industry 109/1; treaty town 107/4
Hannibal Carthaginian general 30/2
Hannover (Hanover)
Hanoi (*form.* Thang Long) N Vietnam trade centre 71/2; Japanese occupation 127/5; 1945-75 war 148/3
Hanover (*Ger.* Hannover) former state of N Germany industrial development 98/3, 99/2; unification with Germany 115/2; WW1 119/2; WW2 133/2
Hanseatic League N Europe 59/2
Haraiva (*a/c* Aria) region of C Afghanistan satrapy of Achaemenid Empire 21/5
Harappa N India early urban settlement 9/5, 16/1
Harauvatish (*a/c Arachosia) region of C Afghanistan* satrapy of Achaemenid Empire 21/5
Harbin Manchuria railway 127/4; Russian occupation 107/4; Russo-Japanese war 127/4; industry 123/4
Hare sub-arctic Indian tribe of NW Canada 63/1
Harfleur N France 56/5
Harlech N Wales castle 53/7
Harmozia (*later* Ormuz *or* Hormuz) S Persia Alexander's Empire 23/3
Harold Bluetooth King of Denmark 52T
Hartlepool NE England WW1 119/3
Harwich E England Industrial Revolution 98/1; WW1 119/3
Harz mountains of N Germany prehistoric metal-working 14/2
Hasdrubal Carthaginian general 30/2
Hassuna N Mesopotamia early farming village 7/4
Hastings S England Norman castle 36/3
Hatra (*mod.* Al Hadhr) Mesopotamia Roman Empire 31/3
Hattin Palestine⚔40/3
Hattushash (*mod.* Boğazköy) C Anatolia early urban settlement 16/1; Hittite Empire 20/2
Hausa States (*a/c* Hausaland) *Nigeria* 60-61
Havana (*Sp.* La Habana) Cuba imperial trade 66/1; Spanish base captured by British 86/1
Havelte N Germany megalithic tomb 15/3
Hawaii state of USA military base 149/1 (inset)
Hawaiian Islands (*f/c Sandwich Islands) C Pacific* early Polynesian settlement 10/2; annexed by US 100/2, 110/4; war in the Pacific 135/1
Hawkes Bay province of N Island, New Zealand 112/2
Hay W England Industrial Revolution 98/1
Hay-Pauncefote Agreement 111/1
Hazor N Palestine Levantine city 21/1
Hebrides (*form. Nor.* Sudreyar) Scandinavian settlement 37/1; acquired by Scotland 72/1
Hebron (*Ar.* Al Khalil) Palestine city of Judaea 26/3; West Bank 141/3
Hecatompylos (*a/c* Qumis) on Silk Road 25/1; ancient city of Persia 25/1; Alexander's route 23/3
Heijo (Pyongyang)
Hejaz (*Ar.* Hijaz) region of W Arabia centre of Islam 41/1; under Abbasid sovereignty 41/2; Ottoman sovereignty 124-5
Helenopolis W Anatolia Byzantine Empire 43/1
Heliopolis (*mod.* Baalbek) Syria Roman Empire 31/3
Heliopolis (*Bibl.* On) Lower Egypt 17/3; Alexander's route 22/3; conquered by Arabs 41/1
Hellespont (Dardanelles)
Hellespontine Phrygia country of NW Anatolia 22/3
Helmantica (Salamantica)
Helsinki (*Sw.* Helsingfors) S Finland Swedish port 77/3; WW2 133/2
Helvetia (Swiss Confederation)
Helvetic Republic (*mod.* Switzerland) state under French protection 89/3
Hembury SW England site 15/1
Hemeroskopeion Spain Ionian colony 18/4
Hemudu (Ho-mu-tu)
Henegouwen (Hainaut)
Hengyang SE China industry 123/4
Henry I King of Saxony 54T
Henry II King of England 52/1
Henry IV German king 54T

Henry VI German king 54T
Henry VIII King of England 72T, 73/4
Heptanesus (Ionian Islands)
Heraclea Pontica (*mod.* Ereğli) N Anatolia Greek colony 19/4
Heracleopolis Lower Egypt 16/1, 21/1, 38/1
Heraclius Eastern Roman Emperor 42T
Heraeumteichos W Turkey Greek colony 19/4
Herat (*anc.* Alexandria Areion) C Persia early archbishopric 39/1; Muslim conquest 41/1; early trade 59/3; Safavid conquest 48/2
Herculis Monoeci N Italy Greek colony 19/4
Hereford W England Norman castle 36/3; Industrial Revolution 98/1
Herero people of SW Africa 61/2
Hermopolis Egypt Roman Empire 31/3
Hermunduri western Germanic tribe 30/3
Hernández de Córdoba Spanish explorer 64/3
Herrerías N Spain Palaeolithic art 5/3
Hersfeld principality of C Germany 79/1
Herstal W Germany Frankish royal residence 34/4
Hertford S England Industrial Revolution 98/1
Heruli tribe on N borders of Roman Empire 31/4
Herzegovina SE Europe Ottoman vassal state 48/1
Hesse (*Ger.* Hessen) prehistoric metal-working 14/2; Anglo-Saxon missionaries 38/3; Electorate and Duchy of N Germany 91/4; Reformation 75/1; unification with Germany 115/2
Hesse-Darmstadt Landgraviate of C Germany 79/1
Hesse-Kassel Landgraviate of C Germany 79/1; Reformation 74/4
Hevelli early Slav tribe of Germany 54/2; 55/1
Hexham N England bishopric 38/3; ⚔33/3, 73/4
Hexhamshire franchise of N England 56/4
Hibernia (*mod.* Ireland) Roman Empire 30/3
Hidalgo province of C Mexico 97/1
Hieraconpolis Upper Egypt Old Kingdom city 17/3
Hierapolis A Anatolia archbishopric 27/2
Hierosolyma (*Eng.* Jeruslaem *Heb.* Yerushalayim *Ar.* Al Quds) Palestine Roman Empire 31/3
Hiiumaa (Ösel)
Hijaz (Hejaz)
Hildesheim N Germany bishopric 79/1
Himachal Pradesh state of N India 105/5
Himeji W Japan 126/2
Himera Sicily Greek colony 19/4, 23/2
Hinduism 27/1
Hipponium (*mod.* Vibo Valentia) S Italy Greek colony 19/4
Hippo Regius (*Sp.* Bona *Fr.* Bône *mod.* Annaba) Algeria Phoenician city 19/4; Roman Empire 24/2, 30/3; early bishopric 26/2
Hippo Zarytus (*mod.* Bizerta) Tunisia Phoenician city 19/4
Hiroshima city and prefecture of W Japan 126/2; bombed by US 135/2, 3
Hirsau SW Germany monastery 34/4
Hispalis (*mod.* Seville) S Spain Roman Empire 24/2, 30/3; archbishopric 26/2
Hispania (*mod.* Spain and Portugal) Roman Empire 30/2
Hispaniae Roman province 31/4
Hispaniola (*mod.* Dominican Republic *and* Haiti) island of West Indies early exploration 64/2, 65/3; settled by French and Spanish 66/4; early trade 66/1
Hit Mesopotamia early city 17/4
Hitchin S England Industrial Revolution 98/1
Hittite Empire Asia Minor 21/1
Hjaltland (Shetland)
Hobart Tasmania penal settlement 113/1
Ho Chi Minh City (Saigon)
Ho Chi Minh Trail Vietnam/Laos 148/3
Höchstädt W Germany ⚔81/5
Hodeida (*Ar.* Al Hudaydah) Yemen early trade 58/3
Hódmezövásárhely Hungary site 15/1
Hoggar region of N Africa rock painting 11/1
Hohenfriedeberg (*mod.* Dąbromierz) W Poland ⚔78/2
Hohenlinden S Germany ⚔91/1
Hohenlohe county of C Germany 79/1
Hohenstaufen German dynasty 54/3
Hohenzollern German dynasty 79/1
Hojo clan territory of C Japan 51/3
Hokitika S Island. New Zealand founded 112/2
Hokkaido (*form.* Ezo *a/s* Yezo) N Island of Japan 127/2
Hole-in-the-Wall C USA ⚔95/2
Holkar region of C India Maratha state 87/3
Holkham E England agricultural revolution 98/1
Holland Black Death 57/1; Burgundian possession 73/3; province of Dutch Republic 77/1; kingdom under French protection 90/3, 91/4; WW1 118-119; WW2 132-3. See also Netherlands
Hollandia (*n/c* Jayapura) N New Guinea Allied landing in WW2 135/2
Holme C England Industrial Revolution 98/1
Holmegaard (Novgorod)
Holme's Bonfire North Sea English naval victory 81/3
Holstein region of N Germany medieval German Empire 55/3; under Danish rule 72/1; Reformation 75/1; in German Confederation 115/2; divided between Denmark and Germany 128/2
Holstein-Glückstadt (former state of N Germany 79/1
Holstein-Gottorp former state of N Germany 79/1
Holt N England Industrial Revolution 98/1
Holyhead NW Wales port 98/1
Holy Roman Empire Mongol invasion 46/2; Black Death 57/1; Thirty Years War 74/4
Homestead Florida US Air Force base 149/5
Homildon Hill N England ⚔56/4
Homs (*anc.* Emesa) W Syria occupied by French 125/3
Ho-mu-tu (*a/s* Hemudu) E China early settlement 8/2
Honan region of C China T'ang province 50/1; Ming province 51/4; Nien rebels 107/3; 1911 Revolution 122/1
Hondschoote NE France ⚔89/2
Honduras country of C America early exploration 64/2, 3; independence 91/7; political development 142-3
Hong Kong acquired by Britain 101/1, 2; 107/4; occupied by Japanese 134/1; British colony 139/1; trade and industry 123/4
Honshu the main island of Japan 126/1, 2
Hopeh region of N China T'ang province 50/1
Hopewell early Indian culture USA 12/3
Hopi indian tribe of SW USA 63/1
Hormuz (Ormuz, Harmozia)
Horn, Cape S America first rounded 642
Horncastle N England Industrial Revolution 98/1
Horseshoe Bend SE USA ⚔95/2
Horthaland district of Norway 53/5
Hortus S France site of early man 3/3
Hotin (Khotin)
Hotung N China T'ang province 50/1
Housesteads (Vercovicium)
Hov N Denmark megalithic flint mine 15/3
Hova early state of Madagascar 60/2
Hoya county of N Germany 79/1
Hrvatska (Croatia)
Hsi C China Western Chou domain 9/6
Hsien C China Western Chou domain 9/6
Hsien-jen-tung (*a/s* Xianrendong) SE China early settlement 8/2
Hsien-pi tribe of NE Asia, invade China 33/1
Hsing N China Western Chou domain 9/6
Hsing-t'ai (*a/s* Xingtai) N China Shang city 8/4
Hsiungnu tribe on northern borders of China 28/1, 2; 33/1
Hsü E China Western Chou domain 9/6
Hsuantu NE China Han commanderie 29/3
Hsün N China Western Chou domain 9/6
Huainan E China T'ang province 50/1
Huaiyang C China Western Chou site 9/6
Huamachuco Peru on Pizarro's route 68/2
Huamanga Peru on Pizarro's route 68/2
Huan E China Western Chou domain 9/6
Huancayo Peru on Pizarro's route 68/2
Huang C China Western Chou domain 9/6
Huang Ho (*Eng.* Yellow River) Shang sites 8/4
Huaráz Peru on Pizarro's route 68/2
Huari Empire C Andes 12/4, 5
Huastec Indian tribe of N Mexico 12/2
Huayna Capac Inca emperor 62T, 63/3
Huddersfield N England Industrial Revolution 98/1
Hudson, Henry explorer 64/2
Hudson Bay N Canada exploration 64/2; fur trade 68T/5
Hudson's Bay Company N Canada 68/5, 69/3, 92/1
Hue S Vietnam 1945-75 war 148/3
Huelva SW Spain Civil War 129/4
Huguenots 76/2
Huichol Indian tribe of C Mexico 63/1
Hui-hsien (*a/s* Huixian) N China Shang city 8/4
Hukwang C China Ming province 51/4
Hull N England medieval trade 59/2; Industrial Revolution 98/1; WW2 132/1
Hunan province of C China Manchu expansion 106/1; 1911 Revolution 122/1; Taiping advance 107/3; Hsin-hai revolution 122/1; warlord control 123/3
Hunchun NE China treaty port 107/4
Hundred Years' War 56/5
Hungarians migration after WW1 129/3
Hungary conversion to Christianity 38/2; early kingdom 56/2; Mongol invasion 46/2; medieval Christian state 49/1; Black Death 57/1; empire of Mathias Corvinus 72/1; acquired by Habsburgs 78/3; Reformation 75/1; under Ottoman control 48/2; Habsburg-Ottoman frontier 72/1; movement for independence 88/1; short-lived Soviet Republic 120/3; independence after WW1 128/2; inter-war alliances 128/1; economic and socio-political development 131/3; Axis satelite 132/1; occupation of SE Czechoslovakia 129/5; WW2 132-3; Warsaw Pact and Comecon 137/2; end of Communist rule 137/4. See also Austro-Hungarian Empire
Hungchao N China Western Chou site 9/6
Hungnam N Korea 1950-53 war 148/2
Huns tribe on borders of Roman Empire 31/4; invasion of Europe 32/1
Huntingdon C England Norman castle 36/3
Hupeh province of C China Manchu expansion 106/1; 1911 Revolution 122/1; Taiping control 107/3; Hsin-hai revolution 122/1
Huron Indian tribe of NE Canada 62/4, 63/1
Hussites Bohemia and Moravia 75/1
Hwicce early people of W England 35/3
Hyderabad city of NW India 105/3
Hyderabad (*f/c* Nizam's Dominions) former state of C India 104/1, 105/3, 5
Hyogo prefecture of W Japan 126/1, 2
Hyrcania (*mod.* Gorgan *a/s* Gurgan) region of N Persia Alexander's Empire 23/3

Iadera (*mod.* Zadar *It.* Zara) Yugoslavia Byzantine Empire 42/1
Iaşi (Jassy)
Ibadan S Nigeria 103/3; Biafran War 140/2
Ibaraki prefecture of C Japan 126/2
Iberia ancient country of Caucasus 43/1
Ibero-Celts early people of Spain 18/4
Ibiza Balearic Islands Spanish Civil War 129/4
Ibo people of Nigeria 61/2; Biafran war 140T/2
Iceland Norse settlement 37/1; joins Union of Kalmar 72/1; Reformation 74/1; independence from Denmark 128/2 (inset); NATO 137/2; economy 150/1
Iceni ancient tribe of Britain 30/3
Ice Sheets 4/1
Ichang C China treaty town 107/4
Icheng N China Western Chou site 9/6
Ichou SW China Han commanderie 29/3
Iconium (*mod.* Konya) C Anatolia early city 16/1; Roman Empire 25/2; early archbishopric 27/2; Byzantine Empire 43/1
Icosium (*mod.* Algiers *Fr.* Alger *Sp.* Argel) Algeria Roman Empire 30/3
Iculisma (Angoulême)
Idaho state of W USA Depression 130/2; population 111/5, 145/1
Idalium (*mod.* Dhali) Cyprus Phoenician city 19/4
Idfu (Edfu)
Idrisids Muslim dynasty of Morocco 40/2
Ieper (Ypres)
Ife Nigeria Iron Age site 11/1; early state 60/1
Ifni region of NW Africa Spanish colony 102/5; ceded to Morocco 138/1
Igbo-Ukwu Nigeria Iron Age site 11/1
Ihsun Sinkiang Han expansion 28/2
Ilchester SW England Industrial Revolution 98/1
Ilebo (Port-Francqui)
Ile de France region of N France 52/3
Ileret Ethiopia early site 3/3, 11/1
Ili region of C Asia Chinese protectorate 106/1; ceded to Russia 107/4
Ilipa Spain ⚔30/2
Ilium (Troy)
Il-Khan Empire Persia 46/3
Illiberris (*mod.* Elne) S France bishopric 26/2
Illinois state of C USA industry 110/2; Depression 131/2; population 111/5, 145/1
Illinois Indian tribe of C USA 63/1
Illyria ancient country of Adriatic 22/3
Illyrian Provinces Adriatic under French protection 91/1
Illyrians ancient people of Adriatic 19/4
Illyricum Roman province of Adriatic 31/3
Ilmen Slavs E Slav tribe 44/1
Ilorin early Hausa state of Nigeria 103/3
Ilva (*mod.* Elba) island of W Italy Etruscan city 19/4
Immidir S Algeria rock painting 11/1
Imola C Italy member of 1167 League 55/3
Inca Empire Peru 63/3; conquest by Spain 68/2
Inchon (*a/c Chemulpo Jap.* Jinsen) S Korea Russo-Japanese war 127/4; US landing in Korean war 148/2
India agricultural origins 7/2, 5; early trade routes 25/1; early urban centres 29/4, 5; early civilisations 9/1, 5; centre of Buddhism and Hinduism 27/1; invaded by Alexander 23/3; early empires 29/4; introduction of Christianity 39/1; spread of Islam 41/4; first seaborne European visit 65/2; Mughal Empire 48/2; growth of British power 87/3; Anglo-French rivalry 87/2; trade 59/3, 66/2, 67/1, 83/5; Mutiny 104/1; industrialisation 108-9; under British rule 101/1, 2; anti-British uprisings 104/4; Japanese offensive 135/2; independence 138/1; partition 105/5, boundary dispute with China 141/1; economy 150/1
Indiana state of C USA industry 110/2; Depression 131/2; population 111/5, 145/1
Indian Ocean early trade routes 59/3; European discovery 65/2; British control 100/3
Indo-China French colony early trade routes 25/1, 101/1; occupied by Japanese 127/5; 1945-75 war 149/1
Indonesia (*form.* Dutch East Indies) independence 139/1; political developments 141/1; economy 151/1
Indore C India 105/3
Industrial Revolution 98-99
Ingalik Arctic Indian tribe of Alaska 63/1
Ingelheim W Germany Frankish royal residence 34/4
Ingombe Ilede early state of SC Africa 60/1
Ingria region of Baltic Russia under Swedish rule 77/3
Inishmurray NW Ireland Viking settlement 37/1
Inner Mongolia N China Manchu expansion 106/1; Japanese occupation 134-135
Innocent IV pope 54T
Inönü W Turkey Greco-Turkish War 125/4
Insubres early people of N Italy 30/1
Invercargill S Island, New Zealand founded 112/2
Iolcus E Greece Mycenaean settlement 19/1
Iona island of W Scotland monastery 38/2, 3; Scandinavian settlement 39/1
Ionia ancient region of W Anatolia 23/1, 2

Ionian Islands (*anc.* Heptanesus) W Greece occupied by France 89/3; ceded to Greece 116/1
Ionians early Greeks 18/3
Iowa state of NW USA Depression 131/2; population 111/5, 145/1
Ipswich E England medieval trade 59/2; Industrial Revolution 98/1
IRA Ireland 137/6
Iran (*f/c* Persia) Baghdad Pact 148/1, 4; oilfields 150/4; economy 150T/1; overthrow of Pahlevi dynasty 141/1
Iraq (*form.* Mesopotamia) British mandate 125/1; political disturbances 140/1; independence 138/1; Baghdad Pact 148/1, 4; Gulf war 150T
Ireland (*anc.* Hibernia *Ir.* Eire) expansion of Christianity 38/2, 3; Scandinavian settlement 37/1; English and Norman overlordship 53/6; English kingdom 72/1; Reformation 74/1; English control 73/4; attempted French invasion 90/3; revolt against England 88/1; trade and industry 82/4; socio-political change 130/3; neutral in WW2 132/1; EEC 137/2. See also Irish Free State
Irian Jaya (Dutch New Guinea, West Irian)
Irish Free State (*created 1922, since 1937* Republic of Ireland) 128/2
Irkutsk Siberia founded 84/2, 3; industry 147/1
Iroquois Indian tribe of NE USA 63/1, 624
Isandhlwana Zululand, SE Africa × 103/2
Isauria C Anatolia district of Byzantine Empire 43/1
Isca (*mod.* Caerleon) S Wales Roman Empire 24/2
Isenberg county of C Germany 79/1
Isernia (Aesernia)
Isfahan (*f/s* Ispahan *properly* Esfahan) C Persia early bishopric 39/1; early trade 58/3
Ishikawa prefecture of C Japan 126/2
Ishim Russ. C Asia founded 84/2
Isiro (Paulis)
Iskenderun (Alexandretta)
Islam 40-41, 48-49
Island Arawak Indian tribe of the Caribbean 63/1
Island Carib Indian tribe of the Caribbean 63/1
Island No 10 C USA × 92/1
Ismailia E Egypt war with Israel 141/3
Isonzo (*S. Cr.* Soča) *river* Italy-Yugoslavia battles of WW1 119/3
Ispahan (Isfahan)
Israel (*form. part of* Palestine) at time of David 21/2; independence 138/1 war with Arab States 141/3; economy 150/1
Issus E Anatolia × 21/5, 22/3
Istanbul (*form.* Constantinople *anc.* Byzantium) W Turkey Ottoman Empire 48-49
Istria region of NW Yugoslavia Byzantine Empire 42/1; conquered by Franks 35/4
Istrus Bulgaria Greek colony 19/4
Isturits SW France Palaeolithic art 5/3
Italia Roman province of S Italy 31/3, 4
Italian East Africa (Ethiopia, Eritrea)
Italians inter-war emigration to France 128/3
Italian Somaliland (*now S part of* Somalia) colony 101/1, 102/5, 103/3, 129/5
Italy Mycenaean trade 18/2; Greek colonisation 19/4; growth of Roman power 30/1; Visigothic and Ostrogothic invasions 32/1, conversion to Christianity 26/1; in medieval German Empire 33/4; Norman kingdom in south 36/2; 14C 56/3; Black Death 57/1; Renaissance 73/5; peasant emancipation 82/1; states established by Revolutionary France 89/3; under Napoleon 90/1; industrial revolution 99/2; unification 114/3; colonial empire 101/2; growth in armaments 117/3; WW1 118-9; inter-war alliances 128/1; S Tyrol regained 128/2; socio-political development 131/3; expansion 1934-39 129/5; WW2 132-3; NATO 137/2, 149/1
Itil N Caspian Khazar city 45/2
Ivan III Emperor of Russia 72T, 84T, 85/1
Ivory Coast (*Fr.* Côte d'Ivoire) country of W Africa French colony 100/2, 103/3; independence 138/1; economy 150/1
Iwate prefecture of N Japan 127/2
Iwo Jima Japanese island of N Pacific × 135/2; US base 149/1 (inset)
Ixtacmaxtitlan Mexico on Cortés route 68/1
Izmir (*form.* Smyrna) W Turkey 125/3, 4
Izmit (Astacus, Nicomedia)

Jablines N France megalithic flint mine 15/3
Jackson SE USA × 92/5; civil unrest 144/3
Jaffa (Joppa, Yafa, Yafo)
Jaipur E India 105/3
Jajce Bosnai acquired by Ottomans 48/1
Jakarta (Batavia, Djakarta)
Jalapa Mexico on Cortés' route 68/1
Jalisco province of C Mexico 97/1
Jamaica island of West Indies British colony 66/4, 69/4, 100/2, 97/1; independence 139/1 (inset); economy 150/1
James Island Gambia, W Africa British settlement 60/1
Jamestown E USA × 92/1
Jammu and Kashmir native state of British India 105/3; disputed with Pakistan 105/5
Jämtland old province of E Sweden acquired from Norway 77/3
Jankau Bohemia × 74/4
Japan Buddhism and Shintoism 27/1; Chinese cultural influence 51/1; attacked by Mongols 47/1; early trade 66/2; 15-16C civil war 51/3; invasion of Korea and China 51/4; industrialisation 108/1; Russo-Japanese war 127/4; modern development 101/2, 126/1, 2; expansion in Asia 127/3, 5; WW2 134-5; US bases 149/1; economy 141/4.
Jarmo N Mesopotamia early farming site 7/4
Jarrow N England monastery 38/3
Jarvis Island US island of C Pacific 139/1 (inset)
Jassy (*Rom.* Iaşi *Turk.* Yaş) NE Romania Ottoman attack 48/2; WW2 133/2
Jauja Peru × 68/2
Java (*Indon.* Jawa) island of C Indonesia early man 8/3; early sites 8/3; Muslim expansion 40/5; spread of Buddhism and Hinduism 27/1, 70/1; Mongol expedition 51/2; Dutch expansion 71/4; early trade 71/2; Dutch possession 71/4; occupied by Japanese 134/1
Java Sea naval battle of WW2 134/1
Jayapura (Hollandia)
Jebel Irhoud Morocco site of early man 3/3
Jebel Moya Sudan Iron Age site 11/1
Jedda (*a/s* Jidda) W Arabia Red Sea trade 58/3; early Chinese voyages 58/3
Jehol former province of Manchuria Boxer uprising 107/3; occupied by Japanese 123/3
Jemappes Belgium × 89/2
Jemdet Nasr N Mesopotamia Sumerian site 16/2
Jena E Germany × 91/1; WW1 119/3
Jenne (*Fr.* Djenné W Africa town of Mali Empire 60/1
Jenne-jeno W Africa Iron Age site 11/1
Jenny Lind W USA mining site 94/1
Jericho (*Ar.* Ariha) Palestine site of early village 7/4; town of Judaea 26/3
Jerusalem (*anc.* Hierosolyma *Roman* Aelia Capitolina *Heb.* Yerushalayim *Ar.* Al Quds) Israel Mycenaean trade 18/2; Levantine city 21/1; under Alexander 22/3; centre of Christianity 26-27; patriarchate 27/2; town of Judaea 26/3; early Jewish community 39/4; Muslim conquest 41/1; Byzantine Empire 43/1; Kingdom of 40/3; early trade 58/3; Ottoman Empire 49/1; WW1 125/2; in Arab-Israeli conflict 141/3
Jewish AR E USSR 146/2
Jews in medieval Europe 39/4
Jeypore district of E India ceded to Britain 87/3
Jhansi N India Indian Mutiny 104/1
Jiangxi'an (Chiang-hsi-an)
Jibuti (Djibouti)
Jidda (Jedda)
Jinsen (Inchon)
Jivaro forest Indian tribe of S America 63/1
Jo C China Western Chou domain 9/6
Jodhpur NW India 108/1
Jogjakarta (Yogyakarta)
Johore state of Malaya 71/5
Joppa (*mod.* Jaffa *Ar.* Yafa *Heb.* Yafo) Palestine Philistine city 19/4; Levantine city 21/1; early bishopric 27/2; town of Judaea 26/3
Jordan independence 138/1; conflicts 141/3, 148/4; economy 150/1. See also Transjordan
Jordhøj N Denmark megalithic tomb 15/3
Juan-juan (*a/c* Avars) tribe of N China 33/1
Judaea Palestine 26/3; Roman province 31/3; independent Jewish state 26/3
Judah kingdom 21/2
Judaism 38-39
Judeirjo-Daro N China Harappan site 9/5
Jui China Western Chou domain 9/6
Juikin S China centre of Kiangsu Soviet 123/4
Jülich duchy of W Germany 79/1
Juliomagus (Angers)
Julius Caesar Roman Empire 30T
Junan C China Han commanderie 29/3
Junction City C USA cow town 94/1
Jund-i Shapur NW Persia early archbishopric 39/1
Justinian Roman Emperor 31/4
Jutes Germanic tribe, invasion of Britain 32/2
Jutland Denmark × 118/3

Kaarta early state of W Africa 60/2
Kabáh E Mexico Mayan centre 12/2
Kabardino-Balkar ASSR Caucasus 146/2
Kabul Afghanistan Achaemenid Empire 21/5; Muslim conquest 41/1; Mongol conquest 47/1; conquered by Babur 48/2
Kadambas tribe of S India 29/5
Kadero Sudan early site 11/1
Kadıköy (Chalcedon)
Kaesong C Korea Russo-Japanese war 127/4
Kaffa (*It.* Caffa *Turk.* Kefe *anc.* Theodosia *mod.* Feodosiya) Crimea Mongol conquest 46/1; Ottoman conquest 48/2
Kaga N Japan anti-Bakufu domain 126/1
Kagawa prefecture of W Japan 126/2
Kagoshima city and prefecture of W Japan 126/1, 2
Kaifeng N China Ming provincial capital 51/4
Kaingang Indian tribe of S Brazil 63/1
Kaira district of W India no tax campaign 104/4
Kairouan Tunisia Muslim conquest 40/1
Kalambo E Africa Iron Age site 11/1
Kalanay C Philippines Iron Age site 8/3
Kalémié (Albertville)
Kalenberg duchy of N Germany 79/1
Kalgan N China 107/4
Kalgoorlie W Australia goldfield 113/1
Kalibangan N India Harappan site 9/5; early agriculture 7/2
Kalimantan (Borneo)
Kalinga region of E India 29/4
Kalinin (*until 1932* Tver) C Russia industry 147/1
Kaliningrad (*form.* Königsberg) W Russia industry 147/1
Kalka River S Russia × 44/3, 46/1
Kalmar, Union of Scandinavia 72/1
Kalmuks (*Russ.* Kalmyki) tribe of C Asia, conquered by Russia 85/1
Kalmyk ASSR S Russia 146/2
Kalpi N India Indian Mutiny 104/1
Kaluga W Russia 1905 Revolution 120/1; Bolshevik seizure 121/2; industry 147/1
Kalumpang Celebes, E Indies Neolithic site 8/3
Kalundu S Africa Iron Age site 11/1
Kamarupa region of NE India under Guptas 29/4, 5
Kamchadali native people of Kamchatka 84/2
Kamchatka territory of E Russia 84/2
Kamenets (*later* Kamenets-Podolskiy) Ukraine 45/2
Kamerun (Cameroon)
Kamina Zaire Congo crisis 138/4
Kaminaljuyú E Mexico Mayan site 12/2
Kamnama E Africa Iron Age site 11/1
Kampala Uganda Speke's journey 102/1; taken by British 103/3
Kampen Netherlands Hanseatic town 59/2
Kampuchea (Cambodia)
Kanagawa city and prefecture of C Japan 126/2
Kananga (Luluabourg)
Kanara district of SW India ceded to Britain 87/3
Kanchow NW China early bishopric 39/1; Ming frontier defence area 51/4
Kandahar (*a/s* Qandahar *anc.* Alexandria-Arachaton) Afghanistan trade 59/3
Kandesh district of W India civil unrest 104/4
Kandy Ceylon Buddhist site 27/1
Kanem-Borno early empire of NC Africa 60/1
Kanesh (*mod.* Kültepe) C Anatolia early urban settlement 16/1; early trade 17/4
Kanli Kastelli early Cretan palace, 19/1
Kano Nigeria Hausa city-state 60/1, 61/2; Barth's journey 102/1; taken by British 103/3
Kanpur (Cawnpore)
Kansas state of C USA Depression 131/2; population 111/5, 145/1
Kansas City C USA cow town 94/1; population 111/5
Kansu province of NW China 50/1; Manchu expansion 106/1; Muslim uprising 106/3; 1911 revolution 122/1
Kapisa (Begram)
Kapovaya C Siberia Palaeolithic art 5/3
Kapwirimbe S Africa Iron Age site 11/1
Karachaevo-Cherkess AR Caucasus 146/2
Karachev town of Novgorod-Seversk, W Russia 45/2
Karachi Pakistan naval mutiny 104/4; industry under British rule 105/3
Karafuto *southern part of Sakhalin* island of Pacific Russia acquired by Japan 127/3; reoccupied by Russia 135/1
Karaganda Russ. C. Asia industry 147/1
Karagwe early state of Uganda 61/2
Karahüyük C Anatolia Hittite city 21/1
Kara-Kalpak ASSR C Asia 146/2
Karakhanids Muslim dynasty of C Asia 41/2
Kara-Khitai Mongol empire of C Asia 46/1
Kara Khoto Mongolia early trade 59/3
Karakorum Mongolia Mongol capital 47/1
Karakoyunlu district of E Anatolia 49/1
Karaman (*anc.* Laranda) S Anatolia early trade 17/3; Turkoman principality 49/1
Karanga tribe of SE Africa 61/2
Karanovo Bulgaria site 14/2, 15/1
Karaova Suya (Aegospotami)
Karasi early emirate of NW Anatolia 49/1
Karatepe SE Anatolia Hittite city 21/1
Karbala (Kerbala)
Karcha Caucasus early archbishopric 27/2
Karelia region of Finland and N Russia to Sweden 77/3; to Russia 85/1; ASSR 146/2
Karenni (*n/s* Kayah State) C Burma 71/2; 104/2
Karikal SE India French settlement 87/2, 105/3 (inset)
Karka (*Lat.* Caria) country of SW Anatolia satrapy of Achaemenid Empire 20/5
Karkamış (Carchemish)
Karkarchinkat W Africa early site 11/1
Karkh Mesopotamia early archbishopric 39/1
Karli W India Buddhist site 27/1
Karl-Marx-Stadt (Chemnitz)
Karlsburg (Alba Iulia)
Karlsruhe S Germany industrial development 99/2
Karmona (*Sp.* Córdoba) S Spain Muslim control 37/1
Karnak Upper Egypt 21/1
Karnata (*Eng.* Carnatic) region of S India 29/1
Kärnten (Carinthia)
Karok Indian tribe of NW USA 63/1
Karos S Aegean burial site 14/2

Kars E Anatolia conquered by Ottomans 48/2; lost to Russia 121/2
Kars and Ardaham Ottoman province of E Anatolia 124/1
Karshi (Nautaca)
Kasai province of C Belgian Congo 138/4
Kashgar Sinkiang silk route 25/1; Han expansion 28/2; early trade 50/1, 59/3; early bishopric 39/1; Muslim risings against Chinese 106/1
Kashmir NW India Mughal conquest 48/2; divided between India and Pakistan 105/5
Kaska sub-arctic Indian tribe of NW Canada 63/1
Kaskaskia C USA French post 67/3; fur station 94/1
Kasmira (*mod.* Kashmir) region of NW India 29/4
Kasogi tribe of Caucasus 45/2
Kastamonu C Turkey revolt against Ottoman rule 48/2. See also Çandar
Kastri S Aegean early settlement 14/2
Kastri S Greece Mycenaean settlement 19/1
Katanga (*now* Shaba) province of S Congo in Congo crisis 138/4
Katarpur N India political disturbance 104/4
Kathiawar group of western Indian states under British rule 105/3
Katsamba C Crete Mycenaean settlement 19/1
Katsina Hausa city-state of N Nigeria 60/1, 60/2
Katuruka E Africa early site 11/1
Katyn Poland 132/1
Kaunas (*form. Russ.* Kovno) Lithuanian SSR WW2 133/2
Kawa Upper Egypt New Kingdom temple 21/1
Kawasaki C Japan bombed by US 135/3
Kayseri (*anc.* Caesarea Cappadociae *or* Mazaca) C Turkey Ottoman Empire 49/1
Kazakhs Turkic people of C Asia, conquered by Russians 84/2, 3; 146/3
Kazakhstan C Asia 147/1; SSR 146/2; independence 151/4
Kazalinsk Russ. C Asia railway 84/3
Kazan C Russia Mongol capital 46/1; 1905 Revolution 120/1; Bolshevik seizure 121/2; industry 147/1
Kazan Mongol khanate of C Russia conquered by Russia 85/1
Kea (Ceos)
Kebarah N Palestine site of early man 3/3
Kedah state of N Malaya tributary to Siam 71/5
Kediri early state of Java 51/2
Keijo (Seoul)
Keilor Australia site of early man 3/3
Kelantan state of N Malaya tributary to Siam 71/5
Kells E Ireland monastery 38/3
Kemerovo S Siberia industry 147/1
Kendal N England Industrial Revolution 98/1
Kenesaw Mountain SE USA ✕ 93/5
Kenora C Canada growth 111/1
Kent early kingdom of SE England 33/3; conversion to Christianity 38/3
Kentish Knock E England English naval victory 81/3
Kentucky state of SE USA Civil War campaigns 93/5; Depression 131/2; population 111/5, 145/1
Kenya (*form.* British East Africa) British colony 103/3, 5; independence 138/1; political development 140/1; economy 150/1
Keraits Mongol tribe of C Asia 47/1
Kerbela (*Ar.* Karbala) Mesopotamia ✕ 41/1
Kerch (*anc.* Panticapaeum) Crimea industry 84/4; WW2 133/2
Kerkira (Corfu, Corcyra)
Kermadec Islands SW Pacific New Zealand possession 139/1 (inset)
Kerman (Kirman)
Kermanshah (*a/s* Kirmanshah) Persia early trade 58/3
Kernstown E USA ✕ 93/5
Kesslerloch SW Germany Palaeolithic art 5/3
Kett's rebellion S England 73/4
Kexholm N Russia conquered by Sweden 77/3
Keyukon sub-arctic tribe of Alaska 63/1
Key West Florida US naval base 149/5
Khabarovsk Russ. Far East railway 84/3, 120/4; industry 147/1
Khafajah (Tutub)
Khakass AR Central Asia 146/2
Khalandriani S Aegean Mycenaean settlement 19/1
Khalkha Mongol tribe 51/4
Khalkidhiki (Chalcidice)
Khanbalik (*mod.* Peking) N China Mongol capital 39/1, 47/1
Khania (*a/s Canea anc.* Cydonia) Crete palace and city 19/1
Khanty-Mansi AR W Siberia 146/2
Khara-Khoja C Asia early bishopric 39/1
Kharkov Ukraine founded 85/1; 1905 Revolution 120/1; Bolshevik seizure 121/2; WW2 132-3; industry 147/1
Khartoum British occupation 103/3
Khazar Empire S Russia 41/1
Khazars Jewish-Turkish tribe of S Russia 44/1, 50/1
Kherson Ukraine founded 85/1
Khios (Chios)
Khirokitia Cyprus early farming site 7/4
Khitan (*a/c* Liao) tribe of Mongolia, raids on China 50/1
Khiva (*a/c Khwarizm anc.* Chorasmia) region of C Asia independent khanate 124/1; People's Republic incorporated into USSR 120/4
Khmer (*mod.* Cambodia) SE Asia kingdom under Hindu influence 50/1; temple kingdom 51/2
Khmer Rouge Cambodian guerrilla movement 141/1
Khoisan people of S Africa 60/1, 61/2, 103/2
Khokand (Kokand)
Kholm (*mod. Pol.* Chełm) W Russia town of Vladimir-Volynsk 45/2
Khorasan (Khurasan)
Khotan Sinkiang silk route 25/1; Han expansion 28/1
Khotin (*Rom.* Hotin) Ukraine Ottoman siege 48/2
Khotylevo E Russia Palaeolithic art 5/3
Khrushchev, Nikita 146T
Khurasan (*a/s* Khorasan) region of C Persia Muslim conquest 41/1, 50/1; under Abbasid sovereignty 41/2
Khuzistan (Susiana, Elam)
Khwarizm (*a/c Khiva anc.* Chorasmia) region of C Asia under Abbasid sovereignty 41/2
Khwarizm Shah, Empire of the Mongol empire of C Asia 47/1
Khyber Pass NW India trade routes 59/3
Kiamusze Manchuria 123/4
Kiangsi province of SE China under the Ming 51/4; Manchu expansion 106/1; Taiping control 107/3; 1911 revolution 122/1; Nationalist control 123/3; Soviet under Mao Tse-tung 123/4
Kiangsu province of E China Manchu expansion 106/1
Kiaochow E China railway 127/4
Kibris (Cyprus)
Kiel N Germany WW1 119/3
Kiev (*Russ.* Kiyev *Ukr.* Kyiv) Ukraine bishopric 38/2; Viking trade 44/1; principality 45/2; medieval fair 59/2; 1905 Revolution 120/1; WW2 132-3; industry 147/1
Kievan Russia 37/1, 45/2
Kii (*a/c* Kishu) S Japan Tokugawa domain 126/1
Kikuyu tribe of E Africa 61/2
Kildare's rebellion S Ireland 73/4
Kilia (*n/s Kiliya Rom.* Chilia-Nouă) Ukraine Ottoman control 49/1
Kilik-Koba S Ukraine site of early man 3/3
Kilizi N Mesopotamia Mitannian city 21/1
Kilkenny S Ireland centre of rebellion 76/4
Killdeer Mountain E USA ✕ 95/2
Kilwa (*a/c* Kilwa Kisiwani) early trade 11/1; Muslim colony 60/1, 612
Kimberley S Africa ✕ 103/4
Kimberley Plateau W Australia goldfield 113/1
Kindu C Belgium Congo Congo crisis 138/4
King's Lynn (*a/c* Lynn) *E England* medieval trade 59/2; Industrial Revolution 98/1
Kingsmills N Ireland IRA 137/6
Kinsale S Ireland ✕ 73/4
Kinshasa (Léopoldville)
Kintampo W Africa early site 11/1
Kiowa plains Indian tribe of C USA 63/1
Kirensk SE Siberia founded 84/2
Kirghiz Turkic people of C Asia, destroy Uighur Empire 50/1; conquered by Russians 84/3; 146/3
Kirghizistan C Asia independence 151/4
Kiribati (*f/c* Gilbert Is) Pacific 139/1 (inset)
Kirillovskaya Ukraine Palaeolithic art 5/3
Kirin province of Manchuria occupied by Russia 127/4
Kirkby Stephen N England rebellion against Henry VIII 73/4
Kirman (*a/s Kerman anc.* Carmana) region of S Persia Muslim conquest 41/1
Kirovograd (Yelizavetgrad)
Kisangani (Stanleyville)
Kish N Mesopotamia Sumerian city 16/2, 17/4
Kishinev (*Rom.* Chişinău) W Russia industry 147/1
Kiska island of Aleutians, Alaska captured by Japanese 134/1; retaken by Americans 135/2
Kistna district of SE India ceded to Britain 87/3
Kithira (Cerigo, Cythera)
Kit's Coty SE England megalithic tomb 14/3
Kittim (Citium)
Kiukiang C China treaty town 107/4
Kiungchow S China treaty port 107/4
Kivu province of E Belgian Congo 138/4
Kiyev, Kiyiv (Kiev)
Kizzuwadna (Cilicia)
Klaipéda (*Ger.* Memel) Lithuanian SSR industry 147/1
Klasies River Mouth S Africa site of early man 3/3
Kleve (Cleves)
Knossos (*Lat.* Cnossus) Crete farming site 15/1; 19/1, 3
Knoxville SE USA ✕ 93/5
Kobe C Japan bombed by US 135/3
København (Copenhagen)
Koblenz (Coblenz)
Kochi city and prefecture of W Japan 126/1, 2
Kohat NW India political disturbance 104/4
Kokand (*a/s* Khokand) C Asia on Silk Road 25/1; conquered by Russia 84/3; Muslim khanate 124/1
Kok Charoen C Thailand early site 8/3
Kok Pleb W Thailand Neolithic site 8/3
Kök Türük (Blue Turks)
Kola N Russia monastery 38/2
Kolberg (*Pol.* Kolobrzeg) N Poland Hanseatic trade 59/2
Kolhapur SW India industry 108/1
Köln (Cologne)
Köln-Lindenthal Germany early site 15/1
Kolobeng S Africa 102/1
Kołobrzeg (Kolberg)
Kolomoki USA early site 12/3
Kolomyya (*Pol.* Kolomyja *Ger.* Kolomea) Ukraine 45/2
Kolubara river of N Siberia WW1 119/3
Komarów S Poland WW1 119/3
Komchen E Mexico Mayan centre 12/2
Komi ASSR W Siberia 146/2
Komi-Permyak AR W Siberia 146/2
Komsomolsk-na-Amure Russ. Far East industry 147/1
Kongo early kingdom of W Africa 60/1, 61/2
Königsberg (*since 1946* Kaliningrad) W Russia founded by Teutonic Knights 54/4; Hanseatic city 59/2; 18C financial centre 82/4; Reformation 75/1; WW2 132/1, 133/2
Königshofen W Germany Mithraic site 26/1
Konjic C Yugoslavia Mithraic site 26/1
Konstanz (Constance)
Konya (*anc.* Iconium) S Anatolia early trade 58/3; revolt against Ottoman rule 48/2
Koonalda Cave S Australia flint mine 4/1
Köprüirmaği (Eurymedon River)
Kopys W Russia town of Smolensk 45/2
Koraput district of E India civil unrest 104/4
Korea (*anc.* Koryo *or* Silla *Jap.* Chosen) spread of Buddhism 27/1; conquered by Chinese 29/2; attacked by Mongols 47/1; invaded by Japan 51/4; invaded by Manchus 106/1; end of Chinese tributary status 1077/4; Russo-Japanese war 127/4; acquired by Japan 101/2, 123/4, 127/3, 5; WW2 134-135; 1950-53 war 148/2; economy 108/1
Korea, North militarisation 149/1
Korea, South militarisation and US bases 149/1
Kortrijk (Courtrai)
Koryak AD E USSR 146/2
Koryaks tribe of Russ. Far East 84/2
Koryo (Korea)
Kosala early kingdom of N India 29/4
Koselsk C Russia town of Chernigov 45/2
Kosogorsk SE Siberia founded 84/2
Kosovo (*properly* Kosovo Polje *a/s* Kossovo *Ger.* Amselfeld) S Yugoslavia ✕ 49/1
Kostienki SW Russia site of early man 3/3; Palaeolithic art 5/3
Köszeg (Güns)
Kot Diji N India Harappan site 9/5
Kotor (Cattaro)
Kovno (*Pol.* Kowno *now* Kaunas) W USSR Hanseatic city 59/2; WW1 119/3
Kowloon S China acquired by Britain 107/4
Kowno (Kovno)
Kow Swamp Australia site of early man 3/3
Kozhikode (Calicut)
Krain (Carniola)
Krak des Chevaliers Syria 40/3
Kraków (Cracow)
Krapina N Slovenia site of early man 3/3
Krasnik C Poland WW1 119/3
Krasnodar (*until 1920* Yekaterinodar) Caucasus industry 147/1
Krasnoi W Russia ✕ 91/1
Krasnovodsk Russ. C Asia on railway 84/3; Revolution 121/2; industry 147/1
Krasnoyarsk S Siberia founded 84/2; railway 84/3; industry 147/1
Kristiania (Oslo)
Krivichi E Slav tribe of C Russia 44/1
Krivoy Rog S Ukraine WW2 133/2; industry 147/1
Kromdraai S Africa site of early man 3/3
Kronstadt (*Russ.* Kronshtadt) NW Russia 1905 Revolution 120/1; WW1 119/3
Krukath (Cyropolis)
Krung Thep (Bangkok)
Krym (Crimea)
Ksar Akil Lebanon site of early man 3/3
Ku C China Western Chou domain 9/6
Kuachou NW China Ming military post 51/4
Kuala Lumpur Malaya occupied by Japanese 134/1
Kuala Selinsing Malaya early site 8/3, 51/2
Kuan C China Western Chou domain 9/6
Kuanghan W China Han commanderie 29/3
Kuannei N China T'ang province 50/1
Kuba early state of C Africa 60/1, 61/2
Kublai Khan Mongol ruler 46T
Kubota N Japan 126/1
Kucha NW China Han protectorate 28/2
Kuei W China Western Chou domain 9/6
Kufa Mesopotamia early trade 58/3
Kuldja (*Chin.* Ining) Sinkiang on silk route 25/1
Kullyspell House NW USA fur station 94/1
Kulmerland region of E Germany occupied by Teutonic Knights 54/4
Kůlna Cave Czechoslovakia site of early man 3/3
Kültepe (*a/c* Kanesh) C Anatolia Hittite city 21/2
Kumamoto city and prefecture of W Japan 126/1, 2
Kumasi Gold Coast, W Africa 103/3
Kumbi Saleh W Africa possible site of capital of Ghana Empire 60/1
Kumul (*Chin.* Hami) Sinkiang early bishopric 39/1

Kunduz (Drapsaca)
Kunersdorf (*now* Kunowice) W Poland ⚔78/2
Kunming W China French sphere of influence 107/4
Kunowice (Kunersdorf)
Kuomintang China 123/3
Kurds people of N Iraq, uprisings 140/1
Kurgan Siberia industry 147/1
Kurile Islands (*Russ.* Kurilskiye Ostrova *Jap.* Chishima-retto) acquired by Japan 127/3; reoccupied by USSR 135/2; disputed with USSR 141/1
Kurland (Courland)
Kurnool district of SE India ceded to Britain 87/3
Kurs early people of Baltic 45/2
Kursk W Russia 1905 Revolution 120/1; WW2 133/2
Kurukshetra region of N Indian 29/4
Kuruman S Africa 102/1
Kurume W Japan 126/2
Kush early kingdom of Sudan 11/1
Kushan Empire S Asia 25/1
Kushiya Egypt satrapy of Parthian Empire 20/5
Kusinagara Tibet Buddhist site 27/1
Kustanay Russ. C Asia industry 147/1
Kutch (*f/s Cutch*) *region of W India* border dispute with Pakistan 105/5, 141/1
Kutchin sub-arctic Indian tribe of NW Canada 63/1
Kut el Amara Mesopotamia ⚔125/2
Kutno C Poland WW2 132/1
Kuwait country of Persian Gulf Ottoman sovereignty 124/1; British protectorate 125/2; WW1 125/2; independence 138/1; economy 150/1, Gulf War 150T
Kuybyshev (*until 1935 and from 1991* Samara) E Russia industry 147/1
Kuzbass industrial region of Siberia 147/1
Kuznetsk S Siberia founded 84/2
Kwajalein Marshall Islands, C Pacific occupied by US 135/2; US base 149/1 (inset)
Kwakiutl coast Indian tribe of W Canada 63/1
Kwale E Africa Iron Age site 11/1
Kwangchow (*Eng.* Canton) S China Ming provincial capital 51/4
Kwangchowan S China acquired by France 107/4
Kwangsi province of SW China under Ming 51/4; Manchu expansion 106/1; Taiping rebellion 107/3, 1911 revolution 122/1; warlords 122/2
Kwangtung province of S China under Ming 51/4; Manchu expansion 106/1; Hakka-Cantonese war 107/3; 1911 revolution 122/1; Kuomintang 123/3
Kwantung Leased Territory NE China 127/3
Kwararafa W Africa early state 60/1
Kweichow province of SW China under Ming 51/4; Manchu expansion 106/1; Miao tribal rising 107/3; 1911 revolution 122/1; Kuomintang 123/3
Kwidzyn (Marienwerder)
Kyakhta S Siberia Russian trade with China 106/1
Kyongju S Korea Buddhist site 27/1
Kyoto C Japan Buddhist site 27/1; early capital 50T/3 city and prefecture 126/1, 2
Kypros (Cyprus)
Kyushu W Island of Japan 126/2
Kzyl-Orda (*form.* Perovsk *earlier* Ak-Mechet) Russ. C Asia industry 147/1

Laang Spean Cambodia early site 8/3
Labastide SW France Palaeolithic art 5/3
La Baume-Latronne SW France Palaeolithic art 5/3
Labrador region of NE Canada rediscovered 64/2; to Newfoundland 111/1
Labuan N Borneo British colony 101/1
Laccadive Islands SW India conversion to Islam 41/4; gained by British 87/2
Lacedaemon (*a/c* Sparta) S Greece Byzantine Empire 13/1
La Chaise SW France site of early man 3/3
La Chapelle-aux-Saints C France site of early man 3/3
La Clape SW France megalithic tomb 14/3
Laconia ancient country of S Greece 18/3, 22/1
La Coruña (*Eng.* Corunna) NW Spain Civil War 129/4
Ladoga, Lake (*Russ.* Ladozhskoye Ozero) NW Russia waterway trade route 45/2
Ladrones (Marianas)
Ladysmith S Africa besieged 103/4
Laetoli E Africa site of early man 3/3
La Fère Champenoise NE France ⚔90/1
La Ferrassie S France site of early man 3/3
La Ferté-Bernard N France French Revolution 89/2
La Frebouchère W France megalithic tomb 14/3
Lagash (*a/c Shipurla*) ancient city of Mesopotamia 16/2
Lagny C France medieval fair 58/1
Lagos S Portugal ⚔87/1
Lagos Nigeria taken by British 103/3; British colony 100/2; Biafran war 140/2
Laguna de los Cerros C Mexico Olmec centre 12/2
La Graufesenque (Condatomagus)
La Habana (Havana)
La Halliade SW France megalithic tomb 14/3
La Hogue N France megalithic tomb 14/3; English naval victory 81/4
Lahore NW India in Mughal Empire 48/2; political disturbance 104/4; industry in British India 105/3; capital of Pakistan Punjab 105/5
La Hoz NE Spain Palaeolithic art 5/3
Laish N Palestine Levantine city 21/1
Lake Albert W USA ⚔94/2
Lake Atitlán C Mexico Mayan centre 12/2
Lake Mungo Australia site of early man 3/3
Lake of the Woods (Fort Charles)
Lake Okeechobee SE USA ⚔95/2
Laldène SW France Palaeolithic art 5/3
Lalibela Ethiopia monastery 39/1
La Madeleine SW France site of early man 3/3; Palaeolithic art 5/4
La Magdeleine SW France Palaeolithic art 5/3
Lamanai Belize Mayan centre 12/2
Lambaesis (*mod.* Tazoult) Algeria Mithraic site 26/1; Roman Empire 30/1
La Mouthe SW France Palaeolithic art 5/3
Lampaka ancient country of NW India 29/4
Lampsacus (*mod.* Lâpseki) NW Anatolia Greek colony 19/4; early bishopric 27/2
Lamu Kenya Muslim colony 60/1
Lamuts Siberian tribe 84/2
Lanchow NW China T'ang prefecture 51/4
Landau W Germany fort 89/2
Langobardi early tribe of NW Germany 30/3. See also Lombards
Lang-t'an-tung E China site of early man 3/3
Languedoc region of S France French Royal domain 52/2, 72/2; revolts 77/2; province of France 80/1
Lanka (Ceylon)
L'Anse aux Meadows Newfoundland Norse colony 13/1; 62/4
Lan-t'ien C China prehistoric site 3/3; Late Chou site 9/6
Laodicea (*mod.* Denizli) W Anatolia Roman Empire 31/3; one of seven churches of Asia 27/2; Byzantine Empire 42/2
Laodicea (*mod.* Latakia *Fr.* Lattaquié) Syria Byzantine Empire 42/2, 43/1
Laodicea in Media (Nehavend)
Laon N France ⚔90/1
Laos country of SE Asia 51/2; kingdom of Luang Prabang 71/2; end of Chinese tributary status 107/4; French protectorate 101/2; independence 139/1; Pathet Lao 141/1, 148/3
La Pileta S Spain Palaeolithic art 5/3
Lapita early people of Melanesia 10/2
Lapland region of Swedish empire 77/3
Lapps people of N Russia 38/2
Lâpseki (Lampsacus)
Lapurdum (Bayonne)
La Quemada Mexico site 62/4
La Quina SW France site of early man 3/3
Laranda (Karaman)
Larisa (*a/s* Larissa *Turk.* Yenişehir) C Greece archbishopric 27/2; Byzantine Empire 43/1
La Rochelle W France 16-17C revolts 77/2; commercial harbour 80/1
Larsa (*Bibl.* Ellasar) Mesopotamia early city 17/2, 4
Las Bela NW India Alexander's Empire 23/3
Lascaux SW France Palaeolithic art 5/3
Las Navas de Tolosa S Spain ⚔37/4, 40/2
Las Palomas S Spain Palaeolithic art 5/3
La Starza S Italy early settlement 14/2
Latakia (Laodicea)
La Tène E France site 15/5
Latin America (America, South)
Latin Empire 43/3
Latini early tribe of Italy 30/1
Lattaquié (Laodicea)
Latvia country of the Baltic independence from Russia 129/2; inter-war alliances 128/1; socio-political change 131/3; WW2 132-3; annexed by Russia 137/4; SSR 136/1, 146/2; independence 137/4, 151/4
Latvians emigration from Russia 129/3
Lauenburg principality of N Germany 79/1
Laugerie-Basse SW France Palaeolithic art 5/3
Laugerie-Haute SW France Palaeolithic art 5/3
Launceston W England 16C riots 73/4
Launceston Tasmania gold 113/1
Laupen W Switzerland ⚔54/5
Lausanne Switzerland 1924 Conference 128/2
Lausitz (*Eng.* Lusatia) region of E Germany acquired by Poland 52/1
Laussel SW France Palaeolithic art 5/3
Lava Beds W USA ⚔94/2
Laval N France 17C revolts 77/2
Lavan Island S Iran oil terminal 150/4
La Venta C Mexico Olmec centre 12/2
Lazaret S France site of early man 3/3
Lazica early country of the Caucasus 43/1
Lebanon district of Ottoman Empire 124/1; French mandate 124/1; political disturbances 140/1, 149/1; independence 138/1; Middle East conflict 148/4; economy 150/1
Lebda (Leptis Magna)
Lechfeld S Germany ⚔37/1, 55/1
Ledosus (*mod.* Lezoux) C France Roman Empire 24/3
Leeds N England industrial development 98/1
Leek C England Industrial Revolution 98/1
Leeward Islands West Indies British and French settlement 66/4
Le Gabillou SW France Palaeolithic art 5/3
Leghorn (Livorno)
Legionum Urbs Wales early bishopric 26/2
Legnica (Liegnitz)
Le Havre N France fortified naval port 80/1
Leicester (*anc.* Ratae) C England Viking base 37/1; Industrial Revolution 98/1
Leipzig E Germany medieval fair 59/2; 18C financial centre 82/4; WW1 119/3; Communist insurrection 120/3
Leipzig (Battle of the Nations) E Germany ⚔91/1
Leith Scotland ⚔73/4
Le Kef (Sicca Veneria)
Le Mans N France French Revolution 89/2
Le Mas-d'Azil SW France Palaeolithic art 5/3
Lemberg (*Pol.* Lwów *now Russ.* Lvov) N Austria-Hungary medieval fair 59/2; WW1 118T, 119/3; E Germany WW2 133/2
Lemnos island of the Aegean Byzantine naval victory 36/2; ceded to Greece 116/1
Le Moustier S France site of early man 3/3
Lenca Indian tribe of central America 63/1
Leninakan (*until 1924* Aleksandropol) Armenian SSR industry 147/1
Leningrad (*form. and again from 1991* St. Petersburg *Russ.* Sankt-Peterburg, *between 1914 and 1923* Petrograd) NW Russia WW2 132/3; industry 147/1
Lens NE France WW1 118/3 (inset)
Lenzen N Germany ⚔55/1
Leo III 34T
León early kingdom of C Spain 37/4; city of N Spain, Civil War 129/4
Léopoldville (*now* Kinshasa) W Belgian Congo 138/4
Lepanto (*mod. Gr.* Navpaktos) C Greece ⚔48/2
Le Placard SW France Palaeolithic art 5/3
Le Poisson SW France Palaeolithic art 5/3
Leptis Magna (*a/s* Lepcis Magna *mod.* Lebda) N Libya Stone Age site 11/1; Phoenician city 19/4; Mithraic site 26/1; Roman Empire 24/3, 31/3; early bishopric 27/2
Lerna C Greece Mycenaean settlement 19/1
Les Bolards C France Mithraic site 26/1
Lesbos (*mod. Gr.* Lesvos *a/c* Mitylene) island of the Aegean Greek parent state 19/4
Lesotho (*form.* Basutoland) S Africa independence 138/1; economy 150/1
Lespugue SW France Palaeolithic art 5/3
Les Trois Frères SW France Palaeolithic art 5/3
Letts people of Latvia, NW Russia 121/2
Le Tuc d'Audoubert SW France Palaeolithic art 5/3
Leubuzzi Slav tribe of C Germany 54/2
Leucas (*mod. Gr.* Levkas *It.* Santa Maura) W Greece Greek colony 19/4
Leucate SW France farming site 15/1
Leucecome early port of W Arabia 25/1
Leucos Limen Red Sea early trading centre 25/1; Roman Empire 25/2
Leuthen (*Pol.* Lutynia) SW Poland ⚔78/2
Leuven (*Fr.* Louvain) town of Spanish Netherlands 76/1
Leu Wiliang W Java early site 8/3
Levant Egyptian cities 21/1
Levanzo Sicily Palaeolithic art 5/3
Levkandi E Greece Mycenaean settlement 19/1; Levantine port 21/1
Levkas (Leucas, Santa Maura)
Lewes S England ⚔53/6
Lewis and Clark US explorers 94/1
Lexington NE USA ⚔92/1
Leyden Netherlands 18C urban development 82/4
Leyte SE Philippines US landing 135/2
Leyte Gulf C Philippines WW2 naval battle 135/2
Lezetxiki N Spain site of early man 3/3
Lezoux (Ledosus)
Lhasa Tibet Buddhist site 27/1
Liang NW China Western Chou domain 9/6
Liaohsi NE China Han commanderie 29/3
Liaotung NE China Ming frontier defence area 51/4
Libau (*Latv.* Liepāja) W Russia WW1 119/3
Liberia country of W Africa independent state 100/2, 102/5; economy 150/1
Libya Arab conquest 41/1; under the Almohads 60/1; under Ottoman Empire 61/2; Italian colony 100/2, 102/5, 124/1; WW2 132-3; independence 138/1; political development 140/1; US base 149/1; economy 150/1
Li-chia-ts'un (*a/s* Lijiacun) NE China Shang burial site 8/4
Liège Belgium bishopric 79/1; urban revolt 57/1; 18C urban development 82/4; Prince-Bishop expelled 88T; WW1 118/3
Liegnitz (*Pol.* Legnica) W Poland ⚔46/2; Reformation 74/4
Liepāja (*Ger.* Libau) Latvian SSR industry 147/1
Ligny Belgium ⚔90/1
Ligor S Thailand Hindu-Buddhist remains 51/2
Ligures early tribe of N Italy 30/1
Ligurian Republic NW Italy state established by French Revolution 88/3
Lijiacun (Li-chia-ts'un)
Lille NE France medieval fair 58/1; 18C financial centre 82/4; gained by France 81/4; WW1 118/3 (inset)
Lilybaeum (*mod.* Marsala) Sicily Phoenician city 19/4
Lima Peru colonised 66/1, 69/3
Limanowa N Austria-Hungary WW1 119/3

Limburg region of Belgium/Holland Burgundian possession 73/3; county 79/1
Limerick C Ireland Viking base 37/1; -81/4
Limoges C France annexed to France 72/2; industrial development 80/1
Limonum (Poitiers)
Limousin region of C France under English rule 52/2; French province 80/1
Li Muri N Sardinia megalithic tomb 15/3
Lincoln, Abraham 92T
Lincoln (*anc.* Lindum) E England Danish Viking base 37/1; rebellion against Henry VIII 73/4; Industrial Revolution 98/1
Lindisfarne (*a/c* Holy Island) N England monastery 38/3; Viking attack 37/1
Lindsey early kingdom of E England 33/3, 35/3
Lindum (*mod.* Lincoln) E England Roman Empire 24/2, 30/3; bishopric 26/2
Lingen district of NW Germany county 79/1
Lingling S China Han commanderie 29/3
Lingnan S China T'ang province 50/1
Lingyuan NE China Western Chou site 9/6
Linyanti S Africa on Livingstone's route 102/1
Linz Austria medieval fair 59/2; WW2 133/2
Lipara (*n/s* Lipari) island of S Italy early settlement 14/2; 19/4, 23/2
Lippe county of N Germany Reformation 74/4; 79/1
Lisbon (*Port.* Lisboa *anc.* Olisipo) Portugal Muslim conquest 38/2, 40/1; colonial trade 66-7; trading port 83/5; 18C financial centre 82/4; ⚔90/1
Liscuis NW France megalithic tomb 14/3
Listem C Ukraine 45/2
Liternum C Italy Roman colony 30/1
Lithuania country of the Baltic conversion to Christianity 38/2; early expansion 56/2; Black Death 57/1; empire of Casimir IV 73/1; acquired by Russia 85/1; Reformation 75/1; independence 129/2; inter-war alliances 128/1; socio-political change 131/3; loses Memel territory to Germany 129/5; WW2 132-3; retaken by Russia 137/4; Soviet Socialist Republic 136/1, 146/2; independence 137/4, 151/4
Lithuanians (*earlier* Litva) people of N Europe.
Little Big Horn N USA ⚔95/2
Little Entente 128/1, T
Littlehampton S England Industrial Revolution 98/1
Little Poland 53/1
Little Rock C USA civil unrest 144/3
Litva (*mod.* Lithuanians) early people of NW Russia 45/2
Liu C China Western Chou domain 9/6
Liverpool N England trading port 83/5; industrial development 98/1; WW2 132/1
Livingstone, David Africa exploration 102/1
Livonia region of NW Russia occupied by Teutonic Knights 54/4, 56/2; conquered by Russia 85/1; Reformation 75/1; under Swedish rule 77/3
Livonian Order NW Russia 45/2
Livorno (*obs. Eng.* Leghorn) C Italy 18C financial centre 82/4; WW2 133/2
Lixus (*mod.* Larache) Morocco, Roman Empire 30/3
Llangollen N Wales Industrial Revolution 98/1
Llewellyn prince of Wales 53/7
Lo C China Western Chou domain 9/6
Locarno Switzerland 1925 Conference 128/2
Lochhill SW Scotland megalithic tomb 14/3
Locri S Italy Greek colony 19/4, 23/2
Locris W Greece parent state 18/3, 19/4, 22/1
Lodi N Italy Lombard League 55/3; Signorial domain 56/3; ⚔91/1
Lodomeria (Vladimir)
Lodz (*Pol.* Łódź) Poland industrial development 99/2; inc Russia 120/1; WW1 119/3
Logan's Fort NE USA ⚔95/2
Lohumjo-Daro N India Harappan site 9/5
Loi N China Western Chou capital 9/6
Lokoja Nigeria taken by British 103/3
Lolan Sinkiang Han expansion 28/2
Lolang N Korea Han commanderie 29/3
Lombards early tribe of S Germany 32/2. See also Langobardi
Lombardy region of N Italy kingdom under Frankish dominion 33/4; under medieval German Empire 55/1; 14C 56/3; medieval trade 58/1; acquired by Habsburgs 72/1; unification of Italy 114/3
Lombok island of E Indies occupied by Japanese 134/1
Lonato N Italy ⚔91/1
Londinium (*mod.* London) S England Mithraic site 26/1; Roman Empire 24/2, 30/3; bishopric 26/2
London (*anc.* Londinium) S England Vikings 37/1; urban unrest 57/1; Hansa trading post 59/2; trade and industry 82/4; ⚔73/4; industrial development 98/1; WW1 118/3; WW2 132-3
London C Canada growth 111/1
Londonderry N Ireland IRA 137/6
Long March by Chinese Communists 122/4
Longwy NE France fort 89/2
Loochoo Islands (Ryukyu Islands)
Lookout Mountain S USA ⚔93/5
Loos NE France WW1 118/3 (inset)
Lord Howe Island W Pacific Australian possession 139/1 (inset)
Lorient NW France 80/1
Lorraine (*Ger.* Lothringen) region of NE France part of medieval German Empire 55/3; acquired by Habsburgs 72/2; Burgundian possession 73/3; German duchy 79/1; Holy Roman Empire 81/2; German Empire 98/3, 115/2; WW1 119/2
Lorsch W Germany monastery 34/4
Los Angeles W USA foundation 69/3; population 110/2; civil unrest 144/3
Los Casares NE Spain Palaeolithic art 5/3
Los Millares S Spain early settlement 14/2
Lostwithiel SW England ⚔76/4
Lothagram E Africa site of early man 3/3
Lothal N India early urban settlement 16/1; Harappan site 9/5
Lothar I King of Germany 35/5
Lothringen (Lorraine)
Loudoun Hill C Scotland ⚔56/4
Loughborough C England Industrial Revolution 98/1
Louhans E France French Revolution 89/2
Louis King of Germany 35/6
Louis XIV King of France 80/1
Louisbourg Nova Scotio captured by British 86/1
Louisiana state of S USA French rule 67/3, 69/3; Spanish rule 92/1; purchased by USA 92/2; Civil War 92/5; Depression 131/2; population 111/5, 145/1
Lourenço Marques (*n/c* Maputo) 103/4
Louth E England Industrial Revolution 98/1
Louth Ireland bishopric 26/2
Louvain (Leuven)
Lovelock Cave W USA site 62/4
Lovewell's Fight NE USA ⚔95/2
Lower Burma annexed by British 104/2
Lower California province of N Mexico 97/1
Lower Ob Gasfield N Siberia 147/1
Lower Palatinate W Germany Reformation 74/4
Lowestoft E England English naval victory 81/3; WW1 118/3
Lo-yang (*als* Luoyang) N China Shang city 8/4; Chou site 9/6; sacked by Hsiung-nu 33/1
Lozi tribe of C Africa 60/1
Lu E China Chou domain 9/6; state 28/1
Lü C China Western Chou domain 9/6
Luanda Angola early trade 67/1; Portuguese settlement 61/2
Luango early state of W Africa 61/2
Luang Prabang SE Asia early political centre 51/2
Luba early kingdom of C Africa 60/1, 61/2
Lübeck N Germany urban revolt 57/1; Hanseatic city 59/2; Reformation 75/1; bishopric 79/1; WW1 119/3; WW2 133/2
Lublin Poland medieval fair 59/2; WW1 119/3
Lubumbashi (Elisabethville)
Lubusi S Africa Iron Age site 11/1
Luca (*mod.* Lucca) N Italy Latin colony 30/1
Lucania region of S Italy part of Kingdom of Naples 56/3
Lucca (*Lat.* Luca) N Italy Republican commune 56/3; independent republic 73/5, 88/3
Lucerne (*Ger.* Luzern) early Swiss canton 54/5
Luck (Lutsk)
Lucknow N India Indian Mutiny 104/1; industry 105/3
Ludendorff offensive 118-9
Lüderitz SW Africa German settlement 103/5
Lugansk (*between 1935-58 and 1970-90 called* Voroshilovgrad) Ukraine 1905 Revolution 120/1
Lugdunensis Roman province of N France 30/1
Lugdunum (*mod.* Lyon *Eng.* Lyons) C France Roman Empire 24/2, 30/3; archbishopric 26/2
Luluabourg (*now* Kananga) C Belgian Congo 138/4
Lumbini Tibet Buddhist site 27/1
Luna (*mod.* Luni) N Italy Roman colony 30/1
Lund S Sweden bishopric 38/2; Danish archbishopric 53/3
Lunda early kingdom of C Africa 60/1, 61/2
Lüneburg N Germany Hanseatic city 59/2
Lungchow SW China treaty port 107/4
Lunghsi NW China Han commanderie 29/3
Lungyu NW China T'ang province 50/1
Luni (Luna)
Luoyang (Lo-yang)
Lusatia (*Ger.* Lausitz) region of E Germany under medieval German Empire 55/1, 3; acquired by Habsburgs 56/2; modern German Empire 79/1
Lushai district of W Burma annexed by British 104/2
Lusitania (*mod.* Portugal) province of Roman Empire 30/1
Lusizzi Slav tribe of Germany 55/1
Lutetia (*mod.* Paris) N France Roman Empire 30/3
Lutsk (*Pol.* Łuck) W Russia WW1 119/3
Lutter W Germany ⚔74/4
Lutynia (Leuthen)
Lützen C Germany ⚔74/4, 91/1
Luxembourg (*Ger.* Luxemburg) Burgundian possession 73/3; German customs union 98/3; German Confederation 114/5; WW1 118/1; EEC and NATO 137/3
Luxeuil E France monastery 38/3
Luxor Upper Egypt 21/1
Luzern (Lucerne)
Luzon island of N Philippines Spanish control 67/1; American occupation 110/4; US landings 135/2
Luzzara N Italy ⚔81/5
Lvov (*Pol.* Lwów) W Ukraine industry 147/1
Lycia country of SW Anatolia 19/4; Roman Empire 31/3
Lydia country of W Anatolia 22/1; Byzantine Empire 43/1
Lyon (Lyons)
Lyonnais region of C France Royal domain 52/2
Lyons (*anc.* Lugdunum *Fr.* Lyon) C France medieval fair 59/2; 18C financial centre 82/4; St Bartholomew Massacre 74/3; centre of French Revolution 89/2
Lys *river* NE France WW1 119/3 (inset)
Lystra S Anatolia early bishopric 27/2

Maastricht town of Spanish Netherlands 77/1
Mabueni S Africa Iron Age site 11/1
Macao (*Port.* Macau) S China early Portuguese trade 67/1; Portuguese settlement 66/2; Portuguese colony 101/2, 107/4, 139/1
Macassar (*Indon.* Makasar) East Indies Dutch settlement 67/2, 71/2
Macau (Macao)
Macclesfield C England Industrial Revolution 98/1
Macedonia SE Europe 19/4; conquered by Persians 22/1; Antigonid Kingdom 22/4; Roman province 31/3; Byzantine Empire 43/1; Ottoman province 124/1; divided between Serbia, Greece and Bulgaria 116/1; Greek-Bulgarian conflict 128/2; independence 137/4
Macedonians Slav people of SE European 115/1
Machaerus Judaea area of revolt 26/3
Ma-chia-ya (*a/s Majiaya*) *N China* early settlement 8/2
Macias Nguema Biyogo (Fernando Po)
Mackay E Australia early settlement 113/1
Macon USA early site 12/3
Macquarie Harbour Tasmania penal settlement 113/1
Macú Indian tribe of S America 63/1
Mada (*a/c* Media) country of NW Persia satrapy of Achaemenid Empire 21/5
Madagascar (*form.* Malagasy Republic) Indonesian settlement 11/1, 60/1, 3; settlement from Africa 61/2; French penetration 103/3; French colony 100/2, 103/3; independence 138/1; political development 140/1; economy 150/1
Madeira island of E Atlantic Portuguese exploration 64/1; Portuguese territory 100/2, 138/1
Madhya Pradesh (*form.* Central Provinces) state of C India 105/5
Madras (*now* Tamil Tadu) state and city, S India British settlement 66/2, 87/2; under British rule 104/1, 4; trade and industry 105/3
Madrid C Spain 18C financial centre 82/4; captured by French 90/1; Civil War 129/4
Madura island of E Indies Dutch control 71/4; joins Indonesia 139/2
Madura S India industry 105/3
Maes Howe Scotland megalithic tomb 14/3
Mafeking S Africa Boer War 103/4
Magadha early kingdom of NE India 29/4
Magdeburg E Germany bishopric 38/2; archbishopric 52/1, 79/1; Reformation 74/4, 75/1; Hanseatic city 59/2; industrial development 99/2; WW1 119/3
Magellan Strait S America first sailed 64/2
Magenta N Italy ⚔114/3
Magersfontein S Africa ⚔103/4
Maghreb (*collective name for Algeria, Morocco and Tunisia*)
Maginot Line E France defence system 132/1
Magna Graecia the Greek colonies of S Italy 19/4, 23/2
Magnesia (*a/c* Magnesia ad Maeandrum) W Anatolia ⚔22/4
Magnitogorsk C Russia industry 147/1
Magnus the Good King of Norway 52T
Magyars invade W Europe 37/1
Maha-Kosala early country of C India 29/4
Maharashtra state of W india 29/4
Mahayana Buddhism 26T, 70/1
Mahdia (*a/s* Mehdia) Tunisia Pisan raids 36/2
Mahé SW India French settlement 87/2 (inset), 105/3
Mahón Minorca, Spain Civil War 129/4
Mähren (Moravia)
Maidstone SE England rebellion 73/4; Industrial Revolution 98/1
Maidum (*als* Meidum) Lower Egypt early agriculture 6/2; pyramid 17/3
Mainake S Spain Ionian colony 18/4
Maine state of NE USA British settlement 67/3; Depression 131/2; population 111/5, 145/1
Maine region of N France 52/2, 72/2, 80/1
Maininskaya E Siberia Palaeolithic art 5/3
Mainpuri N India centre of Mutiny 104/1
Mainz (*anc.* Mogontiacum) C Germany archbishopric 34/4, 38/3, 79/1; medieval trade 58/1
Majapahit Java early Empire 51/2; trade 59/3
Majdanek E Poland concentration camp 132/1
Majiaya (Ma-chia-ya)
Majorca (*Sp.* Mallorca) Civil War 129/4
Majuba Hill S Africa ⚔103/2
Majuro island of Marshalls, C Pacific occupied by US 135/2
Makakam SE Borneo Hindu-Buddhist remains 51/2
Makapansgat S Africa site of early man 3/3
Makasar (Macassar)
Makin Gilbert Islands, Pacific WW2 134/1, 135/2
Makran region of SE Persia Muslim conquest 41/1
Makurra state of NE Africa 60/1
Malabar district of S India ceded to Britain 87/3

Malaca (*mod.* Málaga) S Spain Roman Empire 24/2, 30/3
Malacca (*Mal.* Melaka) district of S Malaya early sultanate 51/2; early trade 59/3, 67/1; captured by Portuguese 70/3; European discovery 65/2; captured by Dutch 66/2, 70/3; under Portuguese rule 71/2; British possession 71/5, 101/1
Málaga (*anc.* Malaca) S Spain 18C urban development 83/4⚔81/5; Civil War 129/4
Malaga Cove W USA site 62/4
Malagasy Republic (Madagascar)
Malao (*mod.* Berbera) N Somalia early port 25/1
Malapati S Africa Iron Age site 11/1
Malatya (*anc.* Melitene) E Turkey Hittite city 21/1; revolt against Ottoman rule 48/2
Malavas people of NW India 29/5
Malawi (*form.* Nyasaland) country of C Africa independence 138/1; political development 140/1; economy 150/1
Malaya Iron and Bronze Age sites 8/3; early trade 25/1; spread of Islam 40/5, 70/1; British control 101/2; occupied by Japanese 134/1. See also Malaysia
Malaysia (state formed by amalgamation of Malaya, Sarawak and Sabah) independence 139/1; economy 150/1; confrontation with Indonesia 139/2
Malay States SE Asia British protectorate 71/5. See also Malaya, Malaysia
Malbork (Marienburg)
Maldives islands of N Indian Ocean conversion to Islam 41/4; acquired by British 87/2; protectorate 101/2; independence 139/1
Mali (*form.* French Sudan) country of West Africa independence 138/1; political development 140/1; economy 150/1
Mali Empire early state of W Africa 60/1
Malinalco Mexico Aztec temple 62/2
Malindi Kenya Muslim colony 60/1; early Portuguese trade 61/2
Mallia Crete palace site 19/1
Mallorca (Majorca)
Mallus W Anatolia Ionian colony 19/4
Malmédy E Belgium ceded by Germany 128/2
Maloyaroslavets W Russia⚔91/1
Malplaquet N France⚔81/5
Malta island of C Mediterranean Norman conquest 36/2; British colony 101/2; WW2 133/2; independence 138/1
Mal'ta E Siberia site of early man 3/3; Palaeolithic art 5/3
Malujowice (Mollwitz)
Maluku (Moluccas)
Malvasia (*a/c* Monemvasia) S Greece Venetian territory 48/1
Malvinas, Islas (Falkland Islands)
Mameluke Empire Egypt/Palestine Mongol invasion 46/1
Mamelukes (*a/s* Mamluk) 40/2
Manassas (*a/c* Bull Run) E USA⚔93/5
Manchanagara district of Java Dutch control 71/4
Manchester N England industrial development 98/1
Manchouli N China treaty town 107/4
Manchukuo (name given to Manchuria as Japanese puppet state)
Manchuria (*called 1932-45* Manchukuo) region of NE China Manchu homeland 106/1; occupied by Russia 107/4; Russo-Japanese war 127/4; Russian and Japanese spheres of influence 127/3; warlord control 122/2; Japanese puppet state 123/3, 4; 127/5, 134/1; reoccupied by Russia 135/2
Manchus people of NE China, under the Ming 51/4; homeland expansion 106/1
Manda E Africa early trade 11/1
Mandalay C Burma trade 71/2; occupied by British 104/2; terminus of Burma Road 127/5; occupied by Japanese 134/1; retaken 134/2
Mandan plains Indian tribe of C Canada 63/1
Mangalore S India industry 105/3
Mang-vu Siam early trade 59/3
Manhao SW China treaty town 107/4
Manila C Philippines early trade 67/1; Spanish settlement 66/2; captured by Japanese 134/1
Manipur state of E India 71/2, 104/2, 105/5
Manisa W Anatolia Ottoman Empire 49/1
Manitoba province of C Canada economic development 111/1; joins Confederation 101/1
Mannheim W Germany industrial development 99/2 WW2 133/2
Mantinea C Greece⚔23/2
Mantua (*It.* Mantova) N Italy Lombard League 55/3; Signorial domination 56/3; 73/5
Manuel I Byzantine Emperor 42T
Manuel's Fort N USA fur station 94/1
Manunggul Cave W Philippines Iron Age site 8/3
Manus Island W Pacific Allied base 135/2
Manzikert E Anatolia⚔42/4, 43/1
Mao-Mao Kenyan guerrilla movement 138/1
Maoris New Zealand tribe 112/2, 3
Mao Tse-tung 122T
Ma-pa E China site of early man 3/3
Mapungubwe early state of SE Africa 60/1
Maracanda (*mod.* Samarkand) Alexander's route 23/3; Achaemenid Empire 21/5; early trade 25/1
Maranga C Andes early site 12/4
Maranhão province of Brazil 97/1
Mărăşeşti Romania WW1 119/3
Marash (*Turk.* Maraş) N Anatolia Byzantine Empire 43/3
Maratha Confederacy N India in alliance with British 87/2; 87/3
Marathon C Greece⚔20/5, 22/1
Maravi early state of E Africa 61/2
Marche region of C France 52/2; annexed by France 72/2
Marches (*It.* Le Marche) province of Italy unification 114/3
Marches, of Wales 73/4
Marcianopolis Bulgaria early archbishopric 27/2; Byzantine Empire 43/1
Marcomanni early tribe of C Europe 30/3, 31/4
Marco Polo route 59/3
Mardi early tribe of N Persia 22/3
Marengo N Italy⚔90/1
Mari Mesopotamia early urban settlement 16/1, 17/4
Mari people of C Russia 44/3, 45/2, 85/1; ASSR 146/2
Marianas (*form.* Ladrones) islands of W Pacific German colony 101/2; US occupation 135/2
Marie Galante island of W Indies French settlement 66/4 (inset)
Marienburg (*Pol.* Malbork) N Poland seat of Teutonic Order 54/4
Marienwerder (*Pol.* Kwidzyn) N Poland founded by Teutonic Knights 54/4; 1920 plebiscite 128/2
Maritime Provinces (*Russ.* Primorskiy Kray) Russ. Far East acquired from China 107/4
Mariupol (*now* Zhdanov) S Russia industry 85/4
Marj Dabik SE Anatolia⚔49/1
Mark W Germany Reformation 74/4
Market Harborough C England Industrial Revolution 98/1
Marksville USA Hopewell site 12/3
Marlborough province of S Island, New Zealand 112/2
Marne *river* NE France WW1 119/2; ⚔118/3 (inset)
Maroc (Morocco)
Marqab Syria 40/3
Marquesas Islands S Pacific Polynesian dispersal centre 11/2; French colony 139/1 (inset)
Marrakesh (*Fr.* Marrakech) Morocco early trade 58/3, 61/2
Marruecos (Morocco)
Marsala (Lilybaeum)
Marseilles (*Fr.* Marseille *anc.* Massilia) S France Mediterranean trade 58/3; galley port 80/1; centre of French Revolution 89/2
Marshall Islands C Pacific German colony 101/2; occupied by US 135/2
Marshall Plan 136T
Marston Moor N England ⚔76/4
Martinique island of W Indies French settlement 66/4, 69/3; attacked by British 86/1; French territory 97/1, 100/2, 139/1 (inset)
Martyropolis E Anatolia early bishopric 27/2
Mary (Merv)
Maryland state of E USA colony 67/3, 92/1; Civil War 93/5; Depression 131/2; population 111/5, 145/1
Masada Judaea Roman siege 26/3
Masai tribe of E Africa 60/1
Masal Hüyük N Anatolia Hittite city 21/1
Masampo S Korea Russo-Japanese war 127/4
Mashdad (Meshed)
Masovia (*a/s* Mazovia *Pol.* Mazowsze) region of Poland 53/1, 54/4
Masqat (Muscat)
Massachusett Indian tribe of NE USA 63/1
Massachusetts state of NE USA British colony 92/1; Depression 131/2; population 111/5, 145/1
Massachusetts Bay NE USA British colony 67/3
Massagetae tribe of C Asia 23/3
Massawa N Ethiopia Ottoman settlement 48/2, 61/2; Italian attack 103/3
Massilia (*mod.* Marseille *Eng.* Marseilles) S France Roman Empire 24/2, 30/2, 3; bishopric 26/2
Masulipatam S India early trade 25/1
Maszycka S Poland Palaeolithic art 5/3
Mataco Indian tribe of S America 63/1
Matadi W Belgian Congo 138/4
Mataram Sultanate of Java Dutch control 71/2
Mathura C India early trading centre 25/1
Mato Grosso province of Brazil 97/1
Matsu *island* SE China Nationalist outpost 149/1
Matsue W Japan 126/2
Matsuyama W Japan 126/2
Matthias Corvinus king of Hungary 72/1, T
Maubeuge NE France WW1 119/2
Mauer Germany site of early man 3/3
Mauern S Germany Palaeolithic art 5/3
Mauretania region of NW Africa conversion to Christianity 26/1
Maurice (Mauritius)
Mauritania country of NW Africa independence from France 138/1; political development 140/1; economy 150/1
Mauritius (*Fr.* Maurice) *island* Indian Ocean early trade 66/2; British colony 101/1, 2
Mauthausen Austria concentration camp 132/1
Maya people and civilisation of C America 12/2, 13/1, 62/2
Mayapán Mayan city of E Mexico destroyed 62/2
Maysville Road C USA settlers' route 94/1
Mazaca (*mod.* Kayseri) C Anatolia Achaemenid Empire 21/5
Mazouco N Portugal Palaeolithic art 5/3
Mazovia (Masovia)
Mazowsze (Masovia)
Mbandaka (Coquilhatville)
Meadowcroft E USA early site 5/2
Meadows, The W USA ⚔94/2
Meath early kingdom of C Ireland 53/6
Meaux N France unrest 57/1; St Bartholomew Massacre 74/3
Mecca (*Ar.* Al Makkah) W Arabia birth of Islam 41/1; early trade 58/3; Ottoman Empire 48/2; Sharifs of Mecca 46/1; WW1 125/2
Mecklenburg N Germany duchy 79/1; Reformation 74/4, 75/1; unification of Germany 98/3, 115/2
Medes ancient people of NW Persia 20T
Media (*a/c* Mada) ancient country of NW Persia 20/4; in Alexander's Empire 22/3
Media Atropatene Hellenised kingdom of NW Persia 22/4
Medina (*Ar.* Al Madinah) W Arabia centre of Islam 41/1; early trade 58/3; Ottoman Empire 48/2; WW1 125/2
Medina del Campo N Spain medieval fair 59/2
Medina de Rioseco N Spain medieval fair 59/2
Medinet Habu C Eygpt New Kingdom temple 21/1
Mediolanum (*mod.* Milano *Eng.* Milan) N Italy Roman Empire 24/2, 30/3; bishopric 26/2
Mediterranean Sea Greek colonisation 18/4; Phoenicians 18/4; Mycenaean trade 18/2; Roman routes 24/2; Saracen invasions 37/1; Norman and Venetian expansion and Byzantine reconquest 36/2; early trade routes 24/2, 58/3; WW2 132-3
Meersen, Partition of 35/6
Meerut N India Indian Mutiny 104/1; riots 104/4
Megara C Greece Greek parent state 19/4
Megara-Hyblaea Sicily Greek colony 19/4
Megiddo Palestine Egyptian fortress 21/1; ⚔WW1 125/2
Mehdia (Mahdia)
Mehemmed I Ottoman ruler 48T, 49/1
Mehemmed II Ottoman ruler 48T, 49/1
Mehi N India Harappan site 9/5
Meidum (Maidum)
Meiji Restoration Japan 126T
Meinarti island of Upper Nile Egyptian fortress 21/1
Meissen district of E Germany 52/1, 55/1, 3
Melaka (Malacca)
Melanesia region of W Pacific early settlement 10/2
Melbourne SE Australia founded 113/1
Melilla (*anc.* Rusaddir) N Morocco Mediterranean trade 58/3; acquired by Habsburgs 72/1
Melitene (*mod.* Malatya) E Anatolia spread of Mithraism 26/1; Roman Empire 25/2, 31/3; early archbishopric 27/2; Byzantine Empire 42/2
Melka Kunturé S Ethiopia site of early man 3/3
Mello N France civil unrest 57/1
Melolo S East Indies Iron Age site 8/3
Melville Island N Australia 113/1
Memel (*Lith.* Klaipeda) NW Russia founded by Teutonic Knights 54/4; WW1 119/3
Memel Territory (*Ger.* Memelgebiet *or* Memelland) region of SW Lithuania annexed by Germany 129/5
Memphis Lower Egypt Iron Age site 11/1; city of Ancient Egypt 17/3, 21/1; Alexander's route 22/3; Achaemenid Empire 20/5; Roman Empire 25/2, 31/3; Byzantine Empire 43/1
Memphis SE USA ⚔92/5; civil unrest 144/3
Mende N Greece early bishopric 19/4
Menes king of Egypt 16T
Mengtze (*Fr.* Mong-tseu) SW China treaty port 107/4
Meniet S Algeria early site 11/1
Mennonites sect 74/2
Menominee Indian tribe of C USA 63/1
Menorca (Minorca)
Menteşe early emirate of SW Anatolia 49/1
Mercia early kingdom of C England 35/3, 38/3
Meremere N Island, New Zealand ⚔112/3
Mérida (*anc.* Emerita Augusta) SW Spain Civil War 129/4
Mérida SE Mexico early Spanish city 66/1
Merimbe Egypt early agricultural site 11/1
Merina early state in Madagascar 103/3
Merkits Mongolian tribe 47/1
Meroë Sudan Iron Age site 11/1; city of Alwa 60/1
Merovingian kingdom 35/2
Mersa Matruh (Paraetonium)
Merse (of Berwick) SE Scotland acquired by Edward III 56/4
Mersin E Anatolia early trade 17/4
Merthyr Tydfil S Wales Industrial Revolution 98/1
Merv (*since 1937* Mary *anc.* Alexandria) Russ. C Asia early trade 25/1, 59/3; spread of Christianity 26/1; early archbishopric 39/1; Muslim conquest 41/1; Safavid Empire 48/2
Mesas de Asta S Spain early settlement 14/2
Mesaverde SW USA site 62/4
Mesembria Bulgaria Greek colony 19/4
Mesen (Messines)
Meshchera E Slav tribe of C Russia 85/1
Meshed (*Pers.* Mashhad) Alexander's Empire 23/3
Mesoamerica classic period 12/2, 13/1
Mesopotamia (*mod.* Iraq) early agriculture 6/2, 7/4; early empires 16-17; spread of Mithraism 26/1; Alexander's Empire 23/2; Roman Empire 31/3; Muslim conquest 41/1; WW1 125/2; British control 125/3

Messana (*mod.* Messina) Sicily Roman Empire 24/2, 30/3, 23/2
Messapii early people of S Italy 30/1
Messenia ancient region of SW Greece 18/3
Messina (*anc.* Zancle *later* Messana) Sicily early bishopric 26/2; Norman conquest 36/2; 18C urban development 82/4; WW2 133/2
Messines (*Dut.* Mesen) Belgium medieval fair 58/1; WW1 118/3 (inset)
Metaurus N Italy ⚔30/2
Methven C Scotland ⚔56/4
Metz NE France annexed to France 151/4; French Revolution 89/2; WW1 119/3; WW2 133/2
Meuse (*Dut.* Maas) *river* NE France WW1 119/3 (inset)
Mexico Aztec Empire 62/2; Spanish colonisation 68/1; imperial trade 66/1; independence 101/1; exports and foreign investment 96/3; population 92/2; US intervention 143/1; political development 97/1; economy 109/1, 142-3, 150/1
Mezhirich' Ukraine Palaeolithic art 5/3
Mezin W Russia Palaeolithic art 5/3
Mi C China Western Chou site 9/6
Miami Indian tribe of C USA 63/1
Michigan state of N USA Depression 131/2; population 111/5, 145/1
Michoacán provice of C Mexico 97/1
Micmac Indian tribe of NE Canada 63/1
Middle Awash SE Ethiopia site of early man 3/3
Middle East (*a/c* Near East) WW1 125/2; Cold War 148/4
Midhurst S England Industrial Revolution 98/1
Midnapore district of NE India ceded to Britain 87/3, 105/4
Midway island of C Pacific US occupation 110/4; WW2 ⚔134/1; US base 135/2, 149/1 (inset)
Mie prefecture of C Japan 126/2
Milan (*It.* Milano *anc.* Mediolanum) N Italy Lombard League 55/3; medieval trade 58/1; Signorial domination 56/3; Duchy 73/5; 18C industry 82/4; industrial development 99/2
Milas (Mylasa)
Milazzo (Mylae)
Miletus W Anatolia Mycenaean city 18/2, 19/1; Levantine port 21/1; Greek parent state 19/4, 22/1; Roman Empire 31/3; bishopric 27/2; Byzantine Empire 43/1
Milev Algeria early bishopric 26/2
Milford Haven S Wales port 98/1
Military Frontier 78/3
Milizi Slav tribe of E Germany 55/1
Milk Creek C USA ⚔95/2
Milwaukee N USA civil unrest 144/3
Minas Gerais province of C Brazil 97/1
Mindanao island of S Philippines Muslim expansion 40/5; Spanish control 70/3; US occupation 110/4; Japanese occupation 134/1; retaken by US 135/2; political unrest 139/2
Minden NW Germany bishopric 79/1
Mindoro island of C Philippines US landings in WW2 135/2
Ming Empire China 51/4
Mingrelia Caucasus princedom under Ottoman Empire 124/1
Ming Voyages 59/3
Minneapolis-St. Paul N USA industry 111/2
Minnesota state of N USA Depression 130/2; industry 110/2; population 111/5, 145/1
Minoan civilisation 18T
Minorca (*Sp.* Menorca) British naval base and ⚔87/1; Civil War 129/4
Minsk W Russia early town of Polotsk 45/2; WW1 119/3; Bolshevik seizure 121/2; WW2 133/2; industry 147/1
Minturnae (*mod.* Minturno) C Italy Roman colony 30/1
Minusinsk SC Siberia founded 84/2
Minyueh region of S China 28/1, 2; Han commanderie 29/3
Mirtos E Crete Mycenaean settlement 19/1
Mirzoyan (Dzhambul)
Misenum C Italy Roman Empire 30/3
Miskito Indian tribe of C America 63/1
Mison C Indo-China Hindu-Buddhist temple 51/2
Mississippi state of S USA Civil War 92/5; Depression 131/2; population 111/5, 145/1
Missouri state of C USA Civil War 92/5; Depression 131/2; population 111/5, 145/1
Mitanni ancient kingdom of Middle East 21/1
Mithraism 26T, 26/1
Mitla Mexico Mixtec site 62/2
Mito C Japan 126/1
Mitylene (Mytilene)
Mixtec early people of C Mexico 12/2
Miyagi prefecture of N Japan 126/2
Miyazaki city and prefecture of W Japan 126/2
Mladec Czechoslovakia site of early man 3/3
Mlu Prei Cambodia early site 8/3
Moab ancient country of Middle East 21/2
Mobile S USA fur station 94/1; ⚔93/5
Moçambique (Mozambique)
Moçâmedes Angola Portuguese settlement 103/3
Moche C Andes site 12/4
Modena (*anc.* Mutina) N Italy Mithraic site 26/1; Lombard League 55/3; Republican commune 56/3; Renaissance Italy 73/5; unification of Italy 114/3
Modoc plateau Indian tribe of NW USA 63/1
Moesia region of Balkans district of Byzantine Empire 43/1
Moesiae late Roman province of Greece 31/4
Moesia Inferior Roman province of the Balkans 31/3
Moesia Superior Roman province of the Balkans 31/3
Mogadishu (n/s Muqdisho *It.* Mogadiscio) Somalia Muslim colony 60/1; early trade 58/3; Italian occupation 103/3
Mogador (*now* Essaouira) Morocco Iron Age site 11/1
Mogilev W Russia Hanseatic trade 59/2; WW1 119/2; WW2 133/2; industry 147/1
Mogontiacum (*mod.* Mainz) W Germany Roman Empire 24/2, 30/3
Mohács Hungary ⚔48/2
Mohammed founder of Islam 40T, 41/1
Mohave Indian tribe of SW USA 63/1
Mohenjo-Daro N India early urban settlement 9/1, 16/1; Harappan site 9/5
Mohi Hungary ⚔46/2
Moira Baths C England Industrial Revolution 98/1
Mojos forest Indian tribe of S America 63/1
Mokhlos E Crete Mycenaean settlement 19/1
Mokpo S Korea Russo-Japanese war 127/4; 1950-53 War 148/2
Moldavia (*Turk.* Boğdan *Rom.* Moldova) region of Romania/Russia Hungarian 56/2; under Ottoman control 49/1; occupied by Russia 91/1; part of Romania 116/1; SSR 146/2; independence (Moldova) 137/4, 151/4
Molino Casarotto NW Italy farming site 15/1
Mollwitz (*Pol.* Małujowice) SW Poland ⚔78/2
Molodovo W Russia Palaeolithic art 5/3
Molotov (Perm)
Moluccas (*Indon.* Maluka *Dut.* Malukken *form.* Spice Islands) islands of E Indies Muslim expansion 70/1; European discovery 70/3; early Portuguese trade 67/1; Dutch control 71/2; independent republic 139/2
Molukken (Moluccas)
Mombasa Kenya Muslim colony 60-61; early trade 61/2, 66/2; British occupation 100/3
Monamore SW Scotland megalithic tomb 14/3
Monastir (*S. Cr.* Bitolj *Maced.* Bitola) S Yugoslavia WW1 119/3
Monastiraki Crete palace site 19/1
Mondovi NW Italy ⚔90/1
Monemvasia (*It.* Malvasia) S Greece Byzantine Empire 43/3; Ottoman conquest 48/2
Mongol Empire 46-47
Mongolia (*form.* Outer Mongolia) 33/1; under Turkish Empire 33/1; unification of Mongol tribes 47/1; Chinese incursions under Ming 51/4; Chinese protectorate 106/1; autonomy 1;07/4; Russian sphere of influence 101/2; People's Republic 120/4; limit of Japanese expansion 127/5
Mong-tseu (Mengtze)
Monmouth W England Industrial Revolution 98/1
Mons (*Dut.* Bergen) Belgium WW1 118/3, 119/2
Mons people of S Burma early kingdom 51/2
Montagnais-Naskapi subarctic Indian tribe of NE Canada 63/1
Montana state of NW USA Depression 130/2; population 11/5, 145/1
Montauban S France 80/1; French Revolution 89/2
Mont Cenis SE France Hannibal's route 30/2; pass 58/1
Montdidier NE France WW1 118/3 (inset)
Monte Albán C Mexico early site 13/1; Zapotec centre 62/2
Monte Circeo Italy site of early man 3/3
Montenegro *S. Cr.* Crna Gora) region of S Yugoslavia independent state 116/1; under Ottoman rule 124/1; 19C alliances 117/2,, WW1 118-9; forms part of Yugoslavia 129/2; WW2 133/2
Montenotte N Italy ⚔90/1
Montereau N France ⚔90/1
Monte Verde S Chile early site 5/2
Montezuma I Aztec emperor 62T
Montezuma II Aztec emperor 62T
Montferrat Renaissance Italy 73/5
Montgaudier SW France Palaeolithic art 5/3
Montgomery S USA civil unrest 144/3
Montmaurin S France site of early man 3/3
Montmirail N France ⚔90/1
Montpellier S France Genoese trade 36/2
Montreal (*Fr.* Montréal) E Canada capture of French fort by British 86/1; industry 111/1
Montreux Switzerland 1936 conference 128/2
Montserrat *island* West Indies English settlement 66/4; British colony 139/1 (inset)
Mooloya Estate C Ceylon political disturbance 104/4
Moravany Czechoslovakia Palaeolithic art 5/3
Moravia (*Czech.* Morava *Ger.* Mähren) region of C Czechoslovakia occupied by Poland 51/2; medieval German Empire 55/3; acquired by Bohemia 56/2; Hussite influence 57/1; acquired by Habsburgs 72/1, 78/3; Reformation 75/1; Margravate 79/1; forms part of Czechoslovakia 129/2
Mordva people of C Russia 44/1, 45/2, 85/1; conquered 44/3
Mordvinian ASSR W USSR 146/2
Morea (*a/c Peloponnese) region of S Greece* Byzantine Empire 43/3; conquered by Ottomans 48/1
Morelos province of C Mexico 97/1
Moreton Bay E Australia penal colony 113/1
Morgarten E Switzerland ⚔54/5
Mori W Japan clan territory 51/3
Morioka N Japan 126/1
Mormon Bar W USA mining site 94/1
Mormon Trail N USA settlers' route 94/1
Morocco (*Fr.* Maroc *Sp.* Marruecos) under Almohads 60/1; Sharifian dynasties 61/2; Spanish conquest 103/3; independent sultanate 124/1; French and Spanish protectorates 100/2; independence 138/1; conflict with Algeria 140/1; US bases 149/1; economy 150/1
Morotai *island* N Moluccas, E Indies captured by Allies 135/2
Mortsani Slav tribe of E Europe 54/2
Moscha (*a/s* Moskha) S Arabia early trading centre 25/1
Moscow (*Russ.* Moskva) W Russia early bishopric 38/2; city of Vladimir-Suzdal 45/2; early trade 58/3; 18C urban development 83/4; captured by Napoleon 91/1; urban growth 146/2; WW1 119/3; Bolshevik seizure of power 121/2; WW2 132-3; industrial development 147/1
Moshesh tribe of S Africa 103/2
Moskha (Moscha)
Moskva (Moscow)
Mosquito Coast C America English settlement 66/4; to Nicaragua 97/1
Mossel Bay S Africa Portuguese exploration 64/1
Mossi early states of W Africa 60-61
Mostar Herzegovina, Yugoslavia Ottoman Empire 49/1
Mosul (*Ar.* Al Mawsil) Iraq early archbishopric 39/1; Muslim conquest 41/1; Ottoman Empire 49/1; WW1 125/2; oilfield 150/4
Mound City USA Hopewell site 12/3
Moundville SE USA site 12/3, 62/4
Mount Isa N Australia copper 113/1
Mount's Bay SW England megalithic axe factory 14/3
Mouri W Africa early Dutch settlement 60/1 (inset)
Mousehold Heath E England ⚔73/4
Mozambique (*form.* Portuguese East Africa *Port.* Mocambique) early trade 66/2; Portuguese settlement 66/2; Portuguese colony 101/1, 103/3; independence 138/1; political development 140/1; economy 150/1
MPLA Angolan guerrilla movement 138T/1; 140/1
Mtskheta Caucasus early archbishopric 27/2
Muchic Andean Indian tribe of S America 63/1
Mudraya Libya satrapy of Achaemenid Empire 20/5
Mud Springs C USA ⚔95/2
Mughal Empire India 41/4, 48/2
Mukden Manchuria capital of Manchuria 106/1; treaty town 107/4; Russo-Japanese war 127/4; Japanese occupation 127/5
Multan district of NW India Muslim conquest 41/1, 4; industry under British rule 105/3
München (Munich)
Mundurucú forest Indian tribe of N Brazil 63/1
Munich (*Ger.* München) S Germany in Thirty Years War 77/5; industrial development 98/2; WW1 119/3; WW2 133/2
Munster SW Ireland Presidency 73/4
Münster N Germany bishopric 79/1
Muqdisho (Mogadishu)
Murad I Ottoman ruler 48T; 49/1
Murad II Ottoman ruler 48T; 49/1
Murban United Arab Emirates oilfield 151/4
Murcia region of S Spain reconquest by Castile 37/4
Murfreesboro SE USA ⚔93/5
Murmansk N Russia Allied occupation 121/2; industrial development 147/1
Muroma E Slav tribe of C Russia 44/1
Murom-Ryazan early principality of C Russia 45/2
Muroran N Japan 126/2
Murviedro (Saguntum)
Murzuk Libya early trade 61/2; Barth's journey 102/1
Musang Cave N Philippines Neolithic site 8/3
Muscat (*Ar.* Masqat) town and district of SE Arabia early trade 58/3; Ottoman siege 48/2
Muscat and Oman (*now* Oman) SE Arabia British protectorate 125/1
Muscovy early principality of W Russia 48/2, 85/1
Mutina (*mod.* Modena) N Italy Roman Empire 24/2, 30/1, 31/3
Muziris S India early trade 25/1
Mwenemutapa early state of SE Africa 61/2
Mycale W Anatolia ⚔20/5, 22/1
Mycenae ancient city of S Greece 16/1, 18/2, 19/1
Mylae (*mod.* Milazzo) Sicily Roman Empire ⚔30/2
Mylasa (*mod.* Milas) SW Anatolia Alexander's route 22/3
Myos Hormus ancient port on Red Sea 25/2
Myra S Anatolia Byzantine Empire 42/2
Mysia ancient country of W Anatolia 22/3
Mysore (*now* Karnataka) region of S India alliance with Britain 87/2 (inset); state under British rule 104-5
Mytilene (*a/s Mitylene) island of Aegean* ceded to Greece 116/1
Mzilikazi tribe of S Africa 102/2

Nabateans ancient people of Palestine 26/3
Nabha N India Sikh demonstrations 104/4
Näfels Switzerland ⚔54/5
Nagano city and prefecture of C Japan 126/2
Nagappattinam (Negapatam)

Nagasaki W Japan early European trade 67/1, 66/2; industry 126/2; bombed by US 135/2, 3
Nagidus S Anatolia Greek colony 19/4
Nagorno-Karabakh AR Caucasus 146/2
Nagoya C Japan 126/2, 135/3
Nagpur C India 104/4, 105/3
Nahuatl Indian tribe of C Mexico 63/1
Naimans Mongolian tribe 47/1
Nairobi Kenya occupied by British 103/3
Naissus (*mod.* Niš) S Yugoslavia Roman Empire 24/2; bishopric 27/2
Najd (Nejd)
Najran SW Arabia early bishopric 39/1
Nakhichevan ASSR Caucasus 146/2
Nakhodka Russ. Far East industry 147/1
Nakhon Pathom S Thailand Hindu-Buddhist remains 51/2
Nakhon Ratchasima C Thailand Vietnam war 148/3
Nambicuara forest Indian Tribe of W Brazil 63/1
Namibia (*form.* South West Africa, *earlier* German South West Africa) German colony 101/2, 103/3; independence from South Africa 138/1, 140/1; economy 150/1
Namsos C Norway WW2 132/1
Namur Belgium Burgundian possession 73/3; town of Spanish Netherlands 77/1; WW1 119/2
Nanchang S China Ming provincial capital 51/4; under warlord control 122/2; anti-Nationalist insurrection 123/4; occupied by Japanese 127/5
Nanchao (*mod.* Yunnan) SW China independent kingdom 50-51
Nan Chihli E China Ming province 51/4
Nancy E France⚔73/3; WW1 119/2
Nanhai S China Han Commanderie 29/3
Nanking N China Ming provincial capital 51/4; treaty port 107/4; Nationalist capital 122/2; occupied by Japan 127/5
Nanning S China treaty port 107/4
Nantes NW France Scandinavian settlement 37/1; 17C revolt 77/2; trading port 83/5; centre of French Revolution 89/2; industrial development 98/2
Nantwich C England⚔76/4
Nanyueh SW China independent kingdom 28/2
Napata Egypt Iron Age site 11/1; fortress 21/1
Napier N Island, New Zealand founded 112/2
Naples (*anc.* Neapolis *It.* Napoli) Mediterranean trade 58/3, 82/4; industrial development 99/2; WW2 133/2
Naples, Kingdom of Black Death 57/1; to Aragon 72/1; acquired by Habsburgs 72/1; to Austria 81/5; satellite of France 91/1; unification of Italy 114/3
Napoleon Emperor of France 90-91
Napoli (Naples)
Naqada Upper Egypt 17/3
Nara C Japan Buddhist site 27/1; prefecture 126/2
Narbo (*mod.* Narbonne) S France Roman Empire 24/2
Narbonensis (*a/c* Gallia Narbonensis) Roman province of S France 30/3
Narbonne (*anc.* Narbo) S France Muslim conquest 40/1; medieval trade 58/1
Nariokotome E Africa site of early man 3/3
Naroch *Lake* W Russia WW1⚔119/3
Narosura E Africa early site 11/1
Narraganset Indian tribe of NE USA 63/1
Narragansett Fort NE USA⚔95/2
Narva Estonia, W Russia 1905 Revolution 120/1; WW2 133/2
Narvik N Norway WW2 132/1
Narym W Siberia founded 84/2
Naseby C England⚔76/4
Nashville SE USA⚔93/5
Nashville Road C USA settlers' route 94/1
Nassau principality of C Germany 79/1; Reformation 75/1; unification with Germany 115/2
Natal province of S Africa annexed by Britain 103/2; British colony 103/4
Natchez S USA Indian tribe 63/1
Natchez Trace S USA settlers' route 94/1
Natchitoches S USA fur station 94/1
Natick NE USA Protestant mission 94/1
National Road C USA settlers' route 94/1
Nations, Battle of the (Leipzig) E Germany⚔90/1
NATO 137/3, 148T
Naucratis Egypt Iron Age site 11/1; Greek colony 19/4
Nauru *island* W Pacific independence 139/1 (inset)
Nautaca (*mod.* Karshi) C Asia on Alexander's route 23/3
Navajo Indian tribe of SW USA 63/1
Navarino (Pylos)
Navarre (*Sp.* Navarra) region of N Spain/SW France kingdom 37/4; acquired by Habsburgs 72/1; acquired by France 80/1
Navas de Tolosa S Spain⚔40/2
Navpaktos (Lepanto)
Naworth Castle N England⚔73/4
Naxos Sicily in Mycenaean world 18/2; Greek colony 19/4
Nazca Andean Indian tribe of S America 63/1
Nazlet Khatir S Egypt site of early man 3/3
Ndeni (Santa Cruz)
N'Djamena (Fort Lamy)
Neanderthal Germany site of early man 3/3
Neapolis (*mod.* Napoli *Eng.* Naples) S Italy Greek colony 19/4, 23/2; Roman Empire 31/3; early bishopric 26/2
Near East (Middle East)
Neath S Wales Industrial Revolution 98/1
Nebraska state of C USA Depression 130/2; population 111/5, 145/1
Neerwinden Belgium⚔89/2
Nefertara N Greece Mithraic site 26/1
Negapatam (*n/s Nagappattinam) S India* Dutch settlement 66/2;⚔87/2 (inset); industry 104/3
Negri Sembilan state off Malaya 71/5
Negroponte (Euboea)
Nehavend (*anc.* Laodicea in Media) W Persia⚔41/1
Nejd (*Ar.* Najd) region of C Arabia 124/1, 125/2
Nellore district of SE India ceded to Britain 87/3
Nelson county and town of S Island, New Zealand founded 112/2
Nelson Bay S Africa Stone age site 11/1
Nemausus (*mod.* Nîmes) S France Roman Empire 30/3 early bishopric 26/2
Nemetocenna (Arras)
Nemours region of N France 72/2
Nenets AR N Siberia 146/2
Neocaesarea N Anatolia early archbishopric 27/2; Byzantine Empire 43/1
Nepal tributary state of Chinese Empire 106/1; 107/4; economy 150/1
Nepala (*mod.* Nepal) tributary state of the Guptas 29/4, 5
Nepete N Italy Latin colony 30/1
Nerchinsk SE Siberia founded 84/2
Nerchinsk, Treaty of 106/1
Nerja S Spain Palaeolithic art 5/3
Nestorian churches 39/1
Nesvizh (*Pol.* Nieśwież) W Russia town of Turov-Pinsk 45/2
Netherlands (*a/c* Holland *form.* Dutch Republic United Provinces) Burgundian possession 73/3; acquired by Habsburgs 72/1; agriculture and land reclamation 8/3; trade and industry 82/4; independence in north 114/5; industrial revolution 98/2; colonial power 100/2; socio-political development 130/3; EEC and NATO 137/3; economy 150/1. See also Belgium, Flanders, Holland
Netherlands, Austrian (*mod.* Belgium) revolt against Emperor 88/1; occupied by French 88/3
Netherlands East Indies (*now* Indonesia) occupied by Japanese 135/1. See also East Indies, Borneo, Java, Moluccas, Sumatra
Netherlands, Spanish (*later* Holland *or* United Provinces; and Belgium) Reformation 75/1; part of German Empire 79/1; Dutch revolt 76/1; territory lost to and gained from France 81/2, 4
Netherlands, United 79/1
Neuchâtel Switzerland Reformation 75/1
Neuengamme N Germany concentration camp 132/1
Neuenheim W Germany Mithraic site 26/1
Neustria the Frankish lands of N France 34/4
Neuve-Chapelle NE France WW1 118/3 (inset)
Nevada state of W USA Depression 130/2; population 111/5, 145/1
Nevers C France independent fief 72/2
Neville's Cross N England⚔56/4
Nevis *island* W Indies English settlement 66/4; British colony 97/1; self-government with St. Christopher 139/1 (inset)
New Amsterdam (*earlier* Fort Amsterdam *now* New York city) colonised by Dutch 67/3
New Britain *island* Papua New Guinea early Melanesian settlement 10/2; retaken from Japanese 135/2; to New Guinea 139/1 (inset)
New Brunswick province of E Canada joins Confederation 101/1; 111/1
New Caledonia *islands* S Pacific early Melanesian settlement 10/2; French colony 101/2, 139/1, US base 135/4
Newcastle SE Australia penal settlement 113/1
Newcastle-under-Lyme C England Industrial Revolution 98/1
Newcastle-upon-Tyne N England medieval trade 59/2; Civil War 76/4; industrial development 98/1
Newchwang Manchuria treaty port 107/4; Russo-Japanese war 127/4
New England NE USA British settlement 67/3
Newfoundland province of E Canada rediscovered 64/2; British settlement 67/3, 86/1; British colony 69/3; joins Dominion 111/1
New France French possessions in Canada 67/3, 86/1
New Galicia Spanish colony of C Mexico 66/1
New Granada (*mod.* Colombia) Spanish colony 66/1, 69/3; vice-royalty in rebellion against Spain 88/1, 97/1
New Grange Ireland megalithic tomb 14/3
New Guinea (*now part of* Papua New Guinea) early settlement 10/2; Dutch/German/British control 101/2; attacked by Japanese 134/1; retaken by Allies 135/2. See also West Irian
Newham N England⚔73/4
New Hampshire state of NE USA colony 67/3; 92/1; Depression 131/2; population 111/5, 145/1
New Haven NE USA founded 67/3
New Hebrides (*Fr.* Nouvelles Hébrides *now* Vanuatu) *islands* S Pacific early Melanesian settlement 10/2; British/French condominium 101/2; US base 134/1; independence 139/1 (inset)
New Holland (*now* Australia) early voyages 65/4
New Ireland *island* Papua New Guinea early Melanesian settlement 10/2; occupied by Japanese 135/1
New Jersey state of E USA colony 67/3, 92/1; Depression 131/2; population 111/5, 145/1
New Lanark S Scotland Industrial Revolution 98/1
New Malton N England Industrial Revolution 98/1
New Mexico state of SW USA ceded by Mexico 97/1; Depression 131/2; population 111/5, 145/1
New Netherland (*now* New York State) Dutch colony 67/3
New Orleans S USA French/Spanish occupation 69/3; Civil War 92/5
New Plymouth N Island, New Zealand founded 112/2. See also Taranaki
Newport S Wales Industrial Revolution 98/1
Newport Pagnell S England Industrial Revolution 98/1
New Sarai S Russia Mongol capital 46/1
New South Wales state of SE Australia early exploration 65/4; settlement and development 113/1; statehood 101/1
New Spain (*mod.* Mexico. C America and Caribbean) early voyages of discovery 65/3, 69/3; Spanish vice-royalty 66/1; rebellion against Spain 88/1
New Territories S China acquired by Britain 107/4
Newton C USA cow town 94/1
Newton C Wales Industrial Revolution 98/1
Newton le Willows NW England Industrial Revolution 98/1
New Ulm N USA⚔95/2
New York (*form.* New Netherland) colony 67/3, 92/1
New York state of E USA Depression 131/2; population 111/5, 145/1; industry 110/2; social unrest 144/3
New York City (*1653-64 called* New Amsterdam *earlier* Fort Amsterdam) 67/3; British naval base 86/1; industry 110/2; population 110/2; social unrest 144/3
New Zealand early Polynesian settlement 10/2, 3; early voyages 65/4; settlement and development 101/1, 112/2, 3
Neyshabur (*a/s* Nishapur) N Persia 17/4
Nez Perce plateau Indian tribe of W Canada 63/1
Ngandong Java site of early man 3/3
Ngaruawahia N Island, New Zealand 112/3
Ngatapa N Island, New Zealand⚔112/3
Ngazargumu W Africa centre of Kanem-Borno 60/1
Nguni (*a/c* Ngoni) tribe of S Africa 61/2, 103/2
Nha Trang S Indo-china Hindu-Buddhist temple 51/2
Niah cave Borneo site of early man 3/3; Bronze Age caves 8/3
Niami W Africa early centre of Mali Empire 60/1
Niaux SW France Palaeolithic art 5/3
Nicaea (*mod.* Iznik) W Anatolia centre of early Christianity 27/2; Roman Empire 24/2, 31/3; Byzantine Empire 43/3
Nicaea NW India Alexander's route 23/3
Nicaragua country of C America early exploration 64/2; independence 97/1; US protectorate 97/1; political development 111/4; Sandanista revolution 142/1
Nicarao Indian tribe of C America 63/1
Nice (*It.* Nizza) S France annexed from Italy 88/3
Nicephorium (*mod.* Rakka) Syria Roman Empire 25/2, 31/3
Nicobar Islands Indian Ocean territory of British India 105/3
Nicomedia *mod.* Izmit) W Anatolia Roman Empire 24/2, 31/3; early archbishopric 26/2; Byzantine Empire 43/1
Nicopolis Lower Egypt 25/2
Nicopolis W Greece archbishopric 26/2; Byzantine Empire 43/3
Nicopolis (*mod.* Nikopol) Bulgaria Byzantine Empire 49/1
Nida W Germany Mithraic site 26/1
Nien rebels N China 107/3
Nieśwież (Nesvizh)
Niger country of W Africa French colony 103/3; independence 138/1; economy 150/1
Nigeria country of W Africa British colony 100/2, 102/5, 103/3; independence 138/1; political development 140/1; Biafran war 140/2; economy 150/1
Niigata E Japan 126/1, 2
Nikki Dahomey, W Africa occupied by French 103/3
Nikolayev S Ukraine founded 85/1; 1905 Revolution 120/1
Nikopol (Nicopolis)
Nile (*a/c* Aboukir Bay)⚔90/2
Nilotes people of E Africa 60-61
Nîmes (*anc.* Nemausus) S France centre of French Revolution 89/2
Nina C Mesopotamia Sumerian city 16/2
Nindowari N India Harappan site 9/5
Nineveh Mesopotamia early farming village 7/4; 17/4; Assyrian Empire 20/2, 3; Mitannian city 21/1; Alexander's Empire 22/3
Ningsia NW China early bishopric 39/1; Ming frontier defence area 51/4
Ningpo E China treaty port 107/4
Ninus (Nineveh)
Nippur C Mesopotamia Sumerian city 16/2, 17/4, 20/3
Nirou Khani C Crete Mycenaean settlement 19/1
Niš (Naissus, Nish)
Nish (*S. Cr.* Niš *anc.* Naissus) E Yugoslavia Ottoman Empire 49/1; WW1 119/3
Nishapur (*Pers.* Neyshabur) W Persia early bishopric 39/1; Muslim conquest 48/2; Mongol conquest 47/4; Muslim trade 59/3; Safavid conquest 48/2
Nisibis (*mod.* Nusaybin) E Anatolia Alexander's route 22/3; Roman Empire 31/3; early archbishopric 27/2, 39/1

Nivernais region of E France Royal domain 52/2
Nizam's Dominions C India 87/2, 3
Nizhne-Kamchatsk Russ. Far East founded 84/2
Nizhne-Kolymsk NE Siberia founded 84/2
Nizhne-Udinsk C Siberia founded 84/2
Nizhniy Novgorod (*since 1932* Gorkiy) C Russia town of Vladimir-Suzdal 45/2; 1905 Revolution 120/1; Bolshevik seizure 121/2
Nizhniy Tagil W Siberia founded 85/1; industry 147/1
Nizza (Nice)
Nkope E Africa Iron Age site 11/1
Noakhali E India riots 104/4
Noemfoor (*n/s* Numfoor) island of NW New Guinea captured by Allies 135/2
Nogai Tartars tribe of C Russia 85/1
Nohmul Belize Mayan centre 12/2
Noirmoutier W France Scandinavian settlement 37/1
Noisy N France megalithic tomb 14/3
Nok W Africa Iron Age site 11/1
Nombre de Dios Panama early Spanish port 66/4
Nomonhan (*a/c* Khalkin Gol) E Mongolia Russo-Japanese conflict 127/5
Non Nok Tha N Thailand early site 8/3
Nootka coast Indian tribe of W Canada 63/1
Nördlingen S Germany medieval fair 59/2; ⚔74/4
Nordmark N Germany region of Brandenburg 55/1
Norfolk Island SW Pacific Australian territory 139/1 (inset)
Noricum Roman province of C Europe 30/3
Norilsk NW Siberia industry 147/1
Normandy region of N France Scandinavian settlement 37/1; French Royal domain 52/2, 72/2; province of France 80/1
Normans in Sicily and S Italy 43/3
Normanton E Australia early settlement 113/1
Northampton C England Industrial Revolution 98/1
North Battleford C Canada growth 111/1
North Carolina state of E USA colony 67/3, 92/1; Civil War 93/5; Depression 131/2; population 111/5, 145/1
North Dakota state of N USA Depression 130/2; population 111/5, 145/1
Northern Cook Islands (Manihiki Islands)
Northern Ireland religious divide and IRA activities 137/6
Northern Rhodesia (*now* Zambia) British colony 100/2, 102/5, 103/3
Northern Sirkars territory of E India 87/2 (inset)
Northern Territory Australia settlement and development 113/1
Northern Wei (Toba)
North Island (*Maori* Te Ika-a-Maui) New Zealand settlement and development 112/2
North Ossetian ASSR Caucasus 146/2
Northumbria early kingdom of N England 35/3; conversion to Christianity 38/3; Scandinavian settlement 37/1
North Vietnam independence 139/1; military growth 148/3. See also Vietnam, Indo-China
North-Western Provinces NW India 104/1
North West Frontier Province N Pakistan in Indian Empire 105/3; joins Pakistan 105/5
Norway conversion to Christianity 38/2; emergence as medieval state 53/4, 5; Black Death 57/1; Union of Kalmar 72/1; losses to Swedish Empire 77/3; union with Sweden 114/4; Reformation 75/1; socio-political change 130/3; WW2 132/1, 133/2; NATO and EFTA 137/2, 149/1; economy 150/1
Norwich E England Scandinavian settlement 37/1; rebellion 73/4; 18C industry 82/4; Industrial Revolution 98/1
Notium W Anatolia ⚔23/2
Nottingham C England Danish Viking base 37/1; Industrial Revolution 98/1
Nouvelles Hébrides (New Hebrides)
Novae Bulgaria Mithraic site 26/1; Roman Empire 24/2
Nova Goa (*later* Panjum *now* Panaji) W India 105/3
Novara N Italy Lombard League 55/3; Signorial domination 56/3; ⚔114/3
Nova Scotia (*form.* Acadia) province of E Canada ceded by France 67/3; British possession 69/3, 86/1, 92/1; joins Confederation 101/1; economy 111/1
Novaya Zemlya region of Arctic Russia discovery 65/2
Novgorod (*Norse* Holmegaard) NW Russia bishopric 38/2; Viking trade 37/1, 44/1; Hanseatic trade 59/2; WW2 133/2
Novgorod Empire NW Russia 45/2; conquered by Muscovy 73/1, 85/1
Novgorod-Seversk early principality of W Russia 45/2
Novibazar, Sanjak of Ottoman province of Yugoslavia 116/1
Novocherkassk S Russia industry 85/4; Bolshevik seizure 121/2
Novokuznetsk (*1932-61 called* Stalinsk) C Siberia industry 147/1
Novonikolayevsk (*since 1925* Novosibirsk) C Siberia on railway 84/3
Novorossiysk S Russia industry 85/4; 1905 Revolution 120/1; Bolshevik seizure 121/2
Novosibirsk (*until 1925* Novonikolayevsk) C Siberia industry 147/1
Novosil W Russia early town of Chernigov 45/2
Ntereso W Africa early site 11/1
Nubia region of NE Africa early settlement 11/1; introduction of Christianity 38/1; Christian kingdom 60/1
Nubt (Tukh)
Nuestra Señora de la Soledad W USA Catholic mission 94/1
Nuevo León province of N Mexico 97/1
Numantia N Spain Roman Empire 30/2
Numfoor (Noemfoor)
Numidia Roman province of N Africa 30/3
Nupe Nigeria early Hausa state 60-61
Nu-Pieds France 77/2
Nuremberg (*Ger.* Nürnberg) S Germany Reformation 75/1
Nuri Upper Egypt Iron Age site 11/1
Nuzi N Mesopotamia Mitannian city 21/1
Nyasaland (*now* Malawi) British protectorate 101/2
Nysa Afghanistan Alexander's route 23/3
Nyssa W Anatolia early bishopric 27/2
Nystad, Treaty of 84T

Oakham C England Industrial Revolution 98/1
Oaxaca province of S Mexico 97/1
Obdorsk (*since 1933* Salekhard) W Siberia founded 84/2
Oberkassel W Germany Palaeolithic art 5/3
Obock E Africa occupied by French 101/2
Oc Eo S Cambodia Hindu-Buddhist remains 51/2
Ochrida (*mod.* Ohrid) Yugoslavia bishopric 38/2; Byzantine Empire 43/3
Oconto N USA site 62/4
Oda C Japan clan territory 51/3
Ödenburg (Sopron)
Odense C Denmark bishopric 52/3
Oder-Niesse line post-war German/Polish boundary 136T, 137/5
Odessa S Ukraine founded 85/1; 1905 Revolution 120/1; Bolshevik seizure 121/2; WW2 133/2
Odessus (*mod.* Varna) Bulgaria Greek colony 19/4; Roman Empire 24/2, 31/3
O'Donnell's rebellion Ireland 73/4
Oea (*mod.* Tripoli) Libya Phoenician city 19/4; Roman Empire 31/3; early bishopric 27/2
Oesel (Osel)
Offa's Dyke 35/3
Ogallala C USA cow town 94/1
Ogasawara Islands (Bonin Islands)
Ohio state of N USA Depression 131/2; population 111/5, 145/1
Ohrid (Ochrida)
Oirots Mongolian tribe 47/1
Oita prefecture of W Japan 126/2
Ojibwa Indian tribe of C Canada 63/1
Okayama city and prefecture of W Japan 108/1, 126/1, 2
Okehampton SW England ⚔73/4
Okhotsk E Siberia founded 84/2
Okinawa *island* SW Japan captured by US 135/2; reversion to Japan 141/1; US base 149/1
Oklahoma state of C USA Depression 131/2; population 111/5, 145/1
Olbia S France Greek colony 19/4
Olbia S Russia Greek colony 19/4; Roman Empire 24/2, 31/3
Old Calabar Nigeria 61/2
Old Chillicothe NE USA ⚔95/2
Oldenburg N Germany 79/1; German unification 115/2
Oldendorf N Germany megalithic tomb 15/3
Old Sarai S Russia Mongol capital 46/1, 3
Old Sarum S England ⚔33/3
Olduvai E Africa site of early man 3/3
Oleshe S Ukraine early town 45/2
Olekminsk SE Siberia founded 84/2
Olisipo (*mod.* Lisboa *Eng.* Lisbon) Portugal Roman Empire 24/2, 31/3; early bishopric 26/2
Ollantaytambo Peru on Pizarro's route 68/2
Olmec States C Mexico 12/2
Olorgasailie E Africa site of early man 3/3
Olsztyn (Allenstein)
Olustee SE USA ⚔93/5
Omagua forest Indian tribe of S America 63/1
Oman region of E Arabia Muslim expansion 41/1; under Abbasid sovereignty 41/2; British sphere of influence 138/1; economy 150/1
Omei Shan W China Buddhist site 27/1
Omo E Africa site of early man 3/3
Omphis early kingdom of NW India 23/2
Omsk W Siberia founded 84/2; on railway 84/3; seat of Kolchak government 120/4; industry 147/1
On (Heliopolis)
Ona Indian tribe of Tierra del Fuego 63/1
O'Neill's rebellion Ireland 73/4
Ontario province of E Canada joins Confederation 101/1; economic development 111/1
Oodnadatta S Australia 113/1
OPEC 150/1
Opelousas C USA fur station 94/1
Ophiusa S Russia Greek colony 19/4
Opis Mesopotamia Persian Empire 21/5, 22/3
Opium War China 106T, 107/3
Opsician Theme W Anatolia district of Byzantine Empire 42/2
Optimacian Theme N Anatolia district of Byzantine Empire 42/2
Orakau N Island, New Zealand ⚔112/3
Oran (*Ar.* Wahran) N Algeria acquired by Habsburgs 72/2; WW2 132/2
Orange principality of S France 80/1; executions during French Revolution 89/2
Orange Free State S Africa 103/2, 3, 4
Orchomenus C Greece Mycenaean palace site 19/1
Ordos Desert N China Palaeolithic sites 8/2
Ordu (Cotyora)
Ordzhonikidze (*form.* Dzaudzhikau *earlier and again from 1991* Vladikavkaz) Caucasus WW2 133/2
Oregon state of NW USA acquired by USA 92/2; Depression 130/2; population 111/5, 145/1
Oregon Trail NW USA settlers' route 94/1
Orel W Russia founded 85/1; WW2 133/2; industry 147/1
Orenburg (*1938-57 called* Chkalov) C Russia founded 85/1; Bolshevik seizure 121/2; industry 147/1
Oriens eastern diocese of later Roman Empire 31/4
Orientale province of NE Belgian Congo /138/4
Orissa (*form.* Jajnagar) region of E India state of modern India 105/3
Oritae ancient people of SE Persia 23/3
Orkney islands of NE Scotland Norwegian Viking settlement 37/1; acquired by Scotland 72/1
Orléanais region of C France Royal domain 52/2; 72/2; 80/1
Orléans C France St. Bartholomew Massacre 74/3, 17C; revolts 77/2; industrial development 80/1
Ormuz (*a/s* Hormuz *anc.* Harmozia) S Persia early trade 58/3; Portuguese base 48/2, 67/1
Orsha W Russia town of Polotsk 45/2
Ortenburg SE Germany county 79/1
Orvieto (Volsinii)
Osage plains Indian tribe of C USA 63/1
Osaka city and province of C Japan 108/1, 126/1, 2; bombed by US 135/3
Ösel (*a/s* Oesel *mod.* Hiiumaa) *island* NW Estonia occupied by Teutonic Knights 54/4; under Swedish rule 77/3
Oslo (*until 1924* Kristiania *a/s* Christiania) Norway Hanseatic trade 59/2; WW2 132/1, 133/2
Osnabrück N Germany Hanseatic city 59/2
Osterburken W Germany Mithraic site 26/1
Ostia C Italy Mithraic site 26/1; Roman Empire 24/2; Roman colony 30/1
Ostpreussen (East Prussia)
Ostrogothic Kingdom S Europe 34/1
Ostrogoths invasion of Europe 31/4, 32/2, 35/2
Ostyaks people of W Siberia 84/2
Oświęcim (*Ger.* Auschwitz) Poland Empire of Casimir IV 72/1
Otago province of S Island, New Zealand 112/2
Otford S England ⚔35/3
Otluk-Beli (*a/c* Tercan) E Anatolia ⚔49/1
Otomi Indian tribe of C Mexico 63/1
Otomo W Japan clan territory 51/3
Otranto SE Italy Saracen raids 37/1; Ottoman attack 48/2
Otrar C Asia Mongol conquest 46/1, 47/4
Ottawa E Canada growth 111/1
Ottawa Indian tribe of E Canada 63/1
Otterburn N England ⚔56/4
Otto I East Frankish King 54T
Ottoman Empire Mongol invasion 47/4; expansion 48-49, 72/1; expansion into Europe 101/1, 2; decline 116/1, 124/1; WW1 118-9, 125/2
Ouadane (Wadan)
Ouagadougou Upper Volta, W Africa taken by French 103/3
Oualata (Walata)
Ouargla (Wargla)
Oudenaarde (*Fr.* Audenarde) Belgium ⚔81/5
Oudh native state of N India 87/3; 104/1
Ouidah (Whydah)
Outer Mongolia (*now* Mongolia) Chinese protectorate 106/1; independence 122/4
Overijssel N Holland Burgundian possession 73/3; province of Dutch Republic 77/1
Overland Stage C USA settlers' route to west 94/1
Oviedo NW Spain industrial development 98/2
Owyhee Forks W USA ⚔94/2
Oxford C England Civil War 76/4; Industrial Revolution 98/1
Oxyrhynchus Egypt Roman Empire 31/3
Oyo Nigeria early state 60-61

Pa C China Han commanderie 29/3
Paardeberg S Africa ⚔103/4
Pachácamac C Andes early site 12/4, 5; Pizarro's route 68/2
Pachacuti Inca emperor 62T, 63/3
Pacheco C Andes early site 12/5
Pacific Ocean early Polynesian settlement 10/2; early European voyages of discovery 65/4; American influence 110/4; WW2 135/1; sovereignty of islands 139/1 (inset)
Pacific Rim 150T
Pacific, War of the Chile-Peru 97/4
Pacy-sur-Eure N France French Revolution 89/2
Padang W Sumatra Dutch settlement 71/2

Paderborn N Germany bishopric 79/1
Padua (*It.* Padova *anc.* Patavium) N Italy 56/3; WW1 119/3
Paeckche Korea early state destroyed by T'ang 51/1
Paestum (*earlier* Poseidonia) S Italy Latin colony 25/1
Paez Andean Indian tribe of S America 63/1
Pagan C Burma Buddhist site 27/1; early empire 51/2
Pahang state of Malaya 71/5
Pair-non-Pair SW France Palaeolithic art 5/3
Paita Peru on Pizarro's route 68/2
Paiute Indian tribe of W USA 63/1
Pajajaran Java early kingdom 51/2
Pakhoi S China treaty port 107/4
Pakistan independence 105/5, 139/1; secession of Bangladesh 141/1; boundary dispute with India 141/1; Baghdad Pact and US alliance 149/1; economy 150/1. (For period before 1947 see under India and/or constituent provinces)
Palaiokastro Crete 19/1
Palatinate (*Ger.* Pfalz) historical region of W Germany Wittelsbach territory 72/1; Reformation 75/1; German unification 115/2
Palau (*f/s* Pelew) SW Caroline Islands, W Pacific occupied by US 135/2
Pale, The Ireland 73/4
Palembang SE Sumatra Hindu-Buddhist remains 51/2; trade 59/3
Palenque E Mexico Mayan site 12/2
Palermo (*anc.* Panormus) Sicily medieval German attack 55/3; 18 C urban development 82/4
Palestine (*Lat.* Palaestina *now* Israel and Jordan) early urban settlement 16/1 Levantine cities and ports 21/1; at time of David 21/2; at time of Alexander 22/3; Roman Empire 24/2; emergence of Judaea 26/3; Byzantine Empire 43/1; Muslim reconquest 40/3; Ottoman province 124/1; WW1 125/2; British control 125/3; WW2 132/1; partition between Israel and Jordan 141/3
Pallavas dynasty of S India 29/5
Palmerston North N Island, New Zealand 112/2
Palmyra (*Bibl.* Tadmor *or* Tamar) Syria Roman Empire 25/2; early bishopric 27/2
Pamphylia ancient country of southern Anatolia 19/4, 31/3, 43/1
Pamunkey NE USA⚔95/2
Panaji (Nova Goa)
Panama Isthmus discovered 65/3; Canal Zone 111/4; independence 97/1; political development 142-3; US base 149/1; economy 150/1; US intervention 1989 143/1
Panama Canal opening 100/2; 109/4
Panchala early kingdom of N India 29/4
Pandya country and dynasty of S India 29/4, 5
Pangim (*form.* Nova Goa *now* Panaji) W India 105/3
Panipat N India⚔48/2, 87/2
P'an-lung-ch'eng (*a/s* Panlongcheng) S China Shang city 8/4
Panmunjom Korea 1953 armistice 148/2
Pannonia C Europe Avar Kingdom 35/4
Pannonia Inferior Roman province of C Europe 31/3, 4
Pannonia Superior Roman province of C Europe 31/3, 4
Panormus (*mod.* Palermo) Sicily Phoenician city 19/4; Roman Empire 24/2, 30/3
Pan-p'o (*a/s* Banpo) C China early settlement 8/2
Pantelleria *island* C Mediterranean WW2 133/2
Panticapaeum (*mod.* Kerch) Crimea Greek colony 19/4; Roman Empire 24/2, 31/3; early trading centre 25/1
Pao W China Western Chou domain 9/6
Pao-an Soviet N China 122/4
Paochi W China Western Chou site 9/6
Papago Indian tribe of N Mexico 63/1
Papal States C Italy expansion 56/3; Black Death 57/1; at time of Habsburg power 72/1, 73/5; Reformation 75/1; unification of Italy 114/3
Paphlagonia ancient country of N Anatolia 19/4, 23/3, 4, 43/1
Paphlagonian Theme N Anatolia district of Byzantine Empire 42/2
Paphos (*Lat.* Paphus) Cyprus Greek colony 19/4; Roman Empire 25/2; bishopric 27/2
Papua Australian territory 101/2
Papua New Guinea SW Pacific independence 139/1; economy 150/1. See also New Guinea
Pará province of N Brazil 97/1
Paraetacene ancient people of NW Persia 23/3
Paraetonium (*mod.* Mersa Matruh) Egypt Alexander's Empire 23/3
Paraguay independence 97/1; political development 142-3; economy 150/1
Paraíba E Brazil Confederation of the Equator 97/1
Paramaribo Dutch Guinea colonised 69/3
Paranilotes people of Sudan 61/2
Parhae (*Chin.* Pohai) early Korean state 51/1
Parihaka N Island, New Zealand early Maori resistance 112/3
Paris N France early bishopric 26/2; 18C financial centre 82/4; St. Bartholomew Massacre 74/3; Fronde revolt 77/2; *parlement* 80/1; centre of French Revolution 89/2;⚔91/1; industrial development 98/2
Parma N Italy Roman colony 30/1; Lombard League 55/3; Signorial domination 56/3; acquired by Habsburgs 78/3; occupied by France 88/3; unification of Italy 114/3
Parpalló E Spain Palaeolithic art 5/3
Parsa (*a/c* Persis) S Persia satrapy of Achaemenid Empire 21/5
Parthenopean Republic S Italy state established by French Revolution 89/3
Parthia ancient country of N Persia 23/3, 4
Parthians ancient people of the Caucasus 31/3
Pasargadae SW Persia Alexander's route 23/3;⚔25/5
Passau SE Germany bishopric 35/4, 38/2, 3, 79/1
Passchendaele NW Belgium WW1⚔118/3 (inset)
Passi di Corvo S Italy farming site 15/1
Patagonia region of S Argentina 97/1
Pataliputra (*mod.* Patna) NE India trading centre 25/1
Patara SW Anatolia Greek colony 19/4; early bishopric 27/2
Patavium (*mod.* Padova *Eng.* Padua) N Italy Roman Empire 24/2
Pathet Lao Laotian Communist movement 140/1
Patna (Pataliputra)
Patras (*mod. Gr.* Patrai *anc.* Patrae) S Greece Byzantine Empire 43/1
Pattala NW India limit of Alexander's journey 23/3
Pau SW France seat of intendant 80/1
Paul, St. journeys 27/2
Paulis (*now* Isiro) NE Belgian Congo Congo crisis 138/4
Pavia (*anc.* Ticinum) N Italy Lombard League 73/5; medieval trade 58/1; Signorial domination 56/3
Pavlodar S Siberia industry 147/1
Pavlov Czechoslovakia Palaeolithic art 5/3
Pavón Mexico early site 12/3
Pawnee plains Indian tribe of C USA 63/1
Paya Indian tribe of C America 63/1
Pearl Harbor Hawaii bombed by Japanese 134/1
Pechenegs tribe of Ukraine, 43/3, 44/1, 45/2
Pechenga (Petsamo)
Pecherskaya Lavra Ukraine monastery 38/2
Pech-Merle SW France Palaeolithic art 5/3
Pechora tribe of N Russia 85/1
Pecsaete tribe of early England 33/3, 35/3
Pedra Branca S Portugal megalithic tomb 14/3
Pedra Coberta NW Spain megalithic tomb 14/3
Pedra Furada Brazil early site 5/2
Peebles county of C Scotland acquired by Edward III 56/4
Pegu early state of S Burma, Buddhist site 27/1; peripheral Mongol control 47/1; early trade 71/2
Pei Chihli NE China Ming province 51/4
P'ei-li-kang (*a/s* Peiligang) NE China early settlement 8/2
Peipus, Lake (*Russ.* Chudskoye Ozero *Est.* Peipsi Järv) W Russia⚔45/2
Peking (*form. Mong.* Khanbalik) N China early trade 59/3; Ming capital 51/4; warlord attacks 22/2; Japanese occupation 127/5; industry 108/1
Pelew (Palau)
Pella Palestine early bishopric 27/2
Pella Macedonia 20/5, 22/3
Peloponnesian War 23/2
Peloponnesus (*Eng.* Peloponnese *a/c* Morea) region of S Greece 18-19
Pelusium N Egypt Alexander's Empire 22/3; Roman Empire 25/2, 31/3
Pelym W Siberia founded 84/2
Pemaquid NE USA⚔95/2
Pemba *island* Tanzania Muslim colony 60/1
Pembina N USA fur station 94/1
Pembroke S Wales Scandinavian settlement 37/1; WW1 118/3
Penang state of Malaya British possession 71/5; WW2 134/1
Peninj E Africa site of early man 3/3
Peninsular War 90/1
Pennsylvania state of E USA colony 67/3, 92/1; Civil War 93/5; Depression 131/2; population 111/5, 145/1
Pennsylvania Road NE USA settlers' route 94/1
Penobscot NE USA founded 67/3
Pensacola SE USA Spanish post 67/3; fur station 94/1
Penuel Palestine ancient capital 21/2
Penydarran S Wales Industrial Revolution 98/1
Penza C Russia founded 85/1; 1905 Revolution 120/1; Bolshevik seizure 121/2
Pepin King of Franks 34T
Pequot Fort NE USA⚔95/2
Perak state of Malaya 71/5
Perath Mesopotamia early archbishopric 27/2
Perche N France fief 72/2
Pereslavets SW Russia 45/2
Pereyaslavl Ukraine bishopric 38/2; early principality 45/2
Pereyaslavl N Russia town of Vladimir-Suzdal 45/2
Pergamum (*Gr.* Pergamon *Turk.* Bergama) W Anatolia Roman Empire 24/2, 31/3; early bishopric 27/2
Perge S Anatolia early archbishopric 27/2
Périgord region of C France English possession 52/2; annexed to France 72/2
Perinthus SE Europe Greek colony 19/4
Perlis state of Malaya tributary to Siam 71/5
Perm (*1940-57 called* Molotov) C Russia founded 85/1; Bolshevik seizure 121/2; industry 147/1
Permians people of N Russia 38/2, 45/2
Pernambuco (*now* Recife) Brazil early Portuguese territory 66/1; Confederation of the Equator 96/1
Perovsk (Kzyl-Orda)
Perpignan S France fort 80/1
Perryville SE USA⚔93/5
Persepolis Persia early trade 25/1; Alexander's Empire 23/3; Achaemenid Empire 21/5; Muslim conquest 41/1
Persia (*now* Iran) war with Greece 22/1; Achaemenid empire 21/5; attacked by White Huns 32/1; expansion of Christianity 39/1; Muslim conquest 41/4; under Abbasid sovereignty 41/2; Mongol conquest 46-7; Safavid Empire 49/1; independent kingdom 125/1; British and Russian spheres of influence 125/3
Persian Gulf (*a/c* Arabian Gulf *or* The Gulf) WW1 125/2; oil 151/4
Persis (*a/c* Fars. Parsa) S Persia Alexander's Empire 23/3
Perth W Australia early settlement 113/1
Peru Spanish colonisation 66/1, 69/2; independence 97/1; war with Chile 97/4; political developments 142-3; economy 150/1
Perusia (*mod.* Perugia) N Italy Roman Empire 30/1, 31/3
Pesaro (Pisaurum)
Peshawar Pakistan industry under British rule 105/3; capital of NW Frontier Agency 105/5
Pesto (Posidonia)
Peterborough E England Industrial Revolution 98/1
Petersfels SW Germany Palaeolithic art 5/3
Petra Jordan Roman Empire 25/2, 31/3; early archbishopric 27/2
Petralona Greece site of early man 3/3
Petřkovice Czechoslovakia Palaeolithic art 5/3
Petrograd (*before 1914* St. Petersburg *since 1924* Leningrad) WW1 119/3; Russian Revolution 121/2
Petropavlovsk (*now* Petropavlovsk-Kamchatskiy) Russ. Far East founded 84/2; industry 147/1
Petsamo (*Russ.* Pechenga) NW Russia Russian conquest from Finland 133/2
Pettau (Poetovio)
Pevkakia E Greece Mycenaean settlement 19/1
Pfalz (Palatinate)
Pfalz-Sulzbach W Germany principality 79/1
Phaistos Crete Mycenaean site 19/1
Phalaborwa SE Africa Iron Age site 11/1; 60/1
Phanagoria S Russia Greek colony 19/4
Phan Rang S Indo-China Hindu-Buddhist temple 51/2
Phaselis SW Anatolia Greek colony 19/4
Phasis Caucasus Greek colony 19/4; Roman Empire 33/1
Phazania (*mod.* Fezzan) region of S Libya 31/3
Philadelphia (*mod.* Alaşehir) W Anatolia early church 27/2
Philadelphia (Amman)
Philadelphia E USA founded 67/3; industry 109/1
Philiphaugh S Scotland⚔76/4
Philippi N Greece Roman Empire 27/2
Philippines early sites 8/3; spread of Islam 40/5; early trade 67/1; Spanish conquest 71/2; acquired by US 102/2, 110/4; occupied by Japanese 127/5, 134/1; retaken by Americans 135/2; independence 139/1; political development 141/1; US bases 149/1; industry and economy 150/1
Philippine Sea⚔135/2
Philippopolis (*mod.* Plovdiv *Turk.* Filibe) Bulgaria Roman Empire 31/3; Byzantine Empire 43/1; Ottoman Empire 48/1
Philistia ancient country of Middle East 20/2
Philomelium (*mod.* Akşehir) C Anatolia Byzantine Empire 43/3
Phnom Laang Cambodia early site 8/3
Phnom Penh Cambodia 70/1, 71/2; Vietnam war 148/3
Phocaea W Anatolia Greek colony 19/4
Phocis ancient territory of C Greece 18/3
Phoenicia at time of Greeks 19/4, 21/2; Roman province 31/3
Phoenicians move into Africa 11/1
Phrygia ancient country of W Anatolia 19/4, 22/3; Byzantine Empire 43/1
Phylakopi S. Aegean early settlement 14/2; Mycenaean palace sites 19/1
Piacenza (*anc.* Placentia) N Italy Lombard League 55/3; Signorial domination 56/3; medieval fair 59/2
Piauí state of NE Brazil 97/1
Picardy (*Fr.* Picardie) region of N France annexed from Burgundy 72/2, 80/1; WW1 118/3 (inset)
Picentes early tribe of N Italy 25/1
Pictavi W France early bishopric 26/2
Picton S Island, New Zealand railway 112/1
Picts early tribe of Scotland 32/1, 38/3
Piedmont (*It.* Piemonte) region of N Italy 88/3, 114/3
Pigs, Bay of Cuba CIA invasion 149/5
Pilos (Navarino, Pylos)
Pilsen (*Cz.* Plzeň) Czechoslovakia industrial development 99/2
Pima Indian tribe of N Mexico 63/1
Pindal N Spain Palaeolithic art 5/3
Pinega N Russia town of Novgorod Empire 45/2
Pinkie Scotland⚔73/4
Pinsk W Russia town of Turov-Pinsk 45/2
Piombino N Italy Duchy 73/5; French rule 91/1
Piqillacta C Andes early site 12/5
Pi-Ramesse Lower Egypt Egyptian city 21/1

Piro forest Indian tribe of S America 63/1
Pisa (*anc.* Pisae) N Italy medieval city 55/3; Mediterranean trade 36/2, 58/1; raids and conquests 36/2; Republican commune 56/3
Pisae (*mod.* Pisa) N Italy Roman Empire 30/1, 31/3; bishopric 27/2
Pisaurum (*mod.* Pesaro) N Italy Roman colony 30/1
Piscataway Fort NE USA ⚔ 95/2
Pishpek (Frunze)
Pisidia ancient country of C Anatolia 22/3, 43/1
Pistoia (*anc.* Pistoriae) N Italy medieval city 55/3
Pitcairn Island C Pacific British colony 139/1 (inset)
Pithecusa S Italy Greek colony 19/4
Pit River W USA ⚔ 94/2
Pittsburgh E USA industry 109/1, 110/2
Pityus Caucasus Greek colony 19/4; early bishopric 27/2
Pizarro, Francisco Spanish explorer 68/2
Placentia (*mod.* Piacenza) N Italy Latin colony 30/1
Plassey E India ⚔ 87/2 (inset)
Plataea C Greece ⚔ 20/5, 22/1
Plate River (*Sp.* Rio de la Plata) Argentina explored 64/2
Plevna (*now* Pleven) Bulgaria WW1 119/3
PLO Palestinian nationalist movement 140T
Pločnik S Yugoslavia early settlement 14/2
Ploeşti Romania WW2 133/2
Plovdiv (Philippopolis)
Plussulien NW France megalithic axe factory 14/3
Plymouth SW England naval base 87/1; Industrial Revolution 98/1; WW1 118/3; WW2 132/1
Plymouth NE USA founded 67/3
Plzeň (Pilsen)
Poço da Gateira S Portugal megalithic tomb 14/3
Podolia region of S Ukraine acquired by Lithuania 56/2
Poduca S India early port 25/1
Poetovio (*mod.* Ptuj *Ger.* Pettau) N Yugoslavia Mithraic site 27/1; Roman Empire 31/3
Pohai (*Kor.* Parhae *mod.* Manchuria) NE China early state 51/1
Pohang S Korea 1950-53 war 148/2
Point of Rocks C USA ⚔ 94/2
Poitiers (*anc.* Limonum) C France ⚔ 34/4, 40/1, 56/5; 17C revolts 77/2; seat of intendant 80/1
Poitou region of W France French Royal domain 52/2; province of France 80/1
Pola (*mod.* Pula) N Yugoslavia Roman Empire 31/3; WW1 119/3
Polabii Slavic tribe of N Germany 54/1, 2
Poland conversion to Christianity 38/2; under Boleslav Chrobry 52/1; Mongol invasion 46/2; union with Lithuania 56/2; Black Death 57/1; Empire of Casimir IV 72/1; acquired by Russia 85/1; agriculture and peasant emancipation 82/1; Reformation 75/1; Partitions 79/4; revolt against Russia 88/1; WW1 119/3; independence after WW1 120/3; socio-political development 128/1, 131/3; WW2 132/1; territorial changes 136/1, 137/3; Warsaw Pact and Comecon 137/2, 149/1; end of Communist rule 137/4
Poles post-WW1 migration to Poland 128/3; post-WW2 migration to West 136/1
POLISARIO W Sahara guerrilla movement 138/1, 140/1
Polish Corridor 128/2
Polotsk W Russia early city and principality 45/2; Hanseatic trading post 59/2
Polovtsy tribe of C Russia 44-5
Poltava Ukraine town of Pereyaslavl 45/2; industry and urban growth 84/4; 1905 Revolution 120/1; Bolshevik seizure 121/2
Poltoratsk (Ashkhabad)
Polyanye Slav tribe of the Ukraine 44/1
Polynesia islands of C Pacific early settlement 10/2
Pomerania (*Ger.* Pommern *Pol.* Pomorze) region of N Europe acquired by Poland 52/1; medieval German Empire 55/3; acquired by Prussia 78/2; Reformation 75/1; unification of Germany 79/1, 115/2
Pomerania, East part of Germany 79/1
Pomerania, Swedish ceded to Prussia 114/4
Pomerania, West to Sweden 77/3
Pomeranians Slav tribe of N Europe 54/2
Pomerelia (*Ger.* Pommerellen) region of N Europe occupied by Teutonic Knights 54/4, 56/2
Pomo Indian tribe of NW USA 63/1
Pompeiopolis S Anatolia Roman Empire 31/3
Ponce de León Spanish explorer 64/3
Pondicherry (*Fr.* Pondichéry) SE India French settlement 66/2; captured by British 87/2 (inset); French enclave 105/3
Pondo region of SE Africa British administration 102/2
Pons Saravi E France Mithraic site 26/1
Ponthieu region of NE France under English rule 52/2; Burgundian possession 73/3
Pontia (*mod.* Ponza) W Italy Latin colony 30/1
Pontianak W Borneo Dutch settlement 71/2
Pontica region of E Anatolia 31/4
Pontnewydd N Wales site of early man 3/3
Pontus district of N Anatolia 19/4; Roman province 31/4; Byzantine Empire 43/1
Ponza (Pontia) *island* C Italy Mithraic site 26/1
Poona W India industry 108/1
Populonia N Italy Etruscan city 19/4, 30/1
Porolissensis Roman province of E Europe 31/3
Porolissum Romania Roman Empire 31/3
Portage la Prairie (Fort La Reine)
Port Arthur (*Chin.* Lushun *Jap.* Ryojun) Manchuria ceded to Russia and Japan 84/3, 107/4; Russo-Japanese war 127/4
Port Arthur (*now* Thunder Bay) C Canada growth 111/1
Port Arthur Tasmania penal settlement 113/1
Port Augusta S Australia settlement 113/1
Port Chalmers S Island, New Zealand 112/2
Port Elizabeth SE Africa British settlement 102/2, 103/3
Port Essington N Australia founded 113/1
Port-Francqui (*now* Ilebo) C Belgian Congo 138/4
Port Hedland W Australia early settlement 112/1
Port Hudson S USA ⚔ 92/5
Portland S England WW1 118/3
Portland SE Australia founded 113/1
Port Lincoln S Australia settlement 113/1
Port Macquarie SE Australia penal settlement 113/1
Port Moresby SE New Guinea Allied base WW2 134/1, 135/2
Porto Novo SE India ⚔ 87/2
Port Pirie S Australia settlement 113/1
Port Royal Jamaica British naval base 86/1
Port Said N Egypt Egyptian-Israeli war 141/3
Portsmouth S England naval base 87/1; Industrial Revolution 98/1; WW1 118/3
Portsmouth NE USA settlement 67/3
Portugal (*anc.* Lusitania) Jewish migration 39/4; Muslim conquest 40/1; reconquest 37/4; voyages of discovery 64-65; expansion overseas 66-7, 69/2; colonial empire 101/2; WW 1 118-9; NATO and EFTA 137/2, 149/1; US bases 149/1; economy 150/1
Portuguese East Africa (*now* Mozambique) 87/2, 101/2
Portuguese Guinea (*now* Guinea-Bissau) W Africa Portuguese colony 100/2; independence 138/1
Portuguese Timor E Indies annexed by Indonesia 139/1, 2
Porus early kingdom of NW India 23/3
Posen (*Pol.* Poznań) W Poland unification of Germany 115/2; ceded by Germany 128/2
Posidonia (*later* Paestum *mod.* Pesto) S Italy Greek colony 19/4
Potaissa Romania Roman Empire 24/2
Potawatomi Indian tribe of C USA 63/1
Potentia (*mod.* Potenza Picena) N Italy Roman colony 30/1
Potidaea N Greece Dorian colony 19/4
Potosí Peru Spanish silver mine 66/1
Pouey-Mayou SW France megalithic tomb 14/3
Powhatan Indian tribe of E USA 63/1
Powys district of Wales 33/3, 53/7
Poynings Law English rule in Ireland 72T
Poznań (Posen)
Pozzuoli (Puteoli)
Prague (*Cz.* Praha) Czechoslovakia bishopric 38/2; medieval trade 58/1; Hanseatic trade 59/2; industrial development 99/2; Communist coup 136/4
Praia das Maçãs C Portugal megalithic burial site 14/2
Prambanan C Java Hindu-Buddhist temple 51/2
Pravdinsk (Friedland)
Preanger district of Java Dutch control 71/4
Předmostí Czechoslovakia site of early man 3/3 Palaeolithic art 5/3
Pressburg (*Cz.* Bratislava) C Czechoslovakia ⚔ 37/1
Preston N England ⚔ 76/4; Industrial Revolution 98/1
Prestonpans S Scotland Industrial Revolution 98/1
Pretoria S Africa on Boer trek 102/2; ⚔ 103/4
Preussen (Prussia)
Preussisch-Eylau (Eylau)
Preveza C Greece ⚔ 48/2
Primorskiy Kray (Maritime Province)
Prince Edward Island (*form.* St Jean) island of E Canada joins Dominion 111/1
Prince's Town Ghana early French settlement 60/2 (inset)
Principe *island* W Africa Portuguese settlement 61/2. See also São Tomé and Principe
Prizren Serbia WW1 119/3
Prome C Burma Buddhist site 27/1
Provence region of S France Frankish Empire 34/4, 35/2; medieval German Empire 55/3; Arabs expelled 36/2; annexed to France 72/1, 2; revolts 77/2; province of France 80/1
Providence NE USA founded 67/3
Provins C France medieval fair 58/1
Prusa (*mod.* Bursa) W Anatolia Byzantine Empire 43/1
Prussia (*Ger.* Preussen) region of E Germany conquest by Teutonic Knights 54/4; Reformation 75/1; Duchy 77/3; opposition to Napoleon 91/4; unification of Germany 115/2
Przemyśl Austria-Hungary WW1 119/3
Pseira E Crete Mycenaean settlement 19/1
Pskov W Russia town of Novgorod Empire 85/1; Hanseatic trading post 59/2; acquired by Muscovy 73/1
Pteria (*mod.* Boğazköy) C Anatolia ⚔ 20/5
Ptolemaïs Egypt Roman Empire 31/3
Ptolemaïs (*mod.* Tulmaythah *It.* Tolmeta) Libya Roman Empire 31/3; early archbishopric 27/2
Ptolemaïs (*Eng.* Acre *mod.* 'Akko) Palestine early archbishopric 27/2
Ptuj (Poetovio)
Puebla C Mexico early Spanish city 66/1; province 97/1
Pueblo Indian tribe of SW USA 13/1, 63/1
Pueblo Bonito SW USA site 62/4
Puelche Indian tribe of Argentina 63/1
Puerto Rico W Indies Spanish settlement 66/4; conquered by US 97/1
Pugachev uprising Russia 85/1, 89T
Puig Roig NE Spain megalithic tomb 14/3
Pukow E China British influence 107/4
Pundra region of E India 29/4, 5
Punic Wars 30/2
Punjab region of NW India Muslim expansion 41/1, 4, 87/3; state of British India 104/1, 105/3; partition between India and Pakistan 105/5
Puri district of NE India cession to Britain 87/3
Pusan (*Jap.* Fusan) S Korea Russo-Japanese war 127/4; 1950-53 war 148/2
Pushkari W Russia site of early man 3/3
Putaya Libya satrapy of Achaemenid Empire 20/5
Puteoli (*mod.* Pozzuoli) C Italy Roman colony 31/1; Roman Empire 24/2
Puto Shan *mountain* E China Buddhist site 27/1
Pyatigorsk Caucasus 85/1
Pydna C Greece ⚔ 22/4
Pygmies people of C Africa 60/1, 2
Pylos (*a/s* Pilos *It.* Navarino) SW Greece Mycenaean palace site 19/1; Levantine port 21/1
Pyongyang (*Jap.* Heijo) N Korea Russo-Japanese war 127/4; 1950-53 war 148/2
Pyramid Lake W USA ⚔ 94/2
Pyramids, Battle of the Egypt 90/2
Pyrgi C Italy Roman colony 30/1
Pyrgos E Crete Mycenaean site 19/1
Pyu S Burma Buddhist kingdom 50/1
Pyxous, Pyxus (Buxentum)

Qadisiya S Mesopotamia ⚔ 41/1
Qafzeh NE Egypt site of early man 3/3
Qandahar (Kandahar)
Qasr Ibrim Upper Egypt fortress 21/1
Qatar sheikhdom of Persian Gulf 125/1
Qatna Syria Mesopotamia 20/2, 21/1
Qishan (Ch'i-shan)
Quadi Germanic tribe 30/3
Quanterness N Scotland megalithic tomb 14/3
Quban Upper Egypt fortress 21/1
Quebec city, E Canada capital of New France 67/3; captured by British 86/1; population 111/1
Quebec province, E Canada 164/5; joins Confederation 101/1; economic development 111/1
Quechua Andean Indian tribe of S America 63/1, 3
Queen Adelaide Province SE Africa 102/2
Queensland state of NE Australia 101/1, 113/1
Quelimane Mozambique Portuguese settlement 103/3
Quemoy *island* SE China Nationalist outpost 141/1, 149/1
Quentovic (*a/s* Quentowic) N France 34/4; Vikings 37/1
Querétaro state of C Mexico 97/1
Quetta Pakistan 105/3
Quiberon Bay W France ⚔ 87/1
Quierzy N France Frankish royal residence 34/4
Quilon S India early trade 59/3
Qui Nhon S Vietnam 1945-75 war 148/3
Quiriguá E Mexico Mayan site 12/2
Quito Ecuador Inca Empire 63/3, 68/2; colonised 69/3

Rabaul Papua New Guinea Japanese base in WW2 135/2
Rabbath Ammon (Amman)
Rabih's State C Africa 103/3
Radimichi W Russia E Slav tribe 44/1
Rae Bareli district of N India civil disobedience 104/4
Rafah (*anc.* Raphia) Sinai Egyptian-Israeli war 141/3
Raffles Bay N Australia settlement 113/1
Rages (Rai)
Ragusa (*now* Dubrovnik) W Yugoslavia Byzantine Empire 43/1; Venetian conquest 36/2; Reformation 75/1; Ottoman vassal republic 48/1
Rai (*anc.* Rhagae *Bibl.* Rages *Gr.* Europus) N Persia early archbishopric 39/1; Muslim conquest 41/1; Mongol conquest 46/1; early trade 58/3
Rainy Lake (Fort Pierre)
Rajasthan (*form.* Rajputana-Agency) state of N India 105/5
Rajputana region of NW India Mughal conquest 48/2; in alliance with Britain 105/3
Rajputana Agency (*now* Rajasthan) state of British India 105/3
Rakka (*anc.* Nicephorium) Syria 49/1
Raleigh E USA ⚔ 93/5
Ramesses III pharaoh 18T
Ramillies Belgium ⚔ 81/5
Ramla Palestine ⚔ 41/1
Ramsey E England Industrial Revolution 98/1
Ramshög S Sweden megalithic tomb 15/3
Rangiriri N Island, New Zealand ⚔ 112/3
Rangoon (*anc.* Dagon) Burma Buddhist site 27/1; early trade centre 71/2; occupied by Japanese 134/1; retaken by British 134/2
Rangpur NW India Harappan site 9/5
Ranians E Germany Slavonic tribe 54/2
Ranjit Singh territories of Lahore, NW India 104/1

Rann of Kutch region of W India boundary disputes with Pakistan 105/5, 141/1
Rapallo N Italy 1922 Conference 128/2
Raphanea Syria Roman Empire 25/2
Raphia (Rafah)
Ras Hafun Somalia Muslim colony 60/1
Ras Shamra (*anc.* Ugarit) Syria Mycenaean trade 18/2
Rataria Bulgaria early archbishopric 27/2
Ratisbon (*Ger.* Regensburg) S Germany ⚔91/1
Ravenna N Italy Roman Empire 24/2; early archbishopric 26/2; exarchate 42/1; captured by Venice 36/2; medieval city 56/3
Ravensberg N Germany Burgundian possession 73/3; county 79/1
Ravensbrück N Germany concentration camp 132/1
Reading S England Industrial Revolution 98/1
Reate (*mod.* Rieti) N Italy Roman Empire 30/1
Rechitsa W Russia town of Turov-Pinsk 45/2
Recife (Pernambuco)
Recuay early people of C Andes 12/4
Redarii N Germany Slav tribe 54/2
Redwood Ferry E USA ⚔95/2
Reformation 74-75
Regensburg (*anc.* Castra Regina *obs. Eng.* Ratisbon) S Germany bishopric 38/2, 79/1; Frankish royal residence 35/4
Reggio (*a/c* Reggio di Calabria *anc.* Rhegium) S Italy Norman conquest 36/2; Ottoman siege 48/2
Reggio (*a/c* Reggio Emilia *anc.* Regium Lepidum) N Italy Republican commune 56/3
Regina C Canada growth 111/1
Regium Lepidum (Reggio Emilia)
Reichenau S Germany monastery 34/4
Reii S France early bishopric 26/2
Reims (Rheims)
Remedello N Italy burial site 14/2
Remi (*mod.* Rheims) N France early bishopric 26/2
Rennes NW France 17C revolt 77/1; French Revolution 89/2
Rethel NE France independent fief 72/2
Réunion (*form.* Bourbon) *island* Indian Ocean French colony 101/2
Reval (*Russ.* Revel *mod. Est.* Tallinn) NW Russia German colonisation 54/4; Hanseatic city 59/2; Swedish Empire 77/3
Rewardashur Persia early archbishopric 27/2, 39/1
Rhaetia (*mod.* Switzerland) Roman province 30/3
Rhagae (*Per.* Rai *Bibl.* Rages *Gr.* Europus) N Persia Alexander's Empire 23/3
Rhegium (*mod.* Reggio di Calabria) N Italy Greek colony 19/4, 23/2; Roman Empire 24/2, 31/3
Rheims (*Fr.* Reims *anc.* Durocortorun *later* Remi) N France sacked by Vandals 37/1; archbishopric 34/4; ⚔91/1; industrial development 98/2; WW1 118/3; WW2 132/2
Rheinland (Rhineland)
Rhenish Prussia W Germany unification of Germany 115/2
Rhesaenae E Anatolia Roman Empire 25/2
Rhine, Confederation of the Napoleonic creation 91/1
Rhineland (*Ger.* Rheinland) region of W Germany remilitarised 128/2, 129/5
Rhode Island state of NE USA colony 67/3; Depression 131/2; population 111/5, 145/1
Rhodes (*mod. Gr.* Rodhos *Lat.* Rhodus *It.* Rodi) *island* SE Aegean in Mycenaean world 18/2; Greek state 19/4; archbishopric 27/2; ⚔41/1; under Knights of St John 49/1; Ottoman conquest 48/2. See also Dodecanese
Rhodesia (*form.* Southern Rhodesia, *now* Zimbabwe) British colony 101/2; independence (UDI) 138/1
Rhodus (*mod. Gr.* Rodhos *Eng.* Rhodes) *island* SE Aegean Roman Empire 24/2, 31/3
Ribe Denmark archbishopric 52/3
Rich Bar W USA mining site 94/1
Richmond N England rebellion against Henry VIII 73/4
Richmond E USA burned 93/5; industry 109/1, 110/2
Ricomagus (Riom)
Rieti (Reate)
Riga Latvia, NW USSR founded by Teutonic Knights 54/4; Hanseatic city 59/2; early trade 58/3; Swedish Empire 77/3; short-lived Communist control 121/2; WW2 133/2; industry 147/1
Rijkholt S Holland megalithic flint mine 15/3
Rimini (*anc.* Ariminum) N Italy Lombard League 32/4, 54/3; Signorial domination 56/3; WW2 133/2
Rio Barbate Spain ⚔40/1
Rio de Janeiro Brazil colonised 69/3; state 97/1; guerrilla activity 143/1
Rio de la Plata (*mod.* Argentina) early Spanish colony 69/3; vice-royalty in rebellion against Spain 88/1
Rio de Oro (*later* Spanish Sahara *now* Western Sahara) NW Africa Spanish colony 100/2, 103/3
Rio Grande do Norte state of N Brazil Confederation of the Equator 97/1
Rio Grande do Sul state of S Brazil 97/1
Riom (*anc.* Ricomagus) C France seat of intendant 80/1
Rio Muni (*a/c* Spanish Guinea *now* Equatorial Guinea) W Africa Spanish colony 102/5
Rio Negro state of W Brazil 97/1
Ripabianca C Italy farming site 15/1
Ripon N England Industrial Revolution 98/1
Rivoli N Italy ⚔91/1
Roc des Sers SW France Palaeolithic art 5/3
Rochdale N England Industrial Revolution 98/1
Rochefort W France naval base 80/1
Rochford E England Industrial Revolution 98/1
Rockhampton E Australia early settlement 113/1
Rocroi NE France ⚔74/4
Rodez region of S France 72/2
Rodhos (Rhodes)
Rodi (Rhodes)
Rogoźnica (Gross-Rosen)
Rogue River W USA ⚔94/2
Rohri N India Harappan site 9/5
Rojadi N India Harappan site 9/5
Roma (Rome)
Romagna region of N Italy unification of Italy 114/3
Romanelli S Italy Palaeolithic art 5/3
Roman Empire 24-25, 30-31
Romania on break-up of Ottoman Empire 116/1; independence 124/1; WW1 118-9; inter-war alliances 117/2, 128/1; acquisition of Transylvania 128/2; emigration of Hungarians and Turks 129/3; economic and socio-political development 131/3; WW2 132-3; Warsaw Pact and Comecon 137/2; end of Communist rule 137/4. See also Moldavia, Wallachia
Roman Republic 88/3
Rome (*anc.* Roma *It.* Roma) C Italy Celtic settlement 15/5; Roman Empire 24-25, 30-31; early trade 24/1; arrival of Christianity 26/1; economy under Empire 24/2; sack by Vandals and Visigoths 32/1; patriarchate 26/2; Jewish community 39/4; Magyar raid 37/1; papal patrimony 55/3; papal schism 57/6; 18C urban development 82/4; under French rule 90/1; annexed by Italy 114/3; WW2 133/2
Romeral SE Spain megalithic tomb 14/3
Romilly (-sur-Seine) N France French Revolution 89/2
Roncesvalles N Spain ⚔34/4
Roosebeke Belgium class unrest 57/1
Rosebud C USA ⚔95/2
Rostock N Germany Hanseatic city 59/2; WW1 119/3
Rostov (-on-Don) S Russia industry 147/1; WW1 132/1, 133/2
Rotomagus (*mod.* Rouen) N France Roman Empire 24/2; archbishopric 26/2
Rotterdam Netherlands industrial development 98/2; WW2 132-3
Rouad (Arwad)
Rouen (*anc.* Rotomagus) N France Scandinavian settlemennt 37/1; archbishopric 34/4; urban revolt 57/1; medieval fair 59/2; 18C financial centre 82/4; St Bartholomew Massacre 74/3; 16-17C revolts 77/2; *parlement* 80/1; French Revolution 89/2
Rough and Ready W USA mining site 94/1
Round Mountain C USA ⚔95/2
Roundway S England burial site 14/2
Roussillon region of S France acquired from Spain 72/1
Roxburgh county of S Scotland acquired by Edward III 56/4
Roxolani tribe of E Roman Empire 31/3
Royale, Ile (*now* Cape Breton Island) E Canada French settlement 67/3
Ruanda-Urundi (*now* Rwanda *and* Burundi) C Africa Belgian colony 101/2
Ruapekapeka N Island, New Zealand ⚔112/2
Ruffec C France French Revolution 89/2
Rugi Germanic tribe of E Europe 32/2
Ruhr region of NW Germany industrial expansion 99/2; occupied by French 128/2
Rumelia (*mod.* Bulgaria) Ottoman vassal state 49/1
Runnymede S England 53/6
Rupar N India Harappan site 9/5
Rupert House N Canada Hudson's Bay Company post 67/3
Rupert's Land region of N Canada Hudson's Bay Company 68/5, 69/3; British possession 67/3
Rusaddir (*mod.* Melilla) Morocco Roman Empire 30/3
Rush Creek C USA ⚔95/2
Russell N Island, New Zealand first capital 112/2
Russia (in Europe); Palaeolithic art 5/3; conversion to Christianity 38/2, 3; Jewish immigration 39/4; Kievan Russia 45/2; Mongol invasion 44/3, 46/1; Viking trade 44/1; Black Death 57/1; expansion 84-5; opposition to Napoleon 91/1; industrial revolution 99/2; expansion into Asia 84/2, 3; growth in armaments 117/3; 19C European alliances 117/2; 1905 Revolution 120/1; WW1 118-9; Revolution 121/2; Allied intervention 121/2; WW2 132-3. See also USSR and Russian Federation
Russia (in Asia) expansion 84/2, 3; acquisition of Maritime Province from China 107/4; 19C spheres of influence 101/2
Russian Federation free elections 137/4, 151/4
Ruthenia region of SW Ukraine acquired by Poland-Lithuania 56/2; incorporated into Czechoslovakia 128/2 occupied by Hungary 129/5
Rwanda (*form.* Ruanda) early state of C Africa 61/2; independence 138/1; political development 140/1; economy 150/1
Ryazan C Russia early bishopric 38/2; town of Murom-Ryazan 45/2; acquired by Muscovy 85/1; industry 147/1
Rye SE England Industrial Revolution 98/1
Rylsk C Russia town of Novgorod-Seversk 45/2
Ryojun (Port Arthur)
Ryukyu Islands (*f/c* Loochoo Islands) E China Sea acquired by Japan 127/3

Saaifontein (Zaayfontein)
Saar (*Ger.* Saarland *Fr.* Sarre) district of W Germany industrial development 98/2; League of Nations mandate and plebiscite 129/2
Saavedra Spanish explorer 64/2
Saba Dutch island of W Indies 66/4, 97/1
Sabah (*form.* British North Borneo) incorporated into Malaysia and claimed by Philippines 139/2
Sabini early tribe of C Italy 30/1
Sabrata (*a/c* Abrotonum) Libya Punic city 19/4; Roman Empire 24/2, 30/3; early bishopric 27/2
Saccopastore Italy site of early man 3/3
Sachsenhausen C Germany concentration camp 132/1
Sacramento City W USA mining site 94/1
Sadowa (*a/c* Königgrätz) Bohemia ⚔115/2
Saena Julia (Siena)
Safavid Empire Persia 49/1
Saga prefecture of W Japan 126/1, 2
Saguntum (*med.* Murviedro *mod.* Sagunto) E Spain Greek colony 18/4; Roman Empire 30/2, 3
Sahara region of N Africa trade routes 61/2
Sahel SE Asia landbridge 4/1
Sahel region of W Africa early settlement 11/1
Sa Huynh C Indo-China Iron Age site 8/3
Sai island of Upper Nile Egyptian fortress 21/1
Saïda (Sidon)
Saidor E New Guinea Allied landings in WW2 135/2
Saigon (*n/c* Ho Chi Minh) S Vietnam early trade centre 71/2; Japanese base in WW2 134/1; 1945-75 war 148/3
St. Albans (Verulamium)
St. Anthony Egypt monastery 38/1
St. Augustine (*form.* San Agostin) SE USA Spanish fort 86/1
St. Barthélemy W Indies French settlement 66/4
St. Bartholomew Massacre 74/3
St. Catherine, Cape W Africa Portuguese discovery 64/1
St. Césaire W France site of early man 3/3
St. Christopher *island* W Indies English settlement 66/4
St. Christopher and Nevis W Indies British colony 86/1, 97/1; 139/1 (inset)
St. Cirq SW France Palaeolithic art 5/3
St. Clair's Defeat NE USA ⚔95/2
St. Denis N France medieval fair 58/1, 59/2
Saint-Domingue (*now* Haiti) French colony 66/4, 69/3, 86/1
St. Eustatius *island* West Indies Dutch settlement 66/4; colony 97/1
St. Florentin C France French Revolution 89/2
St. Gallen Switzerland monastery 34/4
Ste. Geneviève C USA fur station 94/1
St. Helena *island* Atlantic British colony 100-101
St. Helens N England Industrial Revolution 98/1
St. Ives SW England medieval fair 58/1
St. James's Day Fight SE England English naval victory 81/3
St. Jean, Ile (*Eng.* Isle St. John *now* Prince Edward Island) E Canada French settlement 86/1
St. Jean-d'Acre (Acre)
St. John Novia Scotia growth 111/1
St. Joseph C USA fur station 94/1
St. Lawrence River E Canada exploration 64/2
St. Louis C USA fur station 94/1
St. Louis Senegal French settlement 61/2, 102/1, 103/3
St. Lucia *island* W Indies disputed between French and English 86/1; British colony 97/1; self-government 139/1 (inset)
St. Macarius Egypt monastery 38/1
St. Malo N France naval base 80/1
Ste. Marie Madagascar French settlement 87/2
St. Martin (*Dut.* Sint-Maarten) *island* West Indies French settlement 66/4; shared by French and Dutch 139/1 (inset)
St. Mary, Cape SW Africa Portuguese discovery 64/1
St. Michel-du-Touch France site 15/1
St. Mihiel NE France WW1 119/3 (inset)
St. Nazaire WW2 132/2
St. Neots C England Industrial Revolution 98/1
St. Omer N France medieval fair 58/1
Saintonge et Angoumois region of SW France under English rule 52/2
St. Pachomius Egypt monastery 38/1
St. Petersburg (*1914-24* Petrograd *1925-91* Leningrad) W Russia acquired by Muscovy 85/1; 18C urban development 82/4; founded 85/1
St. Pierre et Miquelon Newfoundland French colony 86/1, 100/2
St. Pol N France fief 72/2
St. Quentin NE France WW1 118/3 (inset)
St. Riquier N France monastery 34/4
St. Samuel Egypt monastery 38/1
St. Simeon Egypt monastery 38/1
St. Vincent *island* West Indies disputed by French and English 86/1; British colony 97/1; self-government 139/1 (inset)
Saipan *island* Marianas. C Pacific Japanese base in WW2 134/1, 135/2
Sais Lower Egypt Iron Age site 11/1

Saitama prefecture of C Japan 126/2
Saka Haumavarga C Asia satrapy of Achaemenid Empire 21/5
Sakas early people of W India 29/5
Sakata N Japan 126/2
Sakhalin (*Jap.* Karafuto) *island* Russ. Far East north acquired by Russia 84/3; south acquired by Japan 127/3; south reoccupied by Russia 135/2; claimed by Japan 141/1
Saksiny tribe of S Russia 45/2
Sala Morocco Roman Empire 30/1
Saladin Muslim conqueror 40/3
Salahiyeh (Dura-Europos)
Salamanca N Spain ⚔90/1
Salamantica (*a/c* Helmantica *mod.* Salamanca) N Spain Roman Empire 30/3
Salamis (*later* Constantia) Cyprus Greek colony 19/4; Roman Empire 31/3; archbishopric 27/2
Salamis C Greece ⚔20/5, 22/1
Salankayas people of SE India 29/5
Saldae (Bougie)
Salé N Morocco site of early man 3/3
Salekhard (Obdorsk)
Salem district of S India ceded to Britain 87/3
Salernum (*mod.* Salerno) S Italy Roman colony 30/1; Byzantine port 36/2
Salinelles SE France megalithic flint mine 15/3
Salisbury S England Industrial Revolution 98/1
Salisbury (*n/c* Harare) S Rhodesia 103/3
Salish House NW USA fur station 94/1
Salonae (*a/s* Salona) Albania Mithraic site 26/1; Roman Empire 24/2, 30/3; early archbishopric 27/2; Byzantine Empire 42/1
Salonika (*a/s* Salonica *a/c* Thessalonica *Gr.* Thessaloniki *Turk.* Selanik) N Greece bishopric 38/2; occupied by Ottomans 49/1; 18C urban development 83/4; WW1 119/3
Saltillo N Mexico early Spanish city 66/1
Salt Lake City W USA early trails 94/1
Salzburg Austria bishopric 34/4; archbishopric 38/2, 3, 79/1
Samara (*1935-91* Kuybyshev) C Russia founded 85/1; on railway to east 84/3; Bolshevik seizure 121/2
Samaria region of C Palestine 26/3
Samarkand (*anc.* Maracanda) C Asia on Silk Road 25/1; early archbishopric 39/1; Muslim conquest 41/1; Timur's Empire 47/4; early trade 59/3; Soviet Union 147/1
Samarobriva (Amiens)
Samarra N Mesopotamia early farming site 7/4
Samatata early state of E India 29/4, 5
Sambor Prei Kuk Cambodia Hindu-Buddhist temple 51/2
Sambre *river* NE France WW1 119/3 (inset)
Samoa *islands* S Pacific early settlement 10/2; German colony 101/2; annexed by US 111/4. See also Western Samoa
Samogitia (*Lith.* Žemaitija) region of NW Russia occupied by Teutonic Knights 54/4; by Lithuania 28/2, 56/2
Samory's Empire W Africa 103/3
Samos *island* Aegean Sea Greek parent state 19/4; bishopric 27/2
Samosata E Anatolia Roman Empire 25/2; Byzantine Empire 43/1
Samoyeds people of N Siberia 45/2, 84/2
Sampford Courtenay W England ⚔73/4
Samrong Sen Cambodia early site 8/3
Sana SW Arabia early bishopric 38/1
San Agostín (*now* St. Augustine) SE USA Spanish fort 66/1
San Antonio S USA early Catholic mission 94/1
San Antonio SE USA Spanish fort 86/1
San Candido (Aguntum)
Sanchi C India Buddhist site 27/1
San Cristóbal W Cuba Soviet missile base 149/5
Šandalja N Yugoslavia site of early man 3/3
Sand Creek C USA ⚔95/2
San Diego (*form.* San Diego de Alcalá) SW USA early Catholic mission 94/1
Sandinista revolt Nicaragua 143/1
Sandwich Islands (*now* Hawaii) C Pacific discovered 65/4
San Felipe S USA early Catholic mission 94/1
San Fernando Rey de España W USA early Catholic mission 94/1
San Francisco (*form.* San Francisco de Asis) W USA Spanish settlement 69/3; early Catholic mission 94/1
Sanga C Africa Iron Age site 11/1; tribe 60/1
San Gabriel Arcángel SW USA early Catholic mission 94/1
Sangela NW India Alexander's route 23/3
San Gimignano C Italy Republican commune 56/3
Sangiran Java site of early man 3/3
San José Magote C Mexico Olmec centre 12/2
San Juan del Puerto Rico W Indies Spanish fort 66/1
Sankt Peterburg (St. Petersburg)
San Lorenzo C Mexico Olmec centre 12/2
San Luis Obispo de Tolosa W USA early Catholic mission 94/1
San Luis Potosí state of C Mexico 97/1
Sansapur W New Guinea taken by Allies 135/2
San Sebastián N Spain Civil War 129/4
San Stefano, Treaty of 125/3
Santa Barbara W USA early Catholic mission 94/1
Santa Catarina state of S Brazil 97/1
Santa Cruz W USA early Catholic mission 94/1
Santa Cruz (*n/c* Ndeni) Solomon Islands WW2 ⚔135/2
Santa Fe SW USA on trail west 94/1
Santa Fé de Bogotá (*n/c* Bogotá) Colombia Spanish capital of New Granada 66/1
Santa Marta Colombia Spanish port 66/1
Santa Maura (Leucas)
Santander N Spain Civil War 129/4
Santa Rita E Mexico Mayan centre 12/2
Santa Severina S Italy Saracen occupation 37/1
Santiago Chile founded 66/1
Santiago de Compostela NW Spain bishopric 38/2
Santiago del Estero Argentina early settlement 66/1
Santimamiñe N Spain Palaeolithic art 5/3
Santo Domingo (*now* Dominican Republic) W Indies Spanish colony 66/1, 4; 69/3
Santorini (Thera)
Santuao E China treaty port 107/4
San Xavier del Bac SW USA early Catholic mission 94/1
São Jorge de Mina (Elmina)
São Paulo S Brazil state 97/1
São Tomé *island* W Africa Portuguese colony 103/3
São Tomé and Príncipe *islands* W Africa united as independent republic 138/1
Saracens invasion of S Europe 37/1
Saragossa (*anc.* Caesaraugusta *mod.* Zaragoza) N Spain bishopric 38/2; ⚔90/1; captured by French 90/1; Civil War 129/4
Sarai S Russia early trade 58/3. See also New Sarai, Old Sarai
Sarajevo C Yugoslavia captured by Ottomans 49/1; Ottoman administrative centre 49/1; WW1 119/3; WW2 132-3
Sarandib (Ceylon)
Saratoga NE USA ⚔92/1
Saratov C Russia founded 85/1; Bolshevik seizure 121/2
Sarawak country of N Borneo British protectorate 101/2; occupied by Japanese in WW2 134/1; incorporated into Malaysia 139/2
Sarcee plains Indian tribe of W Canada 63/1
Sardes (Sardis)
Sardica (Serdica)
Sardinia (*It.* Sardegna) *island* W Mediterranean Muslim conquest 40/1; Saracen attacks 37/1; Byzantine Empire 42/1; Pisan conquest 36/2; to Aragon 72/1; rebellion against Piedmont 88/3; Kingdom 114/3
Sardis (*a/s* Sardes) W Anatolia Alexander's route 22/3; Roman Empire 31/3; one of seven churches of Asia 27/2; Byzantine Empire 43/1
Sargon King of Akkad 16T
Sarkel S Russia ⚔44/1
Sarmatians (*Lat.* Sarmatae) tribe of Caucasus and S Russia 19/4, 31/3
Sarmizegetusa Romania Mithraic site 26/1; Roman Empire 31/3
Sarnath E India Buddhist site 27/1
Sarnowo Poland early site 6/2
Sarre (Saar)
Saruhan early emirate of W Anatolia 49/1
Sasanian Empire Western Asia 29/5
Sasebo W Japan 126/2
Saskatchewan province of C Canada economic growth 111/1
Saskatoon C Canada growth 111/1
Satala NE Anatolia Roman Empire 25/2, 31/3; early archbishopric 27/2
Satara district of W India 104/4, 105/3
Satavahana ancient kingdom of India 29/4
Satricum C Italy Latin colony 30/1
Satsuma old province of W Japan 126/1
Saturnia N Italy Roman colony 30/1
Saudi Arabia Kingdom of Arabia 140/1, 149/1, 151/4
Sauk Indian tribe of C USA 63/1
Sault Ste. Marie C Canada French fort 67/3, 86/1
Saumurois region of W France 52/2
Savannah SE USA evacuated 92/5
Savenay NW France French Revolution 89/2
Savignano N Italy Palaeolithic art 5/3
Savoy (*Fr.* Savoie *It.* Savoia) region of France/Italy medieval state 55/3; Calvinism 75/1; annexed by France 88/3; ceded to France 114/3
Saxon March 34/4
Saxons Germanic tribe of NW Europe 34/4, 32/1
Saxony region of N Germany conversion to Christianity 38/3; Frankish Empire 34/4; medieval German Empire 55/1, 3; Black Death 57/1; Wettin territory 72/1; Reformation 75/1; Electorate and Duchy 79/1; unification of Germany 98/3
Say W Africa occupied by French 102/1, 103/3
Sayda (Sidon)
Saylac (Zeila)
Saylan (Ceylon)
Sayn country of C Germany 79/1
Scandia (*mod.* Scandinavia) region of N Europe 30/3
Scandinavia (*anc.* Scandia) Viking invasions of Europe 37/1. See also Denmark, Sweden, Norway
Scania (*Sw.* Skåne) region of S Sweden acquired from Denmark 77/3
Scapa Flow N Scotland WW1 118/3
Scarborough N England WW1 118/3
Scarpanto (Carpathos)
Schism, Great (Western) 56T, 57/6
Schlesien (Silesia)
Schleswig (*Dan.* Slesvig) S Denmark bishopric 52/3; Reformation 75/1
Schleswig-Holstein region of N Germany unification of Germany 98/3, 115/2
Schlieffen Plan WW1 118T, 119/2
Schooneveld I and II S North Sea Dutch naval victories 81/3
Schouten and Le Maire explorers 64/2
Schwaben (Swabia)
Schwarzburg county of E Germany 79/1
Schwarzerden W Germany Mithraic site 26/1
Schweizerbild Switzerland Palaeolithic art 5/3
Schwerin N Germany WW1 119/3
Schwyz Switzerland original canton 54/5
Scodra (*mod.* Shkodër *It.* Scutari) Albania Roman Empire 31/3
Scone S Scotland Edward I's campaign 53/6; Civil War 76/4
Scotland (*anc.* Caledonia) Scandinavian settlement 37/1; Anglo-Scottish wars 56/4; Black Death 57/1; acquires Shetland, Orkney and Hebrides 72/1; Reformation 75/1; in English Civil War 76/4
Scots 31/1
Scots Celtic tribe of N Ireland 52/2
Scupi (*mod.* Skoplje *Mac.* Skopje *Turk.* Üsküb) early archbishopric 27/2; Byzantine Empire 43/1
Scutari (*mod.* Shkodër *anc.* Scodra) Albania conquered by Ottomans 49/1
Scythia ancient country of C Asia 23/3
Scythians ancient tribe of S Russia 19/4, 22/3
Scythopolis N Palestine city of Decapolis 26/3
SEATO 148T
Seattle NW USA ⚔ 94/2
Sebaste Palestine bishopric 27/2; town of Judaea 26/3
Sebastopol (*Russ.* Sevastopol) Crimea. S Russia 1905 Revolution 120/1; WW1 119/3; WW2 132-3
Sebta (Ceuta)
Sech S Ukraine 85/1
Sedan N France ⚔115/2; WW1 119/2; WW2 132/1
Segesta Sicily ally of Athens 23/2
Segontia (*a/c* Segontium *mod.* Caenarvon) Wales Mithraic site 26/1; Roman Empire 30/3
Ségou (*Eng.* Segu) French Sudan 102/1, 103/3
Segovia C Spain Roman Empire 30/3
Segu (*Fr.* Ségou) early city-state of W Africa 61/2
Seibal E Mexico Mayan centre 12/2
Seila Lower Egypt pyramid 17/3
Seistan (*a/s* Sistan) province of E Parsia Muslim conquest 41/1
Selangor state of Malaya 71/5
Selanik (Salonika)
Seleucia (*a/c* Veh-Ardashir) Mesopotamia early trade 24/1
Seleucia (*a/c* Seleucia Tracheotis) SE Anatolia early archbishopric 27/2; Byzantine Empire 43/1
Seleucia-Ctesiphon Mesopotamia early trading centre 25/1; early patriarchate 27/2, 39/1
Seleucian Theme S Anatolia province of Byzantine Empire 42/2
Seleucid Kingdom Anatolia-Persia 22/4
Selinus (*mod.* Selinunte) Sicily Greek colony 19/4, 23/2
Seljuks Turkish Muslim dynasty of Middle East 41/2, 43/3, 46/3
Selkirk county of C Scotland acquired by Edward III 56/4
Selymbria SE Europe Greek colony 19/4; Byzantine Empire 43/1
Semendre (*mod.* Smederevo) N Serbia conquered by Ottomans 49/1
Semgallen (*obs. Eng.* Semigallia) region of NW Russia occupied by Teutonic Knights 54/4
Seminole Indian tribe of SE USA 95/2
Semipalatinsk S Siberia founded 84/2
Semna Upper Egypt fortress 21/1
Sempach C Switzerland ⚔54/5
Sena Mozambique Portuguese settlement 61/2
Sendai N Japan 126/2
Senegal W Africa French colony 100/2, 101/2, 103/3; independence 138/1; economy 150/1
Senegambia region of W Africa source of slaves 61/2
Sennar Sudan early town 61/2
Sennones early people of N Italy 30/1
Sens NE France archbishopric 34/4
Seoul (*Jap.* Keijo) S Korea Russo-Japanese war 127/4; Korean war 148/2; population 151/1
Sepphoris town of Judaea 26/3
Septimania ancient region of S France, part of Frankish Empire 34/4
Serbia (*now part of* Yugoslavia) country of SE Europe conversion to Christianity 38/2; Byzantine Empire 43/3; Mongol invasion 46/2; empire under Stephen Dushan 56/2; Black Death 57/1; Ottoman province 49/1; independence 116/1, 124/1; industrial development 98/2; WW1 118-9; forms part of Yugoslavia 129/2; WW2 133/2
Serbs Slav tribe of SE Europe 32/2, 33/5
Serdica (*a/s* Sardica *mod.* Sofia) Bulgaria Mithraic site 26/1; Roman Empire 24/2, 31/3; early archbishopric 27/2; Byzantine Empire 43/1
Serpukhov C Russia town of Muscovy 85/1

Sesamus (*later* Amastris) N Anatolia Greek colony 19/4
Sesebi Upper Egypt fortress 21/1
Sesheko S Africa on Livingstone's route 102/1
Sestus SE Europe Greek colony 19/4; Roman Empire 24/2
Settiva Corsica megalithic tomb 15/3
Sevastopol (*Eng.* Sebastopol *med. Turk.* Akhtiar) Crimea acquired by Muscovy 85/1
Severyanye E Slav tribe of S Russia, 44/1
Seville (*Sp.* Sevilla *anc.* Hispalis) S Spain Emirate of Cordoba 37/1; reconquered from Muslims 37/4; 18C urban development 82/4; Civil War 129/4
Sèvres, Treaty of 125/3
Seychelles *islands* Indian Ocean captured from French 87/2; British colony 101/2
Shaba (Katanga)
Shaheinab Sudan early site 11/1
Shahr-i Sokhta C Persia early urban settlement 16/1
Shama W Africa Dutch settlement 60/2 (inset)
Shanghai E China treaty port 107/4; Nationalist control 123/3; occupied by Japanese 127/5; industry 123/4
Shanidar Persia site of early man 3/3
Shannan Hsitao C China T'ang province 50/1
Shannan Tungtao C China T'ang province 50/1
Shansi province of N China Ming province 51/4; Manchu expansion 106/1; Taiping northern expedition 107/3; 1911 revolution 122/1; warlord control 122/2
Shan State(s) Burma annexed by British 104/2; part of India 105/3
Shantung province of E China under Ming 51/4; Manchu expansion 106/1; 1911 revolution 122/1; Japanese influence 123/3; warlord control 122/2
Sharm-el-Sheikh S Sinai Egyptian-Israeli war 141/3
Sharon SE USA ⚔ 95/4
Sharpsburg (*a/c* Antietam) E USA ⚔ 93/5
Sharqat (Ashur)
Shavante forest Indian tribe of NE Brazil 63/1
Shawnee Indian tribe of E USA 63/1
Shawnee Trail C USA cattle trail 94/1
Shechem Palestine ancient capital 21/2
Sheffield N England Industrial Revolution 98/1
Shefford C England Industrial Revolution 98/1
Shen C China Western Chou domain 9/6
Shensi province of N China under Ming 51/4; Manchu expansion 106/1; 1911 revolution 122/1
Shetland (*form.* Hjaltland) NE Scotland Norwegian settlement 37/1; acquired by Scotland 72/1
Shiga prefecture of C Japan 126/2
Shih-lou (*a/s* Shilou) N China Shang burial site 8/4
Shihr S Arabia early Chinese trade 58/3
Shikoku island of SW Japan 126/1, 2
Shillong NE India capital of Assam 105/3
Shiloh (*a/c* Pittsburgh Landing) SE USA ⚔ 92/5
Shilou (Shih-lou)
Shilsk SE Siberia founded 84/2
Shimane prefecture of W Japan 126/2
Shimazu clan of W Japan 51/3
Shimonoseki W Japan
Shipibo forest Indian tribe of S America 63/1
Shipurla (Lagash)
Shiraz S Persia trade 59/3
Shizuoka (*form.* Sumpu) C Japan 126/2
Shkodër (Scodra, Scutari)
Shoa tribe of Ethiopia 103/3
Shongweni S Africa Stone Age site 11/1
Shoshone Indian tribe of NW USA 63/1
Shrewsbury W England Industrial Revolution 98/1
Shu SE China Western Chou domain 9/6
Shubat-Enlil (Chagar Bazar)
Shuo-fang N China Han commanderie 29/3
Shu Pa state of E China conquered by Ch'in 28/1
Shuruppak (*mod.* Fara) Mesopotamia Sumerian site 16/2
Shuswap plateau Indian tribe of W Canada 63/1
Sialk Persia 16/1, 17/4
Siam (*now* Thailand) spread of Buddhism 27/1, 70/1; conquests 71/2; under Japanese influence 127/5; occupied by Japanese 134/2
Sian N China early trade 59/3
Siberia Russian expansion 84/2, 3; industrial development 147/1; labour camps 147/1
Sicca Veneria (*mod.* Le Kef) Tunisia Roman Empire 30/3; early bishopric 27/2
Sicily (*Lat. and It.* Sicilia) *island* C Mediterranean Mycenaean trade 18/2; Greek colonisation 19/4; Muslim conquest 36/2; Saracen raids 37/1; Byzantine Empire 42/1; German attacks 55/3. Norman conquest 36/2; to Aragon 72/1; to Savoy 81/5. Kingdom of the Two Sicilies annexed to Piedmont/Sardinia 114/3; WW2 133/2
Sidama Kingdoms E Africa 103/3
Side S Anatolia Greek colony 19/4; Roman Empire 25/2
Sidi Abderrahman Morocco site of early man 3/3
Sidi Barrani Egypt WW2 132/1
Sidon (*mod.* Saïda *Ar.* Sayda) Lebanon Mycenaean trade 18/2; Assyrian Empire 20/3; Phoenician city 19/4; Levantine city 21/1; Alexander's route 22/3, early bishopric 27/2; Crusades 40/3
Siena (*anc.* Saena Julia) N Italy medieval German Empire 55/3; Republican commune 56/3
Sierra Leone country of W Africa Portuguese exploration 64/1; British settlement 103/3; British colony 100/2, 101/1; independence 138/1; economy 150/1
Siirt (Tigranocerta)
Sijilmassa Morocco trans-Saharan trade 58/3
Sikhs people of N India 105/3
Sikkim country of Himalayas British protectorate 107/4 dependency of India 105/3; annexed to India 139/1
Silesia (*Ger.* Schlesien *Pol.* Śląsk) region of Germany/Poland acquired by Poland 52/1; medieval German Empire 55/3; acquired by Habsburgs 56/2, conquered by Prussia 78/2, 3; unification of Germany 115/2; divided between Germany and Poland 129/2
Silistria (*Bulg.* Silistra *anc.* Durostorum) Bulgaria Ottoman control 49/1
Silla *Eng.* Korea *Kor.* Koryo) occupied by T'ang 50/1
Simbirsk (*since 1924* Ulyanovsk) C Russia acquired by Muscovy 85/1; industry 147/1
Simferopol (*early Turk.* Ak Mechet) Crimea acquired by Muscovy 85/1; Bolshevik seizure 121/2
Simhala (Ceylon)
Sinai Egyptian-Israeli war 141/3
Sinaloa state of N Mexico 97/1
Sind province of NW India Muslim expansion 41/4, Mughal conquest 48/2; British rule 104-5; joins Pakistan on partition 105/5
Sindhia Maratha state of N India 87/3
Singapore (*earlier* Tumasik) S Malaya British possession 71/5; early trade 71/2; occupied by Japanese 134/1; independence 139/1, 2; economy 150/1
Singara Mesopotamia Roman Empire 25/2, 31/3
Singhasari early state of Java 51/2
Singidunum (*mod.* Belgrade) Roman Empire 24/2, Byzantine Empire 43/1
Sinkiang province of NW China early trade 25/1; part of Han Empire 106/1; cession of territory to Russia 107/4
Sinope (*mod.* Sinop) N Anatolia Greek colony 19/4; Roman Empire 25/2, 31/3; early bishopric 27/2; Byzantine Empire 43/1
Sint-Maarten (*Fr.* St. Martin) *island* W Indies shared by French and Dutch 139/1 (inset)
Sinuessa C Italy Roman colony 30/1
Sion Switzerland megalithic tomb 15/3
Sioux plains Indian tribe of C USA 63/1
Sipontum S Italy Roman colony 30/1
Sippar N Mesopotamia early city 16/2, 17/4
Siracusa (Syracuse)
Siraf Persia early trade 59/3
Sirionó Indian tribe of S America 63/1
Sirmien (Syrmia)
Sirmium (*mod.* Sremska Mitrovica) Yugoslavia Roman Empire 24/2, 30/3; early bishopric 27/2
Siscia (*mod.* Sisak) Yugoslavia Roman Empire 31/3
Sitagroi-Fotolivos NE Greece early settlement 14/2
Sitifis Algeria Roman Empire 30/3
Siti River C Russia ⚔ 44/3
Sivas E Anatolia early emirate 49/1; Ottoman centre 48/2
Siwa Egypt Muslim trade 58/3
Skåne (*Eng.* Scania) region of S Sweden under Danish rule 53/3
Skanör S Sweden medieval fair 59/2
Skopje, Skoplje (Üsküb)
Skudra region of SE Europe satrapy of Achaemenid Empire 20/5
Śląsk (Silesia)
Slave Coast W Africa 61/2
Slavkov (Austerlitz)
Slavonia province of early Hungarian kingdom 78/3
Slavs movement in Europe 32/2; expansion 32/5
Sleaford E England Industrial Revolution 98/1
Slesvig (Schleswig)
Slim Buttes N USA ⚔ 95/2
Slovakia prehistoric metal-working 14/2; short-lived Soviet republic 120/3; forms part of Czechoslovakia 128/2; occupied by Hungary in WW2 132/1; independence 137/4
Slovenes Slav tribe of S Europe 32/2
Slovenia and Yugoslavia 128/2; independence 137/4
Sluys (*n/s* Sluis *Fr.* Ecluse) Netherlands ⚔ 56/5
Smaldings Slave tribe of E Europe 54/2
Smederevo (Semendre)
Smolensk W Russia bishopric 38/2; Hanseatic trade 59/2; captured by Napoleon 91/1; Bolshevik seizure 121/2; (principality) 45/2; acquired by Lithuania 56/2; industry 147/1
Smyrna (*mod.* Izmir) W Anatolia Roman Empire 31/3; one of seven churches of Asia 27/2; Byzantine Empire 49/1; Ottoman Empire 49/1; Greek occupation 125/3, 129/2
Snaketown USA early site 12/3
Soba Sudan monastery 38/1; early town 60/1
Sobibor Poland concentration camp 132/1
Society Islands (*Fr.* Iles de la Société) S Pacific Polynesian settlement 10/2; European discovery 65/4; French colony 139/1 (inset)
Soča (Isonzo)
Socotra *island* Arabian Sea early bishopric 38/1; acquired by Britain 101/2
Soerabaja (Surabaya)
Soest W Germany Hanseatic city 59/2
Sofala Mozambique early trade 66/2; Portuguese settlement 61/2
Sofia (*anc.* Serdica *a/s* Sardica *med.* Sredets) Bulgaria Ottoman control 49/1; 18C urban development 82/4; Communist uprising 120/3; WW2 133/2
Sogabe clan territory of W Japan 51/3
Sogdiana (*a/c* Sogdia, Suguda) ancient region of C Asia limit of Alexander's Empire 23/3; Chinese protectorate 50/1
Sogdian Rock C Asia besieged by Alexander 23/3
Söğüt NW Anatolia Ottoman centre 49/1
Soissons N France monastery 34/4; WW1 119/2
Sokoto N Nigeria city and sultanate 60-61; occupied by British 103/3
Soleb Upper Egypt fortress 21/1
Sole Bank E England Dutch naval victory 81/3
Solferino N Italy ⚔ 114/3
Soli SE Anatolia Greek colony 19/4
Solms former county of C Germany 79/1
Solomon Islands SW Pacific British protectorate 101/1 (inset); occupied by Japanese 134/1; retaken by Allies 135/2; independence 139/1 (inset)
Solovetskiy N Russia monastery 38/2
Somali people of NE Africa 60-61
Somalia (*form.* British and Italian Somaliland) independence 138/1; political development 140/1; economy 150/1
Somme *river* NE France WW1 offensive 119/3 (inset)
Songhay early empire of W Africa 60/2
Sonora Pass W USA 94/1
Soochow E China in Ch'ing economy 107/2; treaty port 107/4; industry 123/4
Sopatma S India trading port 25/1
Sopron (*Ger.* Ödenburg) Hungary Hallstatt site 15/6; to Hungary after plebiscite 129/2
Sora C Italy Latin colony 30/1
Sorbs Slavic tribe of C Europe 33/5, 34/4, 54/2
Soshangane tribe of SE Africa 102/2
Sotho tribe of S Africa 102/2
Sotka-Koh NW India Harappan site 9/5
Sousse (*anc.* Hadrumetum) Tunisia Ottoman Empire 124/1
South Africa Union 101/2; immigration from Europe and India 109/2; Republic 138/1; political development 140/1
Southampton S England Industrial Revolution 98/1; WW2 132/1
South Arabia (South Yemen)
South Australia settlement and development 101/1, 113/1
South Carolina state of SE USA colony 67/3, 92/1; Civil War 93/5; Depression 131/2; population 111/5, 145/1
South Dakota state of N USA Depression 131/2; population 111/5, 145/1
South-East Asia early civilisations 8/3; Mongol attacks 51/2; 1511-1826 70-71; post 1945 conflicts 141/1, 148/1, 3
Southern Rhodesia (*now* Zimbabwe *f/c* Rhodesia) British colony 101/2, 103/3
South Island (*Maori* Te Waipounamu) New Zealand settlement and development 112/2
Southland province of S Island, New Zealand 112/2
South Moluccas E Indonesia republic suppressed 139/2
South Ossetian AR Caucasus 146/2
South Tyrol (*Ger.* Südtirol *It.* Alto Adige) region of Austro-Hungarian Empire acquired by Italy 128/2
South Vietnam independence 139/1; war 148/3. See also Vietnam, Indo-China
South West Africa (Namibia)
South Yemen (*also called* People's Democratic Republic of Yemen *form.* Federation of South Arabia *earlier* Protectorate of South Arabia *earlier* Aden Protectorate) independence 138/1; political development 140/1; economy 150/1; union with north Yemen 138/1
Soviet Union (USSR)
Sowerby Bridge N England Industrial Revolution 98/1
Sozopol (Apollonia)
Spa Belgium 1920 Conference 128/2
Spain (*anc.* Hispania) Palaeolithic art 5/3; prehistoric metal-working 14/2; Celtic penetration 15/5; early invasions 32/1; conversion to Christianity 38/2; Jewish migrations 39/4; Muslim conquest 41/1; Umayyad caliphate 40/2; Reconquista 37/4; Union of Castile and Aragon 72/1; Habsburg possession 72/1; voyages of discovery 64-5; overseas expansion 66-69; overseas settlements 66/4; colonisation of America 86/1; Reformation 75/1; War of the Spanish Succession 81/5; opposition to Napoleon 90/1; colonial empire 88/1; 19C alliances 117/2; 20C socio-political change 131/3; Civil War 129/4; US bases 149/1; economy 98/2, 150/1
Spalato (*anc.* Spalatum *mod.* Split) Yugoslavia Byzantine Empire 43/1
Spalding E England Industrial Revolution 98/1
Spalding's Mission NW USA 94/1
Spanish-American War 111T
Spanish Guinea (*now* Equatorial Guinea) W Africa colony 101/1
Spanish March 34/4
Spanish Sahara (*a/c* Western Sahara *includes* Rio de Oro) NW Africa Spanish colony 103/3; partition between Morocco and Mauritania 138/1, 140/1; economy 150/1
Spanish Succession, War of the 80T, 81/5
Sparda (*Lat.* Lydia) region of W Anatolia satrapy of Achaemenid Empire 20/5
Sparta (*a/c* Lacedaemon) S Greece Mycenaean palace site 19/1; Peloponnesian War 23/2; Roman Empire 24/2, 31/3
Spartalos N Greece ⚔ 23/2
Spasinou Charax Mesopotamia town of Achaemenid Empire 21/5
Sphacteria S Greece ⚔ 23/2

Spice Islands (Moluccas)
Spiennes NE France megalithic flint mine 15/3
Spion Kop S Africa ⚔ 103/4
Spirit Cave N Siam early site 8/3
Spiro S USA Mississippian site 12/3
Split (Spalato)
Spokane House NW USA fur station 94/1
Spoletium (*mod.* Spoleto) N Italy Latin colony 30/1; Dukedom 42/1
Spotsylvania E USA ⚔ 93/5
Spy Belgium site of early man 3/3
Sredets (Sofia, Serdica)
Sredne-Kolymsk NE Siberia founded 84/2
Srem (Syrmia)
Sri Ksetra S Burma Hindu-Buddhist remains 51/2
Sri Lanka (Ceylon)
Srinagar N India capital of Kashmir political disturbance 104/4; 105/3
Srivijaya E Indies early empire 51/2
Stabroek (*now* Georgetown) Guyana Dutch settlement 66/4
Staffarda N Italy ⚔ 81/4
Stafford C England Industrial Revolution 98/1
Stalin (Varna)
Stalin, Joseph 146T
Stalinabad (Dushanbe)
Stalingrad (*until 1925* Tsaritsyn *since 1961* Volgograd) S Russia WW2 132-3
Stalino (Donetsk)
Stalinsk (Novokuznetsk)
Stamford C England Viking base 37/1; Industrial Revolution 98/1
Stanley, Sir Henry Morton African exploration 102/1
Stanleyville (*now* Kisangani) S Belgian Congo Congo crisis 138/4
Starčevo Yugoslavia early site 15/1
Stargard E Germany Hanseatic trade 59/2
Stavanger S Norway WW2 132/1
Stavropol (*1940-44* Voroshilovsk) S Russia industry 147/1
Stavropol (Tolyatti)
Stębark (Tannenberg)
Steiermark (Styria)
Steinheim Germany site of early man 3/3
Stentinello Sicily farming site 15/1
Steptoe Butte NW USA ⚔ 94/2
Sterkfontein S Africa site of early man 3/3
Stettin (*now* Szczecin) N Poland Hanseatic city 59/2; Swedish Empire 77/3; WW2 133/2
Stillman's Defeat N USA ⚔ 95/2
Stirling Bridge C Scotland ⚔ 56/4
Stobi S Yugoslavia Roman Empire 31/3; early archbishopric 27/2
Stockholm Sweden Hanseatic city 59/2; 18C urban development 82/4; in Swedish Empire 77/3
Stockport N England Industrial Revolution 98/1
Stockstadt W Germany Mithraic site 26/2
Stoke-on-Trent C England Industrial Revolution 98/1
Stone Tower C Asia on Silk Road 25/1
Stony Lake N USA ⚔ 95/2
Stormberg S Africa ⚔ 103/4
Stourbridge W England medieval fair 59/2; Industrial Revolution 98/1
Stowmarket England Industrial Revolution 98/1
Stralsund N Germany Hanseatic city 59/2
Strasbourg (*Ger.* Strassburg *anc.* Argentoratum) E France centre of French Revolution 79/2; industrial development 98/2
Strassburg (*Fr.* Strasbourg) SW Germany royal mint 54/1; medieval fair 59/2; 18C urban development 82/4; Reformation 75/1; gained by France 81/2; bishopric 79/1; WW1 119/3
Stratford-on-Avon C England Industrial Revolution 98/1
Strathclyde N Britain medieval kingdom 33/3, 38/3
Stratonicea W Anatolia Roman Empire 31/3
Stresa N Italy 1935 Conference 128/2
Stuttgart S Germany industrial development 98/1; WW2 132/1
Stutthof (*now Pol.* Sztutowo) NE Germany concentration camp 132/1
Styria (*Ger.* Steiermark) province of SE Austria medieval German Empire 55/1, 3; acquired by Habsburgs 56/2; Duchy 79/1
Suakin E Sudan Ottoman settlement 61/2
Suceava (Suczawa)
Suczawa (*n/s* Suceava) Romania under Ottoman control 49/1
Sudan region of N Africa 60-61
Sudan (*form.* Anglo-Egyptian Sudan) Mahdist state 103/3; British control 124/1; Anglo-Egyptian condominium 103/3; independence 138/1, 140/1; economy 150/1
Sudbury E England Industrial Revolution 98/1
Sudbury NE USA ⚔ 95/4
Sudetenland C Europe German annexation 129/5
Suebi (Sueves)
Suessa Aurunca (*mod.* Sessa Aurunca) C Italy Latin colony 30/1
Sueves (*Lat.* Suebi) early tribe of SW Europe 32/2, 34/1
Suez (*Ar.* As Suways) N Egypt Egyptian-Israeli war 140/3
Suez Canal N Egypt opening 109/4; Egyptian-Israeli war 141/3; Anglo-French attack 140/1
Su-fu-t'un NE China Shang burial site 8/4
Sugambri early tribe of NW Europe 30/3
Suguda (*a/c* Sogdia *or* Sogdiana) C Asia satrapy of Achaemenid Empire 21/5
Suhar E Arabia Muslim conquest 41/1
Sui C China Western Chou domain 9/6
Suifen NE China treaty port 107/4
Suiyuan former province of N China 123/3
Sukhothai C Thailand Buddhist site 27/1; major political centre 51/2
Sukhum-Kale (*mod.* Sukhumi *anc.* Dioscurias) Caucasus conquered by Russia 85/1
Sulawesi (Celebes)
Suleiman Ottoman ruler 48T
Sumatra (*Indon.* Sumatera) E Indies spread of Buddhism 27/1; Muslim expansion 40/5; early sites 8/3; early trade 59/3; Dutch possession 101/2; occupied by Japanese 134/1
Sumba island of E Indies occupied by Japanese 134/1
Sumer Mesopotamia 17/2, 3
Sumerians ancient people of Mesopotamia 16/2, 17/3
Sunda SE Asia landbridge 4/1
Sunda Kalapa (*mod.* Jakarta) Java Islamic town 70/1
Sunderland NE England Industrial Revolution 98/1
Sung N China Chou domain 9/6; warring state 28/1
Sungchou C China T'ang prefecture 50/1
Sung Empire China conquered by Mongols 47/1, 3
Sungir N Russia site of early man 3/3; Palaeolithic art 5/3
Sungkiang E China British attack 107/3
Süntel N Germany ⚔ 34/4
Sun Yat-sen Chinese president 122T
Suomussalmi C Finland WW2 132/1
Surabaya (*Dut.* Soerabaja) Java trading centre 71/2; occupied by Japanese 134/1
Surakarta district of Java Dutch control 71/2
Surashtra early state of W India 29/4
Surat NW India Mughal port 59/3; Ottoman siege 48/2; industry 105/3
Surgut W Siberia founded 84/2
Surinam (*Dut.* Surinam *form.* Dutch Guiana) country of S America 142-3
Susa SW Persia early urban settlement 16/2, 17/4; Assyrian Empire 20/2, 3; Alexander's route 22/3; Persian Royal Road 21/5
Susiana (*a/c* Elam *mod.* Khuzistan) region of SW Persia province of Alexander's Empire 22/3
Susquehanna Indian tribe of NE USA 63/1
Sussex early kingdom of S England 35/3, 38/3
Sutkagan-Dor NW India Harappan site 9/5
Sutrium N Italy Latin colony 30/1
Suvar E Russia early town 45/2
Suzdal C Russia town of Vladimir-Suzdal 45/2
Sverdlovsk (*until 1924 and again from 1991* Yekaterinburg) C Russia industry 147/1
Swabia (*Ger.* Schwaben) region of S Germany province of medieval German Empire 55/1, 3
Swakopmund SW Africa German settlement 103/3
Swanscombe England site of early man 3/3
Swansea S Wales Industrial Revolution 98/1
Swartkrans S Africa site of early man 3/3
Swatow S China treaty port 107/4; Japanese occupation 127/5
Swaziland country of SE Africa British protectorate 101/1, 103/4; independence 138/1; economy 150/1
Sweden conversion to Christianity 38/2; Viking expansion 37/1; emergence as a state 53/5; Black Death 57/1; Union of Kalmar 72/1; Reformation 75/1; empire in the Baltic 77/3; losses to Russia and Prussia 114/4; industry 98/2; loss of Denmark and Norway 114/4; 20C economic and socio-political development 131/3; EFTA 137/2; economy 150/1
Swift Creek / Santa Rosa Group early Indians of USA 12/3
Swindon W England Industrial Revolution 98/1
Swiss Confederation (*a/c* Helvetia) formation 54/5
Switzerland medieval cantons 54/5; Reformation 75/1; Industrial Revolution 98/2; neutral in WW1 118/1; EFTA 137/2; economy 150/1; neutral in WW2 132/1
Sybaris S Italy Greek colony 19/4
Sydney SE Australia founded 113/1; Allied base in WW2 135/2
Sydney Nova Scotia growth 111/1
Syene (*mod.* Aswan) Upper Egypt 38/1
Sykes-Picot Agreement 125/3
Syktyvkar (*until 1930* Ust-Sysolsk) N Russia industry 147/1
Sylhet district of Bengal votes to join Pakistan 105/5
Synnada W Anatolia early archbishopric 27/2; Byzantine Empire 43/1
Syracusa (*a/s* Syracusae *mod.* Siracusa *Eng.* Syracuse) Sicily Greek colony 19/4; Roman Empire 24/2, 31/3; ⚔ 31/2; bishopric 27/2; Byzantine Empire 43/1; Norman conquest 36/2
Syria earliest settlements 7/2; centre of ancient civilisations 16-17; Mitannian cities 21/1; at time of Alexander 22/3; expansion of Christianity 38/1; Arab conquest 41/1; Ottoman province 124/1; WW1 125/2; French control 125/3; WW2 132/1; independence 138/1; war with Israel 141/3; economy 150/1
Syriam S Burma early trade centre 71/2
Syrmia (*S. Cr.* Srem *Hung.* Szerém *Ger.* Sirmien) district of Austria-Hungary *now part of* Serbia WW1 119/3
Syzran C Russia founded 84/2
Szczecin (Stettin)
Szechwan province of W China under Ming 51/4; Manchu expansion 106/1; Taiping rebellion 107/3; politically fragmented 122/2; Nationalist control 123/3
Szemao SW China treaty town 107/4
Szerém (Syrmia)
Sztutowo (Stutthof)

Taanach N Palestine Levantine city 21/1
Tabasco state of S Mexico 97/1
Tabennesis Egypt monastery 38/1
Tabert Algeria Arab conquest 40/1
Tábor Moravia Hussite centre 57/1
Tabora E Africa Livingstone's travels 20/1
Tabriz NW Persia early archbishopric 39/1; occupied by Mongols 46/1; early trade 58/3; conquered by Ottomans 48/2, 49/1
Tabun Israel site of early man 3/3
Tadcaster N England Industrial Revolution 98/1
Tadmekka NW Africa early town 60-61
Tadmor (Palmyra)
Taegu S Korea 1950-53 war 148/2
Taejon S Korea 1950-53 war 148/2
Taganrog Crimea acquired by Muscovy 85/1; industry 85/4; 1905 Revolution 120/1
Taghaza NW Africa trans-Saharan trade 60-61
Tagliacozzo C Italy ⚔ 55/3
Tahiti *island* S Pacific Polynesian settlement 10/2; European discovery 654
T'ai-hsi-ts'un (*a/s* Taixicun) N China Shang city 8/4
Taimyr AR N Siberia 146/2
Taiwan (*a/c* Formosa) Mesolithic sites 8/2; early settlements 8/2; contested by Dutch and Spanish 71/2; rising of aboriginals 106/1; acquired by Japan 107/4, 123/3, 127/3; seat of Chinese Nationalist government 141/1
Taixicun (T'ai-hsi-ts'un)
Taiyuan N China T'ang city 50/1; Ming provincial capital 51/4; French railway 107/4
Tajiks people of C Asia 146/2, 146/3
Tajikistan C Asia independence 151/4
Takeda C Japan clan territory 50/3
Takedda NW Africa trans-Saharan trade 60/1
Takla Makan Desert 25/1
Takoradi W Africa early Dutch settlement 60/2 (inset)
Takruo early empire of W Africa 60/1
Takua Pa S Thailand Hindu-Buddhist remains 51/2
Talas *river* C Asia ⚔ 41/1
Talavera C Spain ⚔ 90/1
Ta-li C China site of early man 3/3
Tal-i Ghazir W Persia early city 16/2
Tal-i Malyan W Persia early city 16/2
Tallinn (*Ger.* Reval *Russ.* Revel) Estonian SSR industry 147/1
Talladega SE USA ⚔ 95/2
Tamanrasset S Algeria Saharan trade 61/2; French occupation 103/3
Tamar (Palmyra)
Tamaulipas state of N Mexico 97/1
Tambov C Russia founded 85/1; 1905 Revolution 120/1; Bolshevik seizure 121/2
Tamluk (*a/c* Tamralipta) E India early trade centre 25/1
Tamsui N Taiwan treaty port 107/4; Anglo-French attacks 107/3
T'an E China Chou domain 9/6
Tana S Russia Mongol conquest 47/4; early trade 58/3
Tanais S Russia Greek colony 19/4
Tanana sub-arctic Indian tribe of Alaska 63/1
Tananarive (*n/s* Antananarivo) Madagascar centre of Merina kingdom 103/3
Tancáh E Mexico Mayan centre 12/2
Tanganyika (*form.* German East Africa *now part of* Tanzania) independence 138/1; political development 140/1
T'ang Chi-yao Chinese warlord 122/2
Tangier (*a/c* Tangiers *Fr.* Tanger *Sp.* Tánger *Ar.* Tanjah *anc.* Tingis) Morocco international control 103/3
Tanguts tribe of S Mongolia 47/1
Tanis (a/c Avaris) Lower Egypt 21/1
Tanjah (Tangier)
Tanjore district of S India ceded to Britain 87/3
Tannenberg (*Pol.* Stębark) E Prussia ⚔ Teutonic Knights defeated 54/4; ⚔ WW1 119/3
Tannu Tuva (*now* Tuvinskaya ASSR) C Asia Russian protectorate 107/4, 120/4
Tantu E China Western Chou site 9/6
Tanyang E China Han commanderie 29/3
Tanzania (formed by amalgamation of Tanganyika and Zanzibar) 140/1. See also German East Africa
Tao C China Western Chou domain 9/6
Taochow W China Ming military post 51/4
Taoism 27/1
Taoudenni NW Africa French occupation 103/3
Taprobane (Ceylon)
Tara W Siberia founded 84/2
Tarabulus al Gharb (Tripoli)
Tarabulus ash Sham (Tripoli)

Tarahumara Indian tribe of N Mexico 63/1
Tarakan NE Borneo Allied landing in WW2 135/2
Taranaki (*a/c* New Plymouth) province of N Island, New Zealand 112/2
Taranto (*anc.* Tarentum) S Italy Saracen occupation 37/1
Tarapacá S Peru acquired by Chile 97/4
Tarasco Indian tribe of C Mexico 63/1
Tarawa Gilbert Islands, S Pacific ⚔ 135/2
Tarentaise SE France archbishopric 34/4
Tarentum (*mod.* Taranto) S Italy Greek colony 19/4; Roman Empire 24/2, 30/1, 31/3
Tarim Basin C Asia occupied by China 50/1, 106/1
Tarnopol (*now Russ.* Ternopol) E Austria-Hungary WW1 113/3; WW2 133/2
Tarnow (*now Pol.* Tarnów) E Austria-Hungary WW1 119/3
Tarquinii (*later* Corneto *mod.* Tarquinia) C Italy Etruscan city 19/4
Tarracina (*earlier* Anxur *mod.* Terracina) C Italy Roman colony 30/1
Tarraco (*mod.* Tarragona) NE Spain Greek colony 19/4, 24/2, 30/3
Tarraconensis Roman province of N Spain 30/3
Tarragona (*anc.* Tarraco) NE Spain Civil War 129/4
Tarsus S Anatolia early city 16/1; early trade 17/4; Assyrian Empire 17/4; Mycenaean trade 18/2; Hittite city 21/1; Alexander's route 22/3; Roman Empire 25/2, 31/3; early archbishopric 27/2; Byzantine Empire 43/1
Tărtăria N Romania early settlement 14/2
Tartars (*a/s* Tatars) Turkic people of E Russia 47/1, 84/2, 146/3
Tartu (Dorpat)
Taruga C Africa Iron Age site 11/1
Tarvisium (Treviso)
Tashkent Russ. C Asia Alexander's journey 23/3; Mongol conquest 47/4; centre of Bolshevik activity 120/4; industry 147/1
Tasmania (*until 1856* Van Diemen's Land) island state of SE Australia settlement and development 113/1 (inset)
Tassili Massif N Africa rock painting 11/1
Tatanagar NE India industry 108/1
Tatar ASSR W USSR 146/2
Tatars (Tartars)
Tatung N China early bishopric 39/1; Ming frontier defence area 51/4
Tauchira Libya Greek colony 19/4
Taung S Africa site of early man 3/3
Taunum W Germany Mithraic site 26/1
Taurasia (Turin)
Ta-wen-k'ou (*a/s* Dawenkou) NE China early settlement 8/2
Taxila NW India early trading centre 25/1; Alexander's route 23/3
Tayadirt N Morocco megalithic tomb 14/3
Tazoult (Lambaesis)
Tbilisi (*f/s* Tiflis) Georgian SSR economy 147/1
Tchad (Chad)
Teate (*mod.* Chieti) C Italy Roman Empire 30/1
Tebessa (Theveste)
Teheran (*Pers.* Tehran) C Persia 124/1
Tehuelche Indian tribe of S Argentina 63/1
Te Ika-a-Maui (North Island)
Tekke SW Anatolia region of Ottoman Empire 49/1
Tel-Aviv C Israel 141/3
Tell Abu Hureira Syria early farming site 7/4
Tell Agrab Mesopotamia Sumerian site 16/2
Tell Asmar (Eshnunna)
Tell Aswad N Mesopotamia Sumerian site 16/2
Tell Brak E Syria early farming village 7/4; Mitannian city 21/1
Tell el-'Ubaid S Mesopotamia Sumerian site 17/2
Tell es-Sa'idiyeh Palestine Levantine city 21/1
Tell-es-Sawwan Mesopotamia early farming village 7/4
Tell Halaf Mesopotamia early farming village 7/4
Tellicherry SW India English settlement 66/2
Telloh C Mesopotamia Sumerian city 16/2
Tell Ramad Lebanon early farming site 7/4
Tell Tayinat NW Syria Mitannian city 21/1
Tell 'Uqair N Mesopotamia Sumerian site 16/2
Tell Wilaya C Mesopotamia Sumerian site 16/2
Telo Martius (Toulon)
Tembu region of SE Africa 103/2
Temirtau W Siberia industry 147/1
Tempsa S Italy Roman colony 30/1
Tenasserim district of S Burma British control 71/2; annexed by British 104/2
Tenetehara forest Indian tribe of NE Brazil 63/1
Teng N China Chou domain and city-state 9/6; warring state 28/1
Tengyueh SW China treaty town 107/4
Tennessee state of SE USA Civil War 93/5; Depression 131/2; population 111/5, 145/1
Tenochtitlán Mexico Aztec capital 62/2; conquest by Spaniards 68/1
Teotihuacán early culture of C America 12/2
Tepehuan Indian tribe of N Mexico 63/1
Tepe Yahya S Persia early settlement 16/1
Tepic state of N Mexico 97/1
Te Porere N Island, New Zealand ⚔ 112/3
Terebovl W Russia town of Galich 45/2
Teremembé forest Indian tribe of NE Brazil 63/1
Terezín (Theresienstadt)
Tergeste (*mod.* Trieste) N Italy Roman Empire 30/3
Ternate Moluccas, East Indies Islamic town 70/1; Portuguese settlement 70/3
Ternifine Algeria site of early man 3/3
Terracina (Tarracina)
Terranova di Sicilia (Gela)
Tertry N France ⚔ 34/4
Teruel E Spain Civil War 129/4
Teschen (*Cz.* Těšín *or* Český Těšín *Pol.* Cieszyn) city and district divided between Poland and Czechoslovakia 129/2; Czech part retaken by Poland 129/5
Teshik-tash C Asia site of early man 3/3
Těšín (Teschen)
Tete Mozambique Portuguese settlement 61/2; Stanley's travels 102/1
Teutonic Order Baltic 45/2; conquest of Prussia 54/4 territory lost to Poland 72/1
Teverya (Tiberias)
Te Waipounamu (South Island)
Tewkesbury W England Industrial Revolution 98/1
Texas state of S USA independent 97/1; Depression 131/2; population 111/5, 145/1
Texel I and II N Netherlands English/Dutch naval battles 81/3
Teyjat SW France Palaeolithic art 5/3
Thailand (*f/c* Siam) early Iron and Bronze Age sites 8/3; Theravada Buddhism 70/1; US bases 149/1; political developments 141/1; economy 150/1. See also Siam
Thais people of SE Asia, expansion 51/2
Tham Ongbah W Siam early site 8/3
Thames N Island, New Zealand gold rush 112/3
Thamugadi (*a/c* Timgad) Algeria ancient city 30/3
Thang Long (*mod.* Hanoi) N Indo-China major political centre 51/2
Thapsacus (*Bibl.* Tiphsah *mod.* Dibse) Syria Alexander's route 223; Achaemenid Empire 21/5
Thapsus Tunisia Punic city 19/4; Roman Empire 31/3
Thara N Persia Alexander's route 23/3
Tharro NW India Harappan site 9/5
Thasos *island* N Greece ancient city 19/4
Thaton S Burma early Hindu-Buddhist temple 51/2
Thebes (*mod. Gr.* Thivai) C Greece Mycenaean palace 19/1
Thebes (*Lat.* Thebae *earlier* Diospolis Magna) Upper Egypt Iron Age site 11/1; 21/1; Roman Empire 25/2, 31/3
Thenae Tunisia Punic city 19/4
Theodosia (*mod.* Feodosiya) Crimea Greek colony 19/4; Roman Empire 31/3
Theodosiopolis E Anatolia early bishopric 27/2; under Seljuks of Rum 43/3
Thera (*mod.* Thira *a/c* Santorini) island of S Aegean Greek parent state 19/4
Theresienstadt (*now Cz.* Terezin) C Germany concentration camp 132/1
Thermopylae C Greece ⚔ 20/5, 22/1
Thessalonica (*a/c* Salonika *Gr.* Thessaloniki) N Greece Roman Empire 31/3; Byzantine Empire 43/1
Thessaly (*Gr.* Thessalia) region of C Greece 18/3; district of Byzantine Empire 43/1; ceded to Greece 116/1
Thetford E England Industrial Revolution 98/1
Theveste (*mod.* Tebessa) Algeria Roman Empire 24/2, 30/3
Thionville (Diedenhofen)
Thira (Thera)
Thirteen Colonies N America 69/3, 86/1, 88/1
Thirty Years' War 77/5, 74/3
Thivai (Thebes)
Thomas Quarries N Morocco site of early man 3/3
Thom Buri Thailand early trade centre 71/2
Thorn (*Pol.* Toruń) N Poland founded by Teutonic Knights 54/4; Hanseatic city 59/2
Thrace (*anc.* Thracia) region of SE Europe divided between Bulgaria and Turkey 116/1; East occupied by Greece 128/2
Thracesian Theme W Anatolia district of Byzantine Empire 42/2
Thracia (*Eng.* Thrace) SE Europe Roman province 31/3, 4; Byzantine Empire 43/1
Three Days Battle S England English naval victory 81/3
Three Forks NW USA fur station 94/1
Thule Greenland sites 62/4
Thunder Bay (Fort William)
Thurii Copia S Italy Latin colony 30/1
Thuringia (Thüringen) region of E Germany Frankish Empire 35/2; medieval German Empire 35/4; amalgamation of petty states 91/4; German unification 98/3, 115/2
Thyatira (*mod.* Akhisar) W Anatolia one of seven churches of Asia 27/2
Tiahuanaco Empire C Andes site 12/5, 13/1
Tiberias (*Heb.* Teverya) Israel town of Judaea 26/3
Tibesti Massif N Africa rock painting 11/1
Tibet (*anc.* Bhota) C Asia spread of Buddhism 27/1; early expansion 33/1; unified kingdom 50/1; part of Mongol Empire 46/1, 3; Chinese protectorate 106/1; British sphere of influence 107/4; absorbed by China 139/1
Tibur (*mod.* Tivoli) C Italy Roman Empire 30/1
Tichitt W Africa early site 11/1
Ticinum (Pavia)
Ticonderoga (*Fr.* Fort Carillon) NE USA British capture of French fort 86/1
Tidore *island* Moluccas, E Indies Islamic town 70/1; Portuguese settlement 70/3; Dutch settlement 71/2
Tien early state of W China 28/1
Tienshui NW China Han commanderie 29/3
Tientai Shan *mountain* E China Buddhist site 27/1
Tientsin NE China treaty port 107/4; Boxer uprising 107/3; Japanese occupation 127/5
Tieum N Anatolia Greek colony 19/4
Tievebulliagh N Ireland megalithic axe factory 14/3
Tiiflis (*n/c* Tibilisi) Caucasus Muslim conquest 41/1; Mongol conquest 47/4; Ottoman conquest 48/2; urban growth 146/2
Tighina (Bender)
Tiglath-Pileser I King of Assyria 20/3
Tiglath-Pileser III King of Assyria 20/3
Tigranocerta (*mod.* Siirt) E Anatolia Roman Empire 31/3
Tikal E Mexico Mayan site 12/2, 13/1
Timbira forest Indian tribe of N Brazil 63/1
Timbuktu (*Fr.* Tombouctou) W Africa trans-Saharan trade 60/61; occupied by French 103/3
Timgad (Thamugadi)
Timor island of E Indies early Portuguese colony 67/2; Dutch/Portuguese control 101/2; occupied by Japanese in WW2 134/1; joined Indonesia 139/2
Timucua Indian tribe of SE USA 63/1
Timur's Empire Persia 47/4
Tinian island of C Pacific US base in WW2 135/2
Tingis (*mod.* Tangier) Morocco Roman Empire 24/2, 30/3; early bishopric 26/2
Tingitana NW Africa region of Roman Empire 30/3
Tinian *island* Marianas, C Pacific occupied by US in WW2 135/1
Tinnevelly district of S India ceded to Britain 87/2
Tipasa Algeria early bishopric 26/2
Tiphsah (Thapsacus)
Tippecanoe NE USA ⚔ 94/2
Tippera district of E India riots 105/4
Tippermuir C Scotland ⚔ 76/4
Tippu Tib's Domain E Africa 103/3
Tipton C England Industrial Revolution 98/1
Tirana Albania Ottoman Empire 124/1
Tirguşor Romania Mithraic site 26/1
Tirol, Tirolo (Tyrol)
Tîrpeşti Romania farming site 15-1
Tiryns S Greece Mycenaean palace 19/1
Tirzah Palestine ancient capital 21/2
Tiszapolgár Hungary burial site 14/2
Tito Bustillo N Spain Palaeolithic art 5/3
Tiverton SW England Industrial Revolution 98/1
Tivertsy Slav tribe of W Russia 44/1
Tivoli (Tibur)
Tjeribon (Cheribon)
Tlaxcala region of C Mexico early kingdom 62/2; defence against Cortés 68/1; modern state 97/1
Tlemcen NW Africa early trade 58/3
Tlingit coast Indian tribe of NW Canada 63/1
Tmutarakan S Russia 44/1
Tobago island of W Indies French rule 66/4; dependency of Trinidad 139/1 (inset)
Tobolsk W Siberia founded 84/2; on railway to east 84/3
Tobruk (*Ar.* Tubruq) N Libya WW2 132/1
Tochigi prefecture of C Japan 126/2
Todmorden N England Industrial Revolution 98/1
Togo (*form.* Togoland) country of W Africa independence 138/1; economy 150/1
Togoland W Africa German colony 100/2; 103/3. *For French mandate see* Togo
Tokushima city and prefecture of W Japan 126/1, 2
Tokyo (*form.* Edo) C Japan industrialisation 126/2; WW2 135/3
Toledo (*anc.* Toletum) C Spain Muslim conquest 41/1; Civil War 129/4
Toletum (*mod.* Toledo) C Spain Roman Empire 24/2, 30/3; archbishopric 26/2
Tolmeta (Ptolemais)
Tolosa (*mod.* Toulouse) S France Roman Empire 24/2, 30/2; archbishopric 26/2
Toltecs early people of Mexico 62T
Tolyatti (*until 1964* Stavropol) C Russia industry 147/1
Tomassee SE USA ⚔ 95/2
Tombos Upper Egypt fortress 21/1
Tombouctou (Timbuktu)
Tomi (*now* Constanta) Romania Greek Colony 19/4; Roman Empire 24/2, 30/3
Tomsk C Siberia founded 84/2; on railway to east 84/3; industry 147/1
Tonbridge SE England Industrial Revolution 98/1
Tonga island kingdom of S Pacific early settlement 10/2; British protectorate 101/2; independence 139/1 (inset)
Tongking (*Fr.* Tonkin) region of N Indo-China Hindu-Buddhist state 71/2; tributary state of China 106/1
Tongking, Gulf of Vietnamese war 148/3
Tønsberg Norway Hanseatic trade 59/2
Toowoomba E Australia early settlement 113/1
Topa Inca emperor 62T, 63/3
Torhout Belgium medieval fair 58/1
Torino (Turin)
Torki people of S Russia 45/2
Torone N Greece Ionian colony 19/4
Toronto E Canada growth 111/1

Toropets W Russia early town of Smolensk 45/2
Torres Strait Australia/New Guinea European discovery 65/4
Tortona (*Lat.* Dertona) N Italy Lombard League 55/3
Toruń (Thorn)
Torzhok W Russia early town of Novogorod Empire 45/2
Toscana (Tuscany)
Totonac Indian tribe of C Mexico 63/1
Tottori city and prefecture of W Japan 126/1, 2
Touat (Tuat)
Toul NE France annexed 72/2
Toulon (*anc.* Telo Martius) S France naval base 87/1; executions during French Revolution 89/2
Toulouse (*anc.* Tolosa) S France Muslim conquest 41/1; St. Bartholomew Massacre 74/3; *parlement* 80/1; French Revolution 89/2
Toungoo C Burma 51/2
Touraine region of C France French Royal domain 52/2
Tourane (*mod.* Da Nang) C Vietnam early trade 71/2
Tournai region of Belgium Burgundian possession 73/3
Tours (*anc.* Caesarodunum *later* Turones) C France archbishopric 34/4; 17C revolts 77/2; seat of intendant 80/1
Townsville E Australia early settlement 113/1
Toyama city and prefecture of C Japan 126/2
Trabzon (*Eng.* Trebizond *anc.* Trapezus) NE Anatolia 49/1
Trachonitis ancient district of N Palestine 26/3
Trafalgar S Spain ⚔ 90/1, 3
Trajectum (*mod.* Utrecht) Netherlands bishopric 26/2
Tra Kieu C Indo-China Hindu-Buddhist temple 51/2
Transjordan country of N Arabia Ottoman province 124/1; British mandate 132/1
Transkei region of SE Africa annexed by Cape Province 103/2; independent Bantustan 140/1
Transnistria SW Russia WW2 133/2
Transoxiana ancient region of C Asia, Muslim conquest 41/1, 2
Trans-Siberian Railway 127/5
Transvaal S Africa Boer republic 103/2, 4
Transylvania region of Hungary/Romania prehistoric metal-working 14/2; early trade with Greece 18/2; Empire of Mathias Corvinus 72/1; part of Austro-Hungarian Empire 128/2
Trapezus (*mod.* Trabzon *Eng.* Trebizond) NE Anatolia Greek colony 19/4; Roman Empire 25/2, 31/3; early bishopric 27/2
Trasimeno C Italy Palaeolithic art 5/3
Trasimenus C Italy ⚔ 30/2
Travancore former state of S India 87/2, 3; 104/1
Traverse des Sioux N USA fur station 94/1
Trebia N Italy ⚔ 30/2
Trebizond (*Turk.* Trabzon *anc.* Trapezus) NE Anatolia Byzantine Empire 43/1; early trade 58/3; Ottoman Empire 49/1
Trebizond, Empire of NE Anatolia 42/4, 49/1
Treblinka Poland concentration camp 132/1
Trelleborg Denmark circular fortification 52/3
Trengganu state of Malaya tributary to Siam 71/5
Trent (Trient)
Trent, Council of 75T
Trentino (Trient)
Trento (Trient)
Tres Zapotes C Mexico Olmec site 12/2
Treves (Trier. Augusta Treverorum)
Treviso (*anc.* Tarvisium) N Italy Signorial domination 56/3
Trévoux E France seat of intendant 80/1
Trianda Rhodes Mycenaean town 19/1
Trichinopoly S India ceded to Britain 87/3; ⚔ 87/2
Trient (*It.* Trento *or (district)* Trentino *Eng.* Trent *anc.* Tridentum) S Germany bishopric 79/1
Trier (*Eng.* Treves *Fr.* Trèves *anc.* Augusta Treverorum) W Germany archbishopric 34/4, 79/1
Trieste (*anc.* Tergeste *S. Cr.* Trst) WW1 119/3; WW2 133/2
Trincomalee Ceylon captured by British 87/2
Trinidad island of W Indies discovery 65/3; Spanish settlement 66/4; British colony 97/1; independence 139/1 (inset)
Trinil Java site of early man 3/3
Trío Indian tribe of S America 63/1
Triple Alliance 81/4, 117/2
Triple Entente 116T
Tripoli (*Ar.* Tarabulus al Gharb *anc.* Oea) N Libya Muslim conquest 48/2; trans-Saharan trade 61/2; Mediterranean trade 58/3; Italian occupation 103/3
Tripoli (*Ar.* Tarabulus ash Sham *anc.* Tripolis) Syria Roman Empire 31/3; early bishopric 27/2; Byzantine Empire 43/1; Venetian trade 37/2; Crusaders 40/3
Tripolitania N Africa district of Byzantine Empire 43/1; under Almohads 60/1; Italian occupation 103/3
Tripura district of NE India Partition 105/5
Tristan da Cunha S Atlantic British colony 100/2
Trizay W France burial site 14/2
Troas (*Eng.* Troy) W Anatolia early archbishopric 27/2
Troesmis Romania Roman Empire 31/3
Trois Rivières Quebec French post 67/3
Troitskaya Lavra N Russia monastery 38/2
Troitsko-Pechorsk N Russia monastery 38/2
Trondheim (*f/c Nidaros) C Norway* bishopric 38/2; Hanseatic trade 59/2; WW2 132/1
Tropaeum Traini Romania Roman Empire 31-3
Trou Magrite Belgium Palaeolithic art 5/3
Troy (*Lat.* Ilium *Gr.* Troas) NW Anatolia early city 16/1, 18/2, 3, 19/1
Troyes NE France medieval fair 58/1; St. Bartholomew Massacre 74/3
Trst (Trieste)
Trucial Coast (*later* Trucial Oman, Trucial States *now* United Arab Emirates) E Arabia British control 125/1; WW1 125/2
Truckee W USA ⚔ 94/2
Truk Caroline Islands, C Pacific Japanese base in WW2 134/1, 135/2
Ts'ai N China Chou domain 9/6
Tsangko SW China Han commanderie 29/3
Tsangwu S China Han commanderie 29/3
Tsaritsyn (*1925-61* Stalingrad *now* Volgograd) S Russia founded 85/1; urban growth 146/2; industry 147/1; Bolshevik seizure 121/2
Tselinograd (*until 1961* Akmolinsk) Kazakh SSR Russ. C Asia industry 147/1
Tsimshian Indian tribe of NW Canada 63/1
Tsinan N China railway 107/4
Tsinghai province of NW China incorporated into Manchu (Ch'ing) Empire 106/1
Tsingtao E China German treaty port 107/4; Japanese occupation 135/1
Tsitsihar Manchuria 122/4
Tsou N China Chou site 9/6
Tsunyi C China on Long March 122/4
Tsurugaoka (Shonai)
Tswana tribe of S Africa 102/2
Tuat (*Fr.* Touat) Sahara early trade 58/3; 60-61
Tubruq (Tobruk)
Tucano Indian tribe of S America 63/1
Tuchi N China T'ang prefecture 50/1
Tucson SE USA on trail West 94/1
Tugursk Russ. Far East founded 84/2
Tukh (*a/c* Nubt) Upper Egypt pyramid 17/3
Tukharistan region of C Asia Chinese protectorate 50/1
Tukulti-Ninurta I King of Assyria 20/3
Tula Mexico Toltec centre 62/2
Tula C Russia industrial and urban growth 146-47
Tulagi Solomon Islands US base in WW2 135/2
Tulmaythah (Ptolemaïs)
Tulúm Mexico fortified site 62/2
Tumasik (*now* Singapore) Malaya 51/2
Tumbes Andean Indian tribe 63/1
Tumbes Peru Pizarro's landing 68/2
Tunes (Tunis)
T'ung SE China Western Chou domain 9/6
Tungirsk SE Siberia founded 84/2
Tungusy people of Siberia 84/2
Tunhsi Western Chou site 9/6
Tunhwang W China early trade and silk route 25/1; Buddhist site 27/1; conquered by Han 28/2
Tunis (*anc.* Tunes) N Africa early trade 58/3; acquired by Habsburgs 72/1; Ottoman conquest 48/2, 61/2; French occupation 103/3
Tunisia under the Almohads 60/1; autonomy under Ottoman Empire 124/1; French protectorate 103/3; under Vichy control 132/1; WW2 132/2; independence 138/1; economy 150/1
Tupinambá forest Indian tribe of E Brazil 63/1
Turckheim W France ⚔ 81/4
Turfan NW China silk route 25/1; administrative centre of Later Han 28/2
Turin (*It.* Torino *anc.* Taurasia *later* Augusta Taurinorum) N Italy Lombard League 55/3; 18C urban development 83/4; ⚔ 81/5
Turinsk W Siberia founded 84/2
Turkestan region of C Asia spread of Buddhism 27/1; during T'ang Empire 50/1; Chinese protectorate 106/1
Turkey on break-up of Ottoman Empire 124/1; war with Greece 125/4; Greek occupation of west 129/2; European alliances 128/1; neutral in WW2 132/1; Baghdad Pact and NATO 148/4, 149/1. See also Anatolia, Asia Minor, Ottoman Empire
Turkmen tribe of C Asia, conquered by Russia 84/3, 146/2
Turkmen SSR C Asia 146/3
Turkmenistan C Asia independence 151/4
Turks tribes on China's northern borders 50/1; invasion of Anatolia 41/2; movements after WW1 129/3. See also Ottoman Empire
Turks and Caicos Islands W Indies British colony 100/2
Turnhout Belgium medieval fair 58/1, 59/2
Turnu-Severin (Drobetae)
Turones (*mod.* Tours) C France archbishopric 26/2
Turov-Pinsk early principality of W Russia 45/2
Turukhansk C Siberia founded 84/2
Tuscany (*It.* Toscana) region of N Italy medieval German Empire 55/3; unification of Italy 114/3
Tuscararas SE USA ⚔ 94/2
Tustrup N Denmark megalithic tomb 15/3
Tutchone sub-arctic tribe of NW Canada 63/1
Tutub (*mod.* Khafajah) N Mesopotamia Sumerian site 16/2
Tuva ASSR C Asia 146/2
Tuvalu (*form.* Ellice Islands) C Pacific British colony 193/1 (inset)
Tver (*1931-91* Kalinin) W Russia early town of Vladimir-Suzdal 45/2
Two Sicilies kingdom 114/3
Tyana C Anatolia early bishopric 27/2; Byzantine Empire 43/3
Ty Isaf S Wales megalithic tomb 14/3
Tynedale N England Franchise of 56/4
Tyras (*mod.* Akkerman *since 1944* Belgorod-Dnestrovskiy *Rom.* Cetatea-Alba) S Russia Roman Empire 31/3
Tyre (*anc.* Tyrus *Ar.* Sur) Lebanon early trade 17/4, 18/2; Phoenician city 19/4; Levantine city 21/1; besieged by Alexander 22/3; Roman Empire 25/2; early archbishopric 27/2; Crusades 40/3
Tyrol (*Ger.* Tirol *It.* Tirolo) region of W Austria medieval German Empire 55/3; acquired by Habsburg 78/3; County 79/1; peasant revolt 88/1; South Tyrol to Italy 128/2
Tyrus (*Eng.* Tyre *Ar.* Sur) Lebanon Roman Empire 25/2, 31/3
Tyumen C Russia founded 84/2; on railway to east 84/3; industry 147/1
Tzintzuntzán Mexico Tarascan site 62/2
Tz'u-shan (*a/s* Cishan) N China early settlement 8/2

Uan Muhaggiag SW Libya early site 11/1
Ubangi-Shari (Oubangui-Chari, Central African Republic)
Udaipur former state of C India 104/1
Udinsk S Siberia founded 84/2
Udmurty people of C Russia 85/1; ASSR 146/2
Udon Thani N Thailand Vietnamese war 148/3
Udyana region of NW India 29/4
Uesugi E Japan clan territory 51/3
Ufa C Russia founded 85/1; industry 147/1
Uganda British protectorate 101/2, 103/3; independence 138/1; political development 140/1; economy 150/1
Ugarit (*mod.* Ras Shamra) ancient city of Syria 16/1; Mitannian city 21/1
Uighurs Turkic tribe of C Asia 47/1, 50/1
Ujiji C Africa meeting of Livingstone and Stanley 102/1
Ukraine region of SW USSR post-WW1 independence 129/2; WW2 132-3; industrial development 84/4; SSR 146/2
Ukrainians people of S Russia, emigration to West 129/3, 146/1
Ulan Bator (*Mong.* Ulaanbaatar *form.* Urga) Mongolia 120/4
Ulan-Ude (*until 1934* Verkhneudinsk) E Siberia industry 147/1
Ulithi island of C Pacific US base in WW2 135/2
Ulm S Germany ⚔ 90/1
Ulster province of N Ireland early kingdom 73/4; IRA 137/6
Ulu Leang Celebes, East Indies Neolithic site 8/3
Ulyanovsk (Simbirsk)
Umatilla NW USA ⚔ 94/2
Umayyads Muslim dynasty, Caliphate 34/4, 40/1
Umbrians Italic tribe of C Italy 30/1
Umma Mesopotamia Sumerian city 16/2, 17/4
Unao N India Indian Mutiny 104/1
UNITA Angolan guerrilla movement 138T, 140/1
United Arab Emirates (*form.* Trucial States *earlier* Trucial Oman, Trucial Coast) federation of sheikhdoms. Persian Gulf creation 138/1; economy 150/1
United Arab Republic name given to union of Egypt and Syria 1958-61, retained by Egypt after dissolution until 1972
United Kingdom socio-political development 131/3; NATO and EEC 137/3, 149/1; economy 150/1. See also England, Scotland, Wales, Great Britain, Ulster
United Netherlands 79/1
United Provinces (*now* Uttar Pradesh) state of N India 105/3
United Provinces (*a/c* Dutch Republic) occupied by France 81/4
United States Thirteen Colonies and revolutionary war 86/1; War of Independence 92/1; industrialisation 110/2, 109/1; westward expansion 94/1; Indian wars 95/2; railway development 95/3; Civil War 92-3; population 111/5; Great Depression 130/3; 20C economic and industrial development 144-5; WW2 in Asia and Pacific 135/1; WW2 against Axis in West 132-3; involvement in Latin America 111/4, 143/1; in Cold War 148-9; NATO 148/1
Unsan N Korea 1950-53 war 148/2
Unterwalden original Swiss canton 54/5
Upper Burma annexed by British 104/2
Upper Emigrant Trail S USA settlers' route 94/1
Upper Palatinate S Germany Reformation 75/1
Upper Volta (*Fr.* Haute-Volta *n/c* Burkina) country of W Africa independence 138/1; economy 150/1
Uppland E Sweden early kingdom 53/5
Uppsala E Sweden bishopric 38/2
Ur (of the Chaldees) S Mesopotamia early farming village 7/4; Sumerian city 17/2, 4
Urals *mountains* industrial region of USSR 147/1
Urartu (*mod.* Armenia) state of ancient Near East 20/4
Urbs Vetus (Volsinii)
Urewe E Africa Iron Age site 11/1
Urfa (Edessa)
Urga (*mod.* Ulan-Bator *Mong.* Ulaanbaatar) Mongolia seat of Lamaistic patriarch 106/1
Urgench C Asia Muslim trade 59/3
Uri original Swiss canton 54/5
Uruguay part of Brazil 97/1; independence 97/1; political development 143/1; industry and economy 142/2, 3; 150/1